OPPENHEIMER AND SON

Oppenheimer and Son

ANTHONY HOCKING

McGRAW-HILL BOOK COMPANY, JOHANNESBURG

Düsseldorf, Kuala Lumpur, London, Mexico, Montreal, New Delhi,
New York, Panama, São Paulo, Singapore, Sydney, Toronto

ISBN 0 07 091255 6

ISBN 0 07 091264 5 Limited Edition

Set in Monotype Baskerville 10 on 12 point
Printed and bound by Printpak (Cape) Limited,
Dacres Avenue, Epping, Cape

To the Vicarage

Contents

Man sets his hand to the granite rock
  and lays bare the roots of the mountains;
he cuts galleries in the rocks,
  and gems of every kind meet his eye;
he dams up the sources of the streams
  and brings the hidden riches of the earth to light.
But where can wisdom be found?
  And where is the source of understanding?

Job 28: ix-xii.

SOUTHERN AFRICA IN 1910

Stilton Cheese

GREAT RHODES was dying. For years he had suffered from heart trouble, and now it was taking its final toll he was too far gone to resist. For weeks his condition had been much the same: one day he felt better, only to be ill again the next. He spent the nights in his little cottage by the sea not far from Cape Town, and the days in his magnificent home Groote Schuur under the firs of Table Mountain. But suddenly he took a turn for the worse, and was compelled to remain in the cottage.

From the nature of his illness he had great difficulty in breathing. He was most comfortable in an upright position, sitting on the edge of the bed with his hands under his thighs and leaning against a broad band stretched along the wall. Sometimes he struggled for breath; then, worn out by the effort, he would let his head sink so low that his chin touched his chest.

It became quite chilly in the evenings, but he did not heed the cold. Even when his friends swathed themselves in rugs and overcoats he sat before the open window in thin pyjamas. All the time he complained there was too little fresh air. Eventually his friends knocked a hole in the wall opposite the window to create a strong draught across the room. They cut holes in the ceiling too, and put tins of ice under the iron roof, and rigged up a fan which they kept going day and night.

The cottage stood in enclosed grounds, back from the road that followed the shore and in normal circumstances private enough. But in their curiosity crowds hundreds strong gathered outside in the evenings, and forced their way up to the house to glimpse the great man in his distress. There were many callers, but none were admitted except his closest friends who remained with him night and day: the faithful Dr Jameson; Smartt, Stevenson, Michell and Walton; his

1

brother Elmhirst; and his secretaries Grimmer, Jourdan and Le Sueur.

During Rhodes's last days Jameson drove himself relentlessly. He did what he could for his friend for hours on end, then stole away for a few moments' much-needed rest on the truckle bed in the next room. Rhodes would miss him, and call out 'Where is Jameson?' The little Scotsman would dutifully reappear for another spell. Towards the end he almost went to sleep on his feet.

Telegrams of inquiry and sympathy came from all corners of the globe, for Rhodes's progress was a matter of world-wide concern. Even Queen Alexandra sent a message of sympathy, which Rhodes much appreciated. But his friends kept from him all but the most heartening news, even arranging a special edition of the local newspaper so that he could see news of his supposed good progress in print.

Ridiculous though it seemed in the circumstances, Rhodes had set his heart on returning to England. He felt that, away from the cruel torture of the Cape summer heat, he would surely regain his strength. His doctors knew such a trip would be suicidal, but his secretaries booked his passage. Though in great pain, he was looking forward to it. Those with him were surprised to hear him quoting some lines from Tennyson's *In Memoriam*, over and over again: 'So much to do, so little done . . .'

Against all the odds, he seemed to be rallying. His secretaries left him for a time, wondering if the old lion was to surprise them after all. But it was not to be. He suddenly called for Jameson in a loud voice. Then quietly he repeated the names of his friends, and asked Grimmer to turn him over. Facing the wall, he was dead: Wednesday, March 26 1902, at three minutes to six in the evening.

His friends had made ready a coffin of Matabele timber, and in the night hauled it the long miles along the roads which skirted Table Mountain until at last they reached Groote Schuur. They stood silent around the coffin in the hallway, until with a sob someone threw a sprig of white flowers upon its top.

There was a public lying-in-state at Groote Schuur over the weekend. The people of Cape Town filed slowly past the coffin: a continuing stream from every walk of life and of every colour, united in homage to the man whose thinking had dominated their lives. In all more than 35 000 people passed through.

A contingent of Cape police escorted the body into Cape Town, for a second lying-in-state at the Legislative Assembly where Rhodes had ruled as Prime Minister. Thousands more filed past the coffin, now covered with a Union Jack, the Chartered Company's flag and a white ensign with the inscription: 'Farewell, Great Heart'. Upon the coffin rested three wreaths: Queen Alexandra's at the head; in the middle a wreath 'From sorrowing brothers and sisters'; and at the foot a tribute from Jameson, with the single word 'Friendship'.

The crowds gathered early in the streets of Cape Town. In places they stood eight deep on the pavements, all in black, with heads bared and in silence. Mounted police headed the cortège through the streets from the parliament buildings to the Anglican cathedral. The coffin was borne on the carriage of Long Cecil, the great gun made by De Beers artisans two years before during the Siege of Kimberley. With the military units involved and the scores of mourners' carriages, the procession was so long that it took 22 minutes to pass a single spot.

The cathedral was packed, the archbishop himself taking the service with his text 'Know ye not that there is a prince and a great man fallen this day in Israel?' The mourners filed from the cathedral, bound for the railway station. The body was loaded aboard a train for its last journey to the north, six coaches with the foremost of them the De Beers directors' coach in which Rhodes had travelled so often. Now it was to serve as a chapel with cross and candles. Two troopers of the Cape police mounted guard over the bier with arms reversed.

The journey would take a week. The train rolled on, from Cape Town with all its memories; past the fruit farms and wine estates of the Western Cape; up the winding mountain passes to the great plateau of the dry Karoo, the nothingness in South Africa's heart; through the stunted bush, the herds of game, the wheeling birds of prey. At every station of any importance the train stopped, and a guard of honour paraded on the platform to the grim music of death.

South Africa was still at war, though there was talk of an armistice. Imperial forces had crushed Boer opposition in the towns, but in the country it was almost stalemate. To guard the railway to the north, the British had built a chain of blockhouses manned by tiny garrisons on watch for trouble. At each the men were drawn up to attention with arms reversed. Most poignant of all, the train passed a single saluting soldier in the depth of the veld as dusk came. He was silhouetted by the sunset.

The train reached Kimberley, the city of diamonds. Here Rhodes had made his fortune, and given so much in return. The townsfolk had not forgotten and queues of mourners filed past the funeral coach to glimpse his coffin. After seven hours the train continued to Vryburg, accompanied now by an armoured train riding closely in its wake with searchlights sweeping the veld on either side. The harsh reality of the war was brought home even more sharply at Mafeking, where the trains encountered the remnants of Lord Methuen's column. It had been worsted by a Boer army only days before.

They travelled through Bechuanaland, Britain's protectorate, and at last reached Rhodesia: mile after mile of green trees and shrubs on either hand. Now and again the bright purple of mopani trees flashed out against the brighter green of camelthorns, while great violet foxgloves bordered the line.

At Bulawayo they lifted the coffin from the funeral car in solemn silence, and carried it to the Drill Hall where again it would lie in state. It was the turn of Rhodesia's pioneers to do honour to their country's founder, and they did not let him down. World's View, where Rhodes was to be buried, was the top of a huge, solid granite koppie, ringed round with half a dozen boulders each 10 feet high. At dawn the next morning, the team of oxen hauling the bier on the final ascent set off for the summit with the mourners in its wake.

On the way up to the grave, not far from the summit, they passed several thousand Matabele tribesmen from all parts of their country. The Matabele had known Rhodes as Mla'mlakunzi, Separator of the Fighting Bulls, the man whose personal bravery at the time of the Matabele Rebellion had saved them from destruction at the hands of the white man. Now they gave him their royal salute: 'Bayete.' Never before had they honoured an outsider in this way: only Umziligazi, the founder of their nation, and their great chief Lobengula.

The procession reached the summit, and halted round a deep hole gouged in the rock. Those who had been closest to Rhodes in life now stood silent as the coffin was lowered into the rock grave with its three wreaths. 'Earth to earth, dust to dust and ashes to ashes,' but now there were only granite chips to throw into the grave. Slowly, silently, a great slab of rock was eased into place to seal it, with a plain brass plate riveted upon its face: *Here Lie The Remains of Cecil John Rhodes*, as directed in his will. And that was all.

The mourners turned to go. Again, the Matabele saluted: 'Bayete, Nkosi.' And Rhodes was left alone, so close to the cave in which Umziligazi himself was entombed. 'So let them lie in the Matoppos, almost side by side – the founder of the Matabele nation, and its conqueror . . . Umziligazi the drinker of blood, Mla'mlakunzi the mediator, they lie in peace – in the silence of that mighty land, the stillness of the African night, amongst their own people, whom they loved so well.'

2

CECIL JOHN RHODES was 49 when he died. He had come to South Africa 32 years before, not to dig for diamonds but to join his elder brother Herbert who was farming cotton in southern Natal. He had been a weak child, and there were fears for his life. In the bracing climate of South Africa he was soon showing signs of dramatic improvement.

The earliest diamond discoveries had been made by the wandering inhabitants of the South African interior during the later 1860's, and at first they were greeted with scepticism. Everyone knew diamonds occurred only in India and Brazil, it was said. The reports from South Africa must be a hoax. But diamonds turned up in ever-increasing numbers as more people learnt to recognise them, and before long prospectors were at work in earnest. They found the richest deposits lay along the banks of the Vaal River, so it was in this area that the first diamond diggers pegged their claims.

There were already a good many mining men in South Africa, the survivors of a great copper mining boom in Namaqualand some years earlier. These swarmed to the new diggings and brought with them their mining know-how if not knowledge of diamonds. Most, in fact, were abysmally ignorant of the sparkling little stones. But soon there were others from further afield, including experienced diggers who had learnt their skills on the diamond fields of Minas Gerais and Golconda, and the newcomers shared what they knew with the others.

Before long the river diggings were being worked to capacity, both banks pegged for tens of miles and digging camps swarming with a population drawn from all over the world. Later comers and those without luck on the river turned their attention inland, following a number of chance finds which showed prospects were quite bright. The first goals were the farms Koffiefontein and Jagersfontein in the Orange Free State, but before long the diggers discovered the fields in the neighbourhood of what is today Kimberley: bare veld supporting a few scattered farmers and their families, scratching a living from the inhospitable surroundings. To such men the sums offered for their properties by the eager diggers seemed a fortune indeed, a gift from heaven.

In a matter of weeks these barren farms – Bultfontein, Dutoitspan, Dorstfontein, Vooruitzicht – were a mass of tents, a swarm of diggers, buyers, traders, African labourers, camp followers. Finds were swift and rich, far richer than those on the river diggings. Ever greater numbers of men gathered on the new fields from all over South Africa, and from much further afield. Whole convoys of passenger ships brought diggers from Europe, America and Australia. Haulage contractors made fortunes in transporting these men and their belongings and supplies across the weary miles from the coast to the diggings.

It had all happened remarkably quickly, and those involved felt there was no time to be lost. A diamond is forever, but not a diamond mine. Nobody knew the geology of diamonds: that they had properties of carbon metamorphised under untold heat and pressure, to be spewed to the surface through great geysers of lava from the earth's molten interior; that the fields these lucky diggers had discovered were the tops of diamond pipes reaching huge distances down into the earth. For the time the message was dig and dig quickly, for tomorrow you may hit bottom.

Herbert Rhodes was not one to miss an opportunity. Leaving Cecil in charge of the cotton farm he travelled quickly to the new fields, staked himself a claim and began digging. It was 1871, and the fields were coming into their own. His letters were so enthusiastic that he soon persuaded his brother to join him. Cecil arrived at the beginning of 1872, shortly after the discovery of a new mine at the Colesberg Kopje, soon known as the New Rush, which was in time to become world-famous as the Big Hole of Kimberley.

Herbert's claims were in the original mine of Vooruitzicht, known as De Beers' through the name of the brothers who had owned it. When Cecil arrived the mine was already deepening fast: each claim owner worked a patch of ground 30 feet square, gouging out the yellow earth in which the diamonds were hidden. As Cecil wrote home to his mother, it was like a monumental Stilton cheese. He and the others dug deeper and deeper into the exquisite treasure trove, and the hole grew more cavernous every day.

Nearby a town was taking shape. The tents erected higgledy-piggledy among the claims gave way to more permanent structures of wood and tin hauled in from the coast by ox-wagon. Streets appeared, and bars, and banks, and hotels and brothels. The diggers decided they stood no chance of pronouncing Vooruitzicht, so instead named their camp after the British Colonial Secretary of the day, Lord Kimberley. For the settlement which had sprung up at Dutoitspan they chose an even more distinguished name: Disraeli's own, Lord Beaconsfield.

Each mine was worked independently, with its own Diggers' Com-

6

mittee to watch the rights of the claim-holders. As a man made a find, it was for him to sell it to a licensed – or unlicensed – diamond buyer for what he could get for it. He might go to one of the established buyers' offices in Kimberley or Beaconsfield, or he might prefer to make a quick sale to one of the many 'kopje-wallopers', freelance middlemen who wandered the diggings to make what profit they could. That way he could save time and get on with the job. Usually his finds would be relatively small, worth a few pounds only, but every so often he might find a special stone. That would be the signal for real celebration.

As the mines grew deeper, the diggers were faced with huge problems. Everyone was feeling his way as he went, and the most valuable assets were imagination and ingenuity. Men had thought only the yellow ground near the surface bore diamonds and when they hit harder, bluish conglomerate assumed it was bedrock and there would be no more stones further down. Several sold out before it was found the blue ground too contained diamonds, if anything more abundantly than the yellow. The yellow soil was only weathered blueground, or Kimberlite as it came to be called. Engineers and geologists began to appreciate the nature of their diamond 'fields'. Perhaps the mines would last a lot longer than at first expected.

In tune with the mining operations, even the diamond market was growing more complex. Before the discoveries in South Africa diamonds had been found only in India and Brazil, and they were valuable because they were so rare. Now supplies seemed almost unlimited, at least for a long time to come, and there was a very real danger that the value of diamonds would plummet downwards to a point where it was not worth bothering about. Fortunately, the boom in diamond mining prompted a matching boom in diamond fashion in Europe and America, for both men and women. For the time diamonds were safe.

From quite an early stage, then, it was realised competition within the diamond trade was bad for everyone. Both producers and sellers would have to co-operate in keeping the going price of diamonds up to luxury levels. A number of the more far-sighted men suggested schemes for the amalgamation of the individual mines of Kimberley, and eventually of all the diamond mines, but petty jealousies and the self-interests of those concerned prevented them from achieving anything. It was to be the personal tenacity and acumen of Cecil John Rhodes which saw them through.

It took him a long time, chiefly because he lacked capital. Only when he linked hands with a modest, single-minded little diamond buyer called Alfred Beit did he begin to get somewhere. Beit was tiny – 'Beit, you say?' commented an actress after being introduced to him. 'Looks more of a nibble to me.' – but in financial affairs he was a giant. Together, he and Rhodes and their associates bought out the interests of their fellow claim-holders in the De Beers mine until they had complete control of it. Then they turned their attentions to the New Rush, the Kimberley Mine.

It was now that the diamond world's most crucial battle took place. The chief protagonists were Rhodes and Beit on the one hand, and on the other a cheerful young cockney who had arrived in South Africa with hardly a penny in his pocket but had gone on to make one of its biggest fortunes. His real name was Barney Isaacs, though everyone knew him as Barney Barnato. He had progressed from kopje-walloping to buying up 'exhausted' claims in the middle of Kimberley Mine before it was realised the blueground was diamondiferous. Now he had gone on to own virtually the whole mine through his company Kimberley Central – all but a key block of claims near the middle held by the so-called 'French' company.

Barnato was preparing to buy up the French company's holdings for Kimberley Central when Rhodes and Beit began to bid against him. The value of the contested shares mushroomed out of all proportion, and Kimberley could only hold its breath. Barnato's resources were far greater than those of his rivals at De Beers, but with Beit's help Rhodes won the backing of the merchant bankers Rothschilds of London. Besides this, Beit held strong influence with the board of the French company, and urged it to accept De Beers' bid. Rhodes, meanwhile, persuaded Barnato to allow him to buy up the French company's holdings at a reasonable price, on condition he then resold it to Kimberley Central in exchange for a one-fifth interest in its total shareholding.

Barney was cock-a-hoop. He had the French company and that meant the whole mine. But his joy was short-lived. Celebrating with his fellow directors he suddenly realised that he was being attacked from within the gates: the shareholders who should have been behind him were quietly selling out to Rhodes and Beit. Far from resting content with their one-fifth interest, the cunning pair was bidding for majority control. In days it was all over, and Barnato was beaten: halfway through 1889 his precious Kimberley Central fell victim to Rhodes and De Beers.

Barnato was a good loser – particularly as Rhodes had been

deliberately courting his friendship while the battle was in progress and had even put him up for the Kimberley Club. Soon Rhodes persuaded him to stand for the Cape Legislative Assembly as member for Kimberley, in which capacity he was duly elected. Now he saw no reason why he should not join forces with Rhodes in the new company he was forming, De Beers Consolidated Mines. Rhodes would be chairman, but Barney would rank equally with Beit, Rhodes and a third associate as 'life governors' – ahead of the regular directors.

Rhodes had achieved what he wanted. It would not be long before De Beers bought out Dutoitspan and Bultfontein, and also yet another diamond pipe soon to be discovered on the farm Wesselton and initially rushed just as the older mines had been. With this final amalgamation the producers were one. Rhodes could turn his attention to the diamond buyers, who should be brought to heel so that the price of diamonds might be kept high and indeed raised higher.

As a first step, Rhodes arranged a deal with the leading firms, Wernher, Beit and Barnato Brothers, which were, of course, controlled by Alfred Beit and Barney Barnato. Barney was a convinced disciple of his conqueror by this time and ready to back him all the way. Beit remained as staunch an ally as ever. De Beers would drastically cut back production, but what diamonds there were would be sold to Barnatos and Wernher, Beit, with the price rising a shilling per carat each month. By this means De Beers and the two buying firms could force up the price of diamonds – and at the same time hold the other buyers to ransom as they would suddenly find themselves without a source of supply.

The news of the agreement provoked a furious row in the diamond world, and not surprisingly. The trade could never support such outrageous price rises, said the dealers. But at the end of the three months Barnato was ready to sign another contract along similar lines – and far from complaining the other buyers hastily formed themselves into a syndicate as Rhodes now suggested and came to terms with De Beers without further complaint. Again they contracted to buy De Beers' production over the next three months, and again it was agreed the price should be raised a shilling a carat every month. Rhodes left it to the syndicate to settle the exact percentage of the production each should receive.

Besides Wernher, Beit and Barnatos, which were to bear by far the biggest burdens, the firms involved were Mosenthals (15%), Dunkelsbuhlers and Joseph Brothers (10% each) and a number of small companies which would receive five per cent or less. Rhodes's critics said the new system could not possibly work, and certainly he had a lot more difficulty imposing his views on the trade in Europe than he had had in South Africa. But he persisted for more than six months, forcing the price of diamonds as high as he dared, before at last throwing the market open to general competition once again. However, it was soon clear the closed system was more efficient, so from 1893 the Diamond Syndicate became a permanent feature of the trade.

As Rhodes and Beit worked towards the amalgamation of the mines, those defeated in the struggle lost interest in Kimberley and turned their attention to the little Boer republic across the Vaal. Years before veterans of the old goldfields of California and Australia had found typical gold deposits in the hills of Lydenburg, though the 'gold rush' which resulted had, of course, been completely overshadowed by the rush to Kimberley. As the years passed Barberton, Pilgrim's Rest, Mac Mac and the other camps that developed in the area made fortunes for some and ruined many others, as is always the case with opportunist mining. Now most of the gold had been worked out, and what remained was tied up by a handful of companies. The independent miners spread further afield in hopes of finding new deposits of their own.

This had been going on for years, and gold turned up in the most unlikely places: all over the Transvaal, in fact, and even in the Free State, though rarely in payable amounts. Always the prospectors panned for gold in the traditional way: many years passed before any of them realized the gold was in fact associated with the rock and they could recover much more by crushing the conglomerate and running it over zinc plates to separate it out. Once they had tumbled to this, however, it was only a matter of time before a chance discovery revealed gold in an odd layer of rounded pebbles caught in quartz like nuts in toffee. Prospectors even called it 'banket', for an Afrikaner delicacy it resembled.

The discovery was made in 1886, but it was some time before anyone realised its true significance. For one thing, to exploit the new field would involve a huge amount of capital. Prospectors swarmed to take options on the farms that contained the strange 'banket' against the time they could sell for a profit, and some of the more enterprising went down to Kimberley to try and raise money to open the deposits themselves. These last even provided a public demonstration in the Kimberley market place, with one of the prospectors panning the crushed conglomerate in the age-old tradition.

The diamond magnates sat up and took notice, though they could hardly credit the stories they were told. As Alfred Beit put it, 'I could not believe there could be another place as rich as Kimberley on the same continent.' He hired J B Robinson, an erstwhile rival he and Rhodes had helped to ruin, and sent him to investigate the discoveries on the spot and, if necessary, take out options. Robinson travelled on the same coach as Rhodes's representative – though each was supposed to be making the trip in secret.

When they got to the Witwatersrand as the Boers called the area, Robinson began buying claims as fast as he could. Rhodes's man, on the other hand, was expected to report back to Kimberley before taking any options. In the event Rhodes preferred to visit the goldfields in person to see what was happening at first hand. Beit was off to a flying start on the Reef, though as it turned out the deposits were so extensive that there was room for all. To his great chagrin Rhodes was a slow starter but more than made up for it later; and there was even scope for Barney Barnato who arrived long after mining had started and the new town of Johannesburg had been established.

The three magnates each bought extensive interests, and formed mining houses to finance and administer them. First to be inaugurated was Beit's Central Mining, to which he later allied another holding company he called Rand Mines. Next came Rhodes's Gold Fields of South Africa. Barney Barnato's Johannesburg Consolidated Investments was not only involved in mining but in many other facets of the Reef's development, and particularly in property. Other mining financial houses were formed at this time, but the big three from Kimberley were to maintain their position at the forefront of all that was happening for a long time to come.

In this period, Rhodes was embroiled in the projects which were to make his name as the greatest imperialist, 'the greatest man now living' as Kipling described him. For some time the magnates of Kimberley had had their eyes on the great lands of the Matabele and their serfs the Mashona, as yet free of the white man's yoke. It was supposed they were richer in gold and precious stones than any lands so far developed: from the time of the earliest pioneers it was supposed the fabulous kingdom of Monomotapa lay to the north. Rhodes's men spent months at the kraal of the Matabele's king Lobengula at Bulawayo, seeking concessions to search for minerals in his lands.

Competition from rival parties was intense, but in the end Rhodes's party was successful in winning rights to develop Mashonaland. Through De Beers' influence in Britain Rhodes procured an extraordinary royal charter from Queen Victoria, enabling him to establish

11

the British South Africa Company with vast powers to exploit the new concessions. He was permitted to occupy territory, create a police force, embark on military expeditions and enter into diplomatic relations with other powers. Before long he raised a Pioneer Column, drawing men from all parts of South Africa to colonise Mashonaland and 'civilise' the area. Each of its members was to be granted free and in the neighbourhood of the little outpost they established, Fort Salisbury, so named after the British Prime Minister.

More settlers arrived, and gradually the charter company's influence spread further afield: into the territory of the Matabele to the south, which was not calculated to please Lobengula and soon precipitated a war in which his power was crushed; and over the Zambezi to the north. Before long the BSAC's territory was known to the world as Rhodesia, with Rhodes's great friend and confidant Leander Starr Jameson as its administrator and chief executive.

Rhodes was returned to parliament at the Cape, and was made Prime Minister. Always his dream was of a united South Africa: of 'One land from Lion's Head to Line,' from the Cape to the Zambezi. In his view, those not born or at least bred in the shadow of the British flag were to be pitied. He did what he could to compensate later generations, in fact in South Africa and in spirit in the rest of the world. That was the rationale behind his pioneering ventures in Rhodesia. He governed the Cape, and Britain controlled Bechuanaland. As Prime Minister he annexed Pondoland to the east of the Cape Colony's borders. Natal was under British rule, too, and there was the prospect of buying the barbaric territories of Lourenco Marques and Delagoa Bay from the impecunious Portuguese. All that stood in his way were the prickly little Boer Republic of the Orange Free State, and President Paul Kruger's South African Republic over the Vaal.

Kruger! What an image Oom Paul enjoyed throughout the world: the patriarchal, Bible-punching champion of God's chosen people, as the Transvaal Boers were accustomed to see themselves. What menace he represented to Rhodes's dream. The Free State was as nothing: poor, primitive, undeveloped and unsophisticated. But the Transvaal was another thing altogether. Far from being ready to co-operate with his imperialist neighbours, Kruger seemed to be doing all he could to alienate them. His own *burghers* were considerably outnumbered by the *uitlanders* or foreigners who had come to mine the Witwatersrand and other likely sites: but far from allowing them full say in the state's affairs, he refused them even the prospect of the franchise. On the

12

other hand, he taxed them without mercy: they were fair game when it came to trying to fill coffers which had been empty virtually from the start. No amount of representation made any difference: 'Oom Paul's' heart was hardened against them, as he believed they threatened the very survival of his people and was not prepared to take chances.

There was another side to Kruger's position. Rhodes's dreams of a united Southern Africa had developed into an even more ambitious plan. Short of seeing the whole map of Africa painted red for British rule – even he realised this might be impractical – he planned to build a railway link from the Cape to Cairo, and a telegraph line too. For that he would need a corridor of land up the middle of Africa, through the territory that was as yet unclaimed. However Kruger was seeking to expand his influence to the north, while at the same time the Germans had rather belatedly developed colonial ambitions: they had annexed a slab of territory nobody else wanted, north of the Cape Colony on the Atlantic coast, an empty desert they called South West Africa. The German Kaiser was making overtures to Oom Paul and if Rhodes was not careful there was a chance the two might consolidate the territory between their respective spheres of influence, and block his route to the north.

These were the factors which made Kruger the greatest thorn in Rhodes's flesh, and made the imperialist all the more eager to crush his rival's power at the first opportunity. It came, not surprisingly, through the *uitlanders*. Their position was growing more difficult virtually by the week, as Kruger's *Volksraad* slapped ever more oppressive legislation on them to make their continued presence in the Transvaal as unpleasant as possible. They were screaming for relief, and Rhodes decided it should be granted.

In great secrecy the most prominent *uitlanders* organised a Reform Committee which had as its aim the overthrow of Kruger's regime. Openly they continued to make overtures to Pretoria which seemed to be having some effect: Kruger's own supporters wondered if he was not courting disaster to take so hard a line with them. But behind the scenes they were plotting revolution. Rhodes, Beit, Barnato and De Beers were in on the plans, and were already smuggling quantities of arms and ammunition to Johannesburg from Kimberley. It was arranged the Reformers would rebel on New Year's Day, and after seizing Johannesburg would march on Pretoria. They would be supported by an armed incursion from across the border in Bechuanaland, led by Jameson and a number of men from the BSAC and supposedly

13

riding to the aid of *uitlander* women and children whose lives were endangered by the fighting.

Jameson and his men were to cross the Transvaal border three days before the date set for the rebellion. But suddenly there was a change of plan. The Reform Committee found Kruger was bowing to pressure and was ready to negotiate a franchise for the *uitlanders* and a reduction in taxation. The uprising was called off, and word was sent to Jameson to hold his horses. It arrived too late. The fiery little doctor would hear nothing of postponement. Union Jack to the fore, the column advanced on Johannesburg.

Several times the Reform Committee sent messengers imploring Jameson to withdraw. The news reached Rhodes, and he too sent instructions. But they had no effect. Jameson was cast in heroic mould, and in the best tradition of his age determined not to reason why, pledged himself to do or die. In Cape Town, Rhodes was in despair. He would have to bear the whole responsibility of Jameson's action. 'My friend for twenty years, and now he rides in to ruin me.' In Pretoria Oom Paul was all smiles. As a present from heaven, the British had played into his hands and the Reform Committee's case was spent.

The Raid ended in disaster. All the way on its hopeless ride to Johannesburg Jameson's column was harried by the Boers. At last, in an ideal spot, the column was ambushed. The fighting went on all day, the British in the open and the Boers hidden behind the surrounding rocks. The column's artillery blasted at the rocks until most of its ammunition was spent and succeeded in killing one man, though its own losses were appalling. The Boers could snipe at their targets virtually at will. At last Jameson could continue no more. Trembling uncontrollably he surrendered his sword to the Boer general, Piet Cronje.

It was an event which provoked reaction around the world. The Kaiser of Germany sent a telegram congratulating Oom Paul, which provoked a fierce backlash in Britain. Rhodes had to resign. There were rumours that the great British Colonial Secretary himself, Joseph Chamberlain, was strongly implicated. Jameson was handed over to the British for punishment. The leaders of the Reform Committee were tried in Pretoria, and four of them were sentenced to death.

The sentences were commuted and the four were made to pay huge fines instead, but the point was made. There could be no trifling with Oom Paul. It had seemed the old man was losing his grip. Instead, it looked now as if he would survive for ever. Rhodes was in virtual despair. How could he hope to unseat the South African Republic?

14

His dream was as farseeing as ever, but never so far from realisation. Where before the world had feared the British, now it was laughing. Jameson had made the Empire an object of ridicule and done more than any man to bring about its end.

Oom Paul had tweaked the lion's tail and got away with it. In a few years he was in action again, this time fighting the lion tooth and nail and more than holding his own. The South African War was to bring humiliation on the British, with crack forces from all over the Empire tied down in years of frustrating conflict with the light-as-air commandos of the little Boer republics. It was en eye-opener for the more jealous of Britain's rivals, particularly Germany and France. The days of the lion's supremacy were numbered.

Rhodes did not recover. A friend had offered a bet that he would regain his previous strong position within a year of the Jameson Raid. Rhodes told her to forget the bet, and said instead it would take him ten. But though there were already signs he would return to power sooner than that, it was too late to put his theory to the test. In 1902, exhausted by the strain and at last overcome by his failing health, he died in Muizenberg.

3

IT WAS Rhodes's proud boast that the machinery he and his colleagues had created to regulate the diamond trade was so efficient that the *status quo* would remain for years to come. The arrangements were perfect, he claimed. All but a tiny proportion of diamond production was controlled by De Beers, and all but a fraction of sales were handled by a single sales organisation. De Beers and the Syndicate were so interlinked that they seemed inseparable. It was the most impregnable monopoly in the world.

The chairmanship of De Beers passed to Sir Lewis Michell, a Rhodes protégé who could be counted on to maintain existing policies through what proved a trying time: the reorganisation of the diamond trade in the wake of the South African War. Other disciples of Rhodes were with him on De Beers board, and could be expected to support his decisions. In London, the Syndicate continued much as before. Its member firms co-operated in dividing its responsibilities among themselves, and were content to share its business in proportion to their size and importance.

The dominant position in the Syndicate was maintained by Barnatos, Wernher, Beit and Mosenthals, as had been the case since the reorganisation of 1893. The other firms were smaller, but each contained personalities highly thought of among their colleagues, and all co-operated in building the diamond trade to new levels of prosperity through the dingy corridors of their offices in Holborn and Hatton Garden. Representatives of the diamond cutting establishments of Amsterdam and Antwerp visited them at regular intervals to view the 'sights' at which the goods were sold, parcel by parcel and with no come-back if a customer was not satisfied: if, that is, he wanted to be invited back.

Among these merchants was Anton Dunkelsbuhler, a veteran of the earliest days on the diamond fields. Like so many of the others, he was from Germany. He had gone out to South Africa in 1872 to represent Mosenthals in Kimberley. Before long he won a reputation as one of the biggest spending and most generous buyers on the fields. Sir David Harris, Barney Barnato's cousin and himself once a kopje-walloper, left a description of Dunkelsbuhler in his autobiography.

'The quickest mental arithmetician I have ever known,' he wrote. 'He could calculate correctly a given number of carats at any figure long before the ordinary business man could even work them out on paper. Those in the habit of doing business with him accused him of sleeping with a ready reckoner.'

Dunkelsbuhler remained on the diamond fields until 1876 when he returned to Europe on long leave. He had decided to leave Mosenthals and set up on his own, and before leaving Kimberley invested all he had in buying up stocks of stones to sell in London.

'To Diggers!' ran an advertisement in the Kimberley *Diamond News*. 'Mr Anton Dunkelsbuhler intending to leave for Europe in February next, is prepared to buy previous to his departure, all classes of diamonds: Fine Glassy Stones, Pure large Yellow Stones and Large Cleavage are particularly required. Highest Market Rates Paid.'

The profit he made gave him the wherewithal to establish A Dunkelsbuhler and Company with offices on Holborn Viaduct, and soon another office in Kimberley where he employed a resident representative buyer and staff to assist him. It was in this way he took on a young man related to him through his wife, a first cousin of a first cousin: Bernhard Oppenheimer, eldest son of a cigar merchant in a little town near Frankfurt, Friedberg in Hesse, and over the river Rhine from the famous wine-producing area of Oppenheim which gave the family its name.

Bernhard, or Bernard as he was known on the diamond fields and

16

later, had left home when he was 13. His parents, Eduard and Nanny Oppenheimer, were not altogether poor, but no more were they well off. They had a big family, six boys and four girls, and in the troubled conditions of Central Europe in those days they realised their children would have better prospects outside Germany than at home. Already several relatives of theirs had left for South Africa and made good on the river diggings and in Kimberley. Bernard wanted to try his luck with them and he was so obviously determined that his parents gave in and let him go.

He reached Kimberley in the years of the great take-over battles involving Rhodes, Barnato, Beit and the rest of them. These were fascinating times, though also depressing. One by one those beaten in the struggle packed their bags and set off for the newly discovered gold-fields of the Eastern Transvaal and the Witwatersrand. But it was the claim-owners and diggers who were affected, not the diamond buyers. Bernard learnt the business and prospered, and became Dunkels-buhlers' chief representative. When Rhodes triumphed over Barnato and forced through the amalgamation of De Beers and Kimberley Central, Bernard was one of the signatories to the first contract between De Beers and the Diamond Syndicate.

By this time there was a second Oppenheimer in Kimberley – Bernard's younger brother Louis. He had arrived in 1886, at the age of 16. Bernard taught him what he knew, and after a while could safely leave him in charge of the Kimberley office while he himself moved up to the Reef to develop business interests there on Dunkelsbuhlers' behalf. There he fell in with two young Russians fast building a fortune out of property and coal mines, Isaac Lewis and Sammy Marks. They had interests in diamonds too: a few small deposits had been found round Pretoria. They persuaded Bernard to leave Dunkelsbuhlers and come over to them.

Louis remained on in Kimberley several years before himself moving to the Reef and then to London to manage Dunkelsbuhlers' head office. There he arranged a job for his favourite brother, ten years his junior and fourth in the family heirarchy. Ernest Oppenheimer reached London on May 22 1896. It was his sixteenth birthday.

4

AT DUNKELSBUHLERS Ernest started at the bottom. Obviously he was at a considerable advantage in being related to Louis, for there

17

was every prospect that he would follow in his footsteps and become a really accomplished diamond evaluator one day. But for the time he was office dogsbody, with no more responsibility than making the tea and keeping his seniors supplied with stationery.

Though Louis kept a close eye on him, like the rest of the staff he stood in dread of the boss, or Old Dunkels as they all called him behind his back. In physical appearance Dunkels was a little man by now in later middle age, blind in one eye with a spreading girth and a mighty expanse of bald head. He was at his desk one day, with Ernest standing over him to fill an inkwell. Suddenly, disaster. Ernest tipped the well, and the ink splashed down upon Old Dunkels's pink pate.

'Diamond expert!' the great man exploded. 'Diamond expert! Why, you wouldn't even make a good waiter.'

Ernest's starting salary at Dunkelsbuhlers was only £1-0-0 a week. Of this 17s 6d went on his board and lodging, an upstairs room at 10 North Villas, Camden Town, with breakfast and supper. That left half a crown to pay for whatever else he needed. He had to save for new clothes as he grew out of the old, and the £5-0-0 bonus he received each Christmas was earmarked for a new suit and a new pair of boots. One useful economy he was able to make was on fares to and from work. He walked both ways.

Ernest soon progressed in the Dunkelsbuhlers hierarchy, and displayed a natural talent for sorting stones. To him, each had a personality of its own: there was a glow in his eyes as he explored it. No two were the same. He literally fell in love with diamonds, and that is quite a rare thing to happen with men who handle them day in, day out – especially when they are in their rough state, before they have been cut and their inner fire is released. Diamonds were Ernest's first love and the affair would continue for the rest of his life.

A fascinating glimpse of Ernest in these years survives in an article by the leading diamond evaluator, Etienne Fallek of Paris. He joined Dunkelsbuhlers in 1900 at the age of 17, one of the first Frenchmen to work for the Syndicate. Louis was managing the Dunkels office by this time, and was the Syndicate's chief evaluator. He put Fallek to work at the sorting table by the desk from which he directed operations. The newcomer found himself next to Ernest, now twenty years old. The two young men worked side by side for two years.

In these years Dunkelsbuhlers specialised in a particular grade of triangular stones called macles, Fallek recalls. The remaining stones were sent over to the offices of other members of the Syndicate – crystals and octahedrals to Wernher, Beit, misshapen and broken stones to

18

L and A Abrahams, which was now representing Barnatos. Curiously there was little market for the biggest diamonds in those days: buyers made their profits from goods of between three and ten carats, and found they lost on big stones and little stones. The buyers were prepared to sell bigger diamonds for ten per cent less than their value in terms of the series. Louis – 'a true gentleman', Fallek comments – allowed the sorters working for him to buy these big goods on their own account. Fallek later took full advantage of this, buying two or three white stones each month. Ernest, on the other hand, preferred the 'fancies' – the coloured diamonds of interest only to real connoisseurs. He began his collection as soon as his salary warranted it.

Dunkelsbuhlers received a great deal of mail from the mines in South Africa and particularly from Leon Soutro, its representative in Kimberley. Louis handled all this correspondence, but passed it on to Ernest who studied it with extraordinary appetite. Not only that, but Fallek recalls he was never without a selection of sixpenny exercise books in which he painstakingly wrote down everything which might conceivably be of use to him one day. He later transferred the contents of the exercise books to a comprehensive register. In this he kept all the statistics of mine production, outputs, depths and returns, together with many other observations.

When he was 'busy' like this Ernest would pass the diamonds he was supposed to be sorting down the table to his companion with the simple words: 'You don't mind, Fallek.' But he did not appreciate it when Fallek teased him sometimes, telling him 'You will emulate Cecil Rhodes!' He was irritated by the invasion of his privacy, and in any case the taunts came closer to the bone than he cared to admit. He held the magnate and all he stood for in unstinted admiration, particularly after glimpsing him on one of his trips to London.

One particularly interesting period for Ernest would have been the South African War, which, of course, threw the affairs of all the Syndicate firms into some confusion: for four months at the beginning Kimberley was besieged by a strong Boer army with Rhodes himself trapped in the town. Ernest and Louis would have wondered what was happening to Bernard, who was also in Kimberley at this time and serving in the local volunteer force, the Kimberley Regiment.

There were some remarkable goings on in Kimberley in this period – not least thanks to Rhodes, who regarded the military commander of the garrison as completely incompetent and went over his head to send a chain of runners to the British forces demanding immediate relief. More helpfully, he put the De Beers foundry to work making guns –

including Long Cecil – and shells to fire from them, and sheltered women and children down the Kimberley mineshaft during enemy bombardments. The town was relieved in February, 1900, and survived the rest of the war unscathed as Roberts and then Kitchener chased the elusive Boer commandos round the countryside.

It was all so far away, and yet so close: the war filled British newspapers, and a great deal of everyday conversation too. Tiny, remote settlements like Mafeking and Ladysmith and Colesberg became household names – Mafeking even found its way into the dictionary – and for a time South Africa seemed to be the centre of the world. This quickened Ernest's interest in the territory all the more, even if he was not already longing for the chance to visit the country himself.

On the other hand, for all this determination and ambition, Ernest was no sourpuss. There was a feeling of close camaraderie among the fifteen sorters at Dunkelsbuhlers. Fallek conjures up a picture of what happened on foggy days in Holborn: the lamps turned on outside in the street and in the offices, and the young men playing heads and tails 'like little boys' – but with golden guineas.

Twice a week the sorters had dinner together. The meals were not over-extravagant: no wine to drink, for instance, only schnapps and lager beer. But there were cigars in plenty, and certainly there was no shortage of gaiety with jokes and puns flying freely. Fallek says he took enormous pleasure in watching Ernest on these occasions, doubled up with laughter at the table and with tears rolling down his cheeks. Ernest, he says, was regarded by one and all as 'a jolly good fellow'.

By this time five of the Oppenheimer brothers were in England. Besides Louis and Ernest their brothers Gustav and Otto had now arrived and Bernard was home from South Africa. Gustav, between Louis and Ernest in the line of brothers, entered the diamond trade but was not destined to make a great impression on it. Otto, on the other hand, would soon follow in the footsteps of Bernard, Louis and Ernest, joining Dunkelsbuhlers as a sorter and given his initial tuition in diamonds by Etienne Fallek.

A photograph taken soon after the turn of the century shows the five brothers together in a garden in Maidenhead, with Bernard's young son Michael. They are posed in the stiffly 'casual' style that was typical of the age. Bernard is in the centre of the group, with an unfortunately cynical, rather calculating look on his face. He was now an important figure in the diamond world. Beside him, heavily moustached and rather remote, is Gustav.

Louis sits on the lawn and stares the camera in the eye, but coldly and sadly. Young Otto, in contrast, lounges in a deckchair, hat on head and hand in pocket, evidently not giving a damn. Ernest looks distinctly uncomfortable in a high, stiff collar and his best clothes, but meditates quietly with an open book on his lap and another in his hands. By design or otherwise, the picture provides a quite uncanny insight into the brothers' very different characters.

For Ernest to be caught with books in his hands was by no means untypical at this stage. He was spending all available spare time 'improving' himself, trying to catch up on what he now saw as a deficient education. He had left school before his sixteenth birthday, after all. It was up to him to read everything that he could put his hands on, a systematic quest for knowledge that he was to pursue most of his life. It was the kind of dedication that led Fallek to speculate: was this the hint of things to come, the gestation of the future great captain of finance?

Fallek had a more specific notion. Ernest, he was sure, had set his eyes on a particular position: Leon Soutro's in Kimberley. The men at Dunkelsbuhlers had no great respect for the ponderous Frenchman, Fallek suggests: a boring man, and what was worse, 'sans esprit'; the kind of man who spent his time working hard to build his personal fortune with ever greater numbers of shares in De Beers, sending his stock exchange orders through Dunkelsbuhlers in London. All that Fallek could find to say about Soutro was that each time he made the three week voyage between England and South Africa, he stocked up in advance with great quantities of Gallia milk.

Louis Oppenheimer no doubt shared the low regard his firm had for Soutro. Certainly it was he who decided that Soutro should be replaced, and that the right man for his job would be Ernest. All arrangements were made. Ernest would go out to Kimberley for three years, at a salary of £500 a year, and would then be due for a six-month vacation at home before embarking on a second term in South Africa. Soutro was informed.

The representative was rather put out, it may be imagined. Here he was, middle-aged and experienced, superseded by an unknown youth of twenty-two whose single qualification appeared to be his close relationship with the boss. Soutro made no bones about his irritation, complaining bitterly to his staff in Kimberley. But there was nothing else he could do but make the best of the situation. He pulled himself together, and when Ernest's ship docked in Cape Town sent him a warm telegram welcoming him to South Africa.

He was not amused when a message reached him in reply, apparently from Ernest but in fact from his junior office staff: 'Your telegram received: meet me at station to look after luggage.'

5

ERNEST REACHED Kimberley in November, 1902. Rhodes had died eight months before. It is not recorded whether Soutro overcame his displeasure in time to meet Ernest at the station. If he did, he must have had a surprise. Far from the overbearing, arrogant young man he was expecting he would have found a shy, nervous, self-conscious youngster looking rather fewer than his 22 years, conservatively dressed and most apprehensive about all that lay ahead of him. Diamond city or no, Ernest was out of his element.

Ernest had arrived in Kimberley with his personal luggage and £50 in his pocket: all he had in the world. He was to lodge with a relative, at any rate for the time being. There was nothing to detain him from starting work at the first opportunity: like anyone else in a new situation, he wanted to establish himself without delay, as if to prove to everyone that he really did belong. Shyly he went down to the offices of the Syndicate in the diamond market, and after meeting his new colleagues set to work on the diamond tables.

In her book *Diamond* Emily Hahn records an amusing anecdote told by one of the diamond sorters of Ernest's first days in Kimberley:

'I recall the day I first saw Ernest. It was in the sorting room where he was working in Kimberley. He had just got to town, and I noticed him immediately; it was a little place and you always did look twice at strangers in those days. It was 1902, and a warm summer day. His sleeves were rolled up and I noticed his arms immediately. I thought I'd never seen such muscular arms on any man. . . Well, I asked the man in charge of the office, "Who's that fellow with the big arms?" and he said it was a new man, Ernest Oppenheimer, who'd just been sent out from London. He said, "I don't think very much of him from what I've seen so far. He's terribly shy, and he doesn't seem to be very bright".'

The judgment was not very perceptive, but there was little about Ernest in those early days to contradict the impression he created. The others left him largely to himself, or when they did talk to him tended rather to patronise him. He seemed a poor sort of fish to occupy the relatively important position he held.

Ernest was worried by the attitudes shown by the others, and wondered what he ought to do about them. One day he was talking to a guest at the house where he was lodging, rather a famous guest. It was none other than Jameson, who always stayed in the house on his frequent visits to Kimberley.

Ernest explained how worried he was by his relationship with the rest of the staff. They seemed to have no regard for him at all: a pipsqueak, after all, certainly no older than they were themselves and indeed younger than most.

'Every day I go there, and I work as hard as anybody in the firm, if not harder,' he told Jameson. 'I sit down and sort diamonds with them. Yet somehow they don't respect me.'

'That's the trouble,' the wily doctor replied. 'Of course they don't respect you for working hard. Don't sort diamonds: let them do the sorting.'

Ernest followed the advice. The problem was soon resolved.

Public Servant

IN CHARGE of the Diamond Syndicate's operations in Kimberley during those years after the South African War was a middle-aged German called Fritz Hirschhorn, who had been out on the diamond fields since the early days. He had made his fortune on the river diggings, then moved to Kimberley to represent Wernher, Beit. After some years in Kimberley he was invited to join the board of De Beers, first as Alfred Beit's alternate and latterly as a full director in his own right.

Hirschhorn was stocky and square-built, with a powerful frame and bull-like head: a quiet, rather gentle sort of man, with a generous nature that won him friendship and respect in every section of the Kimberley community. He was a bachelor, living alone in a big house opposite the Sanatorium built by Rhodes before the Siege, just off the road to Beaconsfield.

Though he lived alone, he cannot have been lonely. He delighted in the gracious social life that marked Kimberley in those days: the dinners and dances, the evenings at the Theatre Royal and at the Kimberley Club, the expeditions to Alexandersfontein Estate each week-end. Besides, he had a great sense of humour. On one occasion he invited a number of friends to his house, only to tell them when they arrived that they had come on the wrong night. The house was bare, and he had nothing to give them. Magnanimously he offered to try and salvage their wasted evening by taking them to a nearby hotel for a simple dinner. When they reached it they found he had organised a lavish banquet for them with orchestra in attendance.

Hirschhorn was Kimberley's greatest authority on diamonds at this time and was naturally closely involved in company politics. Visitors to Kimberley made a point of calling on him, and many had a standing invitation to stay at his house. Alfred Beit, Leander Starr Jameson, Solly Joel: all these were his guests. So were all those involved most closely with De Beers itself: Gardner Williams, the De Beers consulting engineer; Sir Lewis Michell, Rhodes's successor as chairman; Francis Oats, who would soon succeed Michell; William Pickering, the company's secretary, who lived across the road.

But however full his life, it is clear Fritz Hirschhorn was more than usually pleased when told that his young cousin Ernest would soon be coming to Kimberley. Ernest was related to him through his mother, who was herself a Hirschhorn. Fritz had already played host to Bernard and Louis when they lived on the diamond fields, but that had been ten years before. How well he knew their brother is a moot point. He and Ernest would no doubt have met in London on one of Hirschhorn's visits on long leave, but there would have been little to hold them together. Apart from the considerable age group, both were uncommonly shy.

But whatever the relationship, it was quickly decided that Ernest should move into Hirschhorn's house. In fact, he lodged there for three years, until it was time for him to return to England on long leave. He was lucky in more ways than one. Not only was he living in surroundings far more luxurious than he could have afforded on his salary, but at the same time he had the chance of learning all Fritz Hirschhorn could teach him about the diamond business. On top of that, he had an immediate introduction to the men who made Kimberley tick, and indeed the men who made South Africa.

One of the first he got to know was David Harris from the East End of London, a cousin of Barney Barnato and his brother Harry. Harris had preceded them to the diamond fields, and persuaded them to join him on the strength of the fortune he made there. What he did not tell them was that it came not from diamonds but from a roulette wheel. Though he had never gambled in his life before, one night a friend took him into a canteen where a game was in progress, with the object of having a quick 'flutter, win or lose a tenner'. The proprietors were offering free drinks to those playing, and Harris's friend called for a small bottle of champagne and had it poured into two glasses. He gave one to Harris, who told the story in his autobiography.

'Up to this time I had been only a disinterested spectator, being determined not to risk my money at gambling. However, just as I had finished drinking my glass of champagne, one of the proprietors remarked significantly that some men only visited the rooms for the purpose of getting free drinks. This remark aroused my ire, as I thought it was meant for me. So purely out of pique, I put a sovereign on number thirteen with the intention of losing it and clearing out. But, strange to tell, the ball eventually rolled into this number, which paid 35–1.

'Well, to cut a long story short, I played on till 1.30 in the morning, and punted with such luck that I broke the bank. I eventually left the premises I was so loath to enter, with £800 in cash, and a cheque for £600 – £1 400 in all. At last I thought my fortune had been made, for I never dreamt of possessing such wealth. I have never entered a gambling house since.'

David Harris went to London on his winnings and when he returned to South Africa he took Harry Barnato with him. Barney went out a few months later, and the brothers were soon calling for their nephews Jack, Woolf and Solly Joel. This side of the family made money hand over fist and did not let their cousin go short. Harris later enrolled in the military to fight in the Kaffir Wars and subsequently arranged Kimberley's town defences during the siege, in command of the Town Guard.

But of all the interesting acquaintances Ernest made through Fritz Hirschhorn the most important was Jameson. The little doctor was one of the most glamorous characters in all South Africa's history, though to look at him you would not have guessed it. Small, neat, good-looking, dapper, informal: he was likely to drop off to sleep at any moment, sprawled out on a rocking chair in the afternoon heat.

This was the man who had been Rhodes's best friend, who shared his hopes and his dreams and who on his death pledged himself to continue the work Rhodes had begun. From 1902 he was leader of the Opposition in the Cape Parliament, the Progressive Party. Two years later, thanks largely to the disenfranchisement of those Cape Boers who had rebelled against the colonial government, Jameson's party was elected to office. Not ten years after the raid which had brought him disgrace and disrepute all over the world, Jameson was Prime Minister of the Cape Colony.

It was an outstanding achievement, and it may be imagined how it appeared to Ernest when the modest little doctor arrived in Kimberley on his periodic visits, and came to stay with Hirschhorn. Ernest and Jameson would have had much to talk about.

One thing, however, they would not mention: the Raid itself. In Jameson's mind it had become a blank spot, after all the disgrace and suffering it had brought him. About this time Sir Percy FitzPatrick, who had such success with his book *Jock of the Bushveld*, wanted to write a full account of what happened. Several times he sounded out

Jameson, only to meet with an explosive reaction: 'What's the use of talking? Who knows the whole truth? Let it go at that.'

Then one evening FitzPatrick tried for the last time. Jameson had been talking without reserve, and the writer thought he would succeed. But again there was disappointment.

'Jameson nodded slowly and began quite calmly and deliberately, but in less than a minute he stopped and I saw the blood rush to his face, and his eyes began to glow, and suddenly he leapt from his chair. His frail but intensely nervous frame shaking with the storm of feeling and with both hands clenched to his side, he blazed out, "God in Heaven, what's the use of talking!" And in a second he was out of the room.'

A key to Jameson's character lay in his reading habits, and in the fantasy of his daydreams. 'I remember him sitting on the stoep, his right leg crossed over his left, reading about swashbucklers,' Ernest told an interviewer in later years. The swashbucklers were characters in the novels of Sir Walter Scott, which were the only books Jameson had any time for. If in leading the raid he was thinking of himself as a Scotian hero, much of its glorious folly can be understood and the whole affair looks a good deal less sinister.

That, certainly, was what the British public saw in Jameson and what appealed to many South Africans as well. Kipling, for a long time Rhodes's protégé as the poet of Empire, is supposed to have based one of his best-known poems on Jameson:

> '*If you can make one heap of all your winnings,*
> *And risk it all on one turn of pitch-and-toss,*
> *And lose, and start again at your beginnings,*
> *And never breathe a word about your loss. . .*'

The poem was *If*, and its conclusion was '. . . *you'll be a man, my son.*' It was a poem of message, and the young diamond buff took it to heart.

Ernest listened carefully to everything Jameson told him, and indeed to everything anyone told him. He admitted later it was Jameson who set him thinking that he should aim to head his own organisation one day, rather than work for others. This rather cut across the ambitions he had had before coming out to Kimberley: to save £50 000, invest it and live on the proceeds the rest of his life. That way he could devote himself to what he most enjoyed: burying himself in books and catching up on what he had missed through his rather stunted education. For the time, though, both of these aims were as remote as the moon: he was earning just £10–0–0 a week.

With his rather studious tastes it may be imagined Ernest was not to

28

be found painting Kimberley red. He had never learnt to dance: in fact, he never did learn his whole life through. There was gambling at Kimberley's hotels and the Kimberley Club, in particular poker and faro. But Ernest was not to be tempted into such activity: he preferred to save his money for more important things. On the other hand, when there was a party he enjoyed himself. Standards of entertainment in Kimberley were high, and at such parties the champagne flowed freely. Ernest learnt to drink it, and promised himself that when he could afford it he would drink nothing else. It was one of his sadnesses that by the time he had enough money he had come to prefer whisky and soda.

Another taste he acquired in this period was for biltong, the sun-dried venison that had traditionally been the staple diet of Boer adventurers in the veld and is as distinctively South African as the song *Sarie Marais*. Outsiders can hardly believe that the bonehard, unattractive strings of meat can be edible: but its devotees prefer it to anything else. Certainly Ernest made it a rule later in life to have a special supply made up for him in Kimberley every year – and some would say that from this time he could be accounted a true South African.

But life was not all leisure and there was work to be done. The firms belonging to the Syndicate each had offices in the diamond market, not far from the famous Big Hole. The offices were next door to each other in an L-shaped block: Wernher, Beit on the corner, with Dunkels-buhlers and L and A Abrahams which represented Barnatos on one side and Mosenthals and some of the smaller firms on the other. There were more buyers' offices across the street, little glass-fronted shops, really no more than booths, and next to them more offices catering for the alluvial diggers and debris washers who still abounded round Kimberley.

The Syndicate's agreement was to buy the whole production of the De Beers mines. It was handed over when the head office at De Beers collected something like 50 000 carats, provisionally sorted already according to size, quality and colour. The diamonds were packed in tin despatch boxes and carried to the Syndicate's offices under armed guard. Now the sorters had to divide the goods among the firms participating according to the percentages laid down in the agreement. To this end they pooled their resources, with most of the sorting done by their combined staffs on the first floor of Wernher, Beit.

Here the diamonds had to be sorted all over again, this time not so much to evaluate them as to establish what was available, and make it possible to divide them fairly between the different firms. They had first to be sieved, to establish their size according to eleven grades; then classified according to quality; and lastly examined for colour.

There was an intriguing vocabulary in the sorting room, a relic of the earliest days on the diamond fields. 'Close goods' were the pure, well-shaped stones, the prize finds; 'spotted stones' were the crystals slightly flawed, but not so badly that they could not be cut; 'rejection' stones, on the other hand, were too badly spoilt to be workable. Broken stones, anything but the pure octahedral shape of the ideal diamond, were 'cleavage'; 'flats' were distorted octahedrals, and 'macles' triangular stones which were really two stones joined together. 'Rubbish' was the refuse material, only a little better than the lowest grade of all, the 'boart' which was used for cutting and polishing workable crystals.

Once the stones were sorted, the staff at Wernher, Beit's gathered them in 'parcels' to be despatched to London, a fixed quota of stones of different sizes, qualities and colours in each. In all some 350 to 400 parcels were made up from each consignment of gems delivered by the company. The parcels were put into specially marked papers carrying descriptions of their contents, then bundled in tin boxes securely wrapped in cloth-lined paper, carefully sealed and delivered to the post office to be forwarded to England.

Ernest was Dunkelsbuhlers' representative, and as such in charge of an independent office. But with the Syndicate's firms working in such close co-operation it was clearly in the general interest to simplify administration. Rather than stand on his own rights Ernest was happy to place himself under Fritz Hirschhorn and his assistant E W Weatherby as the Syndicate's chief representatives in Kimberley. His staff co-operated with the sorters of the other Syndicate firms in making up the parcels to be despatched to London.

Ernest would have been happy if it were not for one major snag. He found himself with too much time on his hands. The Syndicate's operations in Kimberley were run to a formula, and left Ernest and the other representatives with nothing more than administrative responsibility. He was glad, then, when Hirschhorn invited him to sit in on meetings of the De Beers directors from time to time, helping to take the minutes.

Here as nowhere else he could catch the atmosphere of the world of Rhodes and Barnato and Beit and the other pioneers: the austere board room looking out on the little courtyard behind; the twin fire-places, one at each end; the long table with its round-backed leather chairs; the walls hung with photographs of directors who had died or retired; on one mantelpiece the cheque for £5-million odd which De Beers had paid to the liquidators of the Kimberley Central; and dominating the room from the other end a photograph of Rhodes. What decisions had been made, what plans laid in this room!

Ernest had time to make up his own mind about the personalities on the De Beers board, all so different. The one that impressed him most was Barnato's nephew Solly Joel, an imposing hunk of a man with a rich growth of nautical beard. Now his uncle was dead, his elder brother Jack was living permanently in England and his younger brother Woolf had been shot dead by a blackmailer, Solly was virtually in sole charge of the great Barnato empire: not Barnatos alone, with its huge interests in De Beers and the Syndicate and Jagersfontein which it controlled, but also Johnnies on the Rand with its great gold mines and big property investments.

Solly Joel lived in the tradition of the Randlords, dividing his time between his palatial residences in London and Johannesburg, with a steam yacht named after his daughter, a string of racehorses, sporting interests in every sphere and the great and the famous among his friends. He did not often attend these board meetings in Kimberley, but when he did it was a red letter day. The other directors fussed round him like so many flies – particularly David Harris his cousin, who, of course, relied on Joel's support for his continued influence.

It was quite usual at these meetings of the board for the directors to bring with them some glittering new prize from the mines, to be handed round and admired and perhaps envied. At one meeting Solly Joel dipped in his pocket and proudly produced a huge chunk which he duly passed across to the others.

'How much do you think it's worth?' he asked them.

They passed it from hand to hand, each increasing the estimates that had gone before. All agreed it was something very special indeed. At last it reached Ernest. He looked at it, but said nothing. Solly Joel glared at him.

'Well, Oppenheimer? What's its value?'

'Nothing. It's not a diamond.'

'What do you mean?' roared the magnate.

'It's glass.'

'You prepared to put £50 on that?'

Ernest swallowed hard. With the state of his finances as they were £50 was a lot of money. But he was sure he was right. At this time a noted diamond evaluator was visiting Kimberley from London, and it was left to him to decide the matter. He agreed with Ernest. It turned

31

out Solly Joel's diamond was a lump of broken bottle glass, retrieved from the gravel of the river diggings where it had lain for years and assumed a beautiful shape which made it look just like diamond. Joel paid up, and learnt a respect for the precocious young German which he did not forget later in life.

'Best £50 I ever earned,' Ernest used to say.

No doubt the windfall came in very handy at this stage of Ernest's career. But he would have gained more lasting benefit from the actual deliberations of the directors, which became quite heated at times. These successors of Rhodes were far from united in their interpretation of his policies, and their views of how they should be put into effect. One area where this was especially apparent was in respect of several new diamond deposits discovered in recent years, which seemed to be more than usually important.

It had never been Rhodes's policy to set out to win control of all diamond production regardless: he had happily tolerated small companies working diamond pipes like the Roberts Victor Mine and Blauwboschfontein in the Free State, and of course Jagersfontein and Koffiefontein. Their production was tiny in comparison with what emerged from the pipes in Kimberley, and in any case the individual buyers dealing with these companies and with independent diggers were happy to follow De Beers policy on prices as they were for the good of all.

The new discoveries were in the Transvaal, in the neighbourhood of Pretoria. They had seemed insignificant in comparison with the gold finds further south, so nobody had bothered about them. But one of the mining houses on the Reef, Lewis and Marks, had been investing heavily in the discoveries on the recommendation of Ernest's brother Bernard, who was now heading a full diamond wing of the organisation.

Now came news that a really important deposit had been uncovered: a diamond pipe much bigger than anything found in the Kimberley district, in fact more than six times as big. Its discoverers were calling it the Premier Mine, and the company they formed induced the Transvaal colonial government to take a 60 per cent interest in the project to help raise enough capital to bring it into production.

A number of Kimberley men by now living in Johannesburg went to see what was happening at the new mine, and returned with widely divergent reports. Many thought there was nothing to it: that the stories of its potential were ludicrous exaggerations. Others took them more seriously. It is said Alfred Beit was so horrified by what he saw that he had a stroke which contributed to his death a few years later.

Not only mining men but Syndicate representatives went up to have a look, and among them Ernest. It was his first trip to the Transvaal, and must have been exciting in view of all he had heard about it. Bernard had quickly appreciated the importance of the new mine and negotiated a contract with the company to buy its production for Lewis and Marks. He will have passed on his opinions to Ernest, who in turn told Louis. On the strength of them Dunkelsbuhlers bought a healthy stake in the operation even before it came into production – at a time when other Syndicate fiims and certainly De Beers were lukewarm at best and in several cases downright scornful.

Three years after operations started, the mine manager at the Premier, a man called Wells, spotted a telltale glint in the side of the open pit and hopped down to investigate. It looked like diamond, and he gouged out the stone with his penknife. He must nearly have fainted. What he had discovered was the biggest diamond the world has ever seen, no fewer than $3\ 024\frac{1}{2}$ carats of almost flawless blue-white which could barely be grasped in one hand. On the urging of General Smuts, who had made his name through the South African War, the Transvaal government bought the stone and sent it to King Edward VII as a mark of loyalty. The king sent it to Amsterdam to be cut into several stones. These were set in the British Crown Jewels, where they remain to this day. Named the Cullinan Diamond after the Thomas Cullinan who was the man behind the mine, the astonishing stone set the Premier firmly on the map.

Ernest's dreams lived on. He was learning all the time: learning about diamonds, though this was a labour of love; learning about gold, which was so crucial for this new country; even learning of the prospects outside the mining industry: he visited the Bechuanaland Protectorate and the Northern and Southern Rhodesias divided by the Zambezi, still united under royal charter by Rhodes's British South Africa Company, and as many other parts of South Africa as he could.

His first three-year term in Kimberley was nearly over, and he was due to take long leave in London. Louis had already confirmed that if he wished he could return to South Africa. He had thoroughly enjoyed his life on the diamond fields and had already half made up his mind he meant to settle in South Africa permanently. Certainly the opportunities seemed brighter than any England could offer.

To Ernest as he set sail from Cape Town the prospect of six months in London must have appeared attractive indeed. He would have the chance of looking up all his relatives and friends, and of going over to

Germany to visit his parents. They were not getting any younger. But what he looked forward to most of all was visiting Mary Pollak, or May as he knew her.

He had met her not long before he set out for Kimberley in 1902, at Louis's wedding reception. Louis was marrying Charlotte Pollak, May's elder sister. They were the daughters of a wealthy stockbroker, a past president of the London Stock Exchange. Young Ernest was captivated by May, at this time only sixteen years old, and when he told her of his fate in being sent out to the darkest continent for the eternity of three years she said she would keep in touch with him.

All this time May had made good her promise, and she and Ernest had been in close contact. Now he would be seeing her again. It was a thought that alarmed him a little. She would have grown up. She had left school, and would soon be going up to Girton College in Cambridge. Ernest, of course, had not attended university. Would they have anything in common?

He need not have worried. May was as he remembered her. In no time he overcame his initial reticence and decided he wanted to make her his wife. He proposed and she accepted. Her father agreed to the match, and they began planning the wedding. It was all rather rushed. Ernest would soon have to return to South Africa, and he intended to take May with him. That meant she would have to forget Girton, but it was a sacrifice she was ready to make.

When they reached Kimberley, Ernest and May lodged with Fritz Hirschhorn for a time; but clearly they would have quickly to move into a home of their own. The best Ernest could find was an apartment in the town centre, in a fairly new block called Siege Buildings. It was not over-comfortable, but for the newly-weds it was adequate. In due course they would have a house of their own, but that could wait.

2

THERE WAS a distinct change in Ernest's fortunes. He had been careful to save all he could of his salary in the years that had passed and now had quite a useful nest-egg. Besides, May was relatively well off in her own right. After a few months in Kimberley she and Ernest decided they would build a house. They chose a site not far from Fritz Hirschhorn's, down the street which had now appeared in what had been open veld and was called Lodge Road. Building began that year, with the promise that the house would soon be completed. The project took on new urgency when they found May was expecting.

In business, Ernest's fortunes appeared quite stable. The De Beers machine was working smoothly with the five mines in regular production and the Syndicate's member firms in close co-operation. Sales were going well and the only disquieting feature of the trade was the challenge offered by the Premier away in the Transvaal. Its production had been rising spectacularly from 750 000 carats in 1904 to nearly 1 900 000 by 1907 – very nearly as much as De Beers itself.

Ernest had a close interest in what was happening at the Premier, not only through the Dunkelsbuhlers shareholding but because its production was handled by Lewis and Marks. Things were going so well that Bernard had been made a partner in the firm, and had formed a full-scale organisation called the South African Diamond Corporation in direct competition with the Syndicate. Besides the various Transvaal producers he had added Roberts Victor and Blaauwboschfontein in the Free State to his belt and now represented a considerable challenge to the other merchants.

By now De Beers realised the significance of the threat offered by the Premier, though the directors did not know how to counteract it. The Syndicate was equally impotent. The firms knew Rhodes would have worked for amalgamation, as he had in Kimberley. But if they followed such policies they would have to deal with the Transvaal government, and that was a very different proposition from Barney Barnato. The best the Syndicate could do was negotiate a special sales contract to buy £193 000 worth of diamonds from the Premier each year, compared with their £450 000 from De Beers. But that still left the bulk of production in the Diamond Corporation's hands – as much as it could handle. Bernard was now selling direct to the United States.

Then, so unexpectedly that the trade had no time to prepare for it, there was an international slump in 1907 and the demand for diamonds almost dried up overnight. The Syndicate was left with £3-million worth of stock on its hands and no chance of getting rid of it. Three member firms went to the wall. The remainder had to take drastic action, going back on their agreement with De Beers and the Premier and refusing to buy more stones. Between themselves the firms agreed to freeze the greater part of their accumulated stock, and release only small quantities of stones each month in a bid to keep up the price.

De Beers was in a tight corner. A contract was a contract, but in the circumstances there was nothing the directors could do. They could hardly offer to sell to the Diamond Corporation, though Bernard showed

35

no sign of co-operating with the Syndicate in freezing his stocks. Rather, he was allowing his prices to fall. Mining at the Premier and elsewhere was a lot cheaper than at Kimberley, for the open pits were not really all that deep as yet, and there was no question of underground mining. But De Beers was forced to cut back on production at all five of its mines and to close Dutoitspan altogether. Hundreds of miners were thrown out of work and thousands more were affected: the depression hit the whole community.

Ernest was in Kimberley at this stage and saw the hardship for himself. For the first time he could appreciate the dangerous position of an industry based on a luxury trade, and the delicate economic balance that could net fortunes at one minute and the next throw thousands into misery and poverty. With May, he played a big part in organising relief soup kitchens for those out of work – many of them not De Beers employees at all but drawn from peripheral occupations which depended on the prosperity of the mines.

The fate of the unemployed made a considerable impression on Ernest. As a result he soon determined to play a rather bigger part in public life, and seek election to the Kimberley Town Council. When a vacancy occurred early the next year, he was nominated and in due course elected. He took his seat at the council's horseshoe table in the town hall.

Kimberley was in chaos, the whole confidence of the industry undermined. De Beers had cut back production, but it looked as if the sacrifice might be in vain. Far from co-operating for the mutual good, the Premier had actually *increased* production so that it was now well ahead of De Beers' and still rising. Bernard had to get rid of it all somehow, and was left with no alternative but to let prices drop even further. From an average 23s a carat in 1904 they had fallen to 14s 9d in 1908 and the next year to 12s 6d. The price cuts affected the Syndicate's business too, and even the important firms with their interests spread in many areas were finding the going tough. Bernard was not popular.

As if all this was not enough, there was news of a blow from a completely unexpected and unprotected quarter: the discovery of huge new diamond deposits in a new area, not in South Africa at all but across the border in German South West. Suddenly the British monopoly of the diamond trade was in jeopardy, and the market became vulnerable to the kind of competition which could spell ultimate ruin.

Not that De Beers was immediately concerned by the new threat. Reports rather understressed the importance of the finds. It was said

36

only a few alluvial stones were involved, found by a labourer working on the railway near Lüderitz. He recognised them as diamonds because he had previously worked in Kimberley, and showed them to his supervisor who promptly had them tested. When it was proved they were indeed diamonds the supervisor took out prospecting claims all over the area, and as soon as possible began digging in earnest. The new fields were declared a public diggings, and miners streamed in from all over the world.

Strange stories filtered down to the Cape. They said it was just like the boom days in Kimberley. Bars and gambling joints seemed to grow out of the ground to serve the diggers' needs. A man wanting a drink might pay for it with a diamond, and after a little luxury like this the bartender might get choosy and reject all but the best stones. Fritz Hirschhorn led a De Beers delegation to investigate the discoveries. But its report did little to change the opinion of the new chairman, Francis Oats, that the discovery represented only a small threat to the trade which would soon fade as the deposits were exhausted. Cecil Rhodes had always insisted alluvial diggings had a limited life however rich they appeared at first, so could safely be disregarded.

In Kimberley Ernest was watching the position with interest, though no doubt he was as confused about the situation as most people. All they could do was sit and wait for matters to resolve themselves. The German authorities soon decided to form their own selling organisation, the Regie, which took complete charge of all diamond buying on the fields and marketed their production through Berlin. In London, the Syndicate decided to take no action, or at least not for the present.

In South Africa, the trade struggled on. Sales picked up as the recession eased, though with prices so low it was difficult even to recover costs let alone make a profit. However De Beers top management retained its optimism. The company had seen and weathered many such crises: they could even work out a timetable to show that these occurred on average every seventh or eighth year. Yet always the trade had seemed to come through more strongly than before. Now the Syndicate firms and the Diamond Corporation worked together to restore prices to their old levels. Bernard was not unreasonable.

For the Oppenheimers, however, there were other things to think of. Safe in her new house May gave birth to Ernest's son and heir on October 28 1908. They named him Harry Frederick.

3

ERNEST FOUND local politics to his liking. He could immerse himself in the affairs of the community, and was now generally accepted as one of Kimberley's leading citizens with his views widely respected. His speeches at council debates were accorded generous space in the *Diamond Fields Advertiser*, and it was clear his fellow councillors admired him greatly. It was a sad blow, then, when he fell seriously ill and had to give up his interests in business and local politics. May took him to Cape Town to recuperate. They were there several months. When they returned to Kimberley in mid-February, 1909, Ernest attended the next council meeting and promptly tendered his resignation.

It was a necessary step, he explained. He and May were due to set off for England in a month's time, on long leave. He would be away eight months. He felt it would not be fair to the ratepayers he represented to be absent so long. Better, he felt, to resign for the time and perhaps seek re-election on his return.

Ernest used the opportunity to present a broad survey of the many wrongs he felt the council should put right, from providing pensions for its long-service employees to pushing through the amalgamation of the twin townships Kimberley and Beaconsfield; from the waterworks question to a recommendation that the relief soup kitchen, which he had organised at the time of the diamond slump, should be discontinued as it might encourage men to shun employment.

Ernest sat down, and it was the turn of each councillor in succession to make a few remarks regretting his resignation. Some pressed him to withdraw it and to continue as a councillor even when on long leave. But Ernest insisted it was not fair, and said he would take his chance again when he returned.

'The Mayor spoke in hearty appreciation of Councillor Oppenheimer's services to the town, and expressed the sincere regret of the Councillors that he was compelled to take such a step. He would be welcomed on his return to the Council, and he was sure that if there was no opening for him in Ward 3, some other ward would be pleased to have the benefit of his valuable services. Councillor Oppenheimer had given a good deal of his time and attention to the affairs of the Council, and had thoroughly studied every question with which he had to deal in a practical manner. They appreciated

The Oppenheimer brothers together in Maidenhead, Berkshire, at about the turn of the century. *Back from left:* Gustav, Bernard and Ernest; *front from left:* Louis, Bernard's son Michael and Otto. *Anglo American Corporation.*

The Oppenheimers' home in Friedberg, Hesse. Ernest was born here in 1880. *Anglo American Corporation.*

The Mayor of Kimberley. Ernest was elected to this office in 1912, and remained mayor until his resignation in 1915. *Kimberley Municipality.*

his valuable work, and they hoped it would not be long till they had him back around the horseshoe.'

Ernest duly set off for England, and with him went May and Harry. They returned towards the end of the year for Ernest's third term on the diamond fields.

Barely were they back in Lodge Road than it was time to celebrate Harry's first birthday party. Ernest and May hired a marquee for the garden, and invited all the children in the neighbourhood – including William Pickering's daughter, now Dolly Farrer, who was at this stage eleven years old and lived across the road. She remembers the party well. The guest of honour could not be expected to play a leading part, but the other children had a great time hunting treasure trove and playing all the other games of the day, and eating bread and butter covered with 'hundreds and thousands'.

Important things had been happening while the Oppenheimers were in England. Delegates from the Cape Colony and the old Orange Free State, the Transvaal and Natal had attended a 'National Convention' to evolve a formula for the unification of the four colonies. At last their work was complete, and the British Parliament passed the South Africa Bill. From May 31 1910, South Africa was one land, with General Botha of the Transvaal appointed as the first Prime Minister and a cabinet which included elements of all the old colonial parliaments.

There were some ticklish problems to deal with. In trying to circumvent impassioned local prejudices the negotiators recommended no fewer than three capitals for the new country: Cape Town for the legislature, Bloemfontein for the judiciary, and Pretoria for the executive. Each of the old colonies became a province with its own laws and administration. There was provision for the eventual inclusion of Northern and Southern Rhodesia and the protectorates of Bechuanaland, Swaziland and Basutoland within the framework of Union – so long as all sides were agreed on policies of mutual benefit.

Ernest, meanwhile, had been fretting to rejoin the Kimberley Council, but had to wait until June, 1910, before there was a chance to return to the horseshoe. He must have felt he had never been away. All the old problems lingered on – the waterworks question, the soup kitchens for the unemployed, pensions for the aged, and the old perennial of the relationship between Kimberley and Beaconsfield which were administered as separate municipalities though only three miles apart. Ernest returned to battle with each of these burning questions, but now made a point of interesting himself much more in the community as a whole and all that was involved in it.

39

There was, for instance, a new attraction at Alexandersfontein: magnificent men in flying machines. The African Aviation Syndicate – Captain Guy Livingstone, Evelyn Driver and Cecil Compton Paterson – had reached South Africa in time for an 'aviation fortnight' in Cape Town some months before, equipped with a Bleriot monoplane and a Gnome biplane. Their aim was to foster an interest in aviation throughout South Africa.

De Beers offered the aviators a large tract of ground at Alex 'eminently suited for testing purposes'. There the intrepid trio gave a series of displays in their fragile craft – when, that is, the machines were in flying order. Driver's monoplane gave endless trouble, and it was left to Paterson to provide most of the excitement and stir local interest. Kimberley folk out at Alex each week-end applauded enthusiastically as the biplane swooped precariously overhead.

One event in particular caught local imagination – a race over six miles between Paterson's biplane and a motor-cycle. 'Mr Arthur Wright, riding a $3\frac{1}{2}$ horsepower Bradbury motor-cycle, essayed to race Paterson with his 50 horsepower Gnome engine-fitted biplane', reported the *DFA*. 'The race was from scratch for a gold medal. From the word "go" the airman asserted his supremacy over the motor cycle, and encircling the course at an average rate of two minutes for each twelve furlongs, he finished the race in eight minutes dead – five furlongs ahead of his rival.'

That was not all. 'Mr Paterson terminated an afternoon's display demonstrating the utility of the biplane in warfare. Ascending to "giddy heights" the airman attempted with remarkable success to drop "bombs" on to an imaginary camp marked off on the course by a large tarpaulin. The "bombs" were of the harmless variety, being nothing less than small musk melons. Thus terminated the most brilliant aviation display ever seen on the Diamond Fields.'

But there was trouble. Disagreement between the three members of the Syndicate forced their company into liquidation in September. Livingstone and Driver left Kimberley, though Paterson remained to arrange the disposal of their assets. It was as well he did. The syndicate's efforts in Kimberley had not been in vain. Local residents decided the aviation business was just what Kimberley needed, and formed a new company – Paterson Aviation Syndicate Ltd. Its directors were the men who provided the money to set the scheme on its feet: Tom Hill, who himself bought Paterson's biplane to enable him to continue flying; Alpheus Williams, David Harris's son Herbert, Charles May, George Ronaldson, David Macgill – and Ernest Oppenheimer.

40

The Paterson syndicate was no flying circus, whatever the quality of its early exhibitions. The young Englishman had serious ambitions for his new school. 'We came to this country with a purpose and object in view,' he told the *Diamond Fields Advertiser*. 'Namely, to interest the Government in aviation, so that when they decide to form their defence scheme, they will probably agree to form an aviation corps.'

It was not long before the South African Defence Force was duly brought into being. Paterson began badgering the Union government with his ideas – greatly helped by Fritz Hirschhorn who provided him with his most important contacts. They persuaded General Smuts himself to visit Kimberley to see what was happening. When he returned to Cape Town he recommended the cabinet to enrol ten pupils to be trained as military pilots. These eventually constituted one of the earliest air forces in the world. With the private pupils already under tuition, it seemed the school's future was assured.

Paterson invited a fellow aviator, E W Cheeseman, out from England to assist him. Soon after his arrival Cheeseman crashed the precious biplane and when malaria complicated his injuries died in Kimberley Hospital – the first fatality in South African aviation. The ten military pilots were sent elsewhere, Paterson returned to England, and Kimberley's flying school, South Africa's first and hopefully greatest, closed down for good. It was one of the few ventures in which Ernest interested himself to end in failure, though certainly not for lack of prescience. Far from it, the investment provided a foretaste of his far-sighted views of the future.

But in spite of this disappointment, there was much to compensate Ernest in other directions. For one thing, his family was growing. On October 17 1910, May had borne their second son, Frank Leslie. Another new member of the household was May's younger sister, as yet unmarried but extremely attractive and more than enough to tempt Fritz Hirschhorn. Each evening the gouty old bachelor came courting, though without notable success. The sister eventually married an officer in the Indian army.

Ernest and May enjoyed a fairly modest social life. Ernest had long been a member of the Kimberley Club, but had no great patience with the all-night gambling sessions each week-end which were the club's chief diversion. His creed was early to bed, early to rise. But he did take May to the occasional dances held there, and regularly to the theatre. Sometimes they took Harry with them to the theatre as a special treat. Dolly Farrer remembers he used to chew sweets right through the performance.

The Oppenheimers were an attractive couple, modest and accomplished, and were popular guests everywhere they went. On the other hand, May immersed herself in all Ernest's affairs, well able to keep pace with him and give timely advice when needed. There was, for instance, the old perennial of amalgamation. All talk in South Africa was of union, Ernest liked to point out, so surely this was the time to bring about the amalgamation of Kimberley and Beaconsfield. All the objections came from Beaconsfield, or so the Kimberley councillors insisted. Their counterparts in the Beaconsfield Council were worried by what had all the trappings of a take-over. What would happen to Beaconsfield's name? But more important, would they retain any say in the running of a combined council?

Ernest had patiently to make the point again and again, that the plan was for union, not annexation. Beaconsfield's name would be retained, as it is to this day. Beaconsfield would continue to elect its own councillors, but they would serve on the combined Kimberley Town Council, sharing equal rights with the councillors representing Kimberley proper.

At last all the details were agreed. The new council was to come into being from the beginning of 1912. Each ward voted in its new representatives and together they elected the first mayor of the combined municipalities of Kimberley and Beaconsfield. Their choice was unanimous, and fell on Ernest.

4

IF ERNEST had influence before, now he had responsibility: two years to do what he could to make Kimberley South Africa's model city. He started with many advantages: the goodwill and co-operation of De Beers, the support of his fellow councillors from both Kimberley and Beaconsfield, some of the best public services in South Africa brought through the prosperity of the diamond fields. But there were problems too, particularly in trying to fit together the quite separate elements that were the two communities.

There was, for instance, the pressing question of the tramways. Until now several independent systems had existed side by side, catering for the different parts of the twin townships. They had charged inordinately high fares to cover their costs. Now the municipalities were united Ernest could press home a scheme by which the different companies handed over their assets to De Beers for appropriate compensation.

After the take-over there was a marked upsurge in efficiency and a spectacular drop in fares.

At the same time, Ernest's commitments to the diamond industry were as full as ever. He was acknowledged as one of the most accomplished diamond buyers on the fields, second only to Fritz Hirschhorn and sharing his reputation. De Beers frequently called on him for advice in the handling of its business, though he was still outside the company and no part of its organisation.

Against that, he was involved elsewhere. At Jagersfontein in the Free State he was elected as an alternate director and seemed set to take his place on the board. However, he found himself frustrated by the intervention of David Harris, as he later discovered. The veteran had taken a dislike to him for some reason, no doubt jealousy, and persuaded others on the board that he should on no account be re-elected. It was a slight he did not forget.

From time to time De Beers sent its representatives to watch developments over the border on the Lüderitz fields. At this stage the German operations were the only real threat to the stability of the South African trade, as Bernard was now co-operating with the Syndicate and the Premier was in agreement with De Beers. On the German fields the different companies were selling their production to the Regie, a government-controlled body operating from Berlin on which the mining companies, the merchants and the cutting industry were represented.

The German authorities were offering their production on tender to the highest bidder. In 1913 there was a major economic boom all over the world, and diamonds were in great demand all over again. The Syndicate put in a bid for half the Lüderitz production, and this was accepted. De Beers stirred uneasily, as it was possible the Syndicate would prefer to do business with the German companies rather than with the South African. The Union government realised this too, and urged De Beers to come to terms with the Germans and organise some sort of agreement with them over production control.

De Beers decided to accept this idea, and arranged to send a delegation to Lüderitz. Initially it was planned to include Hirschhorn, who had already visited the South West fields on several occasions. But he was forced to drop out through an attack of gout. Instead De Beers commissioned Gardney William's son to head the mining investigation, and invited Ernest to look into the business aspects of the Lüderitz operation. Each would be accompanied by several assistants.

The team travelled to South West in the early part of 1914, and was given a warm welcome by the Germans who realised it would be in their interests to come to terms with De Beers and the Syndicate. The Lüderitz fields were no rest cure, as Ernest soon found. Sand and dust were everywhere, the heat and the humidity intense and conditions often unpleasant with the heavy mist that blanketed the coast. Supplies were always short, and prices ridiculous. Beer was more plentiful than water. When Ernest wanted to wash, he found he was required first to scrub off the worst of the dust with a paper towel hanging in a roll in his hotel room, then gingerly use the small ration of precious water.

The investigating team travelled all over the diamond fields, and saw enough to make them realise the deposits were a lot richer than De Beers had ever guessed. The days of the most spectacular discoveries, when it was enough to scour the sand for diamonds and pick them from the surface without even having to dig for them, were fading. Only the rich Idatal valley could produce the sight of a gang of African labourers on their hands and knees, covering the sand inch by inch. But it was clear that there were more diamonds in the ground than had been taken from it, and at least the bigger companies could expect handsome returns for years to come.

When they returned to Kimberley, Ernest and Alpheus Williams drafted a comprehensive report on their findings. It was published in June, 1914. After summarising the activities of all twelve companies mining the different concessions they reached these conclusions:

(1) Ever since the discovery of the diamonds in German South West Africa extensive prospecting operations have been carried on both within the diamond area referred to in this report and the country for a considerable distance north, south and east of the diamondiferous area. Up to the present no additional diamondiferous fields have been discovered in any part of German South West Africa; and, therefore, one can safely assume that the future alluvial production will be confined to the area referred to in the report.

(2) During the next five years certain companies will be worked out completely, while the output from other companies will gradually diminish; but the two larger companies, viz., the Koloniale Bergbau Gesellschaft and the Deutsche Diamanten Gesellschaft will increase their production, and it can be safely assumed that for the next five years the present production of 115 000 carats per month could be maintained.

(3) The quality during the next five years will undoubtedly fall

44

off as the richer portions of the gravel are worked out. The average size of the stones will decrease as the better treatment by up-to-date machines will extract more of the smaller stones.

(4) At the end of five years the whole aspect of the fields will be altered because, if the production be continued at the present rate, Pomona will probably be exhausted, and the output will then depend almost entirely on the Koloniale Bergbau Gesellschaft and the Deutsche Diamanten Gesellschaft.

There were other points, each showing that while it was difficult to determine exactly how extensive the Lüderitz deposits would prove they should certainly not be ignored. On the other hand, the way things were going in Europe it looked as if it would make little difference whether De Beers took the alluvial deposits seriously or not.

Dark clouds of war loomed on the horizon, with the powers of the Triple Alliance, Germany, the Austro-Hungarian Empire and Italy, ranging themselves against France, Russia and Serbia. Whether in the event of war Britain would join the war or elect to remain neutral was the question of the hour. Whatever the case, it looked as if there were troubled times ahead for the diamond industry. The De Beers directors prepared for the worst.

On August 1 William II, Kaiser of Germany, declared war on Russia, and two days later on France. Belgium was invaded, in accordance with a plan for the conquest of France and in complete disregard of the country's neutrality. In reaction, Britain declared war on Germany the next day, August 4, and in the days that followed on Austro-Hungary, while Serbia declared war on Germany. Acting on a secret pact with France, Italy dropped out of the Triple Alliance and pleaded neutrality, as did Roumania. The stage was set for what they would call 'The Great War'. General opinion both among militarists and the public at large was that it would last a few months at the most. How wrong they were.

45

The Catalyst

E RNEST WAS in Johannesburg on a business trip when war broke out in Europe. He was coming to the end of his second term as Kimberley's mayor, and would soon have to resign and hand his robes and chain of office to his successor. He felt he had done all he could for Kimberley and now he intended to take a long holiday overseas with May and the boys. Anyway, he was due for his regular long leave.

Instead, he changed his mind and returned to Kimberley without delay. Already there was talk of closing the mines, and for the diamond city that spelt problems. As Ernest returned, the decision was taken and production was cut off. The greater part of Kimberley's population was thrown out of work.

Wildcat rumours swept the town. Kimberley was on the verge of anarchy, there were 16 000 Africans thronging the compounds, and with nothing to do they were sure to cause trouble. There were not enough police in Kimberley to contain the menace. Ernest quietly went to work, recruiting extra police and arranging to have thousands of the Africans sent back to their homes. Many of the whites departed too, for it looked as if the situation would continue.

With De Beers' help, Ernest established a Mayor's War Relief Fund for those out of work. In return for their labour on public works projects, the unemployed were paid a living wage. Before long 250 whites and 350 Africans were at work under the scheme, not De Beers employees alone, for the company was making its own arrangements to relieve distress, but townsmen in general. Ernest provided staff from the Syndicate's offices to administer the fund and supervise the works projects.

The weeks went by, with Ernest and his fellow councillors hard at work. Ernest still intended to resign once the initial problems of the war situation were overcome. He was at the end of his term, and he felt he had done enough. Instead, there was pressure on him to stand for election again, if only to guide Kimberley through the troubled times ahead. It would be irregular, but at the same time it was practical. Ernest allowed the others to persuade him. First he would have to stand in the municipal elections, and a week later stand for mayor.

The mayor-choosing was to be public, following a meeting of the caucus of the new council at which the various issues would be thrashed out in private. The meeting was in the committee room at the city hall, with a full turn-out: Ernest, John Orr, Thomas Pratley, Fred Hicks, William Sagar, Blacklaws, Schmidt, Gunning, Greatbatch, Senier and Wood, and the town clerk, Hopwood Thorp.

The private session over, the councillors trooped into the vaulted council chamber. Several ratepayers were there ahead of them, on the public benches at the back of the room, and so was the *Diamond Fields Advertiser's* reporter. Ernest presided from the elevated mayor's throne while the minutes of the last meeting were approved, then vacated the chair for the election. John Orr took his place. Let the *DFA*'s reporter take up the story:

'Cllr Sagar formally moved the re-election of Cllr E Oppenheimer as Mayor, and Cllrs Blacklaws and Greatbatch rose to second the motion. The chairman asked if there were any further nominations, and none was forthcoming.

'Cllr Hicks said he very much regretted to speak in opposition to the appointment of Cllr Oppenheimer, and he assured the Council that he did so with no feeling of personal animosity. But he felt that Cllr Oppenheimer, if elected, would be placed in an invidious position, temporarily, at any rate. He felt—

'Cllr Orr: Have you any other nomination?

'Cllr Hicks: I am speaking to the proposition. I feel that in appointing Cllr Oppenheimer as first citizen it is not just to the citizens of Kimberley.

'Cllr Senier, intervening, said he thought Cllr Hicks should not be allowed to continue with such remarks.

'Cllr Orr asked if it was the wish of the Council that Cllr Hicks should proceed, as he would like to take the feeling of the meeting on the point.

'Cllr Sagar: He says he is speaking to the proposition, whereas it is evident he is not. He takes exception to the nomination. I rise to a

48

point of order. Unless he wishes to move an amendment he cannot speak against it.

'Cllr Orr said he did not think this was the time to make such remarks. If there was an amendment to the nomination he was willing to hear it. If there were to be any as to personalities they should not be allowed.

'Cllr Hicks said there were no personal feelings in the matter, but he felt that temporarily – while the Empire was engaged in this tremendous struggle – it would be a graceful act if Cllr Oppenheimer would stand on one side.

'Cllr Oppenheimer interposed at this stage with the remark: "I am as much a citizen of the British Empire as Cllr Hicks. (Applause) My stake in the British Empire is far greater, and my interest in every section of the community better founded than that of Cllr Hicks. (Hear, hear.) Even to start such a speech is insulting. Every Councillor and the town knows I have done my level best to alleviate the suffering and to assist the Government in every way possible. For any Councillor, whether he favours my nomination or not, to get up here and start such a speech, and to make suggestions of this kind, is so ill-natured, so rude, and so impertinent that I am sure the public of Kimberley will regret that a man of such a calibre has seen fit to utter them." (Applause, in which many of the ratepayers on the public benches joined.)

'Cllr Orr said he could not allow Cllr Hicks to proceed along the lines he had indicated.

'Cllr Hicks: Blood is thicker than water, but there is no personal feeling, and I feel when the war is over I should be the first to say Cllr Oppenheimer should be chief citizen of the town. He thought, however, it would be graceful on his part if he retired at the present juncture.

'Several councillors protested against Cllr Hicks proceeding with such remarks, and Cllr Orr said that all treated Cllr Oppenheimer in good faith, the same as every other member of the community. He could not allow Cllr Hicks to proceed on the lines he had indicated. He (Cllr Orr) thought it would be very bad form, and very rude on the part of Cllr Hicks to introduce such a matter on an occasion like the present.

'Cllr Hicks: It is a question of opinion with regard to rudeness.

'Cllr Wood thought the Chairman should call for a vote, and Cllr Hicks could vote against the motion if he liked.

'Cllr Orr said he could not allow Cllr Hicks to proceed on such lines.

49

'Cllr Hicks: In that way you stifle discussion.
'Cllr Orr: I cannot allow personal matters to be brought in.
'Cllr Hicks: That is your ruling?
'Cllr Orr: Yes.
'Cllr Hicks: I don't think much of it.
'Cllr Orr: Thank you.'

No other nominations were made, and the motion was then carried 'with acclamation' – though Cllr Hicks voted against. Ernest donned his now familiar mayoral robes once again, and returned to his throne at the end of the horseshoe.

After a scene like that, the *Diamond Fields Advertiser* was not going to mince its words. The next day the newspaper carried a fighting leader.

A REGRETTABLE INCIDENT

In the light of experience, it is scarcely possible to feel surprise at any fresh *faux pas* that may be perpetrated by Councillor Hicks. His whole municipal career has been a succession of evidence of a want of good taste – to put it mildly – that have given him in this respect a local record undoubtedly unique. Even so, the public, we venture to say, will be both staggered and disgusted by his egregious display of 'bad form' at the Mayoral election yesterday, which once more places him in characteristic isolation from the otherwise universal popular sentiment. Locally the incident will be appraised at its true value, but it is perhaps just as well to place on record, for the edification of those at a distance, that there is only one person in Kimberley who could have been guilty of such an outrage upon the proprieties, viz Councillor Hicks. But even from Councillor Hicks, it might be expected that having gone to the meeting, as he must of course have done, with the preconceived intention of taking up such an attitude, he had not at least the common decency afforded him by the preliminary discussion which it is well known is always held in the privacy of the Committee-room on these occasions, prior to the formal election, rather than, as he seems to have done, kept silence until he was able in public to subject the Mayor to what everyone else on the Diamond Fields will feel to have been a peculiarly gross and offensive, and entirely gratuitous, uncalled for and unjustified personal attack. The innuendo underlying the suggestion that Councillor Oppenheimer should stand aside, for which no shadow of justification was or could be offered, will be deeply resented by the entire community, whose only feeling will be one of mortification and regret that an elected representative of the ratepayers could thus bring unmerited discredit upon the general body of citizens whose interests he professes to serve. If Councillor Hicks had contented himself with making an alternative nomination, as he was of course perfectly entitled to do, he could have tested the feeling of the Council in an unexceptionable way. As usual he chose the disagreeable course that none but himself would have dreamt of adopting. . . We can only hope that Councillor Hick's constituents will mark their estimation of his conduct in due course.'

Two days later the paper published a letter from the local branch of the Labour Party.

Sep 11, 1914

Sir,

I have been instructed by my executive to forward you the enclosed resolution, passed at a general meeting of the local branch held on Wednesday, the 9th September, 1914.

I have the honour to remain, yours, etc.

J. DAVIDSON, Hon Secretary

Kimberley, September 10

'Resolved (i) That this meeting of the Kimberley branch of the South African Labour Party, whilst affirming the right to the ordinary privileges of citizenship to all British subjects of alien birth, herewith registers its protest against the appointment for the coming year as Mayor of Kimberley of a citizen of German nationality, and in view of the barbarism inflicted on non-combatant British subjects in German territory, and the recent exposure of German machinations involving prominent naturalised as well as unnaturalised Germans, this meeting entirely approves the protest made by Councillor Hicks at a City Council meeting on September 8th, and registers its contempt for the scurrilous personal attack on Councillor Hicks in the editorial column of the *Diamond Fields Advertiser* of September 9th, 1914. (ii) That a copy of this resolution be forwarded to the Mayor, and to the editors, "Diamond Fields Advertiser", "Rand Daily Mail", "South African Review", and "The Worker".'

The editor had his own comment:

'If British subjects of alien birth are entitled to the ordinary privileges of citizenship, it follows that they are entitled to the same confidence in their honesty and sincerity, as British fairplay extends to all others of His Majesty's subjects, unless good cause to the contrary can be shown. The treatment of non-combatant British subjects in German territory, vague charges against Germans generally, naturalised or unnaturalised, or statements as to what may be going on in the actual theatre of war, have nothing to do with the case. The terms of the naturalisation paper signed by persons of foreign birth on taking the oath of allegiance state that they shall "be entitled to all political and other rights, power and privileges, and be subject to all obligations, to which a natural-born British subject is entitled or subject." We protest against the term "scurrilous" in reference to our criticisms of Councillor Hicks, but are content to leave the matter to the judgement of the public.'

But there was more trouble in store. It came at the next council meeting, a few days later. Ernest was in the chair, with the full council and a small group of ratepayers on the public benches. This is the report that appeared in the *DFA*:

'When the Mayor, in accordance with the usual routine of agenda, asked if there were any questions, Councillor Hicks arose and said: Yes, Mr. Mayor, I rise for the purpose of protesting against you being placed in the position of first citizen –

'Mayor (sternly): I ask you to resume your seat.

'Cllr Hicks: I am going to speak.

'The Mayor: The position is, are there any more questions?

'Cllr Hicks: I intend to speak, Mr. Mayor.

'The Mayor: I ask you to resume your seat.

'Cllr Hicks (with feeling): As a Britisher, I have a right to speak, and I am going to speak. Come now!

'The Mayor was ruling Cllr Hicks out of order, when the latter continued: I am going to speak. I am a Britisher and I am going to speak. Come now!

'Cllr Orr: Surely this is quite out of order!

'Cllr Hicks (who was leaning over the table to face the Mayor): I am going to speak. Do you wish to retire from the chair and put Cllr Pratley in?

'The Mayor: The Mayor is placed here to maintain order.

'Cllr Hicks (raising his voice): I have a right to speak. I am a British subject, and I say I am going to speak!

'The Mayor, failing to get Cllr Hicks to obey his ruling, then moved that the Council should be adjourned.

'Several Councillors rose to second, and Cllr Pratley formally did so, and the motion was thus carried, and the members rose to disperse. Cllr Hicks continued to make remarks, some of a personal character, such as "Your compatriots have proved themselves to be barbarians", and "It is a German ruling, not a British."

' "You are not British in the way you are behaving," remarked Cllr Pratley.'

Kimberley was outraged. Whatever the feelings of the Labour Party, most citizens were solidly behind the mayor. At the next meeting of the council there was a deputation from the Ratepayers' Association. Two of its members stepped forward and explained they had come to make a special presentation to Ernest: a message of congratulation from the ratepayers as a body. The message was on the town clerk's table and he read it out.

'We, the undersigned residents of the City of Kimberley, humbly and respectfully desire to express our most heartfelt congratulation on the occasion of your election for the third time to the honourable position of Mayor of this City.

'The arduous labours which, so ungrudgingly, you have undertaken for the advancement of this city have been productive of far-reaching and beneficial results, whilst the ready manner in which you organised and conducted the various works for the relief of the distress in the city consequent upon the present crisis still further enhances your fitness for the post, and is additional proof of your unselfish interest in the welfare of the city and its inhabitants.

'We desire further to express our entire and unabated confidence in you and our fullest approval of your present assumption of office and we beg to assure you of our great personal esteem.'

Besides the message, the town clerk had before him a bulky parcel. It contained sheets of paper bearing 5 000 signatures. The sheets were gummed together, and when laid out end to end stretched for fifty yards.

2

THERE WAS a war on, and if at first it all seemed a long way from South Africa the impression was soon corrected. Reports from the fronts in Europe crowded the newspapers daily, and fanned a feeling of bitterness in the former Boer republics which lingered from the South African War. Many Boers made it only too plain they were not prepared to support the Allied cause – particularly when their renowned 'prophet', Niklaas van Rensburg, forecast the downfall of the British Empire. Matters came to a head when Botha announced that the Union was to mobilise and invade German South West.

Even as the nascent South African Defence Force enthusiastically formed in centres all over the country, rebellion broke out. Several big names from the South African War were involved – notably the world-famous Christiaan de Wet in the Free State, General Beyers, commander of the Union forces in the Transvaal, and General Manie Maritz, the idol of Boers in the Northern Cape. But though the rebellion broke out in several centres at once, there was little if any co-operation between the leaders, and General Botha and his men soon mopped up all but a few pockets of resistance. Only Maritz's force in the Northern Cape survived to fight again, with the direct support of the Germans across the border.

Meanwhile, the Kimberley Regiment was in training: its men were called up to camp on the Kimberley showgrounds. Many were veterans of the Kaffir Wars in the Eastern Cape frontier and of the South African War. They were, of course, to a man for King and Country. Soon they were to travel to the coast, to embark on the invasion convoy bound for Lüderitz and Walvis Bay. It was arranged that the men should be given a rousing send-off, and by curious coincidence the day appointed was the day of the mayor choosing. Ernest's first official duty after the election was to wish the men God-speed as they entrained for the Cape.

His feelings on this occasion may be imagined. He had been subjected to a direct personal attack which clearly affected him deeply: the suggestion that he was less than loyal to the Empire's cause, when he had made it his own to the extent of rejecting the land of his origins. Whatever his emotions, he put a brave front on them, and with his fellow councillors in full regalia and the directors of De Beers as well prepared to inspect the troops.

The men were drawn up in regimental order on the showgrounds under their honorary colonel David Harris. Rather unkindly, the more sophisticated referred to the commander-in-chief as 'The Duke of Plaza Toro' from his unerring preference to lead his men from the rear. 'They made a gallant body, keen, alert and soldierly', said the *DFA*. 'Their bearing was much admired, and everyone was proud of the men, who, it was felt, were a credit to the city.'

Ernest was first to address the troops, and explained he had made it his first duty after the election to come and wish them well. Kimberley knew the regiment stood for bravery and pluck, and their fellow citizens would follow their movements and be proud of them. 'We know you will be a credit to Kimberley,' he said. 'And to the Empire of which Kimberley is a part.'

The crowds at the showgrounds, several thousand strong, gave the

W L Honnold

H C Hoover

H C Hull

Ernest's first wife and Harry's mother: May Pollak, the daughter of a London stockbroker. She died of a heart attack in 1934. *Star Master Series, Johannesburg.*

Bernard Oppenheimer

Louis Oppenheimer

Leslie Pollak

The De Beers directors in December 1929: the day Ernest was elected chairman of the board. The photograph captures expressions of extreme displeasure on the faces of Sir David Harris, the acting chairman (*front row, centre*) and Fritz Hirschhorn (*front row, second from right*). *De Beers Consolidated Mines.*

men three cheers, and then all gave three cheers for the king. The regiment boarded the train, though without undue haste. 'The men seemed to have relish for the journey, and were a bright and cheery crew.' Before dusk the train pulled out on its long haul to the coast. The men waved their caps and the crowd produced a sea of handkerchiefs in response. As the train moved round the crescent towards Beaconsfield, the soldiers cried out the question that was the rallying watchword of the Allied forces in Europe.

'Are we down-hearted?' they cried as the train pulled into the sunset. And with the heavy vibration of a thousand male voices, the answer came: 'No!'

Ernest plunged into his official activities with renewed vigour, determined that his self-imposed responsibilities should not be neglected. No sooner had the men of the Kimberley Regiment left for the front line than he set up the Mayor's Parcel Service to provide 'comforts for the troops'. He took the closest interest in the news filtering through from Kimberley men on active service. To mark the first Christmas of the war he sent individual Christmas cards to every one of them, showing the Union Jack and the arms of Kimberley and each personally signed by himself and by May.

Soon after this he organised a public meeting to rouse Kimberley's patriotism. He arrived to chair the meeting in his full robes and chain of office, and promptly invited the Belgian Consul in Kimberley to join him on the platform. It was a popular gesture, after what had happened to the helpless little country, and earned enthusiastic applause.

General Botha and his troops were in South West by this time, and it was plain that the relatively weak German forces were being driven back on Windhoek, though fighting every inch of the way. There was a major scandal when it was discovered the Germans were poisoning wells as they retreated: it had been assumed they would fight as gentlemen, and it would be a gentleman's war. The poisoning was a hint of the poison gas warfare that was to cause such havoc later on the Western Front. Already, however, General Botha had decided his new Defence Force was not big enough. He would require thousands more men, he said, and suggested they should be recruited according to local quotas. They would form a number of new regiments, to be trained at the coast. Kimberley and Bloemfontein, he said, should co-operate in raising 700 men between them.

It was a most unfortunate recommendation. If the old rivalries of the South African War were not enough in themselves, there was the newer factor of the support in the Free State of Christiaan de Wet's rebellion.

55

The old antipathies between the two communities could not be swept aside, particularly at a time like this. The diamond fields could not bury the hatchet, much less actually co-operate with the old capital of the Free State Republic as if nothing had happened.

Ernest himself was only too well aware of the difficulty, and fought it in principle. Besides, he had set his heart on quite a different plan: that Kimberley should raise a second body of men on her own account, a second battalion for the Kimberley Regiment. He began lobbying the authorities in Cape Town, urging besides that the men should be trained in Kimberley.

Waiting for the decision, he sponsored a series of recruitment questionnaires in the *DFA*:

DO YOU WISH TO RESPOND
TO GEN BOTHA'S CALL?

If so, fill in this form.

Those who wish to respond to the call for Volunteers for Active Service should fill in the underneath form and forward it to the Committee Room, City Hall. (A $\frac{1}{2}$d stamp will suffice if you do not close the envelope.) All forms received will be forwarded to the Director of War Recruiting.

Full Name

Residential address

Postal address

Married or Single

If married, particulars of family

Particulars of present employment

Age

Can you ride?

Can you shoot?

Are you a member of

  (1) the Active Citizen Force?

  (2) the Citizen Force Reserve?

  (3) the National Reserve?

Give full particulars of previous military service

Give particulars of any special military qualifications which you possess, such as farriery, musketry, signalling etc.

In the event of my being selected, and subject to my being found medically fit, I am willing to serve as a Volunteer in response to General Botha's call inside or outside the Union of South Africa.

DATE: ....   SIGNATURE.............

Completed forms flooded in. There were soon many more volunteers available than were required. It was made a rule that only those with previous experience of warfare were acceptable – those, in fact, who had fought in the South African War.

At last the authorities agreed to Ernest's requests. Kimberley should be allowed to raise a second battalion, four companies with a total strength of 517 men of all ranks. Not only that, but they were to be trained locally. It did not take long to organise the new battalion for training. Most of the men were from Kimberley, though an unexpected feature was the presence of 100 men from Bloemfontein, as well as a contingent from Mafeking.

For Ernest is was a personal triumph, and it did not go unmarked in Kimberley. But however great his efforts on the Allies' behalf, the smear campaigns continued. The latest was a handbill bearing a reprint of an item in the *Rand Daily Mail*.

KIMBERLEY'S MAYOR
LESSON IN MANNERS FOR MR OPPENHEIMER

The London 'Times' of September 9 reports that at a private meeting of the Coventry City Council a letter received from the Mayor, Councillor Siegfried-Bettmann, stated that he had come to the conclusion that it would be in the best interests of the city if he retired from the mayoralty on November 9, and a deputation was appointed to express to him the Council's appreciation of his services, and their regret that circumstances had arisen which precluded him from being nominated. Mr Bettman is a native of Nuremberg and a naturalised Englishman.

Ernest's position in Kimberley was growing increasingly uncomfortable. The tempo of the war was increasing and with it the intensity of anti-German feeling. Ernest had patience in abundance, but the way things were going it would take only a straw to break the camel's back. The crisis was not long in coming.

3

ON MAY 2 1915, world newspapers carried a story cabled from New York: 'The latest manifestation of German frightfulness is a prominent advertisement in the American papers, warning passengers by the British and Allied ships that they must accept risks in the war zone. This was followed by a deluge of faked telegrams addressed to the passengers by the *Lusitania*, sailing from New York on Saturday, containing threats that the vessel would be torpedoed by a German submarine. The British and French Ambassadors in Washington called the attention of the United States Government to the advertisements, which the German diplomats admitted were inserted in accordance with instructions from Berlin.'

The threat was disregarded. There had been many threats before, all part of the 'frightfulness' propaganda campaign. German U-boats had wrought havoc with allied merchant shipping, it was true. But they could never hope to account for a vessel as fleet as the *Lusitania*, one of the fastest in the world. Besides, even the Germans could never stoop to waging war against defenceless women and children. Intending passengers who received the telegrams simply smiled and tore them up. None of them cancelled his passage.

The great liner set sail, speeding across the Atlantic at an average speed of 21 knots, and with 1 900 people on board. Some passengers had been rather apprehensive at first, but nothing had happened and already the coast of Ireland was in sight. It was May 7, a clear day, warm and sunny. There had been a bit of a scare in the morning, when several passengers spotted what looked like the hump of a U-boat conning tower a long way off. The captain was taking no chances, and the *Lusitania* was proceeding in a wild zig-zag at 16 knots to thwart any others that might be lurking. The passengers had just finished lunch, and many of them were on deck gazing at the glimpses of County Cork on the horizon.

Suddenly, several of them spotted another conning tower a thousand yards off. It was visible only for a moment, then the U-boat dived. Heading straight for the ship were first one, now two, now three white streaks that marked the rushes of torpedoes. The first missed. But the second struck the ship square amidships, a huge explosion that ripped the hull's steel plating like paper and lifted it crumpled into the air. As quickly the third torpedo hit home, and the ship was doomed.

There was no panic. The officers and crew efficiently marshalled the survivors they could find on the plunging decks, now listing heavily to port as the sea poured in through the gaping holes in the hull. Many of those on board, particularly those in the first-class accommodation, had been killed outright in the initial explosions. Those that remained were shepherded to the few boats that could be launched, on the starboard side. 'The *Lusitania* continued to send wireless messages to the end,' it was reported. 'Great courage and self-sacrifice were shown on board the liner. Britons and Americans showed the world they could go to their deaths unflinchingly.'

There were several stories told of the heroism shown by celebrities on board. Alfred Gwynne Vanderbilt, heir to the vast fortune of Cornelius Vanderbilt, fastened his lifebelt to a solitary old woman who was passing. He was not seen again. Charles Frohman, the Broadway impresario who put J M Barrie on the map, refused to enter a lifeboat. 'Why should I fear death?' he asked his sister-in-law. 'It is the most beautiful adventure in life.'

The great ship tilted so far that her rudders and propellers were high out of the water, and sank in twenty minutes. It was the worst moment of all. As the passengers and crew who had remained behind jumped screaming into the water, five lifeboats filled with survivors were sucked down into the vortex as the ship slid beneath the waves. Watching the scene were the men of the submarine. They had surfaced again, and a Canadian journalist in one of the lifeboats reported he heard them cheering enthusiastically as the *Lusitania* sank. Then he heard a shout in the silence: 'Will you sing Tipperary now?' It was the last insult. The U-boat disappeared.

The survivors were picked up by other ships and carried to Kinsale and Queenstown in Cork. Six hundred were saved. Thirteen hundred had perished. This was the news which greeted readers the next day: Saturday, May 8. The *Diamond Fields Advertiser* carried the full story.

Ernest's first move on hearing of the disaster was to call on Thomas Pratley, his deputy mayor, to discuss his personal position. He explained his own reactions: his indignation at the outrage, his horror at the dimensions of the tragedy. He said it would be perfectly understandable if feeling against anyone or anything even remotely connected with Germany was revived and intensified in South Africa and other parts of the Empire. All things considered he should resign.

The decision was not made on the spur of the moment. The attacks made on Ernest at the outset of the war had subsided, but the hostility had continued. He was aware of the dark talk behind his back, the unceasing opposition of the Labour Party and others.

But his formal letter of resignation made no reference to the efforts of his opponents. Instead, it goes a long way towards supporting the idea put forward by his son Harry in later years: that in fact the situation acted only as a catalyst. Ernest had done all he could in Kimberley. He needed the excuse for a change.

The Town Clerk,
Kimberley.
Dear Sir,

   With reference to my personal notification to the Deputy
Mayor and yourself yesterday that I had (after careful consideration) decided to resign both my position as Mayor and my seat
on the City Council, I desire to place before you a few points in
connection therewith.

   As you know, my second term of office terminated when,
owing to the declaration of war in Europe, the very serious crisis
in the affairs of Kimberley commenced.

   At the urgent request of ten of the 11 of my brother Councillors, I agreed to remain temporarily in office, as I felt it would
be lacking in public spirit on my part if I declined to do so under
the very adverse conditions then existing.

   My action in this matter must have met with the approval of
the vast majority of the ratepayers, as I subsequently received
a most flattering memorial signed by no less than 5 000 of the
citizens.

   Needless to say, I valued very highly the honour thus accorded,
alike by the Councillors and citizens of Kimberley, as it gave me
the opportunity of proving my interest in public affairs, and also
(if only in a small way) my appreciation of the benefits I enjoyed
as a citizen of the British Empire.

   The confidence reposed in me by the Council and the citizens
stimulated my efforts to do all in my power to avert as far as
practicable, and to assist where possible, all classes of distress
among the inhabitants of Kimberley which were placed before
me. To this end the Mayor's War Relief Fund was inaugurated,
and in this connection I desire to place on record the very generous
financial assistance I received from the De Beers Company, the
commercial and general community of Kimberley, without which
it would have been impossible to carry on a work that at one time
involved a very large outlay.

   I feel that the local distress, consequent on the war, has now
been considerably alleviated, and the financial position of the
Relief Fund is such that I can hand it over to my successor with
every confidence that he will be satisfied with the position, and I
am able to promise that the clerical assistance rendered by

Mr H E Clark and other members of the Syndicate will be continued for the present.

The finances of the city are in a satisfactory condition.

The improvement and extension of the tramway system, together with the great reduction of fares (a work to which I devoted much time, and in which I took a keen interest) have now become an accomplished fact.

The position being as above stated, I feel there is nothing to prevent the placing of my resignation in the hands of the Council.

In doing so, I would like to add the expressions of my very sincere gratitude for the kindly assistance I have at all times received from my fellow Councillors, and my appreciation of the hearty co-operation of all members of the municipal staff.

I am, dear sir,

Yours faithfully,

(sgd.) E. OPPENHEIMER

Mayor of Kimberley

The letter was printed in the *Diamond Fields Advertiser* on the same day as the news that General Louis Botha had entered Windhoek. It looked as if the campaign in German South West was all but over, with victory for the Union forces complete. Ernest's last official act before stepping down was to send a cable 'From Mayor and Council, Kimberley, to General Botha, Windhuk. We beg to convey to you and the troops under your command heartiest congratulations on the good news just received that your arduous operations have culminated in the successful occupation of Windhuk.'

4

AN INQUEST on the victims of the *Lusitania* disaster was held without delay. The jury returned a terse verdict: 'This appalling crime is contrary to International Law and the conventions of all civilised nations. We charge the officers of the submarine, the Kaiser and the German Government with the crime of wilful and wholesale murder.'

An American paper suggested that if the United States President, Woodrow Wilson, ordered the arrest of the German Ambassador in Washington and had him electrocuted, it would be a splendid blow for humanity. The *New York Herald* forecast: 'A brilliant white light of indignation will flash throughout the neutral world at this cold-blooded, premeditated outrage and callous disregard for human sensibilities. It makes one turn sickened as one does from the work of the wholesale butchers of the middle ages.' Wilson's predecessor in the presidency, Theodore Roosevelt, labelled the outrage 'pure piracy – the vastest piracy the world has ever known – this warfare against innocent women and children, against American men and women. It is inconceivable that we refrain from taking action.'

President Wilson, however, was not to be drawn into the war – not yet, anyway. But the man in the street was shattered. In New York, crowds watched for bulletins as they were pinned up outside newspaper offices. They were 'in breathless silence, broken only by the sniggers of German-Americans, who recalled German warnings. One man belonging to this group was pummelled into insensibility.'

From Liverpool, the *Lusitania's* home port, came stories of the wholesale wrecking of shops supposed to belong to Germans. The rioting spread to other cities in Britain, and soon to cities in the Empire. In British Columbia the authorities proclaimed martial law. Spurred on by inflammatory leaders in the papers, there was rioting in Johannesburg: on three successive nights the mob rampaged the city's streets, burning and breaking and pillaging anything they imagined tarred with the German brush. In the first night alone the mob accounted for a quarter of a million pounds' worth of damage.

The rioting spread to other cities of South Africa: 'spontaneous' demonstrations carried out for the most part by young hooligans determined to teach the unfortunate German residents, naturalised and unnaturalised alike, a lesson in 'frightfulness'. In all this Kimberley was to the fore, as was reported in the *Diamond Fields Advertiser* the next day:

Rumours that rioting, after a similar character to that which has occurred in Johannesburg, was to take place in Kimberley were rife in the town early last night. These proved, as the hours sped, only too true, though the disturbances grew from small beginnings until they achieved considerable magnitude. Until nine o'clock the town was absolutely quiet, without signs of the coming storm. About this time a careful observer could detect a knot of people gathered at the corner of Market Place and Dunell St, and this was the nucleus of all the night's trouble. The group openly made known their intention of smashing the shop of Mr Pfeffer, a hairdresser in Dunell St. A number of police were in the vicinity, and this prevented them carrying out their intention at the moment. The little party moved into Jones St where they remained until the Vaudette Theatre emptied at half past ten.

In the meantime a soldier in uniform harangued the party at the corner of the Central Hotel. About ten o'clock one of the party entered the Vaudette Theatre, and calling 'Who is ready?' created some alarm among the audience. The rest of the time was spent in singing 'Rule Britannia' and other songs, and occasionally halting a passing conveyance. The little group had assumed much larger proportions as the Vaudette doors were opened and the audience began to emerge. Their ranks were now swollen to some extent from the audience, and the united throng proceeded to the Market Place. A great many people followed them, purely out of curiosity, and the streets gradually became thronged with sightseers.

The disorderly group proceeded straightaway to Mr Pfeffer's shop in Dunell St, and the windows were quickly smashed in with stones. Some of those taking an active part in the mischief were in Defence Force uniforms. Having spilt blood, metaphorically speaking, the crowd proceeded with an increasing eagerness for mischief to the African Lion Bar; and here the much larger windows were smashed to atoms, and also the great lamp outside the premises. The doors were next burst open, and the rioters rushed in, and crash after crash was heard as bottles, mirrors, etc, were broken to bits. The place was thoroughly wrecked, outside and inside. Men in khaki again took part in doing the damage.

The rioters then proceeded to a stall on the Square, kept by F Wagner, and familiarly known as the 'Day and Night'. The fact that the Union Jack was flying over the stall had no weight with the visitors, who proceeded to haul it down. The canvas around the stall was torn and cut to shreds, food was pitched on to the ground and crockery broken. One man could be seen trying to set fire to the torn canvas. The stall was in a very decrepit condition, with all its lights extinguished, before the rioters moved away. They went to the barber's shop, formerly kept by a German, in Transvaal Rd, and left not a bit of glass intact. The police at that point appeared, but they were helpless to prevent the damage. Some of the constables went so far as to draw batons, but they were not used, and the scene ended with the rioters cheering the police.

The crowd then expressed their intention of proceeding to the Grand Hotel, but on arriving there found a notice at the bar entrance as follows: 'The proprietor is Russian born, and a British subject.' It may be stated that the proprietor has lived for 20 years in South

Africa, and he has two sons who are officers of the Union Defence Force, while a nephew is serving in the Kimberley Regiment. The rioters on seeing the notice, passed the house without harming it. They next moved into Stockdale St, and Rolfes Nebel and Co's warehouses were visited. Amid cheers the windows were broken, and the doors were later on forced. The crowd surged in, and rampaged about for some time, and they were aided in their work of destruction by the electric light being suddenly turned on. By some means or other this was then turned off, and the place was plunged in darkness, on which the rioters left after doing considerable damage.

A visit was next paid to Leinberger and Co, wine and spirit merchants, Stockdale St, and here the greatest amount of damage was done before midnight took place. The windows were broken, and the doors forced. A man in uniform clambered up to the balcony and smashed all the windows in the upper storey. The crowd rushed in through the open doors in the premises, and smashed and destroyed in all directions, while looting also took place.

One man was seen carrying away half-a-dozen bottles apparently filled with whisky, and another was seen with cigars. Inside the building a fire was kindled of boxes and other inflammable material. Handcarts and boxes were also brought outside, and a bonfire made of them. Vessels containing spirits were smashed, and these ran down the gutter as far as Main Street, and, owing to the fires, caught alight. The fire inside the building seemed likely at one period to threaten the store's total destruction, and simultaneously a great bonfire roared and crackled in the street outside. Some police were near the building, and about half-a-dozen mounted men stationed themselves at the corner of Main Street.

The fire brigade was summoned, and a jet of water was quickly directed on to the flames, which were soon extinguished. A terrible mess had been made of the property. While the fire brigade were still carrying out their duty, the crowd moved off to work further damage. In Dutoitspan Rd the plate glass windows of O Vihrog, tobacconist, were broken. The demonstrators proceeded across the way to the American Stores, but the police formed up in a cordon before them, and later the mounted men also took up positions in front of the store.

The reporter had it wrong – no doubt deliberately. The mob was not marching on the American Stores, but on the Oppenheimers' home in Lodge Road. Its threats were all too alarming. The crowd, hoodlums

64

and renegades drunk with loot from the bars and warehouses they had wrecked, was determined to burn down the Oppenheimer home about the family's ears.

At No 7, not to mention the other houses in Lodge Road, all was confusion. Ernest himself appears to have seen the threat as very real indeed – and to have had little confidence in the loyalty of the police sent to head off the trouble. Swiftly he organised his family's evacuation to the safety of the Grimmers' House, No 11. Hirschhorn from No 13 joined them there, himself a likely target for attack.

But all was well. The police stood firm and held back the mob, trapping them in the town centre. Thwarted, the crowd tried to reach Lodge Road by another route. Again they were driven back to the American stores.

'The police and mounted men were booed at and hustled, but tactfully carried out an invidious task. They pushed back the crowd at one point, but it returned again. Despite the utmost efforts to prevent damage, stones were thrown at the windows, and a crash was occasionally heard. One daring individual ascended the balcony and hoisted a Union Jack, amid cheers.'

The mob was on the way to the diamond market. If they could not raze Ernest's house, they could at least wreck havoc at his business. Gathering at the corner, stones were thrown through the windows – not of Dunkelsbuhlers, but of the offices next door. As so often the case in the *Lusitania* riots in South Africa and elsewhere, the mob hit the wrong target. More appropriately, they tore down two brass plates on the wall outside: 'F Hirschhorn' and 'E Oppenheimer'. Again the police arrived before more damage could be done.

The crowd headed again for Rolfes Nebel and Co, 'which on this second occasion was served similarly to Leinberger and Co's, a fire being started. The doors were entered, and a quantity of boxes etc were brought out, and a bonfire lit. The fire brigade was again summoned, and arrived quickly on the scene, and soon succeeded in putting out the flames. . .

'There was an expressed determination on the part of a portion of the crowd to visit Beaconsfield, and a move was started in that direction, but a halt was made, and there was some haranguing.

'Eventually about one o'clock the crowd said they would seek no more diversion that night. The majority began to disperse, leaving only small knots at the corner.'

At the earliest opportunity next morning Ernest smuggled May, Harry and Frank to the station, and put them on the train for Cape

Town. Then he made arrangements to have a permanent police guard set on his own house and on the houses of his neighbours.

Later in the day he was being driven through the centre of Kimberley when he was recognised by several of those who had been involved in the rioting the night before. Seizing stones from the roadside they hurled them at his car, and broke the windscreen. Ernest was cut by the glass, and blood poured from a wound in his forehead. Blindly he staggered out. The crowd was after him now, gathering more stones to throw at him, yelling obscenities at his back. Where was he to go? The Kimberley Club was only a little way up the street, but too far away to reach before they caught him. Instead, he ran into the first building he found.

It was a convent, the sanctuary of the nuns of the Holy Family. The crowd did not pursue him into such a refuge. Ernest was safe. The nuns bathed his wound, and helped him home. It was a kindness Ernest never forgot.

Now his life was in danger. He could not understand what had happened to bring about such a situation. Recalling it all 40 years later he said: 'I brooded over the change. I had been a hero to the people of Kimberley. Now my very name was hated, it seemed.'

Ernest knew there was no hope of things returning to normal. Feeling ran too strong. He had already resigned as mayor. He would leave Kimberley – for good. There were more riots that night, though better contained by the police. Ernest chatted with one of the guards assigned to protect him and the other Germans. He invited him in for a drink and asked his name.

'Schumann,' said the guard.

Next day Ernest packed his bags, and followed his family to the coast.

There were several letters to the *DFA* deploring Ernest's resignation, but it was regarded as inevitable. He had no option.

Sir,

As one of the old stagers here in Kimberley, a word of praise to Mr Oppenheimer for his work during the Mayoralty. We have had a good many Mayors in our Kimberley Borough Council, but none like him yet. German by birth, but not by heart. If all Germans were like Mr Oppenheimer, I don't think there would be a war cloud over us. Since my time here on the Diamond Fields no other Mayor has done for the city what Mr Oppenheimer has. I hope he will be spared for many years to come, and that at a later date render his valuable services again; also Mrs Oppenheimer, as both of them are level-headed and humane.

I am, etc.
OLD STAGER.

Kimberley, May 18

At the next meeting of the Kimberley council, Thomas Pratley was elected mayor. Each councillor paid tribute to what Ernest had done for the city. Even Fred Hicks had something to say. 'He believed Cllr Oppenheimer had been threatened, as two attempts had been made to burn down his house,' reported the *DFA*. 'His office had also been damaged. This he considered to be totally un-British. (Hear, hear).'

5

IN CAPE TOWN, Ernest and his family took rooms in a hotel in Sea Point, overlooking the sea. Ernest had friends in Cape Town, but he did not turn to them. He was on his own now, an alien in an alien land, his citizenship an embarrassment. His spirit was very nearly broken.

He wanted time by himself, to think out the situation he was in. He took to going on long walks by himself, his emotions boiling within him, and a tumble of thoughts churning in his mind. There was a war on, between the land of his birth and the land of his adoption. He knew without a shadow of doubt where his loyalties lay. Why should his fellow-citizens feel otherwise?

In a way, it was an intensely personal battle he was fighting. In Kimberley he had achieved great things in a remarkably short time. But at heart he was a shy man, reserved and insecure. He was sensitive in the extreme to the opinions of others; and it was this that had hurt him most. He had been rejected by the people of Kimberley, and they had used force against him. Their stones had shattered his confidence.

What did he think of in those long walks on the beachfront? His mind must have worked back over his life, searching for a reason for his troubles. What had gone wrong? It had all been so easy, so solid. Now the heavens had tumbled about his ears. Could it really have happened at all? Had he been such a fool, to be trapped by his own ambitions?

He was bitter over what had happened: having to leave the town whose first citizen he was, to forsake his house, his belongings, his business, his future, everything he had. But it was done, and he could not retrace his steps.

Where, then, was he to go? What could he do? Cape Town was no use to him. His world was diamonds, and diamonds were Kimberley. He could not go to Johannesburg: anti-German feeling was even worse there than in Kimberley. There was no other course open to him but to return to England, and that was his decision. He booked passages, and the family embarked.

At this stage Ernest had no intention of resettling in South Africa. He felt he had turned his back on the Union for good. He was seething with indignation. How *dare* they treat him so? But after thinking about it he reconciled his feelings: perhaps he could understand it after all. In later years he maintained that of all the tales in the Bible, the one that meant most to him was the story of Job.

A New Voice

ERNEST'S BROTHERS were no less loyal to the British Empire than he was. In it they saw their future, and they were as resolutely opposed to the machinations of Kaiser Bill as any other of the king's subjects. In London Ernest found Bernard, Gustav and Louis all embroiled in the complexities of the wartime diamond trade, but at the same time helping the British war effort. Only Otto was absent: but he was on the Western Front, fighting with the artillery.

Of them all, Bernard in particular was deeply involved. His Diamond Corporation had done most of its business with the cutters in Antwerp, so when the Germans overran Belgium he was understandably shocked and upset. He decided to turn his hand to munitions making, and with his British and Belgian partners chartered ships to bring 'the latest and most wonderful machinery' over from America. He built huge works at Letchworth in Hertfordshire and within a few months had 3 000 men at work. Almost all of them were Belgian refugees. The works were in operation by the time Ernest's family reached England, and by the early months of 1916 were producing 10 000 shells a day. Lord Kitchener, the Secretary for War, paid several flying visits to inspect progress and a remark of his was quoted later: 'If we only had a half-dozen Bernard Oppenheimers there could never be a shell shortage at the Western Front.'

Nor were Bernard's interests confined to the war in Europe alone. When it was announced a South African expeditionary force was being sent to the German colony of Tanganyika under General Smuts, he made a rather startling offer: he would give £100 to each of the first four South Africans to win Victoria Crosses, and £50 to each of the first four to be made members of the Distinguished Service Order. What had happened to Ernest must have been a mistake, felt Bernard.

He still regarded himself as essentially South African, even though he had been living in England since before the turn of the century.

The first problem facing Ernest and May in London was to find somewhere to live. For a time they stayed with the Pollaks, who had a big house in Portland Place. But both of them wanted a measure of independence, and decided to take a flat. The one they chose was only a street or two away from the Pollaks, but it gave them an edge of freedom. Once settled in, Ernest wondered what his next move should be. Was he to remain in London, or go somewhere else?

Ernest was still a Dunkelsbuhler employee, for all the independence he had enjoyed in Kimberley. Technically he was still in charge of the office on the diamond fields though in practice it was perfectly safe under his assistant Hirsch, who had grown well used to coping with all its business while Ernest served as mayor. But now they would have to find something else for him to do. It all depended on Louis, once again: he was a partner in the firm now, managing its affairs in conjunction with old Dunkels's nephew Walter.

Louis and Walter Dunkels had considerable problems on their hands at this time, not so much through Dunkelsbuhlers itself as from Consolidated Mines Selection. They had negotiated a strong interest in CMS years before, surrendering all the Dunkelsbuhler interests on the Rand in exchange for a strong shareholding and the right to appoint three directors to the board of eight, of whom one would be the managing director. The problems stemmed from a growing amount of anti-German feeling which had recently taken the form of a virtual pogrom of German-owned businesses.

Among those already under fire was the Reef's A Goerz and Company, in which CMS had strong interests. Goerz's was owned largely by German and French interests, but it was registered in London for tax reasons. Already its five German directors had been obliged to resign, and its German shareholdings had been frozen by the Custodian of Enemy Property. The company was trying to salvage its position, and, apart from appointing some suitably Anglo-Saxon directors, had judiciously renamed itself the Union Corporation.

Now CMS itself was under attack. It too was largely owned from Germany, and four of its directors were German citizens. There was a Press campaign in progress, clamouring for immediate expropriation of its interests throughout the Empire and in London. These included not only the enterprises on the Rand, but also substantial interests in mining ventures in British Columbia, Australia and New Zealand. And there were strong protests about its holdings in the United States.

As far as the Rand went, CMS's holdings were fairly modest: a couple of small mines on a new goldfield well east of Johannesburg which was only now being opened up and had yet to prove itself; a prospecting company active in the same area; reciprocal interests in the Transvaal Coal Trust which held a number of gold and coal prospecting concessions; and participation in various ventures of the Goerz company which were now in any case suspended. Louis's feeling was it would not be worth holding on to such slender interests, in view of the fuss that was brewing. Wouldn't it be better to dispose of them before the Custodian of Enemy Property stepped in and decided the matter?

This was the rather depressing situation that met Ernest when he started work at Dunkelsbuhlers after a few months' breather to find his feet again. For himself, he had had time to get over the traumas of the *Lusitania* riots and to sort out his own feelings. He had promised his family they would never live in Kimberley again. Very well, they would not. On the other hand, he was already missing South Africa. When Louis discussed with him what ought to be done about CMS, he had a suggestion: let him go out and try and assess the situation on the spot. As the CMS board minutes put it: 'Mr E Oppenheimer expressed his willingness to proceed to South Africa in the company's interest and the board accepted this offer, with thanks.'

Ernest travelled out by a rather different route this time, through the Mediterranean and the Suez Canal and down Africa's east coast to land in Lourenco Marques, Mozambique. He was travelling on an Indian ship, and May was worried he would not get enough to eat, but in the event he had no complaints on that score. He took the train to Pretoria, travelling the line Winston Churchill had used to make his famous escape during the South African War. And then he continued to Johannesburg. There was no time to waste, for he knew he would have to move fast to forestall the possible expropriation.

He knew his way round Johannesburg quite thoroughly thanks to several visits he had paid before the war. The CMS offices were in the middle of the business district, on the second floor of the most handsome building on the African continent: the Corner House, nine stories high with a magnificent cupola on the top, completed in the early days of the century as the home of Central Mining and Rand Mines and many other mining organisations too. In charge of the CMS office was F R Lynch, the managing director in South Africa, and his staff was accommodated in three rooms. Besides attending to CMS business, they also looked after the affairs of the Transvaal Coal

71

Trust which was closely linked with all the CMS activities. The directors were largely the same – most of them Dunkelsbuhlers men by this stage – and the only major distinction was that CMS was registered in London while the Coal Trust was registered in Johannesburg.

Mining on the Reef was already organised according to the system which has continued to the present day, with the individual mines organised in 'groups' by the different financial houses. Apart from helping to finance them, these houses acted as their secretaries and consulting engineers and provided other services which they might not be able to afford if cast on their own resources. The 'managing' house did not necessarily own even a majority of the shares in a particular mine – in fact it might own less than half, with other mining houses participating in the venture as well to help spread the financial risk. Besides, Reef mining involved not gold alone but coal and other assets and even fields of activity barely connected with mining at all like property. This again helped spread the house's risk so that each enterprise supported the others, and the failure of one would not bring the whole edifice crashing down.

This was the way CMS operated, though on a minor scale compared with the Reef's giants. At that time the Corner House was the biggest name on the Reef, with its chief company Central Mining now chaired by Alfred Beit's protégé Lionel Phillips. Next came Consolidated Gold Fields (plain Gold Fields for short) and Johannesburg Consolidated Investments (Johnnies or JCI), with the Albus' General Mining, Goerz's Union Corporation, Sir Abe Bailey's S A Townships, the Anglo-French Company, CMS, the Transvaal Coal Trust, Lewis and Marks, Henderson's Consolidated and other smaller fry bringing up the tail.

In the war situation most of these groups were fully employed. The Allies needed all the gold they could get, the mines needed coal and so it went on down the line. But strangely there was no mood of optimism on the Reef: no feeling that 'we've never had it so good'. The Imperial War Cabinet had established a 'gold standard' rather lower than it might have been: a fixed price per ounce of gold. And with production costs escalating faster than expected and the older mines already scraping the bottom of the barrel the future was anything but rosy. It was feared the Reef's payable gold deposits were fast drying up, and that even if new deposits found deep down well east of Johannesburg could be exploited – which was doubtful – it looked as if development costs could be prohibitive. Sceptics were saying that the industry could not last longer than 20 more years at the most and the Reef would grind to a halt.

72

All this was depressingly negative, offset by a single positive factor: the prospect of new deposits of gold well east of Johannesburg – the Far East Rand, as they were calling it. There deposits had been revealed some years before by prospecting boreholes drilled by the Transvaal Coal Trust – in search of coal. But they were so far below the surface – a matter of more than 4 000 feet – that it was very dubious whether it would be economic to exploit them. Anyway, it was not at all clear how extensive they might be.

There was another factor to take into account. Most of the land in this Far East Rand area was owned by the Crown. Normally it would have been declared a public diggings and rushed by prospectors in the usual way: but with the gold so far below the surface this was obviously out of the question. No individual diggers could hope to have the kind of capital to make that sort of operation worthwhile – and anyway, to be payable a mine would have to be spread over a wide area which would embrace claims by the thousand.

That was why the Transvaal government had introduced a special Gold Law in 1908 which made it possible for the state to 'lease' gold mining areas, as an alternative to throwing them open as public diggings. This meant a gold mining house could undertake to develop a particular gold prospect in return for a profit-sharing arrangement with the government – additional to the taxation which would have to be paid anyway. So far only one mining house had been tempted to take the bait: Solly Joel's Johnnies, which had established the Government Gold Areas (Modderfontein) Limited some years before. People had said Joel was mad: how could he expect to make a mine work if all his profits were to be fleeced by a sleeping partner? But Joel believed in his idea, and made up most of the initial £1 million needed to develop the mine from his own pocket.

It would be some time before the Modderfontein mine could come into operation, and the other mining houses were wary of following suit until they saw how it worked. Among them was CMS, which was working a shallow outcrop on the farm Brakpan, further east even than Modderfontein. The Coal Trust's boring programme had shown there were potentially rich deposits at deep level, but for the time they were vested in the state. Several times the government invited tenders for new areas, but there were no takers: and on the one occasion when a mining house did make a bid, it was turned down as unsatisfactory.

In the circumstances, and after exchanging views with Louis and the rest of the CMS board in London, Ernest decided the only thing to do was to try and unload the company's various interests for the best price he could get. He went straight to the top: to Lionel Phillips, sitting in slightly decadent glory in the tradition of the Randlords who had most of them now faded from the scene, but retaining an iron grip on the Corner House and all its interests. Phillips he found charming, urbane – but unhelpful. Pleasantly the magnate explained that his group was faced with difficult times as everyone else was; that far from increasing their interests they were being forced to cut back; that the government had already offered him participation on the Far East Rand and his advisers had told him on no account to invest there. Sorry, but there was nothing he could do.

Thinking about it afterwards Ernest realised this would be the story everywhere: nobody would be interested. On the other hand, further discussion with Lynch convinced him that CMS's assets would prove far from worthless if only they could be exploited properly. Lynch was full of the ideas given him by his old chief, an American mining engineer called William Honnold who had been managing director of both CMS and the Transvaal Coal Trust as Lynch now was but who had returned to America in 1915. Ernest had met him in the course of his various visits to Johannesburg before the war.

Honnold's theory was that the gold deposits under the Far East Rand were part of the Main Reef series linked with those under Johannesburg and Germiston: that the Main Reef stretched all the way from Johannesburg to the Far East Rand and perhaps further. He saw the whole area as a kind of basin: perhaps the bed of a great inland sea that had once existed there aeons ago, with the gold washed into it and deposited in the layers of sediment – the 'banket'. Certainly that would explain the rounded appearance of the pebbles in the banket which looked as if they had been washed by water for long periods. If his theory was right, there might be more gold in the Far East Rand than in the Johannesburg complex. It was just a matter of getting at it.

The notion was exciting – but understandably did not commend itself to conservative Rand mining men who had been brought up on the idea that their gold deposits were really not all that different from the alluvial deposits found elsewhere in the world, and indeed like those in the Eastern Transvaal. In other words, they were to be discovered only in isolated spots, certainly not over an area covering hundreds of square miles. Honnold convinced Lynch that his ideas were right and Lynch soon convinced Ernest, who wasted little time in getting in touch with Honnold and discussing the whole position by letter.

Ernest told Louis of the way his mind was working. His recommendation was that CMS should hold on to the interests, and make something of them. Without delay he began negotiating with the South African government for a lease agreement to work the deep levels at Brakpan: practically the only positive advance on the Rand at this time, apart from what was going on at Modderfontein. After a little haggling with the government mining engineer, Robert Kotze, it was agreed. The conservative CMS directors were rather bewildered by the speed of developments, but grudgingly agreed to Ernest's plans to sink a new shaft.

These operations were expensive, and capital was scarce. Ernest decided to follow the methods of the major mining houses and divide the financial load between CMS and the Transvaal Coal Trust, which were, of course, closely linked with each other anyway. He could see some point in bringing them even closer, and with Lynch organised a complicated exchange of shares and capital giving the Coal Trust the right to share in CMS's new ventures on the Rand over the next ten years, to the tune of up to 25 per cent. To celebrate the Coal Trust's new lease of life they changed its name to Rand Selection Trust.

At this time Kotze proposed a number of changes in the working of the state leases. The system had been a miserable failure so far, he admitted. This was very disappointing, for it was the very time the government wanted to encourage new ventures in the mining field. Rather the state should change the basis of the arrangements to encourage private enterprise to develop the new goldfield as soon as possible.

This was what Ernest was waiting for. He and Lynch had already mobilised their prospecting company to explore all the concession areas held by CMS and put Honnold's theories to the test. Now the government was calling for tenders in terms of the new arrangements for a new State lease area. Ernest was one of the first to bid. However, Solly Joel's Modderfontein was now coming into its own, and realising the potential of the scheme, Johnnies also put in a tender. Understandably the government was inclined to favour a house which had fulfilled its obligations to the letter, so Ernest lost out. But on the results of his prospectors' programme he put in a bid for a lease to mine deep levels on the farm Springs, a concession area in CMS territory. The government agreed to give him his chance, and the way was opened for its development. Again he arranged to share the financial load between CMS and Rand Selection Trust.

Other companies had been watching the activity on the Far East Rand. One of these, Henderson's Consolidated, made an offer for a coal mine called Oogies belonging to Rand Selection, which was involving itself more and more with gold at the expense of coal. Henderson's wanted to know if Ernest would consider swopping Oogies for a gold prospect called Daggafontein.

Ernest knew something about Daggafontein already. Years before Henderson's had started mining there, but halted operations later as the directors refused to tie up capital that might be used elsewhere to greater effect. Their decision had not enhanced the Far East Rand's reputation. However, according to Honnold's theories Daggafontein ought to be payable. Ernest recommended CMS's board to accept the offer and his engineers planned the mine's reopening.

By this time the CMS board was restless. What was Ernest playing at? He had gone out to South Africa, they thought, to sell up all their interests. Yet here he was getting them involved in more and more expense. Where was it to end? They decided to call a halt. As the chairman put it, the board 'was simply not prepared to monkey about with the capital of the company'.

The reaction was not unexpected. The CMS board had a reputation for being rather conservative, to put it mildly. Not the directors alone, but even the engineers and agents showed sometimes absurd caution in weighing up possible investments. Their men in Australia, for instance, had turned down so many promising options over the years that a local paper had dubbed the company Consolidated Mines Rejection.

Such caution had its advantages sometimes, but Ernest felt this was not one of them. He immediately took ship for London to see the directors face to face and discuss the situation. The problem was money? Then that was easy. Everything they agreed to put in, he would match pound for pound. He knew he had the backing of Dunkelsbuhlers. In fact, let them regularise the position immediately: draw up an agreement giving him up to 50 per cent participation in any new business CMS initiated on the East Rand over say the next seven years. CMS would need time to set its house in order, so let it be from a date several months hence as yet: June 8 1917.

It was all agreed, and justified to the shareholders as being 'in return for valuable services rendered'. Lynch was amused. The way Ernest was going on he would soon run CMS right out of business. With this new arrangement and the Rand Selection Trust's 25 per cent the parent company was down to a quarter holding in its own projects.

Back in South Africa once more – May despaired of him: when was he going to be with her again? Not till the war ended? – Ernest looked around for yet more fields to conquer. He was convinced of the Far East Rand's potential by this time. Already all three of the deep level mines he had brought into being were nearing the production stage. He was on the boards of all three, and on the Rand Selection Trust's board as well.

He was considering ways to utilise his unexpected new rights: who could have expected the CMS directors would have granted them so readily? He hoped he had not taken on too much. Certainly if he was to play his part in the ambitious ventures now in his mind he would have to recruit some outside help. It would probably be wise to take out a company and attract investment that way. He was ready to hand over his new rights to share in CMS's business free of charge and that would see it off to a flying start. Lynch agreed with him when he discussed it, and so did Louis in London who of course liked to be kept in the picture on everything that happened. Though rather taken aback by his young brother's displays of energy he was prepared to back him all the way.

2

ERNEST AIMED high from the outset. He was thinking in terms of a mining house with authorised capital of £1-million, and later raised the initial target to £2-million. This may not seem very much in comparison with the capital of today's great corporations, but at the time it was ambitious. Gold Fields and Johnnies each had authorised capital of £4,5-million, Central Mining of £3,4-million and General Mining of £1 785 000. Union Corporation's was only £875 000 and CMS's and Rand Selection's £600 000 and £550 000 respectively.

The target was set, but where was the money to come from? Louis and Walter Dunkels held out little hope of finding it in Britain. The war had bled every source dry. Nor was there much chance of raising adequate funds in South Africa. What might have remained after the South African government took its cut in taxation was spirited away to Europe and divided among the shareholders. But fortunately Ernest had another trick up his sleeve: the prospect of capital from the United States.

It all depended on Honnold. All this time Ernest had kept him closely in touch with each development. After all, they were the result of the ideas he had outlined so long before. Now Ernest was thinking of floating an entirely new company it was only natural to bring Honnold into the picture: and as it happened his friend was admirably set to raise that missing capital, for he was a leading light in the fund-raising American Commission for the Relief of Belgium.

'The first object I have in view is to secure for our company a fair share in the business offering on the Far East Rand,' wrote Ernest, 'and all my endeavours will, in the first instance, be directed to that end. Once this is accomplished I shall steadily pursue the course of bringing about an amalgamation of Mines Selection and Rand Selection with our own company.

'Yet we must always bear in mind that, however desirable such a course might be, it can never be carried through except with the willing consent of the older companies. We have already travelled, as you know, some considerable distance towards an amalgamation between Mines and Rand Selection . . . Taking all the facts into account, it does not seem too optimistic to think that we shall be able, within a reasonable time, to bring about a willing combination of the three Eastern Rand holding companies, which would straightaway make us the most important gold group in Johannesburg.'

Honnold did not need much persuading. In fact, he was most enthusiastic and full of suggestions about where to raise the money. He had various connections of his own, but it would be a better plan still to approach the relief commission's chairman who was a friend of his and a mining engineer into the bargain, and had even better contacts: Herbert Clark Hoover, who would be visiting Europe in a couple of months' time. Could Ernest get to London and discuss all the ideas with him man to man?

Ernest could and did. In fact, he went one better and took with him his most powerful ally in the venture, Henry Hull, a mining man who had been South Africa's Minister of Finance in Botha's first cabinet. He had since resigned over a cabinet row – 'This Cape Colony gang means to skin us alive,' he complained to friends on the Reef – but was still close to the seat of power.

The two men met Hoover at the Savoy Hotel. Hoover had already half made up his mind, evidently, for Honnold had explained the whole position with great care. Besides, Ernest had himself committed the whole situation to paper, to give Hoover some idea of the way he was thinking.

'If American capital wishes to obtain a footing in South African mining business, the easiest course will be to acquire an interest in our company. Yet, however much as we would welcome American capital,

78

we could not afford to simply sell such shares in the new company to them at par.

'You will have seen from the foregoing that we do not propose to take bonus shares or commissions, etc. Selling shares at par would, therefore, mean parting with a valuable contract – which it has taken years of hard work to obtain – without special consideration. If, after considering the position above described, you feel inclined to make me some proposition, I shall feel free to discuss it with my friends . . .'

The American listened carefully to all that Ernest outlined. For all his humanitarian work, he was a mining man to his fingertips. His profession had taken him all over the world, particularly to Australia and China. In fact, he had been in Peking at the time of the Boxer Rising. Now, stern Quaker as he was, he had subjugated his personal interests to the wider needs of a world in want. Already he showed the qualities that would one day carry him to his country's highest office.

Hoover was able to give Ernest his answer on the spot. Yes, he could help. With Honnold he was arranging American participation in the venture through the Newmont Mining Corporation of New York, its bankers J P Morgan and Company, and Morgans' London offshoot the merchant bankers Morgan Grenfell.

So it was all arranged. Ernest could hardly contain his excitement. Immediately he was on the wire to Honnold in America, to chase negotiations on their way and bring the mining house into being as soon as possible.

Their first task was to decide on a board of directors. The two had already agreed they would each become a permanent director, and with Ernest on the spot in Johannesburg it was obvious he should be permanent chairman and managing director. They would appoint four more directors in the first instance, two for the South African interests and two for the American, and in addition two alternate directors to represent them when they could not themselves be present. But who should they be?

'If our new company is to fulfil the high hopes which we entertain for it, it is essential for us to have a very strong board,' wrote Ernest. 'It will be of special value if the names of the two directors whom your side appoint carry some idea of the influential connections we have secured . . . We shall be careful on our side to nominate substantial men. All of us must take special pains to appoint good alternatives in South Africa. In this connection it will be wise if none of us appoint anyone too closely identified with any of the existing groups. Our aim

79

should be for our company to make its debut as a "new" factor in South African finance.'

For himself he knew already the men he wanted if he could get them: Hull for one – though his friend insisted on thinking it over before committing himself; and a useful contact of Hull's, the Hon Hugh Crawford of the National Bank. Honnold soon came through with the names of his nominees: William B Thompson of the Newmont Mining Corporation, and C H Sabin of the Guaranty Trust Company, representing the Morgan interests. Ernest and Honnold fixed on CMS's managing director Lynch and E S Langerman as their alternates.

There was another matter to be tied up: the question of a name for the new company. In drafting the articles of associations and all the preliminary matter they had been calling it the Far East Rand Trust Limited. But that, Ernest decided, would never do. He had ambitions for his brainchild which would carry it far beyond the limits of the new goldfield. With such a name how could it hope to rank on equal terms with corporations bearing titles like Central Mining, Consolidated Gold Fields, Johannesburg Consolidated Investments, General Mining and Union Corporation? No, they would have to think of something else. The name ought to be changed 'to a title which will make the American connection apparent, but the "Africa" must also appear in the name,' he wrote to Honnold.

'How about Union of South African Mines or United South African Companies?' wired Honnold in reply. 'Either of which in market parlance would probably be abbreviated USA and thereby serve the purpose aimed at.'

Ernest thought the first of these 'acceptable and excellent'. But Hull pointed out it was most unlikely the South African authorities would accept it. He 'urges adopt African American Corporation Limited. Do you approve?'

'African American would suggest on this side our darkskinned fellow countrymen and possibly result in ridicule . . .,' replied Honnold in a frame of mind far out of keeping with the attitudes of today. 'Hope you can secure acceptance of one of names previously suggested.'

By this time, however, Ernest and Hull had the answer. 'After full discussion with Hull consider it very necessary American identity should form part company's title. Suggest the Anglo American Corporation of South Africa, Limited.'

To this Honnold agreed. All that remained was to register the corporation in Johannesburg. However, before leaving London Hull insisted on seeing General Smuts, who was in Britain serving on Lloyd

George's Imperial War Cabinet. It was supposed to be a purely diplomatic appointment, but the South African was more than making his mark. Indeed, thanks to his successes with the South African contingent in Tanganyika a year before and his present revolutionary suggestions about the formation of a League of Nations in which all the states of the world could meet together, his was a name on everyone's lips.

In South Africa, where Botha was not in the best of health, it was obvious Smuts would succeed him and perhaps in the near future. Hull had not forgotten his political ambitions and wanted to hear whether Smuts approved of his joining the board of a new mining house. Would it affect his future chances?

Ernest accompanied him and took the opportunity of telling Smuts what the scheme was all about. Smuts proved most interested, particularly as it gave him the chance of hearing what was going on in Johannesburg at first hand: he had been in London some months now and was rather out of touch. In his next letter Ernest told Honnold all about the meeting.

'I had a private talk with General Smuts some days ago on our new company and I told him that you and I were collaborating in this matter. He welcomes the idea of American financiers taking an interest in South African development, and generally looks upon the formation of our company with considerable favour. The only doubt in his mind was whether it was not a case of taking an interest in a promising business, snatching a profit and clearing out quickly. I satisfied him that this was not the case, as he would see by the personnel of our directorate, and our general arrangements. That on the contrary, we hoped to build up a big South African company, but that, of course, some measure of success in the early years was necessary to establish us firmly... I may add that the Hon H C Hull only agreed definitely to take a seat on our board after he had discussed the position with General Smuts.'

For Ernest this encounter with Smuts was specially significant. The two men could not have been more different: Smuts the Boer patriot, statesman, scholar, soldier; Ernest the German immigrant, diamond expert, self-educated, businessman. But they saw in each other qualities which bred respect, admiration and affection. They had met before, at the flying school in Kimberley and later when Ernest was mayor: but it was now their friendship began, a friendship which was to last as long as Smuts lived.

Everything was settled, and it was time for Ernest and Hull to return

81

to South Africa. Ernest had been with May and the boys these three months – and it was painful to leave her again. But on the other hand he wanted to get going. It was all so exciting. The Anglo American Corporation of South Africa, Limited was registered on September 25 1917.

The announcement shook the mining world like a dynamite explosion. 'American Millions for the Rand', headlined the *Rand Daily Mail*.

'American financiers are so satisfied by the possibilities of South Africa generally and the immediate prospects of the Far East Rand in particular that they have decided to devote a considerable amount of capital to operations in this country. For many years the technical side of Rand mining has largely been controlled by American engineers, but this is the first occasion upon which American capital on a large scale has been definitely subscribed for the exploitation of South African enterprises.'

Even the London *Times* had something to say. 'The link means the beginning of a new epoch, for it is the first occasion on which a definite arrangement has been made for the employment of American capital on the Rand.'

In the event, this feature of the new flotation was to prove relatively unimportant. What mattered was that Ernest was head of his own corporation and equipped to play a completely independent role in the economic Wild West of South Africa's mines.

3

ERNEST PAID several more visits to Europe in the months that followed, and in the course of them will have seen something of another scheme thought up by Bernard. His munitions factories were still going strong, but he wanted to make a contribution in a more peaceful sphere. Planning to establish a diamond cutting industry in which British and Belgian disabled could be employed, he approached a friend who was principal of the Brighton Technical College. With government support they devised a course at the college and enrolled their first trainees. The scheme proved so successful that they opened cutting works not at Brighton alone but in other centres too and came to employ a labour force of more than 2 000 disabled ex-servicemen.

All this time, of course, Ernest had been intimately concerned with the progress of the war. He was in close touch with each development, certainly as it affected South Africa. After all, he enjoyed the complete confidence of General Smuts. But of the actual fighting and its pressures his only experience had been the unfortunate debacle in Kimberley three years before, if that could be counted. It was difficult for him to appreciate what it was like at first hand. He was in for a surprise.

The sinking of the *Lusitania* had provoked anti-German feeling so strong that it was a matter of touch and go whether America would enter the war. In the event she had not, but the Germans could not afford to take chances. The U-boat campaign against passenger ships was suspended. In 1917, however, the interception of the Zimmermann telegram forced President Wilson's hand once and for all, and America was committed to fight. The Germans recommenced the U-boat 'frightfulness' campaign, and sailing the Atlantic became hazardous in the extreme.

It was in this atmosphere that Ernest sailed for South Africa on September 10 1918, after yet more consultations with CMS, aboard the *Galway Castle*. The liner carried 204 crew and some naval ratings; 346 civilian passengers, most travelling third class; and not far short of 400 invalided South African troops, some blind and the others at least partially helpless because of their wounds – all told nearly a thousand people. The liner was to sail in convoy through the narrows of the English Channel, where the U-boat packs lay in wait. The *Galway Castle* duly left Plymouth with 15 other steamers including the armed liner *Ebro*, escorted by two cruisers and several destroyers.

From the start the convoy was impeded by heavy weather and high seas, and progress was slow. Thirty-six hours after leaving Plymouth the convoy was ordered to disperse. The escorting warships returned to Plymouth, the ships heading for the Mediterranean sailed south, and the *Galway Castle* and the *Ebro* sailed a course more to the westward. The *Galway Castle* was instructed to proceed at maximum speed, which meant 11 knots.

All went well that night, but at 7.40 the next morning there was an unpleasant reveille. A sudden violent explosion shook the ship from stem to stern, knocking men right off their feet. One of the U-boats had scored a direct hit. The liner's engines fell silent, all her lights were extinguished, her wireless went out of action. In minutes the great ship wallowed helpless.

Ernest had been in his bath when the torpedo hit home. Quickly he fumbled into shirt and trousers and hurried on deck. Everything was confusion. The torpedo had exploded forward of the boiler room and down by the keel, breaking the ship's back. Now she sagged amidships with the bow and stern rising up. There was the sound of steam escaping from the burst boilers, and metal rending as the buckling decks thrust upwards.

There was no communication between bow and stern, and not all could reach their proper stations. Three of the lifeboats were damaged beyond saving, but the crew managed to get the remaining 18 over the side. Officers tried to marshal the frightened passengers, but it was a chaotic situation. The boats bumped against the hull on the way down and several were badly strained. One broke in half and pitched its terrified passengers into thin air. Others were holed by wreckage from the ship and sank immediately. Many of the passengers still on board could not bear the suspense and jumped into the sea. The crew threw rafts overboard to try and save them, but a number were knocked unconscious by debris and drowned.

Ernest was still in shirt and trousers and nothing else, and wondered what to do. In the end an officer half pushed him into one of the lifeboats, and luckily it reached the water safely. There were eight men and a woman aboard, all of them passengers. They unshipped the heavy oars and pushed away from the ship, and when they were well clear discussed what to do next. Only one of them had any experience of handling small boats: George Pilkington, a yachtsman from Cape Town. Obviously he should be their skipper, and he took the tiller as they rowed as far from the ship as they could. They all remembered what had happened to those in the lifeboats still close to the *Lusitania* when she went down.

Huge seas towered all about them in the grey morning light and threatened to rain wreckage down upon their frail craft. They could hear the terrified shouts of people in the water, but were powerless to help. Occasionally they saw bodies face down. Waves swamped the boat time and again, and those not rowing bailed for their lives.

Pilkington soon had his crew organised in watches, alternately rowing to keep the boat head on to the waves, and bailing to stay afloat. Once clear of the ship they tried to keep position in case there was a search for them, but with the huge seas it was impossible. They were swept far away from the wreck of the *Galway Castle*, out of sight even of the other lifeboats. All day long they tossed uncomfortably in the heavy seas, frozen, sick and miserable. It was getting dark and they were losing hope. What was to become of them? Then, suddenly, the most beautiful sight they had ever seen: through the great valleys of the waves they glimpsed a destroyer approaching at speed.

Pilkington was taking no chances. He produced a handkerchief and tied it to the end of an oar, thrusting it high into the air until he was sure the destroyer had spotted them. Alongside she came, and lowered a ladder for the weary survivors. One by one they clambered up to the deck. As Ernest reached the top he found himself confronted by an officer.

'Are you Mr Ernest Oppenheimer?'

Ernest could hardly have been more surprised.

'Yes, I am he.'

'General Smuts wants to know if you are lost or saved. We are to tell him as soon as possible.'

They had imagined the *Galway Castle* had sunk hours before. But she was still afloat. Her captain, his officers and a number of volunteers from the crew had stayed aboard while the *Ebro* stood by to assist. She had wirelessed news of the disaster to the departing escorts and they had come racing back. It took hours to rescue those in the scattered lifeboats. When the cost was counted 150 were missing, presumed drowned. They tried to take the *Galway Castle* in tow, but slowly she settled in the water until at last she sank from sight.

The Royal Navy made a fuss of its guests. Ernest was led off to a hammock where he could lie down and rest, and make the most of a hot drink. Later the navy issued each survivor with dry clothes. Ernest eventually stepped ashore in the uniform of a chief petty officer.

4

ERNEST HAD lost all that he had with him on the *Galway Castle*, but that seemed petty compared with the trouble some of the others were in. Several of them told him they had been on their way to settle in South Africa with all their possessions, and were now left absolutely destitute. As soon as he got back to London he made arrangements to have them supported until they could get back on their feet.

May was, of course, delighted to have her husband back with her so soon – though it was not to be for long. He had to get back to South Africa: he never quite believed his men could be trusted to get on with their jobs unless he was there to watch over them and make sure nothing went wrong. But at least before he ventured to South Africa he went to see Smuts who had taken such unexpected interest in him. The general was rather embarrassed to realise he knew about it.

One thing he wanted to hear from Smuts was his view on when the war might end. They had heard there was widespread disaffection in the German ranks, fanned by revolutionary elements which wanted to see the regime overthrown. They were in line with the Soviet rebels in Russia, who had brought chaos to the Eastern Front. In the west the German forces were disappointed by what they heard of the trouble behind them, and were falling back before the Allied troops. These had now taken on a new lease of life. The end was in sight. Before long the Ottoman Empire came to terms with the allies, the Austro-Hungarians followed suit a few days later, and the Germans were left to fend for themselves.

Smuts was sure the German Commander, Ludendorff, wanted peace. He would have given up the struggle long ago if it was up to him. But Kaiser Bill would not hear of it. He wanted to continue fighting to the end. Only when his own troops were on the point of open mutiny was he at last prepared to accede to the American President's demands, allowing Ludendorff to sign the armistice. But by this time Ernest was already back in South Africa – without mishap this time.

Things were going smoothly, he found. By the end of 1918 all three mines – Brakpan, Springs and Daggafontein – were in full production, with others being opened around them showing it was as well he had got in early: had he delayed any longer he would have missed the chance and wasted what was now being hailed as the brightest boom the Rand had yet seen. No longer were there grumbles about the amount the mining companies had to pay for their leases. Profits were more than satisfactory.

As soon as he could Ernest brought May and the boys out to Johannesburg. It looked as if they would be living there for good, certainly for some while to come. All this time Ernest had been living in a house he had bought in the pleasant suburb of Parktown, which was where all the Randlords had lived in the early days. But Johannesburg was developing so fast the suburbs already sprawled far beyond what had been open countryside. The house was fairly modest: a single-storied affair along Jubilee Road, called Brenthurst. But as he explained to May it would do for the time, until they could find something more to their taste. May settled in readily, and soon made herself at home. Before long Harry and Frank were attending Parktown School not far away, smart in the bright red blazers and caps of the school uniform.

May was not among strangers. She had visited Johannesburg several times with Ernest before the war. But apart from friends and acquaintances from that time, there was even a member of her own family in Johannesburg – her brother Leslie. During the war he had won a

Military Cross on the Western Front. Now Ernest had brought him out to work at Anglo. One of his first jobs had been to assist in negotiating yet another gold mining lease from the government – this time for West Springs, adjoining the Springs mine already in operation. Ernest's engineers had worked out a useful economy which would enable the West Springs company to use the shafts already sunk for the Springs mine. Leslie Pollak did so well in these negotiations that before long Ernest appointed him Anglo's managing director.

Early in 1919 Ernest was in Europe again, as it happened at the time of the great Peace Conference at Versailles. All the world's powers but the revolutionary Soviet of Russia had been invited to attend – one of the greatest summit conferences the world had known, though it was obvious its chief object was to wreak vengeance on the already humbled Germans. Smuts would be attending as a member of the Imperial War Cabinet, and asked Ernest if he was interested in accompanying him as an observer.

The memory of that great conference was to remain with Ernest all his life, as it did with everyone who was present. It was dominated by Wilson of America, Lloyd George of Britain and Clemenceau of France, three of the greatest statesmen of the period joined in deciding the destiny of the whole world. The other countries involved in the Great War were represented too, with Botha and Smuts stating South Africa's view; and besides them, two of their political opponents, General Hertzog and D F Malan, who had come to put the case of the die-hard Afrikaners for whom the South African War had never really finished and would continue until the hated British were chased from South Africa's shores.

When at last Ernest got back to South Africa there was plenty of work to do. He had a series of consultations with his directors there, inquiring what ideas they had for the future. Hull asked to see him privately as he had a rather special proposal. He had been given a tip by one of his old political contacts. Did Ernest think Anglo was equipped to take over a diamond producer?

Now that, Ernest knew well, would be to cross De Beers. And with the way things were De Beers would be strong enough to crush the upstart without trouble – unless the enterprise was a really big one. If it was, then he might be prepared to consider it. Yes, said Hull, the producer was very big indeed. Ernest knew then he could only be talking of the Lüderitz fields, the diamond deposits of South West Africa.

He had known their fate was in the balance. When Louis Botha's expedition had mopped up all resistance in South West the Custodian of Enemy Property had stepped in and taken over the diamond fields with all the other German businesses. But it had not been clear what would happen to them now the war was over. Since the South African invasion they had continued producing, with their diamonds sold to the Diamond Syndicate in London.

Now the war was over it was supposed the mines would be returned to the German owners and they would continue as before. But Hull had different ideas. From what he had heard the owners were not altogether keen to have them back. The new League of Nations had given South Africa a mandate to administer South West on its behalf, which meant an entirely new system of government would be introduced, with who knew what perils for diamond producers. If a suitable offer was made, they might well be prepared to sell.

Ernest told Hull to go ahead. Yes, certainly they should see the government and sound out its attitude to the idea. In the meantime they had better raise extra capital. If they were to buy out all the German mines that meant negotiating with twelve different companies, and each would name its own price. They brought in Sir David Graaff, a Cape Town businessman who had made a huge fortune from cold storage among other interests, and was a member of parliament. In fact, it was probably he who tipped off Hull in the first place.

Hull and Graaff went to see Botha soon after his return from the Versailles conference. He told them he had no objections to what they proposed, so barely had they emerged from the interview than they were planning a trip to Europe. It was arranged Hull would go and with him the head of the mines office at Lüderitz to give the German owners a first-hand report. After all, they would have little information. But there was a third member of the negotiating team, travelling in some secrecy: Ernest himself, now highly excited by what had all the promise of a major coup. Already they had cabled ahead to warn the Germans they were on their way and had heard their representatives would meet them in the Netherlands.

It was all arranged so cunningly that the first intimation De Beers had of what was afoot came when Fritz Hirschhorn and Ross Frames went to see Botha on just the same business. Hull and his party were already on their way, Botha told them, backed by Graaff and 'certain mining' interests. De Beers rushed a report of this development to its directors in London.

'From their conversation with General Botha, there is no doubt that Hull and Graaff are endeavouring to obtain interests in South West

88

Africa. Botha made no statement what attitude Government will take up to acquiring rights of German holders in South West Africa. It is very important, therefore, that we should be first in the field before Hull arrives, and, if possible, acquire rights from German holders subject to ratification by Union Government.'

London was not impressed.

'German holders under belief they will remain in possession of their property and from our inquiries in Germany these holders are not disposed to sell at present. We think under these circumstances Hull's mission will be a failure.'

In the event, of course, they were in for a nasty shock. The picture Hull and Ernest and the mines' office manager painted was only too pessimistic, so that the owners seemed glad to dispose of their property before it got them into trouble – all but one, that is, though even this brave company later changed its mind and followed the others.

The deal was not cheap. Ernest, Hull and Graaff had a tough time finding the money they would need, and set themselves some awesome problems. Anglo's capital was already invested to the hilt in the Far East Rand, and the mines had barely begun to pay dividends. However, Ernest was given support by Dunkelsbuhlers once again, thanks to Louis; by Morgan Grenfell which was delighted by the success; and by some of Graaff's interests at home. When they returned to South Africa they were able to lay their plans before the government. They proposed amalgamating all the South West producers in one company along the lines of Rhodes's amalgamations in Kimberley: it would be known as the Consolidated Diamond Mines of South West Africa, with Ernest as chairman and managing director, its head office registered in Cape Town and a nominal capital in South Africa of £3 500 000.

De Beers was understandably not pleased. The Kimberley directors in particular felt their noses had been put out of joint, and sounded out their colleagues in London on the possibility of buying an interest in the new corporation. London refused. 'Our opinion is now that control has passed we should do nothing, we do not want a minority holding.'

As managing director Ernest had to work out a smooth scheme for the actual process of amalgamation. This was no easy matter, with no fewer than twelve mines to be brought into line in that desolate stretch of desert along so inaccessible a coast. It gave him any number of headaches, though at least he had the backing of Louis's know-how and advice. This was particularly useful in organising the

89

new corporation's marketing arrangements with the Syndicate.

Ernest organised a special *quid pro quo* in view of the help he and Louis were giving: if through any chance the sales contract broke down the brothers should be given first right to organise a new one through their own companies. This was to prove a trump card later on.

The negotiations took six months. The government eventually gave its formal approval to the arrangement in February, 1920. Before that happened, however, Louis Botha had died: that last strenuous trip to Europe had been too much for him. He was succeeded by Smuts as everyone expected, who soon called a general election. To ensure his position against the rising power of Hertzog and his Afrikaner Nationalists, Smuts formed a coalition with what had been the Opposition. But before the election came off Ernest and May were on their way to the United States to confront the J P Morgan and Newmont Mining directors in person. The Anglo American needed yet more funds, and this would be the best way to raise them.

A trip from South Africa to the United States in those days was a major adventure – a journey almost halfway round the world. Ernest and May made their preparations in great excitement: they would be away three months or more. They decided to leave Harry and Frank behind at Brenthurst, looked after by their friends the Springbok cricketer Fred Susskind and his wife Doff. The couple would be living in the house.

It was a most enjoyable trip. The meetings in New York were perfectly satisfactory if not dramatic, and Ernest achieved what he had hoped: the promise of further funds as time went on. He and May set off on a journey round America to see as much as they could in the time available. There were several old friends to look up – particularly Honnold, who was now living in California, and who was as excited as Ernest was by the success of their venture.

Ernest was able to tell him that all they had dreamed had come true. CMS and the Rand Selection Trust were securely under Anglo's belt now, with Anglo holding a major share in each; and besides the important position the trio occupied on the Far East Rand which was now really coming into its own and producing ever higher percentages of the Reef's total production, they were moving out of gold and into all sorts of other ventures. Honnold was particularly impressed by the coup in South West. He felt it was in the tradition of the great Solly Joel, always regarded as the master of such tricks.

So far away from South Africa there was little news of home, but one thing that pleased Ernest was to hear the result of the South African election. Smuts and his South African Party had cruised home against the Nationalists and the little Labour Party with a majority of 24. He and May were in a small town not far from the Mexican border at the time the result was declared, and he was very bucked to find the local paper carried not only the result but also a big picture of Smuts.

The trip was long and exhausting, and Ernest and May were quite glad to return home. There was plenty to do. Apart from his business commitments, Ernest was involved in public life once more – fairly modestly, but no less usefully: he had been serving as national secretary of the South African War Memorial Fund, which had the task of seeing that every community throughout the Union erected a suitable monument to those who had died for their country.

On New Year's Day, 1921, it was announced that he was to be knighted. The citation read: 'Honorary Secretary to the South African War Memorial Fund. Took a leading part in recruiting of both combatants and labourers for various fronts during the war.'

Congratulations flooded in, not least from Ernest's family. But for the Oppenheimers there was to be a double celebration. The same New Year's Honours List announced that in view of *his* contributions Bernard Oppenheimer was to be made a baronet.

'In Sir Bernard Oppenheimer's Baronetcy, as in his brother Ernest's Knighthood, South Africa has been particularly honoured,' wrote the *African World*. 'For there are few of her old pioneers whose records and careers for the past thirty years will give finer examples of conspicuous personal ability, coupled with very hard work, and yet ready at all times of financial success to share their wealth with their compatriots, collectively, in every public charitable movement or individually in countless acts of private assistance . . .

'In honouring the Brothers Oppenheimer His Majesty has conferred a reward on two of his most esteemed subjects connected with the subcontinent, whose good deeds – both public and private – have never been known as fully as they deserved.'

Sad to say, within six months Bernard was dead of a heart attack.

Ernest, meanwhile, had set about finding himself a coat of arms. He took the central motif from the arms of Kimberley, and with it a development of the city's motto, *Spero Meliora*, or *I hope for better*. His would be *Spero Optima*, or *I hope for the best*. Somehow that crystallised his ambitions.

When he received his knighthood, Ernest could not know that within

91

six years a private member's bill in parliament would end for all time the granting of such honours to South Africans on the recommendation of the Union's Prime Minister. In fact, Ernest was one of the last two South Africans to be knighted in this way – one of South Africa's last links with the tradition of the British Empire.

Rhodes's Mantle

E RNEST was back in the world of diamonds, and it was the world he knew better than any other. He was in a far stronger position than he ever had been before, and he was not going to waste it. From the outset he made it his target to command the leadership of the whole diamond world. He explained his ideas in a letter to Morgans in November 1921.

'From the very start, I expressed the hope that besides gold, we might create, step by step, a leading position in the diamond world, thus concentrating by degrees in the corporation's hands the position which the pioneers of the diamond industry (the late Cecil Rhodes, Wernher, Beit, etc) formerly occupied.

'Such a position is most difficult to attain, requiring intimate knowledge of the diamond trade, pluck and a great deal of patience, but, above all, the support of powerful financial groups who would be prepared to play the part which Messrs Rothschild played vis-a-vis the original leaders, at the time of the De Beers amalgamation.

'It is quite evident to my mind that eventually an amalgamation of the four big diamond producers (De Beers, Premier, Jagersfontein and Consolidated Diamonds) will be brought about, and I see no reason, if we continue our diamond policy, why we should not play a leading role in such an operation.'

For the time, though, it was only too plain how far Anglo had to go. Acquiring a major stake in such an important producer was only the beginning, and all along Ernest had seen it as essentially a means of forcing De Beers' hand. There was an intriguing precedent. Solly Joel had bought out the controlling interest in the Premier during the war years, and sold it to De Beers for a big profit and a handsome increase in his shareholding. Perhaps Anglo could follow suit.

93

In fact, Ernest had very little respect for De Beers at this time. He considered it was run by men who had no real feeling for diamonds, no understanding of the precepts laid down so carefully by Cecil Rhodes. The sooner the regime was toppled, he felt, the better it would be for the industry.

One thing he had noticed, for instance, was an extraordinary increase in production from alluvial fields discovered just before the war in Central Africa: the Belgian Congo and the Portuguese province of Angola over the border. They posed exactly the sort of danger the South West fields had posed when they were discovered and it looked as if the De Beers board was making the same mistake: sitting back and hoping the problem would take care of itself. Far from it, the fields were producing more every year. It was apparent they were far more extensive than even the companies exploiting them had judged, and eventually no fewer than 150 000 square miles were proved diamondiferous.

If De Beers was not going to act, Ernest thought he should. As it happened he had recently come into contact with an Australian-born mining engineer, Edmund Davis, who had big hopes for several base metal concessions in Northern Rhodesia beyond the Zambezi. Davis had connections with the board of the company which held the diamond concessions in the Congo, Société Internationale Forestière et Minière du Congo, or Forminière for short. Ernest negotiated a shareholding and brought in Solly Joel and Barnatos to help spread the financial load, and at the same time contracted to buy Forminière's whole production for Anglo.

This was the first time Anglo had done any diamond buying, though of course this was Ernest's long-term speciality. From the outset he had hoped Anglo would one day win a place in the Syndicate. The most recent firm to be admitted was Central Mining: admittedly closely connected with Wernher, Beit, but no less essentially a gold mining house. On the other hand, time was on his side. He did not want to force the issue and upset the applecart while his key ally Dunkelsbuhlers was safely riding upon it.

The next year Ernest and Solly Joel came to terms with the Companhia de Diamantes de Angola, Forminière's offshoot in the Portuguese territory and in effect working another part of the same field. The two men were acting for themselves, not the Syndicate. For Solly Joel there were rich pickings to be had, but Ernest planned to use the new agreements in bargaining for a place in the Syndicate. Many more deals like these and its members would have no justification for excluding him.

There was news of the discovery of yet more alluvial deposits, this time away across the Atlantic, in British Guiana: similar to the fields later discovered in southern West Africa and no doubt linked to them in primeval time before the land masses split, as the fields of Brazil would have been linked to South Africa's. There was virtually no supervision of these new diggings, and they quickly became a free-for-all. The best Ernest could do was send representative buyers to create what business they could. But with this new production added to what he was getting from the Congo and Angola, not to mention the actual production management in South West, Anglo held a strong stake in the diamond world and Ernest could plan for the future.

For a while he had been rethinking his idea of amalgamating CMS and Rand Selection Trust within Anglo, and decided instead to leave them as separate entities with an independent existence, though of course very closely tied in with the corporation. Already it held nine-tenths of Rand Selection, as the result of a deal made at the time of the CDM flotation. Now Ernest went to London to see CMS, and arranged to have all its South African interests combined and exchanged for a big shareholding in Anglo and a cash payment. But at the same time he increased Anglo's holding in CMS, to bring the two even closer together.

Here lay the seeds of the three-dimensional 'pyramid' structure that was later to be so important to Anglo's organisation, and which was so largely Ernest's invention. It was not a deliberate policy. At the outset Ernest intended 'amalgamation' and it was only by accident that negotiations took a different turn. But there were such considerable advantages in sharing potential business between inter-linked companies which were at the same time independent that Ernest decided to use this as the basis of all his future negotiations.

Ernest was thinking well into the future by now, to the time when Anglo's interests would take in not gold and coal and diamonds alone, but even activities altogether dissociated from mining. He expressed his ideas as early as the ordinary general meeting of 1920.

'I want to reiterate my firm belief in a great industrial and agricultural future for this country, and, in consequence, I am satisfied that the right policy for this corporation to pursue is to investigate any attractive industrial proposition that presents itself and not merely to confine its activities to mining enterprises. The Anglo American Corporation should be, and is, ready and anxious to play its part in the industrial development of South Africa.'

Profits so far had been rather bigger than Ernest had hoped. He had his share of luck, with an improvement in the gold price. At the end of hostilities Britain had found a recession on her hands, and had gone off the gold standard to allow the currency to find its own level and recuperate for better times ahead. Where in those years of war gold had fetched only 85s an ounce on the London market, it was now fetching up to 112s, even as much as 123s at one time. This 'premium' on the London market which still accounted for the greater part of South Africa's gold sales was a useful boon to fledgling gold mines struggling to get off the ground, like Anglo's on the Far East Rand.

Recognising the main line of fortune, Ernest threw himself heart and soul into the development of the four gold mines, and into the development of the townships associated with them. Not so many years before the sites of Brakpan and Springs had been open veld. Now they were flourishing towns in their own right, with their respective populations increasing rapidly: particularly Springs, which it was claimed was growing faster than any other urban area in the world apart from Los Angeles. Already the community was the fifth biggest in South Africa, and was confidently expected to surpass even Johannesburg in due course. Ernest made it his business to keep an eye on the rapid developments in each centre. Planning them was for him almost a hobby, after his municipal experiences in Kimberley. Before long the communities of the Far East Rand were boasting suburbs with names like Pollak Park, Selection Park and even Brenthurst.

But while the gold price rose, so did costs. South Africa's economy was closely linked with Britain's and the Union suffered recession as well. Diamond sales declined – a great disappointment now that Ernest and Louis were trying to reorganise the Lüderitz fields – and in every sphere of the South African economy times were hard. It often worked like that: while gold boomed everything else suffered, and vice versa. That was what economists meant when they talked of the 'flywheel' effect of gold. In a time of depression, the mines were working to capacity and would help the whole economy return to normal much faster than if the industry was not there.

This is what happened now. Things began to return to normal. But as the value of sterling rose, so the gold price dropped until in 1921 it was precisely what it had been in 1914. This time, however, costs were far higher than they had been, and it was clear to a dozen companies operating with a low safety margin that unless they took drastic action their mines would be run out of business. In this spirit the Chamber of Mines approached the government to seek relief. Smuts appreciated the problem and called a conference of management and miners' unions to thrash out a new policy in a bid to save the industry.

The negotiations were heated. The Labour movement was in its heyday, and Marxist influence was strong. The workers were not prepared to tolerate any measures they felt infringed their rights. Besides, to an ever increasing extent the *uitlander* stock of the early days was being superseded by a predominantly Afrikaner body, which had taken to heart the militant propaganda of Hertzog and the Nationalists as well as the Labour Party's demands. This was to the effect that South Africa was to be kept white at all costs. That meant a whole range of jobs had to be protected against the infiltration of black labour, attractive to the employers because it was so cheap. Already the industrial colour bar was established as possibly the most significant plank on South Africa's political stage.

The crunch came with a sudden, even more drastic, drop in the gold price at the end of 1921. A 5s cut per ounce immediately put seven more mines in jeopardy, apart from those which had already gone under. The Chamber of Mines wanted to substitute black labour for white on a number of jobs so far reserved for whites, which it was convinced was the only solution. The coal mines had been seriously hit by the recession and proposed a cut in wages. And if that wasn't enough several major power stations and engineering works also decided on drastic measures to cut costs.

This was all too much for the already militant trade unions, which termed the different proposals 'ultimatums'. They held a meeting to discuss what action to take, and decided to take an immediate ballot on whether or not to strike until the 'ultimatums' were withdrawn. The ballot produced an overwhelming vote in favour of strike action. Smuts and the Chamber of Mines tried in vain to persuade them the changes proposed were all for the best and that in the end they would be the gainers. Already the workers were challenging each other: 'Are you for a white South Africa?' and were convinced the Chamber of Mines was out to break the colour bar.

Just before World War I there had been miners' strikes on the Rand in both 1913 and 1914. Armed strikers had formed commandos similar to those of the South African War, and fought the police in widespread battles through the streets. In 1913 the miners gained the upper hand. In 1914 Smuts sent in strong reinforcements to quell the trouble before it got out of hand. Now the strike committees called their men to arms yet again: commandos to frustrate any would-be 'scabs' or strike-breakers, and oppose force with force if it should be necessary.

Things began in a small way. The men refused to work, so the gold mines, the coal mines and the major power stations closed down in the second week of January, 1922. The strikers formed pickets to obstruct scabs, and the police were mobilised to prevent trouble. On the night of January 18, the first commando to reveal itself surprised two policemen on the East Rand and took them prisoner. This modest success triggered the formation of commandos all over the Reef, and the campaign was in full swing.

Each locality had its own commando, again in line with the old Boer traditions. There was no co-ordination of effort except towards the common goal of overcoming the police and taking control of the whole area. The most ambitious leaders expected to topple Smuts and his government, and bring in a new order pledged to defend white supremacy. But for most of those involved the real fight was against the employers, and with their power so great they sensed an ideal opportunity to hit them hard and teach them a lesson.

There was fighting all over the Rand, in fact right down to Klerksdorp near the Vaal River where there was an isolated outcrop of reef mined by several companies. There were fierce pitched battles in the streets of Johannesburg, but here the police held their own. Far more serious were the events on the East Rand and the Far East Rand. In each scattered town, Boksburg, Benoni, Brakpan and Springs, the local strikers won through to seize possession of the area almost from the start in the face of weak resistance by police detachments isolated from reinforcements. Sometimes outnumbered by 10 to 1, the police were penned in isolated strongpoints as the strikers took absolute control. Now they could march on the mines.

In Benoni and Boksburg, the mine authorities gave in without resistance. In Brakpan, however, the officials were made of sterner stuff. The mine manager, one of Ernest's protégés, was willing to put up a fight. When the strikers arrived they found themselves confronted by a group of 10 special police and some 25 mine officials armed with revolvers. The battle lasted much of the day, but in spite of the gallant defence the odds were too long. The strikers were victorious, with four of the officials and four of the police shot dead, and many more wounded seriously.

The situation was better at the two Springs mines, again governed by Ernest's men. There the officials showed considerable ingenuity, filling time by constructing an armoured car to help send supplies to the beleaguered police bottled up in their barracks. When the officials heard that the strikers were preparing to drive a train into the middle of the mine they sent out a party to blow up the line. And their master-stroke was in rigging up a dummy machine-gun so realistic that it fooled a captive striker. He was allowed to escape, and his report to the strike committee discouraged any further attack.

All this time the government was growing increasingly alarmed. At first it was thought the police would be able to hold the strikers in check, but the movement was a lot stronger than anticipated. General Smuts decided to bring in his armed forces. Several regiments were mobilised and appeals for recruits found a keen response. Supported by artillery, the army advanced to attack.

Smuts had another trick up his sleeve. Only recently the air arm of the Defence Force had been restyled the South African Air Force in its own right. It was equipped with tardy biplanes mounting two Lewis guns and capable of carrying several 25 pounder bombs. Smuts sent them into action, the Air Force's first engagement. The planes dropped the bombs over Benoni, and made several direct hits on buildings occupied by the strikers. There was a number of casualties, including three women and three teenage children not involved in the strike who were killed.

Smuts himself travelled to Johannesburg from the Cape by train to direct operations against the strikers. It was a military campaign, and fought as fiercely. By the end of the fighting, 230 men had been killed – more than in the whole length of Louis Botha's campaign in South West. But the result was the men at last returned to work – in agreement with the proposals made by the Chamber of Mines. Smuts was given full credit for the ultimate success, a development that cost him dear. The initial popularity of the victory provoked a backlash of resentment which centred largely on Smuts himself: he had sent in an army to crush a strike. Soon he would have to pay the penalty.

During the troubles the workers distributed a satyrical pamphlet aimed against the capitalists and featuring as its anti-hero one 'Hoggenheimer the Jew'. The character was supposed to represent the archetypal South African capitalist, and was drawn from a stage musical which had enjoyed considerable popularity at the turn of the century, *The Girl From Kay's*. It was a simple story of a show dancer who made good through her winning ways with a South African millionaire, Max Hoggenheimer.

> *It's very nice to be*
> *A dame of high degree*
> *With blood and reputation beautifully blue.*
> *But folks with cash can get*

Into the smartest set
And that's what I shall proceed to do.
    When driving through the park
    Perhaps you may remark
A silver-mounted perfumed petrol motor trap.
    You'll see me on the box
    In furs of silver fox
With just a few big diamonds in my cap.
I'll marry Hoggenheimer of Park Lane:
    The money he is winning
    I'll set it gaily spinning,
And ev'ry one that sees me will explain
That I'm Mrs Hoggenheimer of Park Lane

    My Thursdays ev'ry week
    Will be extremely chic
As all the papers will remark in social pars:
    When Kubelik comes in
    To play the violin,
    With recitations by dramatic stars!
    I'll build a hospital
    And give a fancy ball
And all the House of Peers to dinner I'll invite.
    And when some noble Lords
    Are on my husband's boards
He won't be long in getting made a knight.
They'll honour Hoggenheimer of Park Lane,
    And I shall be presented
    In style unprecedented.
There never has been seen so grand a train
As that of Lady Hoggenheimer of Park Lane.

    But our aspiring pride
    Will not be satisfied
Unless we make a bid for something bigger yet!
    I feel that I should seem
    A sort of fairy dream
In ermine robes and little coronet!
    I'll get my husband sent
    Right into Parliament,
With friends enough to set his party in a whirl.

And if the voting's near
He may be made a peer,
A baron, viscount, or a belted earl!
He'll be Lord Hoggenheimer of Park Lane,
And prove he is descended
From Norman baron splendid
And I'll have royal blood in ev'ry vein
When I am Countess Hoggenheimer of Park Lane.

The portrait of the millionaire was drawn from the many 'Randlords' who then had houses in Park Lane and its neighbourhood: Alfred Beit, Harry Barnato, Solly Joel, Sir Lionel Phillips, Sir Julius Wernher, Sir Joseph Robinson among them. The surname 'Hoggenheimer' presumably had only coincidental connections with the Oppenheimer brothers – though Bernard at least was already prominent at the time the show was popular. When the name was revived twenty years later, however, there was an obvious and immediate relevance – even if it was largely unjustified.

Newspaper cartoonists, particularly Boonzaier of *Die Burger* in Cape Town, quickly seized on Hoggenheimer as a standard symbol for South African capital, and though the cartoon character bore no resemblance at all to Ernest, the inference was often drawn. Besides that, his opponents openly nicknamed him Hoggenheimer for years afterwards, particularly those on the Nationalist benches in Parliament. He was the fastest rising star of all, as they well understood.

True, he laid himself open to such attacks. Though out of the public eye since the days of his mayoralty in Kimberley, Ernest was preparing to stand for parliament. General Smuts wanted his support, and suggested he stood for Kimberley in the next general election. When Smuts told him he did not necessarily expect him to toe the party line on every aspect of policy, Ernest was half convinced. When he was sent a requisition signed by voters from every section of Kimberley's electorate, and that meant from every colour group, he felt he was left no choice in the matter.

There was another reason, rather wider. Ernest could not have missed the threat to his own interests and to the world he was so fully involved in: gold and diamonds and all the mines. The Nationalists and militant Labourites wanted to nationalise the whole industry. They had heard that threat many times before, but now it was stronger than ever. There were ominous signs that capital would be pulled out of South Africa. Already – and partly on the strength of the disquieting events of 1922 – Morgans had disposed of their holdings in Anglo

101

American, to the point where there was hardly any American involvement left. There was the danger of this small stream of withdrawal developing into a mighty flood, and Ernest wanted to be in Parliament himself to dam it if he could.

It would be a tense election, they all knew. Two years had passed since the revolt on the Rand, and Smuts was fighting for his political life. His handling of the strike, particularly his decision to bomb Benoni, had lost him respect in every section of the population and it was generally supposed his days were numbered. The two opposition parties, General Hertzog's Nationalists and Colonel Cresswell's Labour Party, made a pact to fight the South African Party with their combined resources and with the single object of throwing Smuts out of power. Ernest was backing an underdog, he knew: but Smuts was an old friend and needed him.

From his first election address Ernest made it plain what he stood for. The issue was clear, he said: they were voting not for parties but for a Prime Minister, between General Hertzog and General Smuts.

'I must now explain to you why I support General Smuts. General Smuts has done more than any other statesman to raise the reputation of our country, not only in England and the Dominions, but throughout the whole world. He is not only known in every capital in Europe, but in America also. He is not known only in the capitals but in every town.

'I remember that at the time of the last General Election, when I was in a small place in the United States of America, near to the Mexican border, that not alone was the result of the South African election mentioned, but that a full-page portrait of General Smuts appeared in the local paper. This will show you how great a boon General Smuts is to the Union, and how much he has increased its prestige.

'That is the first reason why I support General Smuts. My second reason is that he is pursuing the policy which is the traditional policy of Kimberley, and which was the policy pursued by Mr. Rhodes . . .'

In fact, it was the second reason that was most characteristic of Ernest's campaign. He went out of his way to associate himself with Cecil Rhodes, and in particular with a single precept of his which was admittedly out of step with official South African Party policy: 'Equal rights for all civilised men.' The idea found its way into all Ernest's campaign speeches, and never failed to win him enthusiastic applause. At this time the Cape voters' roll had included the names of Coloured and Native voters, though the Nationalists promised to disenfranchise them without delay. From Coloured, Indian and African voters alike Ernest won a wide following denied to his opponent.

Apart from the racial question, there was another precept which Ernest took from Rhodes and which he underlined heavily. In the past the Nationalists had repeatedly demanded South Africa's secession from the British Empire and the declaration of a republic. They had now agreed to drop the demand as a concession to Cresswell and the Labour Party, who whatever they proposed at least supported Britain. But as Ernest several times pointed out, there could be no guarantee Hertzog might not revert to his policies if elected.

'You see, Colonel Cresswell does not believe either that the secession movement is dead. But for all that he is willing to bargain about the Imperial connection, and for one reason only, to put General Smuts and the South African Party out of office. I do not pretend that everything the South African Party has done has been correct, but I shall show the electors in subsequent speeches that they have done a great deal and that the faults are small compared with the good achieved.

'If you had a good watch dog and you discovered the dog had fleas you would not drown the dog. But you are asked to kill the South African Party because of a few unpopular measures, which our great leader has already promised to put right.'

The campaign wound on, with most of the excitement contained in the meetings of Ernest's opponent, Advocate Kitchin of the Labour Party. Whatever the party's successes in the country at large, it was having a tough time of things in Kimberley. David Harris, now quite a veteran in parliament, was doing well in the Beaconsfield constituency, and often he and Ernest appeared on the same platform in each other's support. The two had not forgotten their personal differences, but for the length of the campaign these were tacitly swept out of sight. Ernest also spoke at meetings in support of the SAP candidate for Barkly West, Pieter Scholtz. A high point of the campaign was when Smuts arrived in Kimberley to address the electorate, part of his tour of the whole Union.

Ernest and Harris enjoyed the complete support of the *Diamond Fields Advertiser*, both in its reporting of their meetings and in editorial comment. About the Labour Party's candidates, on the other hand, the paper had nothing at all to say. If Smuts and the SAP were to be swept from power, it would not be blamed on Kimberley's newspaper.

One incident from the campaign was recalled many years later by a journalist who was then the *DFA's* late-night duty sub-editor. It was 1.30 in the morning, and he was alone in the offices when he heard determined steps on the stairs. In burst two men, one rather overwrought about something and the other dignified and silent.

103

'Who's in charge here?' blustered the first man. 'This is Sir Ernest Oppenheimer, and we have to get a statement in tomorrow's paper. It's extremely important.'

As it happened, the sub-editor had sent the last page of the edition to the printers and it was all but ready for the presses.

'Now,' said Ernest's companion, 'you see . . .'

'No, that isn't what we mean at all,' interjected Ernest. 'We appreciate the lateness of the hour, and all the difficulty you will have granting us this request, but we feel that there is indeed some urgency about it, and that is why we have come.'

Then, quickly and concisely, and yet without any sign of heat or haste, he explained that his political opponents were making great play with a canard that had been circulated with the idea of doing him a bit of no good on the eve of the election. I needn't recall it, and anyway it doesn't really matter today what it was, because bigger and better canards have been devised by all parties since then. The point at that moment was that it was my duty to expose the canard and see that Sir Ernest's attitude was made clear on a certain point.

'If you can do anything at all,' he said, 'I shall be grateful.'

That was all. No orders. No commands. No blustering that if I didn't do this or that he'd see that my editor knew that he had a bonehead on his night staff. It was just a business call made by a very polished gentleman on one of the world's workers in the middle of the night. Well, I did my stuff, Bill Helfrich and the boys in the works did theirs, and the result was that we came out with a news interview with Sir Ernest on the front page.

All very ordinary? Maybe. But remember that Sir Ernest, even at that time was perhaps the biggest name in diamonds in the world, and that he was confronting someone who, in the newspaper industry, ranked less than the dust. Yet he acted considerately, kindly. It takes a big man to do that, when things aren't going too well for him personally . . . He doesn't shout. He talks, and because he talks common sense in a kindly, understanding way, he gets things done.

On election day itself, Tuesday June 17, the front page of the *Diamond Fields Advertiser* was given over to photographs of the South African Party's candidates in Kimberley, and resumes of what they had said in their campaigns. 'Vote for Oppenheimer: the man you know and trust.' Inside, there were a number of smaller advertisements carrying election slogans.

Vote for Sir Ernest Oppenheimer, the Moderate and Progressive Man.

Vote for the Man you Know: Sir David Harris for Beaconsfield.

Pack Up Your Troubles in Your Old Kit Bag and Vote For Sir Ernest Oppenheimer.

Back the Old War Horse. Vote for Sir David Harris.

Vote for Sir Ernest Oppenheimer. He Stands for Financial Stability.

From an early stage the candidates were out and about, visiting each polling booth in turn and rallying friends and supporters. May and Ernest rode together in an open car driven by E W Weatherby's son Andrew, himself now a budding diamond evaluator for De Beers. With them went Ernest's election agent, the local lawyer Louis Lezard. The booths were busy from an early stage, with voters streaming in on foot and by car. 'Considering the abnormal motor traffic in Kimberley's difficult streets,' wrote the DFA, 'it is pleasing and satisfactory to be able to state that, according to advice from police headquarters, there was not a single accident during the day.'

Long before it was time to announce the result for Kimberley, a large crowd had gathered outside City Hall. Market Square was filled. Soon after 10.30 that evening the civil commissioner emerged and announced the result:

Sir ERNEST OPPENHEIMER   (SAP)   1 934 votes
S B Kitchin (Labour)   925 votes

'A tremendous cheer broke out, and the cheer was intensified when Sir Ernest Oppenheimer mounted the table to address the people. He could not be heard for at least a minute, so great was the cheering, but when he found his opportunity he said he would not attempt to make a speech, as he was so greatly overwhelmed with their kindness.'

Ernest was jubilant. '. . . I thank Kimberley, which gave me my start in business, and which has now given me my start in political life . . . I thank you for having returned me as your representative, and I thank you in every possible way. I have had a very big fight, and I thank you.'

Ernest clambered down from the table to make way for Advocate Kitchin. But just then a group of Ernest's excited supporters caught hold of him and lifted him shoulder high.

'Sir Ernest was carried to the South African Party Club, which was packed to the utmost. A scene of wild enthusiasm was enacted, supporters cheering at the top of their voices . . . Leaning over the

105

balcony of the SAP club, Sir Ernest was asked the majority. "The majority is 1 000" – and the information was greeted with tremendous cheers . . .

'Sir Ernest, who was received vociferously, said, "I would only like to say how happy I am tonight to be elected by so big a majority. It is a clarion cry that will go through South Africa. It will show South Africa and the whole British Empire that we are true to Cecil Rhodes and that we stand for the British Empire. I stand for equal rights for all civilised men. I will try to be worthy of the confidence you have given me. I thank you very, very much indeed."

Now he was safely elected, and the crowd went on to the *Diamond Fields Advertiser's* offices where results were being displayed as they came through. There was good news from Beaconsfield, where Sir David Harris was re-elected with a comfortable majority. But from the country as a whole the picture was black. Labour and the Nationalists were gaining seats in every direction, and there could be no hope of the SAPs remaining in power. Hertzog and Cresswell had achieved their object. But the blackest news of all came from the Transvaal, from Smuts's own seat. A Labour man had won Pretoria West. General Smuts was not only out of power: now he was out of parliament.

2

THE OPPENHEIMERS moved house again. This time Ernest had bought a full-scale family seat. It was quite close to the first house, in fact just up the road: but there the comparison ended. Their new home was a complete estate in its own right called Marion Court, a marvellous mansion standing in nearly 50 acres of exquisite parkland. Quite apart from the beauty of the site, Ernest must have been attracted by its associations: the house was designed by Sir Herbert Baker, the architect established by Cecil John Rhodes.

Ernest soon changed Marion Court's name to Brenthurst, just like the house they had left. Quite why is not clear: probably for a thoroughly practical reason, Harry suggests, like not having to alter his home letterhead. Certainly the other house was also known as Brenthurst, even when it was sold. But whatever its name, the new estate would be a wonderful place for little boys to grow up: acres and acres of hillsides and lawns and woodland and thick undergrowth to do whatever they liked, and at the bottom of the garden even a miniature maze like the one at Hampton Court. True it was not very thick, and you could cheat and crawl underneath if you found yourself stuck: but with assets like this Brenthurst was a paradise indeed. It was all Ernest had hoped for, a place where he could happily spend the rest of his life.

Hardly had the Oppenheimers transferred than Anglo followed suit. All this time the growing organisation had occupied the second floor of the Corner House. That was all very well when you employed only a handful of people, as had been so when the offices housed only CMS and Rand Selection. It had been so small that Ernest could entertain the whole staff at annual garden parties out in Jubilee Road. But now Anglo's personnel were counted in scores. Ernest leased several floors in a new building in Hollard Street, not far from the Stock Exchange and the Chamber of Mines: Anmercosa House, which was to give its name to a whole string of new investment companies. Its most unusual feature was a strange lighthouse-type structure on the roof, which followed the sun automatically and reflected its light down into the board-room.

For all the expansion, Ernest still valued Anglo's close ties with CMS and Dunkelsbuhlers in London. The Anglo office in London shared premises with CMS, and Dunkelsbuhlers was quietly working on the other firms in the Syndicate with an eye to bringing Anglo a share in its activities. Ernest had been planning this for a long time, and meant to use his contracts with the Belgian and Portuguese producers as his trump card. As he expected, their production was far bigger than De Beers had ever guessed it could be, and far from drying up the source looked good for a long time to come.

Louis helped set up the arrangements, and the negotiations went very smoothly and produced the result Ernest wanted so badly. Perhaps he was a mining magnate, but he remained a Syndicate man to his fingertips. Anglo would hand over the Congo-Angola contracts to the Syndicate in exchange for eight per cent of its business. This was a tiny share in comparison with what the senior members controlled, but it was a step in the right direction and when combined with the Dunkelsbuhler interests the Anglo holding wielded fair influence.

Meanwhile, diamonds had been found in West Africa. The first discoveries were made along the Gold Coast, or Ghana as it is today: rich alluvial fields which seemed most promising. And then even richer deposits turned up in the steaming jungles of Sierra Leone, mixed in with the quartz and gravel of the hundreds of rivers and watercourses. Ernest bought his way into the company which success-fully tendered for the right to prospect and exploit these deposits, the

Consolidated African Selection Trust; and besides this he contracted to buy its whole production for the next five years.

Through these negotiations Ernest met Chester Beatty, CAST's chairman. Beatty was an American, but involving himself in British territories to such an extent that he soon took out British citizenship, and was later knighted. He was particularly glad to meet Ernest, for he was on the point of involving himself in an altogether new area which promised big rewards if things went well, but which would require an astonishing degree of capital. He had his eye on the base metal deposits of Northern Rhodesia.

It was not altogether virgin territory, of course: Rhodes's British South Africa Company and others had been mining there since before the turn of the century. But this had been on a small scale, and Beatty was sure there was a million times more copper in Northern Rhodesia than had yet been taken out of it. It was to be found in the distant north of the country – in fact, not far across the border from the Belgian mines of Katanga in the Congo.

Chester Beatty was not the only party interested in these deposits. Ernest had already been involved with Edmund Davis, of course: one of the BSAC's key men in Northern Rhodesia and particularly at the great zinc and lead mine of Broken Hill. Davis had been trying to interest Ernest in the potential of the territory for some time, and encouraging him to invest. When he introduced Ernest to the diamond companies working in Angola and the Congo, the arrangement was that in return Ernest should help him in Northern Rhodesia.

Ernest had to weigh these requests carefully. The problem with base metals was that the market was extremely fickle. One moment it was up, only to plummet down the next. Besides, the whole market was under American control, with the United States far and away the world's biggest producer. On the other hand, it was possible the heavy American influence would in time help to stabilise prices. Certainly this possibility encouraged Chester Beatty to investigate the situation in Northern Rhodesia and prompted Edmund Davis to search for new capital. Each successfully applied for prospecting concessions from the new colonial administration which had recently succeeded the old BSAC, and when these were granted, turned to Ernest. Both were able to tempt him with a glittering prize: the chance of discovering a new diamond field.

There was a very real chance of this happening. Over the border in the Congo the Belgian companies were working some of the world's richest deposits, extending right down into Angola. Was it not at least

108

conceivable that Northern Rhodesia held them too? If Ernest came in and supported the prospecting operations, he would share in the eventual finds. Ernest agreed, though in both instances he made it a condition that Anglo be appointed consulting engineers. More than that, he recruited a new geologist: one of the best that North America could offer, the professor of geology at McGill University in Montreal. Ernest had such faith in Joe Bancroft that he gave him *carte blanche* to recruit his own team. Many of them were former students of his from McGill. Before long they were in the field exploring the new concession areas, working to a grid system which Bancroft devised.

Whatever Ernest's ideas, Davis and Beatty had decided their first priority was copper. Their own geologists got down to work and it looked as if their chances of finding worthwhile deposits were quite bright. The only adverse note were the depressingly sceptical opinions of American engineers who visited the sites. Take the reactions noted by one of Ernest's men who realised how mistaken they were:

'One of these engineers stood with me on the edge of a trench and remarked that we would not find a copper mine there because no deposits of commercial importance had ever been developed anywhere in a similar formation. Three other very well-known copper men from the United States visited Nchanga for a day, and left with the same impression. In fact, their entire conversation when looking at our work was about the danger and likelihood of being bitten by tsetse flies and contracting sleeping sickness.'

But in spite of these discouragements prospecting continued as keenly as ever, and the Anglo geologists began to add substance to the rumours: Northern Rhodesia possessed a mining field likely to achieve greater importance than any other in the British Empire with the possible exception of the Rand. 'And even of this I am not sure . . .' Ernest told Anglo shareholders.

Even the British were sceptical of a claim so bold. After all, it emanated from the darkest corner of the darkest continent. The London *Times* sent out a special correspondent to check its accuracy. Ernest sent him to see Bancroft in his camp at Nkana, a copper prospect near the Congo border. 'You have arrived at the right time,' Bancroft told him. 'I expect one of my boreholes to intersect the reef at any moment – in fact it may have intersected it during the night. Let's go into the bush and see what is happening.'

The *Times* man was immediately on guard. He had no idea of the great accuracy that could be expected of Bancroft. But the two set out for the borehole, and when they reached the site the driller told them he was just pulling up the rods. Sure enough, the core came up in minutes and when they washed it showed good indications of copper. Bancroft beamed happily and told the newspaperman that he thought it would prove a valuable find.

'But how do I know you didn't put that core in the hole before I came here and just hoisted it up for me to see?' the *Times* man asked.

Bancroft said nothing. He drove the man back to camp, passed him over to a subordinate and refused to speak to him again. But the encounter was typical of outside suspicion of the discoveries: after all, there had been downright frauds before. Wasn't this just another trick to encourage the naive investor to part with his hard-won capital?

The deposits had been proved, but it would be a very different matter bringing them into production. It needed years of planning, and the companies concerned would have to make their moves with great care. But from the indications so far the deposits were large enough to justify investment on the grand scale. Beatty and Davis mobilised the forces at their command, and Ernest strengthened his hold on each side. It was a long term project, and Anglo was in on the ground floor.

Gold, diamonds and now copper: the Anglo American had come a long way since 1917. But while all this was happening there had been developments in a quite different direction, away in the Eastern Transvaal. In the very area where the pioneer prospectors had found their first traces of gold, a German geologist had discovered deposits of a metal worth five times as much: in fact, the most valuable and rare of them all – platinum.

At this time the only known sources of platinum were Russia and Columbia in South America, which was what made it so rare. Certainly nobody could have expected to find it in Southern Africa: but then, nobody had expected gold, diamonds and copper. What had happened was a group of amateur prospectors had found traces of a strange white metal none of them recognised. They sent it off to Johannesburg to a geologist they knew there, Hans Merensky. He recognised it, had it analysed to make sure his eyes were not deceiving him, and was told he was right one hundred percent.

Merensky had been born in South Africa, the son of a missionary: but his parents had taken him to Germany as a boy and he had gone to school and university there, and had served in the German army for a time. He returned to South Africa and proved a great success in his early years: but then war broke out, and he was interned in a concentration camp as an alien. Afterwards he had great difficulty finding his

110

feet again, and was by this time virtually flat broke. He did not have the money to do anything about the new platinum deposits himself, so had to look for a backer.

It was a heartbreaking position to be in. Merensky knew there was platinum, but how was he to convince somebody else? All he had was the initial sample sent to him by the amateurs, and that was hardly convincing: they had despatched it in an aspirin bottle. It took him weeks before at last he was successful in persuading several friends of his to put up what money they could. Even then it was hardly enough to launch a prospecting expedition, let alone a full-scale platinum producer.

Once he was in business Merensky did not waste time. He found and confirmed the original deposits discovered by the amateurs, and set about tracing the reef of platinum as far as it went. He could hardly believe it. Before he was through he followed it in a huge arc curving all the way through the Transvaal, from Lydenburg and up round Rustenburg to Potgietersrust in the north. In time no fewer than 2 000 square miles of the Transvaal would prove platiniferous. Once the news was out rivals fell over each other in buying up options on the farms in the area at extraordinary prices. Speculators floated new companies by the score, and the Stock Exchange had seen nothing like the great bubble of platinum shares that threatened to burst even before any mining had begun.

Working quietly behind the scenes, Ernest came to terms with Merensky and his backers, who of course had taken out the key options for themselves, or rather as much as they could afford. Together they and Anglo and Sir Abe Bailey's S A Townships formed Potgietersrust Platinum Mines. At a later stage they brought in Solly Joel and Johnnies, which made another big contribution to the working capital.

At the time it looked as if the platinum mines would sweep all before them. The editor of the London *Financial Times* sent an enthusiastic report to his paper.

'Platinum is right, the era of genuine development now definitely started, will make South Africa's third mining wonder of the world. First came diamonds, then gold, now platinum.'

But there was disappointment. Threatened with competition which might wipe them from the market, the Russian producers unloaded huge stocks of platinum which reduced prices to a fraction of what they had been. However, platinum mining was still immensely profitable, and Rustenburg was to prove the richest platinum field in the world. In the long run the investment paid off handsomely.

111

3

WITH THE election over there was time to squeeze in a short session of parliament before the end of the year. Ernest and May travelled down to Cape Town for the opening. The member for Standerton had stepped down to make way for Smuts, and in the by-election that followed the leader had been duly returned. Now he and the rest of the Opposition were preparing to fight the Pact with all the resources at their disposal. In marshalling his team, he invited Ernest to sit on the front bench.

Ernest must have been greatly excited to take his place in the House of Assembly where so many great men of the mining world had sat before him. Rhodes had been Prime Minister here, and so had Jameson. Barney Barnato had come here to represent Kimberley. Lionel Phillips, Abe Bailey and many others from the Rand had sat here before him. It was organised along the lines of the Mother of Parliaments at Westminster, though it was not so big: and the benches were not benches, but seats with lift-top desks before them, and little galleries like shallow theatre boxes ringed the walls behind.

The Pact men had prepared an ambitious programme of legislation to push through as quickly as they could. Who knew whether they would be able to hold their position at the next election? There were several rather startling pieces of legislation proposed – one of them a bid to establish a full-scale Union Diamond Board which would have the effect of nationalising the diamond industry, and bring in a home-based cutting industry as well. Nationalist and Labour speakers referred to the diamond and gold industries and to the 'wicked power of the capitalists' almost from the first day – taunts clearly aimed at the new member for Kimberley sitting on the Opposition front bench. Ernest was soon on his feet to reply, in the course of his maiden speech. It was all rather tongue in cheek, in view of the fierce mumblings he could sense on the other side of the house.

'I have the honour of being a vice-president of the Transvaal Chamber of Mines, and I hope in the years to come that body will do me the honour of electing me its president. I am also largely interested in the diamond trade, both as producer and merchant, and in spite of these terrible attributes I am not ashamed to address this honourable House. My presence here shows that I put country before business, and that I have only one desire, and that is to be able to render useful service to South Africa.'

Then he launched his attack. First he turned to the Pact men who had urged the nationalisation of the diamond industry: 'It appears to me that the best bowlers are always outside the field. They don't play, they don't intend to play, they don't risk their money.' Then the fuss made about the gold producers: 'The hon member also described the Chamber of Mines as ogres and then went on to say that they should have their wings clipped. The latter remark suggests that they are angels. Well, we are neither ogres nor angels, but just ordinary business-men who object to being made pawns either inside this House or out-side it.'

As maiden speeches go, it was long and involved, but already showed considerable power. Clearly the honourable member for Kimberley knew what he was talking about. The next speaker, a Labour man from Natal, decided to withhold the customary congratulations on a first effort: 'I have not risen to reply to the mining questions mentioned by the previous speaker, but I would like to say that it takes a great deal more courage for a man to go down a mine than it does for a man to sit in comfort on the surface and invest his money in mining enterprises.'

The die was cast. Hoggenheimer sat on the Opposition front bench in person, and was a juicy target for both Nationalists and Creswellites. In fact, he probably united their efforts more than any other man. Nor was he entirely safe on his own side of the House. The Pact men got wind of the ill feeling that existed between Anglo and De Beers thanks to events of the past, and also of the personal ill feeling between Ernest and Harris. There were many references to 'the supposed feud between us', as Ernest several times described it. He, on the other hand, chose to ignore the taunts and concentrated on siding with Harris in defence of the whole diamond industry as then constituted, which was the glittering prize the Pact men had in sight.

Even within the diamond world, the going was tough. The trade had picked up after the post-war recession, but dealers knew the Syndicate had stocks of unsold stones on its hands – and were not prepared to pay high prices. At the same time the producers found costs were spiralling and they had to demand more per carat. Currency problems, notably in Belgium and between Britain and America, made matters all the more difficult. And on top of this there was a serious threat from the least likely quarter: Communist Russia. The revolutionary government was selling off huge quantities of stones looted from the aristocracy at a fraction of their value. The effect on diamond values could have been as drastic as the effect the sudden release of Russian production had on the world's platinum market. Fortunately for the diamond trade, Solly

Joel quickly intervened and bought up most of what was available before its effect on the market could be felt.

The difficulties only underlined the tensions already present in the dealings of the producers and the Syndicate. Both were caught completely unawares, quite unready to cope with the challenging new developments. The Syndicate had been playing around with its prices in a bid to attract more trade, and now the pressure was on had no leeway to reduce them further. The producers, worried by the speeding growth of diamond production outside South Africa, each wanted a greater share in the market.

Matters came to a head in 1924, the year the Anglo American was admitted to the Syndicate. The agreements between the producers had expired, and it was time to renew the contracts between the producers and the Syndicate. There was a good deal of bickering between the parties concerned or particularly through the influence of Breitmeyers, the old Wernher, Beit renamed now it was controlled by Ludwig Breitmeyer. At countless conferences and confrontations which ensued the four main producers – De Beers, the Premier, Jagersfontein and CDM – heaped abuse on the Syndicate, which the latter returned in good measure. Ernest and Louis were involved on both sides of the fence and sadly shook their heads. What was the diamond world coming to?

Though interested in all aspects of the controversy, Ernest's chief concern was CDM in South West Africa. Its current quota in the producers' agreement was 21 per cent, but its importance called for more. At the producers' meetings CDM's case was urged by Sir David Graaff, backed by the South West administration which needed all the revenue it could get. But the other producers would not hear of any increase in CDM's quota, which would of course affect their own shares.

Apart from CDM, however, Ernest had the Anglo American to think of, and at the same time Dunkelsbuhlers where Louis remained as staunch an ally as ever. Neither of the companies held great influence in the Syndicate's activities, however, and of this the brothers were only too well aware. Several times in these difficult months Ernest went so far as to suggest it was time he and Louis cut their links with the Syndicate, and set out to form a new one of their own – ideally in company with Solly Joel of Barnatos. Though they could not be sure, they had an idea Solly Joel was as dissatisfied with the Syndicate's handling of its affairs as they were.

The new Pact government could see no reason for the long delays and the frustrating tactics employed in the negotiations and decided it was time to step in. It could have no influence over the Syndicate, but its authority over the producers was absolute. The Minister of Mines called a meeting of the main producers in Pretoria in November, 1924, and told them to sort out their differences immediately. If they did not he would be forced to take action; in fact he was already considering it.

Sir David Graaff again held out for an increase in CDM's quota, but Ross Frames who was chairman of De Beers refused. He even threatened to revert to open competition if he was called on to sacrifice anything more.

'We would rather give free vent, free exercise to what we consider our competitive capacity,' he said. 'We would rather die fighting if we are to go down.' That was not 'quite the spirit of compromise,' Graaff pointed out. 'We do not want a compromise,' Ross Frames answered bluntly.

Another meeting in December produced some improvement in the position. Ross Frames grudgingly agreed to a modification of the South West quota but made the offer conditional on a satisfactory contract with the Syndicate and on the willingness of the government to attend an international conference to thrash out all the issues involved. This the government refused to contemplate and the offer was withdrawn. The producers were back in square one.

All through the negotiations Ernest had been counting on one provision of the agreement he had made when taking over CDM in 1920. If ever the producers' arrangements with the Syndicate fell through, he and Louis would be given first option in disposing of the South West mines' production. Now, however, a cable arrived from Leslie Pollak with a warning from Arend Brink, the government's technical adviser:

> Brink says Administrator will be at liberty to consider proposals after 1 January and he strongly advises you submit definite proposal without delay . . . He says you should act immediately, otherwise, if an attractive offer made outside source, Administrator will be obliged to consider it on its merits. He hopes you will appreciate his suggestion prompted by his friendly regard for you.

The news must have come as a bombshell. Regardless of the Oppenheimers' rights under the agreement, the Administrator evidently felt free to accept a better offer if one was made. The dangers of production falling into the wrong hands were too fearful to contemplate. At the very least it meant the abandonment of the principle of sales through one channel; at the worst, it might mean opening the way to a new centre of diamond trading outside London, which in the present state of the trade could pose intolerable problems. If Ernest could not persuade the Syndicate to make an offer for the whole production, and quickly, he would have to make an offer on his own account: and that might be ruinous financially.

There was no time to lose. Ernest took ship for London to confront the Syndicate in person, and incidentally to confront his backers too. It was beginning to look as if he would be needing them. Even as he sailed, news came of yet another development. This time it was provoked by the exasperated Minister of Mines who had cabled all the producers an absolute ultimatum giving them precisely six days to sort out their differences with the Syndicate, until 'not later than noon on the twelfth instant, otherwise Government will adopt such course as it may deem fit untrammelled by any negotiations hitherto'.

Perhaps it was a bluff, but it worked. Three days later the producers met again, and at last agreed on the quotas. Now all depended on the Syndicate's approval of the producers' conditions. In London, Louis was working hard to get the Syndicate to amend its terms in compromise, for he was gravely apprehensive of what would happen to the diamond market if the old arrangements broke down. Already, they had heard, the eager Administrator had disposed of the production of a group of small independent producers in South West, to a syndicate in Antwerp. It was not very important in itself, but a bad omen for the trade as a whole.

Ernest arrived in London on January 14, and Louis and he plunged into their campaign to force the Syndicate's hand. Their words fell on dead ground. The old antipathies persisted, and Breitmeyers vetoed every one of their suggestions. No, the Syndicate would not be forced into signing agreements it did not want. It would not be intimidated by De Beers or the Administrator of South West Africa of the South African government or anyone else, and certainly not by Ernest Oppenheimer. The Syndicate would not tender for the production of CDM, and it would not agree to Ernest's tendering on Anglo's behalf.

Ernest tried again. This time he and Louis had a long and intense discussion with Breitmeyer himself and their cousin Gustav Imroth, who was now in charge of all Barnatos' diamond interests. The brothers produced a hundred and one arguments for coming to terms with the government, which was proving dangerously aggressive. There was even the possibility it might try and nationalise the whole

116

industry, as it was threatening with the gold mines. Imroth listened, but Breitmeyer was as stubborn as ever. Only grudgingly would he allow Ernest to cable the Minister of Mines and tell him they were working hard, and ask for more time.

That afternoon a message arrived from CDM. Unless the Syndicate made a satisfactory offer immediately, Brink was going to accept an offer from outside interests. Ernest spent the rest of the day and the next day too trying to convince the diehards of the need to act. But they were not interested: they were not going to be dictated to by anybody – and certainly not in respect of CDM which after all represented another of Oppenheimer's 'fast ones'. Ernest explained that if they were not prepared to do anything, he was, and that was the end of it.

The crisis over CDM precipitated the final drama. The producers were not going to be pressured into accepting the South African producers' terms, and informed the Minister of Mines and De Beers. For Ernest that move signalled the breaking up of the Syndicate, which in turn released his firm and all the others to make their own arrangements. He immediately cabled Brink tendering for the production of CDM: 'Accept to buy for Anglo American diamonds on your minimum terms . . .'

Brink replied the next day: 'Minister of Mines authorizes me to accept your offer purchase on behalf of Anglo American . . . as from 1 March 1925 the 21 per cent accruing to the Consolidated Diamond Mines of South West Africa during 1925 in terms of inter-producers' agreement . . .' Ernest offered to share the business with the other London buying firms, but they were not interested.

Predictably, the other firms were outraged by Ernest's action. In their view he had queered their pitch. They had been resolutely holding out against what they regarded as mere bluff and banter, and the ground was swept from under their feet. Those connected with De Beers – and that meant the majority of them – could not help but remember the previous occasion when Ernest had outwitted them: in gaining possession of the South West fields under their noses. It was time they taught him a lesson.

The remaining members of the Syndicate met to discuss what should be done. Solemnly they announced their decision. Anglo American's action made its continued membership of the Syndicate unacceptable, and as Ernest had throughout been supported by Louis and Walter Dunkels, Dunkelsbuhlers' membership was also forfeit. The brothers 'gladly withdrew'.

117

Ernest was by no means dismayed by the course of events. He afterwards reflected that it was inevitable the Syndicate should split. There could be no future for it under Breitmeyer's leadership. For himself he had decided on a bold course. With the renewed support of his bankers, J P Morgan in New York and Morgan Grenfell in London, he and Louis quietly approached the South African government and offered to buy the whole production of De Beers and the Premier for the ensuing year.

It looked as if he was going to pull off a major coup. The Syndicate was in a shambles of indecision, and it was inconceivable that at this stage it should suddenly come to its senses. But Ernest bargained without what had all the trappings of a conspiracy. The government disclosed the terms of the offer to De Beers, which deliberately or otherwise passed them on to the other buying firms. Acting rather smartly for a change these old members of the Syndicate promptly made an offer on their own account, more favourable than the Oppenheimers' and subsequently agreeing to all the producers' demands. It was a complete about face.

Ernest and Louis had no idea what was going on until it was too late. The government had requested time to consider their offer, asking them to keep it open for ten days. At the end of this period they were told it was unacceptable, no reasons given. Instead, the contract went to the Syndicate, specially revived for the occasion. Louis and Ernest were furious and felt they had a genuine grievance. Louis expressed his feelings in a letter to Ernest:

'I enclose for your information confirmatory copies of the cables exchanged with Ross Frames. I think it essential that you should point out to him that, while we naturally cast no reflections on him or the De Beers board, I am definitely in possession of the fact that our good faith was abused, our offer was disclosed and two amendments were permitted to the others while we were never given a fair chance. It is not possible that houses of the standing of Morgan's, Anglo American and ourselves should expose themselves to such treatment a second time.'

For a time feelings continued to run high, but as Ernest wrote to Louis a few days later, 'I take the line that nothing can be gained by quarrelling. On the contrary all my efforts will be directed to protect the diamond trade, because it is quite evident that in the long run the Consolidated company cannot be prosperous if the other companies are not prosperous.'

The position was that both the South West African and the Union

Michael and Ina, c 1932. Michael worked for Anglo until his death in an aeroplane accident in 1933. *Star Master Series, Johannesburg.*

On holiday in Northern Rhodesia, 1938: Ernest and Harry with their guests General Smuts (*second from left*) and his lifelong friend Deneys Reitz (*centre*). On the right is Roydon Harrison, then general manager of Nkana mine. *Major Tommy Thomas.*

Opening Day at the Brenthurst Military Hospital: Ernest, Ouma Smuts and a patient. *Star Master Series, Johannesburg.*

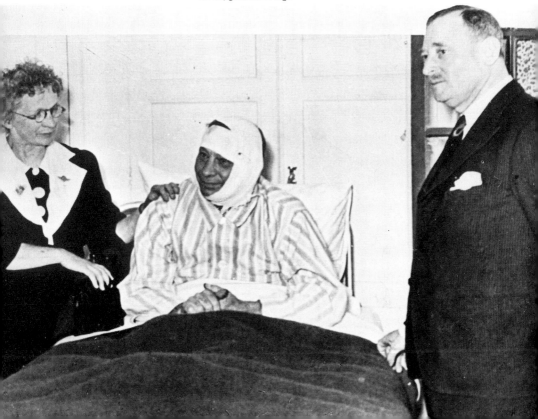

Harry and Bridget on their wedding day: May 6 1943. *Rand Daily Mail.*

producers had contracts until the end of the year. What would happen then was anybody's guess – or rather, there were several possibilities. For the moment, Ernest and Louis concentrated on strengthening their position. By the end of February, Ernest had concluded an agreement with the Administrator of South West by which a five year contract was substituted for the one-year agreement. In London, Louis was working to consolidate the brothers' position as regards the outside producers in the Congo and Angola, and in West Africa. Already Dunkelsbuhlers and Anglo were acting as a syndicate on their own account in concert with their bankers.

Meanwhile, Ernest and Louis were watching Solly Joel, potentially their most valuable ally. They were of course involved with Barnato Brothers in the Congo and West Africa, but was that enough? Ernest had long urged the need for a closer working arrangement with Barnatos: not only for its influence in diamond *buying* with the 45 per cent interest in the Syndicate, but also for the interests in diamond *producing* at De Beers and Jagersfontein, where Solly Joel was the leading shareholder. All the indications were that he was ready for a change. But the wily old magnate was keeping his own council, and nobody could be sure for which side he would eventually declare.

The end of the year was approaching, and so was the time for the renegotiation of agreements with the Union producers. Ernest and Louis were both in South Africa when a message reached them from De Beers.

'The following cable received by Harris from S. B. Joel. Syndicate intend proposing five-year contract. Think it desirable in general interest establish reunion. Tell Sir Ernest Oppenheimer and L. Oppenheimer they should cable offering rejoin. Positive can arrange this if they wish so.'

At an earlier stage, the brothers might have been prepared to rejoin – though, as Ernest commented, it would have been for the Syndicate to invite them, not for them to reapply. Now, however, the tables were turned. Dunkelsbuhlers and Anglo American were in a stronger position than any of the Syndicate members. Not only had they secured the South West Africa contract for five years, and made agreements with the Belgian producers; but they were now preparing to bargain with the Union producers for the 1926 contract on equal terms with the Syndicate.

Solly Joel was getting impatient. When it became clear that the Oppenheimer brothers were not to be talked into rejoining the Syndicate, he let it be known that he would come in with them. He withdrew Barnatos from the Breitmeyers camp, crossed the fence and linked hands with the upstarts. Now things moved quickly. Breitmeyers, representing what was left of the 'old' Syndicate, cabled an offer to De Beers for the whole of its production for 1926. The Oppenheimers were tipped off, and made an offer in their turn. At the end of July, after a period of intense bargaining over profit sharing, the 'Oppenheimer' syndicate's bid was accepted, and the old Syndicate was left out in the cold.

There was jubilation in the Oppenheimer camp. Congratulations poured in from friends, associates and fellow workers. 'Good luck; now we can go ahead,' the two brothers wired Walter Dunkels in London. To Solly Joel they cabled: 'Look forward to closest co-operation in future for mutual success.' Walter Dunkels wrote from London that 'I feel sure that we are all equally delighted at the result of our negotiations and we can all congratulate ourselves on reaching the great aim we set ourselves when the Anglo American Corporation was first formed.' An old associate in London congratulated the brothers 'on your great success which has created a sensation both here and on the Continent'.

With its bid rejected, the heart went out of the 'old' Syndicate. Even before the deadline for the take-over, Ernest and Louis bought out its stocks and took over its business, with the full compliance of De Beers. Breitmeyers and Mosenthals dropped out of the diamond trade for good, while Barnatos, Dunkelsbuhlers and the Anglo American set up new offices in Kimberley. Diamonds were selling briskly again, and the outlay was soon recouped. From the ashes of the old agreements, Ernest and his new Syndicate rose as the phoenix.

4

ERNEST WAS chairman of the new organisation from the beginning, and his prestige in the diamond world was overwhelmingly increased. There was one prize that had so far eluded him, however, but which he had set his heart on years before: a seat on the board of De Beers. He had revealed this ambition as early as 1915, when De Beers had offered him £500 'in recognition of his valuable services to them and the town during his mayoralty and prior to that period'. The De Beers minutes of November 15 1915 record that:

A letter was read from Mr. E. Oppenheimer, dated London, 22 October, saying that the company's offer of a monetary consideration gave him a great deal of satisfaction, and he appreciates it but does not see his way to accept it. On the other hand, as the company evidently desires to show appreciation in some way, he brings forward a request that he be appointed, when the opportunity occurs, a director of the company. Resolved in reply to inform Mr. Oppenheimer that some time ago it was tacitly agreed not to fill up any vacancies in the directorate during the war, and further, that when the time arrives to do so the prior claims of others will have to be first considered.

Ten years had gone by since then, and Ernest's progress had served only to antagonise many of those on the De Beers board: a matter of personal resentment at the rise of a new arrival, and what seemed really nothing more than jealousy. Certainly there could be no place for Ernest on the De Beers board *honoris causa*. He would have to breach the citadel's walls by storm.

He set about the campaign like a general, marshalling his backers and his allies to wage war on De Beers by buying up every share they could. In four months he had so advanced his position that it balanced even Solly Joel's. This was blockbusting stuff, but it served its purpose. Solly Joel was behind him and with his other allies delivered an ultimatum to the rest of the board. In July 1926 Ernest cabled Louis: 'For your private information only De Beers board of directors unanimously agreed appoint me board'.

Meanwhile – and in complete contradiction – Ernest was fighting *alongside* De Beers in the long battle with the Minister of Mines, who still aimed to bring in a government control board to regulate the whole trade and represent it in dealings with the Syndicate and producers at home and in other countries. The ups and downs of the last 18 months had only convinced the minister more firmly than ever that such legislation was needed. He introduced a bill into parliament, and it was for Ernest and David Harris to fight it with every argument they could.

Harris began the onslaught with a direct assault. Ernest planned a more subtle approach, analysing what lay behind the legislation: a fear that the discoveries in other countries were so big that South Africa's pre-eminent position was in danger, so that production had to be controlled and South Africa had to persuade other countries producing diamonds to cut back in sympathy.

'The feeling that has been created throughout the country is that the diamond industry is on the verge of collapse, and that the industry, which was once the mainstay of the Cape Province, is nowadays a most precarious one. Evidently the government has also been convinced that this is the real position of the trade, and this is no doubt the reason why the first part of the Bill exists – the right to control the sale of diamonds. This right of control is clearly meant as a means of protecting the industry.'

Now Ernest gently launched into a complete description of the diamond trade throughout the world, quoting comprehensive facts and figures to show that the reverse was true: 'I do not think that there is any immediate necessity for the control part of the Bill, now that the producers have arranged quotas among themselves. But I know how wearisome the recent negotiations were, how the diamond trade was actually endangered through internal dissension among the producers, and how the uncompromising attitude of the syndicate, secure in the belief that no one could successfully compete with them, lost two months' trade to the producing companies, and thereby considerable revenue to the country.

'I can understand that the Minister of Mines now says: "I will never again run this risk. I want to have the power, if the producers cannot agree among themselves, to step in and settle the matter. If I have the power then these dissensions will not take place and prompt settlements will be arrived at between the producers."

'If I correctly interpret the Minister's intentions, then he ought to make it clear in the wording of the various clauses dealing with control that he will only interfere if the producers cannot agree among themselves. If that were done, a great deal of the objection to Government interference would be removed.'

On the other hand, Ernest thought the whole legislation unnecessary, now the producers had agreed among themselves. But he was more worried about another part of the bill, the section which authorised the government to enter the diamond trade itself and set up a control board.

'If the Government is not alarmed by the experience of the postwar depression . . . and thinks the diamond business so lucrative that they foresee clearly that they could make profits out of it and so relieve general taxation, there is of course no reason why they should not deal in diamonds just as they might decide later on to deal in wool or cotton or any other merchandise. What the country would think of the idea I don't know.'

Ernest conceded point after point, but then he struck home: 'The bill allowed the board to take the diamonds without paying for them in certain circumstances – for instance, where a producer was under contract to sell its production to the board and no-one else, but refused to sell any diamonds at all and stockpiled them.

'That section must have been inspired by the hon member for Troyeville (*evidently noted for his communist sympathies*). I suppose one of his Moscow friends must have described to him how they in Russia deal with diamonds. Does the hon Minister really think that anyone would produce diamonds if they could be taken away from him without payment?'

That one point was more telling than any other he made. Ernest hammered it home. 'I have tried to show that the portion of the bill which makes the Government diamond merchants is risky and, even if passed in its permissive form, it will be a deterrent to capital coming to this country. If it is put into practice we shall see a flight of capital from the Union.'

An HON MEMBER: 'This is an old story.'

Sir ERNEST OPPENHEIMER: 'It may be an old story, but it will be a true story if the Government seizes private property. The hon Minister will admit that I have not indulged in purely destructive criticism. On the contrary I have tried to explain the diamond trade to hon members. But I must repeat that this Act . . . is nothing but confiscation.'

The pleas made little difference: the Act went through, though to be fair with extensive modifications. But there was one issue Ernest had treated in this speech which was to become of extraordinary significance in a short time: the position of alluvial deposits, which the government wanted specifically to exclude from the control enactment, to give small diggers a chance against the big producers.

'I fully admit that one cannot interfere with the alluvial digger who finds to the value of about £50 a month, more or less, and who earns a very precarious living. I maintain, however, that this does not in itself establish the claim that all alluvial diamonds as such should be excluded from the operation of this Bill. This is particularly inadvisable when we remember that all recent discoveries of importance, whether they were South-West Africa, Angola, Congo or British Guiana, have all been big alluvial deposits . . .

'I say no special depression in the diamond trade need be feared from over-production now that all producers of diamonds, with the exception of the river diggings here and British Guiana, voluntarily restrict their output in order to conform to the demand. That being the real position of the diamond trade, I feel that no control Bill meets the case, if the one source of production which is now uncontrolled is to be specially exempted.'

Nobody was to know it, but there was an illustration of just these dangers Ernest had described emerging even now, only 500 miles from Cape Town. Diamonds had been found in Namaqualand, the remote, sandy, wind-blown wilderness up South Africa's Atlantic coast south of the Orange River. The first discoveries were far from dramatic: a few stones found in August 1925, in gravel near Port Nolloth. But they were enough to attract a steady stream of prospectors. Most of these took one look and promptly retraced their steps. But many stayed, and soon the barren shore was pegged for miles.

Leading the field was a number of small syndicates, and it was one of these that precipitated a major boom: a strike in the cliffs north of Port Nolloth. In a week the members of this syndicate found 14 diamonds averaging half a carat each. That did it. With success like this the prospectors poured in, and soon all the land from the Orange River to the Buffels mouth was pegged out and taken under option.

The news reached Kimberley, and the De Beers boardroom. But here it created little stir. The strikes were not impressive, and there were already reports that diggers were finding it hard to make ends meet. In any case, there was another and much more spectacular strike closer to home: on a farm called Elandsputte, near Lichtenburg in the Western Transvaal.

Prospectors and fortune hunters arrived at the new diggings from Kimberley, the Reef, all over South Africa and many countries overseas. It was a Kimberley-style boom all over again, and just as dramatic. These were alluvial fields and soon proved among the richest so far. Not only Elandsputte, but all the neighbouring farms possessed diamonds by millions of carats.

As each new deposit was proven, the government declared a public diggings. Grasfontein, Welverdiend, Hendricksdal, Ruigtedachte: twelve farms were proclaimed in succession. At each site the discoverer had the right to peg the first claims. Then the rush was organised. On one farm the proclamation attracted more than 27 000 men stretched out more than a mile along the starting line in the veld and ready to begin running at the drop of the mining commissioner's flag. When a buck leapt from the grass some way ahead of the line and several boys darted forward to chase it, others thought they had missed the signal and set out on the long run across country to peg their claims. They had to be recalled and started all over again.

124

Right in the middle of the new diggings was the boom town Baker-ville. In a few months it boasted a population of more than 100 000 whites and four times as many blacks. Shebeens abounded, there were some 30 churches and more than 100 shops catered for all the diggers' needs. Each day except Sunday about 400 diamond buyers travelled out from their offices in Lichtenburg to buy what the diggers had produced.

At first it had looked as if diggings like these in the Lichtenburg fields would remain the preserve of the small man, as the government hoped. Instead they proved so rich that they soon attracted the attention of syndicates and indeed companies. It was exactly the kind of production that needed government supervision and control – yet the government's Control Bill had specifically excluded alluvial fields. The other producers could do absolutely nothing, and De Beers at any rate refused to contemplate anybody taking any action. The fields would soon be exhausted, reasoned the directors, and things would return to normal.

Not so Ernest, however. As a first step he sent one of Anglo's geologists to report at first hand. The position was as bad as he feared: the fields were a new phenomenon in the diamond world, with the stones so cheap to recover that in a short time the Lichtenburg production could throw the whole trade out of gear.

Ernest discussed the geologist's report with Solly Joel, who was as concerned as he was. The two decided to move in and buy as many of the alluvial farms as they could, whether proved or unproved. The Minister of Mines had weakly to agree it was for the best – though against that Ernest and Solly Joel would now hold an even bigger stake in the diamond world than they had before.

'We bought the farms with mineral rights so that we can either work them or keep them locked up', Ernest wrote to Louis. 'It is a most valuable purchase, which in the long run must show huge profits. Solly was not inclined, nor was I, simply to hand them over to De Beers. We both felt it was a very useful thing, for bargaining in the future, to have properties of that kind under our control.'

The farms they had bought covered all the really rich deposits: all, in fact, that constituted a threat. But no sooner were they congratulating each other on success then there was a new shock – from Namaqualand. All this time teams of prospectors had been hard at work but achieving disappointing results in comparison with Lichtenburg. But now most of Lichtenburg was tied up and the early 'rushed' claims were largely worked out, there was a steady migration back to the coast. Among those to join it was Hans Merensky, the discoverer of platinum.

Merensky had long expected an important diamond find to rank with Kimberley, and when the first reports of discoveries in Namaqualand reached him he thought this was it. Before World War I he had made a special investigation of the South West fields, and believed these in Namaqualand might well be similar. He was in Europe at this stage, but immediately tried to raise backing to mount a full-scale expedition. The best he could do was persuade a banker friend to lend him £1 000 and make a vague promise to give him £4 000 if he discovered anything.

Nothing daunted, he set off for South Africa, raised a team of prospectors and sent them ahead of him under Ernst Reuning, a German geologist who agreed to take part for the sake of the unusual experience. By this time Merensky's enthusiasm had cooled a little. There were no reports of sensational discoveries as he was expecting, and in any case he heard all available land had been pegged far back from the shore. Before the prospectors left he admitted they were probably off on a wild goose chase.

Reuning and Merensky travelled up and down the coast looking at the different prospecting operations and both noticed one feature in particular. All the richest deposits of diamonds so far discovered seemed to be associated with beds of fossilised oyster shells. Each thought this confirmed his pet theory of where the diamonds came from: Merensky's that they were from an undersea pipe, and Reuning's that they had been washed down long vanished river courses and then scattered along the coast.

At last they decided to concentrate their efforts in the far north, at the inlet of Alexander Bay near the mouth of the Orange River. Claims in this area were held by a syndicate of professional men from the copper mining town of Springbok, who were rather startled when Merensky made his offer to buy them out. After some haggling they quoted a price of £15 000. Merensky said he would have to think about it: after all, the only backing he had was £1 000. Next day, however, the syndicate members raised the price to £17 500, explaining they had forgotten the interests of other important members of their team – their wives. As an afterthought one of them said they held several claims not yet prospected, north of the other they were talking about: he was ready to include these 'as a Christmas present'.

Merensky inspected the whole site and when he came to the 'Christmas present' claims spotted the tell-tale beds of oysters. Always the gambler, he decided to forget the financial problem and accept the syndicate's terms without arguing. Here was the chance to test his theory, and he was not going to throw it up. He had to put down his £1 000 as a deposit, and raise the balance by the beginning of February. He had three weeks.

Merensky set off for Cape Town, leaving Reuning to begin work. His assistant agreed they should start with the 'Christmas present' claims and laid out his trenches. Within days his men found eight diamonds, together weighing 50 carats and the biggest of them a perfect yellow octahedron of 16,6 carats. He quickly sent Merensky news of the success. Merensky had already persuaded two old friends of his to put up the necessary funds, and now brought in Sir Abe Bailey's SA Townships to provide working capital over and above the £17 500 they needed to pay the syndicate. The new partners organised themselves as the H M (for Hans Merensky) Association.

Meanwhile Reuning had been uncovering an Aladdin's cave at Alexander Bay. Within a week of discovering those first stones his men had found 114 diamonds, together weighing 201½ carats. By the time Merensky returned 12 days later they had found 2 762 diamonds weighing 4 309 carats. So far the secret had been kept, but that situation could not last. Merensky applied to the Minister of Mines for permission to start mining in earnest. He asked him if it would be possible to grant not only the discoverers' claims which would be his as of right, but also a lease over the whole Alexander Bay area, along the lines of the State Leases in the gold mining industry. That way they could avoid the danger of attracting thousands of diggers to Namaqualand who would face untold hardship in that terrible place.

What Merensky did not realise was that the minister was trying to bring in various amendments to the Precious Stones Act the government had passed the year before, in a belated attempt to deal with the situation that had developed in Lichtenburg and was now developing in Namaqualand. The most important part of it was that the government would have the right to declare an area a State Alluvial Digging rather than proclaim it a public diggings, or lease it to a particular person or company as Merensky now proposed. There was an ulterior motive: this way the government would have a source of diamonds for the South African cutting industry it so wanted to establish.

These negotiations took a little time, as the minister considered his position. The prospectors had now found no fewer than 12 353½ carats of diamonds, almost all of exceptional quality and size and often occurring in potholes. In one instance 487 diamonds were found clustered in a pocket under a single stone. This was getting too much. Merensky could not afford to wait around until parliament brought in the new legislation. Already rumours were reaching the diggers round Port Nolloth, and if he was not careful he would find a full-scale invasion on his hands and his precious claims overrun.

He soon made up his mind, and drove straight to parliament with the diamonds so far discovered. The house was in session, but dramatically he asked a messenger to summon General Hertzog in person. The Prime Minister soon emerged, rather astonished by such peremptory demands. But when Merensky told him why he had come and showed him the parcel of stones, Hertzog sent messengers to fetch Smuts, Beyers the Minister of Mines and the government mining engineer as well. Together they listened to what Merensky had to say and agreed he was right: they would have to do something. A few days later Beyers issued a proclamation totally prohibiting any more prospecting on Crown Land in Namaqualand until further notice.

Merensky was still in Cape Town, trying to arrange the sale of his first parcels of stones. He had them sorted and arranged on the tables used to handle the production from CDM which was now done in Cape Town as the most sensible centre, before it was sold to Ernest and his associates. Several of the diamond world's leaders were in Cape Town for the parliamentary session, and others went there from Kimberley for this special sight.

Among those to inspect the Namaqualand production on this occasion was Ernest, who needed just one glance to have his worst fears confirmed. This was a threat even bigger than Lichtenburg's. Years later he remembered seeing the reactions of those around him – particularly David Harris's.

'For a long time Sir David stared at the collection. Amazement, admiration and finally a look of horror crossed his face. Raising his hands to his head he turned slowly towards me. "This will ruin us and the whole diamond trade," he said. "We are finished. What about the markets when these new finds start to flood the world?" '

Standing near them was Louis Abrahams, yet another cousin of the Barnatos and the Joels and a veteran of the old Syndicate. His firm had been among those which had dropped out in the recession years before World War I. Now he was the grand old man of the diamond world, and his associates always called him Uncle.

'What can we do?' Ernest asked him.

Uncle grabbed him by the lapels of his jacket.

'Oppie,' he said. That was the nickname familiar to all those who

128

had known Ernest since the earliest days. 'You must buy – and keep on buying.'

It was easier said than done. Where were the funds to come from, if the trade was to keep the price up? But as a first step Ernest bought the whole consignment on his Syndicate's behalf.

Merensky soon applied for his 'discoverer's claims', which were traditionally granted by the Minister of Mines for each new diamond find: a block of up to 20 claims each 30 feet by 30 feet, pegged out by the discoverer before the area was thrown open to the public or for whatever other purpose the minister had decided. There could be no doubt Merensky had found diamonds: but to his dismay the minister now decided they were simply part of one huge alluvial deposit that embraced all Namaqualand. If that was the case, Merensky was not the discoverer at all, but simply following in other prospectors' footsteps.

Merensky fought the decision in court, and won. The government geologist decided that there were in fact five distinct deposits proved in the Alexander Bay area, and discoverer's rights should be granted for each. The H M Association was awarded the rights to two of these, far and away the richest, and on the government's request bought out the owners of the others so that there should be only one organisation operating the claims when the time came.

Up and down the coast the big companies were moving in. De Beers and the Anglo American were buying up as many farms as they could, and Dunkelsbuhlers and Barnatos had acquired many of the claims on the coast itself. Many again had been acquired by a new influence in South African mining, Chester Beatty from the diamond fields in West Africa. He was consolidating the position he had already established in Southern African affairs through his new interests on the copperbelt in Northern Rhodesia.

Ernest decided to try and weld all these diverse interests together in a single organisation. The result was a new company called Cape Coast Exploration. At the same time Ernest sent a team of geologists to survey the area immediately *north* of the Orange River, in CDM's Sperrgebiet. If there were diamonds in Namaqualand, there should be diamonds on the other side of the river as well. He was not disappointed. The prospecting trenches soon revealed deposits just as rich as those at Alexander Bay, and even more extensive.

Meanwhile, Ernest was negotiating for control of the H M Association itself. There were three blocks of shares, two controlled by Merensky and SA Townships, and the third by one of Merensky's friends

129

who had now bought out the other. Ernest and Solly Joel persuaded this friend to part with his holding, which gave them the biggest single interest in the syndicate.

Now he had the right to determine the association's policy, Ernest brought in a young man who had only recently joined Anglo from the Standard Bank, by name Richard Bein Hagart. Two years earlier the chairman at the bank had asked him to draw up some notes on central banking to help Ernest with a speech he wanted to make in parliament. The notes had impressed Ernest so much that when later he needed a man with banking experience he immediately thought of Hagart and though he had never met him, offered him the job. Hagart was pitch-forked into a number of tricky assignments, one of them this secretaryship.

At last the government passed its amendments to the Precious Stones Bill, and was empowered to proclaim Namaqualand or any other new alluvial field a State Alluvial Digging. The way was cleared for the introduction of a diamond cutting industry. There had been several previous efforts to get one going, but they had been rather feeble. The government had blamed Ernest for this, suggesting it was the diamond magnate's deliberate policy to place barriers in its way. Ernest denied it in parliament: 'I suggest to the Minister that the South African Party, the National party and I myself are all anxious to see a diamond cutting industry established in South Africa.'

He had misgivings about the government entering this new sphere of activity. There were many pitfalls for the unwary. But if they were confident they could operate efficiently, he was with them. Nothing daunted by the warnings, the government imported a master diamond cutter from Antwerp, Anton Rausenstrauch, and set him up in a factory in Kimberley almost next door to De Beers' head office. Rausenstrauch brought 50 Belgian journeymen apprentices with him, and the arrangement was he should also have a number of young South Africans on his staff.

Diamonds for the cutting works would come from Alexander Bay, which was now proclaimed the first State Diggings as expected. At last Merensky and his associates could proceed. Those months of waiting were more than compensated when in their first week they found 41 198½ carats in the oyster line claims alone. By the end of six months they had 300 000 carats in the bag. Ernest had by this time negotiated a sales contract to buy the association's whole output for his syndicate. But it made no great difference: the government decided to impound the Namaqualand production against a suitable time for releasing it, in terms of a quota provision in the new legislation.

Two blocks of the discoverers' claims were disappointing, but the others more than made up for them. Evaluators doubled, then trebled their ideas of what the claims were worth. Ernest and Solly Joel decided they needed even greater control. Hans Merensky retained a third interest in the association, and he was their man. After preliminary negotiations Ernest invited Merensky to see him in Johannesburg.

The situation appealed to Ernest's romantic side. Merensky was nearly penniless again, after the protracted negotiations with the Minister of Mines and the refusal of the government to let him release his stones to the Syndicate. He had to sell his shares, or go bankrupt. But he had fixed in his mind the idea that his holding was worth a million pounds, and was determined to stick to his price.

'There is a man coming to see me,' Ernest told Hagart. 'I want you to show him in immediately.' When Merensky departed, Ernest reflected aloud on what had happened: 'It is not often that a man comes in without sixpence in his pocket, and leaves with a million pounds.'

In Namaqualand, mining operations were continuing but with an increasing hazard of theft from the open trenches. It was difficult to impose any form of security on the scattered workings with their large work force of Europeans and Africans, and the only remedy was to step up production in an effort to work out the claims as speedily as possible. This the government encouraged so that it could establish the State Diggings over the whole area and close it to outside interests for good.

All blocks of discoverer's claims were worked out by April, 1929, though originally the H M Association had been expected to span operations over five years in a bid to provide steady revenue for the impoverished Namaqualanders. The association was obliged to hand its whole production to the government for 'safe keeping': 461 444 carats, valued at £5 148 263. The haul was worth a fortune, but now the government had hold of the diamonds it would not let them go. When Merensky submitted a formal application for the release of 100 000 carats of diamonds of two carats or over and excluding rubbish – deliberately chosen to avoid competing with the production of other mines – it met with cold refusal from the government department.

'The Minister regards your request as premature. He certainly never expected within a comparatively few months from the commencement of your production you would prefer such a request.'

Merensky complained bitterly, but it was a long time before Beyers

131

at last agreed to release the 100 000 carats to Ernest's syndicate – and only on condition it took 100 000 carats of State diamonds at the same time. The association made a second application in November, for a further 240 000 carats at a suggested rate of £10 000 worth each month. It was apparent the government was going to be extremely difficult over the whole issue, so as added bait Ernest promised the Syndicate would take 300 000 carats of State diamonds in reciprocation. But the government was not to be tempted.

'The Minister is not prepared at this stage to release any further diamonds belonging to your Association, and will not be prepared to entertain an application for the release of further Hans Merensky diamonds for a considerable time.'

All this was frustrating, and Ernest was not pleased to be left in the air. His relations with the Nationalists were far from cordial: as his business position improved, as it had ever since the beginning of the session, they sought ways to obstruct him. All their attacks centred on him, and when none found their mark the Pact men grew all the more determined to nail him once and for all. If there was a chance to clip his wings, whether in diamonds or gold or in any other field of his activity, they would not hesitate to take it. This was not an aspect of his career to emerge from the little book *Some South African Parliamentarians* which appeared at this time.

'A true South African by adoption,' wrote the commentator, 'he is free from racial prejudices, and is highly esteemed by the Dutch. While he sometimes criticises the opposite side severely on financial grounds, his speeches are never bitter, and he is one of the most popular men in the House. His success is due partly to the fact that he likes Parliament and politics, and does not merely sit in the Assembly because his large interests find it convenient to have a voice there . . . Still a young man, as politicians go, he has qualifications which will carry him far if he concentrates upon politics.'

A more valid glimpse of Ernest the politician is provided by John Cope in an article he wrote after Ernest's death. By that time Cope was himself a member of parliament, but at the stage he is writing of he was a gallery correspondent in the House of Assembly.

I was instructed by my paper to see Sir Ernest on a matter concerning the diamond industry, and I managed to waylay him in the lobby. He was so courteous and so frank in his replies that I was impressed by a quality that will always be my outstanding memory of this unusual man: the strange and impelling form of humility that he possessed.

132

It was not an abasing form of humility, nor did it seem like a mask intended to conceal some other feeling. Without uttering a word, Sir Ernest seemed to say: 'Look here, we're just two people interested in a problem. I'm only too pleased to help you and I'm sure you'd be the last person to let me down. Let's cut out the formalities and get down to the root of the matter . . .'

He gave me all his attention. With a few quick sentences, softly and pleasantly spoken, he opened new windows to the problem. Then at last, when he turned away into the busy throng in the lobby, he seemed to leave an intangible thread linking himself with me.

About this time Cope and other journalists were having coffee with General Smuts at the House. He was giving them a fascinating commentary on current events, when a red-faced member burst through the swing doors in a great hurry, clearly in search of someone.

'Ha!' exclaimed one of the journalists. 'Enter Ernest Oppenheimer's jackal.'

'But what a splendid man to be a jackal to!' replied Smuts quietly.

The others laughed, but then they began to ask Smuts what he thought of Ernest. What sort of man was he? Was he simply a shrewd financier, or did he have something that marked him out above others? What was he driving at, and what was he likely to achieve?

Cope was writing about the conversation years after it took place, and he had forgotten its precise course. But two remarks of Smuts's returned to him: one his verdict that Ernest was 'a man of three dimensions – a combination of intellectual brilliance, unerring instinct and a deep sense of humanism'.

The other remark came when one of the journalists began comparing Ernest with other financiers on the world stage. 'Yes, yes,' interrupted Smuts. 'They make headlines, but Oppenheimer makes history. Wait and see.'

In my profession as a journalist, *wrote Cope*, I have interviewed many different men holding important positions. Many of them at the outset try to convey by some mannerism or even in their opening words that they are important people and that it is a privilege to talk to them.

Sir Ernest did precisely the opposite. His manner conveyed that he was not in the least concerned whether anybody thought him important or not; that there was no such thing as privilege between equals, and that he really was glad you'd bothered to come along and discuss a most important subject with him. He could

133

and did refuse a request or turn down a suggestion as firmly as anyone else. But somehow it never was *his* refusal – merely a kind of joint of decision that flowed inevitably from the series of logical objections that seemed to marshal themselves in overwhelming array.

All this makes 'Hoggenheimer' a good deal less than sinister, of course. But as was to be the case many times in the future, involving not Ernest alone but Harry too when his son took the political stage, the Nationalists found it useful to have a scapegoat when times were hard. Blame their problems on the capitalists, the 'British' or the Blacks, and their own shortcomings were excusable.

Certainly the Pact needed some sort of excuse in these years, for its career had not been noticeably successful. The Nationalists and Colonel Cresswell's Labourites were uneasy bedfellows, and fought each other as much as they fought Smuts and the SAP. Hertzog called a general election for 1928, and agreed to the continuation of the Pact. But this time the Nationalists would be a lot stronger in the field at the Cresswellites' expense; and there could be little doubt that if the Nationalists were as successful as they hoped, and gained the majority they needed, the Pact would be quietly forgotten.

Ernest and May went to Kimberley in plenty of time for the election campaign, which promised to be strangely tame. Kimberley was again one of the seats allotted to the Cresswellites, and was to be contested by a man named Jerry Wills. It did not look as if he was going to present any great challenge: for one thing, it was well known he was not in the best of health.

The Oppenheimers both enjoyed these trips to Kimberley, where the atmosphere was so much more restful than Johannesburg's: more like a village. Ernest used to visit the Kimberley Club, and was never happier than when whiling away an hour or two with the chief steward or some other ordinary soul he would never normally have time to talk to. He felt it brought him into touch with the realities of life, which he could so easily miss if he did not go out of his way to seek them.

Ernest confessed this even in parliament: 'I started life low down on the ladder, and I lived on very little, and I have the greatest sympathy and I have the greatest understanding of the men who have to earn their daily bread.'

May, on the other hand, was a bridge fiend. She had several favourite partners in Kimberley – one of them the same Dolly Pickering who had lived across the road from the Oppenheimers as a little girl.

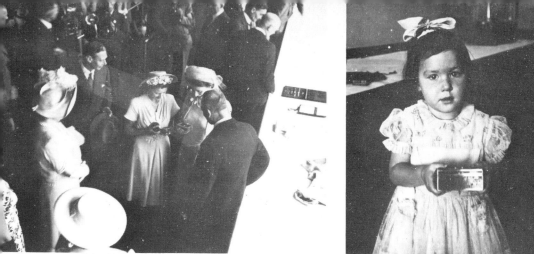

The Royal Visit, 1947: Ernest welcomes the royal party to De Beers, while Mary (right) prepares to present souvenirs of the occasion to the royal princesses. *De Beers Consolidated Mines.*

Ernest explains a special exhibition of diamonds to Their Majesties, King George VI and Queen Elizabeth. *De Beers Consolidated Mines.*

Ernest in the Free State: the opening of the Western Holdings recovery plant. *Anglo American Corporation.*

Harry pours the first bar of gold to be produced by the Anglo American in the Free State. *Anglo American Corporation.*

She was married now with young children of her own: not really in a position to play for high stakes. But May liked some fun out of the game, and insisted on playing for shillings. One day she took several pounds off Dolly, which the young housewife could ill afford: but next morning May arrived at her house laden with presents for her children.

May tried to get Ernest to play bridge, but he had no heart for it and refused to play for more than tickeys. He insisted he was not prepared to gamble in any field but diamonds.

On the day of the nomination court, Ernest and Louis Lezard came face to face with Wills in the City Hall. Both Ernest and Lezard made policy speeches, as was the custom, and then it was Wills's turn to speak. He did not have much to say – only that he appreciated the backing of his supporters in nominating him, but that his doctors had told him on no account to contest the election. He was sorry, but there was nothing he could do about it. Apart from anything else he realised what a disappointment it would be to Ernest to get in without a fight. 'Sir Ernest is a sportsman, we all know that. In fact, we are all sportsmen here. It is a great pity.'

The announcement caused quite a stir. The magistrate checked to see whether Wills was quite definite about not standing. Then, with a minute to go before the closing of the election list, a prominent local Nationalist rose to his feet. He had another nomination, he said: the local chairman of the National Party, A M Hartman. There was no speech to be made – only the payment of the necessary deposit.

Wills protested strongly about the turn of events. How dare the Nationalists presume to put up a nomination in a Labour seat, even if he was not contesting it? Doctors' orders be blowed. He would fight the seat after all – as a matter of principle. The magistrate allowed him a time extension to collect the money he needed for his deposit.

As a front-bencher Ernest was expected to play a full part in the SAP's campaign in centres other than Kimberley, and he did not let them down. In fact, he spent so much time speaking in other constituencies that he made only one really important speech in his own. He attacked not the Pact as such but the Nationalists for all that had gone wrong in the preceding parliamentary term, and then he repeated his support for SAP policy and for Smuts – even though memories were long and the majority of the electorate had not forgiven the old Prime Minister. Ernest knew it too, but he felt he had not lost his own supporters.

'I am generally considered to be a practical man,' he concluded, 'but as a matter of fact I am also a bit of a dreamer, and the dream

135

that is always with me is of the day when South Africa will become a truly great country, and that I shall have been privileged to take some small part in achieving that greatness.'

It had looked as if Ernest would have an easy run for his money. Instead, the Nationalists made a surprisingly strong play for Kimberley. To them it represented their greatest challenge, the bastion of capital built by the hated imperialists. Already the diamond cutting industry they had fostered was bearing fruit. Perhaps they could pull off the final coup and unseat the biggest capitalist of them all. No fewer than three cabinet ministers and even the Prime Minister himself came to Kimberley to help.

Ernest, however, did not have to worry unduly. On election day he regained his seat without trouble, as did the SAP candidate in Beaconsfield. Ernest's majority was not as big as it might have been, for the Nationalist campaign had borne fruit in Kimberley as it had in every other centre and Hartman had done well. Poor Jerry Wills's showing on the other hand was not so impressive.

SIR ERNEST OPPENHEIMER (SAP)	2 044
A H Hartman (Nat)	1 132
J Wills (Lab)	9

The overall position was as predicted. The South African Party improved its position slightly but not at the expense of the Nationalists, who swept all before them and gave Hertzog a clear majority in parliament. Instead, the chief casualties were the Cresswellites, who lost more than half their seats. The Pact was done for, and so was the Labour Party. At last the Afrikaner-backed National Party had the power it had sought so long and could afford to strike out boldly in pursuit of it aims. After more than quarter of a century, the issues of the South African War were finally resolved.

5

NOBODY HAD worked harder than Ernest to defend the diamond trade from the twin assaults of Namaqualand and Lichtenburg. But his efforts were not appreciated. On the one hand the Minister of Mines thought he was acting on his own behalf and for his backers outside South Africa; on the other the rest of the De Beers board resented his success and the personal advantage he now seemed to have. This was in spite of several suggestions by him that they should come in on the transactions. Their criticisms upset him considerably.

136

'Can you imagine my feelings?' he cabled Louis. 'I have done every-thing to control alluvial discoveries and in making suggestion De Beers should take lead have never even asked for profit relying entirely on appreciation of De Beers Consolidated Mines Limited shares for eventual profit . . . Whilst endangering my own political position in order to help trade I am stabbed in the back by my own colleagues.'

What frustrated Ernest most was De Beers' evident malingering in the face of what he considered the most obvious future development of the diamond trade: the unification of all its interests with a single authority controlling every aspect of its activity and powerful enough to withstand the threats which were facing producers and Syndicate alike with disconcerting frequency.

The first step, he insisted, was to pursuade De Beers to take over all producing interests in the sub-continent: not only the alluvial fields held jointly by the Anglo American and Barnatos, but CDM itself and Jagersfontein and other producers too. Quite apart from the practical advantages of the amalgamation it would be perfectly in line with De Beers tradition, as he pointed out in a cable to Solly Joel in 1927.

'Articles of association De Beers show that founders contem-plated securing control other diamond deposits as and when dis-covered, in addition to those already discovered at Kimberley: they also encouraged formation Syndicate in order to ensure sales through one channel. After death early leaders, this policy no longer carried through with energy and by degrees developed into policy belittling new discoveries instead of investigating and, if necessary, obtaining control of them.'

That was where De Beers had gone wrong: tired, uninspired leader-ship; patronising complacency towards the rest of the diamond world: in short too many chiefs and not enough Indians. Left to itself, De Beers was a sinking ship. Ernest saw this clearly, but though he might more profitably have left the old company to its fate he preferred to devote his energies to saving it. To one who had served the trade since his sixteenth birthday De Beers was diamonds, and diamonds without De Beers were unthinkable.

Ernest did his best to keep his ambitions to himself, but it was ob-vious he was after the chair. With extensive interests in all the pro-ducers and undisputed control of the Syndicate he was by far the most powerful figure in the whole trade, and in trying to solve its problems De Beers would be forced to settle with him. At last the board de-cided to act on Ernest's and Solly Joel's suggestion after all and

137

negotiate terms to buy out all the independent producers, but to conclude such deals they needed Ernest's co-operation, and they knew that he would not help unless they made him chairman.

There were two main sources of objection to Ernest becoming chairman. One was impersonal, the fact that he was chairman of the Syndicate. The other directors wondered how they could be sure he would not manipulate De Beers to the Syndicate's advantage. The other source was more dangerous and Ernest felt this much more keenly: a personal antagonism, jealousy of the success he had achieved. And of those who felt this the most significant was his own cousin, Fritz Hirschhorn.

The jeolousy had deep roots. It stemmed from the days in Kimberley before the war, when Hirschhorn had tried to win the hand of Ernest's sister-in-law. When he failed, he must have seen Ernest as partly responsible. He did not forgive him. As a partner in Breitmeyers in the Syndicate after the war, he did his best to thwart Ernest's ambitions for Anglo American. And when in the end it was not Anglo but Breitmeyers itself that was thwarted, his jealousy turned into hatred. From that time he was Ernest's most implacable opponent.

Solly Joel recognised the strong influence Hirschhorn was bringing to bear and the deadlock it had created. De Beers was trying to conciliate Ernest, and as a mark of good faith it was proposed to make him chairman of the Premier company. Joel advised Ernest to speak to Hirschhorn and try and come to terms with him. Ernest described what happened in a cable to Louis.

'I told him Joel has asked me to speak to him, to which he replied that it was useless to say anything at all as his mind was made up, and he continued that, to be perfectly frank with me, he did not admit that I knew any more than he did and, as he had been top dog so long, he was not prepared to sit on any board with me as chairman. I told him that that cleared the position and left it at that.'

When the Premier board voted on the matter in December 1927, Hirschhorn was the only one to oppose Ernest on the grounds that 'being interested in the Syndicate, Sir Ernest would hold a dual position, which should not be in the case of the choice of the chairman.'

Hirschhorn's opposition was to continue, but there were more sinister influences at work. One was the acting chairman, David Harris. In public Ernest had always treated Harris's jealousy as a joke, but he had never really forgiven him that early slight in the Jagersfontein affair, when Harris opposed his nomination to the board after he had served a term as an alternate director. He had taken it personally, and seen no reason to change his feelings later in life.

Harris was all the more dangerous as a relative of Solly Joel's, and in fact a trusted friend of his. It was really rather embarrassing, and made it all the more important for Ernest to keep his feelings to himself. Solly Joel regretted the situation too, and once or twice in recent years he had deliberately kept quiet about a particular issue in which he knew there would be a personal clash between Harris and Ernest. Now, however, he told Louis that he had managed to 'square' David Harris, who would not offer any resistance to Ernest's becoming chairman. Louis told Ernest. The implication was that as acting chairman Harris would have had the right of veto, but would now forebear to use it. Ernest nearly threw a fit.

'For your guidance,' he cabled his brother, 'Sir David Harris's attitude towards me ever since I arrived in South Africa such that I would never agree to leave myself in his hands.'

Solly Joel arrived in South Africa soon afterwards to recuperate from a heart attack. He was a sick man, but active enough to heal the rifts and settle the disputes, and throw open Ernest's route to the chair of De Beers. It was to be some months yet before the election was secured, but in the meantime the interested parties were at last free to negotiate the creation of the buying and selling company which had been mooted for so long.

The idea was really quite simple: a diamond company independent of the Syndicate and of the producers, but in which they were represented. Ideally the new company would maintain control over the whole industry both in South Africa and Europe, and for that matter throughout the world. All were agreed the principle was sound. What was more difficult was to decide on its constitution. Who should be represented on its board, and in what proportion?

Negotiations had been unusually heated. Ernest and Solly Joel and others originally suggested the company's board should consist of twelve members, six from the producers including the chairman, and six from the Syndicate. But De Beers would not agree – or at least its London directors had grave reservations. Obviously Ernest and Solly Joel would expect to have their producing interests represented along with De Beers, but they would hold an additional fifty per cent through the Syndicate. That way they would dominate the situation completely.

It was the revival of a familiar argument, but this time Ernest took it personally. He sent a cable to these directors on his own and Solly

Joel's behalf: 'Your telegram conveys only mistrust and is a direct insult to our honour and integrity.'

He immediately broke off negotiations, and that was the end of the matter for some months. Meanwhile, with the accumulation of ever vaster stocks by the Syndicate and a deterioration in the market, it was obvious something would have to be done. At last Louis and Morgan Grenfells took the lead in reviving negotiations, and presented a number of detailed suggestions. Ernest tore holes in them, but was at least now free to make counter-proposals.

His new suggestions were much the same as his first. This time, however, the De Beers directors offered no resistance. Their bargaining power had dwindled to nothing. The producers' contracts with the Syndicate had soon to be renewed, and with the Syndicate holding huge resources of alluvial diamonds their position was very weak. They needed Ernest's co-operation, and to win that they needed Ernest. On Friday, December 20 1929 they formally elected him chairman, the fulfilment of his life's ambition.

A month later they agreed to the joint buying-selling organisation, which would be known as the Diamond Corporation, a subsidiary of De Beers and registered in London. The name reflected back to Bernard Oppenheimer's South African Diamond Corporation from the time Lewis and Marks had had such strong diamond interests, though those had long since slipped away. Ernest was elected the first chairman, as expected. It meant he was in sole command of the international diamond trade, a position he would retain for the rest of his life. He had assumed the rich mantle of Cecil John Rhodes.

Family Business

THEY MIGHT have known it could not last. For five years the prices of securities had been rising on the stock exchanges of Europe and America, first gradually, then in spectacular leaps. An orgy of buying stocks and shares had swept these countries. As prices went to unprecedented levels more and more people took a hand in the gambling spree. Broking firms contributed by allowing their clients to buy on credit, expecting them to put up as little as ten per cent in cash.

All through these years, but most of all through 1928 and 1929, government officials and leading businessmen again and again put their stamp on the crazy boom. Prices might fall one day, but then recover the next and rise more steeply than before. There was a warning on October 23 1929, a Wednesday. In New York, prices on Wall Street were down. The next day they went down even further, and much faster. There was no improvement during the Friday and Saturday sessions. On Sunday Wall Street was overrun by tourist buses with guides pointing out 'where all that money was lost'.

On Monday the market fell more sharply even than before, and in the final hour selling became frantic. Brokers worked through the night despatching countless telegrams and using every available telephone to demand that clients pay up their loans in cash. At the same time, they were themselves besieged by clients instructing them to sell.

Next day at the start of trading hundreds of brokers swarmed round the trading posts. All the opening prices were down. The declines prompted even more selling, this time the wholesale dumping of shares for whatever price they would bring. Clients were panicking, brokers were selling their own holdings. Wall Street was tumbling down.

There was pandemonium on the trading floor. Hysteria swept America and Europe too as the tickertapes flashed news of the disaster across the world. Member brokers hurried desperately from one trading post to another, pushing, shouting, sweating, suffering. There might be two dozen brokers around a trading post trying to sell a given stock, and not one of them finding a buyer.

This had been the most disastrous day in stock exchange history, and its effects richocheted around the world. Where there had been money to burn suddenly none was available. In the weeks and months that followed the western world gently slipped from plenty and prosperity to penury and unemployment. The Great Depression closed in, an economic Ice Age whose glaciers rolled relentlessly across America and Europe, and more remote parts of the world as well. Among them, inevitably, was Southern Africa.

The glaciers took time. The initial effects were not drastic. There was an overwhelming confidence that the slump was only some ghastly interlude, that before long events would return at least to normal. They might even be better than before. It was this confidence that led governments and industrialists alike to hope for the best, and plan for better times. Certainly this was the attitude Ernest adopted in the areas where he was hardest hit, and the first of these was the copperbelt.

Anglo's initial involvement in Northern Rhodesia had been only speculative, of course: nothing more than a finger in the pie. But as time went on Ernest found himself increasingly heavily committed in Northern Rhodesia, and wondered if he was not being taken for a ride. Edmund Davis 'is trying to sell me something every day,' he complained to Leslie Pollak, who had become Anglo's ombudsman in Northern Rhodesian affairs. 'We are the only mugs. I do not say that these companies will not prove any property; on the contrary I believe properties will be found, of really high value. But prospecting on the scale they do costs a lot of money and they will be hard up again in twelve months' time.'

Ernest was genuinely worried by the very real rivalry developing between Edmund Davis and Chester Beatty. He had a foot in both camps, and would have liked to bring about an amalgamation. But there were serious differences of opinion on just how mining should be carried out. Apart from that there was the question of who should control the resulting company. For all their friendly relations with Ernest, Beatty and Davis envied each other's position. It was stalemate, and Ernest was tempted to cut his losses and escape what might prove a very delicate situation.

But he held his peace. Prices for copper and the other base metals had soared to unprecedented heights before the recession, and were still too high for him to consider opting out. Anglo's prospecting team was still at work, and Joe Bancroft had been filing enthusiastic reports.

'Yes, yes, copper is all very well,' Ernest told him ruefully. 'But it was really diamonds I was after.' Later he admitted to Bancroft: 'I can see copper does for you what diamonds do for me. I suppose I must sympathise.'

By now Ernest was leaning heavily towards Edmund Davis's camp, but retained his healthy stake in Chester Beatty's companies too. What tipped the balance for him was that Davis's was essentially a 'British' organisation while Beatty relied largely on United States capital, for all his personal enthusiasm for the Empire. Ernest could not sit by and see a territory which bore Rhodes's name fall under American domination. When Beatty registered a holding company to administer all his Northern Rhodesian interests, the Rhodesian Selection Trust, Ernest responded by marshalling his powerful allies in Johannesburg and floating a new holding company. They called it the Rhodesian Anglo American, or Rhoanglo for short.

As soon as he could Ernest travelled up to the copperbelt to see what was happening at first hand. With him went advisers from Johannesburg, and the gallant but aging Solly Joel who was in South Africa on business and pleasure, and who had agreed to participate in the venture. They found Joe Bancroft at Nkana and asked him how he was getting on. He explained progress was not spectacular because some new drilling equipment ordered from America had not yet arrived.

'I told them I was disappointed not to be able to show them more drilling results and core samples. Sir Ernest at once said: "That does not matter, what do you think?" I replied that in my opinion we were dealing with one of the world's largest copper mines. He and his party departed by train for Broken Hill and I followed by road, arriving late that night. Next morning when I met Sir Ernest in our Broken Hill office he laughingly said, "You had better live up to what you told me yesterday as I arranged to put up a million pounds this morning." '

The money went to the Bwana Mkubwa company, which held the rights to the Nkana prospect. Ernest wanted to develop the new mine without delay: it was a matter of prestige, for he had heard Chester Beatty was already at work developing two mines in his prospecting concessions, Roan Antelope and Mufulira. There would be a race to see who could reach production first.

British and American involvement on the copperbelt was quite reasonably balanced. There were other mines to be developed in due course, and Ernest hoped to win control of them: but that could wait for the future, when they could see how the initial mines fared. After all, as yet the copper seekers were feeling their way in the dark. Then came startling news: an American company which had so far taken no part in copperbelt affairs was poised to win control of Nchanga, one of the most promising potential mines. Nchanga belonged to the Rhodesia Border Concessions Corporation, a subsidiary of the BSAC in which Ernest had substantial interests.

There had not yet been any thorough prospecting at Nchanga, and to Ernest it was very much an unknown quantity. But he could not afford to take chances. From what he gathered the American company had proposed a financial arrangement which would eventually bring outright control not only of Nchanga but of the RCBC itself. As Davis wrote to him: 'If the transaction goes through as represented, the American Smelting Company will have pulled off one of the most brilliant deals that has ever been put through . . . I take my hat off to the financial genius in the Smelting Company who worked out this proposition.'

But Davis's admiration was tinged with horror. Already Chester Beatty's mines were controlled by American interests. If the RCBC concessions went the same way the British operations would be excluded from the whole copperbelt bar the comparatively slender concessions belonging to the Bwana Mkubwa company.

Ernest reacted quickly. As yet the RCBC had not confirmed the arrangements. Moving swiftly behind the scenes he mobilised strong forces to make a counterbid. Even Chester Beatty gave his support: he was not going to sit by and see such a healthy plum as Nchanga fall into the hands of completely outside interests. It was a close thing, but in the end Ernest's men succeeded in persuading the RCBC Board to agree to their scheme and turn down the American proposals. Nchanga was secure, though there could be no question of developing it for years to come.

The spotlight returned to Nkana and Chester Beatty's mines. The money spent on prospecting them was as nothing compared with what would be spent now. The companies had to set up communications: roads, railways and telegraphs. They had to build towns, housing, hospitals, recreation facilities. They had to set up crushing plants, all the supporting industries that would be needed for efficient functioning of a great mining field. And that was to forget the vast sums they had to spend actually digging out the mine and producing the copper and transporting it to the world's markets.

144

As things stood when the companies took the decision, the venture promised to be more than worthwhile. The price of copper stood at £75 a ton, up £20 in two years and still rising. The capital was pledged and the plans were drawn up and the development was just getting under way when suddenly Wall Street crashed. Down plunged the price of copper along with everything else, to the point where it was most unlikely the new mines could hope to pay their way. The developers were left with a difficult decision: were they to abandon the whole venture now, while they could escape with a relatively minor loss? Or were they to continue and hope for the best?

Ernest had to do some hard thinking. After all, what was he doing in copper anyway? He had gone into Northern Rhodesia in search of diamonds, beyond the magic limits of the Zambezi. Wasn't that rather far from home, and way out of Anglo's proper sphere of operations? Perhaps he should cut losses while he could. On the other hand he knew he could hardly go wrong. However far the price of base metals plunged now there was no demand, it was sure to recover. The world could hardly survive without them. No, Anglo should persevere on the copperbelt, as far as its resources would allow. By the time the mines were ready to go into full production the economic situation should be back to normal.

So that was decided. Ernest could devote his energies to solving what promised to be a far trickier problem: the future of the diamond industry. It was always one of the first to suffer in times of depression for it was essentially a luxury industry. Take all the diamonds away and the world would still go on turning. The trade had faced recessions before, and learnt to weather them by tightening its belt and holding on till better times returned, and by buffering the mines' budgets with cash resources saved from earlier profits. This time, though, the depression was far more extensive than any they had faced before and what resources the trade possessed were already tied up in the huge stocks of unsold diamonds inherited from the Lichtenburg crisis.

Ernest took stock of the position. At the moment all the conference mines were producing to capacity, as they had before the crisis: the three De Beers operations in Kimberley, CDM on the coast, the Premier in the Transvaal, Jagersfontein in the Free State. They all had contracts with the Diamond Corporation, as did the outside producers in Central Africa and West Africa. So long as the Diamond Corporation continued buying, all would be well. But with their resources already tied up, could the member firms keep up the pace?

There was another side to the picture. The government's State

Diggings in Namaqualand were in full production by now, and though many of the diamonds went to the nascent cutting industry in Kimberley, there was a considerable surplus. The government saw no reason why it should not dispose of this without delay and to great profit. Ernest pointed out this might prove rather difficult and in fact dangerous in the present situation; but it was immediately supposed Hoggenheimer was up to his tricks again and trying to thwart his old Afrikaner opponents now they were on equal terms with him. The new Minister of Mines, Adrian Fourie, was determined not to let him get away with it.

In fact it was worse than that. The producers' contracts were coming up for renewal in the near future, and there were dark hints that unless Ernest toed the line the government might have to take a much greater hand in regulating the trade than it had to date. Patiently Ernest tried to explain the industry's case, but the government was on its guard now. Ernest could expect no help or relief from that quarter. There was nothing for it but to proceed with his plans as effectively as he could, praying for time to make the necessary moves before the government realised what he was doing and tried to intervene.

His first thought was of ways to cut down the mines' expenses – particularly in Kimberley, where he thought De Beers had been particularly wasteful. He disposed of the two pleasure resorts that the company had been running at a loss for years, Alexandersfontein Estate and the Belgrave Hotel. Some of the townsfolk interpreted this as his revenge for what had happened in 1915 – particularly when he presented the Belgrave to the nuns of the Holy Family, the convent which had given him sanctuary when he was chased by the mob. But that had nothing to do with it. No more was he punishing Kimberley when he refused to let De Beers continue running the tramways as a subsidised service, and handed them over to the municipality: an ironic move, as it was he who had arranged their transfer to De Beers in the first place.

The Depression showed no sign of letting up, and things were getting worse. As Ernest had foreseen diamond dealers were refusing to pay the prices the Diamond Corporation was asking. Its resources would be strained to the limit if it was to survive: the industry would have to prepare a long-term siege. As a first step Ernest negotiated the acquisition of Jagersfontein for De Beers from Barnatos: its production was relatively small, but could wreak havoc if it fell into the wrong hands. As a corollary to this he arranged the transfer of CDM to De Beers from the Anglo American: a technical move only, but an important consolidation. For De Beers' sake he could afford no loopholes.

But the biggest problem was Kimberley itself. If the town was to survive, De Beers had to keep the mines in operation. Without the mines the population would drift away in search of work elsewhere, for there was nothing for them in Kimberley. It would become a ghost town, and once that happened it could not hope to recover. No more could the diamond trade, for Kimberley was its heart. Preserving Kimberley was for Ernest a personal challenge: if it was not enough to be chairman of De Beers, he was Kimberley's member of parliament. He was not to know that he was committing himself to the greatest battle of his career.

2

ALL THIS time Ernest's sons Harry and Frank had been in England, working their way through school and university. Originally they had been at Parktown School, not far from Brenthurst; but as soon as they were old enough, Ernest entered them for Charterhouse, an old school in the Surrey countryside near Godalming which had long appealed to him. He may even have been attracted by the coincidental connection of its name with Rhodes's 'Charter' company. From there Harry won a scholarship to Christ Church, Oxford: the House, as they called it; and Frank went up to Trinity College, Cambridge.

At school Harry had concentrated on modern languages, particularly French; and it was in French that he won his scholarship. He was 'half bullied and half flattered' into reading this same subject in his first year. 'Then when I got a little bit more confident in my own judgment, I turned to what interested me and what I really wanted to read' – Modern Greats, a course unique to Oxford: Philosophy, Politics and Economics, or PPE as everyone knows it. 'I placed first importance in economics, second in philosophy, and politics only third.' In economics he was tutored by the famous Sir Roy Harrod, a close friend of John Maynard Keynes who pioneered the theory of full employment. But Harry says there were no particular theories or economic precepts which specifically appealed to him at that stage: he kept an open mind.

Harry spent his leisure time quietly. He played some golf, but admits it was very bad. He did not share the prowess of his cousin Raymond, Louis's son, who would later captain the British Walker Cup team. He joined the Oxford Union, but took no active part in debates. On the other hand, he loved talking. For him, meeting people and exchanging and developing ideas was what Oxford was all about. And in that, interestingly, he wholeheartedly adopted the views of Cecil John Rhodes who had gone to such steps to bring men of affairs to Oxford for that very reason.

They were happy years to be at Oxford, the years satyrised in Evelyn Waugh's great novels. Harry himself, like most of his contemporaries, might have stepped straight from the pages of *Brideshead Revisited*. He was not exactly short of money, though he was always pumping Ernest for more. He delighted in taking his friends into the beautiful countryside of Oxfordshire and the Cotswolds on champagne picnics, or visiting the local inns that are so familiar to all Oxford men.

One in particular was a special haunt of his – a hotel called the Spreadeagle, in the little village of Thame. It was distinguished for its publican, a rollicking if rather eccentric character called Fothergill who surprised everyone who discovered he had degrees from Oxford and Leipzig, and from the Slade School of Art. He was later to make his name as an author, but for the present concentrated on making the Spreadeagle something memorable. 'Here I've determined not only to have proper and properly cooked food,' he wrote, 'but to have only either intelligent, beautiful or well-bred people to eat it.'

Fothergill was reputed to charge people 6d extra for a cup of coffee if they failed to come up to scratch. When he discovered people stopping at his inn only to use the Ladies or Gents without so much as a by your leave, he would pursue them down the corridor crying out unmercifully: 'Are you staying for lunch, or is that all you want?' Evelyn Waugh inscribed a copy of his *Decline and Fall* 'to John Fothergill, Oxford's only civilising influence.'

Harry chose the Spreadeagle for his coming-of-age party in October 1929. Ernest and May were in England for the occasion, and among the guests who travelled down to Oxford was General Smuts: Ernest had invited him to propose Harry's health. Smuts confessed afterwards he wondered on the way to the Spreadeagle what on earth Ernest was doing bringing them all out 'into the bush', but once he got there could well understand. Ernest capped a splendid evening by tipping the servants 25 per cent of the bill. John Fothergill had a comment for his diary: 'It is good when the princely and the deserving meet.'

Harry eventually took a second: not the best degree, but perfectly adequate and a fair reflection of the work he had put in, and of the shorter time he had had to complete the three year course. He did not push himself to the limit, by any means: that is not what Oxford is for. But he had enjoyed himself enormously, and got a lot out of it.

Ernest was looking forward eagerly to the time his sons could join his organisation. After all, he had always seen it as essentially a family business. At one stage Harry had wanted to be a diplomat, but realised he was too enmeshed in the machinery of the Anglo American to escape. Now he prepared to work in the London offices of the Diamond Corporation for a short time before returning to South Africa for good. Frank on the other hand had decided he would rather live in England than South Africa: he meant to join Anglo's London office and settle in Britain. The brothers had always had quite different outlooks, and Frank's decision seemed to crystallise the distinction.

When Harry sailed for South Africa he took with him Robin Grant-Lawson, a friend of his from Oxford who would now join Anglo. It was a policy he favoured later on: he liked to have personal friends of his associated with his business life. In this respect he differed strongly from Ernest, who preferred to dissociate business from pleasure.

Ernest wanted Harry to spend time in Kimberley before settling in Johannesburg: he should learn something about diamonds. Ernest still saw the diamond industry as Anglo's corner stone, and wanted his son to feel the same way about it. After a short time in Johannesburg Harry and Grant-Lawson rented a house in Egerton Road in Kimberley, only a stone's throw from the house the Oppenheimers had lived in when Ernest was mayor.

So began what was for Harry a really happy period. True, he took no great delight in sorting and evaluating diamonds: but he did begin to appreciate what made the diamond world tick, and what the experts were talking about. He and his friend put in a good deal of riding, and were frequently to be seen in the Kimberley Club togged up in the fashionable plus-fours. But most week-ends they took the train up to Johannesburg, for Kimberley was not exactly God's gift to high living.

Meanwhile, yet another Oppenheimer was brought into Anglo – Harry's cousin, Bernard's son Michael. He had not had a great deal of luck, and after an embarrassing struggle against long odds had been declared bankrupt. Ernest brought him out to South Africa to help set him on his feet again, and with him his beautiful wife Caroline – Ina for short – and their young son, who was also a Michael. Ernest settled them in one of the cottages on the Brenthurst estate, which he had redecorated and partly rebuilt to house his library. They called it 'Little Brenthurst'.

Michael and his wife were an attractive couple, and soon made their way in Johannesburg society. Ina in particular was a great asset: a noted beauty and very gracious, popular with everyone she met. She was the daughter of an English baronet, Sir Thomas Harvey, and had many amusing stories of her background: like the tales of the visits Queen Mary had paid her family when she was a little girl, and she and her sisters were made to produce samples of their needlework for her approval. She remembered how apprehensive she used to be every time she underwent the ordeal. Ina was not beautiful alone but talented too, and during Michael's difficulties she had helped earn a little extra money with short stories and articles she wrote under the name 'Ina Michael'.

Harry moved back to Johannesburg, and started work at Anglo. Officially he was under the supervision of his uncle, May's brother Leslie, who was proving his worth as Anglo's managing director. But in practice he was soon monopolised by Ernest, who even moved him into his own office, to have him as close by as possible. Harry had to do all his odd jobs for him – 'devilling' as he called it – and among them writing his speeches: he took rather wicked delight in seeing how closely he could match Ernest's very special way of expressing himself. He describes it as 'rather diffuse' in comparison with his own.

But Harry was by no means shackled to the Anglo head office. Several times he accompanied Leslie Pollak to the Rhodesias, to Europe and America in connection with the copperbelt, and gained valuable experience in the complex negotiations then in progress. They were worrying times, for the price of copper was dropping lower and lower: from £75 before the crisis it had come down to £55 by the end of 1929, down to £32 in 1930 and to £26 by the end of 1931. There was simply too much copper available: the fault not of over-production but of 'under-consumption'.

The battle for Nchanga had been won, of course. Ernest and Leslie Pollak had brought in a powerful team of British-backed financial interests to block the American challenge. There were familiar names among them: Rhoanglo, Johnnies, Union Corp, Rothschilds and others. But most significant – and in fact the leading participant – was a mining house which had not been involved in Southern Africa before, though it had strong interests in the copper mines of the Congo: Rio Tinto, most powerful base metal corporation in the British Empire, and an important ally indeed.

Ernest had been keen to bring in Rio Tinto in support of his bid to secure full control of the copperbelt. Anglo by itself could not have managed: its resources were already over-invested as it was, particularly in diamonds. But what was to be the next move? Ernest and Sir Auckland Geddes of Rio Tinto toyed with a number of schemes, each directed towards encouraging co-operation between the different African copper producers and therefore towards making them a far more powerful influence in the world industry. Playing their cards right they could force the American producers to admit their claim to a healthy share of available business. That way they might even establish a stabilised, controlled international base metals industry in just the way De Beers had organised the diamond trade.

Already they controlled Bwana Mkubwa, Nkana, Nchanga and the RCBC concessions, and had substantial minority stakes in all Chester Beatty's mines and concessions. Could they not unify all these interests without delay? They were opposed all the way by the representatives of the American companies still concerned but it was really a foregone conclusion. By substantially increasing RCBC's share capital and making over their interests in the actual potential mine areas to a common pool vested in the enlarged company, all was done. Sir Auckland Geddes became chairman, Ernest and Edmund Davis became deputy chairmen, and RCBC was renamed to signify its much wider operations, all geared to progress on the Nkana mine. So was born the Rhokana Corporation.

Meanwhile, work had been proceeding steadily on the copperbelt's first mines. The race to production was won by Chester Beatty's Roan Antelope which opened only a week or two ahead of Nkana. In the troubled conditions Beatty had cut back the development of Mufulira, and it would not be opening yet after all. But now Rhokana Corporation was in operation, and there were immediate plans to develop the plum which had precipitated all the fuss, Nchanga. For one thing, Ernest had been stung by rumours that the property was hopelessly overrated: American Smelting had been done out of the mine, people were saying, but what a lucky escape.

They began work, and the indications were Nchanga would more than justify their high hopes. But then the American producers proposed a production restriction agreement in an effort to salvage what was left of the market, and to this Chester Beatty and Rhokana agreed. Rhokana's contribution was to stop work at Nchanga, and this seemed only to conform the sceptics' suspicions: the mine was a failure. The taunts annoyed Ernest, but he was in no position to do anything about them for the time: there was no capital to spare, there was no point in producing copper nobody wanted to buy, and anyway he was too involved in a problem far more serious, the fight for the survival of the diamond trade.

For some months the diamond industry had continued as if everything was normal. All the mines were in production, both in South Africa and outside, and the Diamond Corporation had been dutifully buying what it should in terms of the various contracts. But times were bad. The diamond dealers had no customers, so were not going to buy anything themselves. As a result unprecedented stocks of diamonds were building up in Kimberley and London: in Kimberley they were literally storing them in milkchurns. These stocks represented an investment of millions, of course – which would have been justified were there some prospect of selling the stones. But as Ernest himself admitted, things looked bad.

At least in South Africa, the talk was of ostriches. Half a century before there had been a tremendous boom in demand for ostrich plumes in America and Europe, and on the strength of it a mighty industry had been developed in the Eastern Cape to support a trade worth millions each year. But as suddenly as it had come, the fashion disappeared. Most of the birds had to be slaughtered, and the industry never recovered. Wasn't this what was happening to diamonds?

Ernest saw things rather differently. Both diamonds and ostrich feathers were a luxury product, certainly; but there the comparison ended. Thanks to the efforts of Rhodes and his disciples down the years diamonds had an intrinsic value which transcended the fashions of the moment, and certainly the fickle behaviour of the economy. This was diamond's most severe test yet: but if they could safeguard its value until demand picked up again he believed it would be secure for all time.

In this the most crucial factor was the Diamond Corporation. Somehow it had to raise the capital to keep pace with the producers: particularly the outside producers, for once let down they might seek markets elsewhere, the cartel would be broken, and the whole effort would be in vain. It was important too to keep the South African mines in production – for quite different reasons. Ernest did not want to throw any part of the labour force out of work: they would certainly find none elsewhere; and in any case if he allowed the mines to close it might be extremely difficult to reopen them even in a changed economic climate.

Ernest did his best to persuade the shareholders these policies were wise. But they would have none of it. The trade was finished they said: close down and have done with it. The De Beers directors in London shared these views. If the mines continued production and the Diamond Corporation had to find ever greater funds to buy stocks, before long they would face ruin. Even Alpheus Williams, now De Beers general manager in Kimberley, urged Ernest at least to consider cutting back production for the time.

The strain was getting more intense than ever. On Ernest's insistence the Diamond Corporation had tied up tens of millions of pounds in building up stocks. What sales there were had lessened to a trickle, and there was no prospect of improvement. Far from it, things were getting worse all the time. Alpheus Williams drafted a scheme for the cutting back of production in Kimberley. Dutoitspan – most easy to reopen – would close down altogether, and for the rest the working week would be shortened from six to five days and each white miner would work only four days.

But when Ernest put these proposals to the government they were turned down out of hand. It would 'upset the country and the men,' insisted the state mining engineer. Besides, it would cause 'the greatest inconvenience to the government.' The rule was the diamond companies were supposed to give six week's notice of an intention to close. If Ernest forewent this for the time to save the general embarrassment of an announcement, the government would let him close down at a later stage without first giving that notice.

Ernest hung on for a while, but it could not go on. He approached the Minister of Mines, who seemed most put out at the idea of the mines' cutting back. Wasn't the Diamond Corporation spending millions to keep the outside producers in business? Then why should the South African mines be the ones to suffer? It was obvious to him Ernest stood to gain a fortune from these outside producers after all. Didn't he have huge personal interests in those companies? He was out to line his own pockets.

When Ernest asked the minister to hear representations from the industry, he grudgingly agreed. Ernest arranged to bring out several De Beers directors and other key figures from Europe specially for the occasion, and it was agreed there would be a full-scale conference in Cape Town. But even now Fourie was suspicious: he refused to believe the industry was in any danger. Everyone knew what De Beers resources were: it was said they could afford to keep going until doomsday if necessary.

Ernest was incensed. All along he had done his best, he told parliament. But De Beers was heading for ruin, and so were the other producers. Their resources were at an end. At the present rate there would be no money left even to maintain and protect the properties, let alone produce diamonds. They would close down, and the mines would fill with water. If that happened, the mines might be lost for

153

ever. Already the famous Kimberley Mine, the Big Hole, had suffered that fate.

'We have told you that it is our endeavour to help the government and keep our people employed. We were prepared to spend £600 000 and if we got that money in we would keep our people employed; it had to be South African money. We have not got that money in and our financial position has got worse and worse. Regarding the Premier Mine, which is an open-cast mine, if you wanted that mine to fill, it would not do any great damage; Koffiefontein could also be allowed to fill, but in the case of De Beers and Jagersfontein, if we allowed these mines to fill we would be endangering a national asset. It is only fair that De Beers must keep reserves in hand to meet the crisis over a long period. I have been attacked by shareholders for the policy I have pursued. De Beers company cannot afford to have less money in hand. If we do not sell for two years we must keep our mines pumped. I do not know how long the crisis will last. We have reduced our resources to the lowest possible figure. We cannot pay a preference dividend. All along we have done everything we possibly can and then we are told that we are trying to get out of our obligation.'

Summing up, Ernest hit harder still.

'. . . We say that we are so anxious to help the national industry that the producing companies are willing to spend the money they get in order to keep their people employed, but they are not prepared to spend any more. As chairman of De Beers company I might tell you I have had a very worrying time over the diamond industry. I have been attacked from all quarters about spending the company's money and the policy I have pursued is being continually criticized. I have taken the blame just as I will take credit when the trade recovers. I look forward to the time when it can be said in the House that the De Beers company under my guidance kept its people employed while everybody else retrenched. It will be some acknowledgement of what I am doing.'

Mr. FOURIE: It is no use talking about that; appreciation is nothing.

SIR ERNEST OPPENHEIMER: Appreciation is this. There will be some satisfaction in knowing that the Government at least says: 'Here is a South African who stands up for the country and sticks to his guns and who tries to see the thing through.'

The results of the conference were disappointing. Matters stood largely as before: De Beers was ready to close down, the minister believed there was no need. Ernest realised there was no way out, and

154

he would have to give notice of the mines' intention to close.

'It is my duty as chairman of De Beers, and as a man keenly interested in the welfare of this country, solemnly to warn you that a great national industry is in imminent danger of complete collapse.'

He had further discussions with the minister, but nothing could be done. There were no signs of relief from America, and in Europe there was a very real fear that Germany was on the verge of bankruptcy. The diamond market was practically at a standstill. News from the De Beers directors in London was only too definite: 'In view . . . gloomy prospects we are strongly of opinion that we should close down all production of diamonds by all producing companies without further delay . . .'

Ernest was at the end of his tether. At the meeting of the De Beers board on February 16 1932, he took what was probably the most critical decision of his career. The board 'resolved that active mining operations be entirely suspended on 31 March 1932 and all expenditure reduced to an absolute minimum . . .'

'The diamond industry has been struggling against collapse for years,' Ernest told parliament when he announced the decision. 'And that it has succeeded is due to its own efforts. It has preserved the diamond trade in spite of the Minister of Mines but now it can do no more.

'The Diamond Corporation has found more than £13 million to finance its accumulated stocks. The producers have spent vast sums to prevent unemployment. From the Minister, instead of gratitude and help, they have received insults and accusations of bad faith . . . The only conclusion they can come to is that he does not understand the position . . .'

There followed a most unfortunate public row between Ernest and Fourie. The minister responded to the De Beers closure with a series of complaints about the supposedly deceitful way in which the producers had operated. They had given no notice of their intentions, he told a reporter from the *Rand Daily Mail,* and had placed everybody in the most embarrassing position. Ernest wasted no time in ridiculing his remarks, which prompted further bluster on his part and finally the announcement of a commission of inquiry into the whole industry.

In explaining the terms of reference of the commission to parliament, Fourie could not waste a chance to score off Ernest. He was trying to suggest he was directly to blame for the government's stern attitude in wanting to establish exactly what had been going on in the world of diamonds.

'We have had the spectacle in South Africa that there is one man who

155

is chairman of all the producing companies in South Africa, that the same man is chairman of the Diamond Corporation. He alone is the centre of the whole diamond industry, and, moreover, he advocates his own case in this House. The fact is that the Hon Member for Kimberley can juggle, manipulate and deal with all the diamonds as he pleases, and all the men whom he brings over from overseas amount to nothing, because he turns them all round his thumb.'

As it happened the commission was a miserable failure. Only David Harris was prepared to give evidence before it, and he was now retired and out of the picture. Ernest and De Beers had never had such bad relations with the government, but stuck to what they had decided. The mines in Kimberley, the Premier and Jagersfontein closed down as arranged, and soon afterwards the alluvial mines at the coast. Apprehensive for the future as he was, Ernest must have been heartened when the outside producers cut back their production in sympathy. There had been no pressure on them to do so, and the decision was entirely voluntary. It was the first indication Ernest had been given that his efforts were after all appreciated, though in the circumstances it was somewhat hollow compensation.

3

WHILE ERNEST fought for the survival of the diamond industry, he could safely leave his gold mines to look after themselves. It was a strange paradox of economic recession that as other industries were forced to retrench, gold mining prospered. Working costs were lower in relation to the gold price, which made for greater profits. In fact, far from cutting back production Ernest's mines had been working to capacity and making a comfortable profit, and he had even been seeking capital to revive Daggafontein where production had been suspended as unpayable some time before the crash. He sent Hagart to try and raise £50 000 from the banks, promising to repay in three months. But they just did not have it. He eventually raised the money from private sources – and within a few weeks Daggafontein was making more than £50 000 profit every month.

But though the East Rand mines were doing well, and Ernest was wondering whether he should not open more, the same could not be said for the older mines around Johannesburg. Already several had closed, for though they still had gold to mine it was simply not a payable proposition. It looked as if many of the others were going the same way.

Without a substantial increase in the gold price they would quietly die, as many other mines had died before them. Even the government mining engineer took a pessimistic view: after going into the question in great detail he concluded that within 15 years, far from leading the world, the Reef would rank only among the minor producers. But then, this was nothing new: they had expected it from the beginning.

Meanwhile Europe's currencies were tottering on the brink of collapse. It was supposed that of them all Britain's was the most stable, for it had been all along. But suddenly there was a drain on that country's reserves as foreign investors withdrew their holdings without warning, and to avert a national catastrophe the government announced it was abandoning the gold standard and devaluing the pound without delay. The British dominions were left to decide for themselves whether to follow the mother country's example or decide on a course of their own.

South Africa stayed put. The gold industry was perfectly happy about the decision at first, for the gold sold in Britain – and that accounted for most of it – would now earn a handsome premium in terms of the devalued sterling currency. Besides, imported mining equipment would now be appreciably cheaper, so working costs would go down. The mines stood to gain both ways, and in response gold mining shares were booming both in South Africa and Britain.

Then the Gold Producers' Committee, the executive of the Chamber of Mines which controlled the whole industry and on which all the great mining houses were represented, had second thoughts. The long-term disadvantages of remaining on the gold standard were likely heavily to outweigh the short-term benefits. South Africa depended on her economic relations with Britain: the trade amounted to several times as much as the Union's trade with any other country – and certainly with those countries which had remained on the gold standard, like the United States and France. Imports from Britain would now be much cheaper, while exports would be more expensive. Could South Africa afford such a drastic upheaval?

There was another point. Hadn't there been complaints that the Reef's resources were drying up, and the industry would be finished in a couple of decades? Then the present situation provided an ideal chance to save it for years to come: perhaps to double, treble, quadruple its potential. To go off the gold standard and allow the Union's currency to float down would have the effect of *raising* gold profits, so that suddenly all those mines which had been forced to close down or were threatened with closure in the near future would have a new lease

157

of life. Not only that, but there were many deposits nobody had yet tackled which could now be brought into production if this was done.

The GPC put its case to parliament. Smuts and the Opposition were convinced – after all, Ernest was on the front bench. But Hertzog and his finance minister Havenga saw things differently. They were determined to force the economy to find a new level and bring it to a fresh prosperity. Both were convinced they could do it, at the expense of sterling which to them represented the hated British. No, they would not hear of any change. But they were prepared to appoint a special committee to go into the whole question and produce *proof* that the decision was justified – though whatever it concluded, the decision would not sway the government's decision.

It fell to Ernest to state the Opposition's case in parliament, of course, as it usually did on these occasions. He made a strong speech, and was not afraid to admit his own about-face. 'In the first instance I thought we should remain on gold, but then I became doubtful and now I am convinced that the interest of this country will be best served by leaving the gold standard.'

The chief point he wanted to make was that it was time South Africa realised the old gold standard of before the war had broken down and disappeared – never to return. The United States and France were loyal to what they still called the 'international' gold standard, though in practice it was only they who abided by it and their loyalty only served to *lower* its value. Britain was now off it for good, pinning faith instead in sterling which was every bit as significant internationally as the gold standard had been – and which appeared now to be stabilising prices and costs in the countries which had adopted it, and was having a true stabilising effect on their economies.

'The gold system as it was before the war and as it is now is as different as chalk from cheese. That is the point. Today gold brings with it a policy of deflation. We are tying ourselves to an "international" gold currency controlled by the United States. In choosing one currency or another the question is a balance of advantages. We control neither sterling nor the international gold currency. But we do know the results of the two systems. The Minister has quoted them recently.

'On gold, prices continue to fall, and less and less is being received for our primary products. Therefore we have to choose between linking ourselves with one currency which means deflation, and even lower prices, which must result in ruination to our farmers, in crippling our industry, and in slowing up mining development; and on the other hand a currency expressly designed to remedy this state of affairs . . .

'There is no such thing as financial independence, and there is no such thing as a "natural" currency system. At the present time we have to choose between two systems, both of them artificial and both of them outside our control. One of them, the "international" gold standard, is at the moment dominated by France and America, and these countries are pursuing a policy that has led, and is leading, to ever-falling gold prices and the ruin of the primary producer.

'England has broken away from this system, and is managing her currency with the idea of keeping the purchasing power of the pound steady, with the object of increasing the prices of primary products. To follow sterling must increase the price which we get for our products in the markets of the world. Are we to throw away this advantage, the chance of getting better prices for our primary producers and of seeing mining development, simply because we cannot or will not understand that the gold standard, as it existed before the war, has gone never to return?'

The GPC gave evidence to parliament's select committee, with a case even stronger and better reasoned than before. But the government was not to be persuaded. These representations were some sinister trick of the capitalists. They remained obstinately unmoved even when the export markets for just about everything but gold collapsed, when farmers could not sell their wool, their wine or their fruit, when subsidies were being increased out of all proportion, when the railways could not pay their way, even when the South African public began to show its displeasure at the polls and Nationalist candidates were being defeated.

The decisive moment came when a former Hertzog cabinet minister who had been appointed a Judge of Appeal, Tielman Roos, resigned from the bench and began campaigning against the government: the gold standard must be abandoned, he said, if South Africa was not to be ruined. And to save the Union from disaster the two political parties should coalesce: in fact, he offered to serve as their leader. He was welcomed so enthusiastically wherever he went that the government at last realised the degree of ill-feeling it had generated. In days it was all over. South Africa went off gold on December 29 1932.

4

THE CHANGE could hardly have been more dramatic. Like magic there was suddenly money in every direction. Capital poured into the country, the stock exchange had never seen a boom like it, on every side there was prosperity. The unemployment problem seemed to solve itself almost overnight, with tens of thousands of jobs created as employers regained their confidence. South Africa was awakening from the nightmare hibernation to find it was Spring again.

As the Gold Producers' Committee had forecast, it was the gold mining industry which profited most from the change of fortune. Each of the great mining houses was preparing to sink its new-found capital into fresh ventures. Anglo, for one, had already planned a new mine at the Far East Rand next to its existing mines, to be called East Daggafontein: this time under the aegis of Rand Selection Trust. As usual other mining houses were brought into the picture to help ease the financial load – most significantly Gold Fields under Guy Carleton Jones.

Gold Fields was one of the oldest mining houses of them all, founded by Rhodes and in seniority ranking on equal terms with the Corner House and Johnnies. But uninspired management down the years had left it in the wake of its rivals: its mines, once so rich, were being worked out one after the other, and in the years of the Depression there were fears it would fade out altogether.

Now, however, Carleton Jones was in the chair: an imaginative Canadian consulting engineer who had arrived in South Africa before World War I and been with Gold Fields ever since. He was faced with a tough assignment: unless he found new deposits of gold to work his company would be out of business. But he had a hunch that he could lay his hands on more than enough gold to solve his problems: on an extension of the reef *west* of Johannesburg.

All this was happening in the years of recession, when there was little capital to be had. But research into the results of previous prospecting ventures in the area convinced Carleton Jones he was on the right track. Shafts had been sunk and gold found but the reef was buried under dolomitic formations trapping great reservoirs of water, which burst out of fissures as shafts were sunk and made mining extremely hazardous. The mining houses had left the West Rand well alone.

Now – and as it happened entirely by coincidence – Carleton Jones was put in touch with a young geologist recently arrived from Germany who was a disciple of the new science of geophysics. This involved tracing magnetic rock formations far underground, by means of a correlation of great numbers of results taken with a special instrument called a magnetometer. The geologist, Rudolf Krahmann, believed he could trace gold-bearing reef by this means, as the quarz that carried it was always associated with magnetic material. Carleton Jones set him to work.

The result was spectacular. In weeks of criss-crossing the area with his instruments Krahmann succeeded in locating a 24 mile stretch of magnetic quartz which seemed to correspond exactly with the Main Reef series. It was under the dolomite, but great advances in mining techniques meant there would be little problem in getting at the gold if it was there: they would use concrete to fill the fissures and drive out the trapped water before it could do damage. In the depressed conditions Gold Fields needed financial assistance to continue with their programme, and shopped around for help. They found it at Anglo, where Ernest was deeply intrigued by the possibilities. He bought a relatively modest holding in the venture which at least gave him some sort of say.

Prospecting continued, and the boreholes were evidently confirming what Krahmann had said. Ernest was excited, for this was the first new goldfield to be discovered since the Far East Rand twenty years before. If the reef continued thus far, it might go even further. They would have to prospect the new area: in fact, as a first step they would employ yet another new method of survey, this time from the air. Anglo chartered a plane, and hired Major C K Cochran Patrick, ex Royal Flying Corps, to fly it.

Among those most keenly interested in the new developments was Ernest's nephew Michael. By this time he was fully involved in all aspects of Anglo's business, and showing himself to be well equipped for it. Ernest believed he had a strong future. Michael wanted to see for himself how Cochran-Patrick set about his aerial survey work, and one day the two men went out to Baragwanath aerodrome and took off. Cochran Patrick launched into a succession of tricky manoeuvres to show the plane's versatility. All seemed to be well. But then suddenly, to the horror of those watching, the plane nose-dived into the ground and burst into flames. Both men were killed instantly.

Ina was hysterical. How could it happen? He was so young. He was all she had in the world. What could she do now? What would become of her and of young Michael? There was no comforting her, not for days. They did all they could, Ernest, May, Harry and other close friends of the family. But what was there to say?

Gradually Ina recovered herself. She was really a very brave woman. Her son needed her now more than ever. For his sake she had to pull herself together. She wondered if she should return to England: there she had relatives. But Ernest would not hear

161

of her leaving Little Brenthurst: certainly not until she was on her feet again.

It was a good thing she did stay. There was nobody who could look after May as she did. May was very ill, they knew. She had undergone a whole series of operations over the last few years, each serious and for a multiplicity of complaints. She needed careful nursing and she responded to nobody as she did to her young niece. Ina was with her constantly when she was in pain, doing for her all that she could. Ernest was beside himself with anxiety. He was deeply in love with his wife, who had been with him through so much. Friends of May's always maintained her brain was as good and keen as his – a man's brain, as if that was a tribute. She had been behind him in everything he did: he could not bear to see her in so much pain.

These personal worries came at a time when Ernest needed all his powers to cope with further problems in the diamond industry. Closing down the mines had not seen the end of them. As Ernest had promised the demand for diamonds was slowly returning. It could be satisfied for years to come from the huge stocks the Diamond Corporation had built up in those years of depression. Suddenly, however, there was a threat from an unprotected flank. The troublesome Minister of Mines was beginning to sell the production of the State Diggings to whoever was prepared to buy it.

It could have been the last straw. All these years Ernest had carefully nursed the trade through successive crises to the point where it seemed secure. It would be some time before there was any justification for re-opening the mines: but the harm was done now, and anyway those thrown out of work could find it elsewhere. At least they all knew that in due course, when the Diamond Corporation had worked its way through the huge stockpiles, the industry would be revived. Or at least, it would be if the government could be dissuaded from its suicidal course. Selling regardless of the price scale and the time-honoured practice of the trade to deal in terms of series, as Nature produced the diamonds and not as the buyers actually wanted them, could destroy the trade's whole structure. If that happened, they would be back where they started.

Ernest knew there could be no hope of the government's understanding such problems while the Nationalists remained in office. Fourie maintained his extreme suspicion of all De Beers' overtures. Ernest was ready to despair of ever persuading him of the urgent need to reach agreement on a common policy before it was too late. And then, so unexpectedly that it took everyone by surprise, there came a complete

162

turn-about in the political situation which swept away all the difficulties as if they had never existed.

What happened was that Smuts approached Hertzog and suggested
they should link hands. The Nationalists had lost a lot of prestige in the
months of the gold crisis, and were divided in their own ranks. Smuts,
on the other hand, realised that whatever the divisions there was little
chance of his party winning an election. In those circumstances coalition seemed the only answer, not only for their own sake but for the
country's: as Tielman Roos had suggested, in fact. Hertzog formed a
new cabinet with Smuts as deputy Prime Minister and several South
African Party men included, and the two opposing parties were joined
to become the United South African Nationalist Party, or United Party
for short.

Fourie retained his seat in the cabinet, but not as Minister of Mines.
He was replaced by a SAP, Patrick Duncan, who was not surprisingly
wholly sympathetic to what Ernest proposed. Soon negotiations were
under way, with the government men and the representatives of the
conference producers thrashing out plans for what was really the reorganisation of the whole industry.

Now things went smoothly. Though it took some time to work out
the precise details, the general form of the arrangement was soon
agreed. The South African producers – not the conference producers
alone, but also the State Diggings – would join the Diamond Corporation as representing the outside producers in a new organisation to be
known as the Diamond Producers' Association, which would decide all
policy. The DPA would buy all production, and then sell it to a new
Diamond Corporation subsidiary to be called the Diamond Trading
Company, which would dispose of it. This gave De Beers complete
control of the whole industry, but seemed a practical and perfectly
acceptable solution. If the worst came to the worst and disagreement
arose, an individual producer was free to withdraw from the association
once its contracts were fulfilled.

These were the bare bones of what came to be known as the Central
Selling Organisation, with its headquarters in London. It is a complex
arrangement, but it has worked very well down the years and today it
is similar at least in principle to what it was when first formulated.
Ernest personally negotiated new contracts with each of the outside
producers, so that the trade was safe for years to come.

As if to celebrate its new lease of life, the industry produced a windfall. Jacobus Jonker, a poor digger working a small claim in the neighbourhood of the Premier Mine, found a diamond of 726 carats which

163

was the fourth largest discovered up to that time. Caught up in the excitement, Ernest bought it for the Diamond Corporation for £63,000. Proudly he showed it to the staff at Anmercosa House before sending it on to London. He let even the most junior typists handle it, though watched all the time by security men.

Here the strict surveillance ended. At the beginning of the century the Transvaal government had wanted to send the Cullinan diamond to Europe to be cleaved and polished. With great excitement and in a blaze of publicity, a small army of detectives boarded a ship with a carefully sealed package and deposited it in the captain's safe – not realising it contained an artificial 'Cullinan' while the real stone went by ordinary mail. Ernest used the same method, though without employing the detectives: the fabulous stone went ordinary mail, for the total outlay of a couple of shillings.

The Jonker diamond was eventually sold to the famed dealer Harry Winston of New York for £145,000. He had it cut into twelve magnificent stones ranging from 5 to 125 carats, and sold the chief of these to King Farouk of Egypt for a million dollars.

Meanwhile, May had been slowly returning to health, and was nearly her usual self again. Ernest decided to take her to the Cape with him for the opening of parliament. Perhaps the sea air would do her good. He decided they should not stay out at Muizenberg, where he had bought a house called Blue Mountains: if anything went wrong it might be difficult to get hold of a doctor. Instead they stayed at the famous Mount Nelson Hotel on the slopes of Table Mountain.

The atmosphere in the new Parliament was most peculiar, Ernest decided: South Africa was now almost a one-party state. They had had an election a few months before, if you could call it that: with no Opposition to fight them most candidates had been returned without a ballot. Now they were all there as members of the United Party. Only a few extremists from either side had refused to join it, and now sat as an Opposition: you could count them on your fingers.

The Oppenheimers meant to remain in the Cape only a week or so: Ernest had to get back to Johannesburg. But May was enjoying herself so Ernest agreed to leave her in Cape Town while he went home by himself. She could follow in a few days. When at last it was time for her to go a number of friends went down to the station to see her off on the 4 o'clock train. But May did not arrive. They telephoned the hotel to find out what had happened, and were told she had suffered a heart attack.

164

It was not serious, they were told: she would survive it, but for the time she should rest. The hotel contacted Ernest in Johannesburg, and he made arrangements to leave for Cape Town immediately. The doctors looking after May left her alone to sleep for a while, for apparently she was out of danger. But at 10 o'clock that night she had another attack, and this time she did not recover.

Ernest took May's death very badly. He had relied on the strength she gave him, for she was the cornerstone of his career. He wrote to his old friend Honnold, who was still living in California. '. . . I feel very tired and weary and am toying with the idea of retiring. I should not like you to think that I am ill, but I find it very difficult after my bereavement to concentrate on work.'

May had died in February. For a time much of the burden of Anglo's affairs fell on her brother's shoulders. Leslie Pollak was firmly in control at Anglo, with Harry assisting him as intended when his father was prepared to release him. But one night Leslie Pollak was at a dinner party with friends when he suddenly complained he was not feeling well. A doctor insisted he should be taken to hospital without delay, but by morning he was dead. He had been suffering from pneumonia, and nobody had even realised he was ill.

Ernest was in England when this happened, still mourning May's loss: nothing could console him. The next most senior man remaining was Hagart, who had risen fast within the organisation and was already a full director: but he was out of Johannesburg. That left only Harry and one other man who was not much older than he was as the only representatives of senior management. They cabled Ernest in London. Were they to take over the whole company? Ernest said yes; there was no alternative. It was Harry's first taste of top level command. From now on he took a full part in shaping Anglo's policies.

In London at this time Ernest was seeing a lot of Frank, who was working at the Anglo American offices and already showing merit. He was quite different from his brother – tall, fair and extrovert while Harry was dark, intense and intellectual. Frank's one problem was weight: he had been grossly over-eating in the good-time London of those days, and needed to reduce drastically. Two friends had similar problems, and the three decided to go on a crash diet. But they would do it in style: at the fashionable Reed's Hotel in Madeira.

They took the holiday the next year, in April 1935. Ernest had been visiting England again, and decided to plan his return journey so that he could see Frank in Madeira. The three friends were enjoying themselves hugely in the glories of Funchal and its delicious surroundings, lazing in the sun and bathing at all hours of the day. Their one discomfort was hunger: they had virtually given up eating. They eventually decided to give themselves a break and have a slap-up dinner. Afterwards they went for a swim at the bottom of the cliffs. The others got out and went up to get dry, but Frank stayed in the sea. His friends returned for him some while later, and found him drowned: lying face down in six inches of water. Doctors decided it was the result of a heart attack.

The shock to Ernest was almost too much to bear. He was on the ship when the news reached him: it threw him into the depths of despair. He loved his sons: they were his life. All his hopes for the future were pinned on them. He returned to South Africa, but he had no interest in his work. He took himself off to Europe again, to sort out his muddled thoughts. He had guided whole industries through the recession; he had worked so hard all these years; was this his reward? What could it mean? He had not taken any great interest in religion before. Now he turned to it for solace: not the Jewish religion particularly, nor the Christian, but to the Bible itself. And there he came to the Book of Job which was so savagely appropriate. For the rest of his life he was never without a Bible at his bedside, and he read it every day both morning and evening.

Curiously, in discovering the power of religion Ernest came closer to his widowed niece who was herself still in mourning. He and Ina spent much time together in these weeks, discussing the implications of the tragedies that had overtaken them. They drew great comfort from each other, going for long walks through the great gardens of Brenthurst and in the surrounding district: it was a custom Ernest maintained the rest of his life. Some months later, he took Ina with him on one of his visits to London. He proposed marriage, and she accepted.

They were united in a quiet ceremony in the new year. When Ina moved up to the main house, Harry took over Little Brenthurst. Ernest, meanwhile, found himself with a youngster about the house again: his new stepson Michael, now ten years old and the apple of Ina's eye.

But in spite of Ernest's new family commitments it was still Harry who dominated his thoughts. He meant to spend the rest of his working life building the empire he would leave his son. To protect the family interests he formed a new company, which he named simply 'E Oppenheimer and Son.' And that, after all, was the crux of the matter.

166

5

MICHAEL OPPENHEIMER had been killed trying out a plane which would have been used to survey the West Witwatersrand. In the time that had elapsed since then Gold Fields had fully explored its area and the boreholes looked as promising as Anglo had hoped. Hagart and Bancroft were watching the progress of the surveys, and advised Ernest to increase Anglo's stake in the operation. This was in line with his own thinking, for with the abandoning of the gold standard and the increased price of gold the venture was moving out of the 'risk' category into something more solid. The NCGF had discovered an altogether new goldfield, one day to bear fruit as the Venterspost and Libanon mines.

Ernest had been much encouraged by the discoveries on the West Wits line as they were calling it, and decided that the story was not over yet. Before long he ordered the most ambitious prospecting programme ever undertaken in South Africa, using aerial, geophysical and drilling surveys to determine exactly where deposits might lie. For the first time they were to use diamond tipped drilling bores, which were many times as fast as conventional bores. Anglo took out a new company, Western Reefs Development, and bought claims and prospecting concessions over a huge area north of the Vaal River. Eight drills were at work for months – but to the chagrin of Joe Bancroft and Frank Unger, Anglo's consulting engineer, produced not a trace of payable reef. Perhaps they were wrong after all.

Just as Anglo was preparing to call off this ambitious programme Bancroft was approached by Jack Scott, a prospector whose father had developed strong interests in the Klerksdorp area years before – even further west. Scott was convinced there was a payable reef in the area: his father had traced an outcrop they called the Strathmore reef, and it had been exploited long ago by a number of small companies formed to mine it. But the heavily faulted ground in the area had discouraged further enterprise.

Nothing if not game, and acting on Bancroft's advice, Ernest agreed to deploy all eight drilling bores for one last try in the neighbourhood of the Orkney Mine, which was the site that interested Scott most. Sure enough, as he had forecast, they struck payable reef. The ground was very irregular, and it was realised that to establish a mine would be difficult: but having got so far they were not going to turn back. There was a slump in Johannesburg in the mid-thirties and development was slow, but Anglo began sinking shafts against the time they could come into full production. One day Western Reefs would more than justify this confidence.

Anglo's success had encouraged other mining groups to buy their way into the Klerksdorp area – particularly a brand new mining house called Anglo-Transvaal, the Reef's first since Anglo had been founded in 1917, and formed expressly to exploit the abandoned workings that would be profitable now that the gold price was higher. Working in partnership with Scott, Anglovaal helped him pinpoint the exact course of this 'Strathmore Reef' of his, and in the eventual sharing of interests emerged with Hartebeesfontein Mine while he joined forces with yet another financial house, General Mining, and developed three more. Anglo, too, prospected further, and eventually established the Vaal Reefs Mine next to Western Reefs. To manage these holdings and interests in the other properties too Ernest brought into being a financial holding company, West Rand Investment Trust.

Meanwhile, it was not long before the prospectors were looking even further afield – this time *south* of the Vaal to the Orange Free State. Again this was nothing new: there had been a 'gold rush' to the Free State as early as 1855, long before any discoveries elsewhere in South Africa. It was later supposed the area had been salted. There had been a short boom in the 1890's as companies were formed to work shallow gold deposits similar to those in the Klerksdorp area, and desultory prospecting had continued ever since. However, it had all been rather half-hearted: the mining laws of the Free State did little to encourage private enterprise. All rights were vested in the administration.

One of the few ventures making any progress was the work of a new company called Witwatersrand Extensions, taken out by two young amateur geologists to rework an old borehole on the farm Aandenk. The borehole had been sunk by an old prospector years before who had run out of funds before World War I and had been forced to discontinue work: however, he had filled it in and laced it with dynamite to make sure nobody else got at it. Now the amateurs, Allan Roberts and Mannie Jacobson, had raised what capital they could to continue work.

The funds did not last long. However, with Anglo's success across the river at Western Reefs, there was no great problem persuading one of the Johannesburg mining houses, the Anglo-French Company, to take a hand. Unfortunately the company soon decided the borehole held no promise after all, and relinquished its rights. Roberts and Jacobson

168

approached everyone they could think of, but to no avail: the mining laws were more than enough to discourage investors. Then they were put in touch with the hero of Rustenburg and Namaqualand.

Merensky had not touched his prospecting apparatus for seven years: in fact, since his days in Namaqualand. He had turned his attention to quite different fields of activity – forestry and agriculture. But it so happened he had long nursed theories about South Africa's goldfields, as he had about so many aspects of the Union's geology. He was one of the earliest to subscribe to the 'placer' theory: that the reefs of gold were strata of what had been a great inland sea, eroded from gold-bearing rocks in surrounding mountains and washed down by some great primeval river. When he heard of the borehole in the Free State he decided this was a chance to test his theory, so gladly agreed to join forces with Wit Extensions.

There was another aspect to his participation. He had been watching the progress of the new science of geophysics. In fact, it had been he who provided the magnetometer used to prospect the West Wits line. Now he would use the method in the Free State. He did and found promising indications. But the borehole on Aandenk had already gone down 4 046 feet without result. Merensky brought in diamond drills to prospect other areas, but again with no reward. He knew the lie of the land was right, and there was gold: but not in payable amounts.

His entry into the Free State had been greeted with a blaze of publicity – though he was quick to disclaim any chance of making another quick fortune. There were huge problems, he well knew, and all would depend on a measure of luck. He was being watched closely by the big mining houses – and particularly by Anglo, which of course had good reason to be grateful to him for previous inspirations. When parliament changed the Free State mining laws to bring them into line with the Transvaal's, Ernest offered Merensky £35 000 for his options in Wit Extensions, and this he accepted.

Now Anglo moved the team of diamond drilling bores down from Western Reefs, and began a comprehensive survey programme in Merensky's footsteps, with Joe Bancroft in charge. But he had no success. Nor for that matter did two of the other big mining houses which now moved into the Free State, Union Corp and Anglovaal. Each found traces of gold, but that was not enough. With the recession on the stock exchange prospecting operations were called off for the time.

Instead, it was a quite different company which made the first strike: Western Holdings, a subsidiary of Sir Abe Bailey's SA Townships which was prospecting even further south. It had been formed to work

169

a group of concessions taken over from Jack Scott, Roberts and Jacobson. These had not revealed anything, so the company brought in one of Union Corp's geologists who had been experimenting with geophysics. He covered a wide area with his magnetometer and eventually suggested they should concentrate activity in the neighbourhood of a farm called St Helena near the sleepy village of Odendaalsrus.

SA Townships' first borehole was so encouraging that the company approached Joe Bancroft and asked him whether he would be interested in bringing Anglo into the picture. SA Townships was not a gold mining company, and was sorely lacking in technical knowledge which Anglo could provide. Bancroft took just three minutes to dismiss the idea: if there was no reef on Aandenk, how could there be one on St Helena? SA Townships approached P M Anderson of Union Corp instead and he agreed to come in as requested.

Later the boreholes on St Helena duly intersected a payable deposit, even as boreholes drilled by a rival company, Lewis and Marks's African and European, struck the reef on the neighbouring farm, Uitsig. Ernest quickly sent Harry to try and negotiate a share exchange between Western Holdings and West Rand Investment Trust: but he was too late. SA Townships was no longer interested. Ernest would have to think again.

For the moment, however, his attentions were concentrated elsewhere. He was watching the gradual recovery of the diamond market. The Diamond Corporation and the individual producers had accumulated vast stocks of diamonds during the depression years, and gradually they fed these to the Diamond Trading Company which now came into its own. From 1935 sales increased by leaps and bounds.

As the situation improved the mines could begin producing again. CDM was first away: operations were resumed at the beginning of 1935. In Kimberley the first step was to wash the blueground already mined and available on the depositing floors. Dutoitspan eventually resumed production in March 1936, Bultfontein in June 1937. Jagersfontein began washing in July 1936 and continued until February 1937: but by then it was realised that under current conditions that mine was unpayable and it was not worth resuming underground mining in earnest. The same went for the Premier.

The Diamond Corporation paid its first dividend in 1937. The next year Anglo American and Barnatos sold their holdings in the Diamond Corporation to De Beers in exchange for shares. Anglo's went to yet another new holding company, Anglo American Investments, formed in 1936 to handle the corporation's diamond interests. At the same time

170

the capital of the Diamond Trading Company was doubled to take account of a rising phenomenon in the diamond world. Suddenly there was a demand for industrial stones.

It was not an entirely new development. Diamonds had been used for industrial purposes since the 1880's. But it was only now the improvements in technology made them not only convenient but essential. Suddenly there was a demand for boart, the diamond waste which had so long embarrassed many of the producers. Before it had been used in the diamond trade to cut other diamonds: but commercially it had been worthless. Now there was a chance it could be exploited to the gain of all. As early as 1934 the Diamond Corporation established a research wing, the Diamond Development Company, in London. Other companies were formed to exploit the new demand, both in England and South Africa. Suddenly, like a gift from heaven to make up for the hardships of the Depression, the diamond trade found it had two strings to its bow.

The situation on the copperbelt had improved too. Nkana and Roan Antelope were well into their stride by now, and so was RST's Mufulira which Chester Beatty had been quietly developing over the years. This gave him a firm lead over Rhokana, which had done nothing further about Nchanga: almost as if it was keeping the new mine for a rainy day. The real reason for the neglect was of course that there was no justification for developing yet another producer until the copper market was firmly on its feet again.

But the situation produced an unfortunate result. The rumours about Nchanga had continued: it was all a hoax, the mine was barely payable. Rhokana had been done, the Americans were gloating. Chester Beatty's interests were a far better investment prospect. The British corporation's prestige was suffering and Ernest was not pleased. Nchanga was being treated as a joke, he complained to Rhokana's managing director in London, S S Taylor. If they wanted to preserve their position in Northern Rhodesia they should open Nchanga and have done with it.

'It is true other people can produce copper somewhat cheaper, but they would certainly not want to sell it at a price which would show a loss to N'Kana, because such a price would enable nobody to pay any dividends. My attitude is best expressed in the following quotation:

' *"He either fears his fate too much*
Or his deserts are small
That dares not put it to the touch
To win or lose it all." '

Anglo's profits for that year were so large that Rhoanglo's shares

171

could be written right down to 7s 6d and still show a profit bigger than the year before. 'I prefer losing the lot if we are to have no chance of turning our investment into a profitable one.'

Copper prices improved by the end of 1936. The time was ripe, Ernest pointed out to Taylor. They should form a new company to administer the mine, and start producing. Nchanga Consolidated Copper Mines was floated in March 1937. As Ernest told Anglo's shareholders soon afterwards: 'I am satisfied that in due course N'Changa Consolidated Copper Mines Ltd will take its place among the large successful copper producers of the world.' How right he was.

Ernest still hoped to bring about the amalgamation of all the Rhodesian copper interests, though the chances of achieving this seemed progressively more remote. Relations between the two rival groups were cordial: each had feet firmly placed in the other's camps. But there was disagreement over control of the whole. Were the Americans to be allowed to dominate the situation, or should it remain a British concern? Ernest's position was unequivocal as ever: 'British control of the copper-fields is a point for which I have fought from the start and I would on no account take steps which would jeopardize that position.'

As it happened he faced a control crisis not in copper at all, but at Broken Hill. Anglo had been involved in Edmund Davis's lead and zinc producer from the early days, both as chartered engineers and secretaries: Anglo's offices had been at Broken Hill before they were moved to Salisbury. The Depression had hit Broken Hill particularly hard and the mine had closed down. In the years since it had resumed operations, but with disappointing results. The zinc market had not recovered as fast as others. Broken Hill would need drastic financial reorganisation if it was to keep its head above water.

Edmund Davis was based in England now, but was still chairman of Broken Hill. Out of the blue he wrote to Ernest from London telling him Chester Beatty's group was making a proposition. He would inject capital on condition the constitution of the board was changed to give him control. Ernest could hardly believe his eyes. It was the first time he had heard about it. What was Edmund Davis up to? Why had he not asked Rhoanglo first?

The whole situation was rather embarrassing. 'I have not had the chance of looking into the merits of the scheme outlined by Edmund Davis,' wrote Ernest. 'But it at once struck me as odd that he should discuss the matter so fully with the Chester Beatty people without reference to us.'

Davis had to apologise.

'I never had the slightest idea that you would like the Anglo American to look into the business.'

Selection Trust wanted to make a thorough investigation of Broken Hill before exercising its option. Beatty allowed it to lapse, and came up with a second offer. Edmund Davis asked him to give Rhoanglo some sort of participation but this he refused categorically. At the same time Ernest refused absolutely to have anything to do with the scheme if he was to be given only a minority interest, and tendered his resignation from the Broken Hill board. Had it been accepted, relations between Rhoanglo and Selection Trust would have broken down completely, and relations between Ernest and Chester Beatty in the diamond world would have been strained to breaking point. But fortunately things did not go that far.

In the end honour was satisfied and a dangerous impasse averted. The Broken Hill board rejected Selection Trust's new bid and instead eventually accepted a proposition from Ernest's camp, in keeping with the arrangements that had held before. The price of zinc was rising, and there was the prospect of a breakthrough in the price of lead even if for the moment it was unprofitable. Broken Hill should prove a major asset.

If Anglo's affairs were on the up, so was Ernest's personal life. Ina was proving a most charming consort: perfect hostess, attractive companion, accomplished home-maker. Ernest adored her. Already she was established as one of the most popular figures in Johannesburg society: she took to her new role of magnate's wife as if she had been born to it.

Ernest was close to Ina, but if anything closer still to Harry. His son was now comfortably installed in Little Brenthurst, and was full of plans for what he wanted to do with the cottage. Each day he was with his father, listening to his advice, discussing the day-to-day operations of Anglo in all their manifestations. He was preparing for the day he would take over the reins.

Certainly Anglo's progress was impressive. The staff was getting so big that even Anmercosa House seemed cramped. Anglo would have to look for yet more premises. This time Ernest decided they should start from scratch and build their own headquarters from the ground up, to their own needs and with a view to the future. With a touch of whimsy Ernest arranged the purchase of a large plot of ground in a part of Johannesburg rather depressed of late, certainly 'at the wrong end of town.' It was the original site of Ferreira's Camp, where the Reef's first claims had been pegged. What more appropriate site for the head office of the Anglo American?

173

Consulting architects were brought in from London, and in a remarkably short time their designs were approved, the working plans were drawn up, the site excavated – to reveal signs of those old gold workings that made it all the more attractive – and the foundation stone laid. Slowly it rose above the skyscape, a great monument of a building framed in steel and concrete and faced with Ficksburg freestone, simple but attractive, with courtyards inset on each side to allow fountains and lawns, so that each room in the building was outward facing and looked down upon a little patch of blue and green.

At last it was ready: not all that high, only five floors, but comfortable and functional and in the architects' eye good for years to come. There was little decoration bar bronze sculpture in the great doors at the entrance, a frieze carved in the stonework outside, and a great etched glass window in the entrance hall. This decoration was deliberately African in character. Now all that remained was to name the building. Of all the possibilities open to him Ernest selected the postal address – 44 Main Street. Name-choosing had never been his forte.

One result of the increased tempo of Anglo's world was that Ernest had no time for his outside interests. One of the first to suffer had been his parliamentary career: he had not made a speech the whole of the session. True, there had been no great need: the economy was now prospering once again, and in any case the government included several former SAPs who could be relied upon to exert strong influence if the Nationalists pressed any more of their old ideas for nationalisation.

Ernest had enjoyed himself in parliament. He could not attend its sessions as regularly as he would have liked, but that could not be helped. Instead, his contributions in those early years had been definitive: great speeches on financial affairs and trade, gold and diamonds, all the things that really counted in the South African economy. For years he had been without peer in these fields, and when it was known he would be making a speech the House was packed.

He enjoyed the social side of parliament too. He was never too busy or too rushed to enjoy a quiet chat with other members in the dining room or the bar. Some of them were quite taken aback when he came up to them in the lobby, greeted them by name and invited them to join him. This was the biggest magnate of them all, and it might be expected he would have more important things on his mind than remembering the names of people he had met perhaps once in his life.

When they reached the bar or the dining-room Ernest would be able to remember just what they wanted to drink. 'Whisky and water with ice, wasn't it?' or 'You have tea and lemon, no sugar. Isn't that right?'

174

To less prominent members, already overawed in the presence of the famed 'Hoggenheimer', this must have seemed incredible: something to tell their grandchildren. Not surprisingly Ernest was soon credited with phenomenal powers of memory.

These he had, certainly: but there was more to it than that. He admitted to his friends that one of the soundest pieces of advice his father had given him was to learn to remember names and faces. That was the basis of everything in life, he had said. For as far back as Ernest could recall he had been developing this technique. At Anglo, for instance, when he saw a face he did not know, he made a point of going up and asking the newcomer his name, and tried to greet him personally when he saw him again.

Sometimes this backfired. One day Ernest was expecting the American ambassador for lunch at 44 Main Street when he suddenly realised he was short of cigars. He button-holed a man he found walking down the corridor past the directors' dining-room, and asked him to collect a box of cigars from his secretary's office and bring them as fast as he could. Only when the man returned and introduced himself did Ernest realise this was his lunch guest in person.

There were other occasions when Ernest greeted someone in the Anglo building and asked how he was enjoying working for the corporation, only to be told the man had no connection with it at all. But in general his whole approach was perfectly logical. The personal touch helped a new man to feel he belonged, and he would then give of his best.

On occasion, though, Ernest cheated a little and gave himself a flying start. Parliament was one of the places he allowed himself some fun. Each member had a desk inside the debating chamber and Ernest kept a chart in his on which he mapped out all the seats in the house with the appropriate names against their numbers and also telling personal details like the 'whisky and water' touch. During the less gripping debates he would look round the house, memorising the names and faces of all the members in relation to his chart – and choosing who to surprise when next he bumped into him in the lobby.

The one thing that disappointed Ernest in parliament was that there had never been an opportunity for him to achieve cabinet responsibility. For the first ten years Smuts and the South African Party had been in opposition. Even with coalition in 1934 Ernest was left out in the cold, for to Smuts and Hertzog trying to rally Afrikaners to their standard the presence of 'Hoggenheimer' was more of a liability than an asset. Gracefully, with no further goals in his political career, Ernest

175

announced he would not be standing in the general election of 1938.

All this time the world had been watching the extraordinary developments in Europe. Hitler and Mussolini were invading country after country and getting away with it every time. As their successes mounted many of the Nationalists in South Africa became increasingly excited. Should they not ally themselves with the Axis powers and share in their triumphs? Hitler would dominate the world and grant South Africa true independence as a republic outside the sphere of British influence.

These feelings simmered on just below the surface until Hitler invaded Poland, and Britain and France declared war on Germany. Suddenly they came out in the open. There was a debate in the South African Parliament on the question whether South Africa should follow Britain's example and declare war. Already there was disagreement in the cabinet. Smuts said she should, while Hertzog urged neutrality at best and in explaining his views to Parliament seemed to favour the Nazi side. Parliament came out for Smuts and Hertzog resigned, taking many of his followers with him to join forces with a small group of hard-line Afrikaners that had refused to join the coalition. Led by D F Malan, Smuts's political arch-opponent, they were known as the 'purified' Nationalists, the Herenigde Nasionale Party.

The crisis came as rather an anti-climax. Far from the general conflagration that was expected, Europe settled into months of 'phony' war when nothing very much happened. Only when Hitler began his blitzkrieg against France and Britain and Mussolini joined in and sent planes to harass Kenya did Smuts act. Calling for volunteers to serve 'anywhere in Africa' for four years, he hurried men northwards to defend British civilisation in East Africa. The Union was finally committed.

Not long before this Ernest had invited Smuts and his lifelong friend Deneys Reitz to travel to Goma in the Congo for a few days to watch an eruption of the volcano Myamlagyra with a mile-long stream of lava flowing down the mountain into Lake Kivu. Harry went with them, and when they rested for a day at Zomba in Nyasaland he accompanied the general on a walk up a hill behind the town. If the truth be known, he was a little overawed in the presence of the great statesman: he did not yet know him well. At the top there was a magnificent view over a wide lake. The two men were alone.

'I am glad to see more of Africa while there is still time,' said Smuts. 'Evil forces are moving in the world and the Commonwealth will face a great test. I do not think there will be more such holidays for many years to come.'

He looked out over the miles of quiet water to the distant shores on the horizon, and turned again to Harry. He was speaking gently now.

'It is wonderful to be an African.'

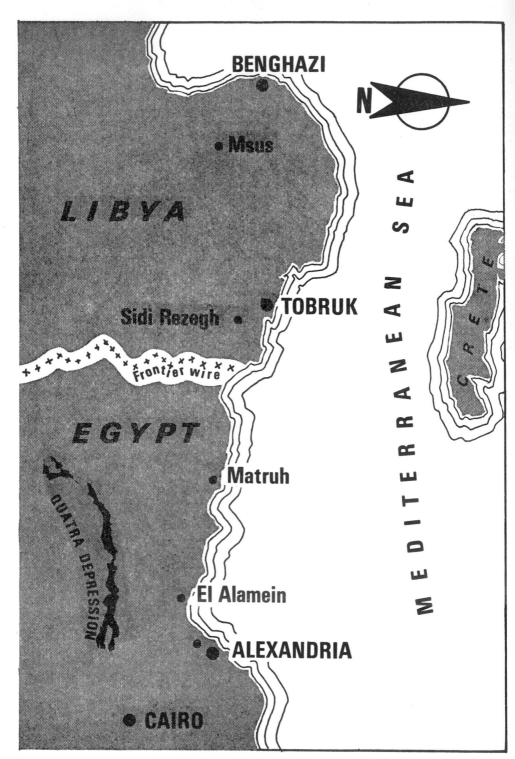

THE WESTERN DESERT

Desert Rat

L IKE THE other Dominions, South Africa was preparing to mobi-
    lise. Among the first to volunteer for service 'anywhere in Africa'
was Harry, who applied for inclusion in the Reserve of Officers, Union
Defence Force, on January 26 1940: 'I Hereby Certify that, to the
best of my knowledge, I am in good health and in all respects fit for
military service.' A few days later he was officially appointed to the
Reserve with the rank of temporary 2nd Lieutenant. As a senior execu-
tive of Anglo and De Beers it was possible he would be left well alone.
Instead, within two months he was called up for full-time duty in the
Defence Force Intelligence Section. He was sent on two training
courses near Pretoria, and emerged with flying colours and a splendidly
South African comment on his lack of Afrikaans: 'Unilingual. Knows
French and German.'

    After several months in the Chief of General Staff's section in Pretoria
Harry applied for a transfer to No 5 Armoured Car Company, South
African Tank Corps, a new body in camp near the Premier at Cullinan.
He wanted to see some action on the fighting fronts, and decided he
would be better off in a mounted regiment than on foot. There were
already three South African armoured car companies in action in East
Africa, fighting the Italians. They had enjoyed great success, and it was
supposed the several companies newly formed would soon join
them.

    The 5th was sent to train in the flat bushveld of Bechuanaland, not
unlike Abyssinia, before at last its orders arrived. It was to proceed to
Durban and embark not for Abyssinia, as Italian opposition had been
virtually wiped out, but for North Africa. Where before the British and
Italians had maintained an uneasy balance on their respective sides of
the border between Egypt and Libya, the situation had changed

radically with the arrival of a full German army secretly shipped over from Europe: General Rommel's crack Afrikakorps.

Harry's company – by now renamed the 4th South African Armoured Car Regiment – sailed for North Africa on board the *Empress of Australia*, with thousands more Allied troops. Disembarking at Port Tewfik at the southern end of the Suez Canal, they were entrained for Alexandria where they soon met their first taste of a world at war. With several important warships in the port, there were heavy German bombing raids each night. After a few days the regiment was taken to El Amiriya in the desert for full-scale training exercises, as desolate a spot as Alexandria was exciting.

The regiment's own officers were left to supervise the training programme. One day Harry was detailed to instruct a squad in handling a machine-gun when a dogfight developed overhead. Two British Hurricanes were pursuing a German JU 88 bomber. They crippled it and the German dived in to hit the ground with a terrifying crash only 200 yards from Harry's squad. The South Africans began running towards the plane with Harry in the middle. He explained later his idea was that if he ran in front it would look as if he was encouraging the men, and if he ran at the back it would look as if he was cowardly. When they reached the JU 88 they found two of its crew were dead, with the remaining two still alive but badly hurt. As Harry arrived he found one of his men holding the head of one of the wounded Germans and trying to comfort him. 'It's all right, we're all friends here.' Harry said afterwards it gave him the idea war was all rather silly.

After the failure of the recent 'Battleaxe' offensive mounted by General Wavell of the 7th Armoured Division, there was now an uneasy stalemate along the 350-mile wire fence erected on Mussolini's orders to mark the border. The Libyan side was held by well-equipped Italian and German armoured divisions and largely responsible for holding the Egyptian side was the famous Desert Rats armoured car regiment, the 11th Hussars. The regiment had been stationed in the Egyptian desert for years, and was best equipped and most mobile of all forces involved in the area. Now it was attached to the 7th Armoured Division, providing both its eyes and its ears. But the Desert Rats had taken a beating in their long patrol and needed a rest. The 4th South African Armoured Cars were sent in to replace them.

Conditions at the front were very different from those the South Africans had trained in. Now they had to survive the heat of the desert with shale, scrub, winds, intense heat by day and intense cold by night, sandstorms and mirages, sudden downpours and relentless insects,

180

landmines and booby traps. The men in the front line had only the most meagre rations of bully beef and biscuits with tinned meat and vegetables as a rare treat, and no opportunity to cook in case the enemy spotted the smoke. Some caught scurvy and their wounds would not heal. Others went down with jaundice or sandfly fever, or developed the uncomfortable 'Gyppo tummy' that was everywhere an occupational hazard. What little water there was went down radiators before throats, and petrol was more plentiful: men used it to wash their clothes. Crews slept beside their cars with one man on watch, but the dew was so heavy that long before the night was over bedding rolls were soaked.

At first there was little for the newcomers to do: long hours sitting on top of their cars scanning the horizon for signs of movement, watching from suitable vantage points on the higher ground at all hours of the day before retiring some distance for the night and returning to their original positions the next day. At times crews would go six or seven days without a single glimpse of the enemy, and even when they did spot movement over the wire it would be at great distance. The only breaks in the monotony were isolated strafings from roving Messerschmitts, or an occasional shell from a tank across the wire.

That was the situation for weeks, and the South Africans had time to settle in to their new role. No longer were they a bunch of rookies from civvy street, but rather an efficient team hardened by the rigours of the desert life. The regiment was organised in four principal parts: three squadrons of four troops each spread along the front line to observe enemy movements, and regimental headquarters some way behind. The troops took turns to patrol the front line a few days at a time, and then rested before returning for further duty. The front cars were in radio contact with a squadron car stationed further back, and the three squadron headquarters were in touch with Harry's radio operators at *regimental* headquarters. It was Harry's job to collate all the information that came through, build a composite picture and in conjunction with the regimental commander (Lt-Col D S Newton-King) and his second-in-command (Major Craig Anderson) decide what should be transmitted to *divisional* headquarters.

Much of the wireless work was in morse cipher, but much again was oral and there was a strong possibility that it might be picked up by the enemy. Harry devised a simple code to confuse the issue in case that happened: for example, Nuts Monkey Sugar for No Movement Sighted. The code was adopted by other units and proved a major help. But wireless interception worked both ways. Harry was able to listen in to enemy transmissions and as he spoke good German easily understood what was being said. It was he who picked up forewarning of what promised to be a major German offensive in mid-September.

The attack came the next night, with the sounds of revving engines beyond the fence at one o'clock in the morning. The armoured cars were instructed to withdraw and keep out of trouble, but at the same time to watch the enemy's every move. At first light the crews boldly advanced to within sight of the advancing tanks and could at last see what they were up against: a whole Panzer division pressing forward in three columns. Had they but known, General Rommel himself was pushing on among the forward troops, as usual keen to direct the manoeuvres personally. It was a reconnaissance in force designed to cut off a large section of the British forces, and open the route to Alexandria and Cairo.

The South Africans had to withdraw, though without losing touch with the enemy. It was the 4th's first experience of an enemy thrust, and it came as a considerable surprise. The enemy was moving forward through the open desert at a speed of 30 mph or more – so fast that in spite of warnings from the forward squadrons regimental headquarters was almost caught napping. Enemy tanks sweeping south nearly cut them off, and when the three squadron headquarters continued to report the enemy's movements Harry had to tell them there was no need to bother: he could see the enemy perfectly well from his own position.

Just then regimental headquarters was shelled, and with the enemy tanks no more than a mile away and advancing fast, Newton-King's armoured car broke down. It had to be set on fire and abandoned. Newton-King and Harry and their driver were lucky to be picked up by a passing 25-pounder from the Royal Horse Artillery and escaped what appeared certain capture. The 4th's orderly room was less fortunate. Its truck broke down shortly afterwards and the staff of three fell into German hands with important documents and cipher material undestroyed. Among the documents was a list of all the men in the regiment. This was sent off to the German propaganda station Zeesen, which soon broadcast all the names with the claim that the soldiers concerned had been captured or killed. Included among these 'casualties' was Harry, but fortunately the news did not reach Brenthurst.

Throughout the day the armoured cars continued to shadow and harry the German tanks, still moving forward in a bid to break the British defences. But it was unsuccessful. The Germans had moved too fast for their own transport columns, and that night the Panzer Division's commander, Von Ravenstein, had to call off his thrust and turn back. The manoeuvre was a failure, and Rommel's troops were back where they had started.

The action had given the 4th its first taste of 'the real thing'. But it revealed the sad inadequacy of its equipment. The armour-plating on the Marmon-Harrington cars was of poor quality, designed to withstand only small arms fire and shrapnel and no match at all for direct shells from tanks and 'needle' bullets from the air. Rumour was that a ·303 rifle bullet could go straight through. By accident the crews had found that at any rate with the 'needle' bullets from raiding aircraft, it helped to pad the outsides of the cars with bedding rolls, mattresses, or anything that would soften the impact and 'mushroom' the bullets. In action the cars sometimes came to look like Chinese laundries.

In all this time the line of demarcation in North Africa had been plain: Mussolini's barbed wire fence, stretching into the interior as far as the eye could see. But there was one thorn in Rommel's flesh which was proving to have more than nuisance value. The harbour fortress of Tobruk, well inside Libyan territory, had been occupied by Allied troops from the outset of hostilities and in spite of intensive siege had so far held out with colours flying. For some time the British had been preparing to attempt the fortress's relief and on the night of November 17 1941, the great land armada of the Eighth Army rolled through the wire into Libya. Operation Crusader was aiming at the destruction of Rommel's armour, the recapture of Cyrenaica and the relief of Tobruk.

The armoured car regiments led the way: the 4th South Africans and the 3rd SA Recce Battalion, the 11th Hussars and the King's Dragoons. Each was heading a division, in line abreast as they swung through the wire for the west, then wheeled right to the north for the move towards the rings of defences laid round Tobruk by the Germans and the Italians. The army was moving on a forty-mile front with the armoured cars instructed to force their way through the enemy lines and pinpoint the chief German concentrations.

Rain was pouring down and scores of vehicles stuck in deep mud. The 4th's squadrons were luckier than most and moved ahead fast, until they came to the lonely tomb of the Moslem saint Sidi Rezegh, a landmark for miles around. At this time the regiment was the furthest westward of any unit in the Eighth Army. Looking down from high ground, the crews could see an aerodrome with 15 planes on the ground preparing to take off. Rushing down the hill with guns blazing they hit plane after plane, some even as they were taking off. It was a notable victory, for before this armoured cars had been regarded only as reconnaissance vehicles.

Soon enemy reinforcements appeared over the hills, and the cars could go no further. They had reached the concentrations of enemy tanks, the great Panzer divisions that would soon spend four days battling with their counterparts in the Eighth Army for the precious ground between Sidi Rezegh and Tobruk. The British tanks arrived and passed through the lines of armoured cars, and the attack was on. Tanks, infantry, supply columns from both sides criss-crossed the desert of the fighting zone, and it was difficult to know which vehicles belonged to which side. Several times the armoured cars were caught unprepared – even regimental headquarters, as recorded by Harry in the diary he kept.

'At 0630 hours Regimental Headquarters, which had just started to move North in order to get closer to Brigade Headquarters, found itself in the path of a dawn attack by the enemy infantry with anti-tank guns. RHQ joined in a general scurry for a short distance east, speeded on its way by a fine display of tracer fire from machine-guns and anti-tank guns.'

The German infantry made another attack at 8 o'clock, this time with artillery cover, but were beaten back by the batteries of the 4th Royal Horse Artillery attached to the 7th Armoured Division.

'RHQ had (rather rashly perhaps) parked next to a battery of 25 pounders, which were shelling the enemy position on the Sidi Rezegh ridge to the north west. This idyllic state of affairs came to an end at 0830 hours when the enemy artillery got the range of these guns (and incidentally of RHQ) with unpleasant accuracy. A rapid move of a few hundred yards became necessary, and such was the urgency of the case that RHQ's tea and sausages, which had just then been prepared, were left to waste their sweetness on the desert air. The 25-pounders were forced to pull out also, but not so fast but that a gunner (evidently a man of unusual presence of mind) contrived to carry off RHQ's breakfast with him. He undoubtedly deserved the tea and sausages, but he might perhaps have left (or anyhow returned) the plates and mugs.'

Most of the day the squadrons of the 4th and indeed of the other armoured car regiments involved could take no great part in the preliminaries to the battle ahead. All they could do was harrass the enemy at intervals and keep a close watch on every aspect of his movements. All was relayed to Harry at regimental headquarters, which was itself involved in violent action. At 1620 hours that day it was attacked by

184

15 Stuka dive-bombers – though as Harry laconically recorded the height at which the pilots pulled out of their dives suggested they were Italian. 'There was much sound, smoke and fury but no casualties, though minor damage was done to a wireless-van and to the Technical Officers' truck. The twin coaxially-mounted Bren in Major Anderson's armoured car was seen in action for the first time and certainly made a fine encouraging noise.'

Next day, November 21, the battle was still fierce. Squadrons of the 4th played cat and mouse with divisions of the enemy, approaching as close as they dared to make an accurate assessment of their strength, and then speeding for the shelter of a convenient wadi or the safety of their own lines.

In the afternoon a new super-offensive got under way, and according to Harry regimental headquarters 'found themselves, as usual, on the fringe of the tank battle and were forced to beat a hasty retreat to the west with shells bursting very close indeed. As they moved west they came under small-arms fire from infantry dug in on the ridge immediately to the north.' The two Command vehicles, Harry in one of them, returned this fire and also opened up on an enemy armoured car.

'All this time the tank battle was raging, and at last 22nd Armoured Brigade appeared from the west, and at 1650 hours were sweeping in majestic waves past Regimental Headquarters as they moved into battle. It was a fine array and at that time it seemed to us that within the next half-hour General Rommel's final defeat would be accomplished. As darkness fell, pierced by the innumerable tracers of the continuing tank battle, we vainly imagined that during the next few days we should be helping to collect the spoils of victory.'

But as sometimes happened in the desert war, organisation on the British side had gone haywire, and with communications between different units fractured beyond hope, Rommel's Panzers regrouped themselves and swept in for what could have been a resounding defeat for the Eighth Army.

The purpose of the whole exercise was to relieve Tobruk, and to that end it was arranged there should be a sortie made by the besieged troops in an effort to link up with the relief column. Two South African brigades, the 1st and the 5th, were detailed to forge the link with Tobruk. The 5th was already in position, but when the 1st tried to move north to make contact it found the way blocked by a strong column of German tanks. The two brigades were cut off. Though the 5th tried to break through the lines of German infantry in making for

Tobruk, it was beaten back and on orders began digging defences in anticipation of an attack from the north.

The battle's third day dawned cold and wet, and continued like that with showers and a biting wind. The Allied formations were becoming increasingly dismayed and confused over what was expected of them. The armoured brigades had taken a bad beating at the hands of the better equipped Panzer regiments, and were in no position to retaliate. 'The fog of battle was dense,' wrote Harry, 'and in consequence the idea of a definitely prescribed line of observation largely lost its significance.'

The confusion reached to the highest levels. At 0750 one of the 4th's troop leaders reported he had come under heavy shelling from a strong enemy column which included 100 tanks. When this information was passed on to higher authority it was suggested the report must be utterly wrong. There could be no column in that vicinity, or at least if there was it could not be hostile. Soon there was ample evidence that the column was only too real and very far from being friendly when it wheeled due west and crashed through the transport echelon of the 5th South African Brigade. It was in fact the 15th Panzer Division. Armoured cars went to investigate what was happening and established beyond doubt that it was an enemy column that was involved. Not only the 4th, but also the 3rd South African Recce Battalion passed regular messages back to headquarters of the 7th Division, warning of the danger to the 5th South African Brigade. The 4th's headquarters was now to the west of the brigade, and Newton-King could see that all preparations had been made in anticipation of an attack from the north. There was heavy shell-fire from that direction, certainly, but he could see the major threat was from the southwest. The guns were pointing the wrong way.

After repeated wireless messages to divisional headquarters Newton-King eventually sent personal runners to the brigade commander to warn him what was happening and arrange immediate evacuation. But still nothing was done: the commander was not prepared to take the warning seriously.

The enemy's tanks were getting closer, heading straight for the brigade's camp. Reaching it ahead of them the 4th found the men it contained entirely oblivious to the danger they were in. Their commander had not told them, still disbelieving the reports. Newton-King's car was flagged down by an officer and he and Harry were asked what they thought they were doing travelling through the camp so fast. Did they not realise there was a 10 mph speed limit?

'At 1505 hours the enemy started to move his tanks north towards the 5th Brigade. In front were 25 tanks in line abreast and behind them embussed infantry and 8 large guns with tractors. The remainder of the tanks and B echelon vehicles were well in the rear.

'Our Regimental Headquarters now moved through the South African camp and took up a position on a ridge about 1 500 yards to the east, from where to report the battle. Shells were already falling in the camp, but there had been a certain amount of shelling all day . . .

'At 1530 hours the enemy tanks were rapidly moving in to attack. Our infantry were lying in shallow slit trenches, which did not appear to be laid out according to any plan. Almost all our artillery was facing north and for the most part the closely concentrated Brigade transport was between the guns and the enemy . . .'

As a fighting unit, the 5th Brigade almost ceased to exist. Its loss was 3 394 men, most of them taken prisoner. But though they went down, they took many Germans with them. The Panzer Division lost more than 60 tanks in the engagement, due to intensive fire from the gallant defenders.

Next day the desert was crowded with swiftly moving enemy columns and an ill-ordered scurry of Eighth Army transport vehicles fleeing before them. The scramble became known as the 'Matruh Stakes', a race to see who could reach the railhead first. In all the confusion the 4th was doing its best to keep in touch with what was happening, at the same time beginning a highly successful campaign against the enemy's 'thin skinned' vehicles in spite of strong coverage from tanks.

Regimental headquarters was not to be left out of the fun, and when it came across a cruiser tank which had run out of petrol but was otherwise sound, secured its crew's co-operation in return for fuel. The tank was a 'cat', named for its sleek appearance. At 1525 the command cars and the 'cat' moved steadily forward towards the enemy column. 'The RHQ plan was for the "cat" to creep up unseen to a victim while the two command cars moved to a prominent place to attract the enemy,' wrote Harry. But the effort was in vain. 'Unfortunately the greater range of the German tank guns defeated our "cat"; but RHQ's part of attracting the Germans' attention was uncomfortably successful.'

Meanwhile the 4th was taking prisoners and these were sent to regimental headquarters for interrogation. They found themselves confronted by Harry, who probably spoke better German than any other officer in the Eighth Army. He was able to extract much information which was to prove invaluable to the Eighth Army at large, quite apart from what he picked up from intercepted wireless messages.

When captured, German soldiers were only too anxious to co-operate. Involved in their units they were disciplined and co-ordinated, but it was not unusual to find that in captivity their morale broke and their loyalties dissolved. 'Rommel', they would curse, and spit upon the ground. In contrast Italians would smile happily when captured, as if relieved to be free of their responsibilities. They would try to make friends with their captors by offering them cigarettes.

General Rommel himself, in the meantime, was attempting a bold thrust towards the British rear. As usual up with the first of his men, he was trying to isolate the British divisions from their transport lines. But he was in trouble. His vehicles were suffering badly, both from the rugged terrain and from consistent attacks by the British. Besides, his own transport lines were broken. Despondently he had to cut his losses and quickly run to the area of Sidi Rezegh and Tobruk. He was too late, and his advantage was wasted. Though badly shaken in the four-day tank battle, the Eighth Army had regrouped and was back to full strength with the arrival of reinforcements.

The units of the Eighth Army were given new roles to play. The 4th was sent on a special mission to the *west* of Tobruk, this time not only to observe what was going on but to do what it could to disrupt communications along the coastal road. After being spotted by a flight of low-flying Stukas, the regiment completed the march by night and took up position in time to make early captures of Italian vehicles. Though a number fell into enemy hands when they were driven off in completely the wrong direction, more than 30 were duly captured and escorted back to the Eighth Army headquarters, with many prisoners. But there was trouble ahead. 'In the early afternoon, enemy reconnaissance planes started methodically quartering the ground, searching for us, and it was plain that our fears of air attack were going to be realised.' The crunch came at about 1600 hours when 'A' squadron was attacked unremittingly for half an hour by eight Me 110's. It was a tricky situation. Now the enemy knew exactly where the Regiment could not hold its ground in the face of such concentrated air attack without its own fighter support or even anti-aircraft guns. After consultation with 7th Armoured Division Newton-King decided it was time to withdraw.

Harry summed up the results of the raid:

'No practicable way down the escarpment was found by our patrols, and the coastal road was therefore never reached. On the other hand the presence of our forces so far west may well have been disconcerting to the enemy, who possibly attached more importance to the Regiment's activities than was really justified.'

The regiment pulled back, but not without heavy casualties. 'A' squadron came in for more heavy punishment from the air, machine-gunned for another half an hour. The troops lost three armoured cars and all their thin-skinned vehicles. After a mauling like that, the regiment needed a rest. In the first week of December it was granted, and the 4th was sent back to Tobruk for what promised to be an extended refit. They would remain at the El Adem repair base for two weeks, and every vehicle would be overhauled.

It looked as if the withdrawal would mark the end of the regiment's part in the Crusader offensive, and the end of its association with the 7th Armoured Division. As a mark of respect for what the South Africans had achieved, the crack British unit awarded them a most unusual battle honour: the right to wear their famous emblem, the Desert Rat, which they had themselves adopted from the 11th Hussars. The evolution was complete, and the Hussars and the Springboks were on equal terms.

When they reached El Adem, the battle front now hundreds of miles away as British reinforcements chased Rommel along the coast, Harry took the opportunity of sending a truck all the way to Cairo and back to pick up a load of luxury items for his colleagues in the regiment. It was a personal gesture, a contribution to the well-being of the regiment as a whole, and entirely at his own expense. He seemed rather embarrassed when others in the regiment tried to thank him.

Meanwhile, Rommel was beaten, or so it seemed. Whatever the losses he had inflicted on the British, his were as great and he could no longer besiege Tobruk. Over the next week he withdrew the German and Italian armies, leaving in his wake isolated frontier garrisons to be besieged in their turn. Back he went and further, the length of the coastal strip between the central plateau and the sea. The British were in fast pursuit, armoured car regiments and tank corps together, but as they progressed further and further away from supplies. Harried by units travelling parallel to his forces but to the south, Rommel and his troops were driven to Benghazi and beyond to El Agheila.

But appearances were deceptive. Just as it had seemed Rommel had the British on the run after the battles of Sidi Rezegh only to be foiled by his own transport problem, now the same thing happened to the

British. As their communications became more and more tenuous, particularly in respect of fuel, Rommel's grew all the stronger. In late January he was able to regroup his battered formations and with reinforcements quickly turned the tables. The Panzers were on the rampage all over again, and it was the turn of the British to withdraw in confusion.

The Germans began their push on January 21. Directly in their path was the British 1st Armoured Division, which had only just arrived in the desert. It was engaged on an exercise at Msus in the interior, a model of an attack destined for El Agheila. The general in command had decided to dispense with armoured car cover for the time as all available regiments were in such urgent need of overhaul. His unsuspecting tank crews had barely settled into their exercise when they suddenly found themselves confronted by a German Panzer division making a reconnaissance in force and routing them in quick time.

Eighth Army flashed a signal to Newton-King, with the 4th Armoured Cars at El Adem and only a few days into the fortnight's rest and recreation that had been promised. The regiment was to report immediately to the 1st Armoured Division.

The road to Msus was crowded with transport vehicles fleeing with tales of speeding panzers and a British rout, but the 4th pressed on. When the cars reached Msus they found the panzers all right, but no trace of the Eighth Army. After many vain attempts regimental headquarters managed to make radio contact with the 1st Armoured Division, 20 miles to the north. Its morale was pitifully low and its commanders were wholly out of touch with the German forces apart from what they now heard from the armoured cars.

But in the end all was well. The Germans did not press their advantage, and with the 4th providing reconnaissance cover the 1st Armoured Division regrouped and made its way back towards Tobruk as rearguard of the whole force. There the British had entrenched themselves along the Gazala Line, a deep belt of complex wire emplacements and minefields and fortified 'boxes' each held by a brigade, reaching down from the coast to a point 40 miles inland.

The 4th came under the wing of the 7th Armoured Division all over again, patrolling the desert to the far south of the Gazala Line with the individual squadrons sometimes as far as 70 miles out into no-man's-land. It was assumed that Rommel would want to penetrate the Gazala Line to win through to Tobruk, and the whole object of the defence was to oppose him. Several commanders warned that he was more likely to try and outflank the line and win through from behind, but they were disregarded on the grounds that it was too bold a plan. Instead, that is exactly what the great general tried to do: the German and Italian forces set out with 10 000 vehicles, tanks and guns. The 4th soon had the measure of them, and realising that something big was afoot kept close watch on every move they made. Though Harry kept up a virtual running commentary over the wireless as the Germans swung round, nobody took much notice. Divisional headquarters was rounded up *in toto* by the advancing panzers, and the division's commanding officer – the general who had been surprised at Msus – was captured in his pyjamas.

Rommel came round the back. His aim was to circumvent the Gazala Line and trap the British and he very nearly succeeded. Only a determined break-out through enemy lines saved whole divisions from falling into German hands. Tobruk was left to its fate, with the 1st South African Division trapped inside and ordered to hold on to the last. As the rest of the Eighth Army pressed on for safety in Egypt the South Africans and their allies attempted a gallant stand against overwhelming odds. But it was in vain. As Harry recorded on June 21, rather laconically: 'An exceptionally hot day. Tobruk fell during the morning, which was an unexpected blow.'

The British fell back over the border and almost to the gates of Alexandria. General Auchinleck, the British commander, had decided to stake everything on a bottleneck the Germans would have to traverse if they were to reach Alexandria and Cairo. To the north was the sea, and to the south was the Qattara Depression, a large area of practically impassable desert and quicksand. That left a line of 35 miles already heavily defended with fortifications built at an earlier stage of the war and now manned by troops fresh to the conflict, with more reinforcements to come. As the battle-worn units arrived after their long withdrawal from Tobruk, they took their places in the elaborate defence network. The 4th was allocated an area to the south of the line, forward of the 7th Armoured Division. The stage was set for the battle which was to turn the tide of the war in North Africa once and for all. The engagement took its name from a tiny hamlet on the railway near the coast. It was called El Alamein.

2

HARRY WAS doing his bit, but then so were the others in his family. Ernest and the enterprises he controlled were key factors in the

British and Commonwealth war effort, as Churchill and Smuts understood only too well: in fact, Smuts was more than a little worried by Harry's absence in the desert war. If anything was to happen to him, who would succeed Ernest? More than once the statesman tried to prevail on Ernest to bring his son back to the Union. It was a matter of crucial importance to South Africa's future.

Ina's contribution to the war effort was along rather different lines. She was thinking of the men absent at the front, and decided to organise a scheme to raise the money to buy them the little luxuries that would make their active service life a little more comfortable. In company with Doff Susskind and her other friends in Johannesburg she initiated what came to be called the Caledonian Market.

It all began in a fairly modest way, but soon mushroomed. More than a hundred volunteer workers were mobilised, manning the basement of Paramount Stores in Johannesburg, which was specially provided by its owner, Sam Cohen. The women set up stalls to sell anything that was presented to them.

Among the first donors was Ernest, who gave Ina a diamond worth £2 000. She and her committee decided to sell it by raffle, and asked for 1s a ticket. When Ernest heard that he could hardly believe it: a shilling for his beautiful diamond? How could they expect to make money if they charged so little? In the event, though, they did not lose, and at least made up the £2 000 the diamond was worth.

It was a different story the next year, when Ina and her helpers were selling 1s tickets for raffles with prizes worth £50 or £25. From a series of these they made £6 000. Ernest naturally wanted to know why they hadn't made that much with his diamond? They couldn't have been working hard enough!

Then Ernest and Ina had another idea. They knew how crowded the Johannesburg hospitals were becoming with men invalided back from the fronts, while they themselves had all that space at Brenthurst. They did not need it: shouldn't they rather give it to someone who did? They moved down to Harry's cottage and handed the big house over to the Red Cross. Brenthurst and its grounds ought to make an ideal convalescent home.

That was the intention, certainly, and when Janet Ford of the Johannesburg General Hospital was made matron she equipped the house accordingly, converting all the bedrooms to wards with equipment bought out of Ernest's pocket and helped by Anglo's buying department until all was ready for the official opening by General Smuts towards the middle of 1941.

The first patients arrived in plenty of time for the opening – not really the type that Ernest and Ina had in mind at all but rather a mixed collection. Many of them had not even left South Africa. Some were suffering from ingrowing toenails provoked by ill-fitting army boots, others were recovering from operations for appendicitis or hernia. On the day of the opening Matron Ford was hard put to persuade them to take to their beds and look convincingly sick as the Prime Minister and the other guests made the rounds.

By this time, though, there were more ambitious plans afoot. Ernest and Ina had been approached by a young army surgeon just back from special training in Britain which he now wanted to put into effect. He had asked the army for the opportunity, but they had decided there was not enough scope: rather take a desk job, they told him, and be promoted. Higher rank held no attraction for him, and when he spotted an item about Brenthurst in the *Rand Daily Mail* he asked his superiors if there was any chance of taking it over. They replied it was nothing to do with them but that he was welcome to approach the Oppenheimers himself and see what they had to say.

The young doctor was Jack Penn, and the training he had been given was in plastic surgery: rather special plastic surgery, in that he had been working with now legendary figures like Gillies, McIndoe, Mowlem and Kilner in treating the casualties of the Battle of Britain and the London Blitz. In sending Penn to Britain the army had intended to establish a plastic surgery unit in South Africa on his return: only now they decided they did not need him in that capacity after all.

Penn was not deterred. He asked Ina for an interview which she readily granted, though when she saw how young he was she had immediate misgivings. Penn did not notice, and plunged into an enthusiastic account of all he hoped to do. Realising Ina could not appreciate it fully unless he showed her some photographs, he asked her to 'hang on' while he went to fetch them. She said later that anyone with confidence like that must have had what it takes. Her mind was already made up, and Ernest fully agreed with her.

The army could hardly back out now. It was decided Brenthurst should be registered as a full military hospital under Jack Penn, but paid for not by the Red Cross or the Defence Force but by the Oppenheimers. They installed an operating theatre in young Michael's old bedroom and Jack Penn began recruiting extra staff: nurses to assist Janet Ford, an anaesthetist provided by the army – though 'Speedy' Bentel had never before carried out an anaesthetic in his life – a dentist to help with jaw surgery and a sergeant who was put in complete charge of administration.

The team's first operation was a rhinoplasty, appropriately enough: reconstructing the nose from a flap of skin brought down from the forehead. It was appropriate because the rhinoplasty operation was really the start of all plastic surgery – known from Hindu writings of 500 BC and earlier, and used for restoring noses cut off in reprisal or in punishment. On this occasion the patient was a young soldier wounded in Abyssinia. Jack Penn had to remove the little that was left of his nose and the scar tissue that had formed, then make an airway with skin taken from the thigh, and lastly bring down a horseshoe of skin from the forehead to make the nose's outer sheath.

That first operation was a success, and the Brenthurst was on its way. Jack Penn went to the military hospital in Oribi in Natal, which was the main clearing house for war casualties invalided home. The registrar was his elder brother, and before long he was sending up a steady stream of patients from the battle fronts. The Straits of Gibraltar were closed, and all serious war casualties south of the Mediterranean were being brought to South Africa. Britons and South Africans from East Africa, Free French, Free Poles, Greeks, Australians, New Zealanders and even a few baffled Italian prisoners-of-war from the Western Desert: all were welcome at Brenthurst.

Before the war was over between 2 000 and 3 000 casualties had passed through the hospital, and Jack Penn had carried out more than 6 000 operations. Many involved startling innovations, for Jack Penn was cast almost entirely on his own resources with no news of the scientific advances being made in other parts of the world. To bring these innovations to the notice of surgeons elsewhere, Jack Penn organised the publication of a quarterly journal he called *The Brenthurst Papers*, sponsored by Ernest. He was not to know it was the world's first journal devoted to plastic surgery, but sent it to plastic surgeons he knew of in England and America. One of Jack Penn's few direct contacts was with an Italian doctor working in Milan – through the International Red Cross in Geneva. He found the Italian was treating South Africans just as he was treating Italians, and again through the Red Cross he was able to arrange the return of some of the South Africans against the repatriation of his Italians. In several cases he was able to continue treatment initiated in Milan, for both he and the Italian had been trained in England according to the same principles.

For all the good work carried out, discipline at Brenthurst was

194

anything but strict. Jack Penn himself was largely to blame, for he had little sympathy with the army's way of doing things. Whenever a visiting 'top brass' wanted to make a tour of inspection Penn would have great difficulty in locating his hat and his cane, for they were never in the same place. Speedy Bentel, the anaesthetist, was even less of a conformist. One day he was sitting on some stairs out of uniform with patients, playing a mandolin and singing, when a brigadier passed him on an inspection round. 'What a very musical orderly,' commented the brigadier to Matron Ford. Another brigadier told her that Brenthurst was the most unmilitary establishment he had ever come across. 'But it seems to work.'

Brenthurst had only 50 beds: far too few to cope with the ever increasing stream of casualties referred to Jack Penn. As time went on he was offered the use of five other large houses in the Johannesburg area and these were turned into convalescent homes. In this way more than 200 casualties were cared for at a time, each staying at one of the convalescent homes to recuperate between operations and admitted to Brenthurst proper only for treatment. One of these houses was later made into an operating hospital in its own right, reserved for those with broken jaws.

Though Jack Penn and his team were at work round the clock in the operating theatre, patients at Brenthurst could hardly have been less aware of it. In the magnificent gardens time stood still: an idyllic fairyland of terraced lawns and shady groves and tumbling streams and ponds, with sunlight winking down and birds singing in the treetops. There was nothing to remind the patients of the war which had landed them in their predicament. If there was anything to disturb them, it was the misery of their own condition and the loneliness many felt at being so remote from their relatives at home.

The unmilitary side of Brenthurst's character extended beyond the gates. The patients, particularly those in more advanced stages of treatment, were allowed and, in fact, encouraged to go out into Johannesburg and mix with the population at large. Under normal circumstances they would have had to wear the regulation 'blues' of military patients, blue battle dress and a red tie. It would have made them all the more conspicuous, and Penn won permission for them to wear their ordinary uniforms.

There was another advantage in the arrangement. As military patients in blues they would not have been allowed to visit bars or other such establishments. If they did they would not have been served, or would have risked arrest. In the case of the Brenthurst patients the rule was waived. Jack Penn soon pointed out to the men that he expected them to behave. If one of them began to disgrace himself in the course of an outing the others were honour bound to look after him and bring him straight back to the hospital. The patients formed a disciplinary committee to order their affairs, and this continued with great effect for the rest of the war. In no instance had Jack Penn to take disciplinary action against any of his patients.

On their visits into town, the Brenthurst patients were often accompanied by nurses from the hospital or by volunteer hostesses recruited by Janet Ford. All were in civilian dress, many of them extremely attractive, and gave the Brenthurst men added confidence in facing up to the world with what were often most unsightly injuries. But deformity is only skin deep. In several instances friendships between nurses and patients blossomed into love affairs. Matron Ford diplomatically turned a blind eye.

All this time, the Oppenheimers were living uncomplainingly down the garden at Little Brenthurst. Ina and her private secretary, Pam Susskind, were running the Caledonian Market on the one hand, and hard at work helping Janet Ford on the other. Ina had grown very fond of the busy and efficient matron, and often invited her for supper by the fire when Ernest was away and, indeed, when he was home. When she went on holiday trips to the Cape she asked Janet Ford to keep an eye on Ernest for her. The matron would go down and have supper with him, and he would tell of the latest financial and mining negotiations he was involved in. She did not have the heart to tell him it was all above her head.

Another friendship that blossomed was between Ernest and Jack Penn. The two had enormous respect for each other, however different their ages and outlook, and in later years Ernest was to give great moral encouragement to the surgeon in all he undertook. Though himself not concerned with the hospital to the extent Ina was, Ernest took pride in all its achievements and tried to make sure every man had what he needed.

Nor was he any less concerned about the staff, so many of them volunteers. He invited them all to gatherings at Little Brenthurst, and sometimes gave parties for all the patients too. When it was announced one of the nurses was engaged he insisted she got married from Brenthurst and paid for the wedding.

Johannesburg people knew what was going on at Brenthurst, but not all of them felt the Oppenheimer role was entirely unselfish. At one party Janet Ford heard a group discussing Brenthurst. A man was saying it was all very well for Ernest Oppenheimer, the whole thing was a tax fiddle.

'It made me boil,' she says. 'If he wanted to, Sir Ernest could have rented half-a-dozen houses for the hospital. Instead he was sacrificing what was probably more dear to him than anything else in the world. He and his wife were giving up their own home.'

3

SLEEPING IN the dew beside an armoured car for months on end was a far cry from the high life of Johannesburg, but Harry remained closely in touch with what was going on at home. Ernest saw to that. Several times a week, all through the time his son was in North Africa, he wrote long letters on everything that was on his mind. He kept carbon copies of these letters in a succession of pads which are preserved in Brenthurst library, and together provide a full account of all that Ernest was involved in during this period.

Much of the material is personal. Ernest was always first and foremost a family man: this was what he lived for. He expected Harry to take an interest too, and gave him full accounts of all that Ina and young Michael were up to. Michael was just matriculating from school, and on his way to Witwatersrand University. He was keen to join up as soon as he could, but Ernest thought it wise for him to wait a year. Clearly he was pleased with his stepson's progress, but he wanted Harry's advice on what was best for him.

Ina was as busy as ever and Ernest told Harry of all her doings. At an American Auction in aid of the Caledonian Market a fur coat worth £50 fetched £2 500. 'About £32 000 has now been raised by Ina.' He was surprised by the speed of developments at the main house. 'To show you how much Brenthurst is now a hospital I walked in yesterday and was stopped by nurses who told me visitors were not admitted after 4.30. I assured them that I once owned the place . . .'

Visitor or no, Ernest could not do enough for his hospital. This was especially clear at Christmas, when he and Ina put themselves out to help everybody have a good time.

'Wednesday was the great day for the Brenthurst Hospital. There was a Christmas tree on the verandah which the men had decorated themselves,' he wrote to Harry. 'We went up to Brenthurst at 7.30. First the patients played various games (not strenuous ones) such as guessing the titles of books and then a most amusing diversion. The sisters had concocted various drinks. The competitors were blindfolded and had to dip a finger into the various beverages and then by licking the finger guess the particular drink. It was really funny, one of the patients ought to become a wine-taster because he guessed 8 out of 10.'

Ernest and Ina decided to have Little Brenthurst redecorated as a surprise for Harry, and for a time moved out to stay in the Carlton Hotel. Harry had several times mentioned plans he had for his cottage, and these were now put into effect. Though it was meant as a secret until Harry returned and saw the improvements for himself, the news leaked out and Ernest had to admit it.

'The changes are those which you discussed with Ina and me on many occasions. We have tried, and I am sure have succeeded, in carrying out your ideas. The house is beautiful. The old dining-room has become the entrance-hall; the gables are pushed out, now have better bedroom and servants' accommodation, even for the Natives. The new dining-room (where the old stoep was) is big enough to seat 35 people . . . I am rather disappointed that some of our friends gave you the information: you know what a talker I am and it was with great difficulty that I abstained from mentioning it in my letters.'

There were other homely touches.

'I had a good breakfast this morning and ate 2 sausages and 2 eggs which Mrs. Kilby had sent in for Michael and me. Mike was late and asked for his breakfast later. Mrs. Kilby then accused "Charlie" of having eaten part of the breakfast. In order to restore peace I had to go into the kitchen and confess to my misdeed.'

There was news of a new ranch Ernest had bought near Gwelo in Rhodesia: Shangani, famous as the scene of the massacre of Wilson's Patrol at the hands of the Matabele in 1893. Ina took personal charge of arrangements for the decor and the furniture. At her prompting too Ernest bought a picnic plot in the Cape, Constantia Hoek, not too far from Blue Mountains.

There was news of friends. The Susskinds featured prominently, with Pam installed as Ina's private secretary. Others mentioned regularly included Claire Unger, Abe Bailey's eldest daughter, and E H Farrer's wife, Ada. Both were seriously ill, and Ernest was clearly most concerned about them. Ada Farrer later died, and so did another old friend from Kimberley days, Lady Rasa Ali.

'I had a terrible experience this morning,' Ernest wrote to Harry. 'Hofing drove me to Lady Rasa Ali's house. As soon as I arrived I was

198

Harry and Bridget took up racing in the years after World War II. With them is Keith Acutt, in later years Anglo's deputy chairman. *Anglo American Corporation.*

Ernest with his comrade and anchor of more than 30 years, R B Hagart. *Anglo American Corporation.*

The hon Member for Kimberley: Harry was elected to parliament in 1948, and represented the diamond city for ten years. With him are Bridget, Mary and Nicky. *Star Master Series, Johannesburg.*

On his way to Oxford's Sheldonian Theatre to receive an honorary doctorate, Ernest processes with the university's vice-chancellor, Sir Maurice Bowra (*centre*) and the Public Orator, Hugh Downie *Anglo American Corporation.*

Ernest and Ina visit Johannesburg's Shantytown to check conditions for themselves. Ernest subsequently organised a loan of £3 million from the mining houses to replace the slums with new townships. *Anglo American Corporation.*

told that her last wish was that the coffin should not be closed before I had seen her. I was with my old father when he died but apart from that I had never seen a dead body before. Imagine my going into the room, Mary in a completely demented state standing at the Head of the Coffin and imploring her sister to speak to Sir Ernest who had come to see her. It was all most upsetting. I must say that Poona (I don't know whether I spelled her name correctly) looked peaceful and pretty, not at all frightening. It was a new lesson for me.'

There were more pleasant social duties. 'On Sunday the Crown Princess of Greece is lunching with us. She is a charming woman. You see your old man is getting famous.' And after the event: 'She is quite young, nice looking and pleasant to talk to. The Crown Prince is in England. She is expecting a baby, do you think Flo could arrange that I can be one of the Godfathers?' Of another guest Ernest wrote: 'She belongs to the oldest profession in the world.'

More than anything, Ernest was concerned with Harry. '. . . You sound a little depressed and whilst I can quite understand it after a long time in the desert, I know it is only temporary and you would not have it really different . . .' 'I cannot tell you how much I miss you. I am fit but there is just no question that one is not so energetic when one is over sixty than one was in one's younger days. I do look forward to the time when you return and take active charge and can play the role of an Elder Statesman.'

He was thinking ahead to the days after the war, when Harry would take an increasingly important part in business affairs. But he expected too his son would involve himself in public life. 'I shall send you the Afrikaans literature tomorrow,' he wrote, promising material which he hoped Harry would discuss with him. And then as an afterthought: 'It is useful to know Afrikaans, particularly if you decide to go into politics after the War, which I hope you will.'

That he was pleased with his son is beyond question. On Good Friday 1942, he was writing: 'The most exciting event this week was the receipt of a letter from your Colonel. I had cabled him when I heard that he had won the DSO and he writes that the honour "was earned by the Regiment as a whole and not least by Harry who has done his job with outstanding courage and good humour under very trying circumstances". I am very proud of you, but I have always been proud of you.'

There were personal matters for Harry's eyes only. 'On the 30th July was your Mother's birthday, I thought of it all day long.' 'Frank's birthday. I know you will be thinking of him and May just as I do.'

'My thoughts are today especially with Frank and your Mother, in the firm belief they are happy and we shall meet again.'

'For the moment I am in a curious frame of mind. Instead of trying to shape business affairs, I feel like letting them drift and shape themselves. This sort of lassitude is quite an Oppenheimer trait and as a rule does not last long . . .'

'You and I look upon things in the same manner. I get the greatest satisfaction out of the fact of having given Brenthurst as a hospital and I contribute liberally to all war funds. I feel that I am entitled to enjoy the luxury of Brenthurst, if during the War I have helped wherever possible.'

'I received your letter of 9th April and had a good laugh about your remark that you doubted whether the Colonel could really manage without you if things flared up and your saying "being your son I can hardly believe it". This idea is in both of us, both a strength and a weakness. It makes us take infinite pains in dealing with every problem, and on the other hand we take on too much work and do not get enough peace of mind to really enjoy life. For all that I cannot and do not want to change my outlook on life. When you are back I shall take it much easier . . .'

Ernest was anxious to avoid writing about the war in his letters: Harry was seeing enough of it already. But on occasion he did allow himself to comment on the way things were going, with characteristic perception.

'What changes we have seen in the structure of the British Empire. The result of the last War was the Statute of Westminster, which turned the Empire into a British Commonwealth of Nations. Once the Allies have beaten Hitler and Japan we shall see a Commonwealth of Democratic Nations in which America will play the leading role.

'I always recall Lord Lothian's remarks when I saw him nearly two years ago in Washington. The important thing he told me is that Democracy and Freedom are preserved and it is less important whether England leads the world or America.'

Apart from personal items, Ernest's letters were not surprisingly brim full of news about the Anglo American. For years he had been confiding all his ideas and thoughts to his son, and he was not going to stop now. It had been his way of developing policy: thrashing out a problem with Harry until the whole thing was straight in his own mind, and then taking action. This is what he tried to do in his correspondence, raising issue after issue in connection with his complex negotiations over gold, diamonds and copper, and as often as not deciding them himself before giving Harry a chance to respond. The result is one of the most scintillating glimpses of the magnate at work.

Ernest had no doubt what his own role ought to be. He was working for his shareholders, certainly: but in the greater context of an Empire at war. Helping the war effort would help his shareholders, and there he saw his duty. There were great profits to be made both in diamonds and copper, he quickly realised: but his responsibility was to keep prices to a minimum, and thereby assist the Allied cause.

This was particularly the case with base metals from the copperbelt, which only now came into their own. Before the war there had been a danger of over-production in terms of world demand. Now the problem was to maintain output at the level desired by the British war cabinet's minister of supply, Churchill's friend Lord Beaverbrook. This was in spite of labour shortages, a shortage of plant and equipment, shipping delays, possible enemy action, closed capital markets and even excessive taxation which made it almost impossible to finance the industry from its own earnings.

'You know from previous letters,' he wrote to Harry, 'that the requests for more and more copper are being pressed by the British Government. Nkana and Nchanga have done their best (without however satisfying Lord Beaverbrook) but poor Roan is in a predicament. Its output has dropped to 5 000 tons in consequence of difficulties in the mine. No doubt it will be put right but will take six months to do so; but the authorities don't quite believe in the difficulties – which is most unfair.'

Certainly there could be little joy for shareholders, but that did not matter. 'In Rhodesia we have only one problem, and that is to produce the maximum quantity of base metals. Only when the war is won can we think again of profits.'

As with copper, so with gold. The Allies needed all they could get, but at the minimum price. Production costs spiralled; there was a labour shortage; and on top of all the other problems the government imposed heavy new taxation on the already over-pressed producers. The mining houses could hold their own, but there could be no question of further development until the war was resolved. Certainly those properties in the Free State which had looked so promising would have to be left in cold storage for a long time yet.

On the other hand, there was no harm in jockeying for position ready for the time when conditions returned to normal. Certainly Ernest was thinking along these lines. With all the disappointments in the Wit Extensions concessions and the successes of others he must have felt he had missed the boat. Anglo was given a minor share in the new company formed to float the St Helena mine in due course, but that was small compensation. The mine would be managed by Union Corporation, and anyway Anglo's share was balanced by similar holdings controlled by Anglovaal and Gold Fields. And as things stood Union Corp would have the right to take charge of any further flotations in the Western Holdings concessions. The company could hardly be expected to surrender what seemed such exceptional opportunities.

The St Helena mine was all prospected and ready for shaft-sinking. Meanwhile in the concessions adjoining the Western Holdings farms African and European was continuing the drilling programme that had already shown considerable promise on the farm Uitzig. In fact A and E was the only company involved in active prospecting at this time. On Ernest's behalf Hagart and Unger went to see Louis Marks of Lewis and Marks, which of course held the controlling interest in A and E. Was he prepared to give Anglo an interest?

Louis Marks gave them cold comfort. He was already heavily committed to other mining houses, and had promised them a chance to participate. Certainly he could give Anglo a share in the business once it was decided to float a mine – but so small that it would hardly be worthwhile. Anglo, of course, was not prepared to come in under those conditions. Ernest and his advisers had to think again.

As it happened, Ernest's fairy godmother was at work once more. Sir Abe Bailey had died the year before, leaving a huge estate which was proving a headache for its executors. How were they to dispose of it all in wartime conditions when nobody had money to spare and certainly not to risk? It looked as if they would have to sell it off piecemeal. Among their first customers was Ernest who bought a strong interest in one of the companies in the Bailey portfolio, Lace Proprietary Mines, which had been involved with Anglo on the Far East Rand.

An ironic feature of the situation was that one of the executors of the Bailey Estate was John Martin, who was chairman of the Corner House group and as such a long-time rival of Ernest's – personal as well as business. Many supposed Martin had slighted Ernest in the past, for the two were notably cool towards each other at times. Now Martin had to find a buyer for the pick of the Bailey interests – his shareholding in SA Townships, and with it the controlling interest in Western Holdings. Martin's Corner House wanted to cream off the considerable coal interests in SA Townships, and had approached Johnnies which seemed a possible buyer. When Johnnies turned the offer down there was no alternative but to approach Ernest, who met the executors in company with Hagart.

'. . . Johnnies – because of the difficult times – have turned down the SA Townships business,' Ernest wrote to Harry. 'I must admit that I was not surprised when I saw the full proposal made to them. They were to buy 354 000 Townships shares at 11s 3d together with the fullest control: that is to say move the company into their offices . . . and generally no obligation to keep any member of the present Townships staff. So far so good, but they had to buy also 1 750 000 Eastern Transvaal Co at 2s 3d with an option on an equal number at 2s 9d they had to exercise or none. The E T C consists of five Barberton properties.

'Well, John Martin came to see me . . . I told him I was interested, but would not buy 1 750 000 E T C at 2s 3d. He was very frank and said he understood my reluctance and that he could not tell me what these shares were worth. He added that the important thing for the estate was not really to sell a big block of these shares which might be good or valueless, but to make sure that someone with an efficient technical staff would look after the properties and advise the estate. He went further and said that they would like to sell some shares together with the Townships deal, so as to give the people who bought the Townships shares a special inducement to look after E T C.'

Ernest laid his cards on the table. He wanted SA Townships, but not E T C. He knew too much about it already: a company with several gold mining concessions in the Pilgrim's Rest area, which would be no use to Anglo. Martin then offered him a free option to 3,6 million E T C shares out of the total 4 million. Not wishing to appear totally unhelpful, Ernest accepted. Ernest and Hagart returned to Johannesburg a few days later, and out of the blue received an altogether unsolicited offer for the option – which they sold immediately at a profit of one shilling a share. Over the next 18 months all the shares were taken up which meant Anglo recouped half the purchase price of the SA Townships shares. Ernest was certainly in luck.

'We are back in the Free State through Western Holdings,' he wrote exultantly. 'Hagart says yes, but the Union Corporation has technical control, to which I reply: that is a pity but one cannot make real money out of technical control, but only out of proper participation in any new business that may come along in the Free State.

'After all the first business is to open St Helena. The next property – if any – will come along in five years' time or so. I am firmly convinced – agreement or no – that the Union Corporation would never insist on

203

becoming Chartered Engineers when the Anglo American is Chartered Engineers of Western Holdings. Such a position was sound when dealing with the Townships but would be ludicrous when dealing with us.'

In the event Union Corp did not see it that way. However, Anglo controlled virtually half the shares in the new company floated to work the St Helena mine. Union Corp had to ask Ernest to surrender some of these to enable it to seek a listing for the new company on the stock exchange. Ernest agreed to this – provided Union Corp allowed Anglo to manage the *next* mine floated on Western Holdings territory, assuming there would be a next mine. That was the best that could be done for the time being.

Meanwhile, Ernest had to attend to the diamond trade. First of all, it was obviously De Beers' job to try and deprive the Axis powers of any source of diamonds. While the Netherlands and Belgium were free this was almost impossible: the cutters were as ready to sell to German buyers as they were to anyone. But with 'blitzkrieg' and the occupation of Belgium and Holland the situation changed dramatically, and Ernest could keep tight control of the situation. With the help of the governments concerned the Diamond Corporation set up new cutting works in New York, Britain and Palestine – staffed chiefly by refugees who had fled Hitler's anti-Semitic persecution.

As with gold and copper, Ernest wanted to keep the price of diamonds as low as possible – or at least the cost of industrial stones. In the war situation it was clear demand would increase dramatically: but he felt it was part of his responsibility to keep prices down to what they had been before. The Diamond Corporation had huge stocks on its hands, and could gradually release these in the months ahead. The mines in West Africa and the Congo were still in production, and would be able to meet the demand. On the other hand, there was no need to keep the South African mines in production: or rather, their labour forces, particularly in Kimberley, could be employed in munitions making. 'One thing is definite,' wrote Ernest to Harry. 'We must not open a mine during the war, but use up the Diamond Corporation stock.'

It all looked quite straightforward and practical. The mines could be reopened after the war, and in the meantime the Diamond Corporation could keep itself going with sales of gemstones, which people might well want to use as a hedge against currency inflation: a use De Beers had been trying to encourage for years. But to Ernest's dismay he found governments clamping down on gemstone sales – for precisely this reason, in case too great a part of their resources was drained off to the Diamond Corporation.

The problem was particularly acute on the one hand in Britain, where the government was trying to clamp down on gemstones, and on the other in the United States, where the government was worried that with all the South African mines closed down the Diamond Corporation was going to run out of industrial stones, so was buying up all it could and demanding a mine should be reopened 'before it is too late'.

Ernest had left it to Louis and Otto to cope with the problems in London, but with the rationing of gemstones they were allowing merchants to pick out the diamonds they wanted, the cream of the crop, while leaving the less saleable stones. That, of course, was inviting trouble.

'Our answer is to my mind quite simple,' he wrote to Harry. 'We should add further qualities to the industrial series and to make good our promises reduce these qualities to pre-war prices. This will increase the quantity of diamonds used for industrial purposes and remove the artificially created fear of a shortage of supply . . .

'The crushing bort position is farcical. The USA Procurement Division has ordered $4\frac{1}{2}$ million carats; all in all we must have sold 10 000 000 carats during the last six or eight months, that is, two tons of diamonds. This quantity cannot possibly be used.'

But the British government would not hear of a change. It was by now thoroughly suspicious of these diamond magnates: 'Our action in selling industrial diamonds at pre-war rates is not appreciated in the smallest way. This in itself should have put a moral obligation on the authorities to help us keep the gem section going. The attitude adopted is quite different.'

There were difficulties at home, too. Ernest was faced with yet another Minister of Mines, this time quite different from any that had gone before. Perhaps with tongue in cheek, Smuts had appointed Colonel Charles Stallard, a colonial of the old school and an archetypal Colonel Blimp. When more progressive members of the staid Rand Club in Johannesburg proposed a rebuilding programme, Stallard promised he would stand on guard at the door and blow the head off anybody who tried to touch it. And he meant what he said.

Now Stallard was in Smuts's government to seal the coalition between the UP, the Labourites and Stallard's tiny Dominion Party, which he had formed at the time of fusion to preserve the British element. But he was not one to regard such a job as a sinecure. Some-

205

how his advisers managed to give him the idea all was not well with the existing arrangements for selling diamonds, and he decided it would be a good thing to revive the idea of a Union Diamond Board in terms of the legislation Ernest had fought back in the twenties. In accordance with the DPA's constitution he gave notice in writing twelve months ahead: the government was not prepared to renew the association's agreement beyond December 1942.

Ernest had been told of the motivation that lay behind this move, and it set him wondering what would happen if Stallard was successful and managed to vest control in the government.

'Let us just examine what can happen if . . . the Government ran the business,' he wrote to Harry. 'We would be driven out and be free to become merchants again. History would repeat itself, we would make outside contracts and slowly arrive back at the point at which we are now. But we would be infinitely stronger in experience . . . and with our cash resources have a much easier task than Louis and Otto and I had at the beginning.

'Therefore let us tender the best advice, do all we can to convince the Government (my colleagues support me absolutely) and if a course contrary to our advice is taken, "wait and see" until we are driven out. I do not want to start a new business, but I would not lay down and become Stallard's doormat.

'It is in that spirit that I shall resume the negotiations with Stallard. It will be the *greatest* fun.'

Before things got out of hand Ernest had a quiet word with Smuts, to try and get him to pour oil on the waters. Smuts promised to watch the situation. But in the meantime Ernest went to see Stallard himself, to try and explain the position. One thing he wanted to clear up was the question of what personal interest he had in the trade. Oppenheimer and Son had taken over the old Dunkelsbuhler interests; but it was only an indirect stake in the various areas, and 'certainly not enough to warp my judgment'.

'I told him that I took so keen an interest in diamonds simply because I had set my heart on preserving a trade with which my family and intimate connections had been identified from the very discovery of diamonds. I concluded by saying that if this position was accepted by him and the Mines Department, all future negotiations would go on more smoothly and everyone would, instead of being annoyed, derive pleasure out of the diamond trade.'

Meanwhile, there were rumblings from the outside producers, which would of course colour the negotiations. In particular, Chester Beatty's

Selection Trust in Sierra Leone was creating problems and refusing to sign a new agreement with the Diamond Corporation except on much better terms. Ernest refused to listen to its counter-proposals and so scared Otto in London that his brother immediately undertook to come to terms with Selection Trust on his own account.

'For all that, what am I to do?' Ernest asked Harry, hardly believing Otto could be responsible for such a monumental mistake. 'Louis and he mean too much to me so I cabled him that if he did find himself in financial difficulties I would, against the security of the diamonds in South Africa, loan him £100 000. I am sure you approve my action. There is no risk, he may never want it, but I wanted to show him my affection had not changed.'

The negotiations between Ernest and Stallard dragged on, with neither side giving ground. Ernest was rather aggrieved by this time: the industry was being subjected to unfair pressure, and his own position was misunderstood and misinterpreted. Even Smuts could not persuade him that there was nothing personal in Stallard's decision to end the agreement. At last Stallard called a conference of the producers in Cape Town.

'I asked him why he had given notice and whether he could disclose his reasons. He was really in a good humour and most polite and proceeded to explain his position. He assured me that he was a convert to "limitation of output to meet the demand of sales through one channel" and that he was anxious to come to a new agreement. I listened patiently and told him that we could not go to any conference before we had consulted our colleagues in London and that this exchange of views had to be by letter as we had reason to believe that the Mines Department saw all our cables. He assured me that he never read them but would not say that under present conditions he could not get copies.'

Ernest and Stallard ranged over the many issues involved, but to no avail. Months passed before they even approached agreement on the complex terms of the new constitution. On the personal level Ernest's relations with Stallard were cordial by this time, though he was from time to time exasperated by the conduct of negotiations.

'I had some more letters from Stallard. I cannot make him out: does he think I am an absolute idiot? He talks of agreement being arrived at when the alterations he suggests have not even been discussed with us . . .'

Ernest was able gradually to bring Stallard round to his way of thinking: the old colonial seemed far out of his depth. With only minor concessions on his side Ernest persuaded him to agree to an agreement not largely different from the one he had terminated.

Ernest's letters to Harry are each pages long, written in longhand and sometimes difficult to decipher, but all with their author's very special touch and all completely topical. They arrived spasmodically, but in great batches. It is entertaining to think of Harry sitting on the sand beside his armoured car so far away from Brenthurst and 44 Main Street, ploughing through them and tucking them away to read again before at last replying in just as considerable detail. He admitted after the war that most of the time life in the desert had been rather monotonous, and the arrival of the letters was a welcome diversion. That was Ernest's intention. He tried to write a letter every day – though with his busy life he had to slacken this schedule as the months passed down to two or three a week. 'There endeth my lesson,' he concluded one of them. 'If it does not do anything else it will have taken your mind off war for a few minutes.'

Ernest was deeply interested in Harry's army career, though always he half hoped Harry would soon be returning home on leave. Instead it looked as if he would be going to Haifa in Palestine, on a captain's promotion course. But what would he do when it was over? Already there were several possibilities. For one thing, Craig Anderson, the 4th's old second-in-command, had asked Harry to join him at the Tank Base Camp in Cairo which he was now commanding. Ernest knew about that one, but told Harry of another idea which obviously appealed to him much more. He had been in contact with an old friend, General Pierre de Villiers, who had been in the desert commanding the Second South African Division.

'Pierre de Villiers rang me up last night to tell me that he has just flown down from up North and that he saw you some time ago and that you were well and fit. He then sang your praises and told me that he was taking up a command in the Union and (although he was not certain as to what would happen) he was asking for you to be put on his staff.

'It must be most flattering to be so much in demand. I suppose you will really prefer to take your Haifa course; on the other hand it will probably depend on what De Villiers offers you.'

What Ernest did not say – and would not dream of saying – was that he thought it was time Harry came home. Fighting in the Western Desert was all very well, but as Smuts had pointed out more than once, it was no place for the heir to one of the world's greatest industrial empires. He might tempt fate once too often: better come home now while the going was good.

The message was not lost on Harry. He understood the implications all too well, and in fact showed the letter to the 4th's new commander, and asked his advice on what he should do. He did not want to leave, particularly at such a crucial time: but on the other hand he was due to go on the course in Palestine anyway, and there was no guarantee he would be sent back to the Alamein lines when it was over.

De Villiers was to set up a new internal defence force to guard South Africa from invasion, to be called Coastal Command. In the end Harry took the decision himself. Yes, he would return to South Africa. Sadly he packed his bags, made the rounds of the men who had shared all those months of little hell, and boarded the flight for the south.

4

SCRAWLED ACROSS a page in Ernest's letter pad is the stark pronouncement: '18th July 1942 Harry rang up at 9 ocl from Johannesburg.'

Ernest and Ina were at their holiday home in Muizenberg. Ernest had gone there deliberately rather than wait for Harry in Johannesburg, he explained, in case there was some delay and he should be disappointed. Instead, Harry was on time. But there was a problem. Arriving in the South African winter straight from the heat of North Africa Harry caught a bad chill. Matron Ford packed him straight off to bed.

But Harry was soon better. He flew down to Cape Town, to meet Ernest again and to report for duty at Coastal Command headquarters. This was Cape Town Castle, the impressive star-shaped fortress built by the Dutch East India Company in their years of occupation. When built it stood on the shore, its bastions washed by the waves. But with years of progressive silting and land reclamation the shoreline has been extended hundreds of yards out into Table Bay, and the castle stands high and dry. It is a place of strong historical associations, linked with the earliest days of South Africa's settlement, and they were not lost on Harry. If he was not fretting to be back in the thick of action, he might have enjoyed himself.

As it was, his work turned out depressingly tedious. The whole point of establishing a strong internal defence force in South Africa was to deter Japan from attempting invasion, and in this General De Villiers's coastal command was to prove wholly successful. In all the war there was to be only one real scare: four Japanese were caught taking photographs from the Hottentots Holland mountains which commanded a panoramic view of Cape Town's surroundings.

This, of course, was exactly what the South African authorities had feared: that the Japanese would attempt the sort of infiltration that had won them half the Far East and was threatening even Australia. The four men had been landed by submarine in False Bay, it was subsequently learnt, and were caught red-handed trying to work out the best means of attempting full-scale invasion. For Harry, their capture was particularly significant: they were concentrating on the vast African Explosives and Chemical Industries dynamite factory near Somerset West, controlled by De Beers in association with Imperial Chemical Industries of Britain and Ernest's direct responsibility as he was the company's chairman. It was evidently their first target.

The capture of the Japanese was kept secret: the government did not want to alarm the South African public, or indeed give the Japanese any idea of what had happened to their men. For a time Coastal Command remained on alert for more Japanese, but none materialised; and as the war with Japan settled down to a stalemate in the Pacific arena and in Burma it became more and more unlikely that South Africa would be involved. Instead, there was more trouble from the Germans: the pilot of a light aircraft flying up the coast from Cape Town was amazed to come upon the crew of a German submarine playing soccer on a remote beach. As soon as they were spotted the crew returned to the submarine and disappeared – leaving behind a single cap to prove the pilot had not been seeing things.

Reports like these only reminded Harry how far he was from the real theatres of war. All the time he watched the progress of his old regiment in the Western Desert; envied them as they entrenched at the Alamein line and prepared for the offensive that they were sure Rommel was plotting; shared with them the triumph of the victory they achieved, as the dynamic General Montgomery brought them the victory that had eluded so many others; exulted as the Allied forces chased Rommel's men back through the desert until North Africa was rid of them for good.

It may be imagined how disappointed Harry was to miss such exciting developments. Fortunately, however, there were other interests to compensate him, particularly an attractive young officer in the Womens' Auxiliary Army Service named Bridget McCall. Ernest and May had been great friends of her parents in Johannesburg years before, but in the meantime Bridget's family had lived in England where she had been at school. Only now had she returned to South Africa with her mother, and she was a lieutenant in the signals sections, stationed on Robben Island, out in Table Bay: the island which has since gained world-wide notoriety as South Africa's maximum security prison for political offenders.

In fact, it was on Robben Island that Harry and Bridget encountered each other. Comparing notes they realised they had probably met before, in Johannesburg. Certainly they knew many of the same people. But as Bridget was quite a bit younger than Harry she would have been so small if they had met before he would hardly remember her. Now, however, it was a different matter. Bridget was tall, dark, attractive and very striking and Harry fell madly in love with her. In fact, it was not long before he proposed.

Bridget had the chance of meeting Ernest and Ina on one of their visits to the Cape. They took to her immediately. But Harry wanted her to see Brenthurst so as soon as possible they made a special trip to Johannesburg. Bridget was a little overawed to be shown round the Oppenheimer estate and to see what she was letting herself in for, but Ernest and Ina did all they could to make her feel at home. Back in Cape Town again she resigned her commission to prepare for her new life.

The wedding was in Claremont, on May 6 1943: a military wedding, Harry in uniform with Michael as his best man and all Harry's brother officers in attendance. Bridget recruited four bridesmaids and four pageboys. She wanted to do things in as much style as the war situation allowed. An aunt of hers lived nearby in a lovely house which she had offered for the reception, and all went off smoothly.

Harry was still in the army, so for a time he and Bridget took a house in the Gardens area. But after a few months he found he was spending an increasing amount of time in Johannesburg where there was a lot happening on the business front, and decided he and Bridget should move north. There was no room for them at Brenthurst so they rented a house along Jubilee Road, a stone's throw away. Harry had taken special leave to allow himself time to attend to Anglo affairs, and at the end of it decided he was better out of the army at this stage and resigned his commission. Apart from anything else, Bridget was expecting.

On Harry's return to 44 Main Street, Ernest immediately made him managing director of the Anglo American. He had been on the board since well before the war, first as an alternate director and then in full capacity; and he had joined the De Beers board in 1937. But the appointment made little difference to his actual status in the organisation. Ernest still wanted him in the same office, as he had been all along.

211

'My father liked reaching his business conclusions by talking with someone who knew about the matters to be discussed, to be able to give an intelligent and considered opinion,' Harry told an interviewer. 'He found my presence in the office a great help to us. But with the growth of the business of the corporation, this arrangement of sharing offices soon became inconvenient, and I had to move out to my own office where I could conduct interviews and talks of my own. But nevertheless we remained intimately associated in all business matters.'

The baby arrived on New Year's Eve 1943, a daughter they named Mary after Harry's mother. If not a son, at least Harry had an heir and Ernest was a grandfather. Ernest and Ina were still living in Little Brenthurst for Jack Penn and his staff were as busy as ever though the stream of casualties from the war fronts was fast diminishing. The success of the operations in Sicily and Italy cleared the Mediterranean and it was more practical to send serious cases for treatment in England or America rather than all the way to South Africa. In any case, it looked as if the war in Europe would soon be over, and Brenthurst's duty would be done. But before that happened the hospital's fate was resolved quite independently. Fire broke out in the main ward.

There was no panic. The patients at Brenthurst knew what to do in an emergency and quietly filed out to safety in the gardens. By the time firefighters arrived most of the damage was done, and a whole wing of the great house was destroyed.

The patients and staff were distributed among the other houses made available to Jack Penn. In one of them he had the operating theatre for work on broken jaws, and he was able to continue work with minimum delay. Before long the military authorities offered him their old headquarters, a magnificent estate called Tara on the border of Johannesburg's northern suburbs, and it was there he worked for what remained of the war.

Ernest and Ina faced the task of bringing Brenthurst back to life from the blackened shell that remained of the wing. This they tackled in a typically energetic way, using the opportunity to improve the house. Jack Penn took a close interest in their progress, though the military authorities had already decided to return Brenthurst to the Oppenheimers and to make no further claim on it. One day Jack Penn was about to leave for the city when Ernest asked him if he could give him a lift to Anglo's headquarters. Ina had already gone to town with the Rolls. Outside in the drive, Ernest looked puzzled as he found himself confronted by two cars: one a sleek Cadillac, the other a beaten-up jalopy.

212

'Which one do I get in?' asked Ernest.

'One belongs to an interior decorator paid by the Oppenheimers,' Jack Penn replied. 'The other belongs to an exterior decorator working for the government.'

Ernest took the hint, and climbed into the right car.

5

ERNEST HAD a foothold in the Free State through Western Holdings, but he was not going to stop there. His men now investigated the situation in other areas round Odendaalsrus, and a clear pattern emerged. Next to Western Holdings on the Odendaalsrus side was an area controlled by the Blinkpoort Gold Syndicate; on the other side a big area controlled by African and European, which had already struck payable reef on the farm Uitsig; and to the north the old Wit Extensions area which had so far been disappointing.

First, the Blinkpoort Syndicate. The company was in a state of suspended animation: its directors had decided not to continue drilling operations but 'rather to conserve its resources pending the results of boring operations being conducted by others'. Now Anglo persuaded the directors to let the corporation share in exploring 5 000 morgen of their territory, particularly the farm Arrarat which looked the most promising. Within a year the two companies drilled three boreholes and began a fourth.

Next, Wit Extensions. Anglo had explored the whole area systematically, but in spite of tantalising glimpses of what was possible, there had been no actual strike. Now, however, Anglo came to terms with New Union Goldfields which held the Roberts and Jacobson interests in the area, and together they restructured Wit Extensions and prepared to continue operations in partnership.

Most important of the three, however, was African and European. This company was already related to Western Holdings through reciprocal shareholdings. Now Anglo bought a substantial holding in A and E, and made arrangements to participate in the exploration of their concessions, Block 7 and Block 8, to the extent of 25 per cent plus an interest in A and E's own participation: all rather complicated, but meaning that Anglo's holding in these areas was now respectably strong.

There were developments all the time. Anglo made a further deal with New Union Goldfields over the right to explore 400 square miles of the Verkeerdevlei area; and at the same time with Lydenburg Platinum to prospect 52 000 morgen of territory south of the Sand River. In each case Anglo would provide the majority of the working capital in any new mining companies to be formed – and that meant eventual control. A definite financial pattern was emerging.

By this time, of course, Anglo's holdings in the Free State were complex and extensive. Ernest formed yet another holding company in the pattern of Rhoanglo, Anglo Investments and WRIT: Orange Free State Investment Trust. It was given control of all Anglo's Free State investments. Even at this stage, reported Ernest at the first general meeting, drilling results on the concessions held by Western Holdings, Blinkpoort Syndicate and African and European 'indicate the probability of at least four separate gold-mining companies being established in due course and in all these new ventures your company will have a very substantial interest'.

On paper things were going well. But Ernest wanted more than a minority interest in each of these schemes. He had already missed out at St Helena, though it was true Anglo would manage the second mine on the Western Holdings land. What was to happen in the north?

The territory Ernest coveted most was African and European's, potentially far and away the richest. Ernest had already angled for full participation in any ventures A and E might initiate, but had been rebuffed by Louis Marks the chairman. Now, however, he was able gradually to improve his stake by buying into companies which controlled important block shareholdings. He scored a major coup by taking over the whole share capital of Associated Mines and Selection Trust, previously controlled by Anglovaal which had big holdings in A and E territory.

Ernest was slowly gaining ground, and the relationship between Anglo and A and E was now so close that already each had two directors on the other's board. A and E was pursuing a vigorous policy: nearly 50 boreholes drilled and a lot more going down – and of the 47 drilled so far 35 of them in the positive area. For Ernest, it was all too exciting. How was he to tip the balance?

His solution was bold. Louis Marks and his brother controlled A and E through their firm Lewis and Marks which was registered in London. It was one of the most important of the smaller mining houses, with its interest chiefly in coal and property. Lewis and Marks and indeed all the London mining houses were having a thin time at present owing to a 100 per cent profits tax imposed by the British government, which hardly encouraged private enterprise. If Ernest had prayed for ideal

Ernest and Ina board a flight for London. *Star Master Series, Johannesburg.*

Ernest was always specially fond of his granddaughter Mary. *Star Master Series, Johannesburg.*

Ernest congratulates his old friend General Smuts on reaching his 80th birthday. *Anglo American Corporation.*

conditions to wage a take-over battle he could not have been granted better: in a few months Anglo could announce the acquisition of 149 850 fully paid shares of a total of 150 000. It cost Ernest rather more than £3 million. Before delivering his cheque he showed it to Jack Penn with pride.

The Marks brothers were not pleased by the take-over – especially when Ernest immediately announced the complete reorganisation of both Lewis and Marks and A and E, with the whole of the existing directorate obliged to resign and Anglo nominees to be appointed in their places. For Ernest, the move was especially poignant: this was the firm with which Bernard had been so closely involved all those years ago. But he was not prepared even to preserve the name, so completely had the company changed. He restyled it Free State Mines Selection Ltd.

The implications of the take-over were at once appreciated in the financial Press. 'When the exploitation of the Orange Free State gold-fields begins,' wrote the London *Statist*, 'the Anglo American Corporation will dominate the situation'. The report went on to draw attention to the immense strengthening of Anglo's position in general.

'The way in which the Anglo American Corporation has expanded its operations in recent times has been rather breath-taking. With its powerful link with the diamond industry on the one hand and the Rand gold-mining industry on the other, not to mention the copper-mining in Northern Rhodesia, the acquisition of the Bailey interests, followed by the acquisition of Lewis and Marks, places it in a formidable position. It is an exercise for a long autumn evening to follow the corporation's manifold ramifications in the mining and industrial world these days.'

If Anglo's ramifications were difficult to follow, they were not as complicated as Ernest's personal interests. His positions as chairman of De Beers and chairman of the Diamond Corporation were altogether distinct from his responsibilities to Anglo, every bit as demanding and even further reaching. On the copperbelt and in gold mining he could speculate and afford to take a few chances. In diamonds one false step might precipitate the ruin of the whole trade: and he was being pressurised into taking it.

The trouble stemmed from across the Atlantic. The American authorities were still worried by what they took to be an acute shortage of industrial diamonds. In fact, though, the Syndicate had stocks enough to last for years without needing to mine another stone. But the Americans were not convinced. They were pressing for the re-

215

opening of a mine 'before it is too late'. Stallard agreed with Ernest that it was 'just nonsense, and there is no risk of a shortage of industrials,' as Ernest explained to Harry in 1942.

'The question of the imaginary shortage of industrial diamonds has again been raised by the American authorities in London and with our Government here. I prepared a memorandum on the whole subject which we cabled to London. I show in my statement that the only method of dealing with the problem (if it exists) is to include better class diamonds and that this will make more industrial diamonds of better quality available than could be obtained if we worked at the three mines in Kimberley and adhered to the present qualities only.'

That was all very well. But Ernest had reckoned without a shortage developing in a quite different direction. Gem diamonds were selling well, especially in America, and with all the South African mines shut down it looked as if the industry would simply not be able to meet the demand. Even with the combined resources of all the outside producers the situation the next year would be even worse. But this problem at least was easy to solve: De Beers reopened Dutoitspan, the mine with the highest yield of gemstones.

But even this was not enough to satisfy the Americans. It now emerged it was not the shutting down of the mines that was upsetting them, but the fact that they could not get as many diamonds as they wanted 'on demand'. Since 1942 they had been asking for permission to be allowed to stockpile diamonds in case the Axis powers gained control of Africa. The Diamond Trading Company had met all requests with a firm refusal, neatly countering the many arguments produced by the Americans and suggesting as a compromise they should build stocks in Canada. It was a move typical of Ernest's loyalty to the Empire.

Exasperated, the United States government at last lost patience and took action which prompted an acid report in *Time* magazine – accompanied by a picture of Ernest looking rather dour in a trilby hat and captioned 'Dignified, mum'.

'Of all the world's tight trade combinations, the British-controlled diamond cartel is the best textbook example of how to control production and fix prices,' said *Time*.

'US businessmen have long been aware that if this cartel could be splintered, diamonds might become cheap enough to: (i) weigh down their wives' fingers; (ii) drastically cut the cost of diamond drills, grinding wheels and other industrial tools. Impressed by these facts, Attorney-General Francis Biddle last week set out to break up the cartel.

216

'In Manhattan, he brought anti-trust charges against famed De Beers Consolidated Mines Ltd., its diamond-selling subsidiary, Diamond Trading Co Ltd, Belgium's "Diamang" and "Forminière", world's biggest diamond miners, and five other British, Belgian and Portuguese companies. Together they supply 95 per cent of the world's diamonds.

'Bigwigs of these corporations live in the far corners of the earth, well beyond the Biddle reach. So he had to content himself with individual charges against seven officials or stockholders near at hand in Manhattan, including Solomon R Guggenheim, aged (84) copper magnate and art collector, and Clendenin J Ryan, lieutenant commander in the Navy and grandson of the late Thomas Fortune Ryan.

'Commander Ryan promptly said that he owned only a small block of stock, that he had nothing to do with running the companies. Another defendant, Herbert H Vreeland of Manhattan, director of Diamang and Forminière (also board chairman of Royal Typewriter Co Inc) died two days after the charges were filed.

'The rest met the charges in the same fashion which the cartel reserves for all complaints – a dignified silence. If De Beers was disturbed by the charges of price fixing, control of production, quotas for diamond merchants, etc, it was comforted by the belief that Biddle had no more chance of denting the cartel than of cleaving a diamond with a butter knife.'

That was true, certainly. But Ernest's personal confidence was considerably shaken by the attack, even if he kept a discreet silence. He had long been aware of hostility from the Americans, but had not realised it could go so far. The attacks came to nothing, of course: but that was hardly the point.

All this time the demand for industrial stones had been booming beyond anyone's wildest expectations. Ernest's brother Otto was largely responsible for the spectacular successes, and was naturally jubilant. Ernest, on the other hand, had serious misgivings. What was to prevent industrial producers such as those in the Congo and Angola from branching out on their own when the war was over?

For the time, all the members of the Diamond Producers' Association were bound by an agreement which was to continue 'until the cessation of the present hostilities'. Once these ended, however, there was nothing to prevent them from going their separate ways. They could negotiate their own contracts with whoever they wished, and there would be chaos all over again.

Trying to forestall such a situation, Ernest and Harry together drafted a memorandum on how they felt the diamond trade should be reorganised after the war, and sent it to everyone who might be interested. First of all they stressed the need for general co-operation in preserving the main features of the trade – for there was no telling what might happen if the established order broke down. But then they made two radical new proposals: one that the South African producers should be guaranteed a fixed quota of the trade like the producers elsewhere, which would help rationalise the whole market; and the other, far more drastic, that the diamond trade should be reorganised into two altogether separate wings, one for gemstones and the other for industrials.

'The increased importance of industrial diamonds makes it necessary to separate this business completely from the gem trade and to make it clear that the maximum quantity of industrial diamonds will always be available irrespective of the state of demand for gems, and that prices for industrials will be fixed in relation to the utility of these goods in industry and will not be affected by changes in the prices of gems.'

Ernest wanted to divide the industry absolutely, to create new buying and selling organisations to handle industrial stones, entirely separate in finance and organisation from the Diamond Corporation and the Diamond Trading Company. Unfortunately Stallard, still the Minister of Mines, did not see the need for it. What would be the point?

It was a ticklish situation. Ernest did not want to show the outside producers how concerned he was: he might give them ideas. In the circumstances the best he could do was gingerly to bring into being a new marketing company, Industrial Distributors (1946) Limited, registered in London and with Otto in the chair.

His luck held. The end of the war saw a slump in the industrial market. It was temporary, they all knew, but the situation reminded the outside producers that they were after all safer within the fold than outside it, and one by one they came to terms with the Producers' Association and signed new contracts. It was all just as it had been before the war. Ernest could breathe freely once again.

Teamwork

ERNEST HAD always maintained that it was not the actual discovery of a new diamond deposit that spelt danger for the
industry, but the way it was exploited. There was no shortage of
examples to prove his point. Now, it seemed, the trade was presented
with the most dangerous yet. Far away in Tanganyika, a lone Canadian
had unearthed the richest diamond pipe of them all.

It had all the makings of a fairy story. John Williamson had arrived
in Africa in 1933, one of the geologists recruited to prospect under
Joe Bancroft. He worked in Northern Rhodesia for two years, then
took leave in Tanganyika and came across the alluvial diamond field
discovered years before. He found some small diamonds for himself,
decided that where these came from there might well be more, and
resolved to resign his job on the copperbelt and go diamond prospecting in earnest.

He was by no means first in the field. It had been known for years
that Tanganyika held kimberlite pipes in abundance. But though a
number of companies had carried out extensive systematic prospecting
campaigns in their respective concession areas, as yet no payable
deposit of diamonds had been discovered. Williamson decided that this
was the fault of the companies, which had been too generous in setting
grids with legs of two miles between prospecting pits; and too lax in
their supervision of individual prospectors, who found it easier to test
the ground of a relatively small area and report back with nothing,
than to make a conscientious exploration of the ground allotted to
them.

Williamson had not known a great deal about diamonds in those
early days: but he was ready to persevere, learning from his mistakes.
With the little money he had he bought a lorry and equipment, and

hired a gang of labourers. With them he travelled far and wide across the barren scrubland of Tanganyika's heart digging prospecting trenches as he went. He had little success – but at least he found enough stones to keep himself alive and his lorry in petrol. When he ran out of funds he was grub-staked by a European garage owner and an Indian lawyer who had faith in him. These were favours he never forgot.

He spent five years like this, and earned the respect of all who came across him. They thought he was mad, but they wished him luck. In fact, he became something of a legend in East Africa at this time, rather as Livingstone had been before him: a lone white man, prepared to forsake the company of his fellows to live close to the bush and drive himself relentlessly in pursuit of a dream.

One day in March 1940, Williamson and his team were camped out under a baobab tree on a gently sloping rise above a plain, hundreds of miles from any big settlement. It was a place local Africans called Mwadui: Williamson had pinpointed its locality as a possible source of diamonds. He was walking a little way from the camp, when there at his feet was a diamond. It seemed too good to be true.

As soon as he could he mobilised his Africans, and began a feverish campaign to dig prospecting trenches. At first he concentrated on the ground further up the hill, imagining his lone diamond must have been washed down. But nothing did he find. Only later did he think of prospecting the plain. But here he was lucky. He had found a classic diamond pipe. In the months that followed he established that it was bigger than anyone's wildest dreams: a positive lake of diamonds, five or six square miles in extent, many times bigger than any pipes previously discovered. Mwadui was potentially the most valuable piece of real estate in the world.

The story reached De Beers, but it was a while before Ernest acted upon it. He needed to be sure the Mwadui discovery was all it was claimed: in the event, it more than surpassed expectations. By the end of the war the pipe was in full production thanks to an injection of South African capital, and showing a better yield of gemstones than any other producer. To leave Mwadui to develop its own marketing organisation unhindered would be a grave risk indeed, and Ernest decided it was time to make a move.

He had always imagined Williamson would be a rather tough sort of man to deal with: those years in the bush must have left their mark. Instead, the geologist was anything but a businessman. Indeed, he seemed rather flattered by all the fuss made of him, and gladly signed an agreement which brought him within the framework of the Producers' Association and established him with a set quota of the trade's total production. It looked as if all was well.

Unfortunately this state of affairs did not last long. It suddenly occurred to Williamson that he would make a lot more money from his diamonds if he sold them himself without going through the Producers' Association. Why should they make all the profit? So he was bound by a contract until the end of 1951? Then he would stock-pile his production until he was free to negotiate his own terms. Time was on his side.

This was something new. Never before had the trade been faced with a problem quite like this – and Ernest handed it straight to Harry. For one thing, it had become clear to those who had seen something of Williamson that he was scared stiff of Ernest himself. He was convinced Ernest wanted to strip him of his mine and indeed everything he had. Ernest's hope was that Harry could soothe him into coming to terms again.

Harry found the situation more difficult than he imagined. Williamson was on the defensive now, determined to give no ground. Harry raised point after point in an effort to make Williamson see reason and agree to come to terms with the rest of the trade. Couldn't he see it was for the good of everyone? But each time Williamson countered with the force of his own logic: he could make more money by operating on his own.

For the time, there was really nothing more they could do. At least the Williamson diamonds were out of circulation. There were several years to go before Williamson was free to do as he liked. They could afford to take stock of the situation a little longer.

This had been Harry's most responsible assignment yet, but in fact he was already in the top echelon at both Anglo and De Beers. He had been on the boards of both since well before the war, and had taken an important part in formulating their policies. Nor was he the youngest of Anglo's executives. Through the years Ernest had assembled a wealth of talent at every level. It was a matter of pride within the organisation that it was never necessary to advertise even junior positions. They could be filled certainly by personal recommendation, if not by invitation.

Many of his top men Ernest picked out himself. There was, for instance, Keith Acutt, who had joined the staff as a young man and in a very junior position, back in the twenties. He had been the first secretary of E Oppenheimer and Son. Since then he had risen quickly, entirely on his own talents and personality, through the different levels of management to the point where he was now a full manager and expected to go much further still.

Ernest's mode of thinking may be seen from the way he hired Sydney Spiro, who had survived the war with a Military Cross to his credit and joined Anglovaal. Now he was seeing a lot of the Susskinds' younger daughter Diny. Ernest had heard a little about him, but did not meet him until one evening he had dinner at the Susskinds. He gathered Doff and Fred were a little worried as they felt Sydney Spiro was rather older than their daughter, and they would have preferred her to choose someone closer to her own age.

Ernest was sitting beside Sydney Spiro at dinner one night and chatting to him, at first cautiously but later with great enthusiasm. At the end of the evening he said he would be glad if Spiro had lunch with him. From this came an invitation to Spiro to join Anglo American. As Ernest explained to Doff Susskind: 'There are only two people in the world who understand what I'm talking about. One's Harry, and this is the second. I think you'd better let him marry Diny. In fact, it's a jolly good idea.' Before long the couple were man and wife.

Ernest liked to bring the sons of fathers he knew into the organisation: for instance the Wilson brothers, Comar and Tony, who had joined Anglo almost fresh from university. Comar, some years Tony's senior, had already proved a great success and it looked as if Tony would follow in his footsteps.

On the other hand, if a man was not a success in the organisation – particularly if his presence affected the rest of the team – Ernest was not ashamed to fire him. There was one incident which involved a man who had been drinking rather a lot, and making a fool of himself in public. Ernest said that if it happened again he would be fired on the spot. It did, and Ernest said his previous decision stood. Hagart tried to put in a word for the man, pointing out that he had problems at home, and it was because of these that he was drinking so much.

'It's exactly at times like those you need all your wits about you,' Ernest replied grimly.

Another incident featured Michael, Ernest's stepson. He had joined Anglo as expected but had soon proved a bit of a square peg in a round hole. Still very young, he could not see why he should accept orders from those higher up the scale. When Ernest heard one of his senior men had resigned on the strength of a tiff with Michael, he decided to send his stepson to England where he could continue his studies at Oxford. Ina was upset, but even Michael agreed this would suit him much better.

Harry was responsible for introducing a good deal of new talent to Anglo – particularly younger talent. Among his first recruits were two old colleagues from the 4th Armoured Cars: Gray Fletcher and Guy Young, who had both been troop leaders. On another level Ernest brought in General Pierre de Villiers, who had become quite a friend of the family, and who now joined the board of De Beers. But the catch which attracted most attention – not in South Africa alone, but all over the world – was Group Captain 'Sailor' Malan, one of the most outstanding pilots of the Battle of Britain.

Sailor Malan was South African, a former merchant seaman who had gained his wings in the RAF before the war and joined the famous 74 'Tiger' Squadron at the outbreak of hostilities. In the Battle of Britain he had shot down 32 enemy aircraft confirmed and a good many more 'probables', and was rewarded with a string of decorations from four countries. At the end of the Battle of Britain the RAF pulled him out of the front line to train other pilots for a time, but he returned to take part in the support effort on the day of the Normandy landings and downed three more planes. That brought his confirmed tally for the war up to 35 – putting him among the top three highest scoring RAF pilots. Now the war was over he was at a loose end, and after meeting Harry in England accepted his offer of a job at Anglo.

At first no function was specified: and nobody had less idea of what would be expected of him than Sailor himself. 'I don't know what it will be until I have a try out and see where I fit in,' he told a friend. 'A change of job is always exciting. I've tried the sea and the air. Now it's time I tried the land.'

When it was announced Sailor Malan was coming home there was great excitement in the Union, not surprisingly: more than anyone he had captured the public imagination. Scores of stories had filtered back, stories of his ruthless determination in the air: they called him a cold, calculating killer; and at the other end of the scale very human stories, like the way he buttonholed Churchill one day at Biggin Hill fighter base and asked if he would be godfather to his new-born son: he said afterwards it was the bravest thing he had ever done.

Certainly he was remarkable by any standard. One day another pilot was asking him which was the best way to shoot down an enemy bomber. Sailor's replies were refreshingly direct: he was simply talking about the job he had to do, and he had tried to think it out logically. 'First of all I kill the rear gunner. Then I come in again and kill the navigator. Then I shoot up the plane enought to make it a write-off, even if it does get back to its base. But the pilot I don't kill. Not right away. I try to damage him enough to allow him to get back and crash-land his plane and finish off the job himself.'

That way, Sailor reasoned, there would be some point in the exercise. If he shot the plane down immediately nobody in Germany would be any the wiser. Better to allow the pilot to fly the crippled plane home and let the people there see for themselves what was being done to 'their boys'.

Malan said he never thought of the men in the planes he shot down, only the planes themselves. But he was not really insensitive. An American suggested that he and his men must have flown without any kind of fear. Sailor told him nothing could be further from the truth. 'We were not without fear. The fellow who was not afraid didn't live very long, and taking a Spitfire into the sky in September, 1940, was rather like entering a dark room with a madman waving a knife behind your back. We couldn't see behind us and the Hun was everywhere, ready to spit his guns.'

Sailor arrived in South Africa in a blaze of glory, with civic welcomes arranged in both Cape Town and Johannesburg. It was not sure what he was to do at 44 Main Street, so for lack of a more appropriate designation he was known as Harry's 'private and political secretary'. In fact he became Harry's personal assistant. The two men got on well, in spite of the considerable differences in their backgrounds: Sailor was born and bred an Afrikaner, one of the first to come within close reach of Anglo's heart.

Once he had found his feet Sailor quite enjoyed himself in Johannesburg, though it was the first time he had tasted life in a business community. He was put up for the Rand Club and joined a number of golf clubs where he brought his handicap down to 12. As for his job, he admitted 'It's fascinating work. There's an awful lot to learn and a chap's got to be on his toes. But it's the greatest opportunity I've ever had. I hope I make good . . .'

There was plenty to occupy him, for there was a lot happening. In the first place, the diamond mines were back in production again. De Beers was working Bultfontein and Wesselton as well as Dutoitspan. CDM was in full operation, and of course the State Diggings south of the Orange River had never closed down.

Ernest decided to reopen Jagersfontein and the Premier as well: they had been closed since before the Depression of the thirties. All this time the little settlements that supported them had been ghost towns, their population drifting away in search of employment elsewhere. But now the people returned, new shafts were sunk and new machinery installed at a cost of millions, and in 1949 both mines were working to full strength.

Jagersfontein's rebirth was a welcome boon to the ailing Free State, which was in dire need of the employment opportunities and extra revenue it would provide. But the development was small, in comparison with the developments further north. Here Anglo and the other gold mining houses were proceeding with their exploration of the new goldfields at full speed. The Free State was buzzing with rumours.

As yet only boreholes had gone down: there was always the chance that the promising results achieved so far had been some terrible freak; that the gold reefs being explored at such huge expense were irregular and unpayable; that to sink shafts on the strength of them would be to throw away efforts accounted in tens of millions of pounds, and for nothing.

But there was no need to worry. Borehole after borehole was coming in with a payable result, not from the basal reef only, which was the one that had caused such excitement, but from three lesser reefs discovered higher up the strata. The engineers and all the mining men involved were convinced they had a rich new field on their hands, perhaps the richest yet. But it remained to convince the investing public. The mining men claimed it was a discovery as important as the diamond fields of Kimberley and the rich deposits of the Rand. But how could they be sure?

It fell to Ernest to make the announcement that tipped the balance. It was a simple announcement, made in April 1946, and concerned the result of a borehole drilled by Anglo in conjunction with the Blinkpoort Syndicate, on the border of the farm Geduld.

'About five miles south-east of Odendaalsrus, Geduld Hole 1, on the boundary between Geduld No 697 and Friedesheim No 511, which is being drilled for joint account by the Blinkpoort Gold Syndicate Ltd and Western Holdings Ltd, has intersected the Basal Reef at a depth of 3 922 feet with a true width of 18,4 inches, assaying 1 252 dwt per ton, which is equivalent to 23 037 inch-dwt . . .'

At first nobody would believe it. The 'payable limit' in the Rand formations was taken at 150 inch-dwt, and with an average of 450 dwt from most of the boreholes drilled so far even this was held to be exceptional. But 23 037 inch-dwt? There must have been a mistake. Senior men at Anglo and the other mining houses checked the result, and decided the bore must have been salted: even Hagart could scarcely believe it. The reaction of newspapers can be imagined: some even refused to print the result.

In plain terms, the result meant that if it had been possible to take a ton of rock from the bottom of the borehole it would have yielded 165,875 ounces of gold, worth about £1 600 at that time. The payable limit in existing mines was £3 worth a ton – so the Geduld borehole went more than 500 per cent better. No wonder the stock exchanges of the world sat up and took notice. In London, New York, Paris and Johannesburg there was a stampede for the shares of any company associated with the Free State goldfield: and that meant practically every mining company in South Africa, for nearly all of them were involved.

This rush of interest was all to the good of the mining companies. Before a sod had been turned a major proportion of their job was done. Investors were only too keen to pour money into the Free State mines, and already their market value was extraordinarily high considering no work had yet been initiated and it would be years before they could come into production. But the die was cast. Union Corp began shaft-sinking at St Helena, and a little later Ernest and Harry went down for the ceremony of turning the first sod on the Welkom mine in Block 7, the A and E concession. Already there were plans to open four more Anglo mines in this area alone: President Brand and President Steyn in what remained of Block 7; Free State Geduld partly on Blinkpoort Syndicate territory and partly on the Western Holdings land; and the Western Holdings mine itself, just north of St Helena. Ernest wanted to begin sinking a new shaft on one or other of these mines every four months or so: the whole of this central goldfield would be brought into production virtually at once.

Nor was that all. Johnnies had control of the Free State Development and Investment Corporation which held the concession areas round Odendaalsrus, and it was here two more mines went down: Freddies North and Freddies South, soon to be united in Freddies Consolidated. And further north, in that area first explored by Allan Roberts and Mannie Jacobson, Anglo re-prospected the Wit Extensions area and at last found the Basal Reef: only 400 feet below the point where Roberts and Jacobson had had to abandon their borehole through lack of funds. Now Anglo prepared to bring into being two mines on the Wit Extensions area, again both named for farms of the neighbourhood: Jeanette and Loraine.

There was excitement too from the area south of the Anglo-Union Corp holdings near Odendaalsrus, where borehole drillings had revealed a great wedge of gold-bearing reef separated from the main body, but big enough to support four mines. Now there were plans to develop them too: Harmony and Merriespruit under Rand Mines, Free State Saaiplaas under Gold Fields and Virginia under Anglovaal. All told, that meant there were plans to develop no fewer than fourteen new mines all at once – all full-scale, and each producing a good deal more than any on the old Central Rand and East Rand.

So far these plans were on paper. It would be years yet before any of the mines were in production. Shafts had to be sunk, machinery put in, headgear and surface plant installed. But more important even than this, accommodation had to be provided, services like power and water and transport laid on, whole communities had to be built up. And the companies were starting virtually from scratch: a couple of sleepy little hamlets in the middle of the bare veld.

So far everyone had assumed that Odendaalsrus would bear the brunt of the astonishing change in the Free State's fortunes. It could not have been less prepared. 'Sandy tracks serve as roads,' wrote the correspondent of the London *Times*. 'In the middle of the village the market square, a piece of grass-covered veld, is lined with trees and has only one building upon it. This is the municipal office, no larger than a single office in a large Johannesburg mining house'.

Property speculators moved in on Odendaalsrus, and land values spiralled. The government was thinking in terms of making this the centre of the new goldfield, especially as it was clear the Free State's own provincial administration felt this was the wisest course. But this was to reckon without Ernest and Harry. In co-operation with Union Corp they engaged a distinguished town planner from Britain and set him to work drawing up designs for an entirely new community in the veld, central to Anglo's five mines and St Helena too. He chose the site of the old drillers' camp at A and E's Uitsig – which boasted eight houses, a boarding house and office block and recreation club. Ernest presented the government with the results, a complete detailed scheme for a brand new city right down to the town's own airport.

The government had begun with the idea of developing a single large metropolis for the whole area, and this was the idea Ernest favoured in outlining plans for his new town. He wanted to avoid the mistake he felt had been made on the East Rand, where the government had allowed a whole string of little towns to develop: a single large community would have been far more effective. But the government found itself under considerable pressure from local political interests which were upset to see Odendaalsrus by-passed. In the event they approved exactly what Ernest had wanted to avoid: no fewer than four little communities, each to be autonomous: Allanridge, Odendaalsrus,

Welkom and Virginia. Anglo was to have responsibility for Allanridge, serving Jeanette and Loraine, and Welkom serving the six mines in the middle of the field; while Odendaalsrus would cater chiefly for Freddies and Virginia for the mines in the south.

In the first instance the manager at Welkom mine had responsibility for all developments on the Anglo properties, and even for the slowly developing village of Welkom itself: a mammoth area bulldozed from the veld with separate sections reserved for civic offices, shopping area, residential area, recreational facilities, all in the eye of the town planner as yet but destined one day to take full shape. Already its first inhabitants were settling in to life in the Free State. The new goldfield was on its way.

2

SMUTS WAS in trouble again. Through the war years he had more than held his own even without Hertzog's support. But his harsh treatment of the more militant Afrikaner nationalists – he had interned a number of them at the disused Koffiefontein diamond mine, along with German and Italian prisoners-of-war – had made him many enemies. When the war was over it was no surprise to find he was challenged from every side: at one extreme the Labour Party and the Dominion Party wanted South Africa to strengthen her ties with Britain, and at the other the 'purified' National Party and the newly formed Afrikaner Party were demanding a republic without delay.

'Oubaas' Smuts was caught in four fires, with his own party rather less than organised and in no position to give him any real support. He was losing by-election after by-election, and when the two Afrikaner parties joined forces to fight him at the next general election it seemed the writing was on the wall.

That was the situation in 1947, when Smuts announced the Union was in for a rather special treat. Appreciating the very real threat of the republican movement, he had gone right to the heart of the matter and invited the British Royal Family to visit South Africa for a 'pleasant holiday'. After all, he reasoned, in nearly 150 years of British rule Afrikaners, in fact South Africans, had never glimpsed a ruling monarch. Perhaps if they saw King George for themselves they might begin to appreciate him.

There was a great outcry from the Nationalists, so great that elsewhere in the Commonwealth there were suggestions that the King should on no account visit a land so torn. His very life would be in danger. However the King was not deterred, and the royal party arrived in Cape Town early in 1947 to be greeted with an ecstatic welcome.

Smuts had promised a 'pleasant holiday'. The King was in poor health, and could well have done with it. But by this time Smuts had gone ahead and organised a full-scale tour for the royal party, taking in every part of the dominion. The way things were going, there might never be another opportunity. On the other hand, Smuts himself was confident the presence of the King, the Queen and the two Princesses would tip the balance once and for all. Even the hardiest republicans could not fail to respond to their magic.

The visit was planned to the last detail, as it had to be: two months of virtually non-stop travelling from city to city, province to province, even country to country as the royal party took in Southern Rhodesia and Bechuanaland. Welcomes varied: English groups went out of their way to show their loyalty, Afrikaners were more tardy. But at least there was never any hint of danger. Whatever their private feelings, South Africans were prepared to give visitors to their country a warm welcome.

Behind the scenes there was considerable intrigue, of course. The editor of an Afrikaans newspaper in Johannesburg, a Dr H F Verwoerd, refused to refer to the royal tour in his columns. Stellenbosch, the citadel of the republican movement, received the royal party in total silence. On the other hand, Bloemfontein was more than gratified when the Royal Family called on the widow of old President Steyn; and Pretoria was genuinely touched when they attended the Groote Kerk on Palm Sunday, and when the King returned President Kruger's family Bible to his heirs.

For the King, the strain was particularly telling. It was later accepted that the tour contributed to the breakdown in his health which led to his death, five years later. But for the time, he was ready to comply with all Smuts wanted of him. And when Smuts took him home to greet his wife at their quaint farm Doornkloof, he and his family were happy to sample the typical Afrikaner life style that must be good enough for them if it was good enough for the Smutses – even when it came to eating from a plain kitchen table covered in linoleum.

With the tour in its last stages the royal visitors began the long trip back to Cape Town and to the battleship *Vanguard* which was to carry them home to Britain. On their route was Kimberley, where they would spend a day before proceeding. For much of it they would be the guests of Ernest and De Beers.

The date set was to be April 18. Ernest travelled down to Kimberley in good time, though without Ina; and with him went Harry and Bridget and young Mary, now three and a half. They had a second child by this time: Nicholas Frank, born on June 8 1945; but they had left him with his nanny at Little Brenthurst. Kimberley was decked brilliantly, flags and bunting on every building and many of them floodlit. Of them all, the De Beers central offices were the most glamorous.

From early in the morning crowds thronged the streets, angling for the best possible view of the royal party. The King's first duty was to inspect hundreds of ex-servicemen drawn up on Market Square; then to visit Kimberley's famous museum of African tribal life, the Duggan-Cronin gallery, where they met the mayors and mayoresses of all the communities of the district, and the members of the Kimberley city council. Among them, now serving as deputy mayor, was the same Fred Hicks who had caused Ernest such trouble in the early days of the Great War.

So far there had been no hint of Kimberley's real character, no reminder that this was the diamond city. Now the impression was to be corrected. It was time to take the royal party to see Kimberley's world-famous tourist attraction, the Big Hole. Ernest preceded them, to be in time to welcome them on De Beers territory; and with him went Bridget who was standing in for the day as first lady of the diamond world.

Ernest and Bridget were driven out to the Big Hole in plenty of time, but were stopped at the gates by a fresh-faced young policeman. 'Nobody allowed on the property today', he told them. 'Only the Royal Family and people with permits signed by Sir Ernest Oppenheimer'.

Ernest was amused, and patiently explained who he was. But the policeman refused to budge.

'Anybody can say he is Sir Ernest Oppenheimer', he said. 'Better you go back the way you came, sir, or I'll have to make trouble for you.'

There were many bystanders near the gate, and they recognised Ernest through the car window and tried to convince the policeman of his mistake. But that only made him all the more determined to send the intruders packing. There was nothing for it but to go back.

Ernest was heartily amused. It was a ridiculous situation. But just then the Kimberley Chief of Police drove up, full of apologies. He

230

would have the man punished, he said. But Ernest would not hear of it. He had not enjoyed a joke so much in a long time.

Bridget and Ernest barely had time to collect themselves before the Royal Party arrived. The Oppenheimers were presented, and then the King and Queen advanced gingerly to the protective rail, and gazed down at the green waters far below them. As Ernest explained to the King how the mine had functioned, the Queen and Princess Margaret picked up stones to throw them down and listen for the splash. Like most visitors, they could hardly believe how long it took. And when it was time to leave it was obvious they were reluctant.

The party returned to the middle of town for a civic lunch at the Kimberley Club. There was a busy afternoon ahead. De Beers had laid on a special exhibition at the sorting offices, probably the most remarkable display of gem diamonds ever seen. In all, the little piles of rough and polished stones spread over the white surfaces of the sorting tables were valued at more than £3 million.

Ernest was host again, and his first job was to introduce the royal party to his directors – among them, of course, Harry. Then they moved slowly along the table, inspecting the neat piles of diamonds as they went. Ernest and Bridget looked after the King and Queen while Harry escorted the Princesses. All the way the King and Ernest talked happily, while the King several times took the opportunity of running his fingers through the little heaps of diamonds. The Princesses picked up individual stones to hold them to the light, and Harry answered all their questions.

At last they reached the end of the table. Little Mary was waiting for them. She had been practising for this moment for weeks past. Ernest beckoned her forward and shyly she approached each of the Princesses and curtseyed as she gave them the diamonds which Ernest handed to her: for Princess Elizabeth a six carat brilliant, for Princess Margaret a four and a half carat emerald cut, each in a casket of polished blue ground surmounted by a coronet of tiny diamonds.

The gift was altogether unexpected. The Princesses were thrilled, particularly Princess Elizabeth who had so far seemed a little glum. Perhaps she was missing Philip Mountbatten back in England. Her engagement was still several weeks away, and in a few months she would be married. But now she came to life.

'Oh, I say, what a wonderful thing to have,' she said. 'I am very grateful.'

The King and Queen were as delighted as their daughters. After looking at the diamonds the King bent down to shake Mary's hand.

Her grandfather watched proudly with a contented smile on his face. Everything had gone off very smoothly.

Three days later it was Princess Elizabeth's 21st birthday. She had not made as favourable an impression on the South African public as her parents, if only because she seemed so reserved. But this was her moment. Cape Town and General Smuts made sure she would not forget it. At her coming-of-age ball at Government House she was showered with a hundred presents, many of them in diamonds. The climax of the evening came when General Smuts presented her with a birthday gift from the Union of South Africa: 87 flawless diamonds from the State Diggings in Namaqualand, matched for a necklace. The great statesman paid his own tribute.

'In this changing world where mankind is once more reaching for new paths to the future, we wish her a place of her own in history. In her father and mother and the beautiful background of her family life she has sure guides in the paths of public duty and unselfish devotion . . . We are glad and proud that one so human and sincere and modest has been given to us as the link to bind together the peoples of our world-wide group in bonds of understanding and co-operation.'

Earlier that evening, alone in a room at Government House before a microphone, Princess Elizabeth had broadcast to the Commonwealth. Not Britain and South Africa alone, but listeners all through Africa, through India and Pakistan and Ceylon, Burma, Malaya, Australia, New Zealand, the South Seas, Canada, Central America, the West Indies: in short, the whole British family of nations which constituted the greatest Empire the world had known, listened to her words.

Quietly, rather shyly, she embarked on her speech. She told her listeners that when her predecessors had attained their majority, it had been customary for them to take their vows of manhood. She could hardly do that: but she could make a contribution in her own way.

'Through the inventions of science I can now do what was impossible for bygone heirs to the Throne. I can make my solemn act of dedication with a whole Empire listening. I should like to make that dedication now.

'It is very simple. I declare before you all that my whole life, whether it be long or short, shall be devoted to your service and the service of our great Imperial family, to which we all belong.

'But I shall not have strength to carry out this resolution unless you join in with me, as I now invite you to do. I know that your support will be unfailingly given.

'God help me to make good my vow, and God bless all of you who are willing to share it.'

232

3

EVEN SMUTS had to agree the Royal Tour was by no means an unqualified success. In many ways the Royal Family had been rather a disappointment: the King tired and rather listless, his daughters shy and reserved – particularly his elder daughter. Only the Queen had won her way into South African hearts: she had quite 'stolen them away' and it was she whose memory lingered longest. But her contribution alone could not persuade South Africans they were better off within the British Empire than outside it.

However, Smuts persevered. Hardly had the Royal Family sailed away on board the *Vanguard* than he was working on parliament again. What was the alternative to British rule? Should South Africa 'go it alone' and trust in the United Nations which Smuts himself had helped bring into being, and whose declaration of human rights he had drafted? No, he said. South Africa could only lose. British rule was 'a safer guarantee of universal peace than the hitherto most disappointing United Nations Organisation.'

It was time to go to the people, and Smuts called a general election for 1948. The parties published their manifestos, and there was a surprise from the Nationalists. Following a close study made of South Africa's racial problems by a group of academics at Stellenbosch University, they had adopted its recommendation of a novel form of segregation. Separate development, they called it: or as it was phrased in Afrikaans, *apartheid*.

There was a strong case to be made for this 'separate development', they claimed: at any rate, so far as the white elements of the population were concerned, and in fact for each of the 'minority' racial groups like the Coloured people and the Indians as well. Left to develop 'naturally' South African society would be overwhelmed by the expanding black African mass: the minority groups would be submerged, and the high order of western society which was operating in South Africa to the good of all would disappear, perhaps never to return. Rather let each section of the population develop along its own lines in its own areas: and let the divisions be made according to race.

In this earliest form the proposals of the Stellenbosch academics were not intended as a strategy for the oppression of the many by the few, but as an idealistic plan for the survival of all. However, the Nationalists were already going further. It was clear from the tone of their manifesto that they were going to use apartheid as a means towards an end. Their aim was to fortify the position of the Afrikaner and his fatherland for all time: and to achieve it, they would allow nothing to stand in their way. The more militant were calling for the nationalisation of the gold mines: an old story, but no less dangerous.

As a first step in this campaign, cried the Nationalists, Smuts and his party would have to go. Not even their most enthusiastic supporters gave the Nationalists any real chance of ousting them at the first attempt: they would need another parliamentary campaign to consolidate their position and indeed prepare themselves for office. On the other hand, they should certainly introduce as many candidates to parliament as they could, even at this stage. The Nationalists set about their election fight with gusto.

Smuts's men were quietly confident: if the Oubaas was not as popular as he might be, at least his deputies were. Jan Hofmeyr in particular, brilliant academic and thinker, had collected an impressive personal following in his short parliamentary career, and some even hoped Smuts would step down from the leadership in his favour. In any case, the United Party had recruited new talent for its ranks, and was fielding a strong team of candidates. Smuts was especially pleased about one of them. As his father had hoped for so long, Harry Oppenheimer was standing for Kimberley.

Harry was nearly 40 now, well versed in all aspects of financial affairs and already a power to be reckoned with in United Party affairs on the Reef – though he confesses he had not previously been at all keen on venturing into active politics. He had always had it in the back of his mind to stand for parliament one day – Ernest had seen to that – but wanted first to consolidate his business position, and make sure he had something to offer and something worth saying. Now he was ready. There could be little doubt that in standing for Kimberley he would sweep home with a big majority: he had been born there, De Beers was as powerful as ever, and Ernest had served the city well when *he* was in parliament. But Harry was not going to leave it to chance.

The Nationalists had candidates in most constituencies but not in Kimberley. Instead, Harry found himself opposed by two independents, both Kimberley men. One, William Trehaeven, was reputed to have the backing of the Nationalists. The other, like Trehaeven a lot older than Harry, was a familiar figure: none other than Fred Hicks.

It would have been distasteful to recall Hicks's bitter contributions to Ernest's early career: they were best forgotten. Instead, Harry contented himself with answering the points made by his opponents at their various meetings. Fred Hicks, for instance, pointed out that

234

twelve years before Ernest had said Kimberley would have to survive by diamonds and diamonds alone. Could Harry stand by that pronouncement when the town was crying out for new industries? Harry asked whether it was fair to expect his father's words to stand twelve years after they were uttered.

More serious were the complaints about his long absences from Kimberley. How could he represent the city when he lived in Johannesburg, three hundred miles away? Harry had an answer. He was going to breed racehorses, he had decided. He would be taking over Mauritzfontein, the old De Beers stud not seven miles from Kimberley. He planned to build a house there, and would certainly spend time in it.

In the course of each campaign speech Harry emphasised his loyalty to Smuts. He stood by United Party policy all the way, he said, except in matters of race relations where he was inclined to be more liberal than the general caucus. He could see some point in residential segregation: it might even be desirable. But any other form of segregation, economic, social, industrial, governmental or whatever, he vehemently opposed. In particular he championed the rights of the Coloured and Indian communities, caught between two fires: they were on the European side of the fence, and should not be stripped of their rights as the Nationalists were demanding.

Harry enjoyed the full support of Kimberley's retiring representative, and of other local dignitaries: it seemed he would win easily. Bridget played almost as full a part in his campaign as he did himself, canvassing house to house with the other party workers. Ernest intended to make several appearances to support Harry, but had to cancel them when taken ill. But he did attend an important meeting at the Kimberley city hall where the guest speaker was the Minister of Health, Dr Henry Gluckman, who would add the cabinet's stamp to Harry's candidature.

'I say to you all: miners, merchants, civil servants, Coloured people,' Ernest told the crowds packed into the hall. 'If you want to make an old man happy, vote for his son.'

The campaign wound on its way. In Kimberley all was under control, but in the country as a whole it was plain the run of play was not in Smuts's favour. But the old leader was not alarmed. Instead, only a few days before the election he took a step which could only harm his chances with potential Afrikaner supporters: remembering a personal pledge made during the war, he announced the Union was recognising the new state of Israel.

Election day came, and with it Sailor Malan. He had offered to travel down to Kimberley in Harry's support and not surprisingly created quite a stir in the quiet community. He was not going to make a speech or indeed say anything: he had come simply to put himself and his car at the disposal of the voters, and drive them to and from the polling booths. That in itself was quite an attraction.

All day long Harry and Bridget – and Ernest too, now thoroughly enjoying himself – drove round the constituency urging on Harry's supporters and encouraging the UP helpers. At last the polling booths closed and they had to endure the long wait. The results were announced later that night: the Nationalist support of Trehaeven had not been in vain, though poor Fred Hicks had taken a beating.

Mr HARRY OPPENHEIMER (UP)	5 543
Mr William Trehaeven (Ind)	3 277
Mr Fred Hicks (Ind)	101
UP majority	2 266

Next day Harry went on a tour of Kimberley to thank those who had voted him in. Bridget and Ernest went too. They appeared on the balcony of the United Buildings in Market Square, and in Beaconsfield town hall. 'I pledge myself to work for you all – for the city, for the United Party and for South Africa', promised Harry.

Kimberley had voted for Smuts and the United Party. Everyone expected this would be the pattern throughout the Union: perhaps the Oubaas was not as popular as he might have been, but that was more than compensated by the general affection for Jan Hofmeyr and the others. But as more results came through, it was clear that the result was going to be very close indeed: and in the final event, incredible as it seemed, the Nationalists had done it. Against all expectations they had won the election, by the tiny majority of four seats. And as a final insult, they had swept General Smuts himself from his seat at Standerton.

For Harry personally, there was a touch of irony in the result. It was exactly what had happened when his father first stood for parliament in 1924. Ernest had gained his seat safely enough – but the South African Party had been defeated by the Nationalists, and Smuts had lost his seat. It had been a surprise on that occasion, and it was a surprise now: members of Smuts's last cabinet had been so confident of victory that they now had to ask their successors for a few days' grace to allow them a chance to pack and move out of their official residences.

Harry was ready to take his seat in parliament, even in Opposition.

He had prepared himself in a rather important respect, in view of the arrival of the Nationalists: he had been taking private lessons in Afrikaans. With his schooling and university years in England this side of Harry's education had been sadly neglected. After all, there had been little encouragement at home. Ernest did not speak a word of Afrikaans, nor could any others of the family, or indeed many Johannesburgers. It was not necessary: they could get by without it. Not so in parliament.

Harry took lessons from Sarah Goldblatt, regarded as the finest teacher of Afrikaans. For many years she had been the secretary of C J Langenhoven, the writer and parliamentarian given chief credit for the establishment of Afrikaans as one of South Africa's official languages at the expense of High Dutch. Harry was also helped by Twinkle Hanekom, the wife of Blaar Coetzee who was himself a member of parliament and who edited the UP journal *Eendag*.

Twinkle was so impressed by Harry's progress that she got him to write a short story, and when Blaar Coetzee saw it he decided to publish it in his magazine under the initials 'HO'. He sent Harry a cheque for half a guinea as an acceptance fee. The gesture so delighted Harry that rather than cash it he stuck it into a scrapbook with a clipping of the story.

Harry started the new session without the services of his political secretary. Sailor Malan had tried hard, but it was clear to both of them he was just not cut out for a career in business. Harry had recently bought Mauritzfontein, as he had promised, so what more natural course than to let Sailor live there for a while and return to the farming life he had been brought up in? In due course he could have a farm of his own.

The parliamentary session would last several months, and Harry and Bridget might well have considered staying at Ernest and Ina's holiday home out in Muizenberg, Blue Mountains. Instead they took a little cottage in the Malay Quarter on the slopes of Signal Hill, the picturesque neighbourhood adopted by Cape Town's Moslem community after the abolition of slavery.

The cottage faced on to a steeply sloping street running down to the city below, with a courtyard behind it shaded by tall trees and cooled with an ornamental pool. Over the wall of the courtyard peeped the dome of a mosque, and beside it the tower from which the muezzin called the faithful to prayer morning and evening, assisted by a high-powered loudspeaker which did little to enhance the district's calm.

Bridget fancied the colour pink, and duly had the cottage repainted. She did the same at Mauritzfontein, where even the outbuildings, right down to the pigsties and kennels, were being painted that same shade. But somehow, for all its unexpectedness, the colour looked right.

Smuts was out of power now and not the man he had been – after all, he was nearly 80 – so the United Party pinned all its hopes on his deputy. Jan Hofmeyr was the visionary to lead the revival of sanity, and bring about the downfall of the Nationalists. But it was not to be. Before the year's end, even before the opening of the new parliament, he was dead. Some said it was from a broken heart.

It would be a tough session, they all knew: tougher now than ever. Smuts had returned, and would be their leader: but morale was low. They knew the Nationalists had been taken by surprise themselves. Not in their wildest dreams had they imagined they could unseat the UP at the first real attempt. But now they were in power they were not going to waste it. Whether their majority was four or forty, it would be the same.

But the UP was not going to let them get away. This was only some ghastly interlude. Fight now, break them and all would be well. As they started the session the UP members' morale was high, and their unceasing attacks seemed to be having effect. Perhaps the Nationalists were divided in their own ranks. The UP front-benchers made hay with what seemed gross incompetence on the part of the fledgling cabinet ministers. Even the backbenchers joined in – among them a rather diffident, dark young man: the new member for Kimberley City.

Harry's maiden speech was on a subject he knew well – the position of gold and diamonds. The occasion was the budget debate, and the new Minister of Finance – no stranger, in fact: none other than the same Havenga who had served under Hertzog when Ernest was in the House – had a lot to say. After all, the Nationalists' manifesto before the election had said they intended to nationalise the gold industry, and presumably the diamond industry too if they got the chance. Here was their opportunity to get their own back after all those years of oppression from the mining capitalists.

Quietly, almost apologetically, Harry began his speech: hands behind his back, nervous at first, but gradually gaining in confidence. It must have been quite an ordeal: never had he been so exposed in his life. If his own natural reticence was not enough of a handicap, Ernest had always encouraged in him the rather unassuming, modest approach which he favoured himself, and which was anything but suited to the cut-and-thrust of party politics. But Harry stuck it out.

First, the diamond situation. It was an anomaly that a special levy on diamond mines should be continued though the Excess Profits Duty

238

had long since disappeared. True, the diamond mines were prosperous and could afford to pay, but the diamond industry was subject to extremes of booms and slumps, and it was very necessary that when times were good, reserves should be built up against future depressions.

All sound stuff, and the House had heard its like before in Ernest's speeches. After all, Harry had helped to write many of them. Now he warmed to his theme and went on to gold. It was essential that gold production should be increased. It would not be fair to use the profits of high grade mines to subsidise low grade producers, as had been suggested. What was needed was a drastic overhaul of the industry: gold mines would survive only if production costs were lowered or the gold price raised. To snatch the profits of the more prosperous mines would discourage the investment of 'risk' capital by the public at large: and such a course was madness. To take an example, how could the Free State field develop if this was the policy to be pursued?

The speech made a favourable impression, and Harry was not slow to make another. Within two weeks of his debut in parliament he was attracting the attention of the gallery correspondents. One of them paid him an unexpected compliment.

'To make a financial debate sparkle with wit and tingle with interest as Mr J H Hofmeyr used to do was not expected of the United Party, grievously weakened in Parliament by the loss of his matchless tongue. Yet a young backbencher of the United Party achieved almost equal success in this most difficult branch of debating last night. Mr H F Oppenheimer (Kimberley City) held the house with a speech on Mr. Havenga's Part Appropriation Bill as candid as Mr Hofmeyr's used to be and in its own way nearly as gripping. For his knowledge of finance comes not from years spent in the Treasury, but from years outside it . . .'

For the remainder of the session Harry confined himself to speaking on economic questions: probably wisely, though he must have been tempted to break new ground. The Nationalists had overcome their initial problems, and were now working boldly towards the fulfilment of their dreams: the protection of South Africa's whites, particularly the Afrikaners, until the end of time. Already they were preparing to disenfranchise the Coloured people, as Africans had already been disenfranchised before the war. Smuts could only say: 'In the evening of my life I have seen the work of fifty years destroyed.'

The Nationalists went further. Now they produced that blueprint of segregation, the ideal of apartheid. In all South Africa's history it had been the accepted way of life in private: but now they wanted to make it official, and give it the rule of law. So this was it: they really meant what they had threatened. The UP, and Harry among them, believed it was madness. At last Harry could speak out in public, at a Junior UP conference in the Transvaal.

'The Nationalist attitude of looking upon the non-European as a means towards the advancement of the European is a negation of the European civilization which they pretend they are supporting. . . It is all very well to be separated from the Natives and walk in separate corridors at Johannesburg station, but while we still have the Native working in our houses and looking after our children that form of apartheid is getting us nowhere.'

When he was invited to address another political meeting in the Transvaal, this time in a Nationalist stronghold in Pretoria, Harry invited a friend to accompany him: Bill Wilson, who had joined Anglo at the instigation of Keith Acutt, and who was now closely involved with Harry and Acutt in opening up the Free State goldfields. Bill Wilson was rather alarmed to note the presence of the notorious Robey Leibbrandt, a former South African heavyweight boxing champion who had espoused Hitler's cause in the war and after special training in Germany returned to South Africa on board a yacht and landed in great secrecy on the desolate Skeleton Coast. It was his intention to build a guerilla resistance force dedicated to the overthrow of Smuts and his government, but he was betrayed and brought to trial. It was expected he would be executed for high treason, but instead he was sentenced to life imprisonment. When the Nationalists came to power, one of their first – and most controversial – measures had been to release him.

Now he had turned up at Harry's meeting, and as Harry spoke he rose from his seat and began pacing the aisle before the platform in most menacing fashion. Bill Wilson expected a brawl to break out at any minute, but was amazed to see that Harry took not the slightest notice of the interruption and instead carried on with his speech as if he was among friends who agreed with everything he said. The incident gave Bill Wilson an insight into Harry's personal courage.

But whatever attacks were made by Harry and others in the United Party, they made no impression on the Nationalists. Broken and disillusioned, Smuts gave up the struggle. 'My old comrades have turned against me,' he complained. But as someone gently reminded him, 'How could they? Your old comrades are all dead.' Now the Oubaas himself followed them. In May 1950, he celebrated his 80th birthday in Johannesburg and Ernest was among those invited to make a special speech in his honour. But Smuts was already a sick man, and a month later came the heart attack that ended his life.

Smuts was gone, Hofmeyr was gone: their followers' morale evaporating in their wake. Unable to fight the Nationalists, the United Party men fought each other. From the chaos of petty ambition that survived Smuts, the UP had to find a leader. In the end they settled on a compromise: J G N Strauss, of whom it could be said that at least nobody objected to him. For the Nationalists, it was all too significant. What had been so strong at the outset, an Opposition determined to drive them not from power alone but out into the political wilderness never to return, was now crumbling into mediocrity.

In this situation Harry came to play an increasingly important part in the United Party's programme, and his progress was not lost on the gallery.

'Arguing with the honourable member for Kimberley City in a financial debate is rather like arguing with the Bank of England,' wrote a columnist in the *Rand Daily Mail*. 'Other members may wonder where the capital influx has gone since the Nationalists came and why it hesitates to come back. Harry Frederick Oppenheimer, though he looks disconcertingly young, does not wonder. He knows. . .

'He has firm well-groomed views on immigration, on racial peace and tolerance, on the equal rights of English-speaking and Afrikaans-speaking South Africans. Inevitably, however, mining and finance are the subjects on which the United Party chiefly calls upon him to enliven debate and enlighten the Government benches – never so lost as in a bread-and-butter discussion. . .

'In these sometimes acrimonious discussions Harry has a manner all his own. Friendly, courteous, witty, highly persuasive, he is a constructive critic, with no wish but to help his country. He never exaggerates. Therefore, his suggestions are peculiarly illuminating and his criticisms of Nationalist policy peculiarly damaging.'

Harry's rise to prominence was not greatly welcome on the Nationalist side of the House, though it was some time before he was openly attacked. Instead he was allowed the calm before a storm. The government was preparing to introduce its most controversial measure yet – the first true token of the apartheid programme it had promised. Its Separate Representation of Coloured Voters Bill, introduced in the 1951 session, would disenfranchise Coloureds from the full voters' roll, and give them instead four white members of parliament to represent their interests.

The move provoked strong reaction from the horrified United Party.

241

Harry was visiting his constituency, and organised a snap public meeting on the steps of Kimberley city hall. Another member of parliament, Hamilton Russell, was with him: but much more important, for the first time Sailor Malan appeared on a political stage. He had taken a mortgage on one of the De Beers farms, Benfontein, and had set himself up with 900 sheep. But the totalitarian attitude of the government had shocked him, and at Harry's request he had come to lend him his support.

'The government aims not at national unity but at national division,' Harry told the crowd. 'It tries to encourage the growth of group sentiment at the expense of national sentiment; and that is a deliberate invitation to Coloured people who have always been patriotic South Africans to concentrate on their national sectional interest only, to the exclusion of the interests of the country as a whole. . .

'There is one reason and one reason alone for this measure and that is the Government's hope of obtaining some political advantage out of it for the Nationalist Party. That is the reason why our Constitution must be torn up. For that reason the rights of decent citizens must be taken away, for no better reason than that racial relations must be embittered and European leadership in South Africa endangered.'

There were protests in other centres. A group in Natal formed an 'Action Committee for the Defence of the Constitution', and there were many ex-servicemen among its members. Several demanded that Natal should secede from the Union. In Johannesburg ex-servicemen laid a full-size coffin containing 'the Constitution of South Africa' at the foot of the Cenotaph. After the ceremony the men agreed to form a 'Rand War Veterans Action Committee' which would organise a torchlight procession through the streets to the city hall to demand 'Hands off the Constitution'. They invited Sailor Malan to come up to the Reef and take the salute.

Even before the march came off there were similar meetings in other centres. In Johannesburg thousands of people joined in the march or stood by applauding. Sailor was expected to make a speech, and made a brave attempt. 'It is good to see this support in protest against the rape of the Constitution and the attack on our rights and liberties as free men. In Abyssinia, at Alamein and a score of bloody campaigns we won the right to a voice in our country's affairs. And we are determined that our voice shall not only be heard but that it shall also be heeded.'

The government took little notice of this movement at first. Cabinet ministers jeered at the torchbearers, suggesting the whole thing was just another United Party fiasco. 'You are beating against an impregnable fortress with nothing more penetrating than a string of anaemic chickens,' they told the Opposition.

But the movement was not to be quenched. The different groups answered a call to unite forces in converging on Cape Town, and protest in the shadow of Parliament itself. From all parts of the country came jeeps, cars and lorries, a 'steel commando' of English and Afrikaans-speaking ex-servicemen determined to oust the Nationalists. Not only Sailor, but many other 'big names' were involved with the movement now. Among them was Keith Acutt, a rising star at the Anglo American. His presence and Sailor's provoked an obvious taunt from the cabinet: this 'Torch Commando', as it was being called, was nothing but a tool of 'Oppenheimer, Ltd'.

The commando paraded in force through the streets of Cape Town: thousands upon thousands of men and women marching with torches held aloft, singing the songs they had sung in war. Tens of thousands more watched them as they passed, applauding loudly but with respect. Excited Coloured 'skollies' from the slum township of District Six followed them as far as they went: and on their way home again met a force of police reinforcements brought in from the country areas with instructions to 'break up the mob'. The police charged with batons. More than 150 of the Coloureds were injured.

Suddenly the government realised the new movement's potential as a rallying point for anti-government factions, and was not slow to react. But the Torch Commando was in its stride. Its members held a full convention a few weeks later, and elected Sailor as national president. He was their figurehead: an Afrikaner, after all, and an Afrikaner legend at that, pledged now to defend his country's constitution.

Sailor was rather bewildered to find himself so much in the limelight. An interviewer asked him what his politics were. Which party did he support? He sucked his pipe and replied: 'The party that believes a man's a man for a' that. How could I think otherwise? In the war I saw many men die for a cause. They were not only white but all shades of the human race. I'm in the Torch Commando because I don't like seeing people pushed around. There was a chap called Hitler who did just that and made a hell of a mess of the world. It mustn't happen again.'

Numbers were increasing all the time. It was claimed 200 000 had enrolled, not from all four provinces alone but even from South West. Each area formed its own commando, drilled and organised in terms of what its men had learnt in the war. 'We are sick of seeing the Opposition using Queensberry rules,' said Sailor. He talked of 'mobile, disciplined units,' but he insisted 'we are militant, not military.'

'Our aim is to defeat the Government, which is Fascist in spirit. But we have a peaceful purpose too – the building-up of a united South African nation.'

The government would not stand for talk like that. 'People contend that the Torch Commando will go a little way and then vanish,' Prime Minister Malan – no relation of Sailor's, incidentally: it is a common name in South Africa – told a meeting in East London. 'That is not my view. The Torch Commando is to be taken seriously because it has a military or semi-military character. Private armies of that nature cannot be tolerated.'

Suddenly the Nationalists discovered a new threat. A group of businessmen had created a secret fund of no less than £1 000 000 which would be used in a bid to overthrow the government: and the man behind it all was 'the honourable mining magnate on that side of the House' – of course, Harry. 'If it comes to a stand-up fight you can come with your money', challenged one of the Nationalists. 'We have extended the hand of friendship to the English-speaking people and it has been rejected.'

The London *Economist* carried an amusing piece about the fuss which resulted: 'The South African Nationalists play a complicated game of politics with only three well-thumbed cards. These are the black bogey, the British connection, and "Hoggenheimer". This three-card trick has, however, had surprising successes. It put the late General Hertzog into power in 1924 and kept a Nationalist Government going from that date until 1933; and it put the Nationalists under Dr. Malan back into power three years ago, just as if there had been no fusion, no war and no General Smuts.

'The black bogey and the British connection are never in discard, but it is sometimes advisable to hold them in reserve for a time. Then it becomes the turn of "Hoggenheimer". The name is the creation of a brilliant cartoonist called Boonzaaier, who in the mid-twenties attached it to a paunchy, cigar-smoking capitalist, obviously purloined from the Labour Press. "Hoggenheimer" represented "money power", which in South Africa has traditionally meant the gold and diamond mines. It is no accident that "Hoggenheimer" rhymes with Oppenheimer.

'The first hint that "Hoggenheimer" was about to reappear on the political stage came some months ago in the form of some ambiguous phrases from the Nationalist Minister of Economic Affairs, Mr Eric Louw, an indefatigable smeller out of United Party plots and strategems. Mr Louw, in the midst of a discourse on import control, rambled into a tirade against businessmen who bit the Ministerial hand that fed them.

'Well used to Mr Louw's grumbles about his constantly nibbled hands, the general public, and even most businessmen, detected no cause for general alarm, even though Mr Louw warned that those who deliberately tried to harm the government could expect no great favours from it. The real eruption came in Parliament, when Dr J H Loock, a former Smuts supporter who had joined the Nationalists, darkly described a mysterious dinner (held either in Johannesburg or in Cape Town: Nationalist versions differ) at which sinister mining magnates decided to contribute £1 000 000 ("What is a million to them?" asked Dr Loock scornfully) towards the overthrow of the Nationalist Government. Dr Loock explained that one part of the plot was to buy over "outstanding Afrikaner intellectuals", and added modestly that he himself had been offered a good slice of the £1 000 000 but had rejected it with contempt.

'The Nationalist campaign then began in earnest. Dr Malan's paper, the *Burger*, protested in the sacred name of democracy against the United Party becoming the "chosen instrument of the money-power". The *Volksblad* (Bloemfontein) spoke, in the same breath, of "sinister money-power" and "£1 000 000 for spreading the doctrine of liberalism". The *Transvaler* went better than either, disclosing to its presumably horror-stricken readers a "dastardly plot" whereby the mining and industrial magnates would dismiss workers, while simultaneously the rich merchants would "withhold scarce commodities and goods essential to the home", the aim being chaos, misery and the climbing back into power of the United Party. "This plan", said the *Transvaler*, "has been framed in close cooperation with the United South Africa Trust Fund".'

Harry replied to the *Transvaler's* attack in a speech at Kimberley a few nights later. Yes, there was a fund. It had been formed 18 months before, a private trust consisting chiefly of business people who 'have taken an interest in the organisation because they are worried about the way things are going on in South Africa, and because they feel that this is one way in which they can help to re-establish a spirit of tolerance and co-operation between the various sections of the people. They have come into the movement as individuals, and there is no question of organised commerce, industry or mining giving their support to the movement.'

They had organised the fund to help build up a mixed European

245

South African nation with democratic ideals, said Harry, and they hoped it would be the basis of the South Africa of the future. There was nothing secret or sinister about it, even if the fund's objects were similar to the United Party's: to promote racial tolerance, uphold Democracy and defend the Constitution.

'If for these aims Mr Oppenheimer at first refused to apologise', wrote the *Economist*, 'he did not deny that as the United Party's programme seemed to fit in with the Trust's aims, it would very likely be eligible for support from the Fund. He did not conceal his personal view that, judged by its present political programme, the Nationalist Party was unlikely to qualify for a share of the £1 000 000.'

The Nationalists hit back. This time their spokesman was J G Strijdom, Minister of Lands. What was the United Party planning to do with this sinister donation from the Trust Fund? No political party could use £1 000 000 within the framework of the Electoral Act, so the money would have to be used in 'a thousand and one devious ways'. One of them, without a doubt, would be to work towards the abolition of the industrial colour bar: and that would be to strike at the very roots of the South African way of life. Why did they hide? Who were they, these conspirators?

Harry duly obliged with a full statement of the position. He was the Trust Fund's chairman. That much they knew already. But now he revealed the names of the eleven trustees besides himself: the list included the names of R B Hagart and other Anglo and De Beers directors. He repeated its position: in view of the sense of insecurity caused by the rapid deterioration in race relations, together with the absence of agreement on how South Africa's grave problems were to be resolved, the Trust Fund would lend its support to those who worked for racial co-operation and the maintenance of democratic principles.

A few days later it was the Prime Minister's turn again. This time he was prepared to connect the fund with the Torch Commando. The government would not hesitate to act against Sailor Malan and his friends, even if they were backed by Hoggenheimer money. 'I ask the United Party, the Torch Commando and its supporters: "What do you aim to do with a semi-military organisation such as the Torch Commando?" I want to ask the supporters of the United Party: "What are you doing? Are you allowing the Torch Commando to create in South Africa a situation bordering on chaos – almost revolt?"

'I have challenged them before, but they have not yet given me a reply. I now demand a clear and immediate reply – why do you fight us with the Torch Commando and the United South Africa Trust Fund, and not with your own party, the United. Party?'

His claims grew bigger and bolder. The United Party was now altogether controlled by 'Oppenheimer Ltd'. The Company had formed the Torch Commando because it felt the United Party was losing its supporters and a new organisation was needed to rally them. Behind the Torch Commando were the country's big capitalists. 'To show how this organisation is controlled by big capital, I need only mention that Group Captain "Sailor" Malan, the National President, is a former employee of Mr Harry Oppenheimer . . .'

'What we have against us is money power, principally under the leadership of Oppenheimer. He has become a power in the land. Oppenheimer – the one who sits in parliament – has control of millions of pounds, and he puts this at the service of our opponents in this struggle. Oppenheimer with his millions exercises a greater influence than, I think, any man in South Africa has ever had.'

A few days later, this time in parliament, Dr Loock returned to the attack with what was intended as the killer blow: a private motion calling for an investigation of the 'secret subsidising' of political parties by big business. He did not pull his punches. The United Party was falling victim to the Trust Fund and the Torch Commando, he said, and that meant to 'Mr Oppenheimer, who is sitting over there, the Anglo American, who has today practically swallowed up three-quarters of the country, and who will swallow up the other quarter as well if we allow him.'

In the past, Loock went on, the United Party had been subsidised by big business: in 1938 by the Jews, in 1943 by the English. In 1948 big business had withdrawn its support to teach the UP a lesson and get it moving again: nobody had imagined for a moment it could actually lose the election, only that its influence would be whittled down and it would have to fight for its life. But the businessmen had gone too far: against all expectations the Nationalists succeeded in winning.

'There that party sits in Opposition. General Smuts is no longer there. There is a Leader on that side who has a hope, or as the saying goes, who has a "snowball's hope" in South Africa to get that party returned to power . . . (Mr Oppenheimer) then thought of another plan. He thought: "I am going to do what Rhodes did: what Rhodes did with Jameson I am going to do with Sailor Malan, but this Government must be thrown out".'

So there it was: the plot revealed. Harry was planning a Jameson Raid to defeat the Nationalists by force, as Loock's seconder went on to elaborate. 'The hon. member for Kimberley City is in such a position as regards financial riches and power that he has reached the same heights as C J Rhodes, and that he now wants to safeguard his riches by means of his political power, and to use his riches to attain greater political power, and for that purpose the United Party is readily available to him.'

Loock again: 'Just imagine, Mr Speaker, that the position is developing in South Africa where that Party, under pressure of the Torch Commando . . . just imagine that such a party may come into power and that Mr Oppenheimer, who has swallowed up three-quarters of this country . . .

Mr SPEAKER: Order! The hon member must refer to the hon member's constituency.

Dr LOOCK: Well then, just imagine that the hon member for Kimberley should then become Minister of Finance. Can you imagine what position this country will then find itself? Then we shall no longer be a nation; we shall be a company town like Welkom or one of the other mining towns in this country . . .'

At last Loock and his seconder were through. 'We should like to warn the responsible members of that party that the forces which were set in motion fifty years ago by De Beers and by the mining magnates, resulting in the Jameson Raid, and which caused such grief and misery in the country in an attempt to break Afrikanerdom, are the same forces they are building up today by means of a party which has abandoned its principles and whose leader has been placed under the control of the Trust Fund and which has a Torch Commando constituted on military lines which wants to do one irresponsible act after another in this country. These same powers are again being set in motion under the leadership of people imbued with the same spirit that prevailed 50 years ago.'

Slowly, almost gently, Harry rose to his feet up on the backbenches. 'It is obvious that it is the formation of the United South Africa Trust Fund which has been the occasion for the moving of this motion. Since I am Chairman of it and since I have received a good deal of notice in the speeches we have just listened to, I think hon members will regard it as appropriate that I should at once give my views.'

Before dealing with the Trust Fund itself, Harry wanted to consider the whole principle of the subsidy of political parties. It was a democratic right of association, he insisted. If a man was free to vote in private, then he should be free to donate funds to a political party without its being made public. In any case, in South Africa both the United

Party and the National Party relied chiefly on the fund-raising activities of their local branches and gained far more from these sources than from 'business interests'. And again, it was not 'business interests' alone which were to be suspected of influencing political parties: what about the farmers who were the strength behind all the National Party's successes?

It took him time to make these points in the fluent, if rather diffident, style of speaking that was now well-known in the House. But the others had not heard it used before to such effect. Harry commanded the attention of both sides, indeed of everyone present, all agog to hear him come to the real kernel of his speech: his defence and explanation of the Trust Fund and all it stood for. At last it was time.

'I intend to come back specifically to the affairs of the United South Africa Trust Fund. That Trust Fund was formed towards the end of 1949 and it was over a year before it attracted the attention of the Nationalist Party and the National Party Press.

An HON MEMBER: Because it was a secret fund.

Mr OPPENHEIMER: I know that the fact of the matter is that they did not know about it, and that was supposed to be a very suspicious circumstance. But Mr Speaker, I cannot accept the proposition that everything the *Burger* does not know is either secret or sinister. Obviously I know very little about how secret societies are run, but subject to correction by the hon the Minister of the Interior, I think they are not run in the same way as the United South Africa Trust Fund. When that fund was formed the first thing we did was to take on staff and rent offices, to have our name put on a nice big brass plate on the door. When the muddle in the Post Office allowed it we even got a telephone. We had our name put in the telephone directory. I see nothing very much like a secret society in that . . .'

Point by point Harry dealt with the attacks Loock and the others had made, then and previously. He had refused to grant an interview about the Fund? Absolute nonsense: he was not even approached by newspapers before the witchhunt was in full swing, and on the two occasions they had approached him it had been to ask specific questions which he had answered on the spot. The United Party was 'dependent' on the Trust Fund? Again absolute nonsense: it so happened the kind of people involved with the United Party was the kind which supported the Trust Fund, the kind which felt dependent on a United Party victory to get rid of a government it felt was a menace to South Africa. That was all there was to it.

Then what was the relationship between the United Party and the

Trust Fund? 'The trouble is that the relationship is so simple that hon members cannot grasp it; it has certain objects which have been published; we have collected a certain amount of money from people who like those objects; and we have interpreted those objects in such a way – and I speak as a Trustee – that we think that by giving assistance to the United Party we are furthering our objects. That is the position and there is no other relationship between the Trust and the party at all.'

Harry did not confine himself to defending his Fund. That had been done. Now he could take the attack into the Nationalist camp: an attack on all the party was trying to do, an attack on the very things he felt were so great a threat to South Africa's future. He ran out of time, but immediately a UP member moved he be given more. Loock objected, but was overruled by the National Party chief whip. Harry continued.

'The formation of an organisation like the United South Africa Trust Fund is, I think, significant in this respect. What has happened is that we have a Government in power with a small majority, a chance majority and it is using that majority to take action on an almost revolutionary basis, and what is happening is that people are waking up and the people who are waking up are not people who previously took any part in politics, but they are people who generally stood outside the political struggle. They are waking up in reaction to what the Government is doing. I don't expect hon members opposite to like that. I can assure them that they will like it a great deal less when the general election comes along, but I do say that this waking up of the people and the association of the people for objects which are legal and to work by means which are legal, is a fundamental part of the democratic system.

'If hon members are honest and genuine when they say that they too also stand for democracy, then they will support the amendment that I move. ("This house wishes to place on record its approval of the democratic right of South Africans to associate together for the furtherance of any objects not contrary to the law of the land".) The motion which the hon member for Vereeniging (Dr Loock) has moved, to my mind, Mr Speaker, in so far as it was not just an opportunity for the hon member of Vereeniging to indulge in his taste for libellous remarks, is an attempt to stifle the democratic process of association which this House, if it is a genuine defender of the freedom of the people, ought to do its best to vindicate.'

They said it was Harry's most effective and courageous speech yet.

250

As he finished and sat down, the United Party cheered him loudly while the Nationalists had nothing to offer in return. The battle was won. But the most significant reaction came from a quiet old gentleman sitting in a public bay immediately behind Harry. As Ernest realised his son's achievement his face broke slowly into a wide grin. There could be no doubt about it. Harry had what it took.

4

HARRY WAS already a household name in his own right, whether he wanted it or not. The Nationalists had seen to that, and when people talked of 'Oppenheimer' these days they thought of Harry first and only then of his father. Ernest was leading an increasingly sedentary life as he had promised himself, leaving all the real spadework to Harry and R B Hagart and their assistants – though of course maintaining his iron grip on the organisation as a whole.

If Harry's duties in parliament were not onerous enough, he was now responsible for Anglo's stakes in the Free State goldfield: he was chairman of each of the new mining companies. All five of the mines round Welkom were nearing the production stage now, and looked most promising: particularly President Brand, richest of them all. In the north Loraine had come up to expectations, but sadly Jeanette had not: operations had to be discontinued – a reminder of how fortunate Anglo had been in all the other mines where the dividends were high. It remained to raise more capital: and that depended on what was basically simple public relations.

That, after all, was what it was all about. Anglo had to convince potential investors that its mines were a worthwhile proposition: that even though it would be years before they could expect any return on their money, when it came it would more than make up for the long delay. Ernest and Harry began an exhausting round of speeches and lectures to whatever organisations were prepared to listen to them. Rotary Clubs, parliament, business groups, chambers of commerce, the Royal African Society, the Royal Empire Society, ex-patriate groups, institutes of management and many more such: to each they spoke of the new goldfield and tried to impress on their listeners one significant aspect, that in importance the new developments ranked with the discoveries of Kimberley and the Witwatersrand.

They found it was far from easy. It was obvious they could not hope to raise all the capital they would need in South Africa alone: they

251

would have to turn to overseas sources. But even in normal times that would have been difficult: and now, with the world war barely over and nations everywhere struggling to set their own house in order, the problem was a lot graver still.

Harry wanted to bring in the Americans, but Ernest was not at all keen. True, it was American capital that had set Anglo on its feet in the first place: but he had soon come to appreciate the degree of control Americans felt was their due – and the lesson had been brought home again by what he had seen on the copperbelt. No, he decided. Rather go short than bring in the Americans.

There was no prospect of raising money in England: that was obvious. Instead, Ernest and Harry turned to a quite different source, as yet untapped by South Africa – and in fact the one country in Europe which was in a position to help: none other than Switzerland. Fortunately the Swiss had no qualms at all about putting money into an untried goldfield, but even this was not enough. Capital was coming in, but far too slowly for Ernest's liking. He would have to think again. Where could he lay his hands on capital to the tune of millions, but without strings? At last he had it. Right under his nose there were millions and to spare: where else but in the golden treasury of the Diamond Corporation?

Thanks to the boom in its sales during the war and after selling the stocks saved in the terrible years of recession, the Diamond Corporation was showing a surplus of £25 000 000. Certainly it was much more than the Corporation could possibly need to tide it over against another such disaster. It seemed a crime to leave all that money idle, Ernest reflected. To him, capital was a tool, and it had to be used. On the other hand, in the last resort it belonged to the shareholders. Ought he to give them a surprise treat and divide it among them?

But Ernest was not inclined to share out the booty, not after the burden his shareholders had made him bear virtually by himself in those years of the slump. He could have cut losses as they had urged and let the whole diamond industry fade into oblivion, perhaps never to return. But he had stuck firm, and the £25 000 000 was there to prove it. No, it was only right to seek to use the money for a definite purpose. After all, that was the sort of thing Rhodes would have done – indeed *had* done in financing his Charter Company and opening up the Rhodesias.

The matter was decided. The Diamond Corporation was split in two with its funds divided equally. One half retained the original name, and the original function. The other became the De Beers Investment Trust, formed to utilise its capital in whatever spheres the trustees decided would be most profitable: in the first resort, of course, the mines of the Free State goldfield.

When it was announced what Ernest had decided there were understandably mixed reactions from the more militant shareholders. It was all summed up in the London *Economist's* comment:

'It is claimed shareholders might have been allowed to decide for themselves whether to invest money in speculative ventures in the Free State, but Sir Ernest will have none of it. He claims he is "reviving the tradition of Cecil John Rhodes". So shareholders of this group follow Sir Ernest pioneering with the mantle of Rhodes around his shoulders whether they like it or not. So far they have come to no harm . . .'

One by one the new mines in the Free State came into production. Now Ernest and Harry had to assure everyone that they were not simply a substitute for the mines of the Witwatersrand, which many claimed were facing extinction. Ernest pointed out that the mines on the Rand were replacing themselves: as the old levels were worked out, more were opened up to take their place. The Free State field was an entirely new element in the South African economy.

As if to confirm Ernest's views about the older mines, there was an impressive windfall which suggested that there was a lot of life in them yet. Since the development of the Atom bomb in World War II and the consequent advances in nuclear energy there had been a worldwide search for uranium. South Africa possessed resources, but it was supposed they were small and of low grade in comparison with the sources so far used: the Congo, Europe and Canada. Now, however, one of the scientists concerned with America's 'Manhattan Project' had discovered the presence of radio-active material in samples of gold-bearing ore from the Witwatersrand. He sent geologists to investigate, and their geiger counters revealed huge deposits of uranium in the Reef which made it probably the biggest low-grade uranium field in the world.

It took some time for researchers to discover the best ways of dissociating uranium from the gold-bearing ore. In the end they settled on the most economic way imaginable: simply reprocessing the slimes left after the gold reduction process, which would otherwise have gone to waste. For negligible extra cost apart from the plant itself there was a huge new industry established for the asking, which would eventually produce uranium to the value of tens of millions of pounds a year.

In this development Anglo was to the fore, particularly through East Daggafontein and Western Reefs which were among the mines

253

first explored for uranium. Though the first plant to come into production was established at General Mining's West Rand Consolidated, East Daggafontein was in production by 1953, with the opening ceremony broadcast simultaneously in both South Africa and Britain through a historic radio link-up involving Ernest on the Rand and Sir John Cockcroft at Harwell.

Anglo's 'man in uranium' was Hagart, who was soon appointed to South Africa's Atomic Energy Board in view of Anglo's booming uranium plants at East Daggafontein, Western Reefs and at the new Free State mines which were quickly roped in. 'As things stand today our position in the field of uranium is of paramount importance to the future,' he told a study conference. 'Even though we may not be the largest individual producer' – South Africa deliberately cut back on production, realising other deposits would soon be worked out and that would leave the Union with a virtual monopoly – 'our position as a source of uranium is assured until at least the end of the century. Politically, this is a very important factor. The world will want our uranium and for that reason South Africa will be regarded as a very important bastion of Western civilisation.'

In the meantime the Free State had been developing as Ernest had hoped. Each of the little communities was finding its feet, but of them all the showpiece was Welkom: now much more than a gleam in the planner's eye. It was already a recognisable town – in fact, one of the most attractively laid out in all Africa. Its new population matched the fresh appeal: everyone was ready to do their bit to get the community on its feet. The new town seemed to have everything, even its own newspaper. Far from the stretch of bare veld the new arrivals expected, the settlement offered wide streets, tree-lined boulevards and impressive modern buildings. Many admitted that far from missing the high life of the cities they had left, they preferred the village-like atmosphere of their new home.

But while Welkom developed, Anglo planners were busy in quite a different direction – in the Sperrgebiet. Mining at CDM had always been hampered by difficult communications. Supplies had to be transported all the way to Lüderitz, quite a journey in itself, then down the long desert miles of the coast road to the mining area. Now, however, there was a bridge across the Orange River, linking the Sperrgebiet with Namaqualand. It was named after Ernest, and he had gone up to open it.

With the new bridge operations could be stepped up considerably. All this time there had been a little collection of huts and shacks here at Oranjemund – literally Orange Mouth. Now these were to be developed into a thriving town, carved from the desert and planned with as much precision as Welkom. The challenge was even greater than in the Free State, of course: this was the Namib Desert, one of the most barren of all, and the mere transportation of materials cost a fortune. Yet slowly but surely a town took shape, and with it the whole structure of the coastal diamond industry that today represents the mainstay of the South West African economy.

Meanwhile, for all the healthy resources of the Diamond Corporation there was the ever-present threat of John Williamson with the world's biggest diamond mine at his disposal. Still he refused to sell any part of his production to the Diamond Corporation in terms of the agreement he had signed. He would wait until its term was run and he could sell freely to anybody he wanted.

All kinds of rumours circulated, not only in the offices of the Diamond Corporation but even among Williamson's own employees. Of course he had plans. He was going to set up his own marketing system, perhaps in England. He had more than enough goods on hand to make a tremendous success of such a venture. Or was he in collusion with an Israeli syndicate, as others insisted? Certainly that was a possibility.

Yet another rumour claimed he had come to an agreement with an American group, and the whole of the mine's production would be flown to the United States to be auctioned on the spot. So the rumours continued, with Williamson refusing to deny or confirm them. That only encouraged more speculation. He seemed to relish the intrigue.

All this time there was no income. The bills mounted up, for labour and for production costs, and the diamonds accumulated in Williamson's strongroom: all but fancy coloured stones, which he liked to collect in jamjars on his dining-room mantelpiece. Not a word of his problems would he breathe to any of his associates: in fact, nobody was on such intimate terms with him. Yet all this time he was building up an overdraft which would have given most businessmen apoplexy.

At last it was revealed that Alan Lennox-Boyd, the British Colonial Secretary, would be visiting the mine. Those in the know realised he would be making a determined effort to persuade Williamson to resolve his differences with the Diamond Corporation, and get the diamonds flowing again. The mine represented Tanganyika's largest single source of revenue, and the territory could ill afford to be deprived of it.

To give the visit a sense of occasion, the mine security officer erected a tall flagpole in the middle of the compound and duly raised the

Union Jack. He was surprised to be summoned by Williamson shortly afterwards and told on no account to repeat the performance. The owner was Canadian, certainly, and he was proud to be a member of the Commonwealth. But he could not tolerate having the Union Jack flying over *his* mine – in short, *his* private kingdom.

Instead, he organised a competition in which the various employees were invited to submit designs for a special Williamson flag. As the winning flag he selected a design with a white diamond on a red background, with the initials 'W D Ltd.' He had a number of these flags made and gave them out. Interestingly, the move met with the approval of the many Afrikaners he had working on the mine, who were of course not noted for loyalty to the British Crown.

That, then, was Williamson's attitude. He had conceived the mine, he had brought it into being, and he had nursed it from the beginning. It was, therefore, his to command. Out there in the wilderness, with the nearest outposts of civilisation hundreds of miles away, his word was law. If money came in for diamonds, he could spend it – and there was nobody to gainsay him.

On the other hand, he was casual to the point of absurdity: in fact, downright irresponsible. He could not care less if diamonds were pilfered from the mine: what he had never possessed, he reasoned, he would never miss. To the despair of his security officers he shrugged his shoulders when he was told diamonds were being smuggled out in tins of butter, in plaster casts, in sorters' navels. Only when the British authorities complained the renegade stones were being sold to finance nationalist agitators would he agree to take a little more care.

It was all rather impressive: Williamson's personal paradise, an oasis in the surrounding desert of featureless bush and baleful baobabs. Here, in little more than five square miles, he had brought a thriving community into being, with comfortable accommodation for whites and blacks, every amenity, sporting facilities, shops and entertainment. There was even a reservoir close by, and on it Williamson sailed a yacht.

So this was the scene that greeted the British Colonial Secretary: a private kingdom, complete with a virtual army of Afrikaner exiles to work the mine and loyal African labourers taught to distrust outside influence. Lennox-Boyd must have been intrigued by the strange figure he now met: recluse, romantic, a bachelor whose every post brought him offers from women wanting to marry him, cook for him, anything – but whom he distrusted to the end: 'They only want me for my diamonds.' But rugged and handsome and a man's man, here in the bush in the middle of Equatorial Africa.

256

The man was a glorious eccentric: Somerset Maugham would have had a field day with him. His home was filled with precious possessions, antique furniture, Persian carpets, a library of first editions – yet everywhere there were mongrel dogs, living a king's life. Among Williamson's pastimes was knitting: and twice in succession he had won the Aylesbury (Bucks) Women's Institute Silver Distaff Award for Needlework.

Lennox-Boyd would soon be told stories of Williamson's odd behaviour. Of his practical jokes, for instance: how when taking visitors round the mine he would tell them that diamonds were so plentiful you could find them just lying on the ground, then scuff his feet in the dust and urge them to do the same. Suddenly a visitor would come across what seemed a huge pink diamond and pick it up in excitement. Only later would he realise it was a hoax: the diamond was plastic, a replica of the beautiful 54 carat stone Williamson had presented to Princess Elizabeth as a wedding present.

Other jokes had been more mischievous. One night Williamson found the Mwadui Club was left open, and with a friend removed all its furniture. Next day he summoned the worried club president, and explained he had a lot of furniture for sale to replace what they had lost. Then again, he liked to carry a pair of scissors in his pocket, and snip off people's ties. The victim would politely laugh at his little joke, hoping Williamson would not forget to send a new one.

Lennox-Boyd could have heard rumours, too, of Williamson's moodiness: how one day his security officer brought in the week's production from the mine, only to find him having a blazing row with his secretary. The diamonds came in only too handy. Williamson picked them up one by one and threw them at her to drive her from the room. Then he hurled the rest at the wall before breaking into tears and rushing to his bedroom and locking himself in. It took the security officer hours to gather the stones together again.

Of course, Williamson would not show such behaviour when distinguished guests were present. Instead, he liked to be the perfect host: well-mannered, considerate, cultured, friendliness and kindness itself. He would attend to every detail of their entertainment, ordering hopelessly exotic food from Nairobi at huge expense, and making sure they did it justice. Certainly a stay at Mwadui was something Williamson's guests did not forget.

But for all his pride, Williamson was a lonely man. His self-imposed isolation had cut him off from the run of contemporary events. He made occasional trips out of Tanganyika, but was always glad to return.

Life in the bush had taken its toll through the years, and he had had malaria and a score of other diseases. And these, with the frequent depressions that overtook him, had turned him to drink. He was a sick man.

There was one most sinister manifestation of his abnormality. Without warning he could relapse into a sudden silence, plunged into a hushed world of his own mind. Nothing could wrench him out of it. His visitors would be shown in to see him, only to find their greetings ignored as the old prospector sat hunched in his chair, staring sightless at the floor.

But these moods were not permanent. He was genuinely pleased to be visited by the Colonial Secretary: he had made his stand. Now he was ready to return to the Diamond Corporation's fold, but if only for his own pride he needed peace with honour. He was not disappointed. Lennox-Boyd passed word to the Corporation, and within a short while a team of De Beers negotiators led by Harry himself flew to Mwadui.

Again Williamson was keyed up. This was to be the most important conference of his life. He had no cards up his sleeve, for all his cunning bluff. There was no fat contract on offer from a rival concern. There was no money left even to run the mine, let alone set up a private distributing organisation. He had to make peace now or not at all. On the other hand, he wanted it understood that he was king and it was his kingdom: and that meant it was his privilege to accept De Beers' terms or reject them.

Harry and his party were accommodated in a guest house on the mine, carefully guarded day and night and supposedly in the greatest secrecy. To further this aim, Williamson liked to call meetings at the oddest hours, sometimes as late as eleven o'clock at night and extending deep into the morning. Harry and Bill Wilson, his chief aide on this occasion, realised it was all in a promising cause and went along with the Canadian's strange quirks.

They enjoyed themselves at the same time. Harry had long been intrigued by Williamson's strange silences, and before a morning meeting told Bill Wilson he would not speak until Williamson did. They entered his office and faced him across his desk. The recluse stared down at the floor. The silence continued for 20 minutes before Harry could stand the strain no more and said something.

The eerie atmosphere continued outside the conferences. Sometimes Williamson would beg Harry and Bill Wilson to leave him alone for a while, as he needed the chance to think. They would go for a walk in the sunshine, pacing the gravel paths of the mine compound. But as they walked they were flanked on each side by tall elegant marabou storks which appeared to be trying to eavesdrop on everything they said. When they reached the end of a path and turned to retrace their steps, the storks would turn too.

It was all for the best. The negotiations were successful, and Williamson emerged jubilant. All past unpleasantness was forgiven and forgotten, and he and Harry had agreed to a new contract that would be fair to all parties.

The success was quite a feather in Harry's cap, of course: for De Beers and the Diamond Corporation it was an important victory. Though Williamson had not actually challenged the established order at any stage, there was always the possibility that he might. Now he was back on their side again.

5

THE OPPENHEIMERS had always liked to be rather private people. They had often been pressed for information about themselves, and after long practice were prepared to reveal so much, but no more: most they kept to themselves. Not that they had a great deal to hide, but they saw no reason why every move they made should reach the newspapers.

But private though they were, that was not the same thing as being introvert. Far from it, they loved entertaining. Ina was Johannesburg's most noted hostess: and when you were invited to a Brenthurst dinner party there was no telling which celebrity you might find there with you. If it was a special occasion, it would be a black tie affair, and the whole evening would go off in faultless style. Ernest and Ina took great pride in doing things properly.

Down the garden at Little Brenthurst life was rather more relaxed. Harry and Bridget saw more of a younger set, and with little Mary and Nicky at home it was not easy to run the household on exactly formal lines. But Little Brenthurst did boast Ernest's remarkably spacious library, which came in very handy for entertaining large numbers of people. Bridget and Harry used it regularly, particularly when as often happened they invited the members of some sporting or cultural group visiting South Africa on tour.

These affairs were relaxed. Servants were in attendance, but well in the background, while Bridget and Harry mingled with their guests to make them feel at home. There might be a speech or two, but they would be kept to a minimum. On one occasion, however, the speechifying led to a rather curious incident which tested Harry's powers of improvisation to the full.

It happened in 1949, when Harry and Bridget had invited the Australian cricket tour party captained by Lindsay Hassett. Harry made a little speech of welcome, and Hassett replied suitably. But when he had finished he suddenly drained his glass, shouted out 'Up the Black Watch!' and hurled it over his shoulder to smash in smithereens.

There was a deathly silence for a moment. But then Harry yelled 'Up the Black Watch!' in his turn, drained his glass and hurled it just as hard. The whole room heaved a sigh of relief, though fortunately the other guests did not follow the host's example.

The Brenthurst library was a rather special place: it contained one of the world's finest collections of Africana in private ownership, and in fact the biggest in Southern Africa. According to the catalogue there were more than 6 000 items, and many of these consisted of 20 volumes or more. This was Ernest's own collection, and he was immensely proud of it. He liked to immerse himself in his books, as he had since those early days in London as a teenager: historical works and biographies, including a huge body of material relating to Napoleon who was his idol; even romantic novels, in fact anything that appealed to him. When he found something he particularly liked he would pass it on to Harry and expect to discuss it with him in due course.

The library included all sorts of items of absorbing interest. Perhaps the most exciting of all was a letter of David Livingstone's, dated March 26, 1856, and addressed to the Rev Mr Freddox in England. It was only four pages long, but was beautifully preserved. Its interest lay in the famous explorer's announcement of the discovery of the Victoria Falls.

There were original despatches sent by Winston Churchill to his paper, the *Morning Post*, during the South African War, in his own handwriting. There was a great deal of manuscript material reflecting on Rhodes's career and on Jameson, including letters written by the notorious adventuress Princess Radziwill who was the bane of Rhodes's later life. In the collection too was an impressive selection of documents relating to Smuts, collected by Sally Richardson who had been his personal secretary for many years: a mass of notes, letters and speeches from a long period and all in the great statesman's handwriting.

By a special arrangement Ernest acquired almost the whole manuscript corpus of two South African writers whose importance seemed assured. Both were personal friends of Ernest's and both let him have as much of their manuscript material as they could: not only what they had written, but even the notes they had made and the sources from which they had worked.

First there was Sarah Gertrude Millin. She had been born in Russia, but brought to South Africa when still a small child, and raised in Kimberley. There Ernest had got to know her, before the Great War. She wrote her first novel, *Mary Glen*, when she was 16. It was never published, though the manuscript was preserved in the collection. In all the manuscripts of 22 of her books were saved, from her many novels to her biographical works on Rhodes, Smuts and others whom she had known and admired.

There there were the works of Smuts's faithful follower from his earliest days, Deneys Reitz. He was the son of the Reitz who had been President of the Orange Free State, forced to resign his position through ill health but later responsible for drafting the South African Republic's ultimatum to Britain which led to the outbreak of the South African War. Deneys Reitz fought with the Boer forces, and drew on these and later experiences for his great works *Commando*, *Trekking On* and *No Outspan* – in due course all regarded as South African classics. Now his manuscripts were in the Brenthurst Collection, paintakingly written out in little exercise books and stored on the shelves in lettered boxes, exactly as they had been returned from the printers.

There were curiosities galore in the collection; for instance, the first copy of the first book written by Edgar Wallace, who had worked for several years in South Africa as a newspaper correspondent and as first editor of the *Rand Daily Mail*. Edgar Wallace had had an unpromising background: discovered abandoned on a doorstep when he was nine days old, and brought up by a Billingsgate fish porter. But from *The Mission That Failed*, a story of the Jameson Raid published in Cape Town in 1898, sprang a great career.

Ernest's interest was not confined to books and manuscripts. Besides these he assembled a valuable collection of historic maps – and displayed them not at Little Brenthurst but at 44 Main Street. Then again he collected paintings and prints – particularly prints – which reflected early South African life. He built up an impressive collection of work by Thomas Bowler, who had flourished in the Cape in the early nineteenth century, and much more besides.

One of the most outstanding features of the Brenthurst Collection was Ernest's corpus of work by Thomas Baines, the famous artist

261

explorer of Rhodesia and the other pioneer territories. Arriving in South Africa in 1842 from Britain, Baines had become official war artist to the troops fighting frontier wars against the Bantu tribes in the Eastern Cape, and would later have accompanied the great Livingstone Zambezi Expedition of 1858 if he had not fallen out with its leader. Instead he visited the Victoria Falls independently, and was the first artist to paint them. Later he befriended Lobengula, great king of the Matabele, and won mining concessions which were to prove very important when later Rhodes arrived in the territory. Most of his paintings were shared in almost equal proportions between two great collections, Ernest's and the government of Southern Rhodesia's. Between them they owned more than 90 per cent of his work.

Ernest co-operated with the Rhodesian government in making the Baines material generally available, and there were plans to publish as much of the work as was practical. Before that happened, however, Ernest was already involved with the Rhodesian government in another project. There was a good deal of vital material in its archives which it wanted to publish. When the Rhodesians asked Ernest if he would be prepared to help them financially, he agreed to sponsor the whole operation of editing the works and to pay for their publication.

The works embraced accounts of explorers' journeys, the efforts of missionaries and pioneers in the territory, the studies of natural historians and anthropologists. When printed and published they were known as the Oppenheimer Series, and soon became most valuable to collectors. The first print of each volume was presented to the Brenthurst Library.

It is difficult to decide whether Ernest ever really appreciated great paintings. As time progressed he collected a number, and he was proud of them: particularly a collection of Reynolds and Romney and other English masters which he hung in the drawing-room, and a pair of Goyas, *Mother* and *Daughter*, in the main reception room. He collected Dutch and Flemish masters too, and the works of Pieter Wenning, a South African artist he wanted to encourage. In Europe he liked to visit art galleries: but perhaps more because he wondered what he had been missing that did so much for others. Certainly friends did not gain the impression the plastic arts meant a lot to him – though he was always glad to show off his collection to visitors coming 'to see how the poor lived', as he put it.

On the other hand, Ernest was always ready to sit for his portrait. This had first happened in Kimberley, when the town council decided to make him a present of his portrait 'for services rendered'.

As Harry says, it was 'so appalling that even my deep filial piety could not persuade me to preserve it'. Later in life Ernest sat for his portrait on innumerable occasions – sometimes more than once for the same artist. Possibly he never felt any of them had quite caught his real character: looking at the results you may well agree.

There was one painting he did admire, however: for its curiosity value. It was the work of the Dutch artist Hans van Meegeren, who was arraigned after the war for 'selling seven works by the masters Vermeer and Pieter de Hoogh to the Nazi leader Goering, for the equivalent of £500 000'. He had collaborated, said his accusers, and he had squandered Holland's national heritage. Not so, said he. The paintings were not old masters at all: he had painted them himself.

He was not believed, of course, especially when he claimed that besides these paintings he was responsible for the celebrated Vermeer *Supper at Emmaus*, which had been discovered in 1937 and authenticated by art experts from all over the world. Van Meegeren realised he had no alternative but to paint another 'old master', this time before experts. The result was *Christ Among the Doctors*. It convinced the experts and the police too – but instead of letting him off the hook, they sent him to gaol for forgery. He died after four weeks.

Van Meegeren had forged the paintings, he said, 'to show up the ignorance of so-called international art experts'. But really he had done it because he regarded himself as a genius unrecognised. He died, but his paintings lived on. Several years later some of them reappeared as the basis of a major security swindle involving a London bank. *Christ Among the Doctors* eventually found its way to South Africa, and into Ernest's collection.

Ernest had much more time to devote to these external interests now. After all, he had turned 70, and his doctors were urging him to slow down. He had been showing signs of heart trouble: in fact in 1949 he had a mild attack, and that was warning enough. It was a sad decision to have to make, but Ernest had no option: it was announced he had resigned from the boards of seven of his companies.

It sounded an ominous development, but as Anglo was quick to point out it was only a matter of form. The seven companies were all within the Anglo group – mining companies like Springs and Daggafontein, and the London investment house Rand Selection Trust. But all those associated with Ernest appreciated how disappointed he must have been: he had served some of these companies without a break since 1917. Two months later he announced his resignation from eight more.

Shareholders were getting worried. Was Ernest pulling out altogether? Not at all, replied Anglo. He was remaining as chairman of all the major companies. But then came news that he was resigning his permanent directorship at Anglo, and that sounded more alarming still. Surely this was the beginning of the end? But it was explained that all he was doing was becoming an *ordinary* director instead: it was really only a financial arrangement, in terms of what had been agreed when he and Honnold founded the Anglo American in 1917.

Ernest knew how to grow old gracefully: he knew he could safely leave the running of the organisation to Harry and to Hagart, who seemed to complement each other's qualities and together made a first-class team. He went in to the office for the morning only, these days. Then he returned home for lunch, the chance of a snooze in his beautiful silk smoking jacket, and probably a long walk in the afternoon. He had always liked these long walks, out of the Brenthurst estate and along the quiet suburban roads with a chosen companion or two, his favourite confidants. Ina did not go on these expeditions: she never could abide such exercise, and anyway she had too much else to do. Her friend Doff Susskind would go instead.

Ernest had a small group of favourite confidants like Doff, most of them friends he had known for years, and who had shared all too many of his problems and worries. But there was a new one, in many ways the closest of them all. He was getting so fond of young Mary that he had almost confiscated her from Harry and Bridget. He seemed determined to spoil her.

'Jump into bed and I'll tell you a dirty story,' he would say when she was staying at Brenthurst while Harry and Bridget were away. It never was a dirty story, of course: only a suitably edited version of some classic tale that Ernest loved himself. But there could be no doubt he adored her. He thought the world of Nicky too, of course, but Mary was his special favourite: after all, she was the first little girl he had had all to himself.

When he was away from Johannesburg there was one rule Ernest always observed: at six o'clock in the morning, as soon as he awoke, he would telephone Bridget at Little Brenthurst to ask after his grandchildren. He wanted to know exactly what had happened since he had last contacted her: what they had said, how they had behaved. Later, when they were a little older, he liked to take Mary away on holiday with him, all by herself. He made her his 'hostess' at Blue Mountains in Muizenberg when he went there at Christmas. Visitors were astonished to find the little girl not yet ten years old asking them what they wanted to drink and looking after them as if she had been born to it.

But then in earlier years Ernest had treated Harry and Frank in just the same way. Harry admits to being outrageously spoilt as a small boy – to the extent that his father could never say 'No' to him. Ernest would explain that he believed it was impossible to spoil anyone who was 'naturally any good', as he put it. And if Harry and Frank were not 'naturally any good', it did not seem important to him whether they were spoilt or not.

When they were very small, Ernest would take them for walks and tell them stories which later Harry recognised as coming from Voltaire's *Zadig* and *Candide*. As they grew older, however, he took to telling them in considerable detail all his business problems and ambitions. He developed his own ideas as he went along – as if the conversation helped him to work out for himself just what he thought.

Ernest spoilt his children and his grandchildren, but at the same time imposed a sort of passive discipline on them with the tacit assumption that as his kin they should be reasonably intelligent, hard-working and responsible. And this, suggests Harry, amounted to pretty effective moral suasion.

Among their other recommendations Ernest's doctors had advised him to take up new interests for his old age, to keep his mind fully occupied. He was not greatly impressed by this idea at first: what was he to do? He was no good with his hands, he was no gardener, he could hardly take up a sport, he certainly could not learn to paint. But he went away and thought about it, and came back with a solution. He would begin collecting coins. It was a joke of his: that way, he reasoned with a twinkle in his eye, he could make another million! But he did begin collecting coins, and soon had the makings of a fine collection.

Ina, meanwhile, was taking great joy in a farm Ernest had bought for her in the Magaliesberg hills, some way from Johannesburg but within easy reach for a few days' fresh air. She had been brought up a country girl, and even with the wide expanse of the Brenthurst estate there were always housetops to be seen in the distance, over the trees. She often persuaded Ernest to go with her on these expeditions, and he always found they did him a world of good: he could walk through the countryside to his heart's content.

Nor was this his only interest in the country. He liked the company of farming folk. Sometimes he and Ina entertained all the farmers of the locality at their farm in the Magaliesberg. But he also farmed on his own account, particularly stock farming in conjunction with Harry.

They had herds at their ranch in Rhodesia, Shangani, and elsewhere as well: and rarely did they enter an agricultural show without winning half a dozen trophies. Yet, however keen Ernest and Harry were on their cattle, there was one interest the father did *not* share with his son. Harry had gone in for breeding racehorses, and that was something Ernest had no feeling for whatsoever.

Where his interest sprang from Harry is at a loss to explain. He did not learn to ride until quite late on: certainly not when he was a small boy. But after returning home from Oxford he had taken up hunting in Johannesburg – not fox-hunting, but the artificial kind where the hounds chase after a drag – and after the war even played polo, 'though not so that you would notice'. He soon preferred riding to his other leisure sports, golf and squash. And from there it seemed quite a logical development to buy a racehorse and see what it was capable of.

It was a modest start, certainly. Harry's first horse was a filly, Donnybrook, and after making various inquiries he handed her over to a trainer who had stables at Boksburg, Major Tim Furness. Donnybrook duly raced. Harry found it was great fun having his own horse in the running and decided to go in for racing in earnest. And besides that, of course, he bought the De Beers stud outside Kimberley and prepared to breed his own horses there as he had promised Kimberley in the election campaign. He appointed an agent in England and gave him instructions to buy up suitable horses for the new stud.

One of the horses bought this way was Lorelei. She was already in foal to Scottish Union at Lord Rosebery's stud at Newmarket, and Ossian was the result. Dam and foal were shipped out to South Africa and Ossian was eventually handed over for training. Early in his career he so far upset Tim Furness that a colleague suggested it was not worth persevering with him. 'I don't think you ought to disappoint Mr Oppenheimer – shoot him now!'

Things improved, though, and Ossian justified his existence. After a number of successes in lesser events Tim Furness entered him for the Johannesburg Summer Handicap, the premier race on the Rand. At a lunch held the day before the race Harry was special guest speaker, and invited Ernest to be present. To his father's great consternation he suddenly announced he was giving him Ossian.

Ernest could barely struggle out a response: 'Some are born great, others have racehorses thrust upon them. I am now the owner of that great horse Ossian, and my advice to you all is that you stick to the Stock Exchange, which has not been unkind to me.'

Next day Ossian took the course, with his new owner more than

266

usually apprehensive. Vic McMurtrey was riding him, and Ernest was delighted to see Ossian well up the field, then overtaking the leader until at last he came in a clear winner. Proudly, and with a great grin of delight on his face, Ernest led his horse into the paddock.

A columnist who had reported Ernest's earlier remarks now sought his reaction to the win. When he rang Brenthurst he had difficulty in getting through to Ernest who was normally not available to outsiders. But his secretary told him who it was, and Ernest came to the telephone.

'I don't normally speak to newspapermen, and I can think of nothing bright to say,' Ernest told him. 'But my door will be open to you at 11 o'clock on Tuesday morning. I shall think of something by then.'

The columnist reported as directed, and was soon shown in to Ernest's office.

'I'm glad you've come,' said Ernest. 'I've thought of something. Ossian is not the first horse I've ever owned. Forty years ago when I was in Kimberley I bought a pony called "Salad Dressing". Kimberley with its usual quickness called him "Mayonnaise". Seventy-five guineas he cost me.

'I entered him for a race, and he won easily, and I made a bob or two. We entered him for another race, and "Mayonnaise" doddled it out. I thought then that racing was a great game, entered him again, and he was beaten by a head. It was then that I realised that racing is a dangerous game – you can't have winners all the time. I swore off, and now my son Harry gives me Ossian, and he wins the first time out too. A dangerous game!'

Ernest's success did not exactly go to his head, but at least it did turn up in his dreams. Not long afterwards Harry entered another of his horses for the premier race in the Cape, the Metropolitan Handicap. There was a great deal of rivalry at these events between horses from different parts of the country, and the chances of a horse from the Rand, 6 000 feet above sea level, winning at the coast were held to be minimal. The bookmakers were quoting Harry's horse, Prince Bertrand, at 33 to 1. But then one night Ernest had a dream that Prince Bertrand was going to win. Nothing if not game, Harry backed him at £5 each way.

The day of the race dawned with Prince Bertrand's odds down to 22 to 1. But he was still a long shot. Harry held no great hopes for him. The crowd of 26 000 was rooting for the two Cape stars, Beacon Light and Quickgrass. As the horses approached the last straight it looked as if Quickgrass had the race in the bag, and the crowd was going wild. But then, from nowhere, Prince Bertrand moved up on the leader and overtook him at the post. The crowd watched in stony silence. Only the bookies and Harry himself were pleased.

Back in Johannesburg, the unexpected victory prompted pungent comment in the *Star*:

> *Sir Ernest dreamed Prince Bertrand won*
> *And thought it worth a bet,*
> *So Harry (MP) backed his horse*
> *With cautious venture, made, of course,*
> *Because Sir Ernest told his son*
> *Prince B would win the Met.*
>
> *And though at 33 to one*
> *His owner's bet was made*
> *Prince Bertrand tossed his noble head*
> *'I'll show these horses how,' he said,*
> *'A fellow from the Rand can run*
> *And put them in the shade.'*
>
> *He thumbed his nose at Beacon Light,*
> *Made Quickgrass prove his pace,*
> *And then he settled down, the teaser,*
> *And tore a strip off Peran-Wisa,*
> *Ran through the final furlong right*
> *Until he'd won the race.*
>
> *The moral of this story is*
> *Dreams need not go by contraries*
> *And next time you've a dream or hunch,*
> *You'd better ask your son to lunch.*

It was the kind of story Ernest liked to tell his guests at the popular dinner and bridge parties Ina arranged at Brenthurst. The only problem with Ernest's stories were that he was so amused by them himself that often he would be helpless with laughter long before he had finished. It was all very infectious, but rather frustrating if you were hoping to catch the punchline.

Ernest was sometimes capable of rather wicked behaviour. At one dinner party a guest pointed out the woman on his left was undertaking a project for adult education, and was in urgent need of funds.

'You must help her, Sir Ernest,' the guest was saying, ignoring the protests of the woman concerned. She was furiously embarrassed and trying to make it clear nothing of the sort was needed. Ernest turned to her and with his slight lisp and gentle German accent asked her softly: 'If I promise not to give you a single penny, please will you tell me all about it?'

As likely as not Ernest later gave her all that she needed. But those who did not know him would go off and tell their friends what a stingy old man he was. Certainly stories like it are still current in Johannesburg. Nothing could be further from the truth. When he gave he was extremely generous.

What *is* true is that Ernest placed great value on thrift. Not for nothing did he present a special Oppenheimer Prize for Thrift to be competed for in Johannesburg schools. One day he was in ecstasies over a particular diamond when those with him asked him why he did not go ahead and buy it if he wanted it so badly.

'How could I?' he said sadly. 'It would cost a lot of money.'

One Christmas the family was gathered at Brenthurst, and Ernest wanted to hear what Harry thought of the present he had given him: a particularly handsome gold cigarette box.

'I liked it very much,' Harry told him.

A little later Ernest asked him again. What did he really think of it?

'It's very fine.'

Even that wasn't enough. An hour later Ernest asked him a third time. This was too much for Harry.

'Papa, do you really not remember that *I* gave *you* that box two years ago?'

But there were times when Ernest wanted to spend money, and found himself frustrated. For instance, there was the matter of General Smuts's house, Doornkloof. It was a remarkable building by any account – a ramshackle, hopefully temporary corrugated iron affair originally used by the British Army as an officers' mess in the South African War and later bought by Smuts for the proverbial song. Even today visitors are astonished that one who ranked among the century's greatest sons could have lived in such a place. However, visiting Doornkloof you feel the Smuts charisma, and you will never forget it. That is what Ernest appreciated, and he did all he could to persuade Ouma Smuts to let him buy the house for the nation. But she would not: it was still her home. She eventually died there, after Ernest himself had died – and for years the house stood derelict until at last a small group of those who remembered Smuts took it in hand and made it a permanent memorial.

Ouma stayed on at Doornkloof, but Ernest looked for other ways to preserve his great friend's memory. At last it was decided to establish a fund to endow a Smuts House at Witwatersrand University: and in the event, when it was found the fund needed £35 000 to reach its target, Ernest undertook to raise this money on top of what he had contributed already.

True, Ernest liked to pick his causes. Usually he went for those that interested him. But when he did put in money, he did not flinch from committing himself completely. Some of his endowments were well known: for instance, the Chair of Oral and Plastic Surgery at Wits, which he had created for Jack Penn after the war. It had not lasted long but that was chiefly due to the failure of the authorities concerned to co-operate with Penn. There were other chairs as well: the Faculty of Engineering at Stellenbosch University, for instance, and a chair of Portuguese Studies at Wits which was endowed by De Beers at Ernest's instigation.

He was always interested in medicine. For years he had been associated in the work of the Red Cross, even apart from its connection with the Brenthurst Military Hospital in the war years. He was the organisation's branch chairman in the Transvaal. So, too, he was deeply interested in the St John's Committee for the Prevention of Blindness, and was its chairman for many years. But Ernest never made any great fuss of these and the many other gifts he had made to charity: it was simply one more aspect of the position he occupied.

One rule he always applied was never to *lend* money. 'People find it so convenient to forget to pay it back,' he explained. He would give absolutely and without strings, or not at all. He received begging letters by the mailbag, not surprisingly, but liked to go through them himself and where possible reply personally. When he found a particularly deserving case he would quietly send a cheque and that would be the end of it. Scores of young would-be students without money to get them through a course were helped in this way.

Ernest's fame had gone round the world by now, though strangely few people even in South Africa knew a lot about him. His achievements were recognised, but the man behind them was a virtual blank in the public mind. The London *Observer* called him 'a Garbo of industry who has always shunned the limelight'. It came as quite a thrill, then, when it was announced Oxford University was preparing to award Ernest the honorary degree of Doctor of Civil Law.

This would be quite a family occasion. Ina went to England with Ernest to be present at the ceremony, held in the historic Sheldonian Theatre in which all Oxford's degrees are given. Harry and Bridget went too, and they were joined by Michael, who had spent the last few years at Christ Church and had just got married, and a number of friends of the family. They sat together on the benches that ranged round the Sheldonian's circular walls, with a good view of the little amphitheatre where the ceremony was to be acted out. All Oxford's dignitaries were there in their colourful robes, and pre-eminent among them the Vice-Chancellor, Sir Maurice Bowra of Wadham.

Ernest came in and everyone clapped politely: a shy figure in the scarlet robes and soft black bonnet of the doctorate, advancing to the centre of the floor. There he was met by the Public Orator, who proceeded to make a speech in Latin. It would not have meant very much to most of those present, but a translation would be available afterwards.

'Prophets may well have foretold that he would be Rhodes's successor,' the orator was saying, had they but known. 'For, like Rhodes, he was convinced that the expansion of South Africa must depend upon the exploitation of its gold and diamonds and other mineral wealth and on stability in the marketing of these commodities.

'With this in view Rhodes had amalgamated the South African diamond companies. Sir Ernest made a combination of all the producers, putting, as it were, a ring of diamonds round the earth . . .'

So he went on: taking in Ernest's contributions in gold and copper mining, in civic affairs and in parliament, proceeding to his services to South Africa and the Rhodesias and to the British Commonwealth as a whole, his charitable work and his contributions to medical research. He was more than complimentary.

For the time all listened in respectful silence. Only when the Orator had done, and the Vice-Chancellor pronounced the Latin formula admitting Ernest to his degree and was reaching down to shake his hand, did they erupt into hearty applause. You had the impression everyone was extraordinarily happy, and none happier than Ernest himself. He was in Oxford's sanctuary, where Rhodes still meant so much and where they could appreciate his own lifework which was really the direct continuation of what Rhodes had begun. They could not have granted him greater honour. It was one of the most moving moments of his life.

Long Shadows

E RNEST HAD never meant to confine the Anglo American to the mining world. As early as 1921 he told the shareholders that he foresaw the time when the corporation would play a full part in the country's *industrial* economy – at that time barely conceived. One day the mines would end: but that was no reason why the corporation should dwindle and die.

It had been a gradual process so far, but step by step the corporation was feeling its way into the industrial sector. De Beers had already pioneered the way, with its involvement in the great explosives company AE and CI which now controlled the biggest dynamite factories in the world. Anglo entered fruit farming, real estate, brick and tile making, ranching, breakfast foods, fertilisers, chemicals and ceramics, even cold storage. So much for South Africa: but the corporation was active outside the Union too – for instance, with railway development and power stations in the Rhodesias, and forestry projects in Swaziland. Each of these ventures prospered, though there were others that did not: an ill-timed foray into the fishing industry ended in disaster.

All these developments were watched over by Harry and by R B Hagart, who ranked equally as the corporation's joint deputy chairmen. Harry concerned himself with Anglo's new ventures and put all his enthusiasm behind them while Hagart provided a conservative restraining influence. For one thing, he did not really approve of Anglo's bolder ventures outside the mining world. All that they did they discussed with Ernest, even though he appeared only for the mornings, and it was rare that he did not take a briefcase of papers home with him.

One new development Hagart did approve of was the fulfilment of

273

an ambition Ernest had conceived some time before: to form a South African merchant bank along the lines of the merchant banks in Europe, which would help create a real national money market in South Africa. They had the resources: the Orange Free State mines were in full production now, and Anglo had liquid capital once again. This was their opportunity.

Ernest's active interest in South Africa's money market stemmed from long before the war, when he became a director of the South African Reserve Bank. Then in 1949 he had given advice when the government was forming the National Finance Corporation which would help make short-term loans available for development, from money that would otherwise have been idle. But that did not go far enough, he felt. Really *big* loans had traditionally been raised overseas, through the merchant banks of Europe and particularly concerns like Rothschilds, Morgan Grenfell, Hambros and Lazards in London. It was time South Africa had a merchant bank of her own, to use the available money to the full – there was a lot more of it than there ever had been before – and to provide all the services that until now had been lacking.

Accordingly the new bank was floated – Union Acceptances, registered in 1955 with Sydney Spiro as managing director, and initially equipped with capital from Anglo and its associates but geared to attract capital from other sources too. Ernest brought in Lazards of London to help organise the bank's affairs in the early days, and even though its role has long since fallen away the British firm has remained closely associated.

Union Acceptances was an immediate success, and fulfilled all Ernest's hopes. There were soon plans to float two new merchant banks – Rhodesian Acceptances in Salisbury and Union Acceptances (Zurich) in Switzerland to link the first two with sources of large funds in Europe. In the latter case the South African Reserve Bank came into the picture, for it had long needed the services this new company could provide.

Even that was not the end of it. Union Acceptances was going so well that in a short time it was obvious there was scope for a separate discount house as a specialised money market institution. Thus Anglo floated the Discount House of South Africa, soon run completely separately from Union Acceptances; and then a special closed-in investment trust, First Union General Investment Trust or FUGIT.

Long before this Anglo had outgrown 44 Main Street. There was now a new building across the street, in the same style but even bigger than the first and known as 45 Main Street. Union Acceptances had a home of its own, a special block with offices for many other concerns besides the bank's which therefore marked Anglo's arrival in the commercial property field, disregarding townships like Welkom and CDM. Before long this side of the corporation's business would boom beyond recognition.

All these developments made it increasingly difficult for Ernest to keep watch on the whole organisation. But at least he could be friendly towards all his staff, greeting them in the lift, smiling as he saw them and shaking hands to wish them the compliments of the season at Christmas. For that they loved him. They could hardly believe how 'ordinary' and accessible he was.

There are many stories to illustrate Ernest's informality. One, for instance, is of a young man starting a job with Anglo but late on his first day. He dashed up the steps of 44 Main Street, into the lift and up to the right floor. He ran down the corridor and was gratified when a slight figure ahead of him stood back and opened the door for him.

'It was a little old fellow in an off-white raincoat,' he said. 'Such a quiet little man, so polite, that I must have thought it was an old servant of the company working in some light capacity to help out his retirement. I just said "Thanks!" in a lordly kind of way and swept on past without a second glance.

'A week later I was with someone else and we saw the little old man and my friend said in a reverent whisper: "Look, that's Sir Ernest Oppenheimer over there." I was so embarrassed I wanted to sink through the floor.'

Ernest was certainly anything but the general image of the mining tycoon. In his own office he had such a distinct hatred of the telephone that he liked to hold meetings as far from his desk as possible, around a plain table surrounded by leather-backed chairs. In fact, very often he preferred not to have his executives call on him, but rather saw them in *their* offices.

'It's much easier this way,' he would explain. 'It means you won't have to carry all those masses of papers. It saves a lot of trouble if I look at them here.'

Ernest adopted this attitude with every member of his staff. As always, he preferred to think of them as working with him towards some mutual goal. His interests were theirs too. He was always ready to listen to other people's ideas, no matter how off beam they seemed or how naive or how junior the man who put them forward. He admitted many of the ideas he listened to were not worth considering. But

275

against that he insisted that if he did not listen to all of them, he might miss some good ones.

This innate courtesy of Ernest's extended to his dealings with servants. One of them, Ernest King, referred to it in his autobiography *The Green Baize Door*.

'In over 50 years of service, I think I have known only three people who had a perfect approach to servants. They were King George of Greece, the Duchess de Talleyrand (formerly Mrs. Ali Mackintosh, formerly Miss Lela Emery, the American heiress) and Sir Ernest Oppenheimer, the gold and diamond millionaire of South Africa. They made working for them a pleasure, they encouraged one to give one's best.'

What makes this testimony the more remarkable is that King was at the top of his profession. Among his previous employers he counted Queen (then Princess) Elizabeth and the Duke of Edinburgh, whose steward he was; King George of Greece; and the Duke and Duchess of Windsor, whom he served as majordomo. King was never on Ernest's staff himself: the regular servants were too loyal for there ever to be a vacancy and most worked for the Oppenheimers until they retired.

It was significant in this connection that ever since the bereavements which had hit him so deeply, Ernest had been a practising Christian. He had been confirmed into the Anglican communion, and worshipped regularly at St George's Church in Parktown. The minister there, Cecil Tugman, became his personal chaplain and a close friend. In later years Tugman visited Brenthurst each week to give Ernest private communion. 'The old legs aren't what they were, and in church I can't manage to kneel,' Ernest told an interviewer. His own bedroom at home contained a large collection of Bibles in many languages, some extremely valuable, and of crucifixes.

Though he came to it so late in life Ernest tried to carry Christianity into business – particularly in the feeling that every man deserved his chance. This was especially noticeable with younger men on his staff: he had so many of them that on his visits to Kimberley people used to refer to 'the Oppenheimer circus'. His feeling was, the man was good whether he was young or old. He could be trusted. Not only that, but Ernest liked to treat even his most junior executives to information which their seniors might feel they should not have. It was all a matter of confidence in their ability, he explained. If they knew the full facts of the matter, they would be able to handle affairs even more efficiently.

But though he trusted his men, Ernest liked to keep in close touch with everything that was going on. When his senior executives arrived at the airport from some overseas business trip, he would go out to meet them himself. That gave him the chance of discussing whatever had happened without delay. Again, when he had something to discuss with an executive he preferred to thrash it out in the course of a walk round Zoo Lake or on the golf course, rather than sitting closeted in his study or an office.

Often Ernest initiated these ideas himself, and would want to discuss them on the spot. 'Many a time he would come into my office as soon as he arrived in the morning,' wrote R B Hagart, 'and begin with the familiar "Hagart, I've been thinking . . .", and then would follow the outline of an idea or scheme relating to the most recent opportunity that had come our way. He would expect me to comment immediately, testing the feasability of the scheme against my knowledge and experience of detailed company practice and the limitations that company law has placed upon forms of finance. It happened quite often that I had to raise this or that objection to his scheme. He would listen intently, there would be a pause while he would look at me with that curious mixture of appraisement and appreciation that was so characteristic of him, and then he would suggest a way in which my objection could be overcome.

'He had a wonderfully quick and penetrating mind and difficulties seemed to stimulate his imagination to evolve a scheme that was "right" in every respect. But there were times, of course, when Sir Ernest would leave my office saying he would have to think again; and the next day he would call for me and propose either an entirely new technique or a modified scheme which would reveal his astonishing resourcefulness. His tenacity of purpose would inspire idea after idea to achieve his main objective; seldom indeed would he accept defeat.'

For all his lack of formality, though, Ernest was regarded by his juniors with something approaching awe. In the mining world at any rate his achievements had made him a legend in his own lifetime, as Rhodes had been. Yet nobody seemed less aware of it than he. He seemed almost surprised at all the interest he stimulated. What kept him going? Had he never thought of retiring? What quality made him shine above all the others? Was it all a matter of luck?

'A man keeps on working,' he told an interviewer at this time. 'It has never occurred to me to retire. It's something I couldn't bear to do. My business is my life and my life is my business. Of course, I'm taking things a lot more easily than I used to, but I still keep very much in touch.'

Then what was it that got him where he was?

'Well, some would say that I am a good negotiator. Nothing could be further from the truth. I'm a rank bad negotiator, because I cannot stop long enough, once my mind is made up, to think of bargaining. I listen to what the other side has to say. I listen to my own experts. Then suddenly, usually while the other side is talking, I can visualise all the arguments they are going to bring out. Many people get the idea that I am influenced by their arguments. I suppose I am in a way, but it is their unspoken arguments which I have sensed that enable me to reach my decisions.

'Call it a matter of hunches if you like. At times I have persisted when all the experts have told me I am wrong. But even when I seem to be going against their know-how I am really activated by what I feel will be best for the company concerned and its shareholders.'

That was Ernest's usual way of describing his route to a decision. He truly believed it was best to reach it by some sort of intuitive process, and refused to admit that it was necessary to have any detailed knowledge of business methods and procedures. Such knowledge was all very well in the lower echelons, he would say, but not when you were in a top position. With this in mind he not only did not encourage Harry from acquiring any technical business training, but actually discouraged him. Harry says it is something he has always regretted. Ernest was only rationalising from his own experience.

'While there is no doubt some sense in what he said, there is a great deal more nonsense,' says Harry. 'His business judgements often looked like pure intuitions to others just as Sherlock Holmes' judgements looked to Dr Watson, because the reasoning that led up to them was not disclosed.

'Businessmen, like all men of action, must be prepared to act on imcomplete evidence and on what appears to them the balance of probabilities. This, it seems to me, is what distinguishes the man of action from the scientist. What my father called intuition was really an ability to make up his mind quickly about the probabilities of a case and to act unhesitatingly on his judgment.

'He liked to say, "If the wise man thinks too long, the fool does some thinking too".'

So that was Ernest's creed. But there was another principle which he frequently brought into play and which seems to have worked every time: a principle he adopted directly from Rhodes and which he saw used most effectively by Solly Joel. It was a matter of giving before taking.

278

Sailor Malan   Sir De Villiers Graaff   Dr Hendrik Verwoerd

Ernest and Ina stroll through the fields at their farm in the Magaliesberg Mountains. *Anglo American Corporation.*

Harry relaxes in his study at Brenthurst. He is an avid reader, and each day devotes hours to his favourite leisure activity. *Johannesburg Sunday Times.*

The Oppenheimers' home since the early twenties: Brenthurst Estate, in Johannesburg's Parktown. Harry and Bridget have other homes: Shangani in Rhodesia, Mauritzfontein outside Kimberley, La Lucia near Durban, and flats in London and New York. *Anglo American Corporation.*

'You must always be ready to concede all that you can,' he told Harry. 'When you want something from a person, think first of what you can give him in return. Let him think that it's *he* who is coming off best. But all the time make sure it is you in the end.'

This was the principle which Rhodes had used to bring about his greatest coup, the conquest of Barney Barnato and the Kimberley Central. Solly Joel had used it time and again. Ernest had used it in bringing the Anglo American into being, and in bargaining for the amalgamation of the mines of South West Africa. He had tried to use it in directing the efforts of the old Syndicate – and when they had refused to go along with him had had to force their hand and run them out of business. And he had used it in bringing off one of his greatest business achievements, buying his way into the Free State goldfields.

But was this all business acumen? Or had all these successes of his sprung from natural good luck? It was a question he was often asked. In fact, he often wondered himself.

'I can't reply honestly with a simple "Yes",' he told an interviewer. 'From my earliest days in London I hoped I would be able to do big things in the new country. In Kimberley I was working to a plan. Since that plan has succeeded in a measure far greater than my expectations, I suppose my answer should be "Yes, I was lucky". But it was the hand of destiny that led me here. People may think it is a strange thing to say but I believe in my heart that I was fated to come to South Africa.'

Fated or lucky, Ernest had admirers far beyond the confines of his companies. He was in his seventies now, and as he modestly put it 'enjoying the privilege of an old man in being given credit for the work of others'. But it was for the work that he had done already, indeed was still engaged in, that he was recognised by bodies far and near.

Oxford had been first to offer him an honorary degree. Now universities in South Africa followed suit. Rhodes University in Grahamstown celebrated the centenary of its founder's birth in 1953 by awarding Ernest the honorary degree of Doctor of Laws. And the same year the University of the Witwatersrand awarded him a similar degree. On this occasion the oration was delivered by the Dean of the Faculty of Engineering, Prof G R Bozzoli.

'In awarding to Sir Ernest the degree of Doctor of Laws, *honoris causa*,' he concluded, 'the university is honouring a South African who by his vision, vigour, enthusiasm and exceptional qualities of character, has carried forward the development of the diamond, gold and copper industries of South Africa to the highest level and has simultaneously by direct participation in public affairs, by his generosity and by his philanthropic acts put himself in the front rank of benefactors to our country.'

Again in 1953, Ernest was appointed honorary colonel of the Kimberley Regiment. But not all the honours went his way. Harry received his fair measure as well. Through a chance remark made to a visiting American at a business lunch he suddenly found himself appointed First Admiral of the Great Navy of the State of Nebraska.

'It is the greatest navy in the history of the world,' said the American when he invested Harry at a special ceremony in Johannesburg, carrying out the instructions of Nebraska's State Governor. 'It has never lost a battle, it has never lost a casualty, it has never lost a capital ship.'

In accepting the commission Harry admitted he had always wanted to be an admiral, but had given up the idea when he found he had to be a sailor first. At least in Nebraska he could hardly get into much trouble, he reflected. The state was in the great middle west, entirely surrounded by land.

De Beers was not to be left behind in honouring its chairman. On December 21 1954 Ernest celebrated his 25th anniversary as chairman of De Beers, and to mark the day flags were flown at all the company's offices and the offices of all the associated companies too. Ernest and Ina were in Europe with Harry, hoping to raise new capital for the Free State goldfields in Switzerland. De Beers laid on a special celebration in the Diamond Corporation's London offices, at which Sir Reginald Leeper, the mining director, presented Ernest with two valuable paintings: *Anemones and Green Bowl*, by Renoir, and Sisley's *Bords de Riviere*. In due course they found their way to Brenthurst.

Sir Reginald pointed out that the presentation called to mind an event of a few weeks before, when they had gathered to pay their respects to Sir Winston Churchill, 'the greatest living Englishman'. They had given him a painting, and now they were giving paintings to Ernest, 'the greatest living South African'.

The visit to London was Ernest's first in many years, and the British newspapers took notice. 'To thousands of British investors,' wrote the *Sunday Times* in a special profile, 'Sir Ernest is familiar as a name, but only intimate friends know the kind of man he is. Others may form an idea of him by adding together gold and diamonds, uranium and copper, high finance and the "mantle of Rhodes"; but Sir Ernest is nothing like the popular concept of a mining magnate. He is short and slight, quiet voiced and modest, impatient alike of pomp and obsequiousness, as courteous to the most junior member of his staff as to his immediate colleagues, and as ready to discuss modern painting as inch-dwts or recovery grades.'

Ernest's colleagues thought it would be a good idea for him to hold a full Press conference now he was in London. But he seemed rather reticent about it. What would he find to say? However, he agreed to go along with their wishes, and they had no further qualms about his reluctance as they knew this was his usual reaction. When the time came he always rose to the occasion as if there had never been any doubt.

Sure enough, when he met the reporters Ernest delivered a splendidly concise statement which he had ready in his head, showing not a sign of the nervousness he had promised. He answered questions promptly and delivered a steady stream of statistics to support each point. The reporters kept him at it for half an hour, and by the time they were through he was completely at his ease and perhaps even enjoying himself. Then, as the reporters were putting their pencils away, he fainted clean away.

'Though what else he could have expected after behaving as he did I don't know,' explained Ina rather crossly later on. 'All that excitement and the bad air. He's not used to the tension of London in any case, and there he stood in a crowded, smoke-filled room for more than half an hour, and he was talking the whole time. Of course it was the smoke. After all, he's an old man, but he's very strong.'

Ernest soon recovered, but it was an unfortunate thing to happen and did his own morale no good. It had been a family joke that when Ernest was ill, he liked to have credit for it: rather than tell him he was looking well, you had to point out that he was looking much better. This time he was really far from well. Five years before he had had a heart attack – a frightening development, for so many in his family had died of heart trouble. They included Bernard and Otto, who had died in 1948; and, of course, May. Even General Smuts had succumbed to the disease.

The year before Ernest had had a second attack. There was special significance, then, in a grant he now made to the South African Institute of Medical Research, for special studies in cardio-vascular disease. He gave them £10 000 to set up a special unit, which was in fact named after him. A year or two later, when the new unit produced some obviously important results, he added a further grant. He made no secret of his very special personal interest in the project.

281

In these years Ernest *did* come very close to death, but not through heart trouble. For years his doctors had realised he was diabetic, and had treated him accordingly. But a new physician had believed this diagnosis was wrong, took him off his injections and prescribed remedies for quite a different condition.

One night Ina telephoned Jack Penn in great consternation. Penn was now long established as one of the world's leading plastic surgeons: not long before the Japanese government had invited him to visit Japan with a special team to do what he could for the victims of Hiroshima and Nagasaki. He was necessarily out of the world of true medicine, but in response to Ina's worried call drove immediately to Brenthurst.

There he found Ernest in a bad way. They could not understand what was wrong. He had been taking his medicine as prescribed: yet the more he took, the worse he felt. Jack Penn immediately organised drastic treatment, and with Ernest back on his proper diet he was restored to health within 24 hours.

It was touching to see how much Ina cared for Ernest when he was not well. She really suffered with him, and would not leave his side for a moment until she was sure he was all right. In a very real sense she was the woman behind the man, as May had been before her. She gave Ernest the strength he needed to persevere and continue with his work, the drive to press home the advantage gained from all those years of struggle and hardship. In return Ernest was devoted to her in a quite selfless way, and altogether proud of everything she was.

Certainly Ernest was still at work. Interestingly, he had returned to the love of his early days. He made it his business to control the Diamond Corporation: in fact he would entrust its affairs to nobody else, not even to Harry. Other sides of the organisation he could happily leave to Harry and Hagart and the other directors. Indeed, he readily admitted they knew a lot more about it now than he did. But one thing he insisted on: he reserved the right to take all the major decisions in the diamond trade.

As never before, he saw his lifework in the tradition of Cecil Rhodes. The diamond world was stabilised, but that was not enough. Rhodes had used the profits he made to great advantage outside the world of diamonds, the development of the great hinterland to the north. It was Ernest's hope that current diamond profits should be used to a similar end: and now the De Beers Investment Trust was in operation there was every prospect this would happen.

'If I might . . . venture to draw a picture of the future,' he told De Beers shareholders in 1953, 'I would say that anyone visiting these mines 100 years hence would, if he pushed his travels further into the interior, recognise the renewal of their life in the great European civilisations of the far north, and that perhaps he would feel a glow of satisfaction at the thought that the immense riches which have been taken out of the soil have not been devoted merely to the decoration of the female sex.

'And so, for my part, when the policy of this corporation is challenged, I always feel that it is no small thing to be able to say that it has devoted its wealth to other things besides the expansion of luxury.'

A year later he developed his theme. 'We believe that our shareholders will derive satisfaction from the knowledge that, in pursuing our enterprises and making our profits, we are helping to increase the general living standards and happiness of the European and African communities in the subcontinent.'

There had been criticism of the De Beers Investment Trust. But the tongues of the shareholders had stilled as the great mines of the Free State came into production, and it was clear that they were set to share in huge profits. The investment trust was used to finance other projects: the expansion of the great African Explosives and Chemical Industries which Ernest had controlled for years and whose chairman he remained, a company founded for the benefit of the gold mines in the Transvaal and now possessing the two greatest explosives factories in the world as well as many other plants; the development of secondary industry in all parts of South Africa; the progress of agriculture in all its forms. Some saw the creation of the investment trust as Ernest's most significant contribution to Rhodes's great company. It meant that even long after diamonds ceased to be De Beers' main interest – if that ever happened – the company would continue to be a big factor in South Africa's economic life.

With the value of diamond as stable as it ever could be and with the producers safe in the shelter of the Diamond Corporation, there was only one more problem to be solved. But it was a big one. For years the activities of international diamond smugglers had been depriving the producers of a considerable amount of revenue.

In South Africa the position was not as bad as in other parts of Africa. For one thing, the South African producers had lived with illicit diamond buying from the earliest days and after 80 years had it controlled if not beaten. De Beers had its own highly trained diamond detectives operating at each of the mines and at the sorting houses, and the South African Police had a specialist IDB branch which had met with considerable success.

Further north, however, the situation had been going from bad to worse. There was a steady stream of illegal stones from Angola and the Congo passing through the Rhodesias and Mozambique; there was little security at the Williamson mine in Tanganyika; and worst of all, there was illegal diamond mining in West Africa which channeled millions of pounds worth of stones through Liberia into markets in direct competition with the Diamond Corporation's.

Ernest had had a lifelong passion for spy and detective novels, and Harry had inherited it. Each liked to end an evening's reading with a dip into a good thriller. Here was a real-life situation which demanded just the kind of treatment described in those books. How would the heroes of Simenon or E Philips Oppenheim, Conan Doyle or Leslie Charteris have coped? Would they not try to take on the international diamond smugglers on their own terms?

Harry came up with the solution. Years before he had met Sir Percy Sillitoe, the world-famous chief of the British anti-espionage branch MI 5 with years of experience in the world of international crime. It would be difficult to think of a more promising candidate than Sir Percy. And only a few months earlier he had retired. Ernest sent instructions to Sir Reginald Leeper, who headed the Diamond Corporation in London, to track down Sir Percy and ask him if by any chance he fancied the idea of a holiday in South Africa. Ernest had something he wanted to discuss.

Sir Reginald traced the famous detective to the little seaside resort of Eastbourne in Sussex, where he was as far from the world of international intrigue as it is possible to imagine. He was in fact serving behind the counter of a sweetshop, dispensing toffee, chocolate and butterscotch to his matronly customers. He had bought the shop for his son, but could not resist taking a hand himself. Sir Percy was content in his new role, but Sir Reginald did not have to twist his arm very hard. He was soon on his way to join Ernest and Ina in Muizenberg where they were themselves on holiday.

The visit was supposed to be secret and under cover. Unfortunately news of Sir Percy's arrival in South Africa was leaked to the newspapers, which were soon in competition to see which could provide the most sensational explanations for his visit. But it did not need any great perception to understand why he was there. Before long De Beers announced the formation of the International Diamond Security Organisation, which would operate throughout Africa and the world.

Unfortunately, Sir Percy was almost totally ignorant of the diamond industry up to the time when diamonds were set into engagement rings. But De Beers could afford to be indulgent. Ernest personally explained to him all he could of diamond mining and marketing and told him where he felt the points of weakness might lie. He then suggested Sillitoe should make a personal examination of the mines themselves all over Africa, then return to Johannesburg and report on the chances of plugging the leaks at source.

Back in London, Sir Percy recruited two agents who had worked with him in MI 5, and set off on an itinerary which in six weeks included all the major producers in West Africa, Tanganyika, the Congo and Angola, then South Africa and South West. The visits opened his eyes: he did not realise the magnitude of his task. From the millions of pounds worth of stones laid out for his inspection at the different mines, he wondered that the amounts stolen were not many times greater. He could only admit real admiration for the various company officials who every day handled stones worth ten times their annual salary.

Sir Percy discussed his findings with Ernest. As the Diamond Corporation realised only too well, the chief leaks were from West Africa. There were leaks elsewhere too, and highly efficient organisations existed to exploit them.

The results were immediate. At all De Beers premises security was stepped up, particularly in special X-ray examinations of those leaving the mine areas and more particularly of their baggage. At the Williamson mine closed-circuit television was installed to keep a close watch on those handling the gems. Sillitoe's men closed in all over Africa to seek out the dangerous world of the diamond smugglers, and through them trap the really big fish who controlled it.

In Johannesburg the word was spread that Sir Percy's men were looking for contacts in the underworld. Practically the first they made was a Londoner called Radley, then managing a dance hall. He did his best to help them, though it was soon plain that after all his contacts were far from important: only the small fry. But Sir Percy's men persevered, and were soon making progress. They had the considerable advantage of De Beers' financial backing, which could not be made available to the police. It meant they could buy their way into their contacts' confidence, in fact become fully involved in the racket until by persistance they could win their way to the top.

At the same time, it was the IDSO's function to advise on every aspect of diamond security, and that included arranging the vetting of new security officers. Among those they turned down was a young Englishman called Donald Miles.

The investigations were paying dividends. Sir Percy's men soon discovered the main routes used to smuggle stones out of Southern Africa: by air from Johannesburg, by sea from Cape Town, Durban, Lourenco Marques and Beira, for destinations in Europe, North and South America and even Asia. Everywhere they recruited informers, and soon unmasked scores of illegal operators in the mines and at the sorting offices – Africans and Europeans alike. A few were quietly imprisoned after trial: most were sacked on the spot and black-listed for the future.

But the greatest challenge was in West Africa: Sierra Leone, where the rivers ran with diamonds to the sea and the diamond area embraced half the country so that it could not possibly be cordoned off. Literally thousands of Africans were involved in illegal digging, selling their finds to smugglers who carried them over the border into Liberia. There the stones could be sold freely to unlicensed buyers and exported to any part of the world under the elaborate fiction that they were from local mines. The trade was worth millions.

Sir Percy's men infiltrated both countries. The chief problem in the former territory was that in spite of the huge abundance of alluvial diamonds virtually there for the taking, only a relative handful of men was licensed to dig for them. Temptation was all too great for those excluded, and the diggings attracted unlicensed diggers not simply from among the local tribesmen, but from all the surrounding territories as well, even from other countries.

In Liberia, the investigators found, the buyers in Monrovia took few pains to conceal the real source of their stones. They were only too happy to find how abundant they were. The smugglers had little trouble in evading the poorly equipped local police in Sierra Leone, who had other problems besides IDB. In Liberia they were seen as an important source of revenue. The single 'mine' actually in operation in Liberia consisted of a tiny swamp area a couple of thousand yards across with a few diggers desultorily sieving the gravel by hand.

Some reports suggested about ten times as many carats were smuggled out of Sierra Leone as produced legally – up to half a million a year. It required little imagination to see the way out of the problem. If the illegal digging could not be stamped out, it would have to be harnessed. The Sierra Leone administration would have to grant licences to all who wanted them, and the Diamond Corporation would have to set up buying posts in each region where the diggers could sell their stones for a fair price.

286

But these measures took time to implement. Still the illegal traffic continued, and there was need of strong police action to bring persistent smugglers to heel. Sir Percy's men recruited the services of a Lebanese-born general dealer in Freetown, by name Fred Kamil. He had been double-crossed by a friend when he stood surety for him in an IDB case, and in revenge turned informer. Now he was given the chance to form his own private army to combat IDB, 15 mercenaries as hard-boiled as himself who waylaid diamond smugglers en route to Liberia through the dense jungle of the border area.

The smugglers used to travel light in twos and threes, but through fear of Fred Kamil's private army soon took to organising themselves in caravans of as many as 20 at a time. But the jungle was so thick and the country so difficult that their choice of routes was limited and the mercenaries could ambush them almost at will. The buyers in Liberia were understandably not happy about the interruption of the supply, and took steps to combat the new menace. In reprisal Kamil laid his own minefield.

All the diamonds recovered by the private army were turned over to the Sierra Leone government, insisted Fred Kamil. His rewards amounted to some £20 000 a year, though of course as word of this success spread and as the measures taken by the Diamond Corporation took effect there was less and less work for him to do. In fact, at quite an early stage Sir Percy publicly announced that the old leak through Sierra Leone had been plugged – with benefit to practically everyone concerned.

'Arrangements made in Sierra Leone are terribly important, not only to my employer, Sir Ernest Oppenheimer, and De Beers, but to the Sierra Leone Government and the Natives there.

(i) the Natives, who only a few months ago were digging these stones illegally, can now do so legally under licence and get a fair price for them instead of being exploited.

(ii) The revenue of the Sierra Leone Government must go up enormously because diamonds which may be worth £4 million a year are now declared to them.

(iii) The Diamond Corporation and De Beers will benefit because we have a buyer in the country and can get these stones for the legitimate markets in the world.'

In all this time, Ernest and Harry were watching spellbound. After all those novels, they had the real thing happening around them. Not only that, but one of the novelists they so revered – Ian Fleming – came south to South Africa to research a new adventure for his hero James

Bond, based on the situation at CDM. The result – *Diamonds are Forever*. A year or two later, when Sir Percy's work was done and the IDSO was disbanded in favour of a security organisation run by the Anglo American, Sir Percy's erstwhile chief lieutenant helped Fleming to write a full account of the operation. He called it *The Diamond Smugglers*, and in it featured a real life account of their number one opponent in the world of IDB. Sir Percy's man called him Mr Diamant, but could not say exactly who he was.

Even the editors of *Punch* took notice. Remembering those thrillers of E Phillips Oppenheim, they published a short rhyme which must have pleased father and son enormously:

> *Fiction's frequently sublime,*
> *But fact is far sublimer,*
> *For fiction may be Oppenheim,*
> *But fact is Oppenheimer.*

Had they but known it, the best was yet to come.

2

IT MIGHT be expected that a family in the position of the Oppenheimers would assemble a formidable collection of diamonds between them. Ernest, of course, had been a collector for years. He had the true connoisseur's love of diamonds for their own sake, and deliberately set out to acquire 'fancies' of every possible colour, and every possible cut as well. The whole collection numbered only a couple of hundred stones at most, but was still one of the finest in the world.

Ernest kept the collection in a black box in his office, and delighted in showing it off to visitors. When there was a lunch party at 44 Main Street, as often happened, he liked to display it in a special glass case. If his guests did not volunteer a comment themselves, he would deliberately ask what they thought of it all. As he handled the stones you could see his eyes light up with pleasure.

The head of the family liked to see his womenfolk in jewellery. He had helped May build up an impressive and valuable collection, and the bulk of it had been handed on to Bridget. Ina too had an awe-inspiring personal assembly. Her taste was for elegant but rather simple clothes, but she liked to set them off with impeccably chosen pieces: rings, bracelets, brooches and necklaces. Rarely was she to be seen without some.

Harry too liked to see women with jewellery, and always encouraged Bridget to wear hers. He had always felt it was a pity jewellery was usually associated with *older* women – though perhaps they were the only ones who could afford it. He wanted to see Bridget in glory while she was still young. With the jewels she had inherited and the items Harry had given her, Bridget's collection was valued at more than £250 000.

There were some startling pieces in the collection, some of them world-famous in the jewellers' fraternity. The most valuable single item was a pure white emerald cut diamond ring insured for £35 000. The diamond weighed more than 23 carats. Next on the list was an emerald cut pink diamond ring with emerald and sapphire shoulders, valued at £26 000. A blue marquise diamond ring was valued at £20 000 and a pure white marquise diamond ring at £17 000. Another ring, made of white gold and platinum and containing a blue-white brilliant of more than 11 carats, was worth £15 000.

There were diamond and emerald necklaces, a black pearl ring, diamond and ruby bracelets, diamond brooches by the handful, and even two Buddhas set in platinum and diamonds. There were halters, ornamental sprays, evening bags set with diamonds. Many of these items were worth a fortune. Yet of all the pieces in her collection the one Bridget treasured most was a relatively modest diamond brooch worth only £700 or so – the first present Harry had given her, in the shape of the badge of the South African Tank Corps.

For all its value Bridget had no great reverence for her collection. Not for her the security of a bank vault. Instead, she liked to have her whole collection to hand – locked in a wall safe concealed in a cupboard by her bed at Little Brenthurst. It was all listed by the insurance assessors and periodically checked, of course, but Bridget had never had any trouble. Far from it, when she went travelling with Harry she liked to take her collection with her, carried loose in her baggage. Often at night she did not even bother to lock it away.

On the evening of December 5 1955 Ernest and Ina invited Bridget for dinner. She would be by herself, for Harry was in the Belgian Congo on a safari trip with two young South Africans who he hoped would help him improve his Afrikaans. In return he had promised them 'the holiday of a lifetime'. Nicky was away at preparatory school in England these days, and that left only Mary at home with Bridget besides the butler and the maid. Mary's nanny was putting her to bed while Bridget got ready, selecting several pieces of jewellery to wear that night. When she made her choice she locked the safe with a key she kept in a bric-a-brac box in the cupboard, filled with oddments like racecourse badges and cigarette holders.

It was a pleasant evening up the garden, and Bridget got home about 10.15. The house was asleep, and she noticed nothing amiss except that one of her pillowcases was missing. The maid must have forgotten to put on a clean one, she decided. Only when she woke up next morning did she go to the safe to replace her jewellery.

Something was wrong. The box with the key was missing, and a piece of green baize cloth which ought to have been inside the safe was lying at the bottom of the cupboard. She fetched a spare key and opened the safe. It was virtually empty: the cream of her collection was gone. Only a few relatively worthless items were left.

Bridget's first thought was for Harry. How could she get hold of him? She was not even sure where he was, within plus or minus a hundred miles. Instead she rang Anglo. What was she to do?

Anglo called in the police. Soon Little Brenthurst was swarming with detectives and special branch men, and a tight-lipped patrol of executives from 44 Main Street. Word soon reached the newspapers and their reporters only added to the congestion. But though the police hunted high and low not a clue could they find: not a footprint, not a fingermark, not the tiniest indication of an intruder. The Brenthurst security guards had noticed nothing amiss, the dogs had not barked, and Mary, safe in the bedroom next to Bridget's, had slept soundly all night.

Soon the whole country was following the case, and speculating on how the robbery had been carried out. The police alerted Interpol, and a careful watch was kept on all points of exit from South Africa. It was supposed the robbery was the work of an international gang – the sort of gang that had been involved in the IDB operations Sillitoe had been investigating. But however hard they tried, the police failed to discover a single clue to the whereabouts of the jewels or the identity of the thieves.

Everything was insured, but that was poor compensation. The assessors decided something like £213 000 worth had been stolen. Four days after the theft the insurance company concerned announced it was offering £15 000 reward for information leading to the recovery of the jewels, and that a top insurance investigator, Dudley Strevens, would soon be flying out from London.

When Strevens arrived some days later his insurance colleagues in Johannesburg could give him little help. More than a week had gone by with the police as baffled as ever. The many theories put forward only served to cloud the real issue. It was generally supposed the theft was an 'inside job' involving the staff at Brenthurst. But repeated interrogation had produced nothing. Instead the only promising lead was persistent badgering from a man with an Australian accent who had several times contacted the insurance company and demanded an interview. He said he had important information which he would keep for Strevens.

The police case was being handled by the chief of the CID on the Witwatersrand, Colonel Ulf Boberg. First thing next morning he visited Strevens at his hotel. He wanted to make it quite plain he would not stand for any private detective work on Strevens's part. Obviously with such a large reward being offered Strevens might discover things the police did not know. If that happened, then he must tell them immediately.

Duly impressed with this warning, Strevens was driven to the Carlton Hotel where the mysterious Australian was staying. With him went one of the insurance assessors who had been dealing with the case. They had to ask for a Mr Pearson, and when they reached his room found a tall, dark, well-built man who soon came to the point. He told them he was in a position to help them recover the missing jewels, but was not interested in the £15 000. It would cost them a lot more, he said. He knew the thieves, and they wanted £75 000.

Strevens said he was not interested at that price. Pearson said he might recover the jewels for £50 000. Again Strevens shook his head. As an assessor he would be compounding a felony if he paid such a considerable amount of money. On the other hand, he was legally entitled to offer about ten per cent of the total value of the stolen goods. That meant he could raise the reward to £20 000. But that was his limit – and he made it a condition that he should bring the police into the picture. Anyway, how had Pearson come by his information?

Simple, said the Australian. He had arrived in South Africa in November – a month before the robbery. He met a man in a hotel bar who told him there was a big job coming off. He left South Africa for London not long after this, and read of the theft in a newspaper. That must be the big job, he decided. Back in South Africa again he contacted his informant who confirmed his suspicions.

Strevens repeated what he had said earlier. He was not in a position to *buy* back the jewels. Pearson said in that case he might have to hijack the jewels on his own account and get them out of the country – then offer them back to the insurance company. But he wanted his £50 000. Nothing doing, said Strevens. In that case, said Pearson, it looked as if they could not do business. And on that note they parted company.

Later that day, when Strevens returned to his office, there was a message from Pearson. He had been thinking it over, he said, and thought he had a way out. Pay him £20 000 down, then put him on the staff of the insurance company with an annual retainer of £5 000. Thoroughly amused by this idea, Strevens promised to contact his London office with the proposal. He said he would see Pearson first thing next morning.

Before he had time to do this, however, he received a second visit from Colonel Boberg. The detective was getting nowhere – but had a shrewd suspicion Strevens was making progress. This time he was not going to beat about the bush. If Strevens held back anything at all, he would have charges brought against him without the slightest hesitation.

Strevens told his story, which made Boberg angry. He said if Strevens was not actually compounding a felony, it was the nearest thing to it he had ever come across. He wanted the Australian immediately. Get him down to the insurance company's offices without delay.

Strevens did as he was told. When Pearson arrived he was not altogether delighted when the colonel introduced himself, but soon recovered his composure, and calmly repeated his story. If the assessors delivered £50 000 to his hotel, he could get the jewellery.

Boberg told Pearson he did not believe a word of it. He had a hunch the Australian was trying to pull a confidence trick and defraud the insurance company. Having collected the reward he would disappear. The detective had a challenge for him: produce just one item of the missing jewellery – the smallest he liked – and he would believe the story. Pearson said he could not do it.

Boberg challenged again. The insurance company could not pay over £50 000, but the police would. He was prepared to give Pearson the whole amount – in cancelled notes. To his surprise Pearson said that would be all right so long as the money looked good enough. He would carry out his side of the bargain if the police undertook to put him on the first available aircraft to Australia.

It was Boberg's turn to back out. He could not allow Pearson to disappear. What was he to do for evidence? What he *was* prepared to do was employ Pearson as a witness for the prosecution, then let him collect his reward and go wherever he wanted without further hindrance. Pearson grinned impudently. The colonel would never get him into the witness box to testify against the others.

Pearson went off to make contact with the thieves, and the colonel got busy. His detectives raced to the Reserve Bank in Pretoria to collect the money, and it was in the insurance offices within two hours, packed in a battered tin trunk. But when Pearson returned he was not impressed. He had told his contacts the money would be in tenners and fivers, not in single pound and ten shilling notes. And how was he to walk into the Carlton with an old tin trunk? The colonel agreed to substitute suitcases, but insisted the money was all right.

The Australian was ready. He said the thieves now believed he had a buyer for the jewels – none other than the old Mafiosa chief 'Lucky' Luciano, a legend in his own lifetime now living in supposed retirement in Naples. Pearson had told them one of Luciano's men was in South Africa to try and obtain the jewels through him. The man would be with him at the Carlton, but was not to be seen by anyone.

The plan was quite simple. One of the thieves would come to Pearson's suite to check for himself the money was there. Then an accomplice would telephone the room, and if everything was all right would be invited to 'Come up for a drink'. The colonel agreed to all this but with one proviso. There would indeed be a man from 'Lucky' Luciano – a detective in the bathroom.

The trap was set that evening. The detective concealed himself in the bathroom well before time, and other detectives were hidden in rooms surrounding Pearson's suite. Outside, the building was encircled by police squad cars in case Pearson changed his mind and tried to escape. The money was to be delivered to the suite *after* the first thief had arrived, and only shortly before the second man was due to telephone.

Everything went to plan. The first man arrived, then the second, and the police waited to pounce. Pearson collected a cardboard box from the second man and went into the bathroom to show it to the detective. It contained what looked like the complete haul from Little Brenthurst. The detective signalled to his colleagues outside, and seven of them rushed into the room with revolvers at the ready.

The surprise was complete. Pearson hurried off down the corridor, leaving his guests bending over the money in the opened suitcases. One was tall, fair and slim, the other shorter, and with his dark hair slicked back. They made no attempt to escape. Instead they stood stupefied, as if they were indignant at the sudden interruption.

The two men were taken to police headquarters. Boberg himself took charge of the loot, packed in the cardboard box with Christmas wrapping paper and a chiffon scarf. He carried it to the insurance offices and telephoned Bridget. Harry was back by now, and he and Bridget were at home playing bridge with friends. They immediately drove to the insurance offices to check through the jewellery. Bridget found six articles were still missing, worth between £7 000 and £8 000. Otherwise everything was accounted for. Bridget wanted to take it all home with her, but Boberg insisted he needed it as evidence.

Back at police headquarters Boberg interviewed the two arrested men, who were both British immigrants. One was Percival William Radley, who said he was credit manager of a small charter flight company operating between Johannesburg and Amsterdam. He had known Pearson some time, he said, and the Australian simply invited him up to his room for a drink. Nobody could have been more surprised than he when the 'bleedin' police' burst in.

The other man's name was Donald Miles, who called himself a private detective but who had been out of work some time. He had been in the Carlton that afternoon when a man he knew only vaguely invited him to have a drink at the bar. He explained he was just leaving Johannesburg, and asked if Miles would mind delivering a parcel to a friend of his upstairs, a little later on. At the arranged time Miles went up to Pearson's room, Pearson invited him in and there he found Radley and the suitcase full of money.

The men stuck to their stories. By this time Pearson had arrived at police headquarters and Boberg called him in. To Boberg's surprise Pearson seemed full of remorse for the part he had played in 'shopping' his contacts. He even demanded to be locked up with the others. The detective tried to get him to change his mind, but he was adamant. Boberg put him under arrest.

Almost all the loot was recovered, and there were three men in the cells. But the police were as far from discovering how the robbery had been carried out as ever. There must be other men involved, they reasoned: perhaps a whole gang. When the question of bail came up, the police vigorously opposed the idea. Who knew where the men might go, and who might not help them? They would have to spend Christmas in gaol.

All this time the men were visited by detectives day after day, questioning and cross-questioning them in an effort to get to the bottom of the matter. But all stuck to their stories. Only on January 3, when Boberg visited them himself, was there the first sign of a breakthrough. Pearson told the detective all he had been afraid of was the publicity he would get if the facts of his involvement became known. Everything had come out anyway, so there was no point in holding

Harry with Charles Engelhard, the precious metals magnate who was for years a close associate of Ian Fleming and who was evidently the model for James Bond's opponent Goldfinger. *Abe Goldstein.*

Nicky grows up. Harry chats with his son at Nicky's 21st birthday party, June 8 1966. *Anglo American Corporation.*

A new member of the family: Gordon Waddell arrives in Johannesburg before the announcement of his engagement to Mary. *Rand Daily Mail.*

out any longer. He was prepared to give evidence against the others after all. Would the police set him free?

Boberg was far from happy about this development. The fact was he did not trust the man. What was to prevent Pearson from skipping the border into Mozambique? And was his evidence all that strong anyway? He decided to see Radley and Miles and find out what they had to say.

Until now he had been able to discover little about the two suspects. Miles had been a security officer with a cinema group until he was fired some months before, and since then he had been out of work. More telling, it was discovered Miles had an impressive war record behind him – first service in France as a secret agent with the Resistance, and later service in Palestine with the British forces in occupation. Now he was out of the forces and in civvy street again, he just could not find his feet.

Radley, on the other hand, had held down a good job in Johannesburg. He was a colourful cockney who had arrived in South Africa some years before, and all the way through had insisted on his innocence. What Boberg did not know – though the news was on its way from London – was that at home in England Radley had a police record stretching back some 20 years.

It came as yet another surprise for Boberg, then, when Radley suddenly offered to turn Queen's Evidence. Pearson was not as guiltless in the affair as the police imagined, he claimed. He told the colonel a story that seemed at last to clarify the whole issue, implicating both Miles and Pearson. The three of them were in it together. Boberg spent most of the day with the Londoner, and after their discussion took him to see the state prosecutor, Dr Percy Yutar.

The prosecutor was faced with a difficult decision. Should he accept Pearson's offer or Radley's, or ignore them both and hope that the police could build a sufficient case without their help? On the face of it, Pearson was more closely implicated than Radley: indeed, the only evidence against Radley was his actual presence in Pearson's suite when the police burst in.

On the other hand, Boberg had heard from the police in Sydney. They had read of the case and recognised in Pearson a man they wanted in connection with an attempted fraud on the Bank of Australia. They described him as one of Australia's cleverest confidence tricksters, a man not to be trusted in any circumstances. Not surprisingly, Boberg and Yutar decided to enlist Radley's help and after a further court appearance the Londoner was released from custody.

Another week went by. Radley proved only too co-operative – though the news of his police record came as a shock. At last all was ready, and the two accused were brought to court for their preparatory examination before a magistrate. They were not expected to defend themselves. Instead, the purpose of the hearing was to establish whether or not there was a case for them to answer, and whether they should be committed for trial.

The courtroom was packed. To start the proceedings Yutar ran through the story the magistrate would hear from witnesses to be called: a story which seemed to account for every aspect of the case which had been so puzzling for so long. The key figure in the whole drama, he insisted, was Donald Miles.

A year before Miles had been employed by a roofing firm which was called in to insulate the roofs of Little Brenthurst against fire while Harry and Bridget were overseas. Miles was working on the job, and had access to every part of the house. One day he was in Bridget's bedroom when he found her safe and opened it with a key he found in the cupboard. With Bridget and Harry away the safe was practically empty.

Miles conceived the idea of helping himself to the contents of the safe when Harry and Bridget returned. He tried to persuade some friends to join him, though without actually telling them which house he wanted to rob. They refused, but one told a contact of his who he knew had had experience overseas – in fact, Radley. In April 1955 this friend brought them together, and after a preliminary discussion Miles and Radley agreed to join forces.

Eventually in September 1955 Radley and Miles went off to Little Brenthurst on a reconnoitering expedition, and though spotted by one of the African security guards pressed on as if they owned the place. They looked over the house from outside, then retraced their steps. A week later they went again and this time walked straight in through the front door, and up the stairs. The house was in darkness, but they spotted light coming from under a door. Radley took fright and insisted they leave immediately. He thought the whole scheme was too dangerous and told Miles he wanted nothing more to do with it.

Then Pearson came into the picture. He arrived from Australia early in November, and he and Radley met in a hotel bar. They soon 'smelled each other out', as the underworld phrases it, and before long Radley told Pearson there was a big job in the offing. He persuaded Pearson to go off to London to meet a man who was said to be a good contact for a job as big as this.

Pearson flew to London as arranged. Radley saw Miles once or twice but heard nothing further of his plan. Only the day after December 5, when Miles went to Little Brenthurst on his own and pulled off the job, did Radley read about the robbery in that afternoon's *Star*. The next morning Miles came to see him and said he was relying on him to help dispose of the loot.

The same day Pearson read about the robbery in a newspaper while flying between London and Amsterdam, and realised immediately that this must be the 'big job' Radley had told him about. He flew straight back to South Africa, and within hours was closeted with Radley. He told the Londoner everything was arranged. He had cabled his partner to join him from Sydney, and on the way south had called on 'Lucky' Luciano who was sending a man to see to the disposal of the jewels. Then followed his double-cross meetings with the insurance assessors and with the police.

This, then, was the prosecution's story. Yutar began calling witnesses to establish each point of his case. Among the first was Bridget, who was needed to identify her jewels. There was not much else she could tell the court, and though the defence counsel appearing for Miles had hoped to cross-examine her she was excused as she was due to fly off to England to see Nicky.

Miles's old employer from the time he had worked at Little Brenthurst gave evidence that he remembered hearing Miles commenting on the lack of security at Little Brenthurst and on the key he had found. And an old workmate of his from the cinema group gave evidence that Miles had later told him of the jewels in the safe and suggested they should go along and steal them. Then he gave evidence that it was he who brought in Radley. The Londoner had hinted he had a rather dark past and had boasted to him that he had worked for Sir Percy Sillitoe in helping to smash the international diamond smugglers.

But all this was tame in comparison with what was to come. Next day Radley was called to the box. He looked cheerful and confident: in fact, as if he enjoyed all the attention he was getting. Led by the prosecutor, he elaborated on each point of evidence in turn. Yes, he had been in league with Miles until the night they entered Brenthurst and saw the light under the door. Yes, he had remained in touch with the case to the extent of persuading Pearson to fly to London and make contact with the fence. Yes, he had an alibi for the night of the theft: he was at the cinema with his fiancée, now his wife of a few days standing as he had married her soon after his release from custody.

The most extraordinary part of his evidence came in explaining how the theft was carried out. The police had not been able to determine how the thieves had broken in without leaving a trace. Simple, said Radley. The front door had a patent spring lock, and he had earlier shown Miles how to use a special tool which opened the door in seconds.

And how had Miles carried out the job? He had reached Little Brenthurst by bus, said Radley. He had broken in, stuffed the jewels into Bridget's missing pillowcase – and returned to town with the bundle tucked under his jacket. Again he had travelled by bus.

Radley had plenty to say about Miles, but on Pearson his evidence was not so full. When he met Pearson the Australian was already planning a big diamond haul from a merchant in Amsterdam, he now revealed. He was on his way to Europe in any case, so Radley suggested he should get in touch with the fence in London. He did this as directed, but when he returned to South Africa suggested it would be best to let 'Lucky' Luciano see to the disposal of the jewels, just as he was preparing to help with the disposal of the haul from Amsterdam.

At the conclusion of the evidence, Pearson's counsel immediately demanded his release on the grounds of insufficient evidence. What offence had he committed? It was agreed he had nothing to do with the actual robbery. And as for being an accessory after the fact, all the evidence showed he had intended to go to an insurance company days before he was arrested.

The Crown, on the other hand, insisted the evidence against Pearson was all too strong. Pearson's attitude was not that of an honest man seeking a reward; it suggested he was implicated to the hilt, at the same time trying to make as much from the deal as he could – even to the extent of double-crossing his accomplices and certainly the insurance company. The magistrate agreed with the Crown. Both Pearson and Miles were committed for trial. Miles had already stated that he pleaded not guilty and wanted to be tried by judge and jury – not by judge and assessors as was possible under South African law. Pearson still insisted he had nothing to do with the robbery.

Both defence counsel asked for bail for their clients, but the magistrate adjourned the hearing until the next day to consider the applications. In the event he agreed to grant bail of £5 000 to Miles, but refused Pearson's application. The Australian was not a citizen of South Africa and had means at his disposal which might help him leave the country. Besides, there was the strong possibility Pearson might interfere with Radley. He had threatened as much.

Miles was free to leave gaol, but could not raise the bail. Pearson, on the other hand, appealed to the Supreme Court and was granted bail of £7 000. It was a lot of money, but his attorneys found it for him. He was due for the reward of £20 000. The attorneys took out an urgent application at the Supreme Court against the insurance company.

There was an intriguing corollary to the application. Some days before this the Receiver of Revenue had served notice on Pearson in the gaol that he was assessed for £8 000 tax. It was a damned cheek, he complained. But in making the order against the insurance company the judge made it conditional on Pearson's handing over the tax as directed. He duly paid – though his attorneys prepared to submit an application for a rebate. Then he was released from gaol and moved into one of Johannesburg's most comfortable hotels.

There he stayed for five weeks, complaining how bored he was and how deadly dull he found Johannesburg. The Crown, in the meantime, tried to gather evidence against him – and got nowhere. The police could make no advance on what they had achieved already, and they knew it was not enough. They had to drop the charges and Pearson was a free man: but he would be required to give evidence in the case of Regina v. Miles.

So now there was one. Radley and Pearson were free – and to the South African public they were the less attractive of the men involved in the trial. Miles, supposed the public, was down on his luck. The others were the professionals, he was the dupe. More than a few hoped he would get off. But the evidence against him appeared only too strong. When the trial opened on April 3 the whole country waited eagerly for its outcome.

The courtroom was crowded from the start. The first stir came with the arrival of a heavy wooden box carried into court by two burly detectives, a specially made display case covered with a sheet of glass a quarter of an inch thick and securely bolted down. In it was all the jewellery recovered from the haul. The public craned forward to look at it, so that Miles's arrival in the dock went virtually unnoticed.

Boberg, Bridget and one of the insurance investigators were the first witnesses to be called. All Bridget had to do was identify her jewellery and this took but a short time. It looked as if she would have to remain for the rest of the trial in case she was needed again, which was a nuisance as she had been due to join Harry on holiday in Italy. But the judge decided it was not necessary for her to stay after all and she was free to go.

The prosecution had few surprises. Only when Radley arrived in the box did Fred Zwarenstein, Miles's leading defending counsel, provide a hint of things to come. When Miles came to give evidence, said Zwarenstein, he would challenge Radley's claims that he had needed special tutoring to open the door at Little Brenthurst. He had learnt that trick when on special duties during the war. Clearly the contention would be that Radley himself had carried out the burglary.

Miles was called to the witness box next day. He looked ill at ease and nervous, and admitted later he would rather have gone through a secret service assignment all over again, dangling from a parachute and caught in enemy fire, than go through that experience of giving evidence.

It was the first time he had told his story under oath. All the way through the police interrogations he had insisted he had never met Pearson or Radley in his life, but he was prepared to change that story now. Yes, he had met Radley before, in April 1955. He had tea with him and in the course of conversation Radley mentioned he was helping Sir Percy Sillitoe's investigations for the Oppenheimer group.

When Radley mentioned the name Oppenheimer Miles told him he had once worked at Little Brenthurst – and that Harry could do with a security officer as there were a lot of valuables and paintings left literally lying around. He mentioned this point as he had already told Radley he was looking for a job as some kind of security officer, which was all he could do.

Zwarenstein jumped to the night of the robbery. Miles claimed he had gone home to his flat disappointed after being turned down for two more jobs. He spent the afternoon writing more applications and went to a hamburger joint for supper. Then he went home to bed and read until he fell asleep.

Next Zwarenstein asked him about the day the trap was sprung. He had gone to visit Radley at noon, he said, to ask for more advice about finding a job. Radley said he might have something for him, and would see him at his flat at seven that night. The Londoner arrived on time with a box in Christmas wrapping paper, and told him it contained uncut diamonds. He was acting for a syndicate which dealt in uncut stones. He and Radley had had to deliver the box to an Australian he did not really know, so would have to be careful. Would Miles help him out?

Miles felt he had little option in the matter. He needed the money. Radley told him he had to take the box to the Carlton and telephone a Mr Pearson in Suite 641 at nine o'clock exactly. Radley would answer the telephone and if the coast was clear would call him up for a drink. He would give him £250 for carrying out the assignment.

Miles did as he was told. When he got to the suite Pearson opened the door and Radley was there and assured him everything was all right. Pearson opened the box and he saw there were scarves inside. Then Pearson went out through another door, and when he came back the police burst in. Miles said he did not realise the box had contained the Oppenheimer jewels until they were on the way to the police station.

Zwarenstein asked him why he had lied to the police. Miles said he realised what a bad position he was in and did not want to associate himself with Radley. Then who had stolen the jewels? Miles was gripping the rail of the witness-box until his knuckles showed white through the skin. It must have been Radley.

Cross-examination did not begin until the next day. The prosecutor followed the course of events step by step. Why had Miles worried about security at Little Brenthurst on the Oppenheimers' behalf? Because if something was stolen while they were working there the roofing firm would be blamed. How had he come to find the key of the safe? He was looking for a way up to a trapdoor that led into the roof. When he opened the cupboard he found the key lying in an open box.

Had he mentioned the key or the safe to Radley? Certainly not. Had he discussed the lay-out of the place? Not at all. Radley had asked him if it was a beautiful home. But of course he now realised Radley's sole purpose in cultivating his friendship was to get information about Little Brenthurst. And all he discovered from him was that it was a beautiful home? Perhaps Radley had got other things out of him.

The first time he discussed the theft with Radley was about three days after it had happened. Radley said it must have been an inside job. At least, there must have been some help from inside: though perhaps the actual job was done by outsiders. But in discussing the case with Radley he still believed the Londoner was an honest man, and nothing he had said had made him suspect anything different.

Miles was not doing well. The case was black against him, and he was scared stiff. His features twitched with nervousness. On many occasions he was tongue-tied, and when his answers were not accepted or misunderstood in some way he grew impatient.

Then what about the night of the trap? How come he had fallen for the story of the diamond syndicate? Maybe he did not go into it too much. Perhaps he needed the money. Fair enough, Radley had warned him that the deal might be a bit shady, but he had no idea just how valuable the haul was. And he had no suspicion the box contained anything but uncut diamonds.

But surely he could not expect the court to believe that? He knew something of stones. Didn't he realise a box that heavy must contain something very special indeed? No, he knew nothing about diamonds. For all he knew they were still embedded in the rock they were found in. As far as he was concerned they might have been worth in the region of £20 000.

The court adjourned for lunch. Miles's evidence was complete. It remained for the prosecution to sum up its case. In the view of most observers it was cut and dried. There could be little hope for Miles even though Zwarenstein told the jury they had to banish from their minds all the publicity that had surrounded the case. They had to forget the idea that the one 'decent fellow' involved had to take the rap for the others. Who said he was involved at all? There was no burden on the defence to prove that Miles had *not* committed the crime. The prosecution had to prove that he had – beyond all reasonable doubt.

It was a long address. Point by point Zwarenstein dealt with the evidence and showed the jury that the case was by no means cut and dried. There were inconsistencies in Radley's story: there was reason to suspect he had deliberately *used* Miles for his own purposes; and there was strong evidence of his own criminal background. Was it not at least conceivable that Miles's story was true, and that it was Radley who carried out the burglary?

Miles had made a false statement to the police, certainly. But many people had done that before coming clean, and yet were not convicted. There were inconsistencies in Miles's story, but not enough to prove the prosecution's case beyond all doubt. The jury would have to find him not guilty, for otherwise a terrible and tragic injustice would have been done.

Then the judge summed up and addressed the jury. They should not feel sorry for an accused person, he told them, or consider the fact that other people ought to be punished too. If a man had committed a crime, he had to suffer for it.

The jury stayed out for 55 minutes. When they returned the clerk of the court called for silence and the judge returned to the bench.

'Gentlemen of the jury, are you agreed on your verdict?'

'We are, milord.'

'What is your verdict?'

The foreman hesitated a moment.

'Not guilty.'

There was a moment's pause, then came uproar. The spectators erupted into a riot of cheering, hand-clapping, stamping and whistling never before experienced in a South African courtroom. Complete strangers slapped each other on the back. Only Miles showed no reaction, slumped down in the dock as if he had not heard.

The verdict was sensational. Three men had been arrested, and one by one they had been let off the hook. What had gone wrong? It looked as if crime paid only too well. One of the three had made his fortune from the insurance reward – the rebate had been allowed, incidentally. The other two sold the rights to their life stories to magazines and newspapers, and made money out of that. And presumably one of them still had the £8 000 worth of jewellery still missing.

The case was raised in parliament, and the Minister of Justice blamed the result of the case on the jury system – though that explained only Miles's release, not the *cartes blanches* granted to Pearson and Radley. Harry sent £2 000 to the police orphans' fund as a thank-you, but it could hardly compensate Boberg. A few years later when he retired he was asked to make a speech and after a few general observations came to the Oppenheimer case. In a way, he said, it was his greatest success. He had recouped the jewels in double quick time, and made three arrests. On the other hand – and he clearly took it personally – the case was his greatest failure.

All three of the protagonists in the case were deported. All three went to England. Pearson and Miles changed their names in a clear attempt to bury their past and start a new life. Radley, on the other hand, arrived in a blaze of publicity and arranged a meeting with the retired Inspector Fabian of Scotland Yard. He announced publicly that it was after all he who stole the jewels – and that he had done it in 45 minutes flat. He was indeed at the cinema that evening as he had claimed, but had carried out the burglary in the course of the show.

It was a case of the boy who cried Wolf, Wolf. Radley had shouted so much before that nobody was prepared to believe him. The police did not trouble to reopen their files, and like the others Radley faded into obscurity. The baffling Case of the Oppenheimer Diamonds remains officially unsolved.

3

LONG BEFORE now the Nationalists had settled on Harry as Number One bogeyman on the Opposition's benches, and with all the mud they had thrown it was inevitable some should stick. Most South Africans genuinely believed Hoggenheimer and his henchmen were indeed up to something, and that all would be revealed in the weeks of campaigning that led up to the next general election. This would be their chance to drive the Nationalists from power, and they had been making preparations for a long time.

But there were no startling new developments: it was rather an anti-climax. The Trust Fund continued to raise funds, which the United Party seemed only to waste. Certainly its candidates made no impression on the Nationalists in by-elections. And though the Torch Commando marched on as determined as ever, it had no further reaction from the population as a whole: it began to look as if its bolt was shot.

True, Sailor Malan came to the fore, and managed to persuade the leaders of the various Opposition parties to come together and form 'the United Democratic Front' – much like the Pact of years before when the single object had been to drive Smuts from power. Now the boot was on the other foot. But though all had agreed to sink their differences, this only served to produce a pitifully negative common policy which had no appeal at all to an electorate by this time hopelessly muddled. As the election approached, Harry found himself invited by a number of United Party candidates to address meetings in their constituencies, and where possible he accepted. One such invitation came from the candidate standing in the country constituency of Porterville in the Cape, with the request that he should speak on the budget, and restrict himself to speaking in Afrikaans.

Besides Harry, the candidate had invited a young Afrikaans-speaking medical doctor who would himself be standing in the election. This was Zach de Beer, who had recently married J G N Strauss's daughter and had incongruously become quite a power in the Cape Torch Commando though he had been too young to fight in the war. Zach de Beer was rather startled when Harry approached him and asked for a lift out to Porterville, explaining that he had no suitable car. The doctor himself ran a less than efficient student-style jallopy, while he knew well Harry possessed a fine Rolls Bentley.

The two men duly arrived in Porterville, and were met by the local United Party chairman who did not recognise Harry in the passenger seat and wanted to know what had happened to Mr Oppenheimer. It was only now Zach de Beer realised why Harry had asked for a lift in his jallopy. To have arrived among the farming folk of Porterville in the opulance of a Rolls Bentley might immediately have alienated their sympathies. Sadly, for all his efforts Harry's expedition was largely wasted. Though his Afrikaans was perfectly acceptable to his audience, his subject was not. The electors of Porterville possessed as much understanding of budget affairs as they had of nuclear physics.

On the way back to Cape Town Harry and Zach de Beer stopped for dinner at a wayside hotel. The young doctor was rather overawed in the presence of the rising magnate, but was gratified to find Harry accepted his offer to pay for the first drink, though Harry later paid for their dinner. This was in contrast with the attitude of others Zach de Beer had met, who preferred rather to flaunt their money before him as if to consolidate their superiority. Though an age gap of 20 years separated the two men, the evening was the start of a personal and political friendship that was to prove all-important to both.

With election day Harry regained his seat with little trouble, while the electors of Maitland in Cape Town returned Zach de Beer as the youngest member ever to sit in the South African parliament. He was only 24. But that was small compensation to the United Party, for returns from the country as a whole showed that far from being driven from power, the Nationalists had substantially increased their majority. They were, of course, cock-a-hoop. What *wouldn't* they do now?

So that was it. All the way through Sailor and the other commando leaders had promised their efforts were aimed at winning the 1953 election for the Opposition. It would be a fight to the death: there were no plans for action once the election was over. The veterans held a few more meetings, but the heart had gone out of the movement. The old torchmen dropped away one by one, and the Nationalists watched gloatingly as the once dangerous commandos dwindled and died for good.

D F Malan had stayed on as Premier, though he was now very nearly 80. He retained most of his old cabinet. One of them, the former leader of the Nationalists in the Senate, had now won a seat in the House of Assembly where he was to make a name which would ring throughout the world: Hendrik Verwoerd, Minister of Native Affairs. This was the chief supporter of Strijdom, the Nationalist with the hardest line of them all: Africa for the Afrikaners. It was known that given their way Strijdom and Verwoerd would lead the Union out of the British Commonwealth without delay and declare South Africa an independent republic.

'I am glad to get this confirmation that Mr Strijdom hopes to be President of the South African Republic,' said Harry in response to a typically hard-hitting speech from this most ardent Nationalist. 'He is the head of a band of extremists who stand for the isolation of the country and domination by a section over the people of South Africa.'

It had been supposed Malan would remain in office only long enough to see the Nationalists returned to power again, and would then retire. This he now did. Interestingly, he tried to have the moderate Havenga made his successor. Even he was apprehensive of what Strijdom might do. But the party caucus would not hear of it. The Lion of the North, as Strijdom was known, was installed as the new Prime Minister of the Union of South Africa.

But strangely enough, nothing happened: not from Strijdom's court, in any event. Suddenly all the fight had gone out of him. Nobody knew it, but he was a sick man. To an ever-increasing extent he left it to Verwoerd to fight the battles of Nationalist policy and force through each measure that would change the face of South Africa. Harry Lawrence, a survivor of Smuts's last cabinet, pointed out: 'Now the total apartheid juggernaut has got into motion the Prime Minister has become a back seat driver.'

The Opposition contested each measure in turn, and not even all the Nationalists were with Strijdom and Verwoerd heart and soul: the two men had several times to reserve special powers for themselves to carry their policies and legislation beyond words into deeds. But Verwoerd was determined. He had been one of those academics who years before had worked out the blueprint of apartheid. Now he would see it through, the realisation of his dreams. Divided as they were, the Opposition had few weapons to raise against him. It was left to a handful to wage what war they could: and of these the most effective was Harry.

Harry had crossed Verwoerd before. But on those occasions he had been on the defensive. Now he could attack. He chose to make his point in terms of the world he understood best, and which he insisted had most to lose, the world of business.

'We should face the facts that only about a third of the Native population lives in the reserves and that the vast industrial development on which we depend for our well-being, our homes, our motor-cars, and our education requires the co-operation of Black and White. We should recognise that there is no chance whatever of South Africa changing her economic pattern. We should accept that no policy will be successful unless it can carry with it the goodwill of the Native people. We cannot have peace and security if the bulk of the people are dissatisfied.'

The millions of Africans who did not live in the rural reserves but in the cities were the most important part of the African population, he insisted. Whites should take steps to secure their goodwill, for on them safety and prosperity depended.

'We do not need to go in for some kind of head-counting democracy which, in the long run, will turn over the Government of the country to Blacks who would be just as nationalistically inclined as some Whites. What we must do plainly, definitely and unequivocally is to recognise the non-European population as a permanent part of our urban population and give them a sense of permanence and of belonging.'

In the House of Assembly Harry challenged Verwoerd openly. 'I do not know why we have to put up with all these absurdities. But I am told it is because the Minister of Native Affairs has decided that apartheid means the gradual approach to complete separation, and that the people of South Africa have voted for apartheid. Well, of course, one can always vote for a thing. Hon members may have heard the story of how a village voted that the world was flat . . .'

There was one speech in particular in which Harry succeeded in disturbing Verwoerd. Previous attacks on his policies had been ideological, assaults on the theory of apartheid. But as Verwoerd was quick to point out they had no practical application. At least his way was an attempt to combat the problems everybody admitted existed. This time, however, Harry came up with a number of *practical* objections.

'This Minister has been associated with the growth of secondary industry, and all credit to him, and in particular he and his party over very many years have taken the line that it is particularly important to encourage the growth of secondary industry, so that the country should not be dependent to an excessive extent on the mining industry, because mining is a wasting asset.

'A very sound point of view. It has always been felt by thinking people in South Africa that it is absolutely necessary to follow such a policy so that when this mining industry comes to an end there should be none of those deserted, derelict towns along the Witwatersrand which have marked the end of mining industries in other countries.

'Now this is not just a distant fantasy, something we need not worry about, very much like the achievement of full apartheid. This is a matter which has got to be taken into account now, because after all, there are already a great many mines which are getting towards the end of their lives. Even a new mine cannot count on a life of more than 30 or 40 years. Therefore while we don't know when the golden age of apartheid will come, we do know that the golden age of the Witwatersrand and the Free State gold mines will come to an end.

'So it is a question whether the hon Minister still sticks to what I regarded as the established policy, that is to encourage the growth of secondary industries in order that they may in due course take the place of the mining industry when that comes to an end. I think it is important to ask this question, because we know that the Minister of Native Affairs is deliberately setting out to slow down industrial expansion on the Witwatersrand and elsewhere in order to advance his ultimate plan of moving industries to, or near, the reserves . . .

'There are a million people on the Witwatersrand and there are going to be some hundreds of thousands of people on the Free State gold fields who are not going to be at all happy when the mines come to an end to be told that it is quite all right because secondary industries are being developed in the Native reserves.'

Harry contrasted Verwoerd's policies with what he understood had been official Nationalist economic policy as put into effect by Havenga, who had recently stepped down. This had involved giving all the encouragement he could to the development of secondary industry in the cities, and that meant bringing in the African labour which Verwoerd wanted to confine to the reserves. Havenga's successor was Eric Louw, and as Harry pointed out: 'He has got to ride both these horses . . . and it seems to me that that is going to be a balancing feat of no mean order.'

Harry was prepared to concede a number of points. 'After all, I think all of us in this House will agree that we must maintain the standard of living of the European people, and it certainly would not help the Natives to lower that standard. I think people would also agree that it is very desirable to have residential segregation. I think everyone in this House is agreed that it is most undesirable to put political power into the hands of uncivilised, uneducated people, as far as we can help it. I think too that in spite of what the hon Minister of Native Affairs says, that the whole population of South Africa is agreed that Native labour has got to continue to be available, to the mines, to our industry, on our farms and in our houses . . .

'But in dealing with these matters, Mr Speaker, people, I hope, will be very suspicious of any rigid system, and especially of systems which do not concern themselves so much with the welfare of individuals as with talk of groups, or races, and of sections . . .'

'I am quite sure that the attempt by systems and theories to determine the history of this country for a hundred years to come is nothing but folly and nothing but arrogance . . . What is needed is not a rigid system, not an attempt to determine the future . . . What we need is to

308

get together to deal with practical problems in a sensible and humane way. I saw two lines of verse the other day which expressed the point of view I am trying to put to you. And what I saw was this—

'Our stability is but Balance, and conduct lies
In masterful administration of the unforeseen.

'That is what I would commend to hon members of this House. The future is unforeseen anyhow, and if we try now to pre-determine the future relations of our peoples we show ourselves arrogant and foolish and inhumane.'

Verwoerd was not in the House to hear it, but members agreed it was the most effective speech yet made against him. He was told about it in the lobby outside, and hurried in to confer with Eric Louw. What were they to say in reply? It would need some thinking about. But Verwoerd said nothing before the Speaker adjourned the House that evening. Next day it was the same. Several Nationalist speakers attacked Harry, but Verwoerd himself said nothing. Not until the end of the day, when at last he rose to his feet. After answering a number of general points raised in the debate he launched into his counter-attack.

'I now turn to the hon member for Kimberley (City). I want to point out that the hon member argued in that nice, suave, friendly way always used by the capitalist when he intends doing something which is in his own interest . . .

Mr LAWRENCE: That shows that you have no reply to his case. Do not be personal.

The MINISTER OF NATIVE AFFAIRS: It is characteristic of all capitalists that when they are looking after their own interests and acting on behalf of their own businesses, they always direct an appeal . . .

Mr LAWRENCE: On a point of order, the Minister of Native Affairs is now replying to the hon member for Kimberley (City).

The DEPUTY-SPEAKER: What is the point of order?

Mr LAWRENCE: Whether he can say that the hon member has a personal interest.

The DEPUTY-SPEAKER: That is not a point of order.

Mr LAWRENCE: My point is this. The hon member for Kimberley (City) is a member of this House and is entitled to express his views. I ask whether the Minister is entitled to say that the hon member has personal motives.

The MINISTER OF NATIVE AFFAIRS: I was saying that the capitalists have well-tried methods by which they usually attempt to serve the interests of their undertakings and of capitalism. This method is to pretend that they are acting in the public interest, in the interest of the community as a whole. Now my accusation is that the arguments used here were raised in the interest of the capitalist groups, but it is presented in such a way as if there is anxiety that the country, Johannesburg, the Rand, the Free State and mining as a whole will be harmed . . .'

There followed a stormy debate in which Verwoerd tried to take his attack into Harry's camp: to suggest that he and those like him were prepared to sacrifice the interests of South Africa as a whole and white civilisation in general for the sake of their profits.

'The reason why the hon member for Kimberley (City) persists in telling the House that I am trying to kill the Reef, is that the mining companies which have already made money from the gold under the ground, want to make more money as land speculators with the surface value when the gold is exhausted. They would like to sell the surface area of their worked-out mines as industrial sites. Now hon members plead so piously for the poor investors and for the poor house-owner who has one or two plots. He will suffer such tremendous losses! The city of Johannesburg will go downhill! All these claims are made to evoke sympathy for wronged persons.

'However, Johannesburg and the Reef will not suffer. The only people who will not have their way are the speculators who want more land approved for industrial development, even where it is unnecessary for future development. They will most certainly not get new industrial areas approved where they are so badly situated in relation to the locations that new evils will arise.

Mr OPPENHEIMER: Aren't you going to send them to the Reserves?

The MINISTER OF NATIVE AFFAIRS: The hon member must not get upset and create a diversion now that I am touching him on the raw. They attack me and I must give them what they deserve. Do hon members want us to throw open new industrial areas near Johannesburg, this same Johannesburg that has to prepare 50 000 sites for the accommodation of Native families for whom it has made no provision although they work there? Would it be responsible action on my part to allow even more industrial areas to arise which would attract even more Natives while as yet these people are not even housed? Where is the United Party's love of the Native, their concern for the Native, their attachment to the Native?'

Verwoerd continued on his way and pulled South Africa behind

310

him. Time and again the UP attacked, and each time he counter-attacked with the argument that what he was doing was in everyone's interest. There could be no half-measures. He was a man of tireless energy and overwhelming confidence in what he was doing, so much so that he was able to disregard even the doubts of his fellow Nationalists.

It was against this most unpromising background that Harry reconsidered what South Africa was all about. He was becoming more and more interested in the Union's constitution, believing that it was here he would find the key to all these problems that appeared so insoluble. The constitution had to take account of every section of the population, major and minor, and guarantee fair rights and privileges to them all.

Discussing his ideas with Zach de Beer, Harry explained he believed it was necessary to make the two houses of parliament equally strong. The lower house, consisting of representatives of the people, should be elected through a common roll consisting of suitably qualified voters of all racial groups. The upper house, the Senate, should be reconstituted so that it could be empowered to block any abuse of the constitution in the house of representatives: in effect, to operate along the lines of the Senate in the United States.

He admitted he only had the germ of an idea, but felt it should be examined further. He needed advice from constitutional experts, and asked Zach de Beer to accompany him on a trip to Britain. There the two met a number of authorities in constitutional law recommended by Sir John Masterman, the Oxford don who had tutored Harry in politics as an undergraduate. At this time constitution making was all the rage in Britain, where the colonial government was preparing to grant so many territories their independence. Harry and Zach de Beer returned to South Africa with a number of recommendations which they immediately put up to the United Party's caucus.

Harry had hoped for a liberal approach to his plan. Instead, the conservatives soon had the measure of it and immediately threw out the idea of establishing a common roll for all race groups, even according to a qualified franchise. They were more responsive to the idea of elevating the Senate – though only because it provided a further means of ensuring that the white man's domination of South Africa might never be disturbed.

This was quite unnecessary in the circumstances, for to deny non-whites any opportunity of voting on the common roll was an adequate solution in itself.

With great solemnity Harry's scheme was adopted as the Graaff Senate Plan of 1957. As Harry put it later: this was a case of hearing the truth twisted by knaves to make a trap for fools.

4

THE PROGRESS of the Nationalists had not affected South Africa alone. It was reflected in reactions from all the surrounding territories, whose policies stood in stark contrast to apartheid and whose traditions were in direct conflict with the Afrikaner's. In Bechuanaland there was a constitutional crisis, with rival chiefs fighting for supremacy. Spurred on by missionaries, a delegation of Basuto chiefs went off to London to see Queen Elizabeth. But perhaps the most startled reaction of all came from the Rhodesias.

For many years, of course, there had been talk of union of the territories, or at least of federation. The Rhodesias were divided by the broad sweep of the Zambezi and by quite different constitutions and social traditions. But with Nyasaland they represented an island of successful British rule in Central Africa, rather like the bloc formed by Kenya, Uganda and Tanganyika up the east coast.

The movement had gone no further than the discussion stage, if only through the apparently irreconcileable ambitions of the respective European populations. In Southern Rhodesia, Godfrey Huggins favoured peaceful parallel development with Rhodes's goal of 'Equal Rights for All Civilised Men'. North of the river, the trade unionist Roy Welensky – 'the Napoleon of Broken Hill' as they called him – was demanding measures designed to protect the European mine workers.

Huggins realised he would have to move quickly if Southern Rhodesia was not to fall under South Africa's growing influence. He felt the territory's only hope was to preserve its essentially 'British' character as against South Africa's Afrikaner-ness. By itself it would not have the strength: it would have to combine forces with Northern Rhodesia, and Nyasaland as well. And almost in secret, he initiated negotiations.

It took a long time. What had seemed the obvious solution to the problem years before, now seemed a virtual impossibility. The Europeans of Northern Rhodesia were taking the hard line, especially in industrial relations. In retaliation the Africans of the territory were opposing any form of federation or union with every weapon they could bring to bear. Nyasaland was dubious as well. Only when the British government took a hand, did the scheme advance. At last all sides were reconciled and with Huggins as Prime Minister the Central African Federation came into being on October 23 1952 – exactly 64 years after the granting of Rhodes's charter.

Curiously, what had taken the politicians so long to bring into being had been anticipated years before by the business community. Eagerly awaiting the federation, many of them had registered offices in Salisbury or elsewhere in the territory. In this Anglo was to the fore:

'At extraordinary general meetings of the Nchanga Consolidated Copper Mines Ltd., Rhodesian Anglo American Limited, Rhodesia Copper Refineries Limited, Rhokana Corporation Limited, and the Rhodesia Broken Hill Development Company Limited, which were held in London during December 1950, it was decided to transfer the seat of control of these companies from the United Kingdom to Northern Rhodesia.'

It did not end there. To transfer the companies Anglo had to sponsor a bill in the Imperial Parliament – the Rhoanglo Group Act of 1953 – and only when it was passed could they be registered. But at last all was in order: from 1955 there was a strong Anglo American team in Salisbury under Keith Acutt.

'Something more should, perhaps, be said about the corporation's links with the Federation,' Ernest told the Anglo shareholders in 1950. 'Circumstances have established strong ties between this group and the territories that Cecil John Rhodes brought into the Commonwealth. An inherited tradition almost demands that the corporation, which had dominant interests in Rhodes's company, De Beers Consolidated Mines, should continue his policy of fostering the development and settlement of the Rhodesias.'

In this regard Rhoanglo was no laggard, particularly in Northern Rhodesia which was where it most counted. Broken Hill and the mines on the copperbelt were prospering, and the corporation had stakes in several new companies which were re-opening old mines or initiating new ones. More significantly, Rhoanglo was preparing to initiate a big new mine to be named after Dr Joe, the geologist who had done so much for the copperbelt: the Bancroft Mine, with a new town nearby of the same name.

But it was not enough to open new mines. As had happened throughout their history, the mining companies were stymied by two great obstacles: shortage of power, and lack of transport facilities. If the copperbelt was to progress, these problems would have to be solved.

And as the administration was evidently powerless to help, it was left to Rhoanglo to take care of them.

First, the power question. Years before the four chief mines had pooled their resources to build a central power station serving the whole copperbelt, with its fuel brought from the great Wankie Collieries of Southern Rhodesia. Now in 1953 Rhoanglo bought a big stake in Wankie, and took control. Anglo was already running a number of collieries in the Union, the property of African and European which was of course now a wholly-owned subsidiary of Anglo's. Wankie was soon developed out of all recognition, with a brand new town built to house the mine-workers involved.

There was an even more interesting scheme afoot. The new Federal Government was showing its worth with an ambitious scheme to dam the Zambezi in a gorge called Kariba. It would make the biggest dam in Africa, and one of the biggest in the world: an artificial lake 180 miles long. Its power would benefit the whole federation and it was being paid for partly by the World Bank, partly by government grants. Then Ernest announced the mining companies would be contributing £20 million. It was quite logical, he insisted. Power shortages had been a problem for years, and with production on the increase the mines were obviously going to need a big new source. Already they had difficulty transporting enough coal to the existing power stations: the railways could barely cope as it was. Hydro-electric power would be much cheaper than coal power, so in the long run the Kariba dam would prove a handsome investment.

The transport problem was quite separate. Here Ernest made a loan of £1 million to help Rhodesia Railways build new lines, and spent another £5 million buying 20 000 new trucks which Anglo would hire to the railways for 25 years. On top of this he formed a new finance house, the Anglo American Rhodesian Development Company, to help promote general economic development in the territories: cash raised wherever it could be found to help finance private undertakings and public works alike. The first money for this fund – £2¼ million – he raised in the Netherlands. As the London *Daily Express* wrote, 'We praise Sir Ernest for his bold Empire scheming'.

All this investment outside South Africa provoked a fresh outburst of criticism from the Nationalists. Spear-heading the attack was Strijdom, in a speech he made opening the National Party congress at Bloemfontein.

'Perhaps it would be a good thing if Mr Harry Oppenheimer would tell the world how many millions of pounds of the capital of all the companies in which he and his father, Sir Ernest Oppenheimer, are interested, have been allowed during the past ten years to be exported to the Central African Federation for the development of the Federation's tremendous copper mining, coal mining and other undertakings.'

This was a chance not to be missed. Almost gleefully Harry provided the figures. Far from sending capital *out* of South Africa, the Anglo American was attracting it *in*. Over the last ten years Anglo had invested £5 600 000 in the Rhodesias but received £10 700 000 in return.

Harry went on to explain that apart from the actual cash profits, there were big indirect benefits from investment in the Federation. Most of it had gone into the copper mines, and the profits from copper had helped the Federation to build up its reserves of foreign exchange so that it could afford to buy more imports from South Africa. In fact, the Union was poised to supplant Britain as the leading exporter to the Federation.

Besides the twin problems of power and transport, there was a third major obstacle to the progress of the copperbelt: the labour question. From the beginning European miners had set out to consolidate their position, and this meant enforcing a rigid colour bar against the insurgent African mine-workers. They wanted a 'closed shop,' a system by which certain jobs in the mines were guaranteed certain rates of pay – and which would not be given to Africans prepared to work for very much less.

To press its point, the European mineworkers' union had proved unusually militant. In the war years the miners had gone on strike for increased wages and the implementation of the 'closed shop' policy. They were successful – but in a hint of things to come the African workers promptly followed their example. With more tolerant attitudes than they would have found further south, they won their case.

It was the same now all talk was of Federation. The Europeans went on strike for more pay and greater security, and no sooner had they succeeded than the Africans followed the precedent. By this time, however, the African labour force was very different from what it had been, and with two well-organised trade unions each tens of thousands strong was well able to make its point. But rather than knuckle under, the employers wanted to formalise the position once and for all. The administration appointed a commission of inquiry into the whole situation.

Before the commission completed its work, Ernest circulated a statement of the position to all employees of Rhoanglo in Northern Rhodesia. He began with a summary of factors which had led to the impasse.

'Half a century ago the population of the copperbelt lived in savagery and fear – helpless victims of slave-raiding, anarchy and disease. Their progress in a half-century has been phenomenal – a rate of progress probably unsurpassed in the world's history. This progress has been solely due to the order and leadership of the European. Its continuance is still completely dependent on this leadership and will be so for the foreseeable future.

'African progress in Rhodesia must continue. It is the duty of the European leadership to see that it does so; and the copper companies are constantly introducing improvements in African housing, pay, leave and working conditions generally. This, however, is not enough. The African has learnt to use simple European tools and to perform tasks that, until a generation ago, he would have regarded, if he thought of them at all, as far beyond his ability.

'The African must be allowed to develop these skills and he must be helped to develop them through European teaching. It is the whole basis of the policy into new Federation that the African should play a fuller part in the industrial economy of the country of which he is a citizen. Without such development there can be no real future in Central Africa.'

But the problem was extreme: the African was knocking on the door of the 'closed shop'. By implication, if he was not admitted freely he might well find himself a battering ram. Better surrender gracefully, hinted Ernest, than stand on untenable rights and come a cropper. Open up the mining industry and allow Africans to find their way into jobs hitherto regarded as exclusively 'European', and co-operate with them and with the employees.

Privately, Ernest had long been dissatisfied with the privileged position of the Europeans on the copperbelt. In his view they ought not to be there at all in a permanent capacity: only to help the Africans on their way, and then get out. As early as 1941 he had visited the copperbelt and seen the way things were going, and complained bitterly to Harry. For instance, there were his impressions of Nkana.

'. . . The people entrusted with the opening of this enterprise did not create a mining camp, not even a mining town, but a mining Utopia. The layout of the town, the houses, the amenities, the free services to our employees do not exist anywhere else. The whole thing is a dream town, something which – if mining is carried on in Paradise – one imagines it to be like . . .'

316

One day a few years later he was walking through the gardens in the middle of Cape Town with Harry, when they passed the famous statue of Rhodes erected there. The great imperialist is pointing north, and the inscription on the statue has him saying 'Your hinterland is there'. Ernest told Harry there ought to be a similar statue on the banks of the Zambezi – but with Rhodes pointing south. He explained that in his view the river marked the boundary between two completely different systems.

Ernest was more diplomatic in public than to suggest the *status quo* was entirely wrong. But fortunately his subtler arguments won the day, and after long and complex negotiations agreement was signed in 1955. Rhoanglo and the Northern Rhodesian European Mineworkers' Union agreed to a new formula by which 24 categories of jobs were opened to Africans.

It was a major breakthrough, and signalled the pattern of things to come. The union's sting had been drawn, and from now on it would be a downhill journey. The confidence of the African mineworkers was raised high, and with the full co-operation of the trade unions representing all sides the copperbelt went from strength to strength.

One result of the new policy was apparent shortly afterwards, when it was time for the new Bancroft mine to go into full production a whole year ahead of schedule. Ernest travelled up to the copperbelt for the first time in many years – he explained his poor health was to blame for his absence – and there were big celebrations as he declared the mine open. But what made the occasion particularly memorable was that the mine authorities invited representatives of all the mining trade unions involved at the mine, regardless of colour.

These developments were not so welcome further south, however, where they had been watched with concern. This was the thin edge of the wedge, it appeared. The employers were showing their real intentions, to replace Europeans in the mines with Africans. How could they believe they would get away with it?

Feeling ran high in the new Free State mines. At Odendaalsrus, for instance, the mineworkers gathered to listen to Gert Lombaard, organiser of their union. He told them a movement was afoot to create such competition between Europeans and Africans in the mines that soon there would not be room for both races. Something had to give.

What was at stake, he said, was the European's exclusive right to a blasting certificate. Giving the African greater responsibility, as was

317

happening on the copperbelt, was only asking for trouble. For some time Europeans had been working with Africans, only to find them incompetent, idle and insolent. Yet if they 'drove' them too hard, they were dragged before the courts.

'I ask Sir Ernest,' continued Lombaard, 'whether there is any part of the mining industry, at present managed by Europeans, which can safely be left to the natural irresponsibility of the native. European mineworkers are appearing daily before the mine courts to account for natives injured while under their supervision. How will the native be able to work without the European if he cannot look after himself even while under the supervision of a European?'

There, of course, lay the root of the problem. As Ernest had appreciated so long before, the two labour systems north and south of the Zambezi were entirely distinct, and needed quite different treatment. In South Africa, there was no question of allowing black labour to supplant white. Even parallel development was a concept for the future.

The Oppenheimer view of South Africa's situation at this time was crystallised in a speech Harry made at Oxford in 1956, addressing the Duke of Edinburgh's Study Conference on Human Relations in Industry. He began by stating what he believed should be the proper objective of policy in Southern Africa: 'to secure the economic, cultural and social development of all the races concerned to the full extent of their capabilities in a manner that will not adversely affect the high standards already established for the Europeans . . .

'No political party in South Africa seeks – in theory anyhow – to deny the Africans the fullest development of which they are capable, but it is the contention of the Government Nationalist Party, the protagonists of the doctrine of "apartheid", that the full potentialities of the Africans will be realised only if the two races live in separate areas of their own and work out their individual destinies in their own way. As a theory this is certainly attractive. The problems of a multi-racial society are intractable and involve grave risks. It is not surprising, therefore, that many people, Black and White, in South Africa feel that, instead of trying to solve these problems, it would be better to abolish them by doing away with the multi-racial society from which they spring. Those of us in South Africa who are on the other side of the fence do not seek to impugn the good faith of those who entertain such ideas. It is not only in South Africa that people are able to believe with passionate sincerity in things that are manifestly untrue.

'But it is quite plain that the separation of Black and White into areas of their own, what in South Africa we call "apartheid", if carried out to any significant extent, would destroy the economy of the country with disastrous results for all the races in it. Nothing is more certain, therefore, than that, no matter which Government is in power, this policy will not be carried out. But just for that reason the refusal of opportunities for development to the Africans in the multi-racial South Africa that exists today, on the grounds that their just claims will be met by racial separation in the future, is calculated to destroy the possibility of inter-racial co-operation. The idea of solving our racial problems by unscrambling the multi-racial society that has already been built is nothing but a dream, beautiful or ugly depending on your taste, but in any case entirely unsuitable as a basis for action. I am assuming, therefore, that the multi-racial society which has come into being in Southern Africa will continue to expand and that our object is to regulate it in the best interests of the races that make it up.'

There were three factors creating the strains and difficulties that faced South Africa, said Harry: they were inter-connected and over-lapping, but each was logically distinct. First there was race-consciousness as such: the belief of most Europeans in the importance of purity of race, combined with an unquestioning faith in their own superiority, and on the other side of the coin a matching emotion on the part of Africans.

Secondly, there was the social and cultural gap that existed between Africans and Europeans. Most Africans were unsophisticated in the extreme, and Europeans looked upon them with complete distaste which was probably returned. The Africans who *did* manage to make good achieved their position by taking up European standards – and Harry suggested that there could never be general economic advancement of Africans until *all* of them decided to forego their traditional ways and accept the European way of life.

The third factor was the Europeans' worry that if Africans were allowed equal opportunities they would be prepared to work for low wages, and would break down the currently high standard of living in South Africa. This was an unjust view, said Harry, but all the same very real. It had to be taken into account, and if the whole industrial system was to be safeguarded the Europeans would have to be shown the Africans were not after all a threat to their livelihood.

'The European population of South Africa is widely condemned in the rest of the world, and it is generally supposed that it is only the

Europeans in South Africa who are inclined to reject inter-racial co-operation. Unfortunately, that is not the case. Racial politics are every bit as popular among Africans as they are among Europeans, and the emergence of Black nationalism is a major danger to the unity, security and prosperity of South Africa. Recent events on the Northern Rhodesian Copperbelt have emphasised this danger. There, with official assistance and encouragement from London, a strong African mineworkers' union was formed some time ago, and it has been able to gain important benefits for African mine workers, both in the form of higher overall wages and by helping secure opportunities for Africans to do more skilled and better paid jobs that had previously been reserved for Europeans. Recently, however, there has been an unmistakable tendency for this African union to allow itself to be used as the instrument of Black nationalists, whose objective is not a fair participation of Africans in a multi-racial society, but the transformation of Rhodesia into an exclusively African country.

'This brings me back to considerations I touched on at the beginning of my speech. We shall not solve the industrial problems or any other problems of a multi-racial society unless we accept the idea of a multi-racial society and plan on that basis. Physically, South Africa offers great opportunities, and, if the necessary capital, organising ability, and technical skill can be made available, should be able to afford a good life to all its inhabitants. It is not any physical difficulty that stands in the way but the psychological difficulty of obtaining goodwill and co-operation. There is no real possibility of turning South Africa or Rhodesia into White countries or Black countries, or of dividing them effectively into White or Black areas. It is significant that the Tomlinson Commission, which has recently examined the possibility of territorial separation of the races in the Union, with an obvious desire to prove "apartheid" feasible, has found that, when all that would be possible and, to my mind, a great deal that would be impossible, had been done to separate the races, the population in what the Commissioners call the "European areas" would be one-third African, one-third other non-European peoples and only one-third European. The essential multi-racial character of South Africa cannot now be changed. Our choice is not whether Black and White should live together or not, but whether, living together, we should quarrel or co-operate. Considerations of morality, economics and common sense all point to co-operation, but there are powerful forces of prejudice, stupidity and political ambition which drive in the opposite direction. These forces of disruption are just as powerful among the Africans as among the Europeans, and are equally dangerous and equally to be condemned wherever they are found.

'I have tried to show that most of the difficulties we meet in industry in Southern Africa are parallel to those which have been encountered with rapid industrialisation elsewhere. Such difficulties are increased by race prejudice but are not caused by it. On the material side, the industrial revolution in Southern Africa has already brought out a tremendous rise in the standard of living of Africans as well as Europeans, and has, at the same time, developed their needs and aspirations. It is plain that, in Africa, we have reached a stage where further physical progress, which is certainly possible, is going to depend more and more on our ability to solve the human problems that have been created. These problems must be faced and cannot be conjured away by assuming that profound cultural, social and racial differences do not exist or are simply a matter of unreasoning prejudice. On the other hand, if we seek to remove the occasion for conflict by a separation of the races, the effect will be not only to prevent further progress, but to destroy the great advance that has already been made.'

That was Anglo's African policy in a nutshell. In the Rhodesias there had been little problem in carrying it into effect. On the copperbelt and at Wankie Rhoanglo had built up ambitious housing schemes for Africans which were probably the finest of their kind on the continent. Ernest's idea here was to make African employees so comfortable that they would not want to leave. Besides, to encourage them to develop skills would benefit the mines considerably simply by having them remain on the spot rather than migrate from one job to another and never really 'belong' at the mine.

Ernest and Harry made gallant attempts to implement this policy in the Union as well, when they opened up the Free State goldfields. From the start they hoped to circumvent the kind of problems experienced on the Rand by building extensive African towns where Anglo's black workers could settle with their families and build lives for themselves as the Europeans did. But in this they found themselves thwarted by Verwoerd.

After protracted negotiations which got the scheme nowhere, there was a show-down in the House of Assembly. Harry asked Verwoerd 'whether he would be good enough to define his attitude in regard to the experiment which is being made on certain of the new goldmines in the Orange Free State by the establishment of villages on the mines for married Native employees'.

Verwoerd was firmly against it. 'Let me give my reasons for this,' he said in reply. 'Within that Free State gold-mining area every mine can then establish its own Native town with married quarters. That will mean a series of Native towns in the vicinity of the big cities to provide housing for the Natives, it will mean that in addition a large number of black spots will be spread out throughout the whole Free State mining area. Now we must bear in mind that when the mines stop working one day that large number of towns will remain there spread out over that area. They may amount to 20 or 30 or 40 within that area . . .'

In the end, Verwoerd's ministry grudgingly conceded the mines would after all need a token number of skilled Africans as a permanent workforce, and granted permission for them to be accommodated – but to an absolute limit of 3 per cent of the total African labour complement of any mine, and even then only when really necessary.

If they could not employ a permanent work force, the Oppenheimers decided, at least they should aim to provide the best possible conditions for the *migrant* labourers that were permitted. At Kimberley, at Oranjemund, in the Free State, on the Rand and everywhere the company was in operation Ernest and Harry set in motion schemes to make African workers comfortable. Again, they pointed out, it was really a matter of self-interest. Contented workers would be more productive.

This was the thinking that lay behind the special mine hospital built in Welkom, named after Ernest and planned as the best equipped mine hospital on the continent: sixteen wards with more than 750 beds and concentrating as much on preventive as on remedial medicine. Already it had been noticed that careful training on the mines was reflected in the life of the miners when they returned to their home *kraals*.

'Only by giving Natives the best hospitalisation, the best accommodation generally, and the best of food and nourishment can we make them contented citizens who will contribute towards making this a very happy country,' said Ernest when he laid the foundation stone.

These were impressive contributions, but Ernest's most inspired intervention in African affairs came about not in reaction to Verwoerd's policies, but through reading a book which he thought grossly exaggerated the situation. The book was Trevor Huddleston's *Naught for your Comfort*, which soon became a best seller outside South Africa, and which Ernest decided was doing his country no good at all.

What peeved Ernest most was that Trevor Huddleston had been quite a friend of the family. He was an Anglican priest, a member of the relatively high church Community of the Resurrection in Britain which maintained several mission stations and special homes in South

322

Africa. Huddleston had come to work at the mission's station at Orlando, not far from Johannesburg, and had concentrated his efforts in helping those who lived in the shanty dwellings of Sophiatown and its neighbouring districts. Several times Ina had helped him raise money for various projects. Once, indeed, she and he had organised a fund-raising fete at Brenthurst.

Now he had written *Naught for your Comfort*. It was concerned mainly with the hardships caused by Verwoerd's wholesale clearance of slums and slum dwellers without provision of substitute accommodation. The way Huddleston described the removals made them sound like the work of a nazistic tyrant. Ernest could not believe it was a fair reflection of the position, but determined to go down and see for himself.

Ina went too. The couple drove to Shantytown and spent the afternoon quietly wandering in the lanes between the miserably poor quarters in which so many thousands lived: drinking in the strange sights and sounds and smells of a world which was so near them and yet so far away. They were relaxed and were enjoying themselves: certainly the Africans they saw were pleased to see them, as is the way with slum dwellers when they realise someone is taking an interest in them and there may be rich pickings. But Ernest had to confess on his return home: Huddleston was right.

In fact, what he saw that afternoon shocked Ernest rigid. He knew something of the background of the situation: how for three years the Johannesburg City Council had refused to initiate new housing schemes for Africans, afraid of possible retaliation by the apartheid-minded Nationalists; how in the meantime the city's African population had swelled considerably, with the surplus forced to seek shelter in emergency breeze-block huts or shanties they built themselves from waste materials; how when it came to its senses the city council found it was expected to clear 'black spots' in white areas before it turned to the problems of the slums.

It seemed there was no way out. Even with all the government loans at its disposal the city council could expect to build only 3 000 houses a year at most: yet 17 800 houses would be required for one group alone, the 100 000 Africans jammed into the breeze-block shelters at Orlando and the emergency shanty camp at Moroka nearby. The government had initiated its own housing scheme to try and help alleviate the distress. But even this was pitifully inadequate – and designed not for the slum dwellers in their misery, but the Africans driven out of white areas.

Of course, the rub of the matter lay in the attitude of Verwoerd. He was not prepared to compromise: with a policy as demanding as apartheid there could be no trifle. Irritated by the slow pace of removals from the city he instructed the council to soft-pedal its housing schemes and instead to concentrate on what he called 'site-and-service'.

Under the new scheme, Africans were to be removed from their 'illegal' quarters in the city to 'serviced' sites in African locations well out of the way – in fact, to vacant plots equipped with water taps and closets as their sole amenities, where they were expected to assemble their own shacks until they or the municipality had money to build houses. The municipality was to provide the 'services'.

Eighteen months of this 'site-and-service' had produced a nightmare wilderness of slums which hopelessly overwhelmed the pitiful efforts of the council to keep pace with the demand for houses. It was the wilderness and the situation of its inhabitants which had prompted Huddleston's book, and which Ernest and Ina now saw for themselves.

Ernest discussed the position with Harry, with friends at dinner, with everyone who was interested. Finally he was put in touch with Boris Wilson of the Johannesburg City Council, who was in charge of the city's department of non-European affairs. Before long the two men agreed to act in concert. It would be Ernest's job to raise the money, Wilson's to build the houses. Ernest was sure he could raise a big loan from the seven great mining groups. In the event they agreed to the idea without question, and contributed £3 000 000.

A special executive committee was established to administer the funds, and this committee formally offered the loan to the city council, though subject to certain conditions. The night the council was to discuss whether or not to accept the loan, the chamber was packed to the doors with specially invited VIP guests. Ernest was there for one, and so was the Administrator of the Transvaal, and Colin Anderson who was that year's president of the Chamber of Mines and chairman of the mining houses' committee.

Boris Wilson explained his idea of how the loan should be used. What was needed, he said, was the total clearance of the slums of Shantytown and Moroka, the most appalling areas, and the rehousing of a large number of African families living in shacks and hovels round the African township of Pimville. Over a period of three years it ought to be possible to build 15 000 houses, and these could be used to re-house the 80 000 Africans currently living in those areas. The city housing division would be reorganised so that it could double its output in these areas; instead of 12 houses a day, no fewer than 24.

The council was unanimous in deciding to accept the loan, and as soon as the verdict was announced the chamber broke into clapping and cheering. Immediately the excited Press reporters herded Ernest and Colin Anderson outside to explain just what it was all about.

'This work must be done immediately,' Ernest began. 'Anybody who has visited the Native areas on the outskirts of this city, as I have done, would be impressed by the urgency of the need for action in clearing away the slums that have grown almost as rapidly as the industrial development of Johannesburg.

'No time must be lost in providing the Native people living in these areas with decent housing and all reasonable amenities. These Native people are, in general, the employees of European citizens. It is no more than enlightened self-interest that we should do what we can to ensure that the conditions in which they live should make for healthy, efficient, law-abiding and contented service.'

Colin Anderson told the reporters that the loan was Ernest's inspiration. But it was made on three conditions.

'We stipulated, first, that the elimination of these slums should not mean the appearance elsewhere of settlements where near-slum conditions would develop. In other words, we asked that the new housing settlements should be properly built townships, fully equipped with normal sanitary and other essential services, and offering communal amenities in conformity with the latest advanced ideas in Native urban settlements.

'Secondly, we stipulated that this large-scale operation should be carried out with the greatest possible speed. Thirdly, we asked that this £3 000 000 slum clearance scheme should be additional to any rehousing schemes the municipality would be carrying out.

'Indeed, we expressed our hope that this new and special project would lead to an acceleration of the rate at which normal housing schemes for the resettlement of the Native population of Johannesburg would be carried out.'

There were two further conditions to be met by the council, though not to satisfy the mining houses. Instead, Verwoerd had entered the picture. His approval was needed before the scheme could be set in motion. First, he wanted assurances that all the houses would be built on the site-and-service schemes already prepared, and more important, that of the 5 000 to be built each year 2 000 would be set aside to accommodate Africans removed from Johannesburg's 'black spots'.

It looked as if work could start immediately, but there was a delay.

Verwoerd was having second thoughts. He was displeased with the council's attitude to a separate demand of his: that servants in excess of a certain number per locality should be moved to special multi-storey hostels the government had built. Instead, the council was trying to fill the hostels with the 'illegal' Africans who ought to be sent out to the site-and-service areas. These Verwoerd considered a separate problem.

There had been frenzied negotiations behind the scenes, with the council protesting that it was simply not in a position to carry out the government's demands. Now Verwoerd demanded that unless the council gave him its 'unqualified assurance' that it would comply with his wishes over the hostels he would have to withhold his approval of the new housing scheme.

It was blackmail, said the council. He was going too far. But in the event Verwoerd was prepared to back down a little after all, and the housing scheme could proceed. In the first four months of operations more than half the first year's quota of houses was erected: simple but adequate shells on each site-and-service plot, incorporating the amenities already present. As each house went up a shanty was pulled down. Within 48 hours of completion, a family moved in.

All Shantytown responded to the new activity. There were still shacks by the ten thousands in the sprawling slum areas, but the sight of so many new houses going up somehow raised the spirits of the whole community. And those who moved into the new houses were ready to make permanent homes for themselves, not new slums. The difference was immediately apparent.

In all this progress there was one strange anomaly. Standing by its agreement to reserve two out of five of the houses built for the 'illegal' dwellers from European areas, the council duly left them empty. And empty most of them remained, for nobody was prepared to seek out 'illegal' dwellers to live in them. Most of these people were being sent to the hostels after all.

Two years after the inception of the scheme, more than 1 500 of the new houses stood unoccupied. Their windows and doors were broken by hooligans and the houses were falling into disrepair. But until Verwoerd changed his mind, empty they would have to remain even though there were still thousands of families in the slum areas of Shantytown and Pimville living under the most abject conditions. Not for months afterwards was the government prepared to reverse its decision, and allow the needy to move in.

In doing all he could for Southern Africa, Ernest was following in

326

Rhodes's tracks. But where Rhodes had staked everything on gaining new territory and influence for the Empire, Ernest's aim was to consolidate and build up its material prosperity. Rhodes is reputed to have called it 'philanthropy plus five percent' while Ernest justified it as 'enlightened self-interest'. Where Rhodes endowed scholarships to bring citizens of the Empire and indeed the world to study at Oxford, Ernest provided the university with money to set up a special centre for colonial studies.

'This is a time of swift and profound change in the cultural, economic and social life of the overseas territories,' a Colonial Office spokesman said when he announced the grants. 'The new forces set free by these changes call for a new means of creating understanding and unity.'

Nowhere were these changes more apparent than in the troubled lands of Southern Africa. In view of the attitudes taken by the Nationalists, there was a subtle irony in the name Ernest chose for the new centre in Oxford. Intended as a memorial to her coronation year and with her gracious permission, it was known from the outset as Queen Elizabeth House.

5

ANGLO'S INVOLVEMENTS overseas were expanding fast, and so were the interests of the Diamond Corporation. In London, both organisations were suffering from lack of space and clearly there was pressing need for a move. It was decided to build a complete new block to house both of them, named with the now characteristic simplicity: 2 Charterhouse Street in Holborn. Ernest went to London specially to open the new offices on his 77th birthday.

Ernest had mastered what he wanted to say at the opening during the flight to London, then delivered his actual speech without once referring to notes. It was a modest address recalling the astonishing progress Anglo and the diamond world had made since those dark days of the Depression when all seemed lost: 'I have always dreamed of seeing the London Office of the diamond group and the Anglo American Corporation under one roof.'

With the ceremony over, Ernest and Ina did not return to South Africa immediately, but instead stayed on to make the most of their visit. Ernest was indefatigable, travelling to the City nearly every day to attend business conferences and negotiations and surprising even those who knew him well. When he did not go to the City he stayed at home and worked there, or went to the Ritz where he had a special office.

But Ernest wanted to enjoy himself too. He attended the annual cricket match between the Diamond Office and the Anglo American staff, and as a result set in motion plans for a joint sports club. He sat for yet another portrait, and went on his inevitable long walks round Hyde Park. There was a heavy social programme too. The highlight was lunch at Buckingham Palace where Ernest and Ina were guests of Queen Elizabeth and the Duke of Edinburgh.

Before setting off on the return journey, Ernest presided at the first London Office dinner. He made a speech without notes – as usual, and to the interest of those present touched on the three ambitions which had guided his life: first, the ambition to advance himself; then, the ambition to prosper his companies; and, third, the ambition to do something for his country.

Harry did not accompany his father on this trip, for he had pressing commitments back in South Africa. Since the debacle of the 1953 election the UP had at last set its house in order, and there were big plans for the campaign which would lead up to the election due the next year. For one thing, not long before Strauss had resigned from the party leadership. There was a strong move to have Harry elected as party leader in his place: but in the end even his own supporters admitted his views were rather over-liberal for most of the UP's members. Anyway, he was still tainted with the inevitable 'Hoggenheimer' tag, which could hardly appeal to the staunch rank and file of Afrikaner electors. Harry was the last to push his case, and instead all agreed on what was taken to be an ideal choice, in fact a close associate of Harry's: Sir de Villiers Graaff.

The close relationship of Harry and 'Div' Graaff was more than coincidental, of course. Div's father, Sir David Graaff, had been a trusted business associate of Ernest's in the early days, particularly in the tricky negotiations which led to the takeover of the diamond mines in South West. And at a later stage their fathers had sat together on the Opposition front bench in parliament, where the sons now sat. Harry and Div had been close colleagues all through the troubled years since 1948 – and more than once Div had been counted among 'Hoggenheimer's lackeys'.

Div soon exerted his control over the UP, and brought all the warring factions together to face their common task together. They had to make an all-out thrust against the Nationalists, particularly in the constituencies of the Witwatersrand which was where they stood the best

328

chance of making their breakthrough. But who was to spearhead the campaign? Who had the popular appeal to tip the balance in this key area of them all?

There was considerable lobbying behind the scenes, of course. It was too important a matter to rush out a snap decision. But when it came the announcement was quite a shock. By unanimous verdict they elected Harry: he would be chairman of the party's executive committee in the Transvaal, and that meant the whole weight of responsibility for this area would rest upon his shoulders.

Until now Harry had been representing a constituency in the Northern Cape. Ironically, all this time his political opponents in Kimberley had been urging that this was altogether unsuitable when he could spend so little of his time there. Now he had taken the hint: he would be moving from Kimberley, and looking for a seat on the Reef.

There was no shortage of offers, most notably from the UP electors in Springs, which was of course a town closely connected with gold mining and the Oppenheimers. Years before their forebears in the SAP had urged Ernest to give up Kimberley and stand for them instead. Now they wanted Harry, and in explaining their stand drew particular attention to his war record. They said it showed his heart was in the right place.

But Harry did not take up the offer. Instead, he accepted an invitation from Johannesburg North, where the sitting member had recently been kicked out of the United Party and was now an independent. The constituency could be regarded as 'safe' UP and ideal for Harry's purposes. From there he could marshal his election forces to drive the Nationalists from the Transvaal.

Harry soon showed his teeth. The first opportunity came with the UP's national congress a month later. He moved a resolution calling on the electorate to reject the political philosophy of the Nationalists. It was narrow, sectional, intolerant and isolationist, he claimed. It had sown strife and discord and had divided the European sections of the community as never before. And worse still, it had caused the non-Europeans to band together against the whites.

The Nationalists were not slow to react to Harry's promotion. The Prime Minister, Strijdom, said that at last Harry was emerging as the real leader of the United Party. 'He is already leader in the Transvaal.' C R Swart, Minister of Justice, declared war on Harry on behalf of the Free State. 'I do not object to his being a rich man, but I do object to his using his money to gain political influence.' The Minister of the Interior, T E Dönges, resorted to the old complaint that the United Party meant to use its 'money power' against the Nationalists.

'With the two rich young men, Sir De Villiers Graaff and Harry Oppenheimer, at its head, the United Party had now become a greater danger to South Africa than ever before . . . The worker will know what he can expect from a party controlled by two such capitalists. The party will move further and further to the left.'

It was a surprising forecast in view of what Dönges had just said, and when Div was asked for his reaction he made the typically laconic comment: 'Frankly, I doubt its political wisdom.' Harry on the other hand, was amused: 'I am prepared to put up with the crime of my riches for the sake of the compliment to my youth.'

But whatever their feelings about Harry, the Nationalists were at least prepared to be charitable towards Ernest. The guest speaker at a special luncheon in Ernest's honour given by the Diamond Producers' Association was the reigning Minister of Mines, Dr A J R van Rhijn.

'Almost all the countries of the world have their industrial kings and mining magnates,' the minister began. 'In the United States the names of Carnegie, Rockefeller and Ford are well known to every schoolchild. In Germany you have the famous Krupp family, and in England the Lever Brothers. As Sir Ernest is a world figure it is perfectly natural that I should compare him with those I have mentioned.'

It was quite a compliment, especially coming from a Nationalist: but there was more. The others, said Van Rhijn, had remained with a chosen industry. Ernest, however, had not been satisfied with only one: starting with diamonds he had gone on to gold and copper and then secondary industries. 'That is why he could render such yeoman service to South Africa. Sir Ernest always studied the requirements of our country and then catered for those needs.'

As if to confirm what the minister had said, Ernest's reply contained references not to the diamond world alone, but to a new gold mining adventure which De Beers Investments, and that meant the whole diamond industry, was helping to bring into being. It would be the most ambitious mining undertaking the world had ever seen – a mine which would in due course produce as much gold each year as the whole South African industry had been producing each month. As he described it: 'This is the most important enterprise ever started in South Africa.'

The new mine was to the south of mines already in production on the Far West Rand, the fabulous Blyvooruitzicht and West Driefontein which had intercepted both the Ventersdorp Contact Reef and the

Carbon Leader Reef. It was known there was gold under the southern boundaries of these farms, and the deposits continued even further. But by this time the reefs were respectively 5 000 and 7 000 feet below the surface. As far back as 1943 Anglo had taken over the concessions in these areas, and formed a new company, Western Ultra Deep Levels, to explore them.

Knowing the gold was there was a relatively small consideration this time. Clearly there was a mine of astonishing richness between the 6 000 and 10 000 foot levels: but to exploit it would require a bigger outlay than any single mining operation in history. And even if Anglo took the decision to go forward, there was always the chance things would not work out. When the stake involved was in the neighbourhood of £20 million, as it was when eventually the first shaft was begun, that was a big risk indeed.

In fact it was not until the late fifties that Anglo could at last consider developing Western Deep. By this time the Free State was in full swing – Welkom since 1951, Western Holdings since 1953, President Brand and President Steyn since 1954 and Free State Geduld since the year before. Anglo was harvesting big profits, and it was these which would provide most of the wherewithal to develop Wes Deep. The Corner House and Gold Fields came in to take minority interests.

Ernest went down for the official sod-turning ceremony in July 1957, now so familiar to him after 40 years in gold mining. As he started the diamond tipped drills he told his listeners he hoped he would be able to look down and see the first gold that came out of the mine. That might not be so far in the future. On the other hand, he told them ruefully, he doubted whether he would live to see the mine in full production. For those who knew him it was a sad admission: it was expected Wes Deep would be working to capacity in six years.

But Ernest had not been enjoying the best of health. The trips to Northern Rhodesia and to England had taken their toll, evidently. He had always been strong, but now he was sick. Not long afterwards, recuperating at the farm in the Magaliesberg, he was out on one of his long walks when he collapsed. It was not a full-scale heart attack, like the ones he had had eight years before and four years later. But it was damaging enough to put him in bed, and serious enough to warrant calling in Sir Russel Brain, a distinguished British specialist then in Cape Town.

The specialist's advice was that Ernest should rest. He was, in fact, far from well. The next six weeks were anxious, for he suffered a series of relapses. Ina insisted on remaining at Ernest's side constantly, and worried all the time. There were fears that she was on the verge of a breakdown. When Ernest felt better again he suggested it was time she went on holiday. She did not want to go at all: she felt she should remain with him. But he was adamant. She made arrangements to go to London and stay with her sister, Lady Balfour of Inchrye, and was soon on her way.

Ernest was on his own for the first time in a long while, but he was well able to keep himself amused. Bessie Holmes, his personal secretary for years, was with him each day, and always there was a nurse in attendance: usually Sister Pam Walton, who had been looking after him for the last ten years. His personal physician, Dr Kaplan, called regularly; and Harry and Bridget dropped in each day.

The Sunday after Ina's departure Ernest went to a dinner party at the Inanda Club, and seemed in fine fettle. He was looking forward to several commitments in the coming week, particularly a meeting in the city the next morning to discuss the progress of the Smuts House appeal.

Ernest's hosts drove him home, and he had a good night. He was up early next morning as usual, in time to see Harry who came up to Brenthurst before driving to work. The two men discussed the way certain business ventures were shaping and Ernest arranged to go to the office the next day. The doctor arrived, and the three chatted for a while before it was time for Harry to leave.

When the doctor went away too Ernest seemed to be in good spirits, commiserating with Sister Walton over her bad luck the day before. It had been her first day off in months, and she had been looking forward to having her son back from school in Cape Town and taking him on a picnic. It had rained solidly all afternoon. They chatted on until at last the servants called Ernest for breakfast. As he went downstairs the sister stood at the top looking over the bannisters.

'We're just like Romeo and Juliet,' he called up when he reached the bottom.

Chuckling still he went on into the dining-room while she went to write up her reports for the doctor. Their patient seemed much better after those months of illness, but he was by no means one hundred per cent.

Ernest sat down to breakfast, his usual boiled egg. A servant was looking after him. Suddenly he cried out and clutched at his chest, his eyes staring. He crumpled down over the table. The servants rushed in from the kitchen.

'Call the sister.'

She came running. Ernest was breathing, still conscious: but he was in terrible pain.

'What's going on?' he gasped out.

The sister knew it was another heart attack. But that was not the thing to say. 'You don't feel very well,' she comforted him.

With the servants she carried Ernest through to the drawing-room, still supported on his chair. Gently they laid him on a couch.

'What's happening?' he asked the sister again, but remote now, weakening. It would not be long. Then suddenly, he gasped in a deep breath, convulsed: and he was dead.

The sister telephoned Dr Kaplan, and he was at Brenthurst in ten minutes. But it was too late. There was nothing that could be done. She telephoned Harry, and he came immediately. Before long Bridget was there too.

A terrible gloom descended on Brenthurst. This was Ernest's home, where he belonged and where he would be missed most of all. The staff, the servants, the gardeners, even the security men at the gates had loved him. Africans in the grounds wept unashamed: the *inkosi* was gone. Each felt a personal loss: they knew a great man had passed.

Harry telephoned Ina in London. He had to be gentle: it would be a terrible shock. And for her the loss would be the more poignant: Ernest had sent her on holiday when he felt better again, after that long illness when she had not left his side. He was her life. What would it be without him? Those in the household were worried stiff about her: they knew she would blame herself for being away. She would never admit it had been at Ernest's insistence.

Anglo made an announcement later in the morning. All South Africa went into mourning. There were tributes from Ernest's friends, his enemies: even from Strijdom, in surprisingly generous terms to the dreaded 'Hoggenheimer' he had professed to despise. Queen Elizabeth sent a message of sympathy to the family. Statesmen and captains of industry all over the world paid their respects. This man who was gone had been one of the key industrialists of all time.

The funeral was arranged for a few days later. Ina flew from London, comforted by her sister. She was in a terrible state, as they had feared she would be: but she was a brave woman, a remarkable woman, and she did all she could to compose herself for the service. Ernest had asked that his body be cremated, and Cecil Tugman from St. George's who had been his chaplain for years carried out the ceremony in Braamfontein. Harry had invited the bearers: all of them old business colleagues of Ernest's. Everyone was there but Hagart: he too had been in England when Ernest died, but so ill that his doctors told him on no account to risk the flight home.

Ernest's will was published a few days after his death. 'I give and bequeath the whole of my estate and property whatsoever situate and of every description to my son Harry Frederick Oppenheimer absolutely,' said its second clause. If there was any surprise it was that the will represented so little: a mere £3 500 000. But then, most of what Ernest had possessed was accounted for long before, tied up in trust for his dependents. A considerable portion of it had gone to Ina.

Even before the will was published, Harry announced the creation of a special fund of a million pounds in accordance with his father's wishes.

'During his lifetime, my father made considerable donations each year for educational, cultural and general charitable purposes.

'He frequently expressed the wish that such donations should continue to be made in future and asked me, in the event of his death, to take such steps and to make such provision for this purpose as appeared to me to be appropriate.

'In order best to carry out my father's wishes, I have decided to form a trust, to be called the Ernest Oppenheimer Memorial Trust, and to donate to this trust the sum of £1 000 000.

'The funds of the trust will be applied by a board of trustees for the benefit – especially in the educational sphere – of the peoples of the Union, South West Africa and of the Rhodesian Federation.'

Harry's contribution represented the largest single charitable donation in South African history apart from the legacy which established the Rhodes scholarships.

There were more tributes. Friends and associates had their say, and even Ernest's old opponents. But perhaps the tribute Ernest would have treasured most was from a man with whom he had not always agreed, often argued. Trevor Huddleston was back in England now, at the home of the Community of the Resurrection at Murfield. On Ernest's death he wrote to the *Times*. Ernest, he said, was a man of a very strongly developed social conscience.

'Only last year, made aware of the appalling conditions in the "shanty towns" of Johannesburg, he went to see things for himself. Immediately he exerted his unique influence on the Chamber of Mines and secured a loan of £3 000 000 for African housing in that area where the squalor was worst.

'But he also had a more intimate compassion, as I know very well, for immediate and personal causes which could make no appeal. So swift was he in sensing a need (a family in poverty, a jazz band without resources, a church congregation in difficulties) that one hardly dared to whisper it in his hearing, the response would be so immediate and generous . . .

'Yet above all it was his simplicity which was always so endearing. He retained a quality of childlikeness which one could hardly have believed possible in one with such vast material concerns.'

There was a tribute too from the Africans for whom Ernest had done so much. From the stone of the old shanties now swept away they built a tower 30 feet high upon a small hill in the middle of the new township area, looking out upon the rows of houses stretching to the horizon in every direction and dedicated to Ernest Oppenheimer.

The tower's design was deliberately based upon the conical tower of the famous ruins of Zimbabwe in Rhodesia, the remains of a once great city whose presence in that part of Africa has puzzled archeologists ever since its discovery. To the Africans, Zimbabwe is a monument of pride to the great African civilisations of the past. The new tower was a replica of the famous conical tower in the middle of Zimbabwe.

Harry was invited to dedicate the new structure. With him went Ina, and the mayor and mayoress of Johannesburg. Crowds gathered to hear them speak at the simple ceremony. Harry recalled the circumstances which had led his father into raising the loan, then drew attention to the four memorial plaques on the tower. Each said the same thing, but in four languages: English, Afrikaans, Zulu and Sotho.

> 'This tower built of blocks from Shantytown commemorates the slum removal scheme inspired by Sir Ernest Oppenheimer, 1957.'

The municipality persevered with its ambitious rehousing programmes, and like a great octopus the new schemes spread across the old slumland. Each district had a name, but for the whole there was no overall description but 'the south-western townships'. They needed a name of their own and the municipality invited suggestions from those interested. There was a strong movement to employ the name by which all Africans throughout the subcontinent knew Ernest: 'Opahama'. But the idea of naming an African settlement after the great enemy of Afrikanerdom could not find favour with the Nationalists. In the end the Johannesburg city fathers adopted a simple abbreviation for the name they had used all along – Soweto.

There were many obituaries of Ernest, but of them all the most touching was written ten years later for a special edition of the Anglo house magazine *Optima*, commemorating the 50th anniversary of the corporation's foundation: 'Sir Ernest Oppenheimer, a Portrait by his Son'. Harry painted his father's career in all its many colours: but the focus of his picture was contained in his closing observations.

'When my father died in November, 1957, he was in his 78th year. He had been a remarkably strong man, with unusual powers of endurance. Physically, over the last years of his life he had become progressively frailer, but his intellectual vigour did not diminish. I have written of his charm and he was certainly able to command the affection, admiration and devotion of those he worked with. He had a vitality, zest for life and courage which delighted and inspired.

'He was very perceptive and had few illusions about human character or motives, and yet he was full of affection, liking people for what they were with all their faults and frailties. He was entirely without self-consciousness, speaking what was in his mind with a freedom which was sometimes startling and, on occasions, perhaps ill-timed. He was not witty, but he was wise and he was gay. He had an essential youthfulness of spirit which remained with him till the end, so that it was difficult for those who knew him well to think of him as an old man.

'He achieved great success and he enjoyed success. He enjoyed money – both making it and spending it – but primarily he enjoyed it as a symbol and measure of achievement. He was often written of as an "international financier", but this was quite wrong. There was nothing international in his thought or outlook, and he saw his financial success as a by-product of his part in building up South Africa. The South Africa he thought of, however, did not stand alone but was a member of the Commonwealth, as the Commonwealth used to be but can never be again.

'I have often wondered how he would have felt about the Commonwealth and Africa today. I do not think that in his old age he would easily have adapted himself to the changes that have come about, and it may be that he was fortunate in his death as his life. He had successfully met the problems of his times and he left behind him, in Anglo American, an organisation deeply imbued with his spirit, with the strength and flexibility to work and build and serve in circumstances he could not foresee. And that surely is as great a share of immortality as a modest man should ask for on earth.'

CHAPTER TEN   1958—1961

The Inheritance

WITHIN DAYS of Ernest's death it was quietly announced that Harry was the new chairman of the Anglo American and De Beers. From where he sat in his office in 44 Main Street, Harry controlled getting on for 40 per cent of South Africa's gold, 80 per cent of the world's diamonds, half of Southern Africa's coal, almost a sixth of the world's copper. He had strong interests in all sorts of other minerals and metals, and fingers in pies which ranged from paper to platinum, from fishing to fruit farms. And besides all that he controlled AE and CI, by now the biggest explosives enterprise in the world.

There was a crisis virtually as soon as Harry took command – on the copperbelt. After some years of reasonable prosperity a comparatively small surplus of production over demand sent world prices plummeting down all over again. In 1956 price levels had been exceptionally high. But by the end of 1957 they were down to £180 a ton, and by March 1958 down to £160. At that level, said Harry, 'in the long run, the world's requirements of copper cannot be profitably produced'.

As it happened, Rhoanglo had a production problem of its own. Bancroft, the new mine opened with such excitement a year before, had proved disappointing. Many things had gone wrong, though this was largely through misfortune rather than mismanagement. In the normal course of events Harry would have ordered a cutback on all Rhoanglo's mines to take account of the production surplus. This time, however, he decided not to interfere with the others, but to cease production at Bancroft altogether. This would give the mine authorities an opportunity to overcome the early problems, and the labour force could be absorbed in the other mines until copper prices improved.

Announcing the decision, Harry pleaded for co-operation among the

337

world's copper producers, in a bid to stabilise the market in the way diamonds and gold were stabilised.

'Mr. Oppenheimer's remarks have given rise to a good deal of speculation,' commented the London *Financial Times*. 'The fact that he apparently spoke for the producers in general, and not for his own company alone, suggested to some dealers that an agreement might actually have been reached between the leading companies to cut back supplies as prices fell to a certain level. The behaviour of copper-mining companies on previous occasions when there have been surpluses does not suggest that these assumptions are plausible.'

That, sadly, was the position. There *had* been cutbacks in the past. But never had companies acted in concert. Instead, it was all too easy for companies to profit from each other's policies. If one cut back production, that was the signal for others to rush in and claim its business. Certainly that was the attitude of the intensively competitive producers across the Atlantic. In the circumstances all Harry could do was encourage mutual co-operation between Anglo, the Selection Trust and the producers across the border in Katanga.

He found it much easier to get his own way in the diamond world, of course. Here he was working closely with his cousin Phillip, Otto's son, who had just been made managing director of the Diamond Corporation with special responsibilities for the outside producers. But the most serious threat was right on De Beers' doorstep: the Administrator of South West was proposing to license an independent company to prospect the areas between high and low water marks on the Sperrgebiet coast. The move precipitated South West's biggest ever court case. More than 1 000 pages of documents were put before the court by CDM, the prospecting company and the South West administration. They referred back to the original agreements over the Sperrgebiet made from the earliest days of the German colony. The case dragged on days and weeks until at last the assessors decided against CDM. It was a worrying development: that coast was the richest source of diamonds in the world.

There were worries in the outside production areas too. In West Africa, for instance, there were still all too many loopholes from the Sierra Leone fields even though the situation had improved beyond recognition since the days of the IDSO. The Sierra Leone government showed no great willingness to help the producers, and it took Philip Oppenheimer long months of negotiation to persuade them to implement a new agreement which covered the licensing of diggers and new marketing arrangements. Even as he was negotiating there were

338

significant new discoveries on the Gold Coast, and a full-scale alluvial rush in French Guinea. From both these territories there was a serious leak to the 'unofficial' markets of America, West Germany and Israel, which could not obtain all the goods they wanted from the Central Selling Organisation. Besides, diamonds from these new sources were a lot cheaper. For the time De Beers was virtually powerless: the Diamond Corporation could only hope for the best.

Then there was Mwadui. Only seven weeks after Ernest's death John Williamson had followed him. He left all he had to his brother Percy and his sisters in Canada, who now held all the shares in the mine apart from a small block held by the Indian lawyer who had helped Williamson in the early days. It was apparent Percy Williamson was not altogether pleased to find himself in control of the biggest diamond mine in the world. Rather than bury himself in the bush as would be necessary, he might be only too glad to opt out – and there was the serious danger he might sell to third parties outside the Diamond Corporation's control and not in sympathy with its monopoly.

After preliminary negotiations by cable Harry and a De Beers mission flew to Mwadui for discussions with Percy Williamson. They soon came to terms. Williamson and the other shareholders would sell all their interests to De Beers for £4 140 000, plus estate duty of £1 500 000. Harry had no lawyer with him, but realised he would have to draft some sort of sales document. He had never had any legal training, but there was nothing for it but to sit up all night hammering a contract into shape. Next day it was duly signed. When Harry got back to Johannesburg he showed it to Anglo's legal advisers, who told him it was 'a little unorthodox, but it seems to hold water'.

There was another side to the negotiations. Harry realised that the political situation in Tanganyika was ripe for change. As yet the territory was still a British mandate, governed from Whitehall with a local administration. But that could not last. As with other territories in Africa, Tanganyika was progressing fast towards independence. That would mean black power before long, and would leave a South African-dominated mining complex which represented the territory's major source of revenue dangerously vulnerable. Rather than hold all Mwadui for De Beers, Harry suggested the Tanganyika administration should participate in the venture on a 50—50 basis, with De Beers providing the loan funds needed. The Tanganyika administration could make up what was owing from the revenue that accrued to it.

The administration grasped the opportunity. As a first contribution it waived the estate duty, which gave it an immediate healthy stake in the mine, and arranged to pay the balance over 20 years. Now Harry had to raise the £4 million needed to pay the Williamsons, and found it in an altogether new source: West Germany. This was the first time a substantial amount of German capital had been sunk into a foreign venture since 1914.

Now came news that the Russians had made an important diamond discovery in Siberia. What made it all so tantalising was that there was no concrete information for a long time – no clue to how it had happened, the extent and character of the deposits, the quality of the stones. But gradually information trickled through. There were indeed several healthy strikes in Russia, a number of diamond-bearing kimberlite pipes in the sub-arctic tundra of Siberia's far north. But their quality was not all it might have been: largely industrial, with only a small proportion of gemstones. Certain the news was not as alarming as it had seemed at first.

All the same, chiefly because of these discoveries, De Beers shares dropped sharply from 114s 6d to 82s in a few months. It was a worrying situation. The threats had to be met. Harry suggested Philip Oppenheimer should go to Moscow and see what he could do. To everyone's surprise he persuaded even these Russian producers to submit to the Diamond Corporation's aegis: the Diamond Trading Company would buy all the stones the Soviet wanted to export to the West.

But there was another threat, this time from across the Atlantic. The Americans had discovered how to make synthetic diamonds. This had always been the diamond trade's biggest bogey: that one day someone would come up with a way of making artificial diamonds for cheaper than it cost to mine them.

After more than a century of serious experiment in different centres, a Swedish laboratory, Allmanna Svenska Elektriska Aktiebolaget, had announced in 1953 that it had produced some 40 synthetic diamond crystals at a cost of more than £150 000. They were tiny and discoloured, and at that cost represented no threat to the trade: the Swedish company did not even trouble to file a patent. But the success triggered great excitement across the Atlantic where General Electric had long been experimenting along similar lines. At last the company succeeded, and by 1955 devised a payable production method to exploit the discovery commercially. The United States government dropped a veil of secrecy over the whole project.

To De Beers and the rest of the established diamond trade the news came as a bombshell. This was what had been feared for so long. There was already a diamond research laboratory in existence at Crown

Mines in Johannesburg, established to explore new uses for industrial diamonds. Harry now gave instructions that it was to develop De Beers' own process for making synthetic diamonds without delay. After three years of work the De Beers laboratory – Adamant, as they had called it – announced it had succeeded. Working along its own research programme De Beers had synthetic diamonds.

Initially, there was no plans to exploit the discovery commercially. The crystals were so tiny they were really only suitable as grit for grinding operations – and the diamond fields of the Congo already produced a perfectly adequate supply to meet world demand. At least, that was the position until increasing nationalist agitation in the Congo proved too much for the Belgian colonists and they prepared to move out. What would happen to institutions like the diamond mines was anyone's guess. Harry decided then it would be worth developing synthetic diamond production on a commercial basis. As a first step De Beers set up a factory in Springs – and soon afterwards another in Eire, at Shannon.

These efforts drew wide praise for Harry. He was every bit as good as Ernest, people were saying: and in many ways the challenges he met were even greater than those Ernest had faced. As if to celebrate the successes De Beers shares rose to more than 200s again.

Harry's authority was felt not in De Beers alone but throughout South Africa's financial world. Here, however, it was no new phenomenon: Harry had been Anglo's managing director since World War II, and had controlled all sides of its business except the diamond interests which Ernest reserved strictly for himself. But even outside diamonds, it was plain a new broom was at work.

The change was most obvious in Harry's reorganisation of the group's financial arrangements. All the way through its history the corporation had retained the links with CMS, Rand Selection and the various other companies formed for one reason or another in the 'pyramid' structure which had proved so successful down the years: each company with a stake in the others, direct or indirect, and the whole an overwhelmingly strong combination in the South African economy with tentacles practically everywhere. Harry decided it could be improved, and began setting plans in motion to upgrade one of the old financial houses and make it 'the largest investment company in South Africa, with a portfolio of exceptional merit both as regards its security and growth potential'.

The choice fell on Rand Selection. 'It seems to me that the economic potential and value to shareholders and to the community of a company such as Rand Selection, as it is at present constituted, is much less than in the past. By modern standards it is a medium sized investment company filling no clearly defined role in the investment field, and though it has an exceptional portfolio, it is not well equipped for raising money on a large scale, and in particular it is no longer favourably placed to bring money to South Africa from abroad . . . Rand Selection Corporation, as expanded in accordance with our proposals, will be in a very different position. It will provide a safe and solid medium of investment in the economic future of Southern Africa. While it will not itself seek to initiate new business, it will be admirably placed, both because of its financial strength and its connections, to participate in business initiated by others.'

Harry's idea was first to increase the capital and assets of the De Beers Investment Trust by transferring certain assets of other mining houses and their subsidiaries in return for shares; and then to hand over the entire capital to Rand Selection, again in exchange for shares. On top of that existing shareholders had the chance to buy further shares in Rand Selection. The result of this was to raise its authorised capital from eight million shares to 35 million, or in terms of cash from £2 million to £8 750 000.

Rand Selection's new-look portfolio held many big fish, including substantial interests in Anglo, De Beers, Johnnies and the BSAC, and in overseas corporations too. But the showpiece of the catch was Central Mining, for so long an apparently indivisible part of the Corner House but rescued from takeover a few years before by a consortium in which Anglo had played a major role. Now the various companies involved in the consortium had ceded their interests in Central Mining to Rand Selection, which gave the new corporation absolute control. It was an odd twist of fate. Back in 1916 Ernest had offered Central Mining all CMS's interests in the Rand, which included the controlling interest in Rand Selection or Transvaal Coal Trust as it was then, virtually on a plate. Sir Lionel Phillips had turned him down flat.

2

AT THE TIME Ernest died Harry was in the throes of transferring his political loyalties from Kimberley to Johannesburg North. The Reef constituency was awaiting Harry keenly, and even more important, he was to be the key figure in the UP's campaign on the Rand in the general election scheduled for 1958. In an interview published a few weeks before, he had stated unequivocally he was prepared to accept cabinet rank under Sir De Villiers Graaff if the UP was returned to power.

Clearly Harry was a man worth marking – as he had been throughout his career in parliament. It was no great surprise, then, when a week after Ernest's death a Nationalist columnist, 'Dawie' of *Die Burger* in Cape Town, swept in to attack. Could Mr Harry Oppenheimer accept the crown of South Africa's greatest financial and industrial empire and still retain his position in the country's political arena? Dawie doubted it.

Harry was carefully trained as Ernest's successor, certainly. But in spite of his training, did he have his father's unique ability to remain a humble man? Harry was a man of high ideals, a quick thinker and a man of intellect. It was, however, difficult to judge whether he was in politics to satisfy his own ambitions, or because he was deliberately pushed into it by Ernest and his friends.

The columnist called for Harry's immediate retirement from politics. Dawie commanded wide attention among Nationalists, so such a call was significant. Here was the chance to rid parliament of the threat of Hoggenheimer – and the very powerful challenge he represented to the government. Dawie and the other Nationalists were not going to waste it.

They need not have worried. Harry's priorities were all too clear. Though extremely saddened by the whole situation, and personally disappointed into the bargain, he felt he had no option but to resign. He soon made an official statement.

'My father's death has brought me heavy business responsibilities which cannot be discharged properly if I remain actively engaged in political controversy.

'I have, therefore, informed the leader of the United Party, Sir De Villiers Graaff, that I will not be available to stand for Parliament at the next election, and that I desire to resign from the offices I hold in the United Party as soon as satisfactory arrangements have been made about my successors.

'I have taken this step with profound regret and only because I am convinced that it is my duty to do so.

'I would like to express my gratitude and loyalty to Sir De Villiers Graaff and to my many friends and comrades in the United Party. My special thanks go out to the people of Kimberley whom I have represented in Parliament for nearly ten years, and to the people of Johannesburg North Division who nominated me as their parliamentary candidate when my work as chairman of the Witwatersrand Executive made it necessary for me to seek a seat in Johannesburg.

'I firmly believe that the United Party is the best hope for South Africa, and in the work before me my party's ideals of national unity and of justice and opportunity for all will continue to guide me.'

That was what Harry said in public. In private, however, he was far from happy with the progress of the party. It was becoming increasingly clear that it was anything but United, particularly in regard to its racial policies. His sympathies lay with the more liberal members of the party – Zach de Beer among them – and he had no patience with the attitudes of conservatives who seemed close to the Nationalists. Before the 1958 general election he made a donation of £5 000 to party funds 'to show there is no ill feeling', but he insisted it would be his last.

The UP did worse in the 1958 election even than it had in 1953. Harry gave his reactions to the result in a speech to the Royal African Society in London a few weeks later.

'The South African general election represented a swing of something like 4 per cent to the Nationalist Party, and was a great victory for them. For the Opposition, it came as a great shock because while no one in the United Party seriously thought they could win the election, they did not expect any addition to Nationalist strength.

'The chief factors which, to my mind, contributed to the Nationalist victory were: Firstly, the identification of their party with the special cultural aspirations and pride of the Afrikaans-speaking majority of the population and, secondly, a widespread belief that the United Party lacked the will, or the ability, or both, to maintain European supremacy in South Africa.

'I hardly think that the views on race relations of the great majority of those who voted Nationalist went beyond that, and I very much doubt whether the ideological background of the Government's policy, the so-called doctrine of apartheid, means very much to the electorate ... What the election did show, however, was a determination not to accept or to compromise with the claims of Black nationalism. And this is the mood, I think, of very many more South Africans than voted Nationalist ...

'On the Opposition side, the most striking feature of the election was the emergence of Sir De Villiers Graaff as a political force. Even after the large swing towards the Nationalists the two parties are of more or less equal size in the country, but in spite of that, the Nationalists obtained 103 seats in Parliament against the United Party's 53. For this there are various reasons, of which the most important is the high concentration of United Party support in the largest urban areas.

'The effects of this situation are, however, serious, and must be faced. It means that with the parties organised on their present basis and the geographical distribution of their strength more or less as it is now, the United Party could not get a working majority in Parliament unless it secured over two-thirds of the votes cast. Now that is clearly impossible, and so the Nationalists must remain in power until there is a fundamental change in the whole nature of our political situation.'

It was a brave admission. But Nationalists or none, Harry's confidence in South Africa was as great as ever:

'Fortunately our politics, which are bitter, uncompromising, based in the past and, in some respects virtually fossilised, do not reflect the real nature of the present situation of the South African people. I think that South Africans themselves often fail to grasp the extent to which they are united about the things that matter most, or how artificial in many ways are the barriers between the parties. It is surprising to how small an extent the economic development of the country has been affected by political controversy.'

For himself, Harry was supposed to have liberal views by South African standards, but he thought the attitude of 'so-called liberal opinion in South Africa as well as outside it' to political rights for Africans was entirely unrealistic. These liberals did not accept that it was necessary to protect the position of the whites.

'They overlook the risk, indeed the certainty, that the Africans, who have almost all the same vices as the Europeans, would wish to use political power, if they had it, not primarily to secure good government, but in the interest of Black nationalism. African politicians would quite naturally put African government as an ideal far above good government. It would not be difficult for any of us to think of parallels from recent history.

'Civilised standards, which were brought to Africa by Europeans, can by no means be reduced to the doctrine of manhood suffrage, and, in South Africa, as we like to think it is in England, a guarantee of individual liberty would lead directly to inefficiency, corruption and tyranny.'

In short, said Harry, South Africa's political dilemma was to find a way of giving a fair share of power to the emergent non-whites without risk to the standards of the state which the whites had built. It was a call he repeated often in the months that followed, showing he had lost none of his old enthusiasm for the driving issues of South African life.

345

'I am still very interested in what goes on in this country,' he told an interviewer. 'I make no secret of the fact that I am missing politics very much. I keep abreast of what is happening.'

He kept others abreast too – not only through his speeches in South Africa and overseas, but through the medium of Anglo's annual reports. This was a custom that had been pioneered some time before, that the report should include an assessment of the situation in South Africa. But in Harry's hands it became a significant feature of South Africa's political life.

Harry was as much concerned with the Federation as with the Union, and kept a careful watch on what was happening throughout the subcontinent. There were indications that the Federation was in danger of breaking up. If that happened, he forecast, 'all this would mean a tremendous material loss to all sections of the population and worse than that, it would bring to an end much of the most promising experiment which is now being made for the establishment of proper race relations in those areas of Africa where there are comparatively large White populations.'

The chief problem in the Federation was of wide gaps fixed between the living standards in the various territories. Africans in Nyasaland were complaining they were not treated like human beings – comparing their fortunes with what they saw of living standards in the prospering Southern Rhodesia and the advancing copperbelt. And by comparison with their European counterparts, all the Africans together were treated badly: even if the charges of 'not being treated like human beings' were arrant nonsense.

'Nevertheless, I believe there is some meaning in this often-repeated catchphrase, and it is this: In Southern Rhodesia Africans are more and more, like Europeans, the victims as well as the beneficiaries of industrialisation.

'They must, like Europeans, work regular hours for regular wages, and are subject to the irksome discipline of a modern industrial community. Such discipline is destructive of traditional African life, with its tribal ways and ceremonies, its simple subsistence agriculture, and above all, its idleness.

'It is only natural that the tribal African should be attracted to his traditional way of life and should wish to preserve it. It is only natural that he should regard the wage economy of a modern state as dehumanised, as a kind of slavery in which he is not treated as a human being. And it is only natural also that this alien way of life should have become associated in his mind with Federation.

'But, here again, we are up against another aspect of the contradiction to which I have already referred. Politically-conscious Africans very rightly want their people to share to the full in the benefits of industrialisation. They press for higher wages and more responsible jobs for their people, but such demands are, in the conditions of Federation, quite incompatible with the political demand for complete independence from the White man.

'The politically conscious African leaders do not themselves, of course, aim at preserving the tribal African way of life, but what they have done is to harness the ordinary African's attachment to his established institutions to their quite different aims and objectives.

'The point which, to my mind, needs emphasis, is that the choice for Nyasaland and the African tribal areas, as a whole, is not between progress inside or outside the Federation, but between progress inside the Federation and stagnation and poverty outside.'

The troubles in Nyasaland were by no means isolated, of course. From all over the African continent came news of disaffection and strife: the prelude to revolution. Following the bloody guerilla tribal campaigns of the Mau-Mau in the mid-fifties – in which only thirteen whites were killed, in spite of all the panic, but in which tens of thousands of Africans were done away with – there had been increasing signs of unrest stirred by African nationalist leaders.

In West Africa there was the illustration of the Gold Coast, where the British bowed out to Kwame Nkrumah. With the colonial dam breached, other territories went the same way. The remaining British territories in West Africa – Nigeria, the Gambia and Sierra Leone – were set on the road to independence. And in their wake the French had little alternative but to follow a similar policy. Indeed, when De Gaulle was returned to power in 1958, one of his first actions was to offer all French territories in Africa a choice between complete independence and interdependent membership of a French 'community', with the mother country attending to each member's external affairs.

This was the wind of change, as Harold Macmillan described it when he visited South Africa not much later. It was blowing harder down the continent, through Central Africa, through East Africa, until in the Congo it found Patrice Lumumba ready to challenge the oppressive paternalism of the Belgians. He succeeded in his aim of winning independence, but only with the continuing support of the Belgian authorities, who were in any case anxious to protect their considerable investments in the huge territory. When the rank and file of the Congolese army realised that the situation was much as it had been before, there was open mutiny. In Katanga with its copper mines, the local authorities realised the way things were going, and declared independence under the reactionary premier Moise Tshombe.

There was bloody war in the Congo, massacre in Portuguese Angola across the border, and the Central African Federation was splitting apart at the seams. In Southern Rhodesia successive prime ministers were showing ever harder attitudes towards African nationalist movements, and, in fact, the Rhodesian African National Congress was banned outright. So was its counterpart in Northern Rhodesia, and its leader, Kenneth Kaunda, was imprisoned in 1959. In Nyasaland the leader of the local African National Congress, Dr Kamuzu Banda, was implacably opposed to the continuance of the Central African Federation. He, too, was imprisoned, and his organisation banned.

In 1960, frustrated by such bold opposition, the British appointed a commission under Lord Monckton to investigate the whole position. The commission recommended an immediate advancement of African suffrage towards eventual full rights. And, in addition, it recommended that each territory should be granted the right to secede if it wished. As a result each protectorate was granted a new constitution and the Federation was doomed.

The movements towards African independence were not confined to the Federation. South Africa too had her troubles, and with them increasingly militant action on the part of the strongest African organisation, the African National Congress. Reacting to the movement, allegedly linked with communism, the Nationalist government ordered the arrest of the ANC's leaders – Albert Luthuli, Nelson Mandela and Oliver Tambo among them – on a charge of treason. Their trial lasted four years, and focused world attention on South Africa's racial problems.

But the flames of opposition were by no means quenched. Strijdom died in 1958, and Verwoerd succeeded to the premiership. He introduced more legislation in his drive to establish apartheid on the grand scale. For a long time it had been obligatory for Africans outside their supposed 'homelands' to carry identifying passes. Now these regulations were applied with considerable severity. Failure to produce the passes on demand would result in summary conviction. The effect was to deprive Africans by the million of any chance to visit urban centres. Black resistance was not long in coming.

The first signs of trouble came in shock reports from a tumble-down hillside location outside Durban called Cato Manor. It was the custom for the Zulu women there to brew kaffir beer for their menfolk, but this had been made illegal in terms of local by-laws – not least in an effort to get the men to patronise municipal beerhalls. Zealous police raids on the shebeens infuriated these rather militant women who were already up in arms over the passes they were now obliged to carry. They took to picketing the beerhalls, and to pelting the men inside with stones.

The police intervened and dispersed them. The women armed themselves with sticks and knobkieries and anything else that came to hand. They picketed the beerhalls again. The police arrived and tried to drive them away by force. The women attacked an African constable and beat him unconscious. Then they turned on the rest of the force. That day four white and five black policemen were clubbed to death.

The shockwave reverberated through the country. For years the prophets of doom had hinted at things to come, a bloodbath to match Kenya's. Could this be it? The whites retrenched, the black nationalists came out into the open. For some time dissatisfied with the ponderous progress of Luthuli and his ANC, a dissident group known as the 'Africanists' had emerged within the movement, led by a young lecturer from Witwatersrand University called Robert Sobukwe. The movement's aim was to create an almost completely African state within South Africa. Only Africans and Coloureds would belong to it as of right, and whites and Asians would be admitted as citizens only if they accepted African authority.

The 'Africanists' had first tried to sway the feelings of the rest of the ANC. When they failed, they organised a separate political movement, the Pan-African Congress or PAC for short. Sobukwe was restless to get things moving, travelling round the cities in a minibus to whip up support and achieving a certain success. It was through discussions he had in each centre that he worked out a way to beat the pass laws: he would call for massive civil disobedience, with his fellow Africans surrendering to the police and admitting they had no passes. They would be arrested, charged, sentenced to gaol. If *everybody* did it there would be absolute chaos.

The ANC watched these developments with disdain. Sobukwe was an irresponsible young idealist, they claimed. The plans would misfire hopelessly: the PAC's leaders would be sent to gaol not for three *weeks*, as they were bargaining for, but for three *years*. What would happen to their movement with its leaders in prison? When Sobukwe made a call for a national protest the ANC leaders decided they would do absolutely nothing to support it.

March 21 1961 was a Monday. According to Sobukwe's call – by now well publicised – Africans all over the Union were to report to their local police stations without their passes and demand to be arrested. It all sounded great fun, and to many seemed a most promising day's sport. But come the day itself, early checks suggested it was going to be a flop. From Alexandra, one of the key Johannesburg townships, reports said only a dozen PAC men had given themselves up. In Durban, it was only thirteen. However, at Philippi in the Cape, no fewer than 1 500 Africans swarmed down to the local police station. The police lined them up in queues, took their names and told them they would appear in court the next week.

Suddenly all eyes turned on Vereeniging, a booming industrial town thirty miles south of Johannesburg, on the Transvaal's border with the Free State. Huge crowds were gathering at a township called Evaton, and the police had opened fire to disperse them. The crowd was in a state of high excitement and was cutting telephone wires. There was trouble, too, not far away at Vanderbijl Park, where about four thousand Africans were gathered at the police station. And there were even bigger crowds gathering at a place called Sharpeville.

At this stage very few people in South Africa had ever heard of Sharpeville, much less known where it was. Vereeniging was growing fast, and townships were springing up in all directions to accommodate the waves of black migrants streaming in to find work: it was exactly the situation Verwoerd so feared. Sharpeville was one of these new townships, relatively well laid out and serviced and with a population of some 15 000 men, women and children.

It had all begun in quite orderly fashion. As at the other Vereeniging townships there was a strong response to Sobukwe's call and crowds had gone up to the police station on the hill, demanding to be arrested. The police refused. The crowd grew more rowdy, taunting the police until some of them were arrested after all, but for disturbing the peace. The police commander called in reinforcements – who arrived in Saracen armoured cars, fully armed, until there were about 150 police at the station. All this time the crowd was getting bigger, spilling down into the large field of tall grass below the police station.

Some of the crowd had thrown stones at the police, and there were everywhere shouts of 'Izwe Lethu', the PAC slogan which meant 'Our Land'. But in general the atmosphere was of a happy feastday, with the crowd in the mood for mischief but more playful than threatening. A very high proportion of them were women, jeering the police and giving them the clenched fist Pan-African salute. For themselves the police were scared out of their wits. It was all too much like the situation at Cato Manor.

The police commander ordered a baton charge to disperse the crowd. It made little impression on the mob, who continued to press round the armoured cars, taunting the police. Their commander broadcast three warnings to the crowd through a loud-hailer, but his voice was lost in the hubbub. Shots rang out some way off, the crowd pushed forward, and he ordered his men to open fire. The Africans began running away down the field. Many of them were laughing, thinking the police were using blanks. Instead, the shooting was in earnest. It was all over in 12 seconds. All that could get away took cover. But in the grass 69 Africans lay dead and dying, and another 180 were wounded.

The story of Sharpeville went round the world, and did more harm to South Africa's reputation than all the other adverse reports put together. Alarmed, Verwoerd's government hastily issued a statement which seemed only to make matters worse.

'According to the factual information now available, the disturbances resulted from a planned demonstration of about 20 000 natives in which demonstrators attacked the police with assorted weapons, including firearms . . .

'The demonstrators shot first, and the police were forced to fire in self-defence to avoid even more tragic results . . .

'The allegation . . . that the demonstrators were unarmed and peaceful is, therefore, completely untrue.'

The furore escalated. There was trouble in other centres too. In Cape Town there was rioting in Langa township and two Africans were shot by the police. In Pretoria Luthuli now entered the fray, publicly burnt his passbook and urged other Africans to do the same. He called them all to observe a Day of Mourning for Sharpeville, which met with widespread response. Two days later young Philip Kgosana led a march of 30 000 Africans from the townships to the centre of Cape Town for a peaceful demonstration outside the police headquarters. The police met them with Saracens, but Kgosana led the demonstrators away peacefully.

Faced with widespread disaffection the authorities moved in, arresting whites and blacks by scores and hundreds. The government introduced retrospective Emergency Regulations which put the country under martial law. On April 8, following another series of dawn arrests, it passed the Unlawful Organisations Act which banned the ANC, PAC and several smaller organisations. They have remained illegal to this day, and a number of those connected with them are still held in prison.

351

The publicity accorded these events ricocheted round the world and South Africa's image stood lower than at any time in her history. There was universal condemnation, particularly as so few people outside South Africa understood the background to the events, which were widely misreported and exaggerated. Anti-apartheid factions throughout the western world did not hesitate to add fuel to the flames. Their efforts were not unrewarded: in the uncertain situation, with a State of Emergency in operation and the prospect of the bloodbath that had been forecast for so long, there was a sudden drain in confidence. Overseas investors pulled out their capital.

It was a dangerous situation. To meet it, a group of businessmen lobbied fellows of theirs with the idea of forming a non-political organisation dedicated to present 'the positive South African story to the world', an organisation embracing the leading talents in the South African business world both Afrikaans and English speaking. It would be known as the South Africa Foundation, and among those who pledged their support from the outset was Harry.

Soon the foundation issued a brochure setting out its aims and objects:

(1) To promote international understanding of South Africa and her people, their way of life, their achievements and aspirations.

(2) To secure for South Africa and her peoples recognition for the contribution they have made . . . towards the progress on the continent of Africa, of a civilisation founded and built on the western way of life and ideals.

(3) To present to the people of South Africa and to the world a true picture of the country, its standard of living, its industrial and social progress . . .

(4) To illustrate the opportunities for investment in South Africa and the present scope and potential of its natural resources.

(5) To help in stimulating the export of South Africa's productions and services.

(6) To reaffirm South Africa's resolution to serve as an active member of the world community of nations.

Soon a list of the foundation's 96 trustees was published – impressive by any standards. Many of them were millionaires in their own right, while almost all the others controlled the sort of enterprises which were the mainstay of South Africa's economy. The foundation was to be the public relations front for South African business, and as such it would be nursed carefully by those whose interests it represented.

Apart from the work done by the foundation as a body – particularly in bringing influential figures from countries overseas to South Africa to see things for themselves – its individual trustees did all they could to boost its campaigns on their own initiative. And in this Harry was at the forefront.

There was, for instance, the interview he gave to the widely read *US News and World Report*. Asked if he was optimistic about the future of private business in South Africa, he replied: 'Yes, I am. Naturally, I know that the Government's policies here are generally disapproved and condemned, and I have made no secret of it that I dislike them myself. But to say that this country is more dangerous for investment than any other African country strikes me as . . .'

Another question interrupted him. But he went on to talk about the outflow of capital from South Africa. It was through 'a failure of confidence in this country, by investors outside the country, and I should have said there were three main factors.

'First of all, people disapprove of what is going on here, rightly or wrongly. They condemn it and think it immoral. That is one factor . . . the government's racial policy. After all, even investors have their feelings about the morality of such things, and that is, I would think, quite a serious factor.

'Another factor is that people think – and I think this is a bit exaggerated – that what is going on here is going to be so unacceptable to the African population that there is going to be some sort of revolution. I think that thought arises largely from the third factor, which, to my mind, causes this lack of confidence in South Africa, and that is an idea that this country is on exactly the same basis as tropical Africa. What the South African government was trying to do in separating the Black and White races was not necessarily immoral as partition had proved the answer to problems in many parts of the world.

'But I do think the economic integration of the race has gone much too far for there to be any successful separation. I therefore think that the South African government's policy cannot be maintained and the effect of trying to follow a policy that cannot be maintained is unfairness in the treatment of the African population.'

Again, speaking to the Institute of Directors at the Royal Festival Hall in London he posed the question: 'Is South Africa a good risk?'

'You will not, I think, be surprised to hear that South Africa is a "good risk" but I do not for a moment suggest South Africa is a "certainty". South Africa is a risk, but a risk well worth taking, and should therefore have a special appeal for this great gathering of the leading protagonists and practitioners of private enterprise.'

South Africa's problems went far beyond the economic field: it was a matter of finding a way for men of different races to live together in happiness and peace. In the 20 years from 1937 to 1957 South Africa's national income had gone up from £357 million to about £2 000 million, which was an astonishing achievement in spite of changes in value over the period.

'The average income of the African population, though still deplorably low, has risen faster than that of the Europeans and is probably higher than anywhere else in Africa. Unfortunately, this great improvement in living standards has not been achieved without creating grave social problems. And all this is taking place at a time when the spirit of extreme nationalism which came near to destroying Europe is sweeping like a great veld-fire across the plains of Africa.

South Africa's social and political problems could be solved by continued economic growth: 'If Africans are to give their support and allegiance to a multiracial state run on European lines, they must share in the material benefits it brings. But they will not be able to do that unless they shake themselves free from the traditional African way of life. That involves the gradual destruction of tribal discipline.

'This is a risk – but it must be faced, and the process of industrialisation and Westernization carried through to the end. Most certainly, for a comparatively primitive people caught up in an industrial revolution, "a little learning is a dangerous thing".'

On the other hand, apartheid in itself was bound to fail, Harry told a joint meeting of the Royal African Society and the Royal Commonwealth Society in London. 'South Africa will have to turn to a policy of unity on a basis of individual merit, in the place of vision on the basis of race. Such a policy would imply that anyone, irrespective of race, who has certain reasonable educational or property qualifications, must be entitled to vote on the common roll.'

Then again, Harry was impressed by the lessons of the Congo. Over the border in Kitwe on the copperbelt he said: 'What has happened in the Congo should be a lesson to all of us, but I should be very sorry if the lesson that is drawn from these deplorable events is that Africans as such are not, and cannot, be fit to govern. Fortunately there are examples in other parts of the continent to contradict such a pessimistic conclusion.

'What the Congo does show is that primitive, uncivilised people cannot be trusted with the running of a modern state, and that the independent democracy is the only possibility if the electorate has reasonable standards of education and civilisation.

354

'I would like to express the sympathy which I know we all feel to the European men and women who have devoted their lives to the development of the Congo, just as so many here are devoting their lives. I think we ought also to feel deep sympathy with the millions of peaceful Africans in the Congo who found themselves abandoned by the Government, on which they had so long relied, to the mercies of African politicians who have already shown themselves to be callous, irresponsible and incompetent.'

Harry's speeches had grown a good deal more outspoken in their criticism of government policies since his emergence from active politics. He was still a member of the United Party, but no longer felt himself obliged to remain loyal to its decisions. Indeed, he was becoming increasingly disillusioned with the party's performance as were many others of similarly liberal views.

The trouble had first arisen in 1955, as a direct result of the Nationalists' efforts to strip the Coloureds of their right to vote on the common roll. This required changes in the South African constitution, and to carry *these* the Nationalists needed a two-thirds majority not only in the lower house of parliament, but also in the South African Senate. They introduced the Senate Act to increase the body's size, and when it was a *fait accompli*, asked Strauss as leader of the UP to explain his attitude. The removal of the Coloureds from the common roll was now in sight. If the UP was one day returned to power, would it accept the *de facto* situation or would it seek to reinstate them?

Strauss was caught unprepared, and to the horror of many of his supporters he began to bluster. It was all too complicated, he said. He could not see his way through the legislative jungle that lay ahead. The United Party would have to consider its stand when the situation arose.

That evening, a number of liberals in the party held a meeting to discuss their position, and agreed that what Strauss had said was patently unsatisfactory. Some wondered if they could afford to continue as members of the party if that was to be its attitude. Jan Steytler, however, not the most senior parliamentarian in the group but the most persuasive, urged the others to take a more moderate line. Rather than take precipitate action and risk splitting the party, they should first see what could be done to remedy the situation. If they were pledged to keep faith with the Coloureds, it would not be very practical to resign. Above all, they should refrain from making any statement to the papers.

This was agreed by most of those present. However, Dr Bernard Friedman of Hillbrow in Johannesburg decided this was not good enough. He decided immediately to make a statement to the Press, announcing his resignation from the United Party. The papers expected the other liberals to follow suit.

Meanwhile, there was another move afoot. Harry and Zach de Beer were no less concerned by the situation than the militants who held the meeting. Together they went to see Strauss, who admitted he had made a mistake. But what was he to do now? Harry and Zach de Beer said he should do all he could to bring the recalcitrants back into line with the rest of the caucus. In response he forthwith appointed a committee to investigate the best means of doing this: Harry and Zach de Beer, the former Smuts minister Harry Lawrence, Hamilton Russell and Gray Hughes, who were effectively the five next most liberal members of the party after the group that seemed poised to secede.

The committee met the next day and hammered out a statement which would make the rebels happy if Strauss agreed to deliver it. They accepted it, and Strauss duly addressed parliament. Then one by one the liberals stood up and publicly stated they believed that when it came to the point the United Party would after all repeal the Nationalists' legislation, and the caucus party later accepted this as a point of view. As for so long, the door to non-European franchise was to be kept open and for the time the impasse was averted.

One of the results of Strauss's mishandling of the Senate Act affair was that before long he was gently replaced as leader by Sir de Villiers Graaff. The succession was a pointer to the increased influence of the liberals in the party, who were slowly finding their way into its key positions at the expense of the conservatives. Then Verwoerd succeeded Strijdom as Prime Minister.

It was in defending his policies in the no-confidence debate at the beginning of the new parliament in 1959 that Verwoerd provoked the controversy that was to split the United Party for good and all. Now his majority was increased and it looked as if Nationalism was in to stay, Verwoerd set out the blueprint of his grand apartheid.

Unexpectedly, he used the occasion to announce an altogether new concept in apartheid which caught the UP entirely by surprise. Every man, he suggested, of whatever colour, race or creed, should have the right to rise to the full extent of his possibilities, both economically and politically. That was not possible in the present South Africa, with the rates of progress of the different elements of the population so disparate. Instead, to give the black man his proper chance, it would be necessary to create a series of mini-states from the African reserves that already existed. Each should be allowed to develop along its own lines and at its own speed towards eventual true independence.

Graaff reacted immediately, saying South Africa could never tolerate such developments. Others in the party, however, were not so sure – as was clear in the frenzied meetings and discussions that followed. Was not this a neat way out of South Africa's difficulties? Set up a chain of little states within a state, and keep everybody happy?

As the discussions continued there was one point which came to dominate them. In 1936, when the initial ideas of African reserves were long formulated, the government of the day had promised it would increase their size. Now Verwoerd was proposing to make these reserves states in their own right, and was intending to grant them that land.

Douglas Michell, leading a group of UP members from Natal which was the province which stood to lose most through the new policies, put his foot down. The United Party would never allow white-owned land to be given away, he said – land which had been won 'in the blood of our fathers'. His speeches rallied support to his side.

That was enough for the liberals. The land had been promised: it was not now to be taken away. Whether or not the Bantustan policy was carried into effect, the Africans should not now be deprived of their rights to the new land.

While this argument was in progress Graaff had appointed a special committee to investigate United Party policy in view of its dismal showing at the 1958 election. What were they to do to make the party more attractive to the electorate? One of this committee's members, Vause Raw, quickly said that the first essential was to abandon further talk of extending voting rights to non-whites, and that he was prepared to split the party on it. Liberals on the committee – Zach de Beer, Boris Wilson and John Cope – said they felt the caucus should take quite the opposite course on the issue, and *they* were prepared to split the party.

There was a great deal to debate, and in the end the issue was referred to the whole caucus. The liberals seemed to be winning their way over the issue of Coloured voting, and Graaff committed himself to an extension of *African* representation in parliament. Harry Lawrence emerged as leader of the liberal group, and with the others prepared the way for the party's annual national congress in Bloemfontein where all these issues would be debated.

In the weeks before the congress several liberals heard rumours

357

that the conservatives in the party were lobbying massive support from the areas in which they held influence, with a view to marshalling mighty delegations which should carry all before them in shows of hands at the national congress. It was difficult to substantiate the rumours, but they sounded alarming. Then a day or two before the conference was due to begin, the *Eastern Province Herald* in Port Elizabeth published a long list of 'liberals' in the United Party, who, it said, were to be ejected from its ranks at the Bloemfontein congress.

The first motion to be debated at Bloemfontein was on the issue of African representation in parliament. 'It should be the policy of United Party that in future Natives should have their rights on a separate roll and not on a common roll.' For the liberals, obviously opposed to any such move, Colin Eglin made a reasoned speech in which he showed that down the years it had been United Party policy to 'leave the door open' on such issues. When he sat down a platteland farmer stood up and said: 'Now that's the short of chap we've got to get out of this party.'

The voting went against the liberals. Graaff voted with them, but had already pledged himself to go along with whatever the congress decided. It was a bad start, and the liberals were uncomfortable. Several returned to their homes, believing that any further participation in the congress would be a waste of time. One or two of the more extreme – notably Helen Suzman of Houghton in Johannesburg – wanted to resign from the party without delay. But others urged them to bide their time, and see if things improved the next day.

This was to be the show-down: the debate over the issues raised by Douglas Michell. He and his supporters did not mince their words, and whatever the liberals said in reply was greeted with derision. The conservatives' lobbying had paid off handsomely. The voting went against the liberals, and one by one they drifted disconsolately from the conference hall, their cause spent. They met in a Bloemfontein hotel, and prepared a statement setting out their position. They were left no alternative but to resign from the UP.

Though they were leaving the party, those concerned in the move had no intention of resigning their seats in parliament. There was talk of their forming a new political party – though not before the provincial council elections which were soon to be held. For the time they would organise themselves as a 'progressive group' within parliament, outside the United Party but not excluding members who decided to remain within the United Party caucus. Their leader, it was decided, should be Jan Steytler.

Annigoni and his portrait of Bridget, 1966. *James Soullier.*

Harry on the copperbelt: meeting some of his thousands of employees in Zambia over a drink in a Chingola mine club. *Zambian Anglo American.*

As chancellor of the University of Cape Town, Harry confers the degree of Doctor of Science on Professor Christiaan Barnard after the latter's historic first heart transplant operation. *The Argus, Cape Town.*

Among those in this 'progressive group', not surprisingly, was Zach de Beer, who wasted little time in travelling to Johannesburg to inform Harry of the new developments. Since Harry's departure from parliament the year before Zach de Beer had been preparing a weekly report on developments, to keep him closely in touch with whatever happened. This was the most crucial development yet.

Harry was in Rhodesia for a few days, relaxing at his ranch Shangani. When he returned to Johannesburg he was interviewed by the papers, and said that while he was sympathetic to the liberals he wanted first to discover more about the situation. After contacting Graaff and finding him securely perched on the fence where he had roosted since the outset, Harry issued a full statement.

'While I have completely retired from public life and have no intention whatever of returning to it, I have naturally followed with close interest the recent developments of the United Party.

'After careful consideration of the issues involved, and of the statements issued by Sir De Villiers Graaff and Dr J Steytler, I find myself in general sympathy with the Progressive Group.

'In the circumstances, I think it would be improper for me to remain a member of the United Party and I have accordingly tendered my resignation.'

The announcement came as a bombshell, though it was no surprise to those who knew how disaffected Harry had become with his old colleagues.

'We have no doubt that the United Party leadership, while regretting his decision, will recognise that it has not been lightly arrived at and will acknowledge the sincerity of his judgment and his consistent pursuit of the ideal of racial justice,' commented a leader in the *Star*. 'It is evident that Mr Oppenheimer has discerned in the emergence of the new progressive group the hope of realising that ideal with a greater sense of urgency than, in the fast-moving tempo of African events, he could detect in the United Party.

'How far such expectations are likely to be fulfilled has yet to be seen. The progressives have still to define their programme: and Mr Oppenheimer himself is clearly marking time.'

The answer was not long in coming. All this time one of the key figures in the issue, Harry Lawrence, had been on holiday on the Italian Riviera. Lawrence, a veteran parliamentarian who had served in Smuts's war cabinet and who had remained close to the centre of things within the party, had not yet openly come out on the side of the progressives. But from the course of the discussions which preceded the break it was obvious he was at least a potential ally. He was a close friend of Harry's, and now that Harry had resigned it was widely expected he would follow suit.

Harry Lawrence did not see eye to eye with Steytler on a number of issues though Steytler was supposedly at the head of the new group. Instead, he had greater faith in the young Zach de Beer, and realising he was in Johannesburg wondered how he was to contact him. He telephoned Harry at Brenthurst. As luck would have it Zach de Beer was there when he telephoned, and the two men discussed what ought to be done. There seemed only one thing for it: they would have to form an altogether new party.

A month later Harry was himself in Europe, addressing a meeting of the Institute of Directors in London. 'These United Party rebels,' he said of the progressives, 'have not yet announced their policy. It looks, however, as though they will press for major constitutional changes with the object of establishing something in the nature of a federation of races.

'They are likely to be more sympathetic than the United Party to the establishment of autonomous African areas but would regard it as essential that they should be linked with the rest of the Union in a federal system.

'To me there seems much to be said for this line of thought, but many people feel, and there is certainly force in the criticism, that a rigid constitution would make efficient government difficult and might make it impossible unless there were a degree of inter-racial goodwill which may not exist.

'All thinking South Africans are very conscious, moreover, that their future and that of their children depends on finding an acceptable solution to racial problems – and in this respect their situation is different from that of their critics in this country.'

When the progressives managed to organise themselves into a properly constituted political party and brought out their first policy statement, it followed these lines quite closely. But it was a long time before Harry publicly aligned himself with the new movement.

3

HARRY AND BRIDGET had remained in Little Brenthurst, where they were comfortably settled while the children were away at school in England. They meant to move up to the big house as soon as it was convenient, but for the moment Ina continued to live there as she awaited the completion of a new house not far away over the kopje, which she was calling Blue Skies. Harry called in a leading landscape artist to redesign the gardens for him: Joanne Pym who by curious coincidence had lived next door when she was a child. She remembered playing in the maze at the bottom of the grounds when she was a little girl.

The development of the gardens was only one of the plans Harry had for Brenthurst. All this time he had been adding to the Brenthurst Africana library, following Ernest's very thorough groundwork. Apart from books, maps and manuscripts – especially material relating to Byron, a special hero of his – he had been buying up china and silverware as well, and already the collection was showing signs of considerable promise. Bridget said she never had any problems finding Harry a suitable present: he was quite happy if she gave him a piece of antique silverware.

He was building a collection of paintings, too, culled from many sources. He particularly admired the work of the French impressionists, and these were his favourites. But the work of many artists found its way into his collection. His only criterion – as with everything – was that it should be of the best.

'I am not one of those collectors who want an example of each type of a particular subject,' he would say. 'I am for instance not a stamp collector. In fact I would hate collecting stamps. I think they are only meant to go on letters. I prefer to collect things which look good about the house.'

Harry was not getting any younger, though of course all of a sudden he was far busier than he had ever been before. Many of his former outdoor interests had to go by the board. Particularly he had to give up squash, and content himself with infrequent riding excursions and rounds of golf – though even these were often founded more on business than pleasure. He did enjoy walking as Ernest had done, particularly long walks along a beach. But these days his most significant leisure activity was simply reading – reading for profit and reading for amusement.

Bridget shared many of these interests of Harry's: in fact it had long been apparent what an excellent wife she was for him, prepared to push herself to the limit to make him more comfortable, and ready to go to any length of trouble. She was out of bed with the dawn to prepare for the busy day ahead, and showed her care in so many little ways – for instance, writing out personal messages in each of the thousands of Christmas cards she and Harry sent off each year, a job which took her

361

weeks. But there was one interest above all which husband and wife shared together, and in which they were to make a formidable team: their joint interest in the Turf.

This had started 12 years before, when Harry bought his first filly, Donnybrook, and contracted Major Tim Furness to train her at his stables in Boksburg. Harry so enjoyed racing Donnybrook that he decided to buy more horses and race them too, until he had a whole string in training. Some he bought locally, others he imported – among them the horse Ossian which eventually established him as a major power on the South African Turf and which he gave to Ernest in time to win the Johannesburg Summer Handicap.

Tim Furness was a former tobacco farmer from Rhodesia, and had set up his training stables only a short time before Harry was put in contact with him. He soon realised that training the Oppenheimer horses was likely to become a very demanding job, and called in his old adjutant from wartime days, John Breval, to assist him. Before long it was clear the rather primitive premises at Boksburg would simply not do, so Furness moved his stables lock, stock and barrel to new quarters near the Newmarket racecourse in Alberton, 20 minutes drive from central Johannesburg.

Meanwhile, Harry had bought Mauritzfontein and installed Tremayne Toms, a veterinary surgeon, as manager. Before long a pattern emerged. Tremayne Toms produced the foals and watched over them carefully until it was time for them to move on to Newmarket as two-year-olds, where Tim Furness and John Breval slowly advanced their training until they were ready for real tests. The horses would remain at Newmarket for the rest of their racing careers, until retired to Mauritzfontein to produce more youngsters in their turn, or otherwise sold off by auction in the annual culling sales.

Harry watched every development. Though new to the racing game he soon picked up what it was all about. From the outset he made it his responsibility to name each new foal. But more than that, from an early stage he liked to decide just which stallion should cover which mare at Mauritzfontein – so that each foal produced should be very much his own conception! When they were born, Tremayne Toms had the responsibility of contacting Harry and Bridget wherever they were and telling them all he could about the new arrival without delay.

It would be years before Mauritzfontein reached its full potential. But for the time Harry persevered with his racing programme, and achieved gratifying success. He was in racing for the fun of it rather than for investment's sake, so not surprisingly took much more interest in feature races than in minor events which were the stuff of the racing calendar. He lived for the chance to win the chief events on the South African circuit, and in particular the Durban July, the Johannesburg Summer Handicap, the Cape Metropolitan and the Durban Gold Cup, which were the most prestigious of all.

Ossian won the Summer Handicap, though in Ernest's colours as Harry had planned. He came close to winning the July as well, but disappointingly broke down. To make up for that, Prince Bertrand won the Met. Then came a succession of great horses like Tiger Fish, Hengist, Open Sea and Haidee which all won classics and carried Harry and Bridget to a prominent position among South Africa's racing owners. Only the Gold Cup eluded them.

There were all sorts of stories behind the races, of course. There was the July of 1958, when it looked as if Tiger Fish had the race in the bag. The jockey, Charlie Barends, did not see Excise closing on him fast until they were crossing the line, neck and neck.

'Did you pull if off?' he shouted across to Johnny Cawcutt, riding Excise.

'I doubt it,' Cawcutt shouted back.

Barends thought he must have won, and rode Tiger Fish into the Number One box. Harry and Bridget came over in great excitement to lead their horse to the winner's pen. Then the stewards announced that on photographs it was plain Excise had won after all.

'How awfully disappointing' said Harry, who is a sportsman on the racetrack as everywhere else. And he and Bridget slipped away in the crowd. He said later: 'Anyway, it was a jolly good miss.'

Tiger Fish should have won that 1964 race. But at least he made no mistake the next year – winning by $2\frac{1}{4}$ lengths. That year, indeed, Tiger Fish was South Africa's leading stake winner with 10 wins – including a dead heat – three seconds and only one unplaced in 14 races, bringing Harry and Bridget five figure winnings which helped make them South Africa's most successful owners that year, as in so many others later on.

Tiger Fish was always a great favourite of Harry's – even when matched with other horses from his own stable. There was one Summer Handicap in Johannesburg when Harry was strongly rooting for Tiger Fish rather than Hengist, also racing in Oppenheimer colours. In the end Hengist won – and though Harry said he was pleased about this, he could not conceal his disappointment about Tiger Fish.

Harry had been as enthusiastic as this all along. But if the truth be known Bridget had initially lagged behind him: in fact, at the outset she had absolutely no interest in racing at all. As time went on, however, and she attended more race meetings and learnt something of what it was all about, there was an astonishing transformation. From being quite indifferent to it all Bridget became passionately involved – so that in the end she took more interest in all that happened than Harry himself. He went to important race meetings where his horses were performing; she went on every conceivable opportunity, wet or fine, weekday or weekend. If she was not there, people wondered why. For years she has reigned as South Africa's Queen of the Turf.

4

A FORTNIGHT after Sharpeville Verwoerd was shot in the head. It happened in Johannesburg, when he was opening an agricultural show and sitting in the stand waiting for the arena events to begin. A white man made his way towards him, pulled a small-calibre revolver from his pocket and fired two shots in his face at point-blank range. It did not seem possible he could survive.

Verwoerd was thrown back in his seat by the force of the shots. Blood streamed from his nostrils and from the wounds on his face and neck. They carried him down the steps and off to hospital. Incredibly, he was still alive. One bullet had hit him in the neck, while the other entered the side of his face below the right ear, touching the hard palate of the mouth and going on down until it too lodged in his neck.

Verwoerd was taken to the Pretoria General Hospital. A month after the assassination attempt, on May 7, they removed the two bullets. On May 15 he went home and five days later broadcast a message to the nation. 'If one is spared it is in order to fulfil further duties. Similarly if a nation has been spared for centuries in a land of hardship but also of great promise it, too, has a task to fulfil. This may be a difficult year for South Africa in many ways . . . her reputation, her prosperity, her orderliness, her institutions, her leaders, are all under attack; and yet, notwithstanding all this, 1960 is also her year of faith and hope . . . I trust that I will be permitted to testify to my conviction that the protection of divine providence was accorded me with a purpose – a purpose which concerns South Africa, too. May it be given to me to fulfil that task faithfully.'

The would-be assassin, a wealthy English-speaking farmer living not far from Johannesburg, was brought to trial some months later and explained he had come back from a visit to Europe to find South

Africa in disintegration. He said that at the showgrounds he had felt 'a violent urge to shoot apartheid – the striking monster of apartheid that was gripping the throat of South Africa and preventing South Africa from achieving his (*sic*) rightful place among the nations.'

But far from defeating apartheid, the attempt on Verwoerd's life only confirmed his standing at the head of the Afrikaner nation. Before, the new Prime Minister had been widely mistrusted: not a born South African after all, but an immigrant brought to South Africa from Holland at the age of two. But now he had shed blood for the fatherland and the Afrikaner cause.

On May 31 Verwoerd appeared again in public, at the celebrations in Bloemfontein to mark the 50th anniversary of Union. It was supposed to be a non-political affair, with everyone taking a neutral line in referring to the achievements of the half-century. Instead, Verwoerd took the opportunity of furthering a cause now supremely close to his his heart, for which he had striven for many years: the cause of republicanism.

It was not altogether a surprise. At the outset of the session that year Verwoerd had given warning it would not be long before he called on the electorate to decide whether or not South Africa's future should be linked with Britain's. But rather than opt for a general election, as he might have done, he had decided there should be a referendum – as in fact there had been a series of referendums before Union was brought about. The republican referendum would be held later that year, and in the week that included Sharpeville he had initiated a campaign to woo the electorate into meeting his hopes.

The attempt on his life, curiously, came as a godsend to his campaign. If before the issue had been in doubt, now there was none. Verwoerd could be trusted, most Afrikaners now believed. He could afford to widen the scope of his campaign. In Bloemfontein he called on English-speaking South Africans to assist him in establishing a republic, asking them to make sacrifices in the interests of the nation. With the advent of a republic 'the divisions of the past would fade into the mists of history'.

There was opposition from the UP and the new Progressive Party, but the republican movement rolled smoothly on. Verwoerd was persuasive, and prepared to concede what was necessary to assure all sections of the population that the change would be in their interests. He willingly gave up plans to withdraw South Africa from the Commonwealth, realising the implicit importance of this link to South Africa's English speakers.

The referendum was set for October 5. Furious campaigning carried Verwoerd the length and breadth of the country, and in the result he was not disappointed. Of the white electorate, a total of 850 458 voted For, and 775 878 Against – a majority of 74 580. In terms of provinces, only Natal had voted against. The others had presented Verwoerd with a resounding vote of confidence. It was arranged that the new republic should be inaugurated on May 31 the next year.

For many, the development seemed unmitigated disaster. Those long links with Britain had been severed, after 150 years of happy association. Verwoerd had promised the Union would remain within the Commonwealth, but was that the same? What would happen if the Commonwealth decided it could do without South Africa?

This depended on Verwoerd's reception at the next Commonwealth Prime Minister's Conference, scheduled for March. He would formally apply for continuing membership of the Commonwealth, along the lines of the precedents created by India, Pakistan, Ceylon, Ghana and Nigeria. But it was by no means a foregone conclusion that the application would be granted. The rising Afro-Asian bloc within the Commonwealth was preparing a hot reception for South Africa.

Among those who deplored the grave developments was Harry, who had already made it plain he considered the results of the referendum a disaster for South Africa. Now all that could be hoped was that Verwoerd would keep his promise, and make absolutely certain that South Africa retained her place among the nations of the Commonwealth.

At last it was time for Verwoerd to leave. Before the conference actually started Harry broadcast a talk on its importance. For 50 years men had been building a united South Africa, he said. Expel South Africa from the Commonwealth, as was being suggested, and those efforts would have been in vain.

'National unity in South Africa is not yet firmly built, and expulsion from the Commonwealth following on the establishment of the republic would expose it to dangerous strains. The English-speaking South Africans, deprived of so much that is dear to them, would feel bitter, let-down and frustrated.

'Afrikaans-speaking South Africans, with their offer of co-operation within the Commonwealth rejected, would surely tend to retreat into a defiant isolation. The non-European majority, excluded through no action or choice of their own from the one great world organisation which is dedicated to the task of working out in practice how best men

366

of different races can co-operate for common aims, would feel affronted and abandoned.

'South Africa certainly needs the Commonwealth, but so does the Commonwealth need South Africa. The Prime Minister has not gone empty-handed, as a suppliant to the London conference. Economically, politically and strategically South Africa is a leading member of our family of nations. Certainly we are not popular at the present time, and the racial policy of our Government is widely misunderstood and almost universally condemned.

'Nevertheless, whatever the rights or wrongs of that great problem may be, it is surely obvious that if the Commonwealth starts expelling members because their governments' policy is disliked by other member states, it will be the beginning of the end of the Commonwealth.

'South Africa has much to offer, and in the long run it may well be that it will not be through our material progress, our mines and factories and farms, that we will make our greatest contribution to human welfare, but precisely through our experience and experiments – bitterly condemned though some of them may be – in the field of race relations.

'All of us, White and Black and Brown, Afrikaans and English-speaking, have got to live together in South Africa. We are all South Africans and have nowhere else to go, and just because we quarrel and just because – whether we like it or not – we belong irrevocably together and can't escape one another, we will eventually learn how to live together in peace and unity. We will find the way, because we've got to do so or perish. And that is how all the best and most lasting solutions to the problems are found.

'Meantime, our destinies are in a special sense in the hands of the Prime Minister in London. If he succeeds in his mission our path will be easier and our journey happier. If he fails we face a longer, harder road. In London he will not speak for a political party, but for South Africa, and here at home it is not a political party but South Africa which is behind him, and wishes him well.'

Verwoerd knew what he was in for. 'I have come to Britain as a friend,' he told the waiting reporters at London Airport. 'It is for Britain to accept our hand of friendship or reject it.' But in the event it was not Macmillan who called the tune, but the leaders of the black African states. They were set to make the most of the opportunity to challenge apartheid, and Verwoerd was as determined to withstand them. It was left to Macmillan to try and find a way out of the impasse.

The talks went on for more than 15 hours over two days, both at the conference table at Lancaster House and behind the scenes in intense lobbying. But it was to no avail. Though Macmillan succeeded in persuading Verwoerd to concede the other leaders' criticisms of apartheid, the most outspoken of them said it was not good enough. South Africa's racial policies would have to be changed drastically. At least half the Prime Ministers attending said they would pursue the matter openly every time there was an opportunity and the most extreme demanded South Africa's immediate expulsion.

Verwoerd listened quietly to these views, then asked for an opportunity to address the conference. He fully understood the predicament of the older Commonwealth members, Britain, Australia, Canada and the others. They were being forced to choose between their old friend South Africa, and the bumptious new offspring of the Afro-Asian bloc. Either way they would lose. In the circumstances, he was not going to ask them to sacrifice their other interests. He was withdrawing South Africa's application for continued membership of the Commonwealth. From now on the Republic would be on its own.

Midas Magic

EVEN THOUGH he was out of public life and out of the United Party, Harry remained a favourite target of the Nationalists. He was, after all, more powerful than ever: and who could tell what evil deeds were plotted in the closed meetings of those who controlled his companies? Might they not be planning the overthrow of South Africa, as they had in the past? Were they not preparing the downfall of the Afrikaner nation? Verwoerd wanted to know, and said as much in parliament on his return from the Prime Ministers' conference.

'Certain business undertakings hold private discussions in the same way as our political parties and in the same way as the Cabinet and in the same way as our Government and other bodies. A business undertaking may be a very powerful machine. One finds large combinations of business undertakings such as the Oppenheimer group – an octopus in the sense that it has branches in all spheres of the economic life of South Africa. It is a huge undertaking which is spread over the whole of the country's economy.

'The directors, when they meet, hold private discussions. In the case of such a powerful body there is also a central body which lays down basic policy. The influence of that central body, to say the least, must be great in our economic life. Nobody knows, however, what they discuss there. In the course of his speeches Mr. Oppenheimer, the leader, makes political statements; he discusses political policy, he tries to exercise political influence. He even supports a political party, which it so happens is not the party of the hon. the Leader of the Opposition. In other words, he has political aims; he wants to steer things in a certain direction. He can discuss those things secretly with groups of people on his boards of directors. He can secretly cause a good many things to happen. In other words, he can pull strings. With all

369

that monetary power and with this powerful machine which is spread over the whole of the country he can, if he so chooses, exercise an enormous influence against the Government and against the State.'

There were attacks outside parliament too. At a National Party congress in Bloemfontein the member of parliament, Blaar Coetzee – by this time he had left the UP and crossed the floor – listed what he termed South Africa's 'most pressing problems – the United Nations, the English Press, the Liberal Party, the United Party and Harry Oppenheimer'. Harry, he explained, was a bitter enemy of apartheid and the sworn opponent of Dr Verwoerd. Oppenheimer was convinced that through economic pressure he could force the government to weaken and make certain important concessions in its policies that would alter its appearance and power.

There were more attacks, but Harry was used to them. In a leader, the Johannesburg *Sunday Times* commiserated.

'Don't worry, Mr. Oppenheimer. They cannot do without you. They know it and you know it. The Nationalist Party, at its congress this week, indulged in one of its periodic outbursts, this time led by the Prime Minister, against the figure they identify with "big capitalism" and the mining industry.

'Perhaps it was the heady influence of the party's jubilee, for there were distinct echoes of its early days, when the mining magnates and big money – "die georganiseerde geldmag" – were the enemy. The fact, of course, is that it is Mr. Oppenheimer and men like him who make the wheels go round in South Africa, who provide it with the sinews of war and enable it to withstand the assaults of the world. Basically, it is they who keep the Government in power – and the Government knows it.'

It was true in a way – though it took a lot of insight to appreciate the fact. On the face of things Harry was Verwoerd's implacable opponent – certainly as regards the racial policies of the Nationalists. The old ideal of apartheid in the grand sense, with hope for all, seemed to be slipping away. In its place was the morass of what people were calling 'petty apartheid' – the finickety rules regarded as a general nuisance by most sections of the population and doing South Africa no good in the eyes of the world.

Harry's quarrel was with Verwoerd and the Nationalists, not with the Afrikaner nation as a whole, as Verwoerd and his supporters so often claimed. Harry, indeed, liked to regard himself as an 'Afrikaner': by his interpretation, following Smuts's, it meant simply that he was a South African. It was imperative for South Africa, he often claimed,

370

that the two white language groups should not allow themselves to be kept in segregation as the Nationalists wanted them to be, but instead to be united. Verwoerd's view of the South African population was of Afrikaners and 'others' – both white and non-white. That, Harry believed, was entirely wrong, and he looked for the chance to show this.

The opportunity was not long in coming. In fact, the germs of the idea had been spread long before. Whereas originally the Afrikaners had been predominantly an agricultural people, leaving it to the English-speaking elements to develop business interests, to an ever increasing extent the Afrikaner was getting involved. One organisation in particular was making a bid for a stake in the industrial pool, especially the mining world which was the most prosperous part of it: a company established by a group of Afrikaner businessmen, and called Federale Mynbou.

The new company's progress had been spectacular. It had been founded some years before on the slender capital of £60 000, with its interests centred mainly on two little collieries. With the signing of valuable contracts to supply government power stations and an oil refinery the company was able to expand further until at last it was amalgamated with a chain of collieries in Natal to become one of South Africa's biggest suppliers. The company acquired control of a blue asbestos mine in the Northern Cape and a salt mine near Port Elizabeth, and then took the step which was to lead to far-reaching results: it began to acquire interests in gold.

True, the initial investments were far from spectacular. Federale Mynbou bought its way into little mines operating not on the Witwatersrand, but in the picturesque regions of the Eastern Transvaal. At this stage the two men chiefly responsible for the company's success, Willem Coetzer, the chairman, and Tom Muller, the soft-spoken managing director, secured an appointment with Ernest not so long before his death in 1957. They wanted him to help establish them in the real world of gold mining.

'We thought then that if we could help it would be the right thing to do,' said Harry later. 'But there were no opportunities at that time.'

Afrikaner interests tried a new approach – this time by trying to gain effective control of JCI through an intensive share-buying campaign. But to Harry this looked a sinister move, particularly in view of the delicate balance of JCI's investments in the diamond world, let alone the gold. He decided to block the effort, and by means of a share deal involving the BSAC and New Rhodesia Investments, made sure control could not pass to the Afrikaner group.

371

A few years later JCI was in a weak position again, and there was another chance for the Afrikaners to move in. This time Harry blocked the development by arranging a share swop between JCI and Rand Selection, and to bolster the 'establishment's' position even more arranged the granting of a further option on 1 100 000 shares which gave his own interests an invincible advantage.

All this frustration would not make the Afrikaners more fond of him, Harry realised well, and in the fiery context of the South African business world, inextricably linked with its political and economic sisters, he needed all the friends he could get. Accordingly, he returned to the same Tom Muller and Willem Coetzer who had approached Anglo years earlier. He had a proposal for them. In partnership they would make a bid, not for JCI – its investments were too closely linked with Anglo's and De Beers – but, instead, for another of the great golden houses, General Mining.

So was born a new company with assets of R22 million – Main Street Investments. Already its holdings included important stakes in General Mining and other gold mining companies, and it held the chance to increase its stake – provided its backers complied. This was a test of the kind of co-operation that Harry was hoping would be possible. If Muller and Coetzer could win the support of powerful Afrikaner financial houses as yet not involved in the gold mining arena, there was the chance of an important new source of capital of extraordinary importance.

Things went perfectly smoothly. Within a year all was ready for a complete takeover. The capital was available, and the conditions were right. Together Federale Mynbou and Anglo announced what had happened: Federale Mynbou had made the takeover, while Anglo took a substantial minority interest.

There was an outcry. On the one hand prominent Nationalists protested bitterly against the 'awful prospect' of future co-operation between the two sections of the nation. On the other, business interests outside the deal were convinced Anglo had emerged the loser: the Afrikaner octopus had wrapped a first tentacle round one of the seven golden houses, part of the very citadel that protected the English-speaking South African's continued presence in Southern Africa.

Gradually, however, the position became clear. Far from losing out, Anglo was gaining. So, for that matter, was the rest of the business world. It was an act of financial statesmanship of remarkable significance, the financial commentators were saying. And all the credit belonged to Harry. In fact, Tom Muller was first to admit it: 'The

372

takeover would probably not have come about but for the integrity and assistance of Mr. Oppenheimer. He has been extremely constructive about the whole thing and has shown a genuine desire to assist in creating an opening for the Afrikaans business world to come into the world of mining and finance. His tact and goodwill have been invaluable in ironing out difficulties.'

Harry was as insistent as ever about the advantages of co-operation between the race groups – not only for South Africa as a whole, but for the business community itself. 'I think this new sphere of co-operation is a definite step in the right direction. It will also be good for the shareholders of General Mining – an aspect which should be emphasised.'

It was all rather disconcerting for some Nationalist politicians. Verwoerd and several members of his cabinet attacked the unexpected coup, claiming it was a Hoggenheimer trick to trap what little Afrikaner capital there was and syphon it off into the Anglo American's coffers. If Afrikaner business was to flourish it would have to beware of such subterfuge.

But it had all gone too far. There was a new light in the Nationalist ranks: one of the new wave of Afrikaners preparing to involve themselves thoroughly in the world of finance and big capital. This was Nico Diederichs, already Minister of Economic Affairs, who came out openly and denied all the criticisms that had been made: far from being swallowed up in General Mining and the Anglo American, Federale Mynbou had won a most valuable stake in a world hitherto out of reach. It could only be to the good of everyone – as Harry had insisted all along.

So the takeover was a *fait accompli*, and the stage was set for ever-increasing Afrikaner involvement in every sphere of the business world. The Afrikaner-backed business houses were not going to waste it, and in any case had the solid backing of all Anglo American's resources and its allies too. As the financial commentators had pointed out in praising Harry, it was all a matter of statesmanship. And as the same commentators soon appreciated, it was not the only current sample of his talents in this department.

The background this time was the ever deteriorating relationship between the lands north and south of the Limpopo – the black lands to the north and the white regimes to the south. As Ernest had pointed out so long before, the two represented quite different systems. Already it was clear that the Central African Federation for which there had been such great hopes at the outset was doomed to destruction. It could only be a matter of time.

Gradually the movement of independence swept down the continent. The countries of East Africa went their separate ways. Soon it would be Central Africa's turn. Kaunda was freed from detention and returned to power a hero in Northern Rhodesia. And in Nyasaland, Kamuzu Banda made the same progress. Independence was theirs for the asking, and it was announced it would be coming in 1964.

Harry would need his statesmanship now as never before. The copperbelt was a rich plum indeed, and far and away Northern Rhodesia's most valuable asset. What was to prevent Kaunda from nationalising the mines on the spot, and ejecting the 'hated racists' from the south without ceremony? Surprisingly, that was not Kaunda's attitude at all – as Harry quickly appreciated. Instead, Harry found he could afford to be a lot more confident of the situation than he had dared hope. Kaunda wanted the white companies to remain in the new republic.

'I am most encouraged by what I have seen there,' said Harry in an interview. 'All contacts with the new government have been good and the African leaders are behaving in a responsible and orthodox manner. Mr. Kaunda and other African leaders have given an assurance that the copper mines will not be nationalised in an independent Northern Rhodesia – and I think one can accept that this will not be done.'

So Anglo's position was secure after all. Harry set arrangements in hand to move the Salisbury offices up to Lusaka, the new capital of what was to be 'Zambia' from now on, and he turned his attention to preparing better relations between Zambia and the countries to the south. They could not succeed in partnership, but perhaps they could help each other now their interests were independent.

Full co-operation between Southern Rhodesia and the countries to the north was essential and possible, he said in a speech in Bulawayo. But in a message intended for white Rhodesians who had not yet followed the ways of the Nationalists in South Africa, he warned that a friendly relationship with Northern Rhodesia, Nyasaland and other African states would not be possible if discrimination based on the colour of a man's skin was tolerated.

It would be very foolish of South Africa not to give careful consideration to the possibility of establishing normal diplomatic relations with the new Northern Rhodesia, he told listeners at Pietermaritzburg in Natal. Kaunda had already won a reputation for moderation and integrity, and could be regarded as a man of his word. No doubt it would be difficult, but the establishment of diplomatic relations did not

Bridget at the racecourse with the Oppenheimer trainer, John Breval of Newmarket. The Oppenheimers rank as South Africa's most consistently successful breeder-owners, and Breval as one of the Republic's most successful trainers. *Rand Daily Mail*.

The magnate's wife at her desk. Bridget has an extraordinarily full social life, but manages to fulfil all her obligations with noted grace and charm. *James Soullier*.

Though for long one of apartheid's fiercest critics, Harry is on good terms with South Africa's Prime Minister John Vorster (*centre*). With them is Tom Muller (*right*), managing director of Federale Mynbou at the time of its takeover of General Mining. *Sunday Times*.

Harry walks the political tightrope across the Zambezi: lunching with President Kaunda at State House, Lusaka. *Times of Zambia*.

Harry and Rhodesia's leader, Ian Smith (*right*), in mourning after a disaster at Wankie Collieries which claimed the lives of more than 400 miners. *Rand Daily Mail*.

imply agreement in all respects – simply the willingness to discuss mutual interests and problems. It might mark the beginning of a dialogue of incalculable value to Africa and the world.

There was an interesting corollary to this suggestion. Contact with Northern Rhodesia was a splendid idea, wrote the Johannesburg *Sunday Times*. But let it be Harry himself who initiated it, on the South African government's behalf. No doubt the suggestion was made tongue in cheek – it would be difficult to think of a more ironic situation than having the hated Hoggenheimer acting for Verwoerd. But as the paper pointed out, there was nobody better qualified.

Harry's talents as a diplomat would have been more useful south of the Zambezi, where there was trouble in the only one of the three old CAF territories *not* granted independence. Since 1962 Southern Rhodesia had been ruled by a new party called the Rhodesian Front which owed its origin to white electors' fears of racial integration in the face of increasingly stringent demands from Britain that Africans should be given their fair share of government. The Prime Minister was Winston Field, with his chief deputy a World War II fighter pilot named Ian Smith. The position had deteriorated so far that their followers were demanding immediate independence from Britain. When Winston Field failed to win this legally and refused to try and seize it illegally, his colleagues forced him to resign and Ian Smith took his place.

Kaunda had been watching the situation from across the Zambezi with increasing dismay and was already demanding armed intervention by the British. There was talk of 'racial war' between black north and white south. It was this factor which made Harry's situation on the copperbelt all the more precarious. Already the two rival nationalist organisations in Rhodesia – Zimbabwe African National Union and Zimbabwe African People's Union – had been deprived of their leaders through a succession of imprisonments and banning orders. As yet Africans had only tiny representation in the government, for very few had the vote. The hard-line Rhodesian Front men wanted to reduce even that and maintain the terms of Land Appropriation which had existed since Charter days and which confined Africans to reserves like those in South Africa.

In Britain the Labour Party came to power and introduced Harold Wilson to the problem which was to prove the bane of his life. At first he would have preferred to leave Rhodesia alone, but soon introduced the first of his 'five point plans' conditional to Rhodesian independence. Smith was not prepared to make the necessary concessions and seeing

375

no way out of the impasse made the famous Unilateral Declaration of Independence on November 11 1965.

Wilson had already said he would on no account use force against Rhodesia unless law and order broke down. Instead he initiated a moderate economic sanctions campaign, which he confidently predicted would bring Smith to his knees 'in a matter of weeks, not months'. But he was not to guess South Africa and the Portuguese in Mozambique would protect Rhodesia as the front line barrier to the African nationalism which had enveloped the rest of the continent. Though neither the South Africans nor the Portuguese saw any need for Ian Smith's drastic move – in South Africa, indeed, it was widely condemned – what was done was done and they had to make the best of the situation. The sanctions campaign, even when stepped up to the point of maintaining a naval blockade off Beira in the Mozambique Channel, was a failure.

While all this was going on – and he disapproved of it more strongly even than most South Africans because it was so unnecessary – Harry was continuing his efforts to reverse the opinion of South Africa generally held overseas. He was still a trustee of the South Africa Foundation, which had now achieved much in stimulating interest in South Africa by sponsoring visits by important figures from politics and business. More than that, he arranged a special tour of South Africa by a group of ten influential financial editors, drawn mostly from Britain, sponsored by the Anglo American. Anglo had done this before with financial journalists from both sides of the Atlantic, but never had it been more important. The Commonwealth countries and Europe had introduced sanctions not against Rhodesia alone, but against South Africa too. The anti-apartheid movements were bearing fruit.

Would South Africa explode in five years' time as had been predicted, they were asking. The idea was complete nonsense, Harry told them. South Africa's economy was much more firmly based than people thought. Even the restrictive policies introduced in many countries to enforce international sanctions against South Africa had failed to hamper the solid development of the country. Anyway, in spite of job reservation there was a great loosening up of the labour situation and Africans were doing jobs they would never have dreamt of undertaking five years before.

Certainly there was a tendency for politics in the country to lose touch with reality. 'In South Africa politics have the habit of going one way – life another,' said Harry. But the government was not after all completely cutting off the flow of non-white labour into industry. All

376

the same, South Africa would have to rethink the whole position of non-white labour. 'When it comes to economic growth, there is no place for traditional concepts.'

With such ideas Harry helped correct the misconceptions about the South African situation so widely held throughout the world. He tended to be more critical of the situation at home than overseas – if only because it was so very complex that anyone having only a rudimentary idea of what it involved could never hope to grasp what he was getting at. Better, he decided, to win South Africa more friends than consolidate the opposition.

The efforts were worthwhile, and won Harry much praise from overseas sources. At home, it was expected of him. But what he said was far from complacent. There was, for instance, a notable speech he delivered at the University of Cape Town in 1964, marking what he termed the loss of academic freedom at South African universities when they were prevented from enrolling non-white students at will. He entitled the lecture 'The Conditions for Progress in Africa', and to the present day it stands as a most important contribution to thinking on the presence of Europeans in Southern Africa, and the benefits that white men have conferred on the continent at large.

The most remarkable thing about Africa as a whole, Harry began, had been its backwardness. With the single exception of Egypt, the continent had failed to develop anything that could reasonably be called a civilised society. Until the Europeans came, Hobbes's famous phrase was almost everywhere a fair assessment of African conditions: 'No arts; no letters; no society; and which is worst of all, continual fear and danger of violent death; and the life of man solitary, poor, nasty, brutish and short.'

'There were those who argued from this general backwardness to some basic inferiority of the Africans. It was suggested that people who had not been able to evolve an advanced political system of their own could not be capable of participating responsibly in those evolved by others; that because they did not succeed in developing a civilised society of their own, it would be useless and dangerous to admit them to the society developed by the Europeans; that because they had not themselves discovered the use of the wheel, it was only reasonable that they should be confined to the doing of unskilled work. Nowadays, the argument is not so often heard in this crude form, but belief in African inferiority based on African backwardness still persists. But surely the facts of the case really point in quite a different direction. It is not only in Africa that the initiation of a period of progress after ages of stagnation had to wait for external contacts and pressures. Indeed, there is good reason to think that this order of things is an historic fact of general application. But what is astonishing about Africa is the unexampled speed of advance of which Africans proved themselves capable as soon as the necessary conditions had been established.

'The period of Africa's rapid progress corresponds with the period of Colonialism and the conclusion is surely irresistible that it was the Colonial system of government that created the conditions for the spectacular progress of which I have just spoken. It is clear also, that for the part of a century anyhow, Colonial government over most of Africa was never seriously challenged and was generally acceptable to the people. I believe it is worth while therefore to consider, firstly, what the conditions of progress were that the Colonial regimes established, and secondly, why, after long years of general acceptance and great achievement, Colonialism should suddenly be so widely regarded with resentment and hatred. If we are able to find answers to these questions, it will then perhaps be possible to estimate what the chances are of maintaining those conditions for progress established by Colonialism in Africa after the Colonial regimes themselves have passed away.'

Harry warmed to his theme. Colonialism had brought stable, efficient, incorruptible government to Africa. It had not brought – could not have brought – democracy. It put a stop to tribal warfare and slave raiding and conferred the inestimable benefit of peace. It opened up communications and applied modern techniques to mining, agriculture, industry and commerce. It tackled the problems of disease – perhaps the greatest single factor accounting for Africa's general backwardness. It imported capital from overseas and provided expanding markets in Europe for African produce.

That much was obvious. But the great colonialist programme brought with it other less easily measured benefits of first importance. For the first time Africa was opened up to individual enterprise by Africans as well as by Europeans, breaking into the closed, harsh, frustrating tribal system and providing social, economic and even political opportunity for the talents of individual Africans.

'Nowadays,' he went on, 'this statement sounds strange and paradoxical because we have learnt to think of Colonialism as a bar to African advancement. And this is not without reason. Colonialism has become associated in varying degrees with colour bars, social, economic and political, but although this may have been implicit in the system from the start, the impact of Colonialism at the beginning, and indeed until comparatively recently, worked in the opposite direction. Generally speaking, the colour bars which are now regarded as both an insult and an injury to Africans were for many years not in serious conflict with African aspirations and capabilities, and it was not until quite recently that they began to act as a brake on progress. It may well be found in the long run that the introduction to Africa under the Colonial system of the concept and practice of individual freedom and initiative was even a more significant change than the introduction of European organisation and techniques.

'Although, therefore, it is true to say that Africa owes all she knows of peace, freedom and plenty for the individual to the initiative of Europeans, it is also true to say that at a certain stage the white rulers imposed a ceiling on the full development of African potentialities. For this there are many reasons. There was race prejudice, pure and simple – xenophobia, the hate of what is different and strange. Related to that there was the desire – by no means an ignoble one – to maintain the integrity of the white tribe and preserve its customs and standards intact. There was the selfishness of those who wanted to preserve the illusory advantage of cheap African labour. There was the understandable fear of the skilled European workers that the advancement of Africans beyond a certain level would threaten their standard of living. There was the idealism of Europeans who believed deeply and sincerely, but contrary to all common sense and historical experience, that the building of a society capable of operating a full parliamentary democracy should come before, not after, the attainment of political independence. There was the idealism of others who, for the best of motives, sought to protect tribal institutions and maintain tribal discipline in the face of the new forces of revolution.

'Here, perhaps, is the crux of the whole matter. The transfer to Africa of the new techniques evolved during the industrial revolution in Europe, together with the political and social changes that went with it, was bound – in Africa as in Europe – to cause a period of conflict between, on the one hand, the new men seeking wider opportunity and eager for change, and on the other hand the traditionalists, the defenders of a long-established way of life based on the land. In this conflict, the traditionalists must go under, and much that is good, wise and beautiful must go with them. That is the price that must be paid to open the way to new opportunities, wider horizons and higher values.'

Thus far, Harry had been considering Africa in general. Now he turned to the particular – the two systems his father had picked out facing each other across the Zambezi. He recognised the 'one party

379

state' system, and decided it was the best possible for countries so new to democracy. To invite the rural populations of such countries to involve themselves in electoral struggles between government and opposition was to introduce the chance of civil war.

'The African nationalists look on Rhodesia with its substantial European population, and South Africa with its large European population, as fortresses of Colonialism. Obviously, however, the white populations of these countries are on quite a different footing to the handful of white officials and traders who controlled the tropical dependencies of the Colonial powers. The white South Africans are just as African as black South Africans. They have no other home to go to, and there is no question of their pulling out or handing over unconditionally to the African nationalists in the same way as the Europeans in the new countries to the north have done.

'The problem here and in Rhodesia is, therefore, quite different to that of the tropical Colonies. Nevertheless, it is admitted by white South Africans of all political opinions that the present situation in which all power is concentrated in the hands of a white minority is much greater absolutely and proportionately than elsewhere in Africa.'

It was a long address, and Harry went into the problems of Africa in careful detail. What was to be the future of Southern Africa? What would happen to the old British colonies now included in the Commonwealth? And what would happen to the Commonwealth itself? These were weighty questions, and Harry admitted that time alone could tell. But even if he provided more questions than answers, few who listened to him can have forgotten his peroration.

'Political systems may change, but the basic facts of geography and of the needs of human beings remain the same. In Africa, the wheel has turned a full circle. The Europeans who first brought freedom and progress to the Africans were unable, for reasons I have touched on in this speech, to carry through to its conclusion the work they had begun. The question that has to be answered in Africa today is whether the African Nationalists are going to prove capable of completing the work of the Colonialists. In these new African countries are individual men and women to become increasingly free to realise their potentialities? Or is Africa, like Europe when the Roman colonial system collapsed, to sink back into the tyranny and chaos from which the Europeans rescued it?'

Harry made many speeches as challenging as this in these years, each pleading a rational approach to South Africa's problems and begging tolerance from outside. Within South Africa he took an active part in trying to develop an altogether fresh approach to the situation. When the Progressive Party commissioned an inquiry into voting rights in South Africa, chaired by the leading advocate Donald Molteno, he agreed to serve on it.

The commission was charged with defining a set of qualifications for the vote in line with modern concepts of democracy in a multi-racial state. That sounded only too simple: but, in fact, the assignment was tough indeed, for there had been no such reappraisal of the South African situation in decades. The commission's eventual report reflected the difficulties facing its members.

'Recommending general qualifications for a non-racial franchise,' said the report, 'is quite the most difficult we have been set. Whatever recommendations we make in this regard will obviously be open to criticism. We are enjoined to recommend qualifications based on a defined degree of civilisation. But this is a very general test upon which opinions may legitimately widely differ.'

In a particularly interesting section the report dealt with the non-white demand for complete adult suffrage – the 'one man one vote' concept which Harry had already several times attacked as so dangerous.

'While fully understanding this attitude we are bound to point out that it bears no necessary relation to personal freedom, the rule of law, ordered progress or any of the other values that Western democracy has conceived in order to foster. Its inspiration is rather non-White nationalism which, like all nationalisms, is ultimately totalitarian in its logical outcome.

'A modern nationalist mass movement naturally rejects voting qualifications that seek to enfranchise the stable elements in society. To the nationalist the vote is a weapon to be used by the masses at behest of an enthusiastic leadership.'

The commission's report had to be considered by the full national congress of the Progressive Party, and in due course became its blue-print for the future. But even as the commissioners set about their work, it was plain there was little chance of their recommendations ever taking effect. Before the last election, called by Verwoerd for 1961, there had been eleven UP rebels sitting in parliament as Pro-gressives. Now they had to contest their seats against new UP candi-dates, with the whole weight of the National Party and the UP stacked against them and dark allegations about what they proposed to do if they gained any sort of power. The odds were high against them, and

381

in the event only one of the 23 Progressives fighting the election retained her seat – Helen Suzman of Houghton.

Helen Suzman had been a lecturer in economic history at Wits before entering politics: a brilliant woman, but at the same time devoted wife and hard-working mother who now found herself the hardest-worked parliamentarian. She and a full-time research assistant were left to cope with the whole weight of the Nationalist advance and with a United Party Opposition whose policies seemed all too similar to those it was supposed to be fighting. But Helen Suzman bravely held her ground, using the power of parliamentary privilege to full effect. She attracted widespread publicity within South Africa and outside, which transmitted her message all over the world.

At first the other members of parliament saw her success as a flash in the pan. Nationalists confidently predicted she would soon be ousted. But when she kept up her own tough pace and gained support the Nationalists began to attack her bitterly and even her old colleagues in the UP took her to task. Interestingly, as the more intellectual members realised her achievement they treated her with considerable respect: and of them all, one commentator suggested the only one who could match her rapier perception was the new Minister of Justice, John Vorster.

An interesting summary of Helen Suzman's presence in parliament appeared in the *New York Times*, towards the end of her first term as the lone Progressive and with a general election in sight. The paper's Southern African correspondent set out to answer the taunts of a cabinet minister who had asked Helen Suzman who she claimed to represent.

'The answer is that she speaks on behalf of her own constituents, on behalf of the Progressive Party (which is likely to vanish from the scene if she loses), on behalf of all those who believe, as she does, in a gradual transition to multi-racial Government and Black majority rule, on behalf of African nationalists who might spurn gradualism – indeed, on behalf of all non-Whites. Put another way, she represents more South Africans than all the 159 other members of Parliament combined.'

It was imperative that Helen Suzman retain her seat. Harry came out publicly in her support. The Progressives were bearers of a great tradition, he wrote. 'Let us be clear what that tradition implies and does not imply. The Progressive Party does not maintain that all men are equal – something which is manifestly untrue. It does not imply that every man, regardless of his natural qualities or education, should

382

have an equal voice in national affairs. What it does maintain is that the rights and privileges of a man should depend not on his race or colour but on his ability and character.

'The Progressive cause has attracted many fine men and women. None of them, however, has shown greater courage and intellectual grasp, greater realism and wisdom, that Helen Suzman. Her wonderful parliamentary record is known and appreciated far beyond the ranks of the Progressives. The electorate of Houghton, in voting Progressive and voting for Helen Suzman, will strike a blow for all that is best in our country. They will vote for a great ideal and for a courageous, intelligent and sympathetic personality.'

Harry's message earned him a sharp rebuke from John Vorster, who was now firmly tipped as the Verwoerd administration's fastest rising star. He was not complaining about what Harry said of Helen Suzman personally, he told an election meeting in Brakpan. 'What I object to is this phase "strike a blow for all that is best in our country". Mr. Oppenheimer's sort want to destroy all we stand for. Our people may work for him, but he does not own their souls. Our workers will not be intimidated by him or any other capitalist in South Africa . . . I want to say to Mr. Oppenheimer: You and yours will never shake the foundation of South Africa as long as the National Party exists.'

The Progressives were contesting 50 seats at that 1966 election: but in spite of several close results no new members did they return. Only Helen Suzman lived to fight again another day: and with an increased majority.

South Africa's status in the eyes of the world had been deteriorating in these years: worse even than at the low point which Sharpeville produced. Black nationalist organisations had been supported by grants from anti-apartheid factions in other countries, and the early sixties had seen a wave of urban terrorism: chiefly rather futile sabotage attempts aimed at government installations. The government assumed this was the work of outside agencies, presumably communist. There followed a systematic investigation of those with known communist sympathies. Many were imprisoned according to new emergency regulations, while others were 'banned': confined to a single magisterial district and not to be quoted in newspapers and magazines under any circumstances.

Helen Suzman spoke out against these measures, but could make no impact on Verwoerd and his mission. South Africa's critics were calling the country a police state, a Nazi legacy, a fascist regime. But Verwoerd himself seemed unassailable, ever more secure in his leadership. In

383

fact, in the first six weeks of the 1966 session of parliament – later than usual in view of the general election – he did not speak on a single occasion.

On the Tuesday of the sixth week, September 6, the House re-assembled after a long weekend and as it was the day Verwoerd's own budget vote was up for discussion it was sure he would break his silence at last. There was a good deal of excitement and it was expected the House would be crowded, for a major policy speech by Verwoerd was an event of considerable importance in South Africa. The chances were it would follow the pattern of previous speeches of his: a long, fluent oration touching on everything then topical, delivered with a minimum of notes and in that confident, determined way that Verwoerd always used, absolutely sure of himself.

Verwoerd entered the chamber during question time with several other members, and made his way straight to his seat on the front bench near the Speaker's. Barely had he sat down when one of the parliamentary messengers rushed towards him across the floor, barging other members out of the way. Suddenly the messenger pulled out a long sheathknife, tore off its scabbard and lunged at Verwoerd across his desk.

Two, three, four times he stabbed at Verwoerd's neck and chest. There were other members close by and they tried to grab him. But he slashed at them wildly with his knife before at last they could drag him away and pin him down. For Verwoerd they were too late. He had lifted his arm as if to ward off the blows. He tumbled back into his seat with what looked like a half-smile on his face. He stayed upright for a minute or two, then sighed and slumped forward over his bench. Blood poured from his neck and chest, down his arm which dangled loosely from the bench until it dripped to the carpet below.

They hustled the messenger from the chamber, screaming as he went. 'Where's that bastard? I'll get that bastard.' There were several doctors among the members, and they did what they could to help Verwoerd. His wife had arrived in the public gallery just after the stabbings, and saw the scuffle that followed. Now she hurried down to be with her husband, only to be escorted away again by those close to him.

They rushed Verwoerd to hospital, but he was dead long before they arrived. The news went round the world. Who was behind it? An international plot to rid South Africa of its 'dictator'? The police were already investigating.

Everything now centred on the messenger. Feverishly the police traced his past, everything they could about him. The picture that emerged was quite a surprise: a new employee taken on for a few weeks, the offspring of a mixed marriage between a Greek and an African woman from Mozambique, a relatively new arrival in South Africa who had globetrotted the world as a merchant seaman and spent time in mental institutions in several countries. His name was Demitrio Tsafendas.

A full commission of enquiry was instituted into the circumstances of Verwoerd's assassination, and produced some curious findings. There was no single overriding motive for Tsafendas's action. He had been in England where he had heard of Verwoerd, and heard people say he should be killed. But much more significantly, evidently, he had visited South Africa on Greek ships when his crewmates had been frustrated by South Africa's immorality legislation, by which they were not allowed to bring Coloured prostitutes on board or have any relations with them. Verwoerd, they said in their anger, should be killed. With a character as unbalanced as Tsafendas's it did not take long for the idea to take effect, and when he found his way into the job at parliament – virtually by chance, as it happened, though the idea was already half-established in his mind – he was in the ideal situation to carry it out. When Tsafendas was tried, it did not take long to convince the court that he should be put away as unfit to stand trial.

So Verwoerd was dead. The man who had stood as a rock of granite in South African life was there no more, and it was immediately apparent that there would be a tremendous void. Verwoerd was an era, and now it was at an end. What could lie ahead?

The National Party caucus met to consider who should be Verwoerd's successor. The most likely candidate was John Vorster, an ardent Afrikaner nationalist who had been interned by Smuts during World War II as a potential security risk in view of pro-German sympathies he had preached from public platforms. As Minister of Justice in Verwoerd's later years he had been responsible for introducing the emergency measures involving detention without trial – the 90 day and 120 day terms which had brought censure on the Verwoerd regime from all over the world, but, as John Vorster pointed out, were not as ruthless as the punishment he and other militant Afrikaners had suffered at the UP's hands during the war when they were detained not for months but years without being brought to trial. English-speaking South Africans generally stood in fear of him, believing he was as resolute and uncompromising as Verwoerd himself. But in days the appointment was announced.

2

IN ALL THESE years of trouble, with the rest of the world predicting a South African holocaust any minute, it seemed impossible that life in the new republic could continue smoothly. But that was the case. There was always a *possibility* the something would happen, that tables would be turned and the African hordes which outnumbered the whites by more than five to one would suddenly rise and drive the white man into the sea. But somehow nobody really believed it could happen: the Nationalists had the country sewn up to such an extent it was unthinkable.

Harry was asked for his own views on the situation by the interviewer Ken Anderson: 'As regards the future of South Africa and the way things are going at the moment ... Well, I'm a professional optimist about this, and I do think it's going to be all right. Africa touches my heart very much – as it does all of us.

'As you know, I'm not very happy about the way things are being handled here but, as they say in the mining industry, it takes an incredibly bad manager to spoil a good mine, and I think that really is the case in Africa. This is a very, very good mine, and it can be managed badly for very many years and it'll still get through. The people who are managing at the moment, I think, have a point of view which is held perfectly honestly and sincerely by them, but I think it's absolutely the wrong one. I see nothing to point to their changing their view – which would suggest they were learning . . . What I would call learning.

'In answer to your question whether, when I could have done so easily, I ever wanted to live in any other country which is more in the centre of things – America, Britain, the Continent. Well, I may have had a theoretical opportunity of doing this, but I was born here, I've always lived here, and it didn't occur to me to live anywhere else. This has always been something my father was tremendously keen on. The Anglo American Corporation is a South African company – it was one of the first big companies which was registered here, and this was something he felt very strongly about.

'If things went very wrong here, would I get out, you ask. Good gracious no, it doesn't occur to me. Unless I'm chased out I'm going to stay here. You remind me that quite recently when things were going badly a lot of people hived off – well, I think that's silly. I think it's not very brave and I think it's bad judgement, too. It's worse than a crime ... it's a mistake.'

Certainly life was running perfectly calmly and peacefully within the Oppenheimer family. Harry's routine was balanced and regular enough: Bridget saw to that. He drove himself to work each morning, spent the day at the office, then drove home again for private discussions with his key men or perhaps a dinner party or a quiet evening at home. There were frequent trips away from Johannesburg: overseas several times a year, 'round the houses' to visit each of Anglo's widening interests; trips to the Cape, to Kimberley for De Beers board meetings, to Durban for the racing, to Zambia for the copperbelt. Usually Bridget went too.

Bridget and Harry were leading a lot less hectic a life than they had – one of the privileges of getting older, Harry liked to feel. In years past they had thrown a full scale ball every year, but that was a thing of the past now. They were simply rather bored with it all: it was the same thing every time. And in any case, they always managed to pick the one evening in weeks when it rained. Instead, they preferred to entertain more quietly: civilised dinner parties and occasional bridge forays, and always dress occasions. Even when they were alone for the evening, Harry and Bridget made a point of dressing for dinner.

There were occasional exceptions, of course. Once a year now Bridget and friends of hers arranged to throw the Brenthurst gardens open for three days, to raise money for the African Children's Feeding Scheme which was Bridget's favourite charity and which she had helped to bring into being. At the first of these open days Harry had looked out on the throng swarming through the grounds with some amazement – though certainly amusement too – before retiring hastily to his study for the rest of the day.

If Harry and Bridget were taking life more easily, that was certainly not true of Ina – grand old lady of the family by this time, and settled into her new house over the hill. Her life was altogether independent of the rest of them, but she was if anything more dynamic than when Ernest was alive. She took up weaving, and developed great skill before at last an onset of arthritis compelled her to stop. She turned to flower arrangements, but had to give that up too. At last she discovered photography, and equipped herself with one of the most formidable darkrooms in Johannesburg. Though she started from scratch, in due course her work came to attract international acclaim: within three years of starting she was elected an Associate of the Royal Photographic Society in London.

All this time Mary and Nicky were away at school in England. Mary was at the fashionable Heathfield in Ascot, and eventually became head girl. Nicky was doing well not at Charterhouse, where Harry and his brother had been, but instead at Harrow in the footsteps of Harry's cousin Philip and his son Anthony. Harry was waiting for the time Nicky could follow him on to Christ Church, not so far in the future.

Mary came to the end of her career at Heathfield and the big question was: what should she do next? There was talk of her going on to Oxford, to the Sorbonne, at least to university. But that could come later. First of all, Harry and Bridget decided, she should do the London season. Bridget travelled to England to be with her daughter during the hectic months ahead. They took a flat in Belgravia, and Bridget made all the arrangements to equip Mary with the extensive wardrobe she would need.

The English season follows a pattern familiar for more than half a century. Its aim is quite simple: to introduce the young debutantes taking part to society – to the 'right' kind of people who will inhabit their world in the years ahead. It is most certainly *not* intended as a straightforward marriage market: in fact, it is more important and more worthwhile for the future if a girl concentrates on making friends not with the young men she meets, the debs' delights, but with the other girls. No longer are debs presented at court as was the case in the past. The chief criterion enabling a girl to take part in the season these days is not ancestral but financial. But the whole thing is intended as a lot of fun for everyone involved – a spectacular launch into the world of high society.

Mary, of course, was one of the debs of her year: she was the only daughter of one of the richest men in the world. Bridget knew what was expected: in fact, she had herself been presented at court years before, even if she had not actually done the season. She was set to enjoy it all – the 'debs' mums' lunches and other such occasions were all an important part of the season, every bit as much as the events organised for the younger set – and it looked as if she would not be disappointed.

Mary fell in with all the traditions: the tea parties for the debs themselves, the initial cocktail parties with the debs' delights, the charity fashion shows and the early dances. And then it was time for the Queen Charlotte's Ball at the Grosvenor, the real 'debut' ball at which the girls parade in stately white dresses, to be presented to some doyen of the season in place of the royalty who would once have been involved. Mary was there – drilled precisely to proceed down the stairs and up the floor in line with the others in the long row, and curtsey in her turn until at last the ceremony was over and people could return to enjoying themselves.

The key months of the season are May, June, July and August, and Mary's own dance was set for the middle of it all – June 9, the day after Nicky's birthday. Bridget arranged to give it in conjunction with an old family friend, Lady Helen Vivian-Smith, whose husband had been one of Harry's best friends at Oxford, at their fine old home near Epsom, in Surrey. They gave a dinner party for 40, among them the South African ambassador and his wife, while the other guests dined at various houses nearby: and towards midnight all 300 converged on the marquee at the Vivian-Smiths for the dance proper: bands, cabaret, champagne buffet, strawberries and cream, bacon and eggs and dancing till dawn.

Bridget and Mary returned to Johannesburg for a while when it was all over. Then it was time for Mary to return to Europe, this time to study at the Sorbonne and to collect herself before progressing on to the next stage. Bridget and Harry still hoped she would want to go on to an English university, but Mary had different ideas. She saw no real point in it. Should she not rather get on with something more *real?*

So it was that a few months later, yet another Oppenheimer arrived for work at 44 Main Street. Mary started in the accounts department, and spent several months there as a clerk battling with figures before she decided it was not her calling. Instead, and Harry readily agreed, she wanted to do something more constructive. Harry made her permanent secretary of Anglo's twin charity funds, the Ernest Oppenheimer Memorial Trust and the Anglo Chairman's Fund which Harry had established to help deserving charities.

Mary soon developed a routine of her own – driving in to work in time to beat the eight-thirty rush from the suburbs, reading all the Johannesburg newspapers as Harry liked to do, answering her correspondence and interviewing would-be candidates for grants. It was not the kind of job that kept her desk-bound for eight hours a day – which was the way she wanted things. It gave her time to concentrate on the pursuit she enjoyed more than anything else in the world – her riding.

It had all begun years before, when Mary was given her first pony to ride round the grounds at Brenthurst. With the spread of Johannesburg the family had had to give up the stables, but Harry had always encouraged Mary's riding. She was specially keen on show jumping now she was old enough to do it properly. She had the pick of the retired Oppenheimer race-horses, and kept them out at a riding school in the northern suburbs run by a young show jumper, Bill Johnson, in conjunction with his identical twin Arthur.

389

But life was not all work and riding. Mary was, after all, far and away the most eligible girl in the sub-continent, indeed one of the most eligible in the world. Johannesburg is a great city for the young, and Mary was all set to make the most of it. Parties, dances, charity dos, all these she took in her stride. Not a week went past without her picture on the social pages, and quite often a write-up to go with it. And she found herself in increasing demand with magazine journalists seeking an interview with one of South Africa's brightest assets. Her answers to their questions were revealing.

'What do I look for in other people? First they must be upright. I don't like sneakery. Then they've got to have a sense of humour – it's very important, and they must be intelligent and well brought up to show manners.

'I hope one day to marry a South African, but I've no preconceived ideas. First he's got to fulfil the normal criteria I call essential, and beyond that he can be any shape or size. He needn't have any cash. A bank clerk with the right background can end up the "right one".'

Life wasn't all a bowl of cherries, though. Being who she was had its problems.

'It's not easy to be an Oppenheimer. People always watch you, even spy. You must always be careful not to say or do the wrong thing. But even this way you can be hurt. My father and mother are always there to give advice. They know what it is to be in the spotlight all the time.'

But most people wished Mary all the luck in the world. She was one of those delightful girls who enjoy everything that's going, and put everything they have into it. There were always tongues ready to wag: Johannesburg society loves a good piece of gossip. Unless she locked herself in a garret, she could hardly escape its eagle eye. But Mary took no notice of the attention and went her own way.

Meanwhile, Nicky was still in England. He was in many ways a lot more quiet than his sister, more reserved, certainly altogether unassuming. He reminded friends of the family of what Harry had been at his age, and indeed what Ernest had been: an Oppenheimer to his fingertips. His career at Harrow had been rather gentle: a gradual progression through his school years in preparation for Oxford, with a useful apprenticeship in that most favourite Oppenheimer recreation after horsemanship – golf.

He went up to Christ Church in October 1963, to read PPE as Harry had done before him. He was even to be tutored by Harry's old mentor, Roy Harrod: the distinguished economist had achieved world renown in the meantime, and a knighthood too. Again Nicky was set for a quiet life: in the distinguished assembly at the House Nicky was only one famous man's son among many, as had been the case at Harrow. For him it was a refreshing situation, after the glare of publicity in South Africa.

Oxford in these years was a very different proposition from what it had been when Harry was up. Much of the tradition lingered, but the university had not lost touch with the times. The social environment was different, even at Christ Church which was still regarded as the prince among Oxford's colleges. Nicky was content with a small circle of friends who shared his interests. He played lots of golf, lots of squash – in fact there was a strong possibility of his winning a half-blue in Oxford's annual match against Cambridge – and did his modicum of work as Harry had done. They were happy years.

There was romance in the air too, as there always is at Oxford. But for Nicky it did not involve a local girl, but instead a friend from Johannesburg initially studying at the Sorbonne in Paris though she later gave up her course to concentrate on skiing in Switzerland. Nicky had known Orcillia Lasch – Strilli, as everyone knew her – since he was 13 and she was 17 and they met on the golf course at the Johannesburg Country Club. In the years following they had remained close friends. Now things were blooming, and there was every prospect they would one day get married.

But it was not Nicky alone who was involved. Back in Johannesburg Mary was caught in the social whirl, and not surprisingly there had been a procession of eligible young men through Brenthurst in these years. Harry and Bridget were not entirely happy about some of them, but let Mary have her own way. Instead it was Ina who ruled with a rod of iron, the dowager from over the hill. If she did not like one of Mary's young men she said so – and loudly. Mary was too strong-willed to take every hint like a lamb, but she had too much respect for Ina to take no notice.

Many of these friends of Mary's were sportsmen – cricketers, golfers, riders, footballers. This was evidently the kind of man Mary most admired. One of her early beaux was none other than her riding instructor, Bill Johnson. By now he was established in the fashionable Bryanston, some miles north of Johannesburg. His business was popular and booming. Mary liked to visit the riding centre every day – sometimes twice a day, if she could. She kept her three horses there – The Gnat, Googlie and Pearly King, all of them retired from the racecourse, and now showing all the makings of fine show-jumpers.

391

Mary saw a lot of Bill Johnson, though they were really only good friends. Bill was her senior by many years, and after all Mary was not yet out of her teens. Each went out with a number of other people, though it was noticeable they seemed ideally suited to each other. But things just did not work out: as these things go, Mary fell in love with someone quite different. He was Scottish, he was handsome and he was a rugby player. In fact he was rather a distinguished rugby player: he had captained Scotland on many occasions and played for the British Lions in South Africa and Australia. His name was Gordon Waddell, the son of a Glasgow stockbroker.

Mary had first met him many years before, as it happened – at London airport, when she and her parents had been introduced to him by mutual friends. Mary was still at school; Gordon was seven years older, just emerged from British national service as a Royal Marine Commando, and in his first year at Cambridge. Next they met in 1961, this time in Johannesburg. Gordon was touring with the Lions: no stranger to South Africa, for before this he had toured with the Barbarians. He and Mary met at a party and went on to the same night club. Mary had never watched a game of rugby in her life, but the next day accepted an invitation from a friend who had tickets with the compliments of Gordon. He was not playing, but instead sat with them on the sidelines. Once he was back in Britain again he and Mary began writing regularly.

He came down from Cambridge with a respectable degree in Economics and Law, and soon enrolled at Stanford University in California for a post-graduate course in business administration. He was still in touch with Mary, and when she visited the United States with Harry and Bridget in 1963, he met her in New York and they had three days together. At the end of the course he flew to South Africa for a few days to stay with Mary at Shangani and ended by staying with the Oppenheimers for five weeks. When Harry and Bridget flew to London a few months later Mary went too. She was there several weeks, and Gordon proposed. She accepted – but it was all very hush-hush: she did not let even Harry and Bridget know about it.

Not until the day before the Durban July and they were all staying at the Edward Hotel in Durban did she tell them: and found to her delight both were overjoyed. They adored Gordon. Now Mary was so happy she could hardly keep the news a secret. Gordon was flying out to South Africa in a few days' time to get engaged officially. Mary told some of her friends and the news was leaked to the papers. Next day Mary was hounded by reporters and photographers – it was the day of the big race, in any case – and to crown it all Harry and Bridget's horse King Willow came in a clear winner.

Gordon was arriving the next Tuesday. Harry flew to Johannesburg in one of Anglo's private jets to fetch him, and Ina was at the airport too. As if to give the proceedings the final accolade news came through that the Oppenheimers' Kimberley Kid had won at Turffontein. Bridget and Mary were at the airport in Durban, and everyone was commenting on how happy Mary looked, more self-assured and confident and simply attractive than anyone could remember seeing her before. Next evening there was a party at the Edward, Gordon slipped an antique three-diamond ring on Mary's finger, and her proud parents could announce they were officially engaged.

Gordon and Mary decided they wanted to live in South Africa after the wedding, but one question that had to be resolved before long was what Gordon was to *do*. It was not to be imagined he would rest content as some sort of Prince Consort. This, of course, was no real problem. With his degree in law and economics, a course in business administration behind him, his father a stockbroker, and experience in investment and even insurance – not to mention that he was a thoroughly nice chap into the bargain – it was difficult to imagine anyone better equipped to join Oppenheimer and Son. The appointment was duly announced.

As the date of the wedding approached Bridget made sure the personal touch would not be missing. Every invitation that went out – rather more than 900 of them – was signed by someone in the family, and in most cases that meant her. She had to arrange all the catering: they decided on a giant marquee in the gardens at Brenthurst, set out as a period dining-room; and there was the church service to think about: she and Harry prevailed on Leslie Stradling, the Bishop of Johannesburg, to take out a licence as a marriage registry official specially for the occasion.

It was a time of tremendous happiness for everyone. Harry was so pleased by it all he decided to give Gordon a special present. Mary led him out of the house blind-fold one morning and when she undid the handkerchief showed him a spanking new golden-bronze Maserati sports coupé straight out of the box, one of the few of its type in the world and certainly the only one in Africa. That was not all. Harry reasoned that rather than expect Mary to continue living in Little Brenthurst he should give the couple a cottage out in the suburbs: it would give them a little privacy. The house he bought was quite small, too small for them to think of raising a family just yet. But it would do for the time being. When they were finished with it Nicky could take it over.

The day of the wedding dawned overcast, inevitably. Bridget had always complained that when an Oppenheimer organised a do for more than eight or so people at a time the heavens opened. Down came the rain as promised, though it cleared in time for Gordon's departure from Little Brenthurst where he had been staying with his best man, Dominic Cadbury of the British chocolate family. The two had shared an apartment at Stanford for two years. They set off for the cathedral, leaving the scene clear for Mary and her attendants, who were leaving from the big house.

Meanwhile, there were extraordinary scenes in the middle of Johannesburg. Since early morning crowds had been gathering on the pavements near the cathedral to obtain the best vantage points. An hour before the ceremony was due to begin there were already more than a thousand people there, with the police and the ushers getting rather apprehensive. Scores more were arriving by the minute, a good nine out of ten of them female. And female crowds, as the police knew only too well, were a lot tougher a proposition than male or mixed crowds.

Bridget and Gordon's parents set off for the cathedral in plenty of time, and it began to rain: no drizzle this time, but a full-scale downpour, rain pelting down to an extent which would normally have cleared Johannesburg streets until it stopped. But the crowd stayed right where it was. Most of the guests were safely in their seats by now, escorted there by a legion of ushers led by Nicky, who had flown back from Oxford specially for the ceremony. Among the others were Gordon's two elder brothers, and the Springbok fly-half Keith Oxlee who had opposed Gordon in a number of rugby matches.

The police reinforcements had brought a number of dogs with them, but they made little difference: the crowd was not impressed. As Bridget and the Waddells arrived at the cathedral entrance the women streamed forward to catch a closer glimpse. The same happened when the bridesmaids and the little pages drew up. Nicky and the other ushers were hard pressed to help the police keep order: they were recognised and came in for the same treatment. One of the cathedral's canons came out to appeal for restraint, but could not even make himself heard above the din.

At last – and ten minutes after the ceremony had been due to begin – the bridal car negotiated the blocked streets. As it reached the awning pandemonium broke out. The thousands of spectators began pushing,

394

screaming, pulling hair, punching, kicking, forcing their way to the front. One elderly woman had her arm broken; many were battered and bruised. Scores lost hats, shoes, handbags. Harry and Mary were separated, surrounded by the hordes of shrieking women trying to touch Mary's gown for luck. 'Mary, let's see you,' they screamed, as she struggled with her 20 foot train. She was getting really frightened.

The police came through, the ushers joined them, and between them half-hustled Mary through to the porch. Harry joined them there, and he and Nicky tried to comfort Mary who was now almost in tears: it was all too much for her. The bishop came forward too, and gently had a few words to help her become herself again. The organ struck up with Purcell's *Trumpet Voluntary*, at last drowning the noise of the baying horde outside. The ushers struggled to shut the heavy studded doors. They barely managed it, and the cathedral was in danger of full-scale invasion. But at last all was well, the wedding could go forward.

The congregation would be talking about it for years: one of the most spectacular processions Johannesburg had ever seen. The vergers, the choir, priests in their robes, then the bishop himself in cope and mitre of scarlet and gold. A long gap, and then what they had all waited to see: Harry with Mary on his arm, the King of Diamonds and the Princess his daughter, solemn and composed now, tiny figures in that huge emptiness under the high vault of the pillared aisle. Softly they stepped down the long red carpet stretching to the high altar in the distance, flanked by its magnificent candles. Behind them, the little pageboys in blue, and the two bridesmaids. And on every side, the cathedral banked high with flowers, carnations, gladioli, agapanthus.

South Africa had disposed of its royal family, and was largely starved of any sort of pageantry. This, then, was the substitute: and the Oppenheimers had not disappointed their public. It was a simple ceremony, with little pomp: no communion service, only the vows, hymns, prayers and the blessing. The register had to be signed, there were kisses of congratulation all round, and with the cathedral resounding with the wedding march Gordon and Mary set out on the long walk down the aisle to the crowd waiting outside. Now Mary was truly radiant: a beautiful bride, one of the most beautiful they could remember, and Gordon also in the best of moods with a grin from ear to ear and Mary so proud of him. They emerged into the daylight, and it was still raining. The crowd was better controlled now: at last the police had control, with a cordon of more than 50 of them linking arms and providing space enough for the couple to manoeuvre.

There was a heavy flow of traffic that afternoon, but the couple reached Brenthurst well ahead of the guests. Already a small army of security men was on guard, ready to repel the expected gatecrashers. The marquee was in position and the caterers ready with a whole regiment of waiters ready to move among the huge assembly of guests that would be coming. It took ninety minutes for them all to file through: Mary and Gordon shook hands with all of them, trying to say something special to each other. From time to time Gordon stopped a waiter to fill a glass of champagne for the two of them, and Mary had eventually to slip out of her shoes. But at last it was done and they hurried in.

The family disappeared eventually for a quiet dinner party in the main house, and Mary and Gordon went to change. They rejoined everyone in the marquee, and at last it was time to go. No-one knew where they were going on honeymoon: it was rumoured they would spend the first night on a farm near Pretoria. But all the guests trooped out on to the lawns up to where Gordon's new Maserati was parked. The ushers, in fact, carried him there on their shoulders, while Mary lobbed her bouquet into the eager crowd waiting to catch it.

They were not going to Pretoria that night. Instead they drove out to the airport. One newspaper had a team waiting there just in case, so they had to take evasive action and reach the tarmac by a back way. They were booked on a flight to Rome under the names 'Mr and Mrs Grant'. The plane took off, and they were on their way: a few days in Rome, the rest of the honeymoon in Beirut and the Lebanon, and then back to Johannesburg in time for Gordon to start his new career with E Oppenheimer and Son.

An amusing story going the rounds when it was all over was that this particular week-end all the hotels in the coastal resorts, Durban, East London, and Port Elizabeth were booked to capacity, filled with Johannesburg socialites who had not been invited to the wedding. This way they could explain they were 'out of town' while the wedding was on, so sadly could not attend.

3

FROM THE START of his chairmanship of Anglo Harry had been in the practice of making considerable donations to charity – through the various trust funds administered through the group or in his own personal capacity. Few of these made headlines, of course. Harry preferred it that way. But as is the way with newspapers, others were picked up and featured in depth out of all proportion to their real significance.

One story to catch public imagination, for instance, was the gift Harry made to Johannesburg in Ernest's memory. He commissioned a sculptor, Hermann Would, to design a special statue which would help relieve the sombre monotony of Johannesburg's functional architecture.

'Johannesburg certainly has developed into a great and imposing city,' said Harry when the statue was unveiled by the mayor. 'But in many ways it is rather forbidding. Its canyons of concrete tell us of hard work and success, but we want to have something visible of beauty and grace as well as the success and power of the industry on which this city is built. I believe this statue will bring back to us the wide sunlit spaces.'

The statue was immediately acclaimed a real inspiration. Would had conceived a trail of impala buck leaping over jets of water in a graceful arc that seemed to represent perpetual motion. 'A hundred years ago impala were running around here and now they are back to claim the ground,' he explained.

Harry received begging letters by the thousand. An interviewer asked Harry how he dealt with them.

'You assume that I'm bombarded, as you say, by every Tom, Dick and Harry and from every corner of the earth for money and charity and how do I deal with this? Well, obviously, there is a bit of that sort of thing, but it's mainly a question of serious thought as to the amount of money you can, or want, to give to charity – how best it can be used. But I do make a little bit of effort to touch up all this commonsense with a little bit of caprice, because I think that's a good thing.

'What I mean is, I think, in the main, you really want to analyse and, if you're going to spend money, to work out the best way to spend it. That is generally a question of some proper organisation or charity or institution you want to help. But it's fun also to exercise a little bit of "chancey" judgement in a rather more casual and less thoughtful way.'

There was a positive deluge of demands on Harry's resources as a result of one news item in particular: a story which placed him firmly among the ten richest men in the world, with the world's biggest fortune outside the United States. The business magazine *Fortune* had listed the top ten Americans – Paul Getty and Howard Hughes, the only dollar billionaires; then Dr Edwin Land (inventor of the Polaroid camera), H L Hunt the Texas oilman, Daniel Ludwig the shipping magnate, and Ailsa Mellon Bruce, Paul Mellon and Richard King Mellon of the banking family, all these above the 500 million dollar mark, and then a group of five on the 300 to 500 million dollar mark. The London *Times* calculated Harry's personal fortune must place him above the $500 million, so set him at least eighth on the list if not a lot higher.

'The Oppenheimer interests, however, are concealed under a wide spread of nominee holdings, as shown by the fact that only 56 000 Anglo American shares are actually listed in the chairman's name. A large part of his fortune is in Ernest Oppenheimer and Son, the family company set up before the Second World War, as a vehicle for investments.'

Harry's comment: 'I only wish it was true.' Or as he put it to the churchwarden of a church in Surrey, England, who wrote to him asking for help with the church's restoration fund and mentioned he had read the *Times* piece: 'I'm not as rich as that article made out, but would you consider it impertinent if I asked you to accept a cheque for £100?'

The Dean of Pretoria, the Very Rev Mark Nye, liked to recall the time he approached Harry with a request for help after the local health authorities had condemned a school's lavatory facilities. Someone suggested he should approach Harry, but at first he had been too alarmed. When his advisers persisted, he at last took his courage in his hands – and after ten minutes in Harry's office emerged 'with six fresh lavatories in my pocket'.

On a different level there was the story of the St Nicholas Home in Johannesburg, a hostel for Coloured boys over the age of nine who would otherwise have nowhere else to go. It was known many of them were professional beggars, sleeping rough overnight – much like the waifs and strays of London rescued by the famed Dr Thomas Barnardo in the last century. The two men behind the idea were given an option on an abandoned hospital building which would house the home, but with only hours to go before their fund-raising deadline were no-where in sight of their target.

It was then suggested they should approach Harry. Both went to see him at 44 Main Street, and found him sympathetic. When he had heard what they had to say, he asked how much they would need. They told him R45 000. He called his accountant in and asked how he was to make the donation. The accountant suggested he should give R20 000 from his personal account and give the rest as coming from Anglo.

But the best story of Harry's philanthropy is apocryphal. It tells of a group of men who approached him each year for funds for a particular worthy cause. Impressed with their persistence he offered to pay half their expenses for the next twelve months, provided they could find someone to pay the other half. A couple of days later they were back, telling him they had been successful. He asked if they would mind telling him who it was.

'Not at all,' one of them said. 'We're getting it from your wife.'

There is a clear pattern to Harry's giving. In particular, he has tended to pay great attention to education. Ernest made a number of sizeable grants to educational institutions and supported many needy students: but without any ulterior purpose. Harry, on the other hand, has seen education as a cultural weapon, which may be used to great effect if properly applied. His various trust funds have poured large sums into Southern Africa's private schools which are the English-speaking world's most effective bastion against Nationalist-controlled State education.

These private institutions are in most cases modelled on English public schools, and are in the direct tradition of the British colonial heritage. In most cases the Anglo American's contributions have been in the form of new science blocks or similar buildings. Besides helping the growth of an English-speaking institution the block encourages science in the school which in the long run benefits Anglo and its companies. But the thinking behind this is that the schools concerned must be supported: allow these to fall away, says Harry, and perhaps South Africa's last hope will be lost.

As with private education, Harry considered it important to arrange generous grants for universities, not only in South Africa but in other countries as well. Most of these grants stem from the Ernest Oppenheimer Memorial Trust and from the Chairman's Fund, and others Harry helps to finance out of his own pocket. Many of the universities have reciprocated by conferring on Harry honorary degrees to cement friendly relations between themselves and his mighty group.

The South African universities were first to honour him. In February 1963, the University of Natal made him a Doctor of Economics and a month later the University of the Witwatersrand made him a Doctor of Laws for services to South Africa as a 'great business leader and innovator'. Two years later it was the turn of a university in England, Leeds in Yorkshire. Harry had helped to establish a Research Institute in African Geology at the university and in return the Leeds Council decided to make him a Doctor of Laws.

The announcement at Leeds triggered a strong protest movement in that university's Students' Union Committee, which was dominated at the time by a number of confessed Marxists and communists. Harry, they decided, was not a 'proven opponent' of apartheid. They would boycott the ceremony at which he was to be honoured, and in fact protest against it taking place.

This move provoked widespread publicity – the more so as it was so palpably ridiculous. In fact, come the day of the ceremony many more students attended than might otherwise have come – and most members of the Students' Union committee were themselves present in their individual capacities. The only sign of any protest was of a group of some 200 anti-demonstrators, who paraded with banners reading 'Congratulations, Mr Oppenheimer, we are not the reds, we are the majority.'

What happened at Leeds set Harry thinking again about the hopelessly ill-informed views many of those outside South Africa had of conditions in the Republic. He invited the Students' Union to select a group of representatives to visit South Africa at Anglo's expense and see for themselves what was happening. It would be a visit just like those organised by the South Africa Foundation, giving them the chance to go where they wanted and meet who they wished, and allowing them to judge for themselves exactly what the South African problem was all about.

Two months later, with the dawn of the long vacation, the selected students duly arrived – four young men and a girl, and all in their early twenties. Harry arranged all sorts of trips for them, the length and breadth of the country, and a chance to meet a number of prominent South Africans. Their reactions at the end of it all were muddled: 'It is all so much more complicated than we imagined'.

Harry enjoyed his excursions into academic life. In fact, many have claimed that given the choice he might well have preferred to take it up full-time. This he has always denied vigorously, though he admits he enjoys it. Certainly, he was pleased when he was asked to stand as Chancellor of the University of Cape Town.

The chancellorship was a largely honorary affair. It involved little more than the responsibility of conferring the university's degrees at ceremonies held twice a year. UCT's first Chancellor had been the Prince of Wales, later the Duke of Windsor. He had been succeeded by General Smuts, and he by the former South African chief justice, Van de Sandt Centlivres, who had just died. Harry told those who had invited him that he would be delighted to step into the breach if the university's convocation wanted him.

What he had not expected was suddenly to find himself pitchforked into a full-scale election battle. Convocation at the university consisted of all its graduates, who of course numbered tens of thousands by now scattered through the world. Other groups within convocation had their own ideas of who should succeed to the chancellorship, and soon there was a number of names in circulation.

When it was known Harry was standing, there were suggestions this was some sort of Progressive Party subterfuge. A group of UP supporters announced it was putting up the name of Sir de Villiers Graaff. The Opposition leader said he had absolutely no intention of standing, so the UP supporters turned instead to a judge, Marius Diemont. When the name of the noted historian Leo Marquard was brought into the picture, it suggested to most people the small Liberal Party.

To their credit the candidates were really rather embarrassed about the whole thing, but there was no holding their supporters. Manifestos were drawn up and circulated to every UCT graduate whose address was available: even the voting was to be by post. Sponsors were found, support groups formed in each part of Southern Africa, letters were written to newspapers in every city and signed by long lists of backers. The election was of national significance. Allegations and counter-allegations made headline news; there was suspicion of intrigue in high places; lifelong friends found themselves barely on speaking terms now they supported opposing candidates.

At last it was time for the election, and the completed forms flooded in: a proportion of well over 50 per cent of old graduates were involved, which showed the extraordinarily high interest taken in the affair. When they were counted up it was found Harry emerged the winner, though the university council was not going to say by what majority. Trying to explain the result an Oppenheimer supporter said Diemont was the most conservative of the three, Marquard the most liberal. That left Harry in the middle – and the ideal compromise for all groups.

Harry was inducted soon after the election, and showed his delight in what he had to say in his inaugural address.

'Of all the honours – deserved and undeserved – that have come my way over the years, there has been nothing to compare with this. I know cynical people say that such distinctions are a sign that a man's capacity for useful work is over. About that time alone can tell. I can at least say that my own university – where I spent some shamefully idle years — has meant so much to me that I certainly shall not under-rate the responsibility of being the formal head and at times perhaps the spokesman of the great University of Cape Town.'

One of the problems confronting the university at this time was the government's restriction of academic freedom. Verwoerd had introduced segregation to higher education in 1959, and in the process deeply affected UCT where it had been traditional to accept students and academic staff no matter what their colour or creed. The university had already made its protest in the strongest terms, and in addressing Convocation on the occasion of the university's golden jubilee, Harry emphasised he was behind the stand.

'We will continue to struggle for this university's right to decide on purely academic grounds what to teach and how to teach it and who to admit to the university: whether to the student body or to the teaching staff. We claim this academic freedom not out of arrogance but because we are honestly and deeply convinced that without it we cannot give out best to the students, to the country and to mankind.'

Many a time in the months to come Harry used language like this to express his views on the university's behalf: and many a time he was attacked by the Nationalists for his continuing political activity. The university could hardly have wished for a stronger champion. He took his responsibilities seriously, and made a point of attending every degree day. In the years since his election he has capped thousands of UCT graduates, each kneeling before him as he smilingly congratulates them and a photographer catches the moment on film.

Among the first degrees he conferred was an honorary doctorate of science on Professor Chris Barnard, professor of surgical research at the UCT's medical school, after his historic successful heart transplant on Louis Washkansky in 1967. Later the university struck a special gold Medal of Merit for Chris Barnard in recognition of his achievements, and it was again Harry who presented it. More than that, he and the Chamber of Mines donated R1 million to the university towards the development of a special research unit specialising in heart disease.

Chris Barnard's rise to prominence prompted an inspired quip from a Nationalist, to the effect that South Africa was now dominated by four kings – Harry, the King of Diamonds; Chris Barnard, the King of Hearts; the golfer Gary Player, the King of Clubs; and Sir de Villiers Graaff, or Grave as it is in English, the King of Spades.

4

IN THESE years teams of prospectors from Anglo and De Beers had been at work all over the sub-continent searching for new deposits

402

of gold, diamonds, copper, platinum or indeed any other minerals or metals that might be worth exploiting. But hardly a worthwhile trace had they found: certainly nothing along the lines of a new diamond pipe or goldfield or platinum reef, which was what the group needed. Harry and his fellow directors were sure something would turn up: it was a balance of probabilities. But should they not rather let their gaze travel beyond Southern Africa's borders, out into the world at large? There were opportunities galore, especially in the newly developing territories, and they were allowing them to slip by while their rivals in the international markets pressed home their advantage.

Both Anglo and De Beers already held substantial interests in other countries, of course: but this was by accident more than design. In most instances they had acquired these outside interests to defend their position in Southern Africa. The Oppenheimers' thinking, both Ernest's and Harry's, had always been national rather than inter-national. Though content to hold these outside interests they had done little to develop their holdings, and certainly not to initiate new business in areas outside their own aegis.

That, Harry now decided, would have to change. Though Anglo was involving itself in South Africa's great boom in secondary industry as had been planned from the outset, that was not enough to prevent the great corporation from stagnating. Anglo and De Beers were mining houses, and needed new mining business. As a start, and initially purely as an exploratory measure, Harry moved into Canada: he bought a 14,5 per cent stake in a big Canadian corporation running a number of prospering lead, zinc and copper mines in the north, the Hudson Bay Mining and Smelting Company of Flin Flon, Manitoba, from the estate of the New York industrialist C V Whitney. This move proved successful and Anglo established an office in New York to handle this and future business. The resident director was soon made chairman and president of the Hudson Bay company.

The stake in Manitoba cost $20 million. In raising it Anglo en-countered difficulties over currency exchange, which served to emphasise Anglo's present disadvantage as regards international finance in being registered in South Africa. If the political situation and the Republic's continuing unpopularity were not obstacles enough in themselves, it seemed the Republic just was not able to provide the huge resources that would be necessary if Anglo was to move outside its accustomed spheres of operation. Harry decided to establish a strong international finance house in London, to operate in its own right but also to give Anglo a better window on the world. To do this, he first considered the old British South Africa Company, which was being forced to hand its considerable assets north of the Zambezi to Kaunda's government. To the old 'chartered' company he would add others which were better deployed together than as separate entities.

The two companies chosen for the merger with Charter were old friends: CMS and Central Mining. Each already held outside interests in abundance, and particularly in Canada which for the moment seemed the most promising field of development. CMS had been associated with British Columbia since before the turn of the century, and was now the largest shareholder in Baffinland Iron Mines which had uncovered vast deposits of base metals in the Arctic; Central Mining was a big shareholder in Western Decalta Petroleum, which gave it a commanding position in the Canadian gas and oil industries. Adding further strength to this, the BSAC had reinvested what it had recouped from Zambia in widespread ventures which included several mineral and metal ventures in Canada. Together the three companies held assets valued at R280 million.

A merger as big as this took considerable planning, of course, and was not done overnight. It took the best part of 18 months to get the scheme off the ground. But at last all was ready and the new corporation was registered with a name which recalled the original role of the BSAC, so close to Rhodes's heart: Charter Consolidated. The first chairman was Hugh Vivian-Smith, Harry's old friend from Oxford days, who had joined Anglo's London office from a firm of stockbrokers in the City a few years before; and the first managing director was Bill Wilson, from Johannesburg.

Paradoxically, though intended as an 'overseas' investment group the biggest share of Charter's revenue came from Southern Africa. CMS, the BSAC and Central Mining all had substantial stakes in Southern African enterprises: a major stake in Union Corp, big holdings in Selection Trust and Rio Tinto, interests in all sorts of South African companies ranging from Cape Asbestos to a handful of gold mines.

Even as Charter was being formed, Anglo and De Beers and their associated companies were expanding their holdings in Canada. The Baffinland iron deposits were looking particularly hopeful: prospecting teams had uncovered several outcrops, with the biggest of them a whole mountain of iron, a deposit 10 000 feet long and 350 feet thick, with the average iron content nearly 70 per cent which was almost the highest yet found in Canada and equal to the richest anywhere. The companies concerned intended to establish a large-scale iron industry in the Arctic, with the ore transported south in bulk carriers during the three-month Arctic shipping season.

Anglo had for some time held interests in a small copper mine at Whaleback, Newfoundland, in partnership with the British New-foundland Corporation; CMS had a long-standing stake in McIntyre Porcupine Mines Selection, the biggest mining investment concern in Canada and in control of the giant base-metal mining house Falcon-bridge; De Beers subsidiaries had long manufactured the Canadian mining industry's carbide drilling bits and other components; and Central Mining and other group companies held great influence in the Canadian gas and oil industry.

The development which caught local imagination most effectively, however, and which seemed to symbolise Harry's move into Canada more than any other factor, was a top secret search for diamond pipes in Northern Ontario, just south of James Bay. Long before this Harry had said: 'I like Canada and I like the people here. That is why I am looking for more business opportunities in this country. We are prepared to look into any worthwhile mining proposition.' This, then, was it. Diamonds had been found in Siberia, so surely there was no reason why there should not be diamond pipes in Canada's sub-arctic too. When diamonds turned up in Wisconsin, it was suggested they must have come from pipes in the great plateau which separated the prairielands from Hudson Bay: hence the present search. Quantities of ground were sent to South Africa for analysis, but sadly nothing was uncovered.

Anglo, De Beers and now Charter were evidently in Canada to stay, and in accordance with the familiar pattern Harry upgraded the group office in New York to become a full-scale affiliate, the Anglo American Corporation of Canada, taking over all the group's assets in exchange for shares. Soon AMCAN was initiating business on its own account, increasing the holding in Hudson Bay Mining and Smelting up to 28 per cent; buying up 40 per cent of Francana Development with its interests in natural resources, bulk trucking and industrial ventures; and taking 26,2 per cent of White Pass and Yukon Corporation with its ship-truck-train transport service between Vancouver and the Yukon territory.

Meanwhile, Anglo was looking at possibilities halfway round the world again: this time in Australia. Like Canada, Australia was ideal territory for Anglo group involvement, for both had so much in common with South Africa. For more than a century the three had acted as the elder sisters of the British Empire and then the Commonwealth, helping Mother England nurse the fledgling developing nations towards the time they could safely leave the nest. The three had quarrelled; in fact to carry the metaphor further they had seemed sometimes not to be on speaking terms, deliberately ignoring each other's presence in the world. Those who lived in Australia were entirely ignorant of Canada and would not have dreamt of taking any interest in South Africa, and so it went on round the circle. It was as if the three were in competition for Britain's favours, and could not afford to yield an inch to the others if they were to hold their own.

Now, however, things were different. The trio had come of age, and realised they were not so incompatible after all but could safely co-operate: in fact, it would be in their interests to do this. There was a great increase in trade between them; the respective populations at last recognised each other's existence, even if their politicians remained largely aloof. From South Africa's point of view, it seemed ideally appropriate that the chief initiative in making approaches to the other territories should be made by Harry, whom so many in both Australia and Canada, and in many other countries too, regarded as the Republic's uncrowned king.

Harry made a great hit when he first visited Australia. The Sydney papers dubbed him 'Happy Harry' after interviewing him about his wealth. He told them he was happy with his wife, his family and his work. He was happy living in South Africa, which was 'a lot happier than people believe'. He was happy to be in Australia, where he had never met such confidence in such a short space of time. But perhaps he was happiest feeling he was achieving more than making millions out of South Africa. 'You know, it can be extremely satisfying to be continually giving the Government situations they have to contend with.'

Anglo was rather a late-comer in the Australian mining world in comparison with other big corporations already active. As a Melbourne paper put it: 'A major Oppenheimer arrival is about the only thing the Australian mining boom is short of.' But now he was there Harry and his men looked keenly for likely investment opportunities: a vehicle to carry their interests and help Anglo and Charter find their feet. The choice eventually settled on Mount Morgan of Queensland, a mining company producing copper, gold, iron and silver. At first Anglo took a 40 per cent interest in the consortium, but later bid for absolute control. At the same time Charter was negotiating for business too: with Rothschilds of London it took a 30 per cent interest in International Pacific Corporation, a Sydney merchant bank; and with Union

406

Minière in a new partnership looking for nickel in tune with the great share bubble in which so many Australian and overseas investors lost all they had put in, before the market at last settled down. On other fronts group companies were looking for tin under the sea off Tasmania, searching for more gold in the old fields of Ballarat in Victoria and prospecting for base metals like tin and copper in Western Australia. As Harry put it: 'Australia is a first class place to look for minerals, and if we find anything we will invest on a very large scale.'

Meanwhile, Anglo's feelers were reaching beyond the usual sphere of influence: for instance, to Malaysia, which held the world's largest resources of tin. Here Charter bought its way into two producing companies, Tronoh Mines and Bidor Malaya Tin Sendirian Berhad, each with several associates, and a mine management company too, Associated Mines (Malaya) Sendirian Berhad. At the other end of the world, Charter was buying a big interest in Beralt Tin and Wolfram Limited, producing wolfram at Panasqueia in Portugal. In conjunction with ICI it was floating a huge potash mine in Yorkshire, Cleveland Potash, which was expected to produce so much that Britain could export the surplus when before she had been obliged to import.

Charter was looking into black Africa too. Harry was already established in the copperbelt, safely enough: though further north the new republic of Tanzania – Tanganyika plus Zanzibar, united since 1964 – had not been so well disposed. In one visit to Dar es Salaam Harry had announced De Beers and Anglo were extending their prospecting activities in the territory, looking not for diamonds alone but for gold, copper and other minerals too.

De Beers continued to run Mwadui in partnership with the government: but in some ways the partnership was uneasy. The *Nationalist*, Tanzania's leading newspaper, and with several cabinet ministers on its board, attacked Harry fiercely. How could Tanzania boycott South Africa 'if we are in partnership with the South African corporation openly supporting apartheid?' Harry had claimed the trade boycott finding favour among other African countries and states further afield would make no difference to South Africa, though he himself would like to see a change. 'These words can only come from a hypocrite and a traitor to the cause of African liberation.' Fortunately Julius Nyerere, Tanzania's President, took a more reasonable view and the South African companies were given full rein in his country: it was to the advantage of both sides.

The next step forward in black Africa came when Anglo researchers developed a revolutionary new means of processing copper ore by means of chemical reaction at ultra high temperatures. It was known as TORCO, for treatment of refactory copper ores, and proved so successful with low-grade deposits that Zambian Anglo American found it was worth re-opening the old Bwana Mkubwa mine, which had been closed since 1931. Within a few months of the announcement the French Government approached Charter with a request: would it be prepared to come in and open copper deposits discovered in Mauretania, a former French colony now independent but very poor, and on the edge of the Sahara Desert?

The news of the Mauretanian copper deposits was nothing fresh: they had been discovered long before. But it had never been economic to exploit them: American, Canadian and French firms had tried to make the mine a workable proposition but failed. With TORCO however there was a chance of success. It was eventually agreed Charter would come in as major backer of the project with the controlling interest.

There was one area in which Harry's involvement had not prospered: perhaps deliberately in view of Ernest's feelings, Anglo had never established a bridgehead in America. Even the initial office in New York was to cater for interests in Canada. The 'American' in Anglo's name had been practically superfluous since the twenties when Morgans had sold its holdings. Harry, however, was less prejudiced against the United States than Ernest: or rather, not so wary of involvement. If an investment opportunity presented itself – as had already happened with groups like CMS and Central Mining – he would not let it pass.

The chance came with a remarkable friendship that sprang up between Harry and the American metals king Charles Engelhard, who so far involved himself in South Africa that he settled in Johannesburg in the fifties and set himself up as a latterday Randlord. He bought himself into the chairmanship of Rand Mines on the break-up of the Corner House group, and joined Harry in the consortium that helped block the take-over of Central Mining. He and Harry got on like a house on fire from the time they first met, and it was not long before Harry began investing large sums in Rand Mines to the account of Anglo and Charter and preparing to co-operate with Engelhard in a number of joint ventures.

The American had a colourful background. His father had emigrated from Germany and established the Engelhard Metals and Minerals Corporation in the America of the 1890s, dealing exclusively in the noble metals. His son first visited South Africa in the late 1940s, looking for a way to import gold direct to America without having to go through the complicated rigmarole of international exchange. At this time there was a blanket ban on doing this through the South African Reserve Bank, so to export gold in the form of bars was out of the question. It was, however, permissible to export gold *objets d'art* and jewellery made in South Africa. Engelhard promptly registered a new company, Precious Metals Development, and established a works making up jewellery which he exported to Hong Kong and melted into gold bars once again.

This bright idea was thought up by the Engelhard's financial advisers in London, Robert Fleming and Company. Through this firm Engelhard met Ian Fleming – long before the then naval officer made his name from the James Bond books. The two took to each other immediately, and theirs was a lifelong friendship. Fleming later used the gold smuggling idea in *Goldfinger* – and based the arch-villain on his friend. Curiously, Engelhard's one business failure came when he went into partnership with Ian Fleming to develop timber estates on the banks of the Zambezi. Fleming's idea was to float the logs down to the railhead, Oregon style. Sadly, he had not realised that in the tree-felling season the upper reaches of the Zambezi are not co-operative. When the two men tried to salvage their investment and grow vegetables instead they met with an even greater problem: the whole crop was eaten by hippos.

Precious Metals Development encouraged Engelhard to look for further investments in South Africa, and he found the pickings rich. After all, he was principally interested in the noble metals, gold and platinum – and particularly the latter. Until now platinum had been used almost exclusively in jewellery, but now Engelhard Minerals established a first-class platinum research wing which was to discover ways the metal might be used in industry. It was through the wing's great achievements that Engelhard came to be known as the Platinum King. Gradually the $14 million company he had inherited from his father expanded into a gigantic corporation whose influence extended over six continents. At home in America he became one of the key figures in the Democratic Party and was a close friend of both President Kennedy and President Johnson. He represented Kennedy at independence celebrations in Gabon, Algeria and Zambia, and at Pope Paul's coronation in 1963.

His own holdings in Engelhard Minerals were in the hands of a private company called Engelhard Hanovia, which operated along the lines of Oppenheimer and Son. Its most significant asset was 44 per cent in Engelhard Minerals, which amounted to a controlling interest.

409

Engelhard decided he wanted to sell, and turned to Harry. He was already on Anglo's board in his own capacity, as an executive director. But it came as a great surprise: commentators could not understand why he chose to sell at a time when platinum's future looked brighter than ever before, thanks to the moves in America towards pollution control. Environmentalists were calling for the petroleum industry to produce only unleaded gasoline, which meant using platinum as a catalyst in the refining process and in pollution-controlling devices in cars and trucks.

The passing of control was only technical: Engelhard remained EMC's chairman and chief executive, and still held a big block of stock. The advantage for EMC was that its entry into Anglo's group made it easier to negotiate access to the raw materials on which EMC depended. For Engelhard, there was no future in Engelhard Hanovia. The tragedy of his life was that in spite of all his beautiful homes around the world, 250 racehorses in different countries, a fleet of private aircraft, companies operating in every corner of the globe and personal assets valued in hundreds of millions of dollars, he had no heir. His wife and he had produced five offspring, but they were all daughters.

Fixed Bayonets

K EN ANDERSON asked Harry if he had any preference between gold and diamonds. 'Yes, diamonds every time,' Harry replied. 'I think people buy diamonds out of vanity and they buy gold because they're too stupid to think of any other monetary system which will work – and I think vanity is probably a more attractive motive than stupidity.' He gave the same answer some years later when two interviewers were asking which side of his business he found most interesting: 'I find them attractive both from the point of business problems involved and also for the diamonds themselves. They were actually the first facet of the business which I learnt about when I returned from my studies in England.'

The situation had changed drastically since those days, of course. No longer were diamonds the virtually exclusive preserve of Southern and Central Africa, for they were now found in greater or lesser quantities all over the world and there was always the possibility of further new discoveries. Yet in spite of occasional difficulties the Central Selling Organisation had retained its overwhelming grip of the trade in the interests of all – something nobody would have dared predict had the full facts been known in advance. World confidence in diamonds had escalated out of all proportion, and prices were climbing steadily. In the mid-thirties De Beers' annual sales were worth about $15 million: by the late sixties they were worth getting on for $700 million.

On the other hand, these years had seen great improvements in production techniques which were presenting the Central Selling Organisation with 10 per cent more stones than it would have bargained for under normal conditions. So far this rise in production had been accommodated by the extraordinary climb in sales since the end of the war. But there were sure signs that it was flattening out; and Harry knew there would soon be an embarrassing surplus if he did not make efforts to combat it. The answer, he decided, was to advertise.

This was nothing new for De Beers. In the early days diamonds had virtually sold themselves, and there had been no need to try and persuade people to buy them. But the Depression had dealt the whole industry a body blow, and in the mid-thirties Ernest had realised De Beers would have to advertise widely to restore confidence in diamonds. He made this Harry's job, and Harry decided that America was his best bet: the United States absorbed more than half De Beers' production at this stage. He went off to New York to reconnoitre the position, and appointed the well-known advertising agency N W Ayer and Son as De Beers' representatives. They came up with the prestige advertising campaign 'A Diamond is Forever', a slogan based on the remark attributed to Solly Joel.

In the years that had passed since then De Beers had spent a fortune on advertising: a deliberate 'soft-sell' campaign to establish the diamond as the eternal symbol of love. The effort spread from America to Europe, with a new angle: a bid to show that diamonds were not necessarily the preserve of the rich; that the man in the street could buy them too. The most important market, not surprisingly, was the engagement ring; and in America at least it was calculated that eight girls out of every ten insisted on a diamond to mark the occasion. Now De Beers turned their attentions much further afield – even to countries like West Germany and Japan where the idea of diamond gifts to mark a betrothal was completely alien.

At the other end of the scale De Beers was working hard to protect its production monopoly. Harry negotiated the take-over of the companies mining the seabed off the South West Diamond Coast, Marine Diamonds and Sea Diamonds. They had not been as successful as hoped, for the stones they produced were rather small when the market was short of larger diamonds. But it was worth bringing them into the fold while it was possible. The market was sure to change. There was a period of difficulty with Selection Trust in West Africa, where Chester Beatty's son – another Chester Beatty – decided he would do better to sell his production direct to Harry Winston in New York rather than to the CSO. In the same way Philip Oppenheimer was presented with serious problems when the Russian producers cancelled their agreements with the CSO in response to political pressure. But in the end all these difficulties were resolved, and the monopoly was more secure than ever.

In South Africa, there was a lucky windfall when two asbestos prospectors, Alexander Fincham and Ernest Schwabel, stumbled on deposits of garnets near Postmasburg, about 130 miles from Kimberley. Such deposits were usually a sign that diamonds were not far away. As they dug more pits in their search for asbestos they kept coming across more garnets, until they found they had delineated the area of what might be a colossal diamond pipe. Besides, the vegetation within the area seemed much denser than what surrounded it which suggested the presence of water trapped in kimberlite: another tell-tale sign. The two partners quickly abandoned all idea of asbestos and took out a permit to prospect for precious stones. When it looked as if their venture would succeed the two founded a company, Finsch Diamonds, and began digging in earnest. Each pit they sank brought up more diamonds, and when Fincham installed mechanised equipment the new mine's yield reached 50 carats a day. The discovery was of importance: the first major diamond pipe to be developed in South Africa since the Premier in 1903 and not far short of it in size.

De Beers had been watching all this closely, and now volunteered to prospect the pipe down to 200 feet. The results were staggering. De Beers offered to buy out the entire share capital of the mine for £2¼ million, most of which went to Fincham as he had already bought out the greater part of Schwabel's interests. Within a short time De Beers developed the Finsch Mine to the point where it produced 2 million carats a year, a quarter of them gem quality.

The Finsch discovery was important because it was in the tradition of the great discoveries of the old days. There had been depressingly few of them in recent years. Like the other mining houses Harry's companies had been prospecting intensively for years. Union Corp had uncovered new goldfields far east of the Rand at Evander and Rio Tinto was developing vast base metal deposits at Palabora. But Anglo teams had had no such luck. Several new gold mines had been opened, adjoining those already developed; there were new stakes in coal, manganese, asbestos and base metals; but these were as nothing compared with the great coups of years gone by.

Instead the corporation's prospectors were moving further afield: in particular to the old High Commission territories which formed little pockets of black rule in the white south. Before the war Hertzog's Nationalists had had every intention of incorporating Bechuanaland, Basutoland and Swaziland within a greater South Africa – and possibly the Rhodesias too. Indeed this was in the context of Rhodes's original conception of the sub-continent's future. After the war the original blueprint for apartheid mentioned the three territories as potential homelands, and cited the great emptiness of Bechuanaland as a territory which would provide Southern Africa's native peoples with adequate land of their own.

The High Commission territories had stood firm, however, particularly through the personal interventions of their leaders and of these most notably Tshekedi Khama of Bechuanaland. All three were desperately poor, but at least had the advantage of a customs union with South Africa which dated back to the years after World War I – in fact the first in Africa. Through this they were sometimes described as 'South Africa's economic hostages', and for their income relied largely on the money their menfolk earned as migrant labourers in South Africa's mines. But politically they stayed aloof, until Britain granted them independence: to Bechuanaland and Basutoland – renamed Botswana and Lesotho – in 1966; and to Swaziland in 1968.

Not Anglo alone, but several other companies were showing interest in these territories. It was not long before they began reaping rich rewards. The first important discoveries were in Lesotho, or Basutoland as it still was. They came through an old friend: Jack Scott, who had been instrumental in setting Anglo on the path to success on the Klerksdorp gold field and in the Free State. Now he had turned his attentions from gold to diamonds, and the extensive fields in the remote mountain strongholds of Northern Lesotho. There were diamonds in plenty, but they were so hard to get at that South Africans had preferred to leave them to lone Sotho prospectors. Now Jack Scott secured a concession to prospect the whole area properly, and came to light with a number of kimberlite pipes. De Beers prepared to go into business with him.

In Swaziland, Anglo's involvement dates from 1958 when Harry formed the Swaziland Iron Ore Development Company to exploit iron deposits turned up in the course of a government survey. There is evidence that there had been copper workings in the Ngwenya mountains as early as 42 250 BC, which makes them far and away the most ancient mine workings on earth. Anglo brought in a leading British steel firm to give technical advice on iron ore mining, then set about an intensive prospecting programme which more than justified expectations. The Hugo Neu Corporation, a New York dealer in iron ore, negotiated an arrangement between SIODC and two Japanese iron and steel corporations, by which SIODC was to provide them with 12 million tons of iron ore over the next ten years.

There were huge problems, of course. Apart from the inaccessibility of the mine itself, Swaziland had no rail link with the sea. The nearest line was four miles over the Swaziland border in Mozambique, linking up with Lourenco Marques. But it was not difficult to raise the necescary cash between SIODC itself, Anglo, the Swaziland government and the Commonwealth Development Corporation. The railway took 27 months to build at a cost of R16,8 million. The Portuguese extended their line to meet the Swazi Railway at the border, and undertook to run the trains. Besides this, they built special deep-sea berths at Lourenco Marques to cope with the newly commissioned bulk freighters which would carry the ore. Two of them were named for Anglo directors: *Marshall Clark* and *Sydney Spiro*.

Botswana holds rather an anomalous position in Southern Africa, a great island of territory completely surrounded by white regimes but for the 'point of a needle' in the Limpopo River which marks the common boundaries of Botswana, South West Africa, Rhodesia and Zambia. This tiny contact is enough to preserve Botswana's lifeline with the black north, and to an ever increasing extent Botswana is emerging as a political force of importance. Though the hills of South Africa are easily visible from the capital, there is no direct diplomatic contact between Gaberone and Pretoria. Besides, from being the country with the lowest per capita income in all Africa – after all, most of it is Kalahari desert – Botswana has made rapid strides towards becoming a country of appreciable wealth.

Not the least reason for the change in Botswana's fortunes has been the activities of Harry's great corporations – Anglo, Charter and De Beers. Years of intense prospecting turned up mineral deposits of extraordinary significance, including a huge copper-nickel deposit in north-eastern Botswana, at Selebi-Pikwe. Anglo and Charter have a big stake in its management, shared with American Metal Climax and the Botswana government. But even more important has been the textbook discovery of the world's biggest diamond pipe after Mwadui, the Orapa mine near Francistown. De Beers geologists uncovered the pipe through an exhaustive survey which has shown indications of other rich pipes on the Kimberley pattern.

At the opening of the Orapa mine Harry made a special plea to the Botswana government, more particularly to President Seretse Khama, in view of the pressures from the black north. 'In all we are doing here I am assuming the Government, for its part, will continue to follow a policy which will allow as to make a real contribution to the country's welfare in such a way that we can also earn fair profits for our shareholders which are commensurate with the risks that are involved.' In other words, he hoped Seretse Khama had no plans to seize the kind of stakes in the new operations that African leaders were demanding elsewhere in the continent.

On another level, Harry was deeply committed to the new independent states in a personal capacity. For one thing, he presented an arts block to the university college which the three established: Oppenheimer Hall, on the campus at Maseru in Lesotho.

Next he transformed a volunteer medical service operating in Swaziland into a fully equipped Flying Doctor operation. For some time a group of Johannesburg specialists had been driving down to Mbabane every second or third week to carry out mercy operations at local hospitals. It was a 500 mile round trip on less than adequate roads, and a good deal of precious time was wasted in negotiating them. Besides, Swaziland's medical facilities were rather primitive: a volunteer physiotherapist had to construct her own crutches and devise wheelchairs from bicycle parts. Harry stepped in with funds and his own private aircraft to fly the specialists to and from Swaziland every second week-end. They were soon dubbed 'Harry's Angels'.

Most of the specialists who served the scheme were in private practice, though others held resident posts at South African hospitals. Different surgeons would make up the team on each visit, but as a general rule each group included a general surgeon, orthopaedic surgeon, anaesthetist and ophthalmologist, and often a plastic surgeon. On occasions they would take with them a gynaecologist, paediatrician, urologist, neuro-surgeon, thoracic surgeon, dermatologist or ear-nose-and-throat specialist. All gave their time and services absolutely free.

As the word of the service spread to the remote Swaziland countryside the week-end Angels found themselves beseiged by would-be patients. Their reputations as healers soon overcame even the deepest tribal prejudices, and witchdoctors were prepared to 'clear' their patients so that they could attend the clinics. Before long the specialists began operating not in Mbabane alone, but also at Hlalputi hospital 200 miles away, to give tribesmen in remote areas the chance to profit from the service.

As a South African venture, Harry's Angels incurred the displeasure of the Organisation of African Unity, as did a similar service in Lesotho which was backed by Anton Rupert, head of the multi-million Rembrandt tobacco organisation with interests in 70 countries and the first Afrikaner to make his mark in international big business. Harry's Angels wanted to visit Botswana too, where the need was every bit as desperate. But here they were rebuffed with polite refusal: the OAU's pressures were having effect.

In Rhodesia, Harry's interests were not as great as they might have been: little more than the great Wankie coal mine, the estates near Bulawayo which included Shangani, and citrus estates in the Mazoe Valley north of Salisbury. There was an iron pyrites mine at Iron Duke near Salisbury, but that was all until in 1966 Anglo bought 85 per cent of the old Trojan Nickel Mine in the Bindura district. Nickel was in demand all over the world, and Anglo was planning a full-scale nickel smelting and refining works at Bindura to handle production from the Trojan mine, which was to be greatly expanded, and from another mine Anglo now bought: Madziwa in the Shamwa district. To hold the whole operation together Harry formed a new company, the Rhodesia Nickel Corporation. Before the operation came into production new shafts had to be sunk with houses and offices erected and, of course, the refinery brought into being. In all it cost more than \$23 million, but it was expected to net Rhodesia \$12 million a year in foreign exchange.

These developments were not likely to win the approval of President Kenneth Kaunda, watching from beyond the Zambezi. Since UDI he had been Rhodesia's sternest opponent, prepared even to close the border between the countries and therefore his chief rail link with the sea. Harry had at least persuaded him to reconsider that move: to maintain his stand would have brought Zambia to bankruptcy. But now Harry was overtly supporting the rebel regime, and Kaunda took a dim view indeed. His Minister of Mines and Lands went so far as to say Anglo's investment was 'an act of faith in the Rhodesian government' and 'was bound to have repercussions here'. More than that, Harry had 'seriously prejudiced the position of the company in Zambia'.

That, of course, had been a possibility ever since UDI underlined the rift between black north and white south. Indeed, it was inevitable that it would happen one day: Zambia could not afford to leave one of Africa's richest assets under foreign control, especially when it represented almost the country's single means of earning foreign reserves. Besides, to Kaunda and most of his colleagues the mining companies represented white power, no matter how great the efforts they made to 'Zambianise' their workings both underground and on the surface, and introduce Zambian participation at every level. For the time, however, it looked as if the mines were safe. As the President told a party congress: 'The mines are big business and too big for us – so we let them alone, though we control their profits'. Against that the

417

Congo's President Mobutu had successfully nationalised the copper mines of Katanga in 1967, and even more recently the new regime in Chile had carried through similar measures.

Significantly, Kaunda was already forecasting major conflict in the area. 'My fear is that the South African struggle will become both racial and ideological and be worse than Vietnam which is only an ideological conflict.' He was also warning western states that unless they ended white rule in Southern Africa, the black states would be obliged to turn to the communists for help. Already the Chinese were preparing to move in and build a rail link from Zambia to the sea at Dar es Salaam, the Tan-Zam Railway: this way Zambia would be able to by-pass the white-ruled Angola, Rhodesia and Mozambique on which she relied so heavily. Besides this 'hundreds' of Africans were leaving the white states in the south for China, to train as 'freedom fighters'. This trend was going to grow, said Kaunda, and the number involved would swell to thousands.

It was all powerful material, and not surprisingly Kaunda soon won himself a reputation as a leading champion of all black Africa, along-side President Julius Nyerere of Tanzania. Along Zambia's borders sprang up camps run by various guerilla organisations pledged to bring down white rule in the territories to the south. The situation left Harry walking a political tightrope across the Zambezi, with his various companies organised according to quite different principles than those employed in South Africa and Rhodesia. As Ernest had realised so long before, the river marked the boundary between two distinct systems. It was an extraordinary position to be in, and when it looked as if he was going to survive it his critics unsympathetically dubbed him 'multi-facial'. In the circumstances this was a compliment.

Of course the external threat was not nearly as dangerous as Kaunda made out. He was decrying the 'White South' in much the way South African Nationalists have liked to introduce 'Hoggenheimer' and latterly 'communists' to their lists of excuses: fine scapegoats for whatever goes wrong within the framework of their policies. In Kaunda's case, he was finding himself increasingly menaced by inter-tribal rivalries in Zambia itself: particularly by the old differences between the Bembas of the copperbelt who were the chief support of his ruling United National Independence Party, and the Lozis of the west who were turning to the opposition African National Congress in ever increasing numbers. The rivalries had been suspended during the years of white administration, but now that Zambians were in charge once again it looked as if they might re-emerge. Even within UNIP Lozis

418

were calling for a show-down with the copperbelt Bembas who seemed to be travelling a road of their own.

Kaunda himself was above the level of these tribal bickerings, which was what made him an ideal President. Though born and brought up in the north, his parents were immigrants from Malawi. Interestingly, he had been at school with the man who was now his Vice-President, Simon Kapwepwe, most powerful of the Bemba politicians and to Kaunda the most dangerous though throughout their career to date they had been loyal to one another. Years before they had joined the army together, only to be summarily thrown out the next day for showing political tendencies. In the years of their rise to power in the early sixties they had seemed inseparable. Kapwepwe had been the ideal foil to the popular Kaunda: he was mysterious, tough and rather sinister. It was he who had summed up the impotence of the old colonial powers when he dismissed Britain as 'a toothless bulldog'. Now he was playing a game of his own, which looked suspiciously like a bid for the top seat.

Kaunda was fighting for the political survival not of his party alone but of all Zambia, and he used every trick up his sleeve. Looking for a revival of national feeling he created a state-owned Industrial Development Corporation, and 'invited' 25 lesser foreign-owned businesses to hand it 51 per cent of their shareholdings. It was an offer they could hardly refuse, and all but one complied: Indeco started life with control of businesses worth R160 million a year. The move was greeted with great glee in Zambia: the white man had dominated the country long enough. But the euphoria was shortlived. In a shock move which seemed to indicate the shape of things to come, Zambia's white chief justice resigned and fled the country.

A month later there was a national council of the UNIP, which promised to produce the showdown so long threatened. Lozi delegates had drawn up a number of resolutions proposing votes of no confidence in various leaders of the Bemba factions, including Kapwepwe. Had these been allowed to go forward it was possible the northerners would have been frozen out of the party, or would have voluntarily walked out. They would have taken a great many blood supporters with them, and that would mean Zambia's being split down the middle, and perhaps even a revival of the tribal wars which had been interrupted 70 years before when Rhodes and his Charter Company arrived. The scene was set for the kind of bloody chaos and anarchy which had so bedevilled the once prosperous Congo across the border.

Kaunda was facing what looked like his biggest challenge yet. To meet it, he produced his ace. Flanked on the platform by the Prime Minister of Swaziland and the second Vice-President of Tanzania, and with the superb sense of timing that has established him as one of the leaders of the Third World, he skilfully diverted all the feeling that existed between rival tribesmen to the foreign interests which held Zambia's precious mineral rights: handed over to Rhodes's men for a few muzzle-loaders, some beads and calico, and always such a sore point in the Zambian mind.

'We have been trying since independence to negotiate with the holders to purchase back these concessions in the interests of the nation. We were faced with demands for amounts of as much as 500 000 Kwacha for some of them. In the interests of the nation . . . I hereby announce that I shall cancel all these concessions.'

Kaunda was always a great orator, and never more effective than now. Those critics of both sides who had seemed to suggest he was 'going soft on Africanism' listened in wonder as he told them: 'I do not think the nation can achieve economic independence without acquiring full control of the existing mines.' And as his words sunk in, the assembly broke into wild scenes of jubilation and tumultuous applause.

'I have recently decided to ask the owners of the mines to invite the Government to join their mining enterprises,' he went on when it was quiet again. 'I am asking the owners of the mines to give 51 per cent of their shares to the State.' And again there was riotous cheering: never had Zambia heard news so exciting.

Kaunda had stamina as a speaker: the present speech lasted five hours. Point by point he explained his proposals. He was not being unfair, he said. He was giving existing mining companies the 'opportunity to prepare plans for mining development for areas which they have already explored where they have located minerals. I am also giving them the opportunity to complete their investigation in areas where they are carrying out prospecting now and to prepare programmes for mining development if they locate mineral deposits. But they will have to surrender, immediately Parliament passes the necessary legislation, all other areas which they hold in perpetuity for ever and ever.'

It was not to be a straight forced take-over. Kaunda was ready to make reparation for the government's new stake. 'I intend to leave it to Indeco to negotiate the terms and value of payment, but it will be a fair value represented by book value. At the same time, I want to make it clear that the Government has no money to pay as a deposit

420

against these shares. It also cannot afford to release part of the mineral tax or income tax in payment. Revenue from tax is badly needed for our development programme. Indeco, therefore, will have to negotiate payment out of future dividends, bearing in mind the advantages shareholders will derive from associating with the State.'

Item by item he spelt out his proposals, as the delegates listened breathless. Those 'perpetual' rights granted by Rhodes were now buried. Instead they were now vested in the state once again: companies would lease their concessions for 25 years at a time. They would be taxed more, and so would all those in the higher income bracket: mostly whites, of course.

There, in all the magic of it, was the answer to Zambia's problem. Kaunda had waved his wand and it was all as easy as winking. Apart from the foreign businesses taken over the year before, now Indeco could control a copper industry bigger than any in the western world besides those in the United States and Chile, and worth R780 million a year. It was to become the biggest industrial power in black Africa after Nigeria. No wonder the starry-eyed delegates readily agreed to the proposal that the council should immediately break up, so that they could return to their constituencies and prepare for the gruelling elections ahead. Kaunda had lived to fight again another day.

'It is important at this trying time that you leaders be with our followers in order to frustrate any attempt to sabotage our march to independence by foreign and domestic ill-wishers.'

Still worried by the threat of serious dissent within his party and within Zambia, Kaunda moved troops to strategic points all over the country. He justified the moves in terms of his economic measures. 'We are virtually at war with powerful vested interests in South Africa, Britain and the United States,' he said. 'This is a time of national danger.'

The UNIP delegates were not the only parties caught on the hop by the surprise announcement. To the mining companies it came as a bombshell: they had received not a whisper of warning. As regards Zambian Anglo American the wires were soon buzzing with questions and counter-questions, but there could be precious few answers. The day following Kaunda's announcement was a national holiday in Zambia, and everything was closed down. The companies would have to take careful stock of their position.

That, in fact, was the way things remained for some days more. Gavin Relly, Zamanglo's managing director, flew to Johannesburg for top-level discussions with Harry, while RST's men consulted with the great American Metal Climax which held 70 per cent control in Anglo's competitor. But there was nothing to be done beyond negotiating the terms of the nationalisation: it was a *fait accompli*, as everybody admitted.

In analysing the results of the takeover financial commentators concluded there was minimal practical benefit to Kaunda: he was gaining very little in new revenue, as the government was already commandeering a huge share of the copperbelt's profits. On the other hand, he was scaring off potential foreign investors which Zambia badly needed: how could they afford to tolerate such high-handed methods? On balance, the commentators said, it seemed a high price to pay for a matter of national pride: if Kaunda and his Indeco wore anything but a velvet glove in their negotiations with the mining companies they stood in grave danger of killing off the goose that laid the copper eggs.

Both Roan Selection and Anglo decided there was nothing to be gained by complaining about Kaunda's action. It was some time before they made any statement on their position, and even then it was only to say that before anything was agreed, there would necessarily be long and complex negotiations which might involve the restructuring of their companies in Zambia. The first important reaction to the move came from the chairman of Amax, which had only recently faced similar problems with two of its mines in Chile: 'Now that the Zambian Government has made its decision to negotiate the purchase of a controlling interest in the Zambian copper industry, we at Amax will support every effort on Roan's part to implement that decision in a manner which will meet the objectives of the Zambian Government and at the same time respect the ownership rights of the private shareholders.'

Anglo's reaction came shortly afterwards, and was similarly cautious: 'Your directors have in the past advocated the principle of Government participation in the share capital of the mining companies. The main issues which arise from His Excellency's request are, first, the establishment of equitable values and payment arrangements, in respect of Government participation and, secondly, in view of the Government's wish to hold a majority position in the companies, the negotiation of a suitable agreement which will ensure the continued operation of the mines on the present efficient basis.'

Negotiations took some three months, and internal reorganisation took the corporations rather longer. As they affected Anglo, the first step was to merge the interests of Bancroft, Nchanga, Rhokana and Broken Hill as well as Rhokana Refinery within Bancroft Mines, which then changed its name to Nchanga Consolidated Copper Mines Limited with the old producers known respectively as the Konkola, Chingola, Rhokana and Broken Hill divisions, each largely autonomous. The Roan group was similarly reorganised, to become Roan Consolidated Mines Limited. In each case 51 per cent in the new corporations went to the new ZIMCO, or Zambia Industrial Mining Corporation, later renamed Mindeco for Mining Development Company. The remaining 49 per cent in Nchanga went to Zambia Copper Investments, a new holding company formed by Anglo and registered in Bermuda which was also given 12,25 per cent in Roan Consolidated. The point of registering the company in Bermuda was, of course, that most of the shareholders in ZCI – notably Rand Selection and Charter and Anglo itself – were domiciled outside Zambia. Zambian Anglo American remained in Zambia to provide specialist services to the various divisions of NCCM, and also to initiate whatever new business it found, notably in the agricultural field.

Already, however, there had been warnings of dangers to come. White miners were not surprisingly alarmed by these developments, and many decided to pull out while they could. Kaunda went out of his way to reassure them that all would be well. 'People of all races are welcome to make a living in this country or, indeed, to make it their home, provided, like any other Zambian, they are prepared to make their contribution to the growth and development of the country while at the same time legitimately adding to their incomes.'

But his words did not check the general exodus. The turnover of white workers rose from about 25 per cent a year to nearly 50 – far too high for comfort. White miners were concerned by the atmosphere on the copperbelt itself, which seemed ripe for revolution. Warning that bloodshed was on the way, and explaining that he was not prepared to be a part of it, Kapwepwe offered his resignation. On top of all that had happened this might have appeared the last straw. Far from merely being party to any threat of bloodshed, many supposed Kapwepwe was largely responsible. Now he was in a commanding position first to test the loyalty of his own Bembas, and perhaps to challenge for the leadership of the country.

In the event, Kapwepwe failed. In the first place Kaunda prevailed on him to remain Vice-President until a suitable successor could be found, and his initial advantage was lost. Then his attempts to organise a new opposition party pledged to sweep Kaunda from power were rewarded with a long term of imprisonment. Before he was released Kaunda introduced new legislation banning any opposition party, and eventually a new constitution which recognised UNIP as Zambia's single authorised political party.

2

HARRY HAD never subscribed to the view that apartheid was morally wrong. In his view it was at root an honest attempt to cope with overwhelming racial problems. 'The government policy is not an attempt to repress but to find a solution. The assumption is that the two races can't get along, and that the black areas will eventually emerge as independent states.' Verwoerd and his successors had tried to 'give it a go', as he put it, but had based their whole approach on the false premise that it was physically possible to separate black from white, when it was manifestly too late. His chief objections to apartheid, then, were on practical grounds: South Africa had gone so far with all her races together that it was not simply foolish but actually dangerous to interfere with the *status quo*.

According to the apartheid plan the Africans or Bantu as they were now known officially – eighty per cent of the population – were being given autonomous control of their homelands, which represented a mere 13 per cent of South Africa's total land area. Each tribal Bantustan – Zululand, the Transkei, the Ciskei, the Tswanas' territory and a dozen more in South Africa and South West, one for each major tribal group – was to have its own constitution and chief minister and legislative assembly, along the lines of those in Botswana, Lesotho and Swaziland. Several of them were already approaching this stage, notably the great Transkei on the Wild Coast in the Eastern Cape. At the same time the government was trying to endorse out Bantu living in 'white' group areas, and settle them permanently in the homelands. To work in white areas they had to apply for permission and had in any case to hold a valid pass which had the same effect within Southern Africa as a passport.

'How can it be safe to deprive the African people who live in the White areas of all sorts of rights which are acceptable as quite normal and necessary everywhere else?' complained Harry. 'And then, having done this, to build up a series of independent states around our borders – not landlocked states, but states able to communicate in every way with our friends and our foes in the outside world?'

South Africa and South West would continue as before with their white populations: but with a vast 'mixed' population too, the

Coloured people of the Cape and the Indians of Natal who were really closer to the Europeans than the Bantu: and – the worst problem of all – the millions of detribalised Africans who swarmed in the townships outside the big cities and elsewhere. The Nationalists tried to give them homelands to go to, but it was a losing battle, and the 'petty apartheid' legislation which forbade sex across the colour line and further limited the relations of the races could never hope to tackle the problem at its roots. Vorster himself was ready to admit in the case of the Coloured people: 'It is a problem for our grandchildren to solve.'

It was a hideously complex situation, and few observers outside South Africa seemed to understand even a part of it. The worst offenders were the more vociferous members of the Organisation of African Unity who urged the forcible overthrow of the present regime and the immediate substitution of black majority rule. Anti-apartheid groups in Europe and elsewhere were not much better, as Harry many times complained. They failed to understand that the white man had as much right to live in Southern Africa as the black: the Afrikaner, for one, had nowhere else to go, even if English-speakers might easily be absorbed into other populations if the worst happened. But even these had to be seen as a permanent feature of the South African scene: they were not to be dismissed as mere expatriates who would shortly move on. Harry explained his views with some frankness to Rene MacColl of the London *Daily Express*.

'I hold liberal views – but in the old-fashioned sense, in that I object to Black dictatorships just as much as I object to White ones. So many modern liberals seem to suffer from a sense of guilt over the colonial past, and to think in a doctrinal way that to expiate that guilt they must support everything Black – including the Black dictatorships.

'Many people are a bit too fearful of the confrontation of world opinion. They will tend to believe that the trouble with South Africa is that we are suffering from a vice. It is not a vice, but simply that South Africa has a problem that it does not know how to solve. What the rest of the world ought to bear in mind is that there are large White tribes in Southern Africa who desire the same rights of self-government as Black tribes. There must be a place in the sun for White South African tribes as well.'

In speaking to MacColl, Harry was thinking of the economic sanctions which the Wilson government in Britain had imposed against South Africa and of the tragi-comic negotiations between Wilson and Ian Smith over black majority rule in Rhodesia. Even though South Africa had been out of the Commonwealth since 1961, her relationship with Britain remained stronger than with any other country – and Harry urged greater ties still.

'People have got to find a way of living and you cannot find a way of living without taking into account all factors. The White tribes of Africa must be dealt with by the British Government with the same understanding which the British Government extends to the Black tribes. They must receive the same help and consideration as the Black tribes – no more, no less. And London must always remember that the White tribes of Africa are not Europeans. They are Africans. That is the most important point. The White Africans do not think like Europeans any more than do the Black African tribes.'

As if to confirm what Harry said, the white Africans' chief spokesman – John Vorster the Prime Minister – was currently calling for closer co-operation between the states of Southern Africa and those of the black North. What was needed, he said, was first a degree of dialogue to bring about understanding of each other's point of view; and ultimately close liaison in the interests of all. Any black African leader who wished to visit South Africa and examine her situation for himself would be accorded a warm welcome.

The invitation came as a bombshell, in view of the unceasing hostility of the members of the OAU who had been demanding the immediate overthrow of regimes in the white South. Their chief complaints had been not so much about South Africa's internal situation as about the threat she represented to their own survival. Now John Vorster had neatly turned the tables and left the most vociferous of South Africa's critics – Gowon of Nigeria, Nyerere of Tanzania, Kaunda of Zambia and Gadalfi of Libya – wondering how they were to stage a counter-attack.

There was only one precedent for what Vorster had in mind: Chief Leabua Jonathan, Prime Minister of Lesotho, had paid an official visit to South Africa when Verwoerd was Prime Minister. It was not a popular move, and Verwoerd's men made no attempt to repeat it. Only when Vorster succeeded was the policy reversed, and South Africa's view turned towards her neighbours to the north. Vorster quickly came to terms with a leader who had earlier figured among the foremost critics of the white regimes, Dr Kamuzu Banda of Malawi. It was arranged that the Republic should provide Malawi with a considerable degree of aid, and exchange ambassadors. For the first time a black diplomat was to figure in the corps accredited to South Africa.

This was the background to Vorster's invitation. What South Africa had done for Malawi she was ready to do for other black states which became her friends. The invitation was sent out through the news media, not through normal diplomatic channels as in South Africa's case there was no direct contact with black states except through the United Nations. To South Africa's delight there was soon a response.

First to express willingness to visit South Africa was the independently-minded President Felix Houphouet-Boigny of the Ivory Coast, who was effectively spiritual leader of the bloc of former French territories in Central-West Africa. Like Vorster, he was content to 'let it be known' he was ready to visit the white south. Prime Minister Khosi Busia also expressed interest, though he was soon to be deposed while on a visit to London. Other leaders made encouraging remarks. However, by this time the Gowons and Nyereres had weighed the situation and decided it was very far from their interests to give Vorster his way. The OAU would be in a position to expel any states which accepted his overtures. In the end the only black African leader actually to visit South Africa was Banda, received in the Republic as warmly as Vorster had promised but immediately branded 'Sell-Out' by the states further north.

Not surprisingly, in pursuing these bold policies Vorster had failed to carry all Afrikaners with him. There had been serious rumblings within Nationalist ranks, even at cabinet level. The hard-line party members were worried by the way he was going: where now the ideals of Verwoerd and Strijdom and Malan and Hertzog? Were the Afrikaners to join hands with the *Engelsmense* and risk submerging the identity which their forefathers had fought so hard and long to establish? Wasn't the whole point of preserving the Afrikaner way of life that these *Engelsmense* were too soft in their attitudes, and before they knew it would be lowering the drawbridge and allowing the Bantu to take over the country?

The rifts were spotted by the political reporter of the Johannesburg *Sunday Times*, J H P Serfontein, who brought the whole situation to light in a series of headline stories published over a period of three years. The two camps were soon labelled *verlig* and *verkrampt*: terms virtually impossible to translate into English, but in essence meaning *enlightened* and *constricted*. The verligtes centred on Vorster; the verkramptes on his Minister of Posts and Telegraphs, Dr Albert Hertzog, who was the son of General Hertzog and whose most notable contribution to South African life had been his steadfast refusal to introduce television.

As the verkramptes gained confidence in their opposition to John Vorster – though for the time it was confined within the party caucus –

427

they sought targets to attack. Among the first, inevitably, were the capitalists: the old stand-by and coming up for the third time. Since his arrival in parliament in 1948 Hertzog had repeatedly called for the nationalisation of the gold mines. Now a noted verkrampt front-bencher, Martiens van den Berg, took the stage with a speech of a kind not often heard in latterday South African politics. He was ready to admit there had been 'a change of heart and outlook' in the upper echelons of the mining industry as a whole; but against that, it contained one tremendous influence which continued to disrupt the country.

'I want to name the man here this afternoon who exercises that tremendous influence,' he told parliament. 'I do not care to mention people's names in this House, but I must mention his name here because he stands at the pinnacle of the fight which has caused so much strife, and still causes it. I refer to Mr Harry Oppenheimer.

'I just want to say that he incessantly brings the mining industry into uproar as the result of his policy of replacing Whites with non-Whites. He expounds this policy in season and out of season. He has no respect for "gentlemen's agreements" made by Ministers and trade union leaders. He refuses to keep to them and to accept for once that this is the policy of the country, and that is the policy which will bring peace and quiet here.'

Van den Berg had figures to support his case. They concerned the incidence of the dreaded miners' lung diseases, phthisis and TB. Since 1957 there had been 24 420 cases of pneumonoconiosis (phthisis) with tuberculosis, and 30 479 cases of TB alone: a total of 54 899 over a period of 11 years.

'These terrible cases of phthisis can be attributed solely to two factors in the mining industry,' he said. 'The one is silica dust and the other is bad air caused by poor ventilation . . . As a result of Mr Oppenheimer's personal policy, which unfortunately still triumphs in the mining industry, the mine managements want to appoint Bantu as samplers and ventilation officials . . . Even today, Mr Oppenheimer is still continuing the battle over these two important aspects – that the technical people in charge of these things, who must protect the health of all the thousands of mineworkers, White and Black, must be Bantu.'

It was a long and fierce speech, and when it was finished the UP spokesman on mining affairs immediately called on Carel de Wet, Minister of Mines and Planning and himself not entirely devoid of verkrampt sympathies, to repudiate what Van den Berg had said. But the minister made no effort to do so. UP spokesmen – and Helen Suzman too – heaped castigation on the Nationalist front bench. 'If Mr Van den Berg is not immediately and effectively repudiated by the Prime Minister we could chalk up his attack as yet another victory for the verkramptes,' said one of the UP men. 'On the other hand it could make no real difference,' he continued. 'Harry would continue with his efforts to build South Africa undeterred. The dogs will bark but the caravan must move on.'

The battle between the verligtes and verkramptes became more fierce, though still largely behind the scenes. Verkrampt speakers were gaining considerable support particularly in the Transvaal, and J H P Serfontein attended a number of their meetings. At one he was surprised to find the speaker, Dr Ras Beyers, a former advocate of the Supreme Court though not himself in parliament, quoting from what he claimed was a secret government investigation into the affairs of the Anglo American Corporation. It was a bulky document, almost book length, and from what Beyers quoted sounded extraordinarily detailed: a full-scale probe of Anglo's sphere of influence in South Africa with far-reaching recommendations for action to be taken against it.

After the meeting Serfontein asked Beyers about the report, and was told it was the work of a government team led by Professor Piet Hoek, assistant general manager of ISCOR, the state-owned Iron and Steel Corporation, and besides that a member of the Council of the University of Pretoria and a trusted figure in government circles who had already served on several important commissions of inquiry. Serfontein telephoned Professor Hoek and asked him if he was chairman of the government commission into the affairs of the Anglo American. Hoek said he was not, and that he knew nothing of any such government appointed commission.

Three days passed, and suddenly there was news that Hoek was making an urgent application to the Supreme Court. He was asking for a court order restraining Beyers from publishing any part of the report, and demanding that he surrender all copies in his possession. In the papers before the court Hoek now admitted he was the author of the report, with the help of others; that it was highly confidential and the original had remained in his possession; and that it was a private document and as author he had the copyright.

The case was becoming more mysterious. Hoek still maintained that the report was a 'private' effort, in no way concerned with a government commission. 'It contains facts I have compiled for my own information,' he said. 'These facts are therefore private and confiden-

tial, and no one has the right to make them public or publish them.'
There was nothing sinister about them, he insisted. He had collected
information in his professional capacity as a businessman and accountant. The facts were just 'facts' but he did not want to make them
available to Beyers or his associates because 'his conclusions and mine
may be completely different' and he did not want to be associated in
the public eye with Beyers's political activities. 'As far as I am concerned the whole matter is a storm in a tea-cup . . .'

But it was not over yet. For one thing, news of the report came as a
complete surprise to the Anglo American. What was it all about, and
what was the idea behind it? Surely Hoek would not have gone to such
trouble on his own account? One thing was sure: 'It certainly was not
done in co-operation with Anglo,' said a spokesman, 'and we don't
even know what it is about.'

Serfontein was still on the trail. Soon the *Sunday Times* carried a
report giving the full story. 'The investigation of the Anglo American
Corporation, I can reveal today, was carried out on the personal
instructions of Dr Albert Hertzog MP, for a long time the spiritual
leader of the verkramptes. Dr Hertzog instructed the Afrikaner Orde,
the secret underground organisation, to carry out the investigation and
to make recommendations on how the "influence" of Anglo American
could be broken by the government.

'Prof P W Hoek, a senior member of the Afrikaner Orde, was given
the mammoth task of launching this secret organisation. He later asked
four or five others verkrampte economists to assist him. At least two of
them were members of the Afrikaner Orde, the others were "fellow
travellers" of the Hertzog Group . . . This so called "Hoek commission", after a thorough investigation lasting several years, completed
its report on behalf of the Afrikaner Orde more than two years ago.
Copies of the report, whose economic and political recommendations
aim at emasculating Anglo American, were then given to Dr Hertzog,
to certain verkrampte MPs and to several public servants who also
belong to the Orde.'

It was an extraordinary story.

'At private study-group meetings of the Hertzog Group and of the
Afrikaner Orde, as well as at many private discussions during the last
10 years, Dr Hertzog has repeatedly stressed the importance of breaking
the "stranglehold" of Anglo American on the economy. Dr Hertzog
argues that Anglo American, because it is politically opposed to the
ideal of separate development, and the hundreds of companies allegedly
under its influence, would thwart the policy of decentralising industrial

development, of stopping the Black stream to the cities and of establishing border industries.

'He repeatedly pointed out that at the tremendous rate of South Africa's growth, Anglo American's share of the economy, especially in the light of its greater participation in industry and production, would by 1975 be far greater than in the early sixties. He used the argument that in America there were nearly 300 large companies "which all shared the economic cake". In South Africa, he said, one group, Anglo American, had by far the biggest share. That is why Dr Hertzog was anxious for a commission of experts to investigate Anglo American and make recommendations about the action which should be taken to reduce its power and influence. . .

'Dr Hertzog's plan was to confront the Government with these findings in the hope that he would force the Government into taking strong action through legislation against Anglo American. More important, Dr Hertzog saw in such a report an important political weapon. Should the Nationalist leadership refuse to accept its radical proposals to use the resources of the State against Anglo American, then Dr Hertzog and his verkrampte followers would be in a position where they could accuse the then Prime Minister, Dr Verwoerd, of protecting the "British-Jewish international capitalists who are controlling our economy".'

The report had been completed in 1967, but the political climate had changed a lot since then: Hertzog stood revealed, and so severe was his clash with the rest of the Nationalist Party that he had now been obliged to resign from the cabinet. He and his followers were being pushed out into the cold, and Hoek and others who had previously been associated with them, were not prepared to follow. That explained Hoek's now considerable embarrassment to find his report being bandied about at verkrampte meetings.

Unfortunately for the verkramptes, John Vorster remained calm in the face of their activities and it was plain things had gone too far: they would have to withdraw from the party. Soon it was done. With great celebration the Hertzog men announced the formation of their own 'Herstigte Nasionale Party' or 'Reborn National Party', in protest against Vorster's verlig policies. The party was to be 'unashamedly Afrikaans', said Hertzog, based on 'the infallible word of God'. Vorster and his men were co-operating with the English, who were too naive politically to be able to guarantee the survival of the white man. Therefore the responsibility must be shouldered by the strict Afrikaners, 'inspired and strengthened by their immutable Calvinist principles'.

431

The new party's leader was Albert Hertzog, not surprisingly. It was ironic to recall that this was exactly the situation which had prompted his father, J B M Hertzog, to break away from Louis Botha's cabinet and form the National Party back in 1913 with exactly similar aims; and that when D F Malan broke from Hertzog at the time of Fusion in 1933 it had also been to preserve Afrikaner purity. He had called his party Herenigde Nasionale Party – 'Reunited National Party', the matrix of the present regime. It was no accident that the Herstigte Nasionale Party's name was so similar.

There was an election only months away, and the HNP lost no time in calling public meetings throughout the country to explain its aims and rouse support. These provoked fierce opposition from the verligtes who had remained true to the National Party proper, and there were amazing scenes at their meetings: brawls on the platform, bloodied noses, a barrage of tomatoes and eggs and other missiles which gave Hertzog and his men double-figure dry cleaning bills. On the few occasions when they were able to make themselves heard their chief target was 'the greatest threat to White South Africa', Harry and the Anglo American.

'I don't know how, but we will have to break Harry Oppenheimer's power if we want to survive as a White nation,' said one of them, a rebel MP who promptly suggested Anglo American should be nationalised. 'The HNP will act effectively against Mr Oppenheimer,' promised another. But the most intriguing attacks came in the HNP's official newspaper which was established in a matter of weeks: *Die Afrikaner*. In a front-page article it featured an in-depth account of the Hoek report.

It came as rather an anti-climax. Hoek's 'revelations' centred simply on the Anglo group's organisation and the nature of its influence through rather more than 900 companies under its direct control. *Die Afrikaner's* report gave some rather vague statistics suggesting the companies did not pay anything like the tax they should; a suggestion that the investigation had been undertaken on the direct orders of Verwoerd – who was the HNP's idol; and an allegation that copies of Hoek's investigations had been duplicated under the personal supervision of the head of the Security Police, General van den Bergh. It was further suggested that the Prime Minister had not lifted a finger to implement the report's recommendations though it had been shown to him in 1967.

Meanwhile there was an election campaign in progress. Harry would be in Australia on Election Day itself, looking into various busi-

432

ness possibilities. But before he went he put in a surprise appearance on the platform at one of Helen Suzman's meetings in Houghton, and made a hard-hitting speech attacking both government and opposition. Nationalist policy, he said, was 'highly dangerous': the government was asking sacrifices not primarily of the white people, but of the African population, which made nonsense of the claim that apartheid was a fair policy as the Nationalists had always claimed. The UP on the other hand was proposing to offer the Africans eight white representatives in parliament, of a total of 166. 'Now that may not be dangerous but it's really plumb silly.' The United Party was the home of many people who were not prepared to face the facts. If voters returned Progressive candidates they would be 'opening a light at the end of a dark tunnel'.

Harry set off for Australia and Bridget went too. Suddenly there was news of a series of demands being made on Harry by the Minister of Mines and Planning, Carel de Wet. He took grave exception to Harry's speech in Houghton, he was saying: Harry had gone out of his way to attack the government's 'border industry' policy – a long standing call on South African industries to establish their factories on the borders of the Bantustans, and so encourage decentralisation of African labour. Harry had seemed to suggest this was wrong, claimed De Wet. Obviously Oppenheimer had been hoping his remarks would be published in other states in Africa. That way he could promote his interests in those countries. But what did he really think? Was he going to support government policy and do what he could to help, as other industralists were doing? Or would he attempt to use his power to hinder the implementation of the policy and bring about industrial integration? He ought to tell the people of South Africa where he stood.

De Wet first raised the point in a speech he made in a small town near Cape Town, and repeated his questions at a meeting in Philippi, Cape, a few nights later. In fact, he posed them in every election speech he made, and drew great applause from Nationalist supporters on every occasion. Hoggenheimer must not be allowed to throw a spanner in the works. But he saved the climax of this personal campaign of his for his own constituency, Johannesburg West. He did not attract a great audience: no more than 50 people. But he more than made up for the empty hall with the front-page news he made all over the world. He told his audience that at previous meetings he had asked Harry: 'Are you going to use your factories to promote integration in South Africa?' But he had so far received no word from him in reply.

'If he does not give me his answer by tomorrow night, I will see to it that his requests for African workers for his factories will be treated differently from those of other industrialists.'

De Wet elaborated his remarks later in the meeting, when questioned from the floor. No, he did not exactly mean he was going to punish Harry. 'It is any government's duty not to discriminate. I do not say I will discriminate against Mr Oppenheimer, but I will treat his requests differently. I will not allow him and the Progressive Party to destroy our policy.' If Harry did not reply by the next evening, he was going to announce what form this 'different' treatment would take.

When Carel de Wet made this demand he was apparently under the impression Harry was at Brenthurst, a mile or two from where he was speaking. Harry would have no trouble making his reply. Instead, of course, Harry was thousands of miles away: not merely in Australia, but in the depths of the Outback, remote from civilisation and touring by car. He was in no position to answer De Wet's questions even if he was aware they had been asked.

The next evening the minister was in Rustenburg, 70 miles from Johannesburg – this time confronted with an audience of nearly 1 000, eager to hear the next round of his cross-the-globe battle with Hoggenheimer. The minister did not disappoint them. He had not heard from Harry so was left with no alternative but to believe the head of Anglo was after all against the border industry policy.

'Mr Oppenheimer has, through his own political affiliations and statements, differentiated himself from other industrialists and placed himself in a category of his own for his own reasons and purposes,' he said. From now on 'each Oppenheimer application' would receive his own personal attention and 'would be treated with the greatest suspicion' unless Harry promised his help in promoting border industries and the decentralisation of African workers. 'The opportunity will be given to him to help us carry out our policy. If he will co-operate it is not too late. My door is not closed to him and his directors as long as he can show that he is in earnest in wishing to help carry out government policy.'

Harry had reached Melbourne by now, and been told of the attacks at home. But as he gently explained to a Press conference, the threats were all part of the election campaign: they would be dropped when it was all over. In South Africa, however, the storm was only now breaking. As the *Star* put it: 'Nothing that has happened in recent weeks has emphasised so starkly the need to vote against the Nationalist Party as this eve-of-poll incident. Nationalism must be halted in its tracks – for South Africa's sake.'

434

For the United Party the minister's remarks came as a great boon: it was the first time since 1948 that the party's showing improved. Helen Suzman held her own in Houghton, and another Progressive, Colin Eglin, came close to winning a seat in Cape Town. The HNP, on the other hand, did not win a single seat; almost all of its 78 candidates lost their deposits. However, the Nationalists retained their two-thirds majority in parliament, and far from being silenced De Wet was shouting louder than ever. He was in earnest about Harry, he said, quite regardless of the election. He meant to stand by what he had said about Oppenheimer's companies: it was an issue that concerned all South Africa and he and Harry had reached the final stopping point. From now on there would be no holds barred.

Harry flew back to Johannesburg with Bridget the next day. There was a Press conference at the airport as soon as he arrived.

'This sort of controversy, judging from the Australian Press, causes tremendous and important interest outside South Africa. If business-men outside South Africa get it into their heads that people in South Africa not only have to obey the law and conventions that govern our industry, but also have to be active supporters of government policies to get a fair deal, it is a very serious thing for this country. I went out of my way in Australia to say that in our experience the government had never discriminated against business people and I do not think that they would do so in the future. But I am sure that the statements of the Minister, although he may not have meant it so, gave that impression. In the national interest the least said about this matter the better.'

If Harry was not impressed, no more was John Vorster. As a first step he immediately deprived Carel de Wet of the key Planning port-folio which would have given him the right to act upon his threats. And a little later, in an extensive cabinet reshuffle, De Wet was quietly bowler-hatted and sent off to London as Ambassador to the Court of St James.

It had all been a storm in a teacup, as Professor Hoek would have put it. South Africa's friends shook their heads in wonder. What ever next? But no real harm had been done, for Harry had soon clarified the position.

'We are only too happy to establish industries in border areas. In fact . . . we have started a border industry in the Mondi district (near Durban). There is much to be said for the policy of decentralisation of industry, but to say that it is a solution to the African problem is nonsense. I have always said and will continue to say that the type of organisation we have in South Africa does not allow us to make the

435

best use of African labour. This is a bad thing for South Africa and I don't think it is fair to the African, nor is it fair to European workers, who can do much better if we have a much more flexible system. But we are certainly not going to do anything dramatic in our industries and we will go on as we always have done.'

So that was that: one more chapter in the apartheid saga, with a more than usually emphatic conclusion. The most important result was the electorate had given John Vorster a mandate to continue with his verlig policies. Perhaps there was hope for the future after all. As Harry had put it to Rene MacColl: 'I am an optimist and I think everything will come out all right in the long run. South Africa has always been a lucky country and I think she will have a wonderfully lucky future too.'

3

NICKY HAD returned from Oxford and gone to do his nine months' South African military service with the Imperial Light Horse near Kimberley – stationed at Alexandersfontein, which had been turned over to the army as a commando training base. An interviewer asked him about his plans for the future. His answers were refreshingly frank.

'I will start at the bottom, sorting diamonds in Kimberley, and work my way up to the top. Eventually I hope to step into my father's shoes as head of Anglo American.'

He was asked too if he had any marriage plans. After all, he was one of the world's most eligible bachelors.

'No. I like pretty girls and, of course, I love miniskirts. But I have no plans yet.'

When he was through with the army and the sorting offices in Kimberley, Nicky was to move into the Inanda cottage which Mary and Gordon had now vacated as they found it was too small for them. Besides, their first baby was on the way. They moved to Little Brenthurst, suitably redecorated as it had stood unoccupied since before Mary's marriage. Mary gave birth to Harry and Bridget's first grandchildren, Victoria Jane in 1968 and Rebecca a little more than two years later.

Gordon was doing well at 44 Main Street. Interestingly, he was picked out by R B Hagart as a young man who had what it took, in spite of the inevitable back-biting from less favoured men in the Chairman's Office who expected him to prove himself. Hagart always saw himself as Scottish, and took to Gordon immediatcly. Before long Gordon was given his first directorship within the group – on the board of the relatively small Anglo American Prospecting – then in due course achieved managerial status and at last a full seat on Anglo's board.

Sadly, though, not all was well with his marriage to Mary. It had been plain for some time they were far from an ideal couple. Gordon had made every effort to care for Mary, but somehow she needed more than his thoughtful gifts – including roses each month on their wedding day. Gordon was finding himself increasingly heavily committed at Anglo while Mary, young and energetic, was concentrating on her horses and her riding. The two were drifting apart.

In this depressing situation Mary was seeing a lot of Bill Johnson, who had always been her riding instructor. He and his twin brother Arthur had worked hard, and their riding schools and other enterprises were going from strength to strength. Indeed, their most important school was on Harry's property Diepsloot, to the north of Johannesburg, and Harry had helped back Bill's prestige Bryanston Equitation Centre. Mary and Gordon had been close friends of Bill and his wife Vivien, a former pupil at one of Bill's schools. But as she drifted away from Gordon, Mary came much closer to Bill, and soon their friendship developed into a more significant bond.

Harry and Bridget realised what was happening, and in an effort to save the marriage Harry had Gordon posted to New York. His idea was that if Gordon, Mary and the children were left to build a new life in another land, away from the pressures of home, all might be well. Instead, even before they started for New York Mary left Gordon and the children and went to live at the family flat in London, in Eaton Place. It was officially announced Mary would be filing papers to initiate divorce proceedings.

This was all incredibly sad. Harry and Bridget worked hard behind the scenes to try to salvage the situation, if only for the children. They were devoted to Gordon, but both admitted privately the marriage was on the rocks. They did, however, persuade Mary to meet Gordon in Rome. The couple had three days together, and two weeks later Mary returned to Johannesburg and moved back into Cloud End, the mansion she and Gordon had bought in Morningside on the outskirts of the city and now in the new town of Sandton. It looked as if it was all on once more. But six weeks later there were fresh rifts and Mary moved out, this time for good. She went to stay in a flat with friends. That was the end of it. The marriage was a complete breakdown, and this time Gordon filed for a divorce.

Inevitably Johannesburg tongues wagged. What was to be Gordon's future, now he was separated from Mary? Would he remain at Anglo, or return to Britain? The question was soon resolved, when it was announced he was being promoted to executive director, one of the key posts in the whole group. Interestingly, he was being promoted at the same time as his friendly rival within the organisation, Julian Ogilvie Thomson, a brilliant and hard-working former Rhodes Scholar of about the same age who had joined Anglo as a junior in 1956, and been appointed manager and then director after serving as Harry's personal assistant.

The divorce took some time to come through. In the meantime Bill Johnson and his wife were themselves divorced, and it was supposed that at the earliest moment Bill would marry Mary. On the other hand, it was well known Harry and Bridget would not approve of such a development. The gossipers could only watch the headlines. In the event, the only matter to be resolved in the Waddell divorce was custody of the children, which was eventually awarded to Gordon. Mary had the right to see the children according to a complicated time-table.

There was better news from Nicky, who was now installed at the Inanda cottage. It had been clear for some time he was likely to marry Strilli Lasch, his sweetheart for years past. She was the daughter of Helli Lasch, an Austrian-born Johannesburg businessman and international-ly-known glider pilot. Now Nicky asked her to marry him and the wedding was arranged. Neither he nor Strilli wanted a wedding on the scale of Mary's. Instead they planned a simple ceremony at the Anglican Church of St. George's, Parktown, attended by relatives and family friends and followed by a reception at Strilli's home.

As often happened at Oppenheimer gatherings, the weather was not kind. The temperature was far below average, and guests arrived in winter clothing. On top of that it poured with rain. But the wedding ceremony and reception went ahead smoothly as planned. Nicky and Strilli quietly went on honeymoon to Australia, in search of more sun-shine than even South Africa could provide. On their return they lived in the Inanda cottage until Mary and Gordon moved out to Morning-side, when the newlyweds transferred to Little Brenthurst. Strilli produced Harry's first grandson, Jonathan Ernest, on November 18 1969. Sadly their second son, Benjamin, fell victim to a serious illness and died as an infant.

Harry and Bridget were by now thoroughly enjoying grandparent-hood – particularly Bridget, who liked to try and see Victoria, Jona-than and Rebecca every day if she could. Harry and Bridget had now

438

Harry in tense frame of mind after returning from Australia in 1970 to hear of Minister Carel de Wet's threats against his companies. *Star Master Series, Johannesburg.*

Topping out Johannesburg's Carlton Centre, one of the most ambitious building programmes in the world. The project is an illustration of the 'creative' investment policies which Harry favours most. *Rand Daily Mail.*

Presenting the De Beers Diamond Trophy, to be awarded to the winner of the King George VI and Queen Elizabeth Stakes at Ascot. With Harry (*right*) and his cousin Sir Phillip Oppenheimer (*left*) is Her Majesty Queen Elizabeth II. *Rand Daily Mail.*

been married nearly 30 years, and were seen as one of South Africa's most ideally and happily married couples. On the actual 30th anniversary in 1973 they held a private party at Brenthurst for their closest friends, and beforehand met a number of reporters whom they invited to share the occasion.

'How do you keep a millionaire man?' one of the journalists asked Bridget.

'You give up a lot of things and learn to live as he likes to live,' Bridget replied. 'It's something you just take on and you simply do it.'

One of the others asked Harry how he made a success of married life. He replied with a twinkle in his eye.

'You pick the right woman and the rest just follows.'

Both Harry and Bridget were now approaching the gentler years, and there was much speculation over their future. Would Harry retire from Anglo and De Beers, and hand over to a younger man? Surely he would not expect to continue in the saddle as long as Ernest had done? Many friends of Harry's believed the time of his retirement might not be far away.

Certainly it looked as if Harry and Bridget were looking for a new home. They had Mauritzfontein and Shangani and used them frequently, but were they suitable for their retirement? When they flew off to the Seychelles with a party of friends, it was supposed they were seriously considering buying Silhouette, a whole island for sale at R850 000. But this did not materialise: it was rather a long way from South Africa, however attractive. Instead, Harry and Bridget were pouring their energies into developing a new holiday 'cottage' they were building on the Natal north coast, near Durban.

The development was at La Lucia, an exquisite strip of land bought by Anglo's new property company, Amaprop. Harry was the first to buy a section of it – 7,6 acres along the beach with fine views of the green countryside, the white sand and surf, and the deep blue of the sea and sky beyond.

When the architect's plans were ready it was clear that far from being a cottage, the new Oppenheimer home would be a luxurious mansion – five luxury suites, ten bedrooms en suite, fifteen bathrooms, half a dozen reception rooms, a separate children's wing with dormitories, a luxury guest wing, a swimming pool half Olympic size, wine cellar, extraordinary kitchens, dairies, laundries, everything imaginable. Even the servants' quarters were twice the size of a normal two-bedroomed house. It was to be a palace indeed, enough to keep up to 30 guests entertained and happy, and at the same time give Harry and Bridget

439

all the privacy they could want, with special suites for their own use undisturbed by the incursions of their guests.

Three years after Harry bought the site at La Lucia the first house party moved in. Harry called the home Milkwood, for Dylan Thomas's work. He and Bridget filled it with exquisite furniture and fine paintings. Initially, they planned to use it for a couple of months each year: the Durban racing season when Bridget lives at Milkwood permanently while Harry commutes to and from Johannesburg.

For Harry and Bridget, Durban is Mecca – if only for the winter racing season. Racing remains their overriding passion, and though Harry does not have as much time to devote to it as he would like, Bridget more than compensates. Wherever there is racing, if Bridget is nearby she attends.

Over the years she and Harry have become quite knowledgeable about their horses. Each Sunday morning when they are in Johannesburg finds them at the stables in Newmarket, in consultation with John Breval who is in complete charge now Tim Furness has retired. The stable boys lead out each horse in turn, while Harry and Bridget sit on the grass with John Breval discussing their plans. Should Wilwyn be entered for the July or the Gold Cup? Should they consider flying King of the Wind to Cape Town for the Met? How are the two-year-olds coming along? Which is the most promising of the yearlings, and is it time to begin racing them? These are discussions both Harry and Bridget enjoy enormously, and make their racing so much more personal than if they left such decisions to their trainer as so many owners prefer.

There is still a definite policy at the Oppenheimer stable: the horses are bred and trained to be raced to the best of their ability, not for investment's sake. Sometimes Harry and Bridget have more horses than they can themselves race. But in these circumstances they refuse to consider selling any of them. Instead, they prefer to lease them to other members of the family, or perhaps to close friends. They retain the overall ownership of the horse concerned, but the lessee looks after it and races it, and pays over a third of its winnings.

This was the background to a horse called Smash'n'Grab, which incidentally brought Harry a strongly worded letter protesting about the name he had given it. He was out to encourage crime, complained the writer. But the name stayed, and Harry decided to offer the horse to close friends, Punch and Kay Barlow. Punch Barlow headed one of the most progressive industrial groups in South Africa, a family business which eventually gained administrative control of the Rand Mines

440

group. The Barlows took on Smash'n'Grab, and decided to stable him with John Breval. The horse did exceptionally well, and Breval recommended that he be entered for the Gold Cup – the race that had proved the bane of the Oppenheimers' turf career as it was the one classic scalp missing from their belt.

To the great chagrin of Harry and Bridget, Smash'n'Grab scored a runaway win. That did it. There was no reflection on their friends, Bridget insisted, but from now on there would be no more leasing except to members of the family. They could not afford to throw up any more chances, especially where the Gold Cup was concerned. Since 1966 the only people racing Mauritzfontein horses besides Harry and Bridget have been Nicky and Strilli, to some extent Mary, and to a considerable extent Gordon, who races in his own colours of dark blue with a white cap.

The Gold Cup remains elusive, but Harry and Bridget have more than compensated in other directions. Down the years they have won two Julys, four Summer Handicaps, five South African Derbys, and most impressive of all, nine South African Oaks in eleven years, as well as countless lesser races. Since John Breval took over, the stables have never been out of the top ten in terms of winnings, and usually in the top five; and Harry and Bridget have figured among the most successful breeders ever since the beginning of Mauritzfontein, though all their rivals run studs as businesses.

Harry has frequently been praised for his contribution to raising the standard of South Africa's racing through the quality of thoroughbreds he had imported from Europe and America. Likely stock is recommended by John Hislop, editor of the magazine *British Racehorse*, who acts as Harry's agent. The imported horses are put to stud with local fillies at Mauritzfontein. Harry prefers not to race fillies after the age of four, or five if John Breval makes a strong plea; and he stops racing colts at five or six. Of these some will be stabled at Mauritzfontein, but most will be sold in the annual clearance sales, which mark the first occasion an Oppenheimer horse is available on the general market.

Inevitably Harry and Bridget have had many friendly rivalries in the racing world. Probably the greatest of them was with Charles Engelhard, who started his racing career in South Africa in the late fifties with the acquisition of a single horse, and went on to build one of the most successful strings of horses in the world, racing in a dozen countries. When he withdrew his South African-bred colt Hawaii to stud in America, he imported the no less famous Ribofilio to make up

441

for him. South Africa had started him in racing, he explained, and in taking Hawaii away the least he could do was make good the loss. In the event, he shared his stallion with Harry at Mauritzfontein.

Harry's rivalries on the turf were crystallised in one race in particular, the Champion Stakes in Durban. This was the race in which the most successful horses of a particular season were bracketed together, and from an owner's point of view could be regarded as more imprtant even than the individual classics.

One year in particular there was a particularly strong field of five horses, including Harry's King Willow and the noted trainer Syd Laird's Sea Cottage and Java Head, two of the most notable horses ever produced in South Africa. As Harry confided to John Breval: 'I'd give anything to win this race.'

Breval told him that King Willow had a good chance of beating either Sea Cottage or Java Head, but that the chance of beating the stable-mates in combination were so remote that he could scarcely conceive it was possible. The horses ran the race, and King Willow won.

Harry was jubilant. Bridget, on the other hand, was mortified. She had missed it, for she was at home in Johannesburg, having her portrait painted. In normal circumstances she would not have dreamt of staying away from so important an event, but the occasion was rather special. She and Harry had called in Pietro Annigoni, one of the most noted portrait painters in the world, and brought him to South Africa to work on the commission. He insisted on a minimum of 16 two-hour sessions and probably even more, and Bridget had to oblige. In the end the portrait more than compensated her for the bad luck in missing the Champion Stakes, but Bridget was all the same upset. To her it was almost as if the Oppenheimer horses were extensions of her family, and it seemed a shame not to share one of their greatest achievements.

All this time Ina had been living over the hill from Brenthurst at Blue Skies, leading a life of her own though always closely in touch with the rest of the family. She remained extraordinarily popular as she had been all through her life, with a close circle of friends old and young and admirers at every level of society. She was as warm as ever, as lively and as interested in everything that was going on around her, though now in her seventies. Apart from anything else she remained one of South Africa's leading amateur photographers, with her work achieving widespread recognition and bringing her considerable praise from those in the know.

Of all the subjects she photographed, her favourites were animals.

She spent hours in Johannesburg and Pretoria Zoos, seeking unusual studies, and also at zoos in Europe. In particular, she loved pandas. But whenever possible she went out into the wilds, to the game parks of South Africa or to Etosha in South West Africa, the biggest wildlife sanctuary in the world. She was so keen that she had a special safari vehicle rigged up, a fully-equipped van with a special turret to help her catch first-class shots of animals without disturbing them.

When the vehicle was delivered her chauffeur spent a couple of weeks getting used to it, driving it around Johannesburg to run it in. Then she and he set off for the Kruger National Park. She meant to spend ten days there, photographing subjects for an exhibition she was planning. It was November 25 1970 – exactly twelve years to the day since Ernest had died.

The vehicle seemed to be running well. Ina was sitting beside the chauffeur, Stanley Rose, in the cab. They had travelled about 40 miles when suddenly the van spun out of control. Rose could not tell what was happening. The vehicle skidded wildly off the side of the road and into a deep ditch, overturned, travelled on for several yards on its roof and finally stopped. Rose had been thrown clear and was only slightly injured. But Ina was unconscious, and badly hurt.

Among the first people to stop at the scene was a former nurse, who did what she could for Ina. Eventually an ambulance arrived, and took her to the H F Verwoerd Hospital in Pretoria. Her ribs were smashed, her lungs were damaged, but far more serious were her head injuries. She was in a coma, and though she regained consciousness for a time she never returned to normal. She was transferred to a Johannesburg hospital where she died on February 2. At the inquest which followed a witness suggested the accident was caused by a loose wheel, though Rose insisted he had noticed nothing amiss until the car slewed off the road. The magistrate decided Ina's death was by misadventure, and nobody could be held responsible.

To the end Ina had maintained her firm influence with the family and they missed her sorely. With her passing went the last real objection to Mary's marrying Bill Johnson, whom she had opposed ever since she first met him.

'We would have married long ago but for two things – opposition from her family and my wanting her to fight for custody of her little daughters,' Bill told an interviewer some time later. 'Although Mary has never been exactly hung on babies her daughters are now at an interesting stage of development and they've begun to mean a lot to her.'

Bill said he had advised Mary to try and get custody if she could, because she would never be wholly happy unless she had it.

'She often cries because she can't see them as often as she'd like. Her parents are against her fighting for custody of her daughters – they told her they disliked the thought of her making headlines. But I've told her her happiness is more important than caring whether she gets splashed in the newspapers. Children like Mary. Mine love her.'

Whatever efforts she made to avoid making headlines Mary could hardly escape them. For one thing, when short of copy newspapers would not hesitate to speculate openly on her marriage plans. At last they were tipped off: Mary was to be married two days before Christmas at the home of Bill's twin, Arthur, in Swaziland. Neither she nor Bill was ready to admit it, and no more would they tell other members of their families what was to happen. Bridget told a reporter she knew no more about it than he did.

Still on the scent, Press cars queued outside Brenthurst when it was learnt Mary was there shortly before her projected wedding date. She had taken Victoria and Rebecca to a children's party there, and they would be picked up later by Gordon. She drove home, followed by the Press cars, and Bill was waiting for her. She was in an awful state by this time, but when she started telling Bill they should call the whole thing off, he told her not to be so stupid. They set off for the airport, Bill driving as fast as he could.

He had reckoned without the tenacity of the newspapermen. The faster he went, the closer they followed. At last even he had had enough. Suddenly he slammed on the brakes, and the nearest car banged into the back.

Bill jumped out, and so did the newspapermen. A photographer began snapping pictures. Bill wanted to hit him, but the photographer dodged away. Mary was crying, demanding that they call off the marriage. Bill was in no mood to listen to anyone, angry because the photographer was still taking pictures. But at last all was smoothed over and Bill and Mary were on their way again.

The wedding was set for two days later. The Swazi Police set a guard on Arthur Johnson's house, and the papers failed to extract any news of what was afoot until it was all over and Arthur announced the marriage had taken place, performed by the local District Commissioner who was an African. Bill and Mary enjoyed a relaxed honeymoon at the Swazi Spa hotel, then returned to their new life in Johannesburg. Bill soon granted an interview, particularly over the attitudes taken by Harry and Bridget.

'I guess they are getting used to the idea, although I don't think they're exactly thrilled about it. I think Mary's mother is the one who likes it least. Mary has always been a dutiful daughter, never doing anything to displease them. She has always cared too much about not putting a foot out of line. But I think I've taught her to be a little more reckless and not to mind what the rest of the world thinks. I've never given a damn about what people think and Mary is coming round to my way.'

Far from shrinking from publicity, Mary accepted an invitation to write a weekly column for the *Rand Daily Mail*, on anything that came into her mind. She could not type, so at first wrote it in long-hand. But then she decided it was time she became a little more professional, and asked Harry for a typewriter from Anglo. She was sent a huge machine which she could barely move, so spent hours sitting on the floor experimenting with it and finding out secrets, such as how to make capital letters. She promised herself that one day she would learn how to use it properly.

With the Mary Johnson Column Johannesburg at last has the chance to find out what South Africa's unwilling Princess was all about. The results are delightful. From an early success in condemning the catering arrangements at the prestige Rand Easter Show, the country's premier trade and agricultural fair, Mary has moved on to all sorts of new targets and appears to find them every time. She deals in a wide variety of subject matter, though even the most enlightened of her readers choked over their breakfast coffee as they read her account of the unexpected moves of the Bloomsbury Group of Victorian London, with Virginia Woolf, Lytton Strachey *et al.* Strachey had helped relieve the others' inhibitions when he asked Virginia Woolf if the mark he noticed on her dress was made by semen, narrated Mary in great glee. The atmosphere dealt a body blow, the whole company then fell to whole-hearted group bedding and never looked back.

Mary's style is not beyond reproach, but the newspaper's sub-editors wisely leave her work largely uncorrected. Her readers love it: for the first time they can meet an Oppenheimer in person. The column is not particularly witty or clever, but that does not matter; there are other columnists to fulfil these demands. Instead, it is down to earth and sensible and above all *fun*. That is what has won Mary a wide following.

The column appears only once a week. The rest of Mary's time is devoted to running the Johnson home in the suburb of Honeydew: not a big house, but exquisitely furnished and enhanced by Mary's fine collection of modern paintings. Her husband loathes most of them, but for Mary's sake has learnt to live with them. Mary entertains now and again, but not nearly so frequently as she did when married to Gordon. Bridget visits her frequently and seems to be getting on much better with Bill. The whole pace of her life is quite different, and those who come across her cannot fail to see how happy she is.

4

ONE OF THE less attractive features of Harry's position is that he is so exposed. If anyone bears a grudge against one of his organisations, they tend to blame Harry personally for whatever has upset them. He is expected to take full responsibility for everything that happens – even when he knows nothing at all about it, and when he has never even heard of the people involved. Anglo and De Beers have excellent security divisions, but even they cannot always protect him from what has sometimes proved considerable embarrassment.

There was, for instance, the case of Fred Kamil: the same Fred Kamil that did such excellent work for diamond security in West Africa in the days of Sir Percy Sillitoe's IDSO. Since that time the Lebanese had continued to work closely with De Beers in different parts of Africa, but after a disagreement moved first to London and then to Beirut, with his South African-born wife Melanie and their infant son. Nursing his grudge against De Beers – a matter of money he claimed he was owed for services rendered – he wrote direct to Harry in Johannesburg. The letter was referred to Tony Wilson, Harry's close associate in De Beers affairs, who knew nothing about Kamil and nothing about his claims. When Kamil wrote again, this time threatening to blow up 44 Main Street if his demands were not met, Tony Wilson was convinced the letter was the raving of a madman and dismissed it accordingly.

The full story emerged only later, for the Lt Col George Visser who had headed security at Anglo and De Beers for many years and who would have known something about it had recently retired. He had been closely involved with Kamil, as had the South African Police who had been using him regularly until 1968 as an IDB trapper, on a commission basis. Kamil had earned tens of thousands of rands from De Beers and the police, in terms of a third of the value of the diamonds and cash involved in the transactions he exposed. He had arrived in South Africa after several years in Tanganyika, working with the police to stamp out diamond smuggling from the Williamson mine which was being used to boost the revenue of nationalist organisations. Latterly, however, he had demanded R50 000 for an operation in South Africa, which the police and De Beers refused to pay as they felt he had not earned it. In high dudgeon he went to live in London.

Visser met Kamil again in 1970, quite by chance. In chatting with him the old question of money cropped up, and Kamil asked when De Beers was going to pay it. The sooner the matter was settled the better, he told Visser: he had information about a much more serious leak within De Beers itself, involving two of the senior executives who had their own private racket smuggling diamonds to the Argentine. Was Visser prepared to negotiate?

Visser was. He paid Kamil a large sum 'on account', though Kamil preferred to regard it as part settlement on the money he claimed De Beers owed him already. Visser was not prepared to argue about it: there was nothing to be gained that way, and if what Kamil said was right he was on the point of uncovering one of the biggest diamond frauds ever.

He met Kamil several times in the next months and each time received highly satisfactory progress reports. It looked as if they would catch the executives – as yet not named – red-handed. Certainly Kamil had already obtained photostats of statements recording huge transactions involving numbered bank accounts in Switzerland and huge sums in Swiss francs and American dollars. He returned to South Africa expecting to hear from Kamil again. But there was no news after June 1971: he did not even hear Kamil and his wife had moved to Beirut. Visser imagined Kamil had hoodwinked him after all. It seemed a sad end to his career as 'Diamond Dick', but he was due to retire on pension and hand over to his successor.

Shortly after this Kamil began making his demands on Harry and De Beers. He wanted more money, and he wanted to know what had happened to Ingrid Sommers, a German girl who had worked with him on a number of cases but had suddenly disappeared without trace. She had gone to South Africa to work on a case in South West, and had sent him a couple of postcards, but there was no further news. Certainly she had not returned to Europe. Could she have been kidnapped by De Beers, and was she being held against her will? Kamil wanted to know.

But he got no reply. Sitting helpless in Beirut – and beginning to run short of cash: De Beers' golden goose had laid him some splendid eggs in its time and he was missing them – he wondered what to do. There

447

was no point in going to South Africa to try to see Harry personally: the chairman would never agree to the meeting. Then he would have to work out some scheme to ensure that Harry agreed to see him: some way of twisting his arm. At last he had it: he would have to interfere with his family. If he was able perhaps to kidnap one of them, Harry would be prepared to meet him anywhere, any time, and pay him any sum he wanted. That, then, would be the plan.

Kamil realised he could not hope to carry off his mission on his own, so rather naïvely looked round Beirut for a partner-in-crime. He knew a security policeman there who had been trained in one of the Lebanese commando groups, Ajij Yaghi, and asked if he would be interested in taking part. Yaghi spoke no English, but seemed to know what he was doing when it came to the rough stuff. His cut would be taken from the money Harry paid over, which might amount to millions of dollars. Yaghi required little persuading and before long the two conspirators were preparing to leave Beirut for a jaunt down Africa. They told friends of theirs – and Kamil's own wife – they were going to Kenya on a big game safari. Kamil was a keen photographer and took with him a good deal of valuable equipment which proved rather awkward to handle as it was so heavy. But he insisted on keeping it beside him all the time.

Kamil had various contacts from his involvement in the underworld, and brought them into the picture with the promise of handsome cuts from the loot. Working in conjunction with one of these – it is not clear which or where – Kamil was told the man to go for was Gordon Waddell, Harry's son-in-law; or rather ex-son-in-law, though Kamil never did realise that. His latest information on the position was two years out of date. It was not difficult to find out that Gordon was in London at this time, and would soon be flying back to Johannesburg; nor was it difficult to establish which flight he would be on. Kamil and Yaghi and their accomplices prepared to hijack his flight.

The two men from Beirut did go to Nairobi, and to many other cities of Africa too; but their chief base of operations was Khartoum in the Sudan, where Kamil had his most useful contacts. Through the grapevine they discovered Gordon's flight would be landing at Salisbury en route for Jan Smuts, Johannesburg. This, then, would be the best place to stage the hijack. They zig-zagged down Africa, passing through Dar es Salaam and Lusaka before flying to Livingstone on the Zambian side of the Victoria Falls and walking across the bridge to catch an onward flight to Salisbury. There they were met by one of Kamil's accomplices, a beautiful blonde ex-girlfriend who gave him a slip of paper with the information he was after: Gordon's flight would be leaving Salisbury for Johannesburg at 10 a m the next Wednesday. Kamil read the note, digested the information and destroyed it.

There were three days to wait in Salisbury before the flight arrived. Kamil's blonde provided the conspirators with sticks of Nobel's 808 high explosive, rather old but still functional, and short enough to be carried in an inside pocket and to escape detection in an airport check. They booked in at a Salisbury hotel, and booked tickets for Johannesburg, though they found their flight left not at 10.00 but at 12.30. It had evidently been put back. Otherwise, all was in order, and they had a restful day in Salisbury to gather themselves for what promised to be an incredible adventure. They would hijack the plane and fly to Khartoum where there was no love for South Africa and they could expect a good deal of sympathy from the authorities. Harry, they would insist, should fly up there in one of the Anglo planes and talk business with them on the spot: and not only that, but he should bring Ingrid with him.

Kamil and Yaghi – with the blonde, who went out to see them off – arrived at the airport in good time. Their Boeing was there to receive them, a 727 of the sort regularly used for South African domestic services. The flight was called and they filed through to the tarmac. The airport authorities did not check their personal baggage: after all, it was only a flight to Johannesburg. Yaghi was carrying a small valise, while Kamil carried his heavy camera bag and a sizable tripod. The air crew checked them on board, with Kamil and Yaghi sitting rather further than halfway down the plane, towards the back. When everyone was sitting down the hostess assigned to their section looked at the equipment on Kamil's knee and joked that she did not like the look of him. She thought he was a hijacker. Kamil tried to laugh heartily, though the hostess recalled later he looked rather green about the gills.

The plane took off, Kamil on the aisle and Yaghi by the window, wearing dark glasses. It was just after noon, and hardly was the plane airborne than the cabin crew began serving lunch. As soon as they had cleared the debris away again Kamil beckoned the stewardess who had earlier accused him of being a hijacker and told her she was quite right. Would she please tell the captain? She thought he was joking and began laughing, and he had to show her the explosives in his pocket. She went forward and knocked at the door leading to the cockpit, and soon disappeared inside.

Kamil had a feeling she was not coming back and in any case perhaps did not fully believe him. He went to the galley where the cabin crew

449

was busy cleaning up and sent one of the junior stewards to tell the captain he was in earnest. He followed the steward down to the cockpit and went inside himself. There he found the flight crew – captain, first officer and flight engineer – and the hostess he had talked to first. He showed the sticks of explosives in case they doubted him. The captain seemed quite calm about the whole thing and asked him where he wanted to go.

'Khartoum.'

'You must be joking.'

The captain, Blake Flemington, explained he barely had enough fuel to get to Johannesburg from where they were, let alone fly anywhere else. But Kamil would not hear of landing at a South African airport. If they could not get to Khartoum he wanted to fly to the Seychelles. Again Flemington explained he had no fuel. Anyway, he did not know the way it was over the sea: he had never been there before. Besides, he had no navigational aids of any sort. The furthest they could get was Salisbury, and even that would be touch and go.

In the end Kamil agreed. They would fly to Salisbury, then refuel and carry on to the Seychelles and perhaps to Khartoum after that. Kamil seemed undecided, certainly very nervous. Flemington informed Jan Smuts control what was happening, and turned back to Salisbury. By this time Yaghi had joined them in the cockpit, and Kamil quickly put him in the picture. Then he demanded that all the passports should be collected. Flemington briefed one of his stewards to do this, and told his crew on no account to let the passengers realise what was happening. They were to be told there was a technical fault and they were returning to Salisbury because of it. For the time they should all move down to the seats at the back of the aircraft.

The steward returned with the passports, and Kamil and Yaghi looked through them. There was no Gordon Waddell. What had gone wrong? But they could not yet make any inquiry, much less make any demands on Harry: certainly not until they were free of Salisbury and Southern Africa. Kamil told Yaghi: it was a blow, but not the end of the world. At least they now controlled the aircraft. Harry could not refuse them while they were in such a commanding position. He would have to fly wherever they wanted him to go, whether to the Seychelles or anywhere else.

Blake Flemington approached Salisbury safely and came in to land. By this time the passengers realised what was happening. Yaghi had produced a stick of high explosive with a detonator and two-inch safety fuse attached, and was threatening to ignite the fuse with a cigarette

450

lighter. With his swarthy skin and dark glasses and wild looks he was very obviously the real thing. He was patrolling up and down the aisle, particularly near the back of the aircraft where the passengers were.

All this time Kamil had stayed close beside Flemington, who was in radio contact both with Johannesburg and Salisbury. Kamil could hear what he was saying, but not the replies from the controllers as the captain received them through headphones. The Rhodesian authorities were asking Flemington what he wanted them to do. Should they immobilise the plane? He said he would rather they didn't as at least this way he still had a bargaining point with the hijackers. His plane was nearly two thirds full, and there was a lot of responsibility on his shoulders. As he landed the Rhodesian authorities directed him to the refuelling point furthest from the airport building, in case the hijackers decided after all to blow up the plane.

All this time the captain had not left his seat. He had been calmly talking to Kamil.

'What am I to call you? I can't call you "sir".'

'Call me captain. Captain . . . uh . . . Z.'

'So you're the captain? Well, you'd better have my seat.'

'No, no, you stay there. You're in command.'

After that exchange Flemington knew he had the upper hand. He quietly reasoned with Kamil, whose name appeared on the passenger list, as did Yaghi's. They were travelling on their own passports. At the moment there were still 70-odd passengers on board, Flemington told them. If Captain Z really wanted to fly up Africa they could go a lot further and a lot faster with an empty plane. Wouldn't it be better to disembark all the passengers in Salisbury? Kamil saw the point of this and agreed to it, but insisted on keeping a number of hostages on board. He went through the passports again and picked out seven from South Africa. The others could leave: they and the stewards, all but the actual crew needed to fly the plane.

The seven hostages were brought up to the front. Two immediately claimed they could not possibly fly on: one said he had heart trouble, the other diabetes. Kamil said they could leave too. The five left stayed at the front while everyone else disembarked. Flemington called for a volunteer from the cabin crew to stay to look after the hostages. After all, they were paying passengers. Every one of the hostesses volunteered, but he selected the chief flight steward, Dirkie Nel. As the others disembarked, two firemen edged their way up the stairs into the plane. The hijackers were not to know they were security men, one of them a sharpshooter with a rifle concealed in his overalls. But Flemington specifically asked that there should be no interference, for the sake of the hostages.

As the passengers walked back to the administration buildings the plane taxied for take-off. Kamil stood in the cockpit with Flemington, his first officer Arnie Schultz and his flight engineer Bert Cheetham; while Yaghi was in the cabin with Nel and the five passengers: Dr Paul Weinbren, an elderly research scientist living in Salisbury; Francis Mellish, a businessman from Cape Town in middle age; David Bryington of Salisbury and Peter Gouws of Benoni who were quite young; and the diminutive Cecil Orren of Johannesburg. They were sitting in the seats immediately behind the cabin door, while Yaghi paced behind them with a stick of high explosive in one hand and his cigarette lighter in the other.

Blake Flemington had virtually no idea of how to get to the Seychelles, but that was where he was heading. The authorities at Jan Smuts had briefed him as fully as they could, but his only navigational guide was a little map of the world Kamil had torn from his pocket book, which showed the Seychelles as tiny dots in the great Indian Ocean. With the map beside him Flemington prepared to fly out over Malawi and Mozambique, to hit the open sea and who knew what lay beyond. To show him the way to Malawi, a Canberra bomber of the Rhodesian Air Force was accompanying the Boeing as far as the border.

Now they were airborne again Kamil made his demands. Flemington was to tell his superiors that he was prepared to negotiate with Harry Oppenheimer and no one else. He was not prepared to explain what business he had with Harry: simply that he wanted him to fly to the Seychelles and bring with him Ingrid, or at least a letter in her hand-writing saying she had 'changed sides willingly', and had not been kidnapped. That, felt Kamil, should do the trick. There was a long delay before word came back from Jan Smuts: Harry was on his remote farm at Shangani, and could not possibly be contacted.

By this time the Boeing was heading out over the coast towards the open sea, and it was getting late. As darkness fell, Flemington pointed out to Kamil he had no idea whatever where he was. How on earth were they going to find the Seychelles in the middle of the night? They did not have the fuel to stay up more than a few hours more. Were they then to come crashing down? Did he really want to die? Shouldn't they fly to some other destination, and make Harry meet them there?

Kamil had now surrendered command to Flemington, who had so

far been rather wary of the hijackers. He did not know how much they understood about flying a Boeing, for instance, let alone how familiar they were with explosives and whether they were really prepared to blow up the plane and themselves with it. The passengers, meanwhile, were sitting tight in their seats, several of them too petrified to move. Yaghi brooded over them, mouthing Arabic obscenities. Now Flemington suggested to Kamil it would be a lot more sensible to head back for land and aim for a new airport where at least they would take on more fuel. Kamil asked if they could go to Mauritius or to Tananarive in Madagascar. He had accomplices there as he had in Khartoum and the Seychelles and Johannesburg. Flemington became suspicious: surely the hijacker could not have accomplices *everywhere?*

Flemington suggested Malawi, which was, after all, a state friendly to South Africa. He had been there before, and knew they could refuel and then take off for the flight north. Or alternatively, Kamil could ask the authorities for a smaller plane which would have a much better chance of completing the trip safely. Didn't he realise what a risk it was taking a South African Airways jet up black Africa? They might be shot out of the sky. Kamil took the point and though reluctant at last agreed: Malawi it would be. Thankfully Flemington wheeled the plane and headed in for Chileka Airport, Blantyre.

All this time there had been continuous comic opera dialogue between the plane and Jan Smuts. Kamil was still demanding that Harry should go to the Seychelles to meet them. Airport control said it was impossible: he could not be contacted. He had to be, said Kamil. If Harry did not meet his demands his accomplices in Johannesburg would blow up 44 Main Street as they had planned all along. On top of that they would kidnap Mary. In conversation with Flemington, Kamil explained there was a whole army of accomplices waiting to help him: they would carry out their appointed tasks, then make their way to the Kruger National Park and cross into Mozambique where they could not be detected, taking Mary with them.

Flemington relayed this information to Johannesburg, where the police set a large scale security operation in motion. They kept watch on 44 Main Street, then looked for Mary and eventually kept round-the-clock surveillance on her house. A security bodyguard was to accompany her wherever she went, following her car in a beach buggy. The police also checked on Gordon Waddell and his children. Gordon had arrived in Johannesburg on a 747 flight earlier that day from London: the flight his would-be kidnappers should have hijacked. The Jumbo had called at Salisbury briefly on the way south, and left at

10 a m. Blake Flemington and his crew had passed it on their way north to Rhodesia that morning.

The 727 reached Chileka Airport about 6.45 p m, and Flemington was directed to park it on an auxiliary runway some distance from the administration buildings. Kamil remained with him in the cockpit, while Yaghi watched the passengers. Kamil carried his camera tripod in the band of his trousers, and now explained this was no ordinary tripod, but a highly sophisticated electronic detonating device. He referred to it as 'the little bomb', while his camera bag was 'the big bomb'. Yaghi had pulled his valise from the luggage rack and retrieved more sticks of high explosive, which he had evidently taped to the inside of the aircraft. Flemington went down the plane to look for them, but though he could see signs of tampering, he could find no explosive. But he was not prepared to take any chances.

Now began a long battle of wits. As soon as the plane landed at Chileka ground crew deflated its tyres and disconnected its front-wheel steering gear, on the personal orders of President Banda. The president, indeed, was highly indignant that the hijackers should have brought the plane to Malawi. Besides, he had an important BOAC flight to catch in two days' time: he was going to London in a private capacity. He was not going to allow these 'fools of the air', as he called them, to disrupt his holiday plans. Flemington knew the plane had been immobilised, but could hardly tell the hijackers. So long as they thought it was still airworthy there was a chance they would delay trying to blow it up.

The hijackers were looking more and more tense as they failed to win their way. Besides, both were suffering from severe headaches. One of the problems of Nobel's 808 is that it gives off highly toxic fumes smelling rather like almonds, and producing painful migraine headaches in anyone who handles it for a length of time. Dr Weinbren, the research scientist from Salisbury, decided to make the hijackers as comfortable as possible. He made coffee for them and with Dirkie Nel's help put relaxing tablets in it and even tots of brandy from the mini-bottles carried in the aircraft, and later massaged Kamil's neck and gave Yaghi an alcohol rub. This ran counter to Blake Flemington's strategy, which was to put the fear of God into the hijackers and persuade them they had no hope of carrying off such an impossible project. Wouldn't they rather live than blow themselves to Kingdom Come?

There was continuing contact with the Malawian authorities in the terminal buildings, and with South African Airways personnel who

Mary has been an enthusiastic horsewoman most of her life. *Johannesburg Sunday Times.*

Mary and Bill Johnson, who were married in Swaziland in 1973. *Johannesburg Sunday Times.*

Nicky married the former Strilli Lasch in 1968. *Anglo American Corporation*.

Harry and Bridget on their 30th wedding anniversary, in May 1973. They toast each other in pink champagne. *Rand Daily Mail*.

had flown to Malawi in another plane and were now in the control tower. South African Airways still insisted it could not possibly trace Harry: in fact, Harry was not at Shangani but at La Lucia. The first he heard about the hijack was on arriving at Jan Smuts Airport. He asked the airport authorities what they wanted him to do, and they said it would be better if they told the hijackers he was not available.

Kamil made Flemington contact the authorities every hour, and now told him to say he and Yaghi were prepared to negotiate with Tony Wilson. As he told Flemington, 'Only Harry and Tony will know what I'm talking about'. He demanded that Tony Wilson should immediately fly up to Chileka and bring with him 'at least a million dollars' which was what he said it had cost to set up the operation.

Meanwhile, Blake Flemington had devised an escape plan. The hijackers appeared so amateur that he was worried in case they exploded the aircraft without meaning to. The flight crew was to escape through two little emergency windows in the cockpit, one by the captain's seat on the left hand side and the other by the first officer's seat on the right. There was a coil of rope above these windows which they could use to slide the 15 feet to the ground. Dirkie Nel was to swing open the main door in the cabin just behind the cockpit, and the passengers were to jump out that way. All were briefed, and though most were obviously very frightened they all seemed to understand what was required of them.

The hours dragged on, the flight crew and passengers tired and weary. Flemington and his crew had been up since the previous morning, and had flown to Durban and back to Johannesburg before flying up to Salisbury for the beginning of this terrible adventure. They had been looking forward to the end of a busy day when they were hijacked. The strain was beginning to tell, as it was with the hijackers who were in a state of increasing tension not improved by their head-aches. Yaghi was prowling up and down the aisle like a caged tiger, yelling obscenities at Kamil whom he blamed for everything going wrong. Kamil admitted to Flemington and the others he was getting increasingly worried by Yaghi's erratic behaviour. Flemington tried to play on the rift that had developed between the two, sympathising with Kamil over his unfortunate predicament. Interestingly Kamil res-ponded, and told Flemington he was rather sorry to have got so many innocent people into trouble. He believed in peace, he said, as Flemington did. He even produced photographs of his son, and admired Flemington's pictures of his own family. He only wanted to get even with De Beers and the Anglo American, he said: not with Harry personally, Flemington understood, for presumably he did not know what his men were doing, but with the organisation which had given him such a raw deal. Talking to passengers back in the cabin he elaborated on what he had told Flemington. He had hijacked the plane to bring 'certain documents' to Harry's attention.

Yaghi was growing increasingly jumpy. He still held a stick of high explosive in one hand and a cigarette lighter in the other, and every time anyone came near him he would menacingly light up and hold the flame perilously close to the fuse. All the time he was shaking like a reed, abusing Kamil more violently than before. He evidently believed all was lost. It was two o'clock in the morning, and all were tired. Suddenly Yaghi screamed loudly and ran halfway down the aircraft. The others froze. They could see him fiddling with the explosive. Kamil ran after him.

'Christ, he is going to do it.'

They could see sparks on the ceiling, then a whiff of bluish smoke. The plane was going up.

'Out!' shouted Flemington from the cockpit. Kamil was grappling with Yaghi, trying to force the explosive out of his grip. Flemington and his crew were already halfway out of the windows in the cockpit. The passengers looked for Dirkie Nel to open the main door. He was fast asleep. In the split second that passed they tried to open it themselves, but it was jammed. Nel woke up and tried to help, but the hijackers were running down the aircraft at them. Thinking quickly, Gouws and Bryington ran through to the cockpit and jumped out after the flight crew. It was a long drop and Bryington broke his arm, while Gouws landed on Flemington's head. They sprinted down the runway ahead of the aircraft, expecting it to blow up any second.

At last they reached cover, a series of ditches well away from the plane. They dropped into them exhausted. Flemington was there first, and watched as the single figures ran up to him in the black night: one, two, three, four and that was it. Arnie Schultz, Bert Cheetham, Gouws and Bryington. The others were still on board. He was desperately afraid they were done for. Had he made a mistake? At last there was a plaintive call through a loudhailer: 'Captain, come back. They want to blow us up if you don't.'

Wearily Flemington began walking down the runway again. Bryington went with him for a way, but dropped out. Instead Cheetham came running up. They reached the plane and Kamil was looking down from the cockpit. He wanted Flemington to climb up the rope, the way he went down. Flemington told him he wasn't a monkey, and he wasn't

456

going anywhere until Kamil gave him his shoes, leather slip-ons he had left behind in the cockpit. They had been hand-made for him, and were only a week old. Incongruously, in this moment of extreme tension Kamil duly passed down the shoes. Then Flemington demanded the hijackers should lower the ladder at the back, and this they did too.

As Flemington returned on board Yaghi wanted to hit him. He began beating wildly at Flemington's chest, but Kamil pulled him back. Both men were furious. Kamil said they should take off immediately and fly to Uganda. He would present the plane and the South Africans to General Idi Amin. Flemington, of course, knew this was impossible, but could hardly tell the hijackers. Kamil made him return to his seat in the cockpit, and even suggested Flemington should show him how to fly the plane and he would fly it up Africa. Flemington told him he could not as they did not have enough fuel and the Malawians were blocking the runway.

Flemington was becoming desperately tired and sick of the whole business: it had gone on too long, and there was no sign of anything happening. Even the South Africans in the control tower would not tell him what was being planned. He had been thinking in terms of a ransom, but they would not hear of it. Nor would President Banda, initially. But Flemington asked Kamil how much he wanted. Would he accept the million dollars he had mentioned, and a light aircraft to carry him up Africa? Yaghi came through, and though he could understand no English, now butted in. 'One – no, no – Five.' He was thinking big, evidently. Besides this, they accepted Flemington's suggestion that they should be transferred to a light plane to continue their flight. The captain returned to his radio and put the proposal to the control tower. The authorities agreed. They would send out the money the men demanded.

In due course Flemington spotted two men approaching through the gloom, one of them Bert Cheetham. He was carrying a vanity case obviously far too small to carry anything like the amount needed. In fact it was full of cardboard with dollar bills pasted to the top layer. Yaghi and Kamil waved Cheetham away, more het-up than ever. They wanted millions of dollars, and would not settle for anything less. But at least they were now prepared to talk terms even without Harry or Tony Wilson.

In the odd moments he was left by himself in the cockpit, Flemington had given the authorities his personal assessment of the situation, and suggested that if they could contrive some sort of diversion he might be able to organise another escape. They promised they would do their best. But before anything happened Kamil came through and said he wanted Flemington to turn all the lights off. They all needed some sleep. Anyway, it would be better if they slept because he was going to have to blow the plane up and they would die more pleasantly if they were already out cold.

This was Flemington's cue to attack Kamil's nerves once more. No, he wanted to be awake when Kamil lit the fuse. He wanted to see it all happening. The passengers looked horrified, and so did Dirkie Nel. The hijackers should get on with it and blow the plane up without further ado, said Flemington. He was tired of all the waiting around. That was enough for Nel. Kamil was just beginning to say he did not really mean it and was not ready to blow up the plane until the last possible moment. But the steward was already quietly sliding through one of the open windows, so gently that for a time nobody realised he was missing. Kamil soon understood what had happened but was so frightened of what Yaghi might do that he told him Nel was in one of the lavatories.

The tension was at fever pitch now. Yaghi was near the end of his tether and Kamil seemed as frightened of him as the passengers were. At last there was a diversion: a South African security man came on board, giving his name as Fourie of the South African Embassy in Malawi. He was there to negotiate terms with the hijackers. How much did they want? They told him, and he left the way he had come. The real purpose of the visit was, of course, to spy out the lie of the land, and gauge the hijackers' vulnerability. From now on Flemington was looking for a chance to escape. He had already briefed the three remaining passengers. When he gave the word he would throw open the little windows in the cockpit and they would all scramble out. Two or three times he signalled that he thought the moment had come, but on each occasion the passengers told him they could not manage. After all, Weinbren and Mellish were both getting on in years and not as fit as they might have been, while Orren was understandably scared out of his wits.

There was a long delay as the Malawian authorities collected all the money they could lay their hands on, in half a dozen currencies. They eventually assembled something like 150 000 dollars from Blantyre's different banks. They packed it in two tin trunks and Fourie drove it out in a small open delivery truck. It was full daylight by this time and the hijackers watched him coming.

When he reached the aircraft he opened the trunks to show them the money was real. Kamil went down to the tail while Yaghi remained in the cockpit, standing over Flemington who was pretending to be fast asleep. The three passengers crouched in their seats at the forward end of the cabin. Kamil lowered the after ladder and he and the security man tugged the trunks up into the aircraft. Fourie went back to the truck while Kamil opened the trunks and began digging into the money to check that it was all real and there was no trap. He was looking to see if there was a false bottom.

Yaghi was watching all this and at last he could contain himself no longer. He checked to see whether the cockpit windows were tight shut, looked again at Flemington who was still lying flat out in his seat, and went down to the tail. Flemington glanced down the aisle and when he saw Yaghi putting the explosive in his pocket and bending down beside Kamil, he signalled to the passengers. Quickly he unfastened the windows and threw out the ropes, and as Mellish came through and climbed out of the first officer's side he slid out of his own window while Weinbren prepared to follow him. His last glimpse as he slid through was of Orren still in his seat, peering round the door, and of the hijackers throwing money into the air over their shoulders. It looked almost comical. He and the others landed on the ground and raced down the runway for cover. This time the plane was going up for sure.

But it did not happen. As they recovered themselves they turned back just in time to see Orren suddenly diving out of the window head first, at the last minute realising there was a rope, grabbing at it in mid-air, turning a half-somersault and falling the rest of the way to land flat on his back. He had stayed frozen in his seat when the others escaped, and saw the hijackers tearing down the aisle to catch them. But as the last pair of heels disappeared Yaghi had thought all four hostages had gone, and returned to the money. Orren realised that he was on his own, and made his move. The hijackers chased down after him, he slammed the door in their faces and leapt out. On hitting the ground he nearly knocked himself unconscious. Fortunately the security man was still nearby and saw what had happened. He raced up, piled Orren into the back of his truck and sped down the runway to pick up the others. He drove them to the administration building, where a thoughtful soul provided each of them with a long, cold beer.

The end was near. By this time President Banda was handling the situation personally, and his chief Secretary of State was in the control tower at the airport and in touch with the Presidential Palace by hot line. Already men of the crack Malawi African Rifles were in position some way from the plane and keeping it under cover. Banda had said

459

there could be no question of bargaining with the hijackers: they should surrender or blow the plane up, and that was the end of it.

The day dragged on. Bert Cheetham and other South African Airways men went out to turn off all the power in the aircraft by means of a remote switch under the fuselage. That meant Kamil and Yaghi had no light and no water. They were left to swelter out the noon heat in an aircraft already hot as an oven. Later they used the loudhailer to call for a priest. The authorities sent one to see them, and after hearing their confessions he arranged for them to be given water. But when the army commandant demanded their unconditional surrender they refused: they were afraid he would hand them over to the South Africans.

The siege continued into the night, with the troops making no move. But before dawn they moved to within 100 feet of the aircraft, and the commandant again demanded surrender. There was no response, and he ordered his men to open fire – deliberately low. Later they fired into the aircraft itself, and within seconds Kamil and Yaghi emerged down the back steps, with their hands up. Yaghi had been hit in the foot. The airport was reopened, and within hours President Banda was on his way to Britain.

Both South Africa and the Lebanon formally applied for the extradition of the hijackers, and it was expected that President Banda would send them to South Africa where they could expect the death penalty in terms of legislation recently introduced. Instead, he bowed to pressure from the Organisation of African Unity and arranged to have them tried in Malawi. Both pleaded not guilty, and though Kamil refused to make any kind of defence Yaghi made out he had never even seen Kamil before, until they met on a plane flying to Africa from Beirut, and Kamil suggested he should join him on his safari. Certainly, he had no idea he would be involved in anything like a hijack. But the judge was not impressed and sentenced both men to eleven years in gaol, with hard labour. The hijackers appealed, but the sentences were confirmed.

5

THE NOTED American business magazine *Forbes* carried a cover story on Harry and the Anglo American, and introduced an important section on mining house management with a sad confession: 'To American eyes, few financial organisations are more bewildering than the group system perfected by South Africa's Anglo American Corp. The Anglo

American group is not really a single corporation. It is a congregation of hundreds of them – operating companies, investing companies, service companies, you name it. There are in fact 560 such companies to which Anglo provides various services, and a grand total of 1 120 to which it provides board representatives.'

Trying to unravel the point of all this complexity, the magazine resorted to an historical survey of South African mining to explain the need for the various houses: the early problems of trying to borrow money to float new operating companies, the need to spread the load widely through equity, and the method of keeping control of the resulting company not through stock majority but through management contracts.

That certainly was the original conception of a Rand mining house. But in the case of the Anglo American first Ernest and later Harry took the notion a good deal further – partly by accident, though chiefly by planned evolution. Far from a single line of control from top to bottom, as in the pyramid structure now familiar in many forms of business finance, the Anglo group is in three dimensions which pose extreme problems for those trying to reduce them to a simple explanation. Apart from anything else, Anglo is no longer a single mining house *per se*, but an amalgam of the interests of many others that used to be its rivals. As the South African *Financial Mail* quipped:

Where have all the houses gone?
Long time passing . . .
Under Anglo every one.

The problem is, the Oppenheimer group is riddled with apparent anomalies. First of all, it should properly be regarded not as the 'Anglo' group, but as 'De Beers'. In terms of market capitalisation the diamond company is two and a half times as big as the gold mining house, and its interests stretch relatively much further. However, since a time soon after Ernest's appointment as chairman of De Beers in 1929, Anglo has held the appointment of De Beers' consulting engineers, so that decisions taken by Anglo's board and offered to De Beers as advice and recommendation radically affect the decisions taken by the De Beers directors. Since that time, too, the De Beers board has included a significant number of Anglo nominees.

For years Anglo's involvement with De Beers was relatively uncomplicated, until Harry's formation of Charter Consolidated suddenly introduced a third element to the picture. The three companies were to be administered separately, with their own chairmen and boards of directors and more significantly their own highly individual bodies of

461

shareholders, each with ideas of its own. Though Anglo was to provide certain advisory services to the others which affected their policies, the characters of the three partners, each linked with the other through minority holdings in equity, were to remain distinct.

Then there was Rand Selection, a masterstroke of investment strategy which demonstrated Harry's completely original approach to the problems he was facing. The company was given a massive portfolio, half the size of Anglo's, with its money drawn largely from De Beers, even if its chief asset was to be the right to share in Anglo's business outside diamonds. Rand Selection was given an important role in the financing of Charter, and served as a key buttress in strengthening the far-flung Oppenheimer empire.

These four giants of Harry's group – Anglo, De Beers, Charter and Rand Selection – are involved to a greater or lesser extent in all its undertakings, whether directly or indirectly through significant holdings in companies which exert *direct* control. Anglo American Canada, Anglo American Australia, Zambian Anglo American, Rhodesian Anglo American are all locked into place through these cross-holdings. So are Anglo American Industrial, which has a firm holding in De Beers Industrial, which in turn controls A E and C I; Anglo American Gold Corporation, formed through the recent amalgamation of the old WRIT and OFSIT and now the biggest gold investment house in the world; Anglo American Investments, controlling Anglo's 19 per cent holding in De Beers which gives Harry his right to the chair of the senior corporation; UAL, Harry's merchant bank; H D Development, with its control of Engelhard Minerals; even Vereeniging Estates with its control of valuable coal mines. All these companies – and scores more, particularly those operating in mining, industry and property – are subject to Anglo's control and therefore to Harry's as the man who controls Anglo. His holding in the corporation is only 10 per cent or so – 13 118 280 ordinary shares of a total 130 million through Oppenheimer and Son with 565 350 registered in Harry's name – but more than enough to retain his position without the breath of a challenge to his authority.

Anglo itself may be understood as two quite distinct operations – 'AAC Fin' and 'AAC Serve'. AAC Fin is an investment house, with a lot of money available to establish companies in which it buys shares or to buy shares in companies outside Anglo's aegis. It makes money either through the dividends these shares earn, or by selling them on the stock exchange. AAC Serve, on the other hand, is a service organisation, a huge enterprise employing people expert in the fields of techni-

462

cal mining, finance, secretarial and legal services or whatever else is needed. AAC Serve makes itself available to AAC Fin and to any of the companies AAC Fin is associated with, and earns its money through the substantial fees paid for whatever it does.

Of course, AAC Fin and AAC Serve are only notionally distinct, for the men who work for one may also work for the other. Those who hold the purse strings of AAC Fin may also be required to give financial advice to the mining or other companies it controls through holding the biggest single block of stock, even if it is a minority interest. Then they are AAC Serve. On the other hand, men who control AAC Serve companies in different parts of the world may also sit as Anglo nominees on boards of companies in which Anglo has substantial holdings. In this case they are AAC Fin.

In principle, it would be possible for shareholders with a controlling interest in Anglo to decide to close down AAC Serve and concentrate exclusively on AAC Fin. They could shut 44 Main Street, dispose of nearly all Anglo's staff, and resolve to rely on AAC Fin's portfolio of investments, which would still bring them a handsome income. In practice, this would never happen while Harry holds the controlling interest through Oppenheimer and Son. He has said more than once that the idea of making money through the stock exchange simply bores him. He has compared the share market with bookmakers on the racetrack: 'a necessary evil'. Given his way, he prefers to do something 'creative' with Anglo's money, even if the inherent risks are greater and the return takes longer to materialise. As he justifies it: 'In the long run you make more from starting something new.'

This is the thinking that has lain behind a good many of Harry's innovations down the years. As he put it in a recent interview: 'We like to do things that are big and difficult. If we go into a new field, we like if possible to go into something which has in it the seeds of expansion. We don't like to make acquisitions. Making acquisitions isn't really very amusing. I like to be in things where you have a possibility of investment, because it's much more difficult to find good business than it is to find money.'

Of late there have been a number of off-beat examples to show Harry's creative policies at work, each involving tens of millions in capital and taking years to come to fruition. They have been supported by a wide range of subsidiary involvements which have given Anglo its know-how in the world of industry outside mining, through the reinvestment of the group's huge cash flow within South Africa in whatever fields appear most promising: construction, real estate, agriculture,

463

vehicle assembly, even computer services; on a portfolio basis, every-thing under the sun. As the *Star* satirised them:

The time has come, the Chairman said,
To talk of many things:
Of cashew nuts and curried prawns,
Of beer and piston rings.

These are trivial investments in comparison with the 'big three' ventures outside mining in which Anglo is currently embroiled. The first of these is Highveld Steel and Vanadium, a vast undertaking initiated as a relatively modest conception in the late fifties: a means of producing vanadium from deposits north-east of Johannesburg. Anglo metallurgists decided that it would be feasible to make steel from iron in the ore that would be mined to produce the vanadium, so Harry decided this was the opportunity for Harry to challenge the government monopoly in South Africa's steel industry. Because this has been heavily subsidised, steel prices in the Republic are relatively low, and it has taken many years for Highveld to show its first profits. Indications are that eventual results will more than justify Harry's decision to stand loyal to his own policies, rather than cut losses and change tactics as many of his critics urged.

The second major venture is Anglo's costly move into forestry and lumber – put into effect only quite recently, though initially urged by Ernest as early as World War II. Anticipating a worldwide shortage of wood fibre in the near future, Anglo has acquired vast tracts of forest and built the paper mill at Mondi near Durban. The enterprise will be based on lumber, plywood and special wood products on the one hand, and printing and fine papers on the other.

The third significant enterprise is the huge Carlton Centre in Johannesburg, initiated in partnership with South African Breweries through its property subsidiary Retco. The scheme was conceived as an answer to New York's Rockefeller Centre and planned from the outset as one of the most ambitious building projects in the world. Adopting the name of the prestigious old Carlton Hotel, built by Barnato but demolished some years ago, the centre is made up of a complex including an international hotel, a mighty office block, exhibition halls, comprehensive shopping centre, restaurants, skating rink and all sorts of other attractions. Long before completion the project far outstripped initial estimates of its eventual cost, and there were fears it would prove a most unfortunate white elephant. The Breweries decided to end its participation, and after leaving Anglo to foot what was left of the construction bill, sold the group its remaining interests. Harry decided to go ahead as planned, and indications are that in spite of general pessimism, the project will justify his hopes.

This is where Anglo's advantage lies. With enormous cash resources in reserve for any emergencies that may develop, Anglo keeps trumps up its sleeve. As Chris Griffith, who heads a number of Anglo's industrial projects, explained to an investigator: 'Anglo looks for a good return as rapidly as possible, but it does have the capability of holding its breath in the development of a project.' Ernest held his breath with De Beers in the thirties, and today Harry holds his as he guides the massive growth of his world-wide enterprise.

To help him, Harry has a formidable team. He is flanked on each side by his deputy chairmen, Sir Keith Acutt and Hagart's successor, Bill Wilson. Both have worked with him long enough to know exactly how he likes to deal with any question that arises. Were he to step aside tomorrow, each would be capable of continuing with his policies for as long as need be. Each sits with Harry on the Executive Committee of senior directors that is at the heart of the whole group and meets three times a week to decide its policies and direct their interpretation.

There are eight others on this Exco, between them representing the whole spread of Anglo's involvement. They include Sydney Spiro and Murray Hofmeyr, respectively now chairman and managing director of Charter and based in London, though frequently visitors to Johannesburg and of course in close touch through telex communication; and Sir Albert Robinson, an Anglo man who is chairman of JCI by virtue of Anglo's strong holding through Rand Selection. Then there are Gordon Waddell and Julian Ogilvie Thompson, the latter particularly useful through his thorough knowledge of diamond affairs; Gray Fletcher, another De Beers director; and Gavin Relly, who has particular knowledge of copperbelt and North American affairs after stints as resident director in Zambia and Canada.

There has been an executive committee at the heart of Anglo since Ernest's day, of course. It was originally largely Ernest's conception, consisting of himself, Hagart, Harry and perhaps two or three others, meeting when necessary to decide matters of policy. In those days its meetings were so irregular and informal that they were called on the spot whenever there was something to be discussed. The committee's secretary gathered as many of its members as he could to attend. Today Exco's meetings remain informal, but are organised on a regular basis. As many members of Exco as are in Johannesburg will be present. They are backed by a central secretariat based at 44 Main Street and known as the Chairman's Office, responsible for the mass of paperwork that each Exco man must digest to keep abreast of group affairs.

Besides the executive directors, there are a number of directors serving on Anglo's full board who have particular responsibility for defined areas of operation. They include, for instance, W S Gallagher, the group's technical director and one of the most influential men in the group with a mighty international army of mining engineers, geologists and metallurgists under his command. There is Philip Oppenheimer, knighted in 1970 'for services to British exports' in regard to the diamond trade, and apart from his positions as director of De Beers and Anglo and managing director of the Diamond Corporation, now deputy chairman of Charter. There is Sir Frederick Crawford, Anglo's resident director in Rhodesia, and N K Kinkead-Weekes, who represents Anglo in Australia. In all there are 19 full directors, apart from Harry and his deputy chairmen, and 19 alternate directors.

Many Anglo directors and alternate directors are termed 'managers' in terms of the administrative hierarchy headed by Harry and his Exco. There are 25 of these, each responsible for a particular sphere of operations and in the last resort answerable to Exco though allowed a wide degree of freedom. The individual managers are expected to keep in close touch with Exco, particularly on matters of high-level financial operations and top personnel appointments. When they want a ruling on a particular question, they will probably attend an Exco meeting and put their case in person. The spheres of their involvement range from Anglo's gold, diamond and coal divisions, through finance, property, industry, agriculture, prospecting and management services, to particular geographic areas like Rhodesia, Zambia, Australia, North America and Europe.

Parallel with the managers there are a number of specialist consultants – accountants, personnel directors, economists, employment practices advisers, public relations men, even medical advisers and architects – and the men who fall under the technical director, again in slowly concentrating fields of responsibility. The technical director has four deputies, each in charge of a particular international geographic area. Then there are legions of consulting mining engineers, consulting mechanical and electrical engineers, consulting geologists and consulting metallurgists, all with their own assistants and staffs, and all in charge of a particular area of operations and responsible to the technical director. All are on the Anglo payroll, effectively working for AAC Serve, and all are deputed to act in whatever capacity is required by the particular companies which have appointed Anglo their secretaries and consulting engineers.

In terms of the group hierarchy, many of those at the top of Anglo's subsidiaries rank as the equals of senior men within head office management: the general managers of the bigger mines, or the divisions of NCCM on the copperbelt; the general managers of the diamond producers, the industrial companies. They may themselves be promoted to full management responsibility within the group, as have many before them. But for the time they rank as king in their world within a world, each with responsibility for hundreds of the tens of thousands of workers who make Harry one of the world's most significant employers.

It is an awesome responsibility, though of course Harry was born to it. He remains at the heart of his organisation, its breath and its lifeforce, with his considerable personal influence extending to its furthest extremities: prospecting operations in the Yukon, the Amazon basin and in the sea off Thailand; nickel in Australia, potash in Yorkshire, tin in Malaysia, oil in Canada; diamond sales in London, the bullion market in Zurich, citrus farming in Rhodesia, beer brewing in Zambia, hotel management in Natal. He is present at least in spirit in all these ventures and a thousand more.

Extraordinarily, though he is not getting any younger, he shows no sign of slowing down. He continues to spend a good deal of his time in aeroplanes, winging from one part of the world to another – usually by scheduled services rather than in one of Anglo's private jets, as he finds the airliners more comfortable. He sets his own pace, and evidently takes pride in making it as tough as he can. Certainly he shows no sign of wanting to retire, and indeed might find himself bored to distraction in enforced idleness.

Apart from having to meet the actual physical demands of his busy life, Harry is subject also to extreme mental pressures. On top of the daily charge of his organisation, he accepts scores of invitations to address meetings on a wide variety of topics, particularly those related to current affairs and the business world. As he makes it a point of honour to write these speeches himself, and to have something important to say, this purely extra-curricular side to his life takes up a great deal of his time. But never does he disappoint his audience, and he remains as great a figure of controversy within South Africa and outside as he was in his years as a backbencher in parliament. It might appear, indeed, that he is more outspoken than ever.

There was, for instance, a speech he made early in 1973 to the University of Cape Town, at a protest meeting called to discuss the government's action in serving banning orders on a number of alleged student revolutionaries. As the university's chancellor, Harry did not mince his words: 'We are justified in believing that the Government has abused its powers. It has trampled our civil liberties underfoot and brought South Africa a long way nearer to being a police state.'

His words brought censure not from Prime Minister Vorster alone but even from Sir de Villiers, Graaff as leader of 'the official Opposition'. Vorster described Harry's speech as 'highly irresponsible . . . and I wish to express my strongest disapproval of his remarks.' Graaff said Harry was 'playing party politics', presumably on the Progressives' behalf. The UP had condoned the banning of the students as being in South Africa's interests. How could 'the official Opposition' do its job if Harry undermined its authority?

Harry has been careful to dissociate his personal views from those he expresses when he is speaking on behalf of his companies. 'I wouldn't hesitate to express views as chairman of the Anglo American that are contrary to what the government believes,' he told *Forbes*. 'But I would be rather careful to base them on economic considerations.' Or as he put it in an interview with the South African *Financial Mail*, to fulfil the role of captain of industry 'You have to try to convince people that you are concerned with economic development and raising the standard of living of the country in which you are operating. You really can't talk politics. I don't express views on what the Zambian government's attitude to South Africa should be, nor on what the South African government's attitude to Zambia should be. You've got to keep out of that sort of thing.'

Interestingly, Harry's moderation has paid off handsomely. Anglo, De Beers, Charter and all the other companies in the group appear to be popular wherever they operate. Certainly in South Africa the old antagonism between Anglo and the Nationalists has virtually disappeared, whatever they say about Harry personally. For one thing, Afrikaners can no longer afford to throw stones at 'foreign capitalists': South Africa now boasts a host of Afrikaans-speaking businessmen who are millionaires in their own right and moving into overseas markets themselves, both in Africa and on other continents. Besides, as Sir Keith Acutt points out, Anglo is the largest private employer of Nationalists in South Africa.

By a quixotic quirk of fate the fiercest attacks on Harry in the recent past have been made by students from the University of Cape Town, protesting against their chancellor as 'the embodiment of racist capitalism.' Following Harry's reaction to the banning of the student leaders, a group of left-wing Jewish students responsible for a campus

468

magazine, *Strike*, denounced UCT as 'a reactionary campus' and university liberalism as 'a myth', suggesting 'the discrepancy between word and deed originates from the top, filtering right from the Chancellor and the Council to the Senate and the Students' Representative Council.'

'When liberals like Oppenheimer speak of the bannings as infamies which have brought South Africa a long step nearer to being a police state,' the students continued, 'they fail to realise that they are in some measure responsible.

'As chairman of Anglo American and De Beers, and as a director of some 70 companies, our chancellor assumes a less progressive facade. Indeed he is an epitome of racist capitalism exemplified by a promised R60 average monthly Black wage in a gold-mining industry whose net profits exceeded R200 million last year.

'This industry, South Africa's politico-economic base, rests on an iniquitous migrant labour system, a system of barrack-like compounds, strict reinforcements of a disintegrated tribalism, destruction of family life and payment of starvation wages . . .'

A few weeks later, other students carried an effigy of Harry in the university's Rag Procession through the streets of Cape Town – though to be fair, they were not representative of student opinion as a whole. They also carried placards demanding that Harry 'Pay A Decent Living Wage', requesting him to 'Give Rights And Money – Don't Give To Charity', and suggesting 'Hunger Breeds Hatred'.

All this was concerned with Harry's supposed support of the apartheid system through Anglo's employment policy of paying wages admittedly far below the Poverty Datum Line. In particular, the complaints centred on the gold-mining industry, where wages were so low that Africans in the Republic preferred to take jobs elsewhere: for instance in the diamond mines where De Beers could afford to pay substantially higher wages than the gold mining companies, which were forced to keep wages low if they were to make gold mining a profitable operation. These companies were forced to recruit up to 80 per cent of their labour force from beyond South Africa's borders. There had been a worldwide outcry against the wages paid to black workers in South Africa, and reappraisal of the involvement of foreign-owned enterprises in the Republic. Anti-apartheid demonstrators in Europe and North America had been demanding that these outside concerns cut their ties immediately.

As it happened, Harry had a practical answer to the demands made by the students. A few days after the protest march he announced

469

Anglo would be voluntarily increasing the wages of the underground workers at Anglo's mines by as much as 60 per cent. Later in the year it was announced that other mining houses would be following suit. It was an immediate result of the dramatic increase in the price of gold on the world's free market, in the opinion of most long overdue in view of the metal's importance as a firm rock in the sea of fluctuating currency values. Nobody could say Harry and his colleagues were not trying. Indeed, when criticised on a visit to London shortly afterwards at the height of the Fleet Street pogrom that sought to force British firms to cut their ties with South Africa, Harry pointed out that the agitators had entered the field late in the day. The reforms were already an actuality, and he hoped they would go a good deal further yet.

That was happening, certainly. Anglo's gold division under John Shilling organised a complete reappraisal of the wages paid to black miners, and of their living conditions, and step by step its recommendations were brought into effect at the individual mines. Over 15 months there were quite unparalleled improvements, with a complete restructuring of black miners' jobs and steady upgrading of their rates of pay as it became clear the improved gold price was likely to remain.

Then, trouble. On September 4 1973, between two and three hundred machine operators – men who drilled the holes for explosives – working down the No 2 Shaft at Western Deep near Carletonville refused to go underground for the early morning shift. The mine management asked what was the matter, and was told the men were dissatisfied with their pay and wanted more money. The management told the men to resume work and promised that their complaints would be thoroughly investigated. All but thirty-six of the men decided to work the shift, and the dissidents were interviewed. When it was plain they could not be reconciled it was decided they should leave the mine.

Management investigated the complaints, and a most surprising picture emerged. The machine workers – the élite of the mine – had had pay rises amounting to 46 per cent over the previous 15 months, bringing their basic wage up to R51,70 a month, plus the food, housing and other benefits in kind received as of right and estimated as being worth R25 a month. However, a grade of miner junior to theirs – the winch drivers, loader drivers and loco drivers underground – had been granted pay rises amounting to 60 per cent over the same period, bringing their basic wage up to R41,60 a month, plus benefits in kind. The machine operators felt that the gap between the respective wage levels had been narrowed, and that their own

470

privileged position was being eroded. Now, therefore, they were demanding even bigger basic wage increases, to make the wage differential as wide as it had been before.

The management discussed these demands, and decided they could not be met. In terms of the restructuring of the jobs, management felt the new rates of pay were fair. In particular, though the difference between *basic* wages had been narrowed, adjustments to *bonus* rates meant that in terms of the wage actually paid over the differential was as wide as before. They called the machine operators at the No 2 Shaft to a meeting in their compound late in the afternoon of September 12, and told them of the decision. During the meeting, a number of the miners showed their dissatisfaction, and when it was over a number of them left the compound and went to hold a meeting on their own on a nearby kopje overlooking their hostel. Amid angry scenes they decided their only course of action was to go on strike, and to picket the No 2 Shaft in an effort to bring the mine to a halt. They went down to the shaft in time to head off the night shift, not all of whom were keen to go along with their demands. Scuffles ensued, stones and half bricks were thrown, sticks and knobkieries produced, and a number of black miners were hurt.

The mine management tried to intervene, but to no effect. The situation was getting out of hand. Miners were running riot all over the compound, smashing windows, raiding the kitchens, at last breaking into the liquor store and making off with its contents. The mine manager and the hostel manager called repeatedly for order, and asked the strikers to send representatives to discuss their grievances. This was not done and management decided to call in the police.

Initially a small force of twelve armed men arrived to restore order. They fired cannisters of teargas at the mob, but could make no impression on it. In all, more than 7 000 miners were in the compound, though only some 300 of these were involved in the rioting and looting. It was getting dark now, towards 8 o'clock in the evening, and as night fell the strikers grew bolder and the threat to life, limb and property greater still.

The police, by this time reinforced with further contingents, tried a baton charge to break up a mob now swelling to face them with pangas, knives and crowbars, sticks and stones. One brick caught a police constable full in the face, and broke his nose and knocked out his teeth. It was at this stage that the police command decided to open fire.

The situation was nothing like Sharpeville. There, the damage had

471

been done with a hail of bullets fired indiscriminately, and it was all over in 12 seconds. Here at Carletonville the police had been trained in riot procedure, in which the universal practice is to immobilise the ringleaders and so discourage their followers. Initially, three shots were fired, then single shots as the police tried to keep order. The riot continued, with a group of some 200 strikers advancing on the mine administration block in an apparent effort to burn it down. The police pursued them, and strikers ran in all directions as the firing continued. The police chased the strikers round the buildings of the compound like so many cops and robbers, and it was two and a half hours before further strong police reinforcements arrived and order was restored.

The cost was high. Eleven miners were shot dead by the police, while one man had been hacked to pieces by the strikers. A further 26 were seriously injured, either by gunfire or through being beaten up by the crowd. Eight men had been arrested by the police for inciting the disturbance, and were later brought to trial. Of the dead, five were from Lesotho, two from Botswana, two from the Transkei, two were Shangaans and one a Zulu.

There was wide publicity of the incidents the next day, not surprisingly. Gold shares tumbled in Johannesburg, London and New York. A party of more than 100 students from Witwatersrand University invaded 44 Main Street, demanding that Anglo pay higher wages to avoid such incidents in the future. Students at the University of Cape Town demanded that Harry should pay higher wages, or reconsider his position as their chancellor. There were big demonstrations outside South Africa House in London, led by the arch anti-apartheid agitator, the South African-born Peter Hain.

It was all most unfortunate, but for a refreshing change the world at large appeared quite sympathetic to the situation. Anglo had been totally honest about the tragedy, explaining the whole affair without holding anything back. Two days after the tragedy, for instance, John Shilling gave a full interview to Carel Birkby of the Johannesburg *Sunday Times*. He concentrated on the suggestion that the chief reason for the disturbances at Western Deep had been failure to explain the terms of Anglo's proposed wage restructuring to the miners concerned.

'The unfortunate events of this week were really a tragedy of misunderstanding. Dispassionate observers seem to have decided that the Africans became ill-tempered because they failed to appreciate the efforts being made and which will be made on their behalf.

472

'How sad it was that they just did not know. And this notwithstanding the steps we took and intended to take to pass on to our black workers, at all levels, the underlying conception of the scheme that we believe is to their ultimate benefit.

'It is terribly sad and ironic that the tragic event of last Tuesday should have occurred on an Anglo American mine. This group was so clearly in the van in introducing a more scientific and more rational system of job structuring and wage pattern. This was directed at raising the wages at lower levels and compensating men more adequately for skill and productivity potential. It may be that if our communications systems had reached a more sophisticated level the tragedy might not have occurred.

'In implementing the policies the instructions to the mines were clear: that whenever a new phase of the implementation of the policy was introduced, the underlying concept should be explained to the men concerned. For this reason we have for some years employed black assistant personnel officers who make direct contact with black employees.

'We have succeeded in setting up communications committees on some mines, but not all. At Western Deep Levels such a committee had not formally been established, but an advisory committee consisting of black assistant personnel officers and senior black staff had been established to advise the management on the implementation of the new job structure and changes in the wage pattern.'

The same day Harry announced that Anglo supported the idea of holding a full judicial inquiry into the shootings, and had launched its own thorough investigation into the events that led up to it. Anglo would appoint an independent body of advisers, both black and white, to assist the corporation to find ways of improving communications between workers and management. He took the opportunity of trying to set the Western Deep tragedy in perspective.

'It is necessary to distinguish between the grievances of one group of employees at one shaft of an individual mine, and the overall policy that we are following with regard to the improvement of the employment conditions for black labour.

'Our policy is to introduce, throughout our group, a proper hierarchy of jobs objectively evaluated and paid, and our ultimate goal is a uniform wage scale related not to colour or race but to responsibility and skill.

'In moving along this road, we were aware that traditional patterns of employment would sometimes be upset, and the traditional habits and attitudes of particular groups of workers would sometimes be disturbed.

'These risks we had to accept. We remain convinced that our policy is right and we shall continue with it, for this is the only way in which South Africa can progress toward a more productive, more prosperous economy offering greater opportunities to all.

'We believe that our decisions relating to changes in the job structure and pattern of wages have been equitable. We accept that communication to our employees of the concepts underlying our policy is vital to its successful implementation.

'We shall continue to seek ways of improving the means of communication that we have developed, so that as far as possible our policy and the decisions we take in executing it are not only understood, but seen to be fair and reasonable by our employees.

'We are infinitely saddened by what has occurred at Western Deep Levels, but we are not discouraged, nor shall we relax our efforts to raise the living standards of all who work for us.'

Harry had been due to fly to London on the Friday following the tragedy, but postponed his departure. When he did reach London, one of his first engagements was to appear live on the BBC current affairs programme *Panorama*, which devoted a full half hour to what had happened at Carletonville. Most significantly, Harry admitted there was no justification for the relatively wide gap between the lowest wages paid to whites, and the highest paid to blacks.

'This is wrong,' he said. 'We must put it right.'

In the course of the interview Harry went out of his way to emphasise a change of heart on the part of the South African government. Earlier in the year, he pointed out, there had been illegal strikes in Durban involving some 50 000 Zulu workers demonstrating in the city's streets. It was feared the strikers could have got out of hand. But the South African government decided not to intervene, and the strikers won the wage increases they demanded through what turned out to be perfectly peaceful methods.

It may be that Harry is right, and the South African government is indeed reconsidering its view of black African rights. Such a change of heart would help bridge the wide gap between the government and South Africa's biggest private employer, always such an anomaly. For the time, though, Harry's position continues to be delicate in the extreme, at least to the hard core of the Afrikaner nationalists. For all the efforts to seal the breaches, the confrontation between Afrikaners and English – by implication still *uitlanders* – is as bitter as ever. Afrikaner-backed private enterprise has made considerable strides in cornering its share of South Africa's markets at home and abroad, but at the same time mighty state-owned corporations have muscled in on what has traditionally been the private sector in South Africa. Harry knows his enterprises are vulnerable to government interference, for instance through a degree of nationalisation or increased taxation. Against that, even Nationalists recognise that South Africa would be the loser if the brains and brawn of the Oppenheimer empire were to be forced from the field. Harry's companies are responsible for more than 10 per cent of South Africa's gross national product, and account for a third of the Republic's exports. All the same, as Harry put it to *Forbes:* 'I'm not certain that, once you get to be pretty big and pretty prominent, your best protection is not to become bigger still, particularly if your views are not those of the government.'

If Harry is in a delicate position in South Africa, how much more delicate is his involvement in countries overtly hostile to South African concerns, most notably Tanzania and Zambia. In Zambia Anglo has survived the upheaval of nationalisation of the copper mines with a remarkably even keel, and has adjusted well to its new role of partnership with the government Mining Development Corporation or Mindeco. Indeed, late in 1973 President Kenneth Kaunda saw fit to lay on a special luncheon at State House in Lusaka in Harry's honour, and to invite the Press and Zambian television to mark the occasion.

'We welcome you to Zambia once again because we consider you to be a sincere friend of Zambia,' the President began. 'Your organisation, which we know to be effective in the various ways in which it has undertaken various tasks, has done a great deal of work for us and with us in this Republic. We know that together with you and your colleagues we are carrying out in this country a very important experiment – an experiment of getting the State to work with private enterprise. I must say that ever since we started on this experiment we have had no cause to regret at all . . .

'It must be understood clearly that one of the principle reasons why this experiment seems to be succeeding is that your leadership of the industry, which you have led almost for the best part of your life, really has been outstanding. We appreciate this very much indeed. We don't only say this in your presence. We say it in your absence. This shows how genuine we are when we speak of your leadership . . . You have given us that leadership in this country which we value very much indeed and indeed the people you have employed in management have done equally well.

475

'We started off from a doubtful point, but as I have indicated already we have been developing from one point of strength to the other. This is very heartening to us and we hope and pray that God will continue to guide you and all those who work with you. I was going to say those behind you, but here in Zambia we don't accept someone being behind somebody, because, if I may depart a bit, we are receiving lots of statements from certain countries, friendly countries, who said they were behind us, but in the end there was nothing that came from those countries. We like them to say they are with us. So in this respect we are saying those with you as your colleagues and partners in this great adventure have done extremely well too and we are happy to say that.'

The reference to 'friendly countries' was concerned with the many states which had promised aid to Zambia to lighten the difficulties she encountered after closing her borders with Rhodesia and refusing to reopen them, but which had so far failed to deliver any. Like many other developing states in Africa, Zambia was discovering that in the long run it is private enterprise which is the better partner in state development, so long as only financial strings are attached. Harry used the opportunity to highlight the thinking behind private involvement in a state like Zambia, which relied heavily on President Kaunda's own philosophy of socialist Humanism.

'You, Sir, are associated with the policy and the work of Humanism to describe what is right in life and of course this goes not only into consideration of public policy, not only into questions affecting those who work in industry, but even in regard to private enterprise.

'This is a phrase which I think to many people suggests great, large, rather soulless organisations. That's a side to it, of course. But one has to remember that large companies really are made possible because lots of small people entrust their money to people who run these corporations; they expect them to be run properly, honestly, humanely; they expect to get fair returns on their money to bring up their children, to pay off the mortgages on their houses, and to do all the innumerable things that ordinary simple people need income for, and that naturally applies particularly to people who look to the returns on their investments when they get old and are no longer living directly on what they earn from their salaries.

'All this we have got to be conscious of, and I could only say that it is an enormous privilege for us to be allowed to take a part in the development of a country where these human considerations are always so much to the fore. Obviously that springs in the first place from you, Sir, and permeates all through the Government which you lead. We are extremley grateful to have our part in this great experiment.'

Sadly, it was a matter of three months before the situation changed dramatically. First of all President Kaunda signed his country's new constitution, making Zambia officially a one party state. The ceremony was attended by the representatives of a number of independent African republics, but in particular by Presidents Nyerere of Tanzania and Mobutu of Zaire. These heads of state were present three days later when the much heralded Tan-Zam Railway reached the border between Tanzania and Zambia, and crossed into Zambian territory. It was supposed the Chinese workers building the line would reach the copperbelt terminus within two years, which would at last provide the independent link with the sea that Zambia had sought for so long.

Now, in a move altogether unexpected, Kaunda announced his government was preparing to take administrative control of the copper mines. The foreign mining houses which had been responsible for managing the mines until that time were, he explained, still milking Zambia of most that she might gain from her copper resources. That had to cease immediately: and to stop it he would have to deprive these outside interests of their privileges and cancel their contracts.

The news came as a bombshell. What could lurk behind it? Was Kaunda responding to pressure from the Chinese, who clearly had their eye on Zambia's natural resources in view of their own needs for the future? What was he proposing to do when Anglo and Amax pulled out?

Whatever the case, it was soon clear that what Kaunda had said in the heat of the moment was not really what he proposed to do. It appeared to observers that he had responded to heavy pressure exerted by a group of clever young 'advisers' from the London School of Economics, left-wing in their sympathies and keen to rid Zambia of her 'capitalists'. Kaunda soon received a number of offers from financial organisations keen to win the management contracts for the copperbelt – most significantly Anglo's keenest rival in Central African affairs, the Lonrho group, and others from Rumania, Hungary, Italy and Yugoslavia. But copper is perhaps the most fickle of all metal markets, and the companies which offered themselves to Kaunda knew precious little about it, and certainly little about conditions in Zambia. With 97 per cent of Zambia's exports at stake, the president could hardly afford to take precipitate action, and there was a noticeable relaxation of his attitudes as he soberly reviewed the situation and re-opened negotiations with Anglo.

In spite of the left wing opposition encountered in Zambia and indeed in Tanzania, Harry has always insisted that an organisation like Anglo can span the split between Africa's black north and white south, and indeed any other supposedly unbridgable gaps between nations. As Harry told *Forbes*: 'You have to confine yourself to doing the one thing that all these countries want – develop the economy and try to raise the standard of living.' In Southern Africa he is seen as a reactionary, north of the Zambezi he is in the direct tradition of capitalist imperialism. But for all these contrasts in image, Harry will not say something in one country that he cannot say in another. He will say only what he believes – or rather, he will decline to say what he does *not* believe. Harry will not tell Zambia that he believes in black supremacy at the expense of white, because he does not; and no more will he tell capitalist South Africa that he believes in socialism, because again he does not.

These apparent anomalies of Harry's position greatly appealed to the man from *Forbes*, who appreciated the sheer physical power Harry could exert if not trammelled by the touchy nationalist governments he has to accommodate, whether black or white. 'In most countries businessmen are the bedrock of the conservative instinct,' wrote the correspondent, 'the supporters of the status quo, the defenders of the existing regime. But not in South Africa. There the leading political maverick, considered in certain right-wing quarters as only slightly less dangerous than Mao Tse-tung or Fidel Castro, is industrialist Harry Frederick Oppenheimer . . .' In another section of his article he produced a telling quote from an Anglo executive who was trying to describe what Anglo was all about: 'Just think of us as the Mafia . . . and Harry as the Godfather.'

As if to bear out this idea – though of course it could hardly be further from the truth – Harry sees his top-management team as 'a band of brothers'. His idea is that any organisation – business or political or anything else for that matter – should be run by a group of men who are so close that they will communicate their thoughts to each other as soon as they form them, without having to pause to consider the effect they may have. The men may regret them later, but it does not matter: their friendship is so close that they can say whatever they want without constraint.

To generate this climate at Anglo, Harry works particularly hard on the social side of his leadership. He and Bridget give as many as five dinner parties at Brenthurst each week, most of them revolving around men in the Anglo group. Harry likes to know not only the

478

names of those who work for him, not only the names of their wives and something of their background, but what they are like as people. Only this way, he feels, can he know what they have to contribute to the group, and what he can expect from them.

The 'brothers' are by no means stereotyped. It is difficult to spot a common denominator linking them together. In former days there were complaints that there were 'too many Rhodes Scholars and Oxbridge graduates, too few MBAs, hard-driving entrepreneurs and nimble-minded market strategists'; that there was 'too much concern with prestige, power and style, not enough with the tough business of cost cutting and profit making.' But recent years have seen an adjustment of the bias, and today the chief consideration in determining the course of a man's career at Anglo is his suitability for the job in hand, and the success he has in carrying it out.

Interestingly, there is no question of any kind of moral pressure on an Anglo man's political views. It might be expected that membership of the Progressive Party would be a prerequisite of any advancement in the organisation. Instead, at Anglo the accent is on freedom of viewpoint. Anglo will grant a man time off to work for a political party, whatever it is, without being penalised.

Harry himself remains a keen supporter of the Progressives, while his great friend Zach de Beer figures among the managers after what has appeared lightning progress up the organisation since he accepted Harry's offer to join Anglo a few years ago: he is currently the group's man in Zambia, a key posting which involves considerable diplomacy on his part in negotiating copperbelt and other affairs with President Kaunda and his government. Gordon Waddell is a committed member of the Progressives too, and now that he has taken out South African citizenship it is possible he will stand as a candidate for parliament in South Africa's next general election. Indeed, the Progressives even approached Harry to stand for parliament once again, for the Parktown constituency which has until now been regarded as safe UP. He turned them down.

'I'm not standing for Parliament. It is quite out of the question,' he said. 'The Progressive Party in many ways is doing very good work and they are obviously looking for candidates, but my other activities make it impossible for me to accept.'

The *Rand Daily Mail* jumped upon Harry's refusal and replied with a leading article: CALLING HARRY OPPENHEIMER.

'At no time in its history has South Africa been more in need of a strong, effective Opposition able to offer a worthwhile alternative

479

which the majority of voters can accept. The Progressives have such an alternative – even Nationalists admit it – but thus far they have been unable to make any real breakthrough: they have not yet been able to overcome the traditional political status quo and adherence to the old UP.

'In this combination of circumstances the Progressives' approach to Mr. Harry Oppenheimer to stand as a parliamentary candidate makes good sense. It is disappointing that he has said 'no', but the matter is of such importance that it cannot be left there. Mr. Oppenheimer has had parliamentary experience and over ten years showed himself an outstanding MP. He left active politics in 1958 upon the death of his father and since then has devoted himself to building up the Anglo American Corporation. Here, too, he has proved his brilliant talents.

'He is now a man of 64, and having brought his business empire to this glittering point, will surely have made sufficient provision for others to maintain it. It should, therefore, be perfectly possible for him to retire from daily involvement and instead to give himself to the wider interests of the country.

'Not only is Parliament in need of men of his nature, but his entry into Progressive politics would have dynamic effects. It would serve to persuade many who will still view the UP as the main vehicle of change that they too should follow their natural bent and give total support to the Progressives. And without doubt, other outstanding individuals would follow his direct political commitment — to the gain of the country.

'For all these reasons, we hope that Mr. Oppenheimer's 'no' decision is not final. It must not be — for the sake of a sane South Africa.'

It is intriguing to consider what would happen at Anglo if Harry decided after all to accept such a challenge. He has been questioned about it before, and has insisted: 'Anglo American can't be a one man band. I regard it as my job, as I am getting on' – 65 in October 1973 — 'to build up a number of people to run the company. It is very important that they should be energetic, and it is also extremely important that they should like one another. They must see in it, not just a means to a livelihood, but a way of life.'

As time goes on, there is increasing interest in what *will* happen at Anglo when Harry goes. Certainly Sir Keith Acutt or Bill Wilson could step into his shoes at Anglo, Sir Keith or Sir Philip Oppenheimer could run De Beers, and Sydney Spiro could continue to run Charter. But these men are each of Harry's generation, and themselves no longer young. What is the position further down the age scale?

Most interest attaches to Gordon Waddell and Julian Ogilvie Thompson, though any suggestion that either is destined one day to take control of the whole organisation is in the realm of pure speculation. Each is young — not yet 40 years old – and currently they appear to be level pegging in terms of the Anglo hierarchy as virtually the group's joint managing directors. Ogilvie Thompson is well known to Harry as a former personal assistant, and has made it his business to learn of every conceivable side of Anglo's operations. Gordon, on the other hand, brings a valuable independent view to Anglo policy after his intense business training in Britain and America. Both are extremely hard-working, practically married to the organisation, and either would be regarded as a worthy successor should Harry step aside.

Where Gordon is concerned, it is interesting to note that Harry still treats him as a member of his family. He retains custody of his daughters, of course; but apart from that he has always been particularly close to Harry, and as Mary complains: 'He is much more of an Oppenheimer than I ever will be!' In this lies a key factor when it comes to considering Anglo's future: for the group remains largely a family business type of organisation, with the stamp of Oppenheimer and Son closely discernible wherever it operates.

It may well be that Anglo has survived and gone from strength to strength where other mining houses have fallen by the wayside largely *because* it is so much a family operation, not *in spite of* continuing in that framework. As Sir Keith Acutt explains it, other mining houses tended to lose direction as links with their founders disappeared: as the original controlling interest was divided and sub-divided between the surviving members of the founders' families, and their interest in its future and feel for its character slowly dissolved. The founders' places at the tops of their organisations were taken by salaried managers, who were obliged necessarily to look over their shoulders all the time and take into account what shareholders wanted, rather than rely on their own convictions.

Anglo, on the other hand, has been an Oppenheimer inspiration from the outset, as have all the companies in the group since their formation or from the time they fell under Anglo control. Even De Beers gained from this for as Ernest several times repeated, he saw his chairmanship and leadership in terms of the aims and ambitions of De Beers' founders, not the whims and fancies of shareholders – though he did admit that in the long run he and the other members of the board were there to make money for them. These were ideas he passed on to Harry, who has not dismissed the possibility that one day he will be succeeded by an Oppenheimer.

'Would you like to see a member of your family succeed you?' an interviewer asked him in 1969. He replied: 'Oh, obviously I would. This is natural, but it's something that may or may not prove possible. I have one son, who is a young man. He is very keen on Anglo American, but naturally it remains to be seen whether he, as he gets older, has the ability for this, and the taste for it. You know it's a bit like being tied to a wheel.'

Nicky's interest in Anglo has increased since 1969. After completing a term as Harry's personal assistant he remained in the Chairman's Office with an office immediately opposite Harry's over the corridor, and with an open door giving him access to his father at any time. It has been noticeable that of late Harry spends more time discussing Anglo affairs with his son as Ernest did with him. Already Nicky serves on a number of Anglo group boards as director or alternate director. It may well be he succeeds his father in due course, and there are more than a few within the organisation and outside who hope that he will.

But for the moment there seems small chance of any such question of succession arising. Harry is in the peak of condition, and indeed it might appear that in the later days of his leadership he is at his best and most dynamic yet. He has succeeded in building a team of men loyal to his leadership and to their companies, superbly able in the jobs they are doing and more than holding their own in an increasingly competitive world. Borne up by the altogether unprecedented bonanza in the price of gold internationally and the continuing success of De Beers' diamond marketing strategy, of increases in the price of copper and other base metals and the success of calculated risks like Highveld Steel and the Carlton Centre, the group is set to reap the rewards.

For most of his life Harry has been 'on show', bathed in a glare of publicity that will highlight any remark of his that sounds at all controversial, and will revel in the chance to create more controversy through the attacks that are periodically made upon him and upon the organisation. But in spite of it, and his admitted international significance, Harry has succeeded in leading an admirably private lifestyle. Even in Johannesburg he is able to wander the city's streets at leisure. People may recognise him and point him out to each other. But to most Johannesburgers he is simply 'Harry', at least behind his back, though to his face he is 'Mr Oppenheimer'.

Senior Anglo men address him as 'Harry' and refer to him as

'HFO' – though at one stage the adoption of heavy fuel oil on the copperbelt caused great havoc in telex abbreviations – while younger men oriented to American business methods refer to him as 'the Chairman'. At De Beers, still steeped in the tradition of 'Mr Rhodes', Harry is 'Mr Harry' to the longest-serving employees, as he is at Brenthurst and his various other homes. Rarely has a tycoon been so informal.

Not long ago Harry was in America and due to catch a scheduled flight to Europe when news came through that the airport was fog-bound, and he and the other passengers would have to transfer to another airport by bus. On the way Harry sat next to a young American student who was anxious to make conversation. One of Harry's aides across the aisle listened in with some amusement. Before long the student wanted to know what Harry did in life.

'Oh, I'm in mining,' he replied.

The younger man pressed him for details. That sounded interesting. What was his job?

'I suppose I'm really rather on the financial side,' Harry told him.

Harry was passing through London's Heathrow Airport one day when an immigration man stopped him.

'Oppenheimer,' mused the official. 'I know that name.'

He was trying to think of the connection, while Harry politely waited.

'I've got it,' the official said at last. 'Don't you breed bull terriers?'

He was thinking of Harry's cousin Raymond, in many quarters far better known than Harry through his reputation as being perhaps the world's leading breeder in his field.

There was another time Harry was mistaken for Raymond, this time when he was invited to open a new golf course in Britain. Local golfers turned out in scores when it was announced the ceremony would be performed by 'Mr Oppenheimer' – imagining this could only be the captain of the British Walker Cup Team as Raymond had been for many years. They watched expectantly as Harry teed up to drive a ball down the first fairway, and swung his club only to slice the ball and send it trickling a few feet to the left. Bridget was thoroughly amused by his embarrassment and the consternation of the onlookers.

The 'private' lifestyle Harry favours is not studied. He is ready to give his time to deserving interviewers from South Africa and elsewhere, and there is rarely any attempt to impose any form of in-house censorship on material they may produce. Harry is an old hand at dealing with interviews, and it is a fair bet that by the end of the allotted time he will have learnt more about the interviewer than the interviewer learns about him.

On occasions Harry has subjected himself to television interviews too, and again he has shown himself admirably suited to the medium. There was, for instance, a lengthy interview broadcast by BBC television in Britain. The noted critic Maurice Wiggin described the programme as 'riveting stuff'.

'Here we have a man who has made one of the world's biggest fortunes out of South Africa. He might have been the archetypal tycoon, and indeed in some respects he is – but politically he is a Progressive with a capital P, friend of the Black African and a resolute opponent of apartheid. He emerged a delightful man, charming without gush, clear-sighted, very decisive but not arrogant.'

Not everyone saw the programme. One Christmas recently Harry was in London at the time of the annual office party at which all those who work in Anglo's London office and at Charter meet to let their hair down. Everyone attends, from top management right down to the lowliest cleaners and canteen workers. Among the latter was a comely cockney lass known to one and all as Mabel.

The party was going well, when to their startled surprise several of those who knew Harry saw him dancing past with Mabel, who looked blissfully happy. A little later in the evening Mabel was near them and they button-holed her.

'Do you know who that was?' one of them asked.

'Course I do,' she said. 'That was 'Arry.'

'But what were you doing dancing with him?'

'I asked 'im, didn' I?' said the girl from the canteen. ' 'E was all by 'isself, so I thought 'e needed cheerin' up. I goes over and I says, My name's Mabel. What's yours? So 'e says Mine's 'Arry. 'Ow d'you do? And I says, C'mon then. You an' me's goin' to dance.'

She paused and gave Harry a little wave across the room. He grinned back, a twinkle in his eye.

'Real gen'lman,' said Mabel fondly. 'Ain't 'e?'

6

OF ALL THE honours that have come Harry's way down the years, the one he treasures most is that conferred by the town of his birth. On September 4 1973, in a simple ceremony on the steps of Kimberley's old city hall, he was granted the Freedom of the City. There to share the occasion were Bridget and Nicky, the mayor and council of Kimberley, the full board of directors of De Beers, a guard of honour and pipe band from the Kimberley Regiment and a good cross-section of the townsfolk.

As he listened to the speeches in his honour, Harry cannot have known of the fights and struggles behind the scenes that preceded the occasion. The idea of granting him the Freedom of Kimberley had first been raised at council meetings before the little town's centenary celebrations two years before, by Cllr Lawrie Shuttleworth. Would it not be the ideal occasion to honour a man who had done so much for Kimberley, the councillor urged, and indirectly the memory of a family which had done more for the city than any in its history? However at that time the city council was controlled by Nationalists, who dismissed the idea out of hand. Honouring Harry Oppenheimer, indeed! Whatever next?

Before long the Nationalists on the council were swept from power – chiefly as the result of a major row over the picturesque city hall, which they proposed to flatten. Leading the campaign for its preservation was Lawrie Shuttleworth, a man with a keen interest in Kimberley's past and as a result conscious of the city's debt to the Oppenheimers. When he was elected mayor the next year he decided one of his chief aims should be to give Harry his due, and brought the other councillors round to his way of thinking.

The plan at last approved, it remained to set a date. The most obvious was that set aside for a full meeting of the De Beers directors, when all would be in Kimberley. Invitations were sent out, a banquet organised at the prestigious new Hotel Kimberley, a guard of honour recruited from the Kimberley Regiment which was itself a Freeman of Kimberley and of which Harry had been colonel in chief since 1963, as Ernest and Cecil Rhodes had been before him. The council had a special citation drawn up, and a casket made to hold it.

The ceremony was set for five o'clock on a Tuesday afternoon. The streets round the city hall were closed to traffic, and seats for invited guests arranged round an open area on which the guard of honour was to parade. The regiment arrived with its pipes and drums, the mayoral party arrived, and on the stroke of five o'clock the crowds made way for Harry, Bridget and Nicky. They took their place on the platform erected before the city hall, an impressive setting with its Doric columns towering over the scene.

Harry's first job was to inspect his guard of honour on parade with

485

bayonets fixed. This he did to the music of a slow march, which as he admitted at the banquet in the evening was 'a little bit frightening . . . There was that business of the slow march, which I'm not really dreadfully good at. I do my best. I was reminded that when I first got married I used to dance with my wife. I was not very good at dancing and she disapproved of the way I danced and she used to count to make me keep in time. This soon stopped me dancing. It's one of the disadvantages of marrying a young wife—there are advantages too . . .'

For the time, though, Harry was far from amused by the proceedings. Instead, it was plain he was extremely moved. As the mayor launched into the speech of praise which preceded the granting of Freedom, all listened carefully and applauded enthusiastically. Those present were aware of the significance of the occasion, and all wished the guest of honour well. As the mayor ended his speech, the town clerk stood to read Harry's citation.

CITY OF KIMBERLEY

WHEREAS

HARRY FREDERICK OPPENHEIMER, Master of Arts of the University of Oxford, Doctor of Economics (*honoris causa*) of the University of Natal, Doctor of Laws (*honoris causa*) of the University of Leeds, Rhodes University and the University of the Witwatersrand, Chancellor of the University of Cape Town, has played a leading role in South African Affairs for 40 years, directs mining, industrial and financial enterprises in many parts of the world and is a distinguished international figure;

AND WHEREAS the said HARRY FREDERICK OPPEN-HEIMER was born in Kimberley in the year 1908, served with the South African forces in the Second World War and is Honorary Colonel of the Kimberley Regiment, was Member of Parliament for Kimberley for ten years, and was elected Chairman of De Beers Consolidated Mines Limited, Kimberley, on 5th December, 1957;

AND WHEREAS he continues to promote the City of Kimberley as the diamond centre of the world;

AND WHEREAS the City of his birth derives honour from his eminence;

NOW THEREFORE BY THESE PRESENTS BE IT HEREBY MADE KNOWN: That the City Council of Kimberley, acting under the powers vested in it by the Cape Municipal Ordinance, 1951, has this Fourth day of September, 1973, conferred on the said
HARRY FREDERICK OPPENHEIMER
the Honorary Freedom of the City of Kimberley.

It was the mayor's turn to speak.

'Mr Oppenheimer, I have much pleasure in presenting to you this citation which is a token of the Freedom of the City, which I hereby confer upon you.'

There was an eruption of clapping and cheering from all sides, a supremely happy and intimate moment as the mayor clasped Harry's hand and Harry smiled widely in gratitude. But soon he was composed again, and as he began to speak in reply to what the mayor had said, his expression was serious and almost strained as if the occasion was too much for him.

'Mr Mayor, Citizens of Kimberley: I am immensely grateful for the great honour that has just been done to me. I am delighted and grateful for your very kind words. Of all the honours and satisfactions, deserved and undeserved, that have come my way over the years, this must surely be among the greatest.

'Kimberley is my home town *(loud applause)*. Here are the roots of my business life and my public life, and at my farm just outside Kimberley my private life is at its happiest and its most peaceful. I am delighted that my wife and my son can be with me on this occasion. My connection with Kimberley is a family connection. I have followed in my father's footsteps as best I could, and I've tried to build on his achievements, and I hope very much that the time may come when my son in his way will take his sort of part in the life and work of Kimberley . . .'

Harry's speech was unusually personal, and though he ranged widely he always returned to the central theme of his close involvement with the city of diamonds. In reviewing his career he resorted to Afrikaans, one of the first times he had done this since emerging from parliament fifteen years before.

'Mr Mayor, the chains which bind me to Kimberley are strong and

487

unbreakable. Sixty five years ago I was born here in Kimberley, and the first memories of my childhood are of Kimberley, its friendly people, its winding streets and the sounds of life here. Forty years ago I began my working life here in Kimberley, and twenty-five years ago the voters of Kimberley gave me my chance to take a part in the public life of our country.

'My father arrived in Kimberley more than seventy years ago, and sixty years ago, Mr Mayor, he was elected to the high office you occupy today. Ten years later – that's fifty years ago – he was elected to represent Kimberley in parliament, and for fifteen years he was MP for Kimberley City.

'You have referred, Mr Mayor, to the important role De Beers has played in Kimberley's past. I would like to say, Mr Mayor, that the relations between the municipality and the De Beers Company are today outstandingly good, and for me that is a wonderful thing. My father and I, the one after the other, have occupied the chair of De Beers for the past forty-five years in succession, and we have always realised the importance of furthering the kinship of the town and the De Beers Company. And I feel that I won't be wrong to do all I can to further the relationship for all time.

'I have never yet returned to Kimberley without feeling that I'm coming home. And that is why I am so grateful to you, Mr Mayor, for the honour you have paid to me . . . My family and I owe much to the City of Kimberley, and what you have done today has for me crowned a long and happy association. For so long as I live it will be my pride and my joy to call myself a Freeman of this great City of Kimberley.'

At the banquet in the evening Harry was in a very different mood. 'Today has been very very exciting', he confided, 'and this dinner is ending it up in the most exciting way, because you know very often being given tremendous honours is a very uncomfortable procedure. But in Kimberley this is not so, for everything is wonderfully arranged and we're having a really splendid party.'

Harry turned to the remarks Lawrie Shuttleworth had made in the course of the evening, especially those relating to the privileges enjoyed by Freeman of Kimberley. One in particular sounded rather exciting: as a Freeman the Kimberley Regiment was allowed to march through the city with bayonets fixed and banners unfurled.

'Now you were telling us, Mr Mayor, of the privileges which go with being a Freeman of the City of Kimberley. I don't think I'm going to get my bayonet out very much and march about through the city (*laughter*), though it's nice to know that I would be allowed to do

488

so if I wished. But I'm told – I'm not sure if it's true – but if you are granted the freedom of a city like this it enables you to double-park wherever you like. I don't know if this is right. But if it's true, Mr Mayor, I'd like to ask a very great favour of you. Would you be prepared to give a sort of proxy to my son?'

It was a very happy occasion, and clearly nobody was more delighted with the proceedings than Harry himself. The atmosphere recalled the circumstances of Ernest's honorary doctorate at Oxford, twenty years before. As Harry put it: 'Mr Mayor, thank you again very much, it's been one of the very great days of my life; as I say, a day which I feel has given me something which I feel I don't deserve, but life would be a miserable thing if you never got more than you deserved.'

Three days later Harry was honoured again, this time in very different circumstances. He was in Mbabane, Swaziland, attending celebrations marking the little nation's anniversary of independence. One of the features of these celebrations was the opening of the Mbabane campus of the UBLS, the University of Botswana, Lesotho and Swaziland; and as part of the programme the university was conferring upon Harry the honorary degree of doctor of literature.

Harry was to be capped, and the ceremony was to be performed by the university's chancellor, King Moshoeshoe II of Lesotho. Explaining the university's decision to confer the honorary degree, the king said that it recognised in Harry's approach to the problems and policies of Southern Africa the approaches it favoured itself: a policy of cooperation and good will, and a guarantee of equal rights.

The occasion was significant in that Harry was being honoured not for the sake of the corporations he headed, but for what he was as a man; and not by fellow whites, but by Africans of the states which neighboured South Africa and were becoming increasingly vociferous in their condemnations of the Republic's policies. Besides Moshoeshoe, King of the Basotho, the ceremony was attended by Sobhuza, King of the Swazis; by Goodwill, King of the Zulus; by the Crown Prince of the Amandebele; and by an assortment of representatives of the royal and ruling houses of tribes all over the subcontinent.

You had the feeling as you watched Harry being capped and rising to accept the congratulations of King Moshoeshoe and the applause of the other crowned heads, that history was in the making. In the footsteps of Cecil John Rhodes, Mla'mlakanzi of the Matabele, Harry Frederick Oppenheimer was in his rightful place among the all-powerful Kings of Africa.

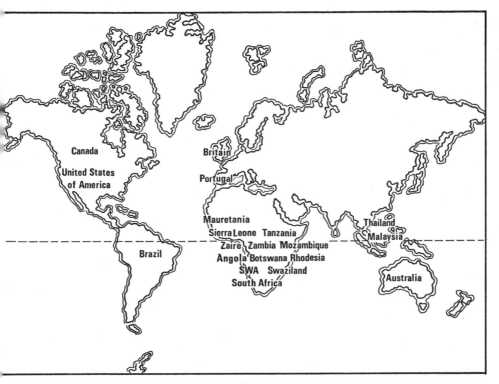

THE OPPENHEIMER EMPIRE

1 **Canada:** Anglo American Corporation of Canada Ltd, interests in Hudson Bay Mining and Smelting; Francana Development Corp; Agnew Lake Mines; White Pass and Yukon Corp; Western Decalta Petroleum, etc.

2 **United States:** Engelhard Minerals and Chemicals Corp, through H D Development.

3 **South America:** prospecting and exploration, especially in Central Brazil.

4 **South Africa:** finance and investment, gold, diamonds, platinum, copper, iron, coal, vanadium, uranium, steel, industry, property, construction, forestry, agriculture, timber, paper, foods, explosives, chemicals, textiles, engineering, transport, computers, merchant banking, etc.

5 **Swaziland:** Swaziland Iron Ore Development Corporation; Swaziland Development Corporation.

6 **South West Africa:** Consolidated Diamond Mines; Marine Diamonds.

7 **Botswana:** Anglo American Corporation Botswana, with interests in Botswana RST, Selebi Pikwe nickel/copper and Morupule Colliery; De Beers Botswana, with control of Orapa Diamonds.

8 **Mozambique:** fishing, agriculture.

9 **Rhodesia:** Anglo American Corporation Rhodesia with interests in coal, nickel, copper, iron, steel, ferro-chrome and allied engineering industries, citrus, sugar, general agriculture, forestry and general timber processing, cement, flour milling, rolling stock hire, property, merchant banking and industrial finance.

10 **Angola:** through De Beers, in diamonds; and through Charter, in oil.

11 **Zambia:** Zambian Anglo American, registered in Bermuda, with interests in Zambia Copper Investments, controlling 49 per cent of Nchanga Consolidated Copper Mines and 12,25 per cent of Roan Consolidated Mines; and industrial and agricultural interests in Zambia.

12 **Zaire:** through De Beers, in diamonds; and through Charter, in copper and cobalt prospecting.

13 **Tanzania:** Williamson Diamonds.

14 **Sierra Leone:** through De Beers, Diamond Corporation.

15 **Mauretania:** Société Minière de Mauritanie, mining copper.

16 **Portugal:** Beralt Tin and Wolfram.

17 **Britain:** Charter, Diamond Corporation, Anmercosa Sales (marketing metals), Cleveland Potash, Covenant Industries (chemicals); also interests in Rio Tinto-Zinc et al.

18 **Thailand:** prospecting for tin.

19 **Malaysia:** Tronoh Mines, Bidor Malaya, Sungei Besi Mines, all tin.

20 **Australia:** Australian Anglo American; mining finance, interests in International Pacific Corp (merchant banking), Tinnabruich (investment) and major prospecting ventures in New South Wales, Queensland, South Australia, Tasmania, Western Australia, Northern Territory and Papua New Guinea.

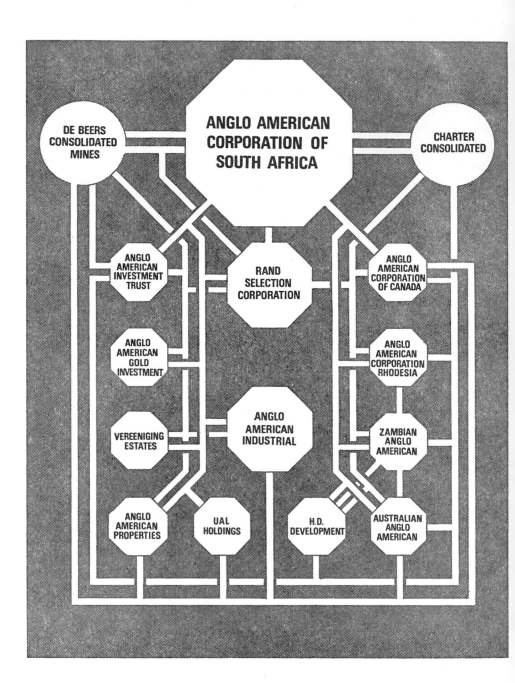

492

STRUCTURE OF THE GROUP

The constituent companies and corporations which make up the Oppenheimer Empire are bound together in a fascinating series of inter-relationships, summarised on the chart opposite. Though there are some notable omissions – for instance, AE and CI – most of the significant elements of the empire are represented. First figures quoted are market values of equity capital as at December 31 1972.

Anglo American Corporation of South Africa: R934 979 000, investments percentage (income from investments in brackets) gold 25 (31), diamonds 26 (19), coal 2 (3), copper 5 (14), platinum 4 (3), other mining 6 (4), industrial 21 (14), property 3 (2), finance 8 (10).

De Beers Consolidated Mines: R244 556 000 producing natural and synthetic diamonds, co-ordinates marketing by De Beers group and other producers, diversified investments outside diamond industry.

Charter Consolidated: £258 827 000, mining finance and investment, distribution of net assets per cent as at March 31 1972 as to mining finance 55,4; diamonds 6,6; gold 2,4; copper and other metals 7,1; tin and wolfram 2,5; industrial, commercial and oil 25,1; long term loans 0,9; geographical distribution per cent South Africa 36,4; rest of Africa 9,9; North America 19,1; Britain 14,4; Australia 15,8; elsewhere 4,4.

Rand Selection Corporation: R156 172 000, finance and investment with interests in great variety of companies in the group and outside.

Anglo American Industrial Corporation: R166 278 000, industrial finance and investment, holdings in De Beers Industrial (with 42,5 interest in AE and CI), Highveld Steel, Vereeniging Refractories, etc.

Anglo American Investment Trust: R575 000 000, major shareholdings in De Beers and diamond trading companies.

Anglo American Gold Investment Company: R455 504 000, substantial holdings in gold and gold/uranium mines of Western Transvaal and all gold mines in the Orange Free State.

The Vereeniging Estates: R61 187 500, property and mineral and coal rights in Transvaal and Orange Free State, and substantial interests in coal mining.

Anglo American Properties: R29 860 000, substantial interests in city centre office and shopping complexes in most major centres of South Africa, townships and marinas, residential apartments and land for future development.

UAL Holdings Ltd: R62 640 000, major force in South Africa in fields of merchant banking finance and related advisory services.

Anglo American Corporation of Canada: C$84 500 000, holding Canadian interests of AAC, De Beers and Charter, especially major holdings in Hudson Bay Mining and Smelting.

Anglo American Corporation Rhodesia: Rhod. $61 400 000, with Rhodesian interest of AAC and Charter in financial and investment companies; citrus and forestry estates; coal and nickel mines; and industrial, prospecting and property concerns.

Zambian Anglo American: £60 171 000, holding interests in ZCI which has interests in Nchanga Consolidated and Roan Consolidated, plus other substantial interests in Australian Anglo American, Anglo American Rhodesia, H D Development, etc.

Australian Anglo American: A$19 646 000, extensive exploration programme, taking advantage of new business opportunities in Australian mining industry.

H D Development: US $249 698 000, holding group's interest in Engelhard Minerals and Chemicals Corporation.

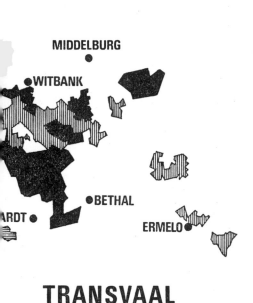

MIDDELBURG

●WITBANK

●BETHAL

ARDT ●

ERMELO ●

TRANSVAAL

● STANDERTON

1	F.S. SAAIPLAAS
2	PRESIDENT BRAND
3	PRESIDENT STEYN
4	WELKOM
5	WESTERN HOLDINGS
6	F.S. GEDULD
7	FREDDIES CONSOLIDATED
8	SOUTH VAAL
9	VAAL REEFS
10	WESTERN DEEP LEVELS
11	S.A. LANDS
12	EAST DAGGAFONTEIN
13	BRAKPAN
14	DAGGAFONTEIN
15	SPRINGS

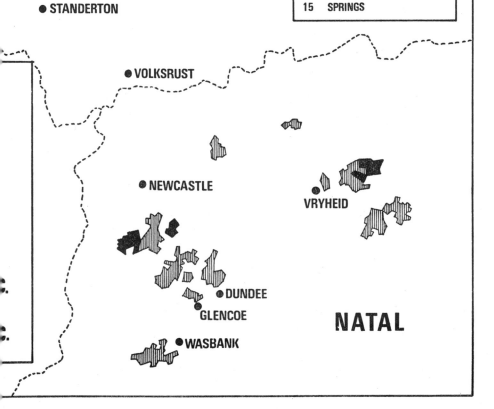

● VOLKSRUST

● NEWCASTLE

VRYHEID ●

● DUNDEE

GLENCOE

NATAL

●WASBANK

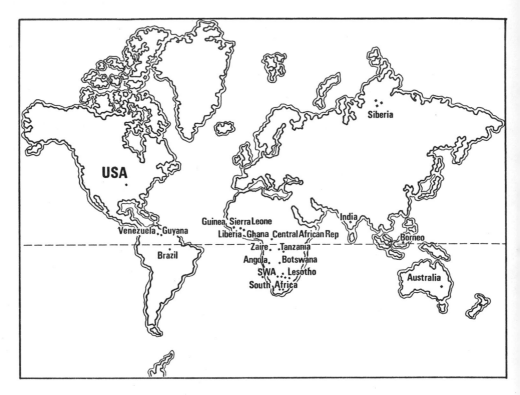

Southern Africa holds the world's richest deposits of gem diamonds, though diamond fields have been discovered as far afield as Siberia, Australia, Venezuela and the United States.

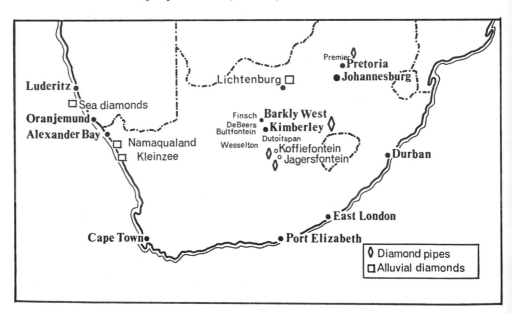

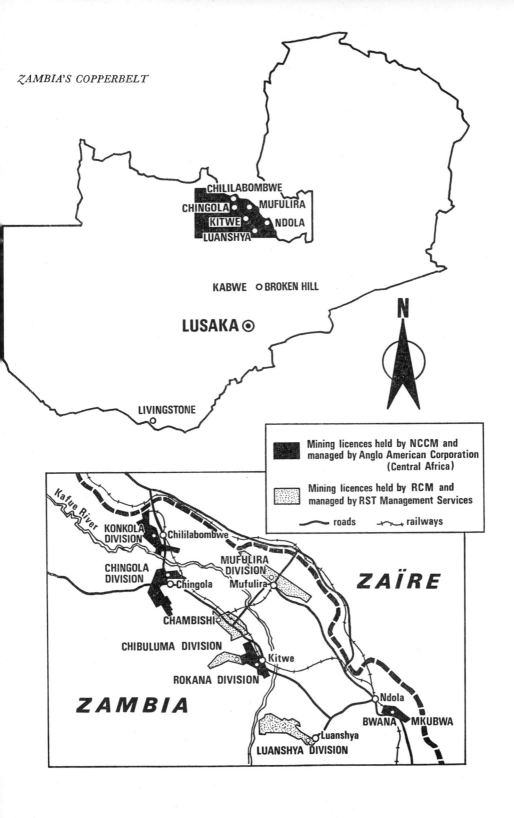

ZAMBIA'S COPPERBELT

CHILILABOMBWE

CHINGOLA   MUFULIRA

KITWE   NDOLA

LUANSHYA

KABWE ○BROKEN HILL

LUSAKA ◉

N

LIVINGSTONE ○

Mining licences held by NCCM and
managed by Anglo American Corporation
(Central Africa)

Mining licences held by RCM and
managed by RST Management Services

roads   railways

Kafue River

KONKOLA
DIVISION   ○Chililabombwe

MUFULIRA
DIVISION

CHINGOLA
DIVISION   ○Chingola   Mufulira○

ZAÏRE

CHAMBISHI

CHIBULUMA DIVISION

ROKANA DIVISION   ●Kitwe

ZAMBIA

●Ndola

BWANA MKUBWA

●Luanshya

LUANSHYA DIVISION

Select Bibliography

A NUMBER of the works cited themselves include select bibliographies, and these are marked with asterisks.

1 Material relating to the life of Sir Ernest Oppenheimer

A GENERAL

Cartwright, A P: *South Africa's Hall of Fame* (Johannesburg, Central News Agency, 1960)

*Gregory, Sir Theodore: *Sir Ernest Oppenheimer and the Economic development of Southern Africa* (Cape Town, Oxford University Press, 1962)

Oppenheimer, Harry: *Sir Ernest Oppenheimer, a Portrait by his Son* (Johannesburg, *Optima*, Sep 1967)

Rae, N and Stanford, G: *King of Diamonds* (Johannesburg, *Personality*, Jun 1957)

B PARTICULAR

pre Kimberley—Fallek, Etienne: *Memories of a Diamond Dealer of the Good Old Days* (Antwerp, *Diamant*, Dec 1960)

mayoralty—*Diamond Fields Advertiser*, Kimberley: council debates and resolutions, 1906–1915; mayoral election 1914, raising second battalion Kimberley Regiment, Aug–Sep 1914; resignation,

Lusitania riots, May 1915. Also cf Kimberley *Mayoral Reports,* 1907–1915

Lüderitz fields—Oppenheimer, E and Williams, A F: *Diamond Deposits of German South West Africa* (Kimberley, De Beers, private printing, 1914)

Galway Castle – African World, London: Jan 23 1933

Knighthood – African World, London: Jan 8 1921

Diamond trade—*Chilvers, Hedley: *The Story of De Beers* (London, Cassell, 1939)

Namaqualand discoveries—Rudd, B J and Watson, V U T: *History of the Namaqualand Diamond Discoveries* (prepared at Sir Ernest's request, Johannesburg, Oppenheimer and Son, 1956). Lehmann, Olga: *Look Beyond The Wind* (Cape Town, Howard Timmins, 1955)

Parliament—Cope, John: *Sir Ernest Oppenheimer* (Johannesburg, *Forum,* Dec 1957); Neame, Elwin: *Some South African Politicians* (Cape Town, Maskew Miller, pref 1929); *Hansard,* South Africa: parliamentary reports 1924–1934

May's death—*Cape Argus,* Cape Town: Feb 6 1934

World War II—Ernest's letters to Harry, 1940–1942 (Johannesburg, carbon copies bound, preserved in Brenthurst Library)

Diamond monopoly—*Time,* New York: Feb 12 1945

OFS goldfields Jacobson, D: *Maize Turns To Gold* (Cape Town' Howard Timmins, 1948); *Cartwright, A P: *The Gold Miners* (Johannesburg, Purnell, 1961)

As magnate: Fortune, New York: *Seven Golden Houses* (reprinted Johannesburg, Libertas, Jan 1947); Joubert, Arrie: *Suid-Afrika se Magtigste Sakeman* (Cape Town, *Die Burger,* May 1957)

see also frequent references in *Rand Daily Mail, Star* and *Sunday*

500

Times, Johannesburg; and in *Cape Times* and *Cape Argus*, Cape Town.

2 Material relating to the life of Harry Oppenheimer

A GENERAL

Anderson, Ken: . . . *And So They Talked* (Cape Town, Howard Timmins, 1963)

Gaskill, Gordon: *South Africa's King of Diamonds* (Johannesburg, *Reader's Digest*, Jun 1964)

Holz, P and Van Eyssen, W: *Harry Oppenheimer* (Pretoria, *SA Panorama*, Oct 1968)

B PARTICULAR

Kimberley—Lawrence, Peter: *Harry Oppenheimer – My Affection for Kimberley* (Johannesburg, *Sunday Times*, Sep 2 1973)

World War II—Klein, Harry: *Springboks in Armour* (Johannesburg, Purnell, pref 1965); letters from Ernest 1940–1942, carbon copies bound, preserved in Brenthurst Library

Parliament *Hahn, Emily: *Diamond* (London, Weidenfeld and Nicholson, 1956); *Economist*, London: '*Hoggenheimer*' *Rides Again* (May 17 1951); *Hansard*, South Africa: parliamentary reports 1948–1957; *Diamond Fields Advertiser*, Kimberley: first election campaign May 4 1948 etc

Diamond robbery—Craig, Dennis and Parkes, Brian: *Drama in Diamonds* (Cape Town, Beerman, 1956)

Relations with Ernest—*Gregory, Sir Theodore: *Sir Ernest Oppenheimer and the Economic Development of Southern Africa*

As chairman, AAC and De Beers—*Financial Mail*, Johannesburg: *Inside the Anglo Powerhouse* (Jul 4 1969); *Forbes*, New York: cover story, Jul 1973

See also frequent references in *Rand Daily Mail*, *Star* and *Sunday Times*, Johannesburg; and *Cape Times* and *The Argus*, Cape Town

3 Material relating to De Beers Consolidated Mines and the international diamond trade

A GENERAL

*Bruton, Eric: *Diamonds* (London, NAG, 1970)

*Chilvers, Hedley: *The Story of De Beers* (London, Cassell, 1956)

*Gregory, Sir Theodore: *Sir Ernest Oppenheimer and the Economic Development of Southern Africa* (Cape Town, Oxford University Press, 1961)

*Hahn, Emily: *Diamond* (London, Weidenfeld and Nicholson, 1956)

*Williams, Gardner: *The Diamond Mines of South Africa* (London, Macmillan, 1902)

B PARTICULAR

Geology—*Williams, Alpheus: *The Genesis of the Diamond* (London, Benn, 1932)

early days—Gregory, Sir Theodore: *Diamonds* (Johannesburg, Anglo American Corporation, not completed); *Herbert Ivor: *The Diamond Diggers* (London, Tom Stacey, 1972)

see also a number of articles in *Optima*, the Anglo American's quarterly journal; the annual reports of De Beers, CDM, Premier and other mining companies; and regular news items and commentaries in South African, American and British financial journals and newspapers.

4 Material relating to the Anglo American Corporation of South Africa, Ltd, and to its gold mining and associated activities.

502

A GENERAL

*Cartwright, A P: *The Gold Miners* (Johannesburg, Purnell, 1962)

Financial Mail, Johannesburg: *Inside the Anglo Powerhouse*, Jul 4 1969. *Gregory, Sir Theodore: *Sir Ernest Oppenheimer and the Economic Development of Southern Africa* (Cape Town, Oxford University Press, 1962)

B PARTICULAR

Namaqualand discoveries—Rudd, B J and Watson, V U T: *History of the Namaqualand Diamond Discoveries* (prepared at Sir Ernest's request, Johannesburg, Oppenheimer and Son, 1956)

Copperbelt—Coleman, Francis: *Northern Rhodesian Copperbelt* (Manchester, Manchester University Press, 1971)

OFS goldfields—Jacobson, D: *Maize Turns to Gold* (Cape Town, Howard Timmins, 1948)

see also a number of articles in *Optima*, the Anglo American's quarterly journal; the annual reports on the Anglo American, Charter Consolidated, Rand Selection Corporation and related companies; and regular news items and commentaries in South African, American and British financial journals and newspapers.

5 Material relating to individual personalities

A GENERAL

*Cartwright, A P: *The Gold Miners* (Johannesburg, Purnell, 1962)

*Roberts, Brian: *The Diamond Magnates* (London, Hamish Hamilton, 1972)

B PARTICULAR

Barnato—*Jackson, Stanley: *The Great Barnato* (London, Heinemann, 1970)

Beit—Fort, Seymour: *Alfred Beit* (London, Nicholson and Watson, 1932)

Harris—Harris, Sir David: *Pioneer, Soldier and Statesman* (London, Sampson Low, 1931)

Jameson—Colvin, Sir Ian: *Life of Jameson* (London, Edward Arnold, 1922)

Joel—Joel, Stanhope: *Ace of Diamonds* (London, Muller, 1958)

Malan—Walker, Olive: *Sailor Malan* (London, Cassell, 1953)

Merensky—Lehmann, Olga: *Look Beyond The Wind* (Cape Town, Howard Timmins, 1955)

Penn—Penn, Jack: *The Right to Look Human* (Johannesburg, the author, private printing)

Rhodes—*Roberts, Brian: *Cecil Rhodes and the Princess* (London, Hamish Hamilton, 1969)

Sillitoe—Fleming, Ian: *The Diamond Smugglers* (London, Cape, 1957)

Smuts—Smuts, J C: *Jan Christiaan Smuts* (London, Cassell, 1952)

Verwoerd—Botha, Jan: *Verwoerd is Dead* (Cape Town, Books of Africa, 1967)

Williamson—Heidgen, Heinz: *The Diamond Seeker*, tr fr German by Isabel and Florence McHugh (London, Blackie, 1959)

Acknowledgements

O F ALL THE people who helped me bring this book into being, I am most grateful to a lady who remains one of Johannesburg's most gracious hostesses as she has been for nearly 60 years: **Mrs Doff Susskind,** who in her lovely home Pellmeadow helped me understand a hundred years of history. She was among Sir Ernest Oppenheimer's closest friends most of his life, and was his favourite confidante. She was close to May Oppenheimer and later to Ina, and counts them among the finest women she ever met. She watched Harry and his brother Frank grow up, and remains as close to the family as ever. To her, my thanks for the valuable information she gave me, but even more for the life she breathed into my story.

Next, my thanks to another dear lady who knew the Oppenheimers in their Kimberley days before World War I: **Mrs Dolly Farrer,** whom Harry still counts among his favourite girl friends! As a little girl she lived across the street from Ernest and May Oppenheimer's house in Lodge Road, Kimberley, and even remembers attending Harry's first birthday party. She was able to recall a great deal of the life-style that characterised Kimberley in the century's early years.

For information on the early days of the Anglo American, I am grateful to **Miss Ethel Gribble**. Miss Gribble joined the staff of Consolidated Mines Selection in 1915, even before the foundation of the Anglo American and the virtual merger of the two mining houses. She has detailed memories of many of the personalities involved at the Anglo American of those early years, and indeed of subsequent years right up to date as she is a member of the staff even today. Her record of nearly 60 years' unbroken service to the corporation is without parallel.

Sir Keith Acutt, who is today one of Anglo's two joint deputy

505

chairmen, provided me with much information on the corporation's activities before World War II, particularly as regards the participation of Oppenheimer and Son and the working of Sir Ernest's embryo Exco. I am grateful also to **Mrs R B Hagart**, for information about her late husband who was for so long Sir Ernest's right hand man, and to **Mr Andrew Weatherby** who helped me with material relating to De Beers and Kimberley.

For my account of Harry's adventures in the Western Desert, I relied heavily on the recollections of three of his former comrades-in-arms who fought with him in the 4th South African Armoured Cars: **Col Robert Reeves-Moore**, South Africa's most decorated soldier, **Mr Guy Young** and **Mr George Sefton**. Mrs Doff Susskind and her daughter **Pam Fordyce** told me much about the Caledonian Market and whatever else was going on in Johannesburg while Harry was away, particularly about the Brenthurst Military Hospital. So did **Dr Jack Penn** and **Mrs Janet Ford**, still together at what is now the famous Brenthurst Clinic in Johannesburg: a private hospital initiated by Jack Penn after the war and named Brenthurst on Ina's suggestion, though without any other connection with the Oppenheimers.

For information on the opening of the Free State goldfields, I am grateful to Sir Keith Acutt and **Mr Bill Wilson**, with Sir Keith today a joint deputy chairman of the Anglo American. The two of them were closely involved with Sir Ernest and Harry in all the complex negotiations which made it possible to develop seven major mines virtually at once. **Dr Pete Freeman** of Zambian Anglo American gave me much information on John Williamson and Mwadui.

As regards Harry's career in parliament, I was given valuable assistance by the late **Harry Lawrence**, who had been a minister in Smuts's last cabinet; and by **Dr Zach de Beer**, whom I interviewed in Lusaka where he is today chairman of Zambian Anglo American. Both Mr Lawrence and Dr de Beer told me of the circumstances leading to the formation of the Progressive Party.

Approaching the present, of the many people who assisted me I want to single out **Mr John Breval**, the distinguished racehorse trainer responsible for the Oppenheimer stable; and **Mrs Madeleine van Biljon**, the well known South African journalist who is a close friend of Bridget Oppenheimer's and Mary's. Both gave me valuable insights into what makes today's Oppenheimers tick! **Captain Blake Flemington**, captain of the South African Airways Boeing hijacked to Malawi, told me his fascinating story; and **Cllr Lawrie Shuttle-**

506

worth, the current mayor of Kimberley, went out of his way to help make the project a success.

I was given a great deal of valuable help by the directors and staffs of South Africa's public institutions: in particular **Dr Roger Liversidge** and the staff of the McGregor Museum, Kimberley; **Mr E Donaldson** and **Mrs Muriel Macey** of the Kimberley Public Library; **Miss Fiona Barber** of the Duggan-Cronin Bantu Gallery, Kimberley; the staff of the Johannesburg Public Library, particularly those in charge of the Strange Africana Collection; the staff of the Johannesburg Africana Museum; and the staff of the South African Library, Cape Town.

Mrs Sheila Loseby, librarian of the Anglo American Corporation and of the Brenthurst Collection, was extraordinarily kind in giving all the help she could. She had a number of suggestions to make on means of collecting what often proved frustratingly elusive information, and I am particularly grateful for all that she and her staff have done to bring the project to fruition.

One of the most useful sources of information was the late Sir Theodore Gregory's definitive group history, *Sir Ernest Oppenheimer and the Economic Development of Southern Africa*. Sir Theodore was assisted by a research department which included **Mr Bill Hefer**, now a manager at Anglo, and **Mrs Catherine Demitriou**. Both were able to help me, and to both I offer my thanks.

I must give grateful credit for direct quotation from the following:

Ken Anderson: . . . *And So They Talked* (Cape Town, Howard Timmins, 1963)

Emily Hahn: *Diamond* (London, Weidenfeld and Nicholson, 1956)

Sir David Harris: *Pioneer, Soldier and Statesman* (London, Sampson Low, 1931)

Rudyard Kipling's poem *If* (London, Macmillan)

Olive Walker: *Sailor Malan* (London, Cassell, 1953)

and for the good work of Dennis Craig and Brian Parkes in writing *Drama in Diamonds* on the diamond robbery from Little Brenthurst. I had necessarily to rely heavily on the information they provided.

The book was typed by my distinguished team of secretaries, who constitute what amounts to a minor cottage industry in Johannesburg's northern suburbs. **Mrs Yvonne Byers** worked wonders with my usually illegible typescript, while **Mrs Joan Nicholson** and **Mrs Sue Story** proved commendably efficient. In editing the material I was assisted by **Mr Eric Lloyd-Williams** of the Anglo American and **Mr Charles Barry** of *The Star*. In organising illustrations I was helped by the photographic sections at Anglo, *The Star*, the *Rand Daily Mail* and the *Sunday Times*, and by **Dave Gaskill** and **Gavin Stuart** who drew the maps.

Last of all, a word of thanks to my victims. I will not pretend they showed any great enthusiasm for the project at the outset, but in the event they have proved more than kind. My experience of them is that they are indeed an extraordinary family: extraordinary in that for the position they occupy they are so approachable, so human and so natural. When you spend a year thinking about a single group of personalities you have plenty of time to decide what you feel about each of its members. In the case of the Oppenheimers, I have grown very fond of them all, and I can only hope my text shows why.

ANTHONY HOCKING
Sandton, Transvaal

Index

509

Botswana 415–416
Britain 327–328
Canada 403–405
Guyana 95
Malaysia 407
Mauretania 407–408
Portugal 407
Rhodesia 313–314, 417
Sierra Leone 107–108
South Africa 77–80, 82, 86–87, 89, 93, 95–99, 107, 111, 114–120, 125, 129, 137, 146–147, 161, 167–170, 173–175, 202–204, 213–215, 251–254, 321–322, 330–331, 372–373, 380, 428–431, 460–475
South West Africa 87–90, 95, 114–120
Swaziland 273, 414–415
Thailand 467
United States 405, 408–410
Zaire 94–95, 119
Zambia 108–110, 142–145, 150–151, 171–173, 201, 313–318, 337–338, 420–423, 465, 467, 475–477
mentioned 101–102
Anglo American Corporation of Australia 405–407, 462
Anglo American Corporation of Canada 405, 462
Anglo American Industrial Corporation 462
Anglo American Investment Trust 170, 214, 462
Anglo American Prospecting Co 437
Anglo American Rhodesian Development Corporation 314
Anglo-French Exploration Co 72, 168
Anglo-Transvaal Consolidated Investment Co, see Anglovaal
Anglovaal 168–169, 202, 214, 227
Angola 94–95, 108, 119, 123, 284–285, 418
    diamonds, see Diamond industry, Angola
Anmercosa House 107, 164, 173
Annigoni, Pietro 442
Antwerp 16, 69, 116, 130
Apartheid 233–234, 239, 306–312, 319–321, 367, 424, 433–435
Arctic Circle 404–405
Argentine 447
Arrarat farm 213
Ascot 387
Associated Mines and Selection Trust 214
Associated Mines (Malaya) Sendirian 407
Atlantic Ocean 58–59, 83–85, 95, 124, 215, 340, 376
Atomic Energy Board, South Africa 254
Auchinleck, Gen C J E 191
Australia 6, 70, 76, 79, 210, 232, 368,

391, 405–407, 432–435, 466–467
Bank of 295
Austro-Hungarian Empire 45, 86
Ayer, N W, and Son 412

BBC 474, 484
BOAC 454
BSAC 3, 11–12, 13, 33, 108, 147, 252, 342, 371, 404, 419
Baffinland Iron Mines 404
Bailey, Sir Abe 72, 111–112, 127, 169, 198, 202
Baines, Thomas 261–262
Baker, Sir Herbert 106
Bakerville 124–125
Balfour, Lady, of Inchrye 332
Ballarat 407
Bancroft, see Konkola
Bancroft, Dr Joe 109–110, 143, 167, 169–170, 219
Bancroft mine 313, 317, 337, 422
Banda, Pres Kamuzu 348, 374, 426, 454, 457, 459–460
'Banket' 10, 74
Bantu peoples, South Africa 233–234, 239, 306–307, 319–321, 345–347, 367, 424, 433–435, 470–474, 489
Bantustan policies, South Africa 306–311, 318–322, 424, 433–435
Baragwanath Aerodrome 161
Barberton 10, 203
Barends, Charlie 363
Barkly West 103
Barlow, Kay 440–441
Barlow, Punch 440–441
Barnado, Dr Thomas 398
Barnard, Prof Christiaan 402
Barnato, Barney 8–9, 11, 13, 15–16, 17, 26–27, 30–31, 35, 112, 128, 279, 464
Barnato, Harry 26–27, 101, 128
Barnato Brothers 9, 19, 29, 94, 114, 116, 120, 137, 146, 170
Barrie, J M 59
Basotho 489
Basutoland, see Lesotho
Beacon Light 267–268
Beaconsfield 6, 7, 25, 38–39, 42, 55, 103, 105–106, 136, 236
Beaconsfield, Lord 6
Beatty, Chester, sr 108–110, 129, 142–144, 151, 171–173, 206–207, 412
Beatty, Chester, jr 412
Beaverbrook, Lord 201
Bechuanaland, British 4
Bechuanaland Protectorate, see Botswana
Beira 286
Beirut 396, 446–448, 460
Beit, Alfred 8, 9, 11, 13, 17, 26, 30, 32–33, 72, 93, 101
Belgium 45, 55, 69, 78, 113, 130, 204, 217

511

512

514

515

516

517

519

520

Orange Free State 5, 10, 12, 32, 35, 39, 43, 54–55, 145, 168–170, 201–204, 213–215, 225–228, 239, 251–253, 274, 280, 283, 307, 317–318, 321–322, 331, 350, 414
   diamonds, see Diamond industry, South Africa, Orange Free State
   goldfields, see Gold mining industry, South Africa, Orange Free State
Orange Free State Investment Trust, see OFSIT
Orange River 124, 126, 224, 254
Oranjemund 255, 322
Orapa 415–416
Oregon 409
Organisation of African Unity 416–417 425–426, 460
Oribi 194
Orkney mine 167
Orlando 323
Orr, John 48–50
Orren, Cecil 452–460
Ossian 266–267, 362
Ostrich farming 152
Ottoman Empire, see Turkey
Oxford University 147–149, 222, 270–271, 279, 311, 318–321, 327, 388–391, 394, 404, 436, 486, 489
Oxlee, Keith 394

Pact, Nationalist-Labourite 102, 106, 112–115, 132, 134–136
Pakistan 232, 366
Palabora 413
Palestine 204, 208–209, 295
Pan-African Congress 349–351
Panasqueia 407
Paris 18, 226, 391
   stock exchange 226
Parktown School 86, 147
Parliament, British 39, 100, 112
Parliament, Cape, see Legislative Assembly, Cape
Parliament, South African
   debates 112–113, 121–124, 153–156, 158–159, 238–251, 305–312, 314–315, 321–322, 328–330, 342–345, 369–370, 383–385, 428–429
   elections 101–106, 134–136, 234–236, 304–305, 344–345, 381–383
   mentioned 132–134, 164, 169, 174–176, 199, 205, 233, 237, 303, 479–480
Parliament, Transvaal 73, 164
Paterson, Cecil Compton 40–41
Paterson Aviation Syndicate 40–41
Paul, Pope 409
Pearly King 391
Pearson 291–303
Peking 79

Penn, Jack 193–196, 212–213, 215, 270, 282
Peran-Wisa 268
Philip, Prince 231, 276, 318, 328
Philippi 350, 433
Phillips, Sir Lionel 72, 74, 101, 112, 342
Pickering, Dolly, see Farrer, Dolly
Pickering, William 26, 39
Pietermaritzburg 374
Pilgrim's Rest 10, 203
Pilkington, George 84
Pimville 324, 326
Pioneer Column 12
Platinum
   prospecting 110–111, 403
   production 111
   value 110–111
   Columbia 110
   South Africa 110–111
   Russia 110–111
   mentioned 408–410
Player, Gary 402
Plymouth 83
Poland 176
Pollak, Charlotte 34
Pollak, Leslie 86–87, 115, 142, 150, 165
Pollak, May, see Oppenheimer, May, Lady
Pondoland 12
Port Elizabeth 358, 371, 396
Port Nolloth 124, 128
Port Tewfik 180
Porterville 304–305
Portugal 407
Portuguese 12, 376, 415
Potgietersrust 111
Potgietersrust Platinum Mines 111
Potmasburg 413
Pratley, Thomas 52–53, 59, 67
Precious Metals Development 409
Precious Stones Act, South Africa 127, 130
Premier mine 32–33, 35–36, 43, 93, 114, 118, 138, 145, 154, 156, 163, 170, 179, 224, 413
President Brand mine 226, 251, 331
President Steyn mine 226, 331
Pretoria
   General Hospital 364, 443
   Zoo 443
   mentioned 13–14, 32, 39, 106, 115, 179, 229, 240, 293, 341, 396, 398, 415
Prince Bertrand 267–268, 363
Progressive Party, Cape 27
Progressive Party, South Africa
   formation 359–360
   elections 433–435
   mentioned 380–381, 401, 468, 479–480, 484
Punch 288

521

Purcell, Thomas 395
Pym, Joanne 361

Queen Elizabeth House 327
Queensland 406
Queenstown, Cork 59
Quickgrass 267–268

RCBC 144, 151
Radley, Percival 285, 294–303
Radziwill, Princess 260
Rand, see Witwatersrand
Rand Club 205, 224
Rand Daily Mail 51, 57, 82, 155, 241, 261, 445, 479
Rand Mines 11, 71, 227, 408, 440
Rand Rebellions 1913–14 97
Rand Rebellion 1922 98–99, 101–102
Rand Selection Corporation 341–342, 372, 423, 462, 465
Rand Selection Trust 75–78, 90, 95, 107, 160, 263, 341–342
  reorganised 341–342
Randlords 31, 74, 86, 101, 408
Rausenstrauch, Anton 130
Red Cross, see International Red Cross
Reef, see Witwatersrand
Reform Committee, Johannesburg 13
Regie, German 37
Reitz, Deneys 176, 261
Relly, Gavin 421, 465
Rembrandt Tobacco Corp 416
Renoir, Auguste 280
Republic of South Africa, see South Africa
Republic Referendum 365–366
Resurrection, Community of the 322, 334
Retco 464
Reuning, Dr Ernest 126–127
Reynolds, Sir Joshua 262
Rhijn, Dr A J R 330
Rhine, River 16
Rhoanglo 143, 150, 171–173, 214, 313–316, 321, 337, 462
Rhoanglo Group Act 313
Rhodes, Cecil John
  career 5–15, 19–20, 32, 37, 93, 112
  death 1–4, 15, 22
  mentioned 17, 25–28, 30–33, 94, 102–103, 106, 108, 140, 148, 152, 160, 247–248, 252–253, 260–261, 271–272, 277, 280, 282–283, 312–313, 317, 327, 404, 413, 419, 483, 485
Rhodes, Elmirst 2
Rhodes, Herbert 5, 6
Rhodes University 279, 486
Rhodesia
  colonisation 11–12
  in Federation, see Central African Federation
  independence 375–376, 425

mentioned, 4, 33, 39, 198, 229, 266 273, 284, 312–313, 335, 346, 348, 359, 362, 375–376, 380, 415, 417–418, 425, 448–451, 454, 466–467, 476, 489
Rhodesia, Northern, see Zambia
Rhodesia, Southern, see Rhodesia
Rhodesian Air Force 470
Rhodesian Broken Hill, see Broken Hill
Rhodesia Congo Border Concession, see RCBC
Rhodesia Copper Refineries 313
Rhodesia Railways 314
Rhodesia Acceptances 274
Rhodesian Anglo American, see Rhoanglo
Rhodesian Development Corporation
Rhodesian Front 375
Rhodesian Nickel Corp 417
Rhodesia Selection Trust 143, 173, 338, 404
Rhokana Corp 151, 171, 313, 422–423
Ribofilio 441–442
Richardson, Sally 260
Rio Tinto Corp 150, 404, 413
Roan Antelope mine 143, 151, 171, 201
Roan Consolidated Mines Ltd 423
Roan Selection Trust 421
Robben Island 211
Roberts, Allan 168–170, 213, 226
Roberts, Lord 20
Roberts Victor mine 32, 35
Robinson, Sir Albert 465
Robinson, Sir Joseph B 10, 101
Rockefeller Centre 464
Rome 396, 437
Rommel, Gen Erwin 180, 182–183, 185, 188–189, 210
Romney, George 262
Ronaldson, George 40
Roos, Tielman 159, 163
Roosevelt, Theodore 62
Rose, Stanley 443
Rosebery, Lord 266
Rothschilds, London 8, 93, 150, 274, 406
Roumania 45
Royal African Society 251, 344, 354
Royal Air Force, 223
Royal Commonwealth Society 354
Royal Empire Society 251
Royal Flying Corps 161
Royal Horse Artillery 182, 184
Royal Navy 85
Royal Photographic Society 387
Royal Typewriter Co 217
Ruitgedachte farm 124
Rumania 477
Rupert, Anton 416
Russell, Hamilton 242
Russia 45, 86–87, 113, 261, 340, 405